CANOEING NORTH
INTO THE UNKNOWN
A RECORD OF RIVER TRAVEL: 1874 TO 1974

CANOEING NORTH INTO THE UNKNOWN

A RECORD OF RIVER TRAVEL: 1874 TO 1974

Bruce W. Hodgins & Gwyneth Hoyle

NATURAL HERITAGE / NATURAL HISTORY INC.

Canoeing North into the Unknown:
A Record of River Travel: 1874 to 1974
by Bruce W. Hodgins & Gwyneth Hoyle

Published by Natural Heritage / Natural History Inc.
P.O. Box 95, Station O, Toronto, Ontario M4A 2M8

Design, typesetting and photo scans: Robin Brass Studio
Maps: Dale van Dompseler
Printed and bound in Canada by Hignell Printing Limited, Winnipeg, Manitoba

Cover photo: Rob Perkins passing through Hawk Rapids on the
Back River, 1988. [Richard Winslow]

Title page: A panoramic view of the George River. [Stewart Coffin]

Canadian Cataloguing in Publication Data

Hodgins, Bruce W., 1931–
Canoeing north into the unknown : a record of river travel, 1874 to 1974

Includes bibliographical references and index.
ISBN 0-920474-93-4

1. Canoes and canoeing – Canada, Northern – History. 2. Rivers – Canada, Northern –
History. 3. Canada, Northern – Description and travel. I. Hoyle, Gwyneth. II. Title

FC3956.H74 1994   917.19'04   C94-932438-8
F1000.5.II74 1994

Natural Heritage / Natural History Inc. gratefully acknowledges the assistance of the
Canada Council, the Ontario Arts Council, and the Government of Ontario through the
Ministry of Culture, Tourism and Recreation.

A SPECIAL ACKNOWLEDGEMENT

In the shadows there is a vast throng of people who are the origin of much that is recorded in this book. These are the people of the First Nations whose ancestors lived in this land long before Europeans reached its shores. They fashioned the boats that were refined into the perfect watercraft of birchbark canoe and skin kayak. Their footsteps marked out the portage trails that are still in use today. Their skills guided the first Europeans who explored the interior of this beautiful land, saved these explorers from starvation, clothed them with garments of deer and caribou, moccasins of leather and taught them the ways of the rivers. A few of their names have come down to us in the journals of the early travellers – from Akaitcho, the Beaulieus, the English Chief to George Elson and Bert Blake of recent times. For every name that is recorded, countless numbers are unnoticed and unsung. We acknowledge with gratitude the priceless gift from the people of the First Nations who led the way.

A photo by Stewart Coffin of a spectacular chute at Twin Islands on the Romaine River. Coffin is the source of many excellent photographs in this book.

CONTENTS

PREFACE 11

INTRODUCTION 14

CHAPTER ONE

JAMES BAY AND BEYOND:
THE ONTARIO CRADLE
OF THE FUR TRADE 29

MOOSE–MISSINAIBI–MATTAGAMI–ABITIBI 29
MISSINAIBI 29
MATTAGAMI 35
ABITIBI 38
PARTRIDGE 43
KESAGAMI 43
ALBANY 43
OGOKI–ALBANY 52
KENOGAMI–ALBANY 54
ATTAWAPISKAT 56
EKWAN 57
WINISK 58
SEVERN 59
FAWN–SEVERN 60

CHAPTER TWO

THE LAND OF THE EASTERN CREE:
QUEBEC'S JAMES BAY RIVERS 63

HARRICANAW 63
NOTTAWAY 65
BROADBACK 68

RUPERT 68
EASTMAIN 75
LA GRANDE (FORT GEORGE) 78
ROGGAN 78
GREAT WHALE 78
LITTLE WHALE 78
HUDSON BAY COAST 79

CHAPTER THREE

HUDSON BAY COAST:
MANITOBA AND KEEWATIN 81

HAYES (INCLUDING ECHIMAMISH AND GODS
RIVERS) 81
NELSON 89
CHURCHILL 91
SEAL 95
THLEWIAZA 96
THA-ANNE 97
MAGUSE 97
FERGUSON 98

CHAPTER FOUR

RIVERS OF THE BARRENS:
THELON AND ITS TRIBUTARIES 99

THELON 99
DUBAWNT 107
KAZAN 109
QUOICH 112

CHAPTER FIVE

**THE ROUTE OF THE EXPLORERS:
THE MACKENZIE WATERSHED** 113

CLEARWATER–ATHABASCA–SLAVE 113
ATHABASCA–SLAVE 118
CREE 123
MACFARLANE 123
PEACE–SLAVE 123
MACKENZIE 130

CHAPTER SIX

**THE RIVER OF MANY WATERS:
WESTERN TRIBUTARIES
OF THE MACKENZIE** 135

LIARD 135
SOUTH NAHANNI 140
NORTH NAHANNI 148
SOUTH REDSTONE 148
KEELE 148
MOUNTAIN 149
ARCTIC RED 150
PEEL 150
OGILVIE–PEEL 151
BLACKSTONE–PEEL 151
HART–PEEL 151
WIND–PEEL 151
BONNET PLUME–PEEL 152
SNAKE–PEEL 153
RAT 153

CHAPTER SEVEN

**EVEN THE LAKES CONTRIBUTE:
EASTERN TRIBUTARIES
OF THE MACKENZIE** 155

HARE INDIAN 155
GREAT BEAR 155
RIVERS FLOWING INTO GREAT SLAVE LAKE 157
MARIAN 158
SNARE 158
YELLOWKNIFE 159
BEAULIEU 160
LOCKHART 160
SNOWDRIFT 162
TALTSON–TAZIN–THOA 162
HAY 164

CHAPTER EIGHT

**THE DESTINATION IS NORTH:
THE WESTERN ARCTIC** 165

FIRTH 165
ANDERSON 166
HORTON 166
HORNADAY 168
CROKER 168
RAE 168
COPPERMINE 168
HOOD 173
BURNSIDE 175
MARA 176

CHAPTER NINE

**QUEEN MAUD GULF AND EAST:
RIVERS FLOWING INTO
THE ARCTIC OCEAN** 177

WESTERN 177
ELLICE 177
PERRY 177
ARMARK 179
SIMPSON 179
KALEET 179
BACK 180
BAILLIE 183
MORSE 184
HAYES 184
KELLETT AND ARROWSMITH 184

CHAPTER TEN

**IN SEARCH OF GOLD:
THE YUKON AND NORTHERN
BRITISH COLUMBIA** 185

THE HISTORIC YUKON 185
HUDSON'S BAY COMPANY EXPLORATION
IN THE YUKON 187
YUKON RIVER 188
BELL–PORCUPINE 193
TATONDUK 199
KLONDIKE 199
SIXTY MILE 200
STEWART 200
PELLY 202
MACMILLAN 204
ROSS 205
BIG SALMON 206

TESLIN 206
ALSEK 207
TATSHENSHINI 208
STIKINE 208

CHAPTER ELEVEN

THE FROZEN LAND: UNGAVA 213

CLEARWATER 213
KOGALUK 215
POVUNGNITUK 215
PAYNE 215
LEAF 216
KOKSOAK 217
LARCH–KOKSOAK 217
KANIAPISKAU–KOKSOAK 218
WHALE 220
GEORGE 221
KOROK 223

CHAPTER TWELVE

THE LAND GOD GAVE TO CAIN:
LABRADOR 225

GRAND OR HAMILTON (CHURCHILL) 225
FRASER 230
KOGALUK 231
NOTAKWANON 232
UGJOKTOK 233
KANAIRIKTOK 234
NASKAUPI 235
GOOSE 236
KENEMU 236

CHAPTER THIRTEEN

SOME NORTHERN WATERS FLOW SOUTH:
RIVERS DRAINING INTO THE
LOWER ST. LAWRENCE 237

ST. PAUL 237
ST. AUGUSTIN 238

PETIT MÉCATINA 238
NATASHQUAN 239
AGUANUS 239
ROMAINE 240
ST. JEAN 242
MAGPIE 242
MOISIE 244

CHAPTER FOURTEEN

THE LAST CANOEING FRONTIER:
RIVERS OF THE ARCTIC ISLANDS
AND MELVILLE PENINSULA 249

BAFFIN ISLAND 249
SOPER 249
SYLVIA GRINNELL 250
AMADJUAK 250
ARMSHOW 250
MCKEAND 250
ISORTOQ 250
RAVN 252
BAFFIN ISLAND FIORDS 252
BANKS ISLAND 252
THOMSEN 252
VICTORIA ISLAND 252
KUUJJUA 252
NANOOK 253
ELLESMERE ISLAND 253
RUGGLES 254
MELVILLE PENINSULA 254
KINGORA 254
AJUQATALIK 254
ARCTIC COAST 254

BIBLIOGRAPHY 255

INDEX TO PEOPLE 261

INDEX TO LAKES AND RIVERS 274

INDEX TO ORGANIZATIONS 277

LIST OF MAPS

NORTHERN ONTARIO 30
MOOSE, ALBANY

FAR NORTHERN ONTARIO 44
ALBANY TO SEVERN

NORTHERN QUEBEC 64
RUPERT, EASTMAIN

MANITOBA AND KEEWATIN 82
HAYES, CHURCHILL

EASTERN ARCTIC AND THE BARRENS 100
THELON, DUBAWNT, KAZAN, BACK

MACKENZIE WATERSHED 114
MACKENZIE, ATHABASCA, PEACE, SLAVE AND
THEIR TRIBUTARIES, LIARD, NAHANNI, PEEL,
SNOWDRIFT, TALTSON

WESTERN ARCTIC 167
COPPERMINE, HOOD, BURNSIDE

**YUKON AND NORTHERN BRITISH
COLUMBIA** 186
YUKON, PORCUPINE, PELLY, ROSS, MACMILLAN,
STIKINE, ALSEK, TATSHENSHINI

UNGAVA REGION 214
KANIAPISKAU, WHALE, GEORGE

**LABRADOR AND ST. LAWRENCE
NORTH SHORE** 226
GRAND OR CHURCHILL, NOTAKWANON,
UGJOKTOK, MOISIE, MAGPIE, ROMAINE

ABBREVIATIONS

CN	Canadian National
CP	Canadian Pacific
ELT	Emergency Location Transmitter
FQCC	Fédération Québecoise du Canot-Camping
FRGS	Fellow of the Royal Geographical Society
GSC	Geological Survey of Canada
HB	Hudson Bay (railway)
HBC	Hudson's Bay Company
MPP	Member of the Provincial Parliament
NAC	National Archives of Canada
NOLS	Northern Ontario Land Survey
NWT	Northwest Territories
ONR	Ontario Northland Railway
RA	Royal Artillery
RCMP	Royal Canadian Mounted Police
RN	Royal Navy
RNWMP	Royal North West Mounted Police
TNOR	Temiskaming & Northern Ontario Railway
WCA	Wilderness Canoe Association

PREFACE

Canada has a rich heritage of exploration and adventure literature, much of it defined by northern rivers. This book concerns itself with northern river travel, for both recreational and administrative purposes, with the canoe as the primary means of transport. It is organized by the principal watersheds, Hudson Bay, Arctic, Pacific, and Atlantic. Within these watersheds the travel on each major river is arranged chronologically with the names of the travellers, the organization they represent, and the route they followed.

The time frame is roughly the century between the exploration by the Geological Survey of Canada and that done by the Canadian Wild River Survey. The former Survey was spread over many decades, but it concentrated on the northern rivers in the 1870s and 1880s. The Wild River Survey, an initiative of Prime Minister Pierre Trudeau, an avid wilderness canoeist, took place between 1972 and 1974. This Survey has evolved into the system of designated Canadian Heritage Rivers.

We have attempted to deal with all northern rivers for which there are records of travel, either for recreational or administrative purposes. Administrative travel includes surveyors, missionaries, Indian Treaty negotiators, official scientific expeditions and police, mounted in canoes not on horseback. Recreational travel has less practical application than other travel and most of it is self-supported. It ranges in scope from continent-crossing expeditions to the vacation-length descent of a single river, and the canoeists run the gamut from youth campers to ornithologists, having in common their love of the wilderness.

Before the Geological Survey and before the earliest recreational trips, most of the great northern waterways of what became Canada were part of the travel routes (*nastawgan* in Algonkian) of the many First Nations. This use continued even as some of the rivers became the highways of the commercial fur trade, with its colourful history and imperial rivalries, involving the three great cultures of the country, the aboriginal, the British and the French. Competition in the fur trade between those operating out of Hudson Bay and those operating from Montreal spurred "exploration" by Europeans of both the far Northwest and the remote Northeast. Ironically the search for the Northwest Passage promoted northern river travel, by Mackenzie and Fraser in the fur trade, and by Franklin, Richardson, Back and others exploring for the British Navy. Almost two centuries before that, De Troyes and others in the service of the French king made similar river trips into the James Bay watershed.

In the opening section of many of our river reports, after a descriptive introduction, we list many of those early epic voyages. When a river was heavily used for aboriginal travel and for the fur trade we make no pretence of being inclusive. From the 1780s to 1821 there were hundreds of canoes each year on the great Voyageur Highway and its tributary side routes. The massive Hudson Bay traffic on the Churchill-Saskatchewan-Hayes route continued to 1870 and beyond. The great changes in the pattern of travel came with the opening of the Canadian Pacific and other trunk railways.

At the other end of our time scale, nearer to the present, recreational travellers on some of the particularly accessible rivers, such as the Albany, the Abitibi, or the central portion of the Yukon, became so numerous that they are unsung and unrecorded. On the other hand, the canoeists' search for new experiences has meant that remote rivers, previously hardly dreamt of, are "discovered" and first descents of these rivers, even after 1974, are recorded in this volume.

Our record of travel includes all significant rivers which flow into the Arctic Ocean, including Hudson, James and Ungava Bays, the North Pacific and the Labrador Sea of the North Atlantic. We also include the northern rivers, from the Moisie eastward, which flow south into the Gulf of St. Lawrence. We do *not*, however, include the upper or western portions of the Churchill or the Saskatchewan (part of the Nelson system), important though they were to the fur trade and, in the case of the Churchill, to recreational canoeing. Similarly we do not include the Rainy River, also part of Nelson waters. South-flowing rivers of the Shield, such as the Temagami and Spanish in Ontario and the Mistassini and Chamouchouane in deep wilderness Quebec, are excluded by definition.

The water-craft are primarily but not exclusively canoes, and where possible the size and type of canoe is recorded. The method of access to the rivers is important and so are the changes which occur with the advent of railways, highways and finally aircraft.

The record contains an extensive bibliography to serve as a starting point for further reading by canoeists and students of history. For the canoeist, the bibliography will be used to appreciate the prowess of others and to dream and plan for future trips. For the historian, it will provide a ready reference to the travels of explorers and adventurers in the North. The record also contains three indexes: the names of travellers, lakes and rivers, and the organizations involved in sending people north.

While the vast literature of northern travel has provided much of our material, this record would not have been complete without the help and cooperation of scores of present and past northern wilderness canoe trippers. The contacts with these people have been consistently rewarding. The annual Wilderness Symposium, held in January in Toronto, sponsored by the Wilderness Canoe Association and organized by George Luste, a great northern canoeist and collector of northern books, has facilitated these contacts. The memory of Eric Morse has been an inspiration. His widow, Pamela, another marvellous tripper and record keeper, has helped us greatly with her notes, letters and her compilation of Eric's extensive files.

We cannot list here the scores of helpers. They appear in the text as "personal communication". All we can do is thank them sincerely and hope that they approve of the result. We must, however, also name Michael Peake, editor of *Che-Mun*, who gave us access to his files; Prof. R.H. Cockburn, who suggested avenues of research; Alex Hall of Canoe Arctic, who commented on some of our Barrenlands material; the daughters of Bill Anderson who loaned us the very fragile record of travel on the Albany River; James Raffan for his ideas and encouragement; the archivist of the Explorers Club in New York and the publishers of *Outdoor Canada* and *Sports Illustrated*, who combed their files for relevant articles; Richard Winslow III of New Hampshire who contributed books, many photocopied articles and lists of names and addresses; Laurie Precht of Edmonton who sent us her thesis and a large package of articles which she had used in her research; Prof. John Wadland, who was always available with practical advice to solve knotty problems. The Frost Centre, Trent University, has supported this project from its inception with a research grant, with the use of its facilities and always with the encouragement of the present director, Prof. John Marsh.

In the early stages of the research we received research assistance from Murray Hodgins and Seana Irvine and later from Shawn Heard, Jennifer McLeod and Katie Hayhurst. The appearance of the book has been enhanced by the maps created by Dale van Dompseler from Gwyneth's thumbnail tracings and by historical photographs taken by Eleanor Underwood.

Throughout, our spouses, Carol and Alex, were most supportive and helpful. Alex Hoyle bravely tackled the mammoth task of copy-editing and in the process learned to appreciate the achievements of the northern canoeists and, incidentally, the spellings of Northern Ontario's rivers. Gwyneth would like to add a note of gratitude to her sons, all of whom encourage her love of canoeing, and particularly to Douglas, who introduced her to the pleasures of the computer, without which this project would have been a very long time in completion.

BRUCE W. HODGINS & GWYNETH HOYLE

INTRODUCTION

The rivers of Canada's North reflect a long history. It is a history of sustenance, trade, commerce, exploration, administration and recreational adventure. The canoe travellers on these rivers, whether they were paddling birchbark *canots de maître* or the latest design of plastic, are all part of that history.

Extensive voyaging by canoes on lengthy river systems had long been the principal means of northern or back country travel and was fundamental to linking our three founding peoples, Aboriginal, English, and French. Canoe travel (including travel by kayak) was important to most of the indigenous peoples of what became Canada. Travelling by canoe then became significant for administrative and scientific work in the North. The canoe in motion, the flow of the river and the awesome nature of the northern landscape are bonded together with the travellers' emotional passage through both space and time.

Who were these canoe travellers? Where on northern rivers did they travel? In what kind of craft? Above all, why did they go on such trips?

THE CANOEISTS

In the eighteenth century, the Cree of the Hudson Bay watershed and people of several other First Nations had been involved in trips of astonishing length ending on the Hayes to York Factory or on the Albany and Moose.[1] Later, in the early nineteenth century, many indigenous people, especially Métis, were voyageurs. Aboriginal people were always heavily involved in trapping and hunting, but the role and numbers of First Nation and Métis people involved in northern river travel are hard to quantify. During the century of this study, long trips by indigenous people were not usual. They involved travel from the village or the fur post to their traditional hunting territories and traplines and back. Winter travel by snowshoe and dog team was perhaps more important.[2]

Before World War II, the fur trade was still extensive, indeed, during the early years of this century it was still expanding northward with great vigour. Canoe travel became essential to the fur trade, whether that trade was organized from Montreal to the *pays d'en haut* or from the Bay to the headwaters and over the divides. During the early part of the century, many of the recreationalists and surveyors took along "Indian guides," mostly Métis who had not previously travelled the entire route. These guides had invaluable bush-lore which the Euro-Canadian and the visitor wanted to learn or at least employ.

Without prompting, the trapper, Indian, Métis, and European made use, as quickly as possible, of outboard "kickers" and of bush-plane drop-ins to their hunting or trapping territory. After all, trapping, fishing, and hunting were their occupations and their livelihood. In the 1960s, they embraced the snow-machine and the all-terrain vehicle. The small motorboat was used in conjunction with the float-plane. Increasingly, it was the Euro-Canadian and American who made the long, remote northern journeys by canoe.

For well over a century, large numbers have travelled on canoe trips, canoeing north-flowing waters as a great mobile recreational activity with a dual heritage and adventure focus. Some of these trips, especially those before World War I, had a veneer of scientific and pseudo-scientific purpose, but sensitive adventure and renewal was often the deeper reason. In the earlier years a very large number were British and American but the majority of recreational canoeists have been Canadian.

One Canadian, through his travels and writings, influenced and encouraged many throughout Canada and the United States to explore Canada's heritage of northern rivers. Eric Morse, addicted to the canoe from an early age and living in Ottawa, began introducing his friends in government circles and the diplomatic corps to the pleasures of the weekend canoe-camping trip. At their urging, the trips became longer and ranged farther and farther afield. Trained as an historian and fascinated by the fur trade, Eric Morse and his companions began retracing some of the old routes, calling themselves "The Voyageurs" and using some of the old terms such as *bourgeois* for the leader and *boisson* for a celebratory drink after a special achievement. Articles by Morse in the *Beaver* and the *Canadian Geographic Journal* and by Sigurd Olson, one of the Voyageurs, in books such as *The Lonely Land*, created immediate interest. Morse's *Fur Trade Canoe Routes of Canada/Then and Now*, published in 1968, became a handbook for many canoeists. In 1962, with his wife Pamela as one of the group, Eric Morse made his first trip into the Barrens, descending the Hanbury and Thelon Rivers. There was a record of previous travel on those rivers, but this was one of the first purely recreational Canadian Barrenland descents. Many northern trips followed for the Morses and many more canoeists followed in their wake.

In Ontario, Algonquin Park was established in 1893 with headwaters preservation, forest conservation, and recreational canoe tripping centrally in mind. By the turn of the century, Temagami, Haliburton, Kipawa, and the area that became Quetico were important havens for canoe travel. As this century progressed, this form of travel became an important recreational activity in the wilderness and quasi-wilderness areas in all the various regions of the country. At that time most canoe trippers did not have the leisure, perhaps not the money, the bush skills, the canoeing abilities for manoeuvring in white water nor the stamina for extensive rough portaging, all requirements to travel the great north-flowing rivers. The image of the canoe tripper is often that of a person with a canoe worn like a great hat over his or her head. For most, the northern river leading down to the Bay, or the sea, was their dream trip. In later life, it became the canoe trip of their armchair – "But I float in my dreams on northern streams that never again I'll see".[3]

A northern trip implies stamina and good health, regardless of age. In the early decades covered by this study, Indian and Métis guides and canoemen lightened the physical effort and those with sufficient leisure who could afford to hire them were often approaching middle age. Young adults, many in their

The northern wilderness trip is filled with days of contrast. A lashing rain which holds the trip windbound beside a seething lake may be followed by a shirtless paddle on glassy-smooth water only just released from the vise-grip of ice: Peter Blaikie and Angus Scott on Lake Kamilukuak in 1968. [Eric Morse/Pamela Morse]

teens, appeared on the rivers early in this century, participating in northern wilderness trips organized by a few of the youth camps, or by relatives. As access and equipment improved, the age span of the canoeists widened and it is now not uncommon to find paddlers in their sixties on remote rivers. The interest and the willingness to undergo the rigours of a northern adventure implies an innate curiosity and high motivation which often equates to higher education. Sylvanna Grimm, in a master's thesis, statistically analysed the users of the Nahanni River in a particular year and found that three-quarters of the canoeists and kayakers had university degrees.[4]

For many decades northern canoe travel was undertaken by people who not only enjoyed it, but as part of their job were paid for it. Many such fortunate souls were paid by government, a few by their church and some by the Hudson's Bay Company. The Geological Survey of Canada (GSC) sent surveyors and scientists on astonishing trips in the far north, usually based on river travel by canoe.[5] Police and Indian Agents in the north often travelled by canoe – and snowshoe.

Early northern travel required a commitment of time and resources that put it out of the reach of many citizens. While few travellers were identifiably wealthy, most came from backgrounds in which financial means provided the time for lengthy canoe trips either involving exploration or adventure. Recently, while improved access decreased the time required to follow a northern river to its mouth, it has not been uncommon to find canoeists seeking sponsors to fund or provide equipment for a particularly long trip.

Between 1890 and 1910 northern river travellers included Warburton Pike and Henry Toke Munn, who came to hunt muskox and discovered that shooting them was not great sport. The Preble brothers, E.A. and A.E., made long exploratory trips on behalf of the U.S. Department of Agriculture and Ernest Thompson Seton joined E.A. Preble on one of these trips. David Hanbury ventured into the Barrens and down the Thelon, making an epic winter journey north and west on a route which crossed many rivers. Books and articles, written by these men and often by provincial magistrates and missionaries served to spark the interest of others in their quest for new experiences. In 1900 the Province of Ontario sponsored and paid for an elaborate summer of canoe travel by land surveyors, forest experts, agronomists and geologists on nearly all the great river waters of Northern Ontario that flow down to the Bay, including the waters of the Albany, the province's northern border.[6]

The majority of canoeists in the early decades of this account were middle-class males. Many of the early trips with a full or a quasi scientific mission were supported by scientific institutions or universities and the participants were exclusively educated men. The few women on northern waters were often the wives of missionaries and traders. There were, however, explorers and adventurers, travelling alone or with their husbands, primarily as passengers. In the years of this study there are many published accounts of women participating in mixed canoe trips on more southern waters. By the later decades of this study, their names occur in many mixed groups, with or without spouses. Recently, it is not uncommon to find women leading northern canoe trips, sometimes with mixed groups, sometimes with groups made up entirely of women.

Ethnically, most were of English, Scottish or Irish descent. In the early decades a majority were British or British born, and many were American. In this century the Canadians, who came from every region of Canada, and the Americans were usually urban based. The civil servants of the Geological Survey heavily increased the Anglo-Canadian component, but apart from this group, French-speaking Canadians were rare in the early decades. Their numbers grew significantly in the 1960s and '70s. In the 1970s, immigrant Canadians, including those from Central and Scandinavian Europe, became proportionately very important.

Some notable canoeists on the Petawawa River in 1967. From the left, Jack Goering, Omond Solandt, Pierre Trudeau, Terk Bayly, Pamela Morse, Angus Scott, Jim Bayly, Eric Morse, Blair Fraser. The photo was taken by Dr. A.R.C. Jones. [Pamela Morse]

During the summers of 1971-74, Prime Minister Pierre Trudeau, himself a keen northern canoeist, initiated the Wild River Survey,[7] under whose auspices small groups of canoeists paddled dozens of remote, and many no longer so remote northern rivers, all in preparation for what later emerged as the Canadian Heritage Rivers System. By the mid-1970s, the numbers of canoeists on north-flowing rivers was vastly expanding, several rivers experiencing a hundred or more travellers in one year, while a few of the most remote rivers were still being descended by canoe for only the first, second or third time. With these exceptions, this study ends at the beginning of that vast expansion.

THE RIVERS

In the early years, the majority of trips were made from point to point or "down and back," sometimes crossing difficult divides between watersheds and until other transportation means were available, involved considerable upstream paddling. The difficulties of access to entry and egress points and the associated costs were the principal factors in delaying and minimizing the number of "first descents". These trips were linear and only rarely were long cross-country circular trips undertaken. Ultimately all the great northern rivers were paddled.

During the 1870s and for a few decades thereafter, the GSC covered the more accessible rivers of the James Bay watersheds in far Northern Ontario, mid-northern Quebec and the Hudson Bay rivers in the region which became northern Manitoba. The survey trips next covered the rivers north of the western prairies and parkland, as well as many of those in the Yukon valley. The construction of the Canadian Pacific Railway, between 1882 and 1886, was the most important single development in making more of the northern rivers accessible to both the GSC and adventurous paddlers. For some time a majority of northern river trips began and often ended at embarkation points on the railway.

Travellers to Moose Factory could now start their canoe journey from the railway station at Missanabie on the CPR line and follow the Missinaibi river route north to the Bay. Or they could indirectly access the Abitibi, the Mattagami, and the mighty Albany by canoeing north from the CPR. In this period there are records of several long canoe journeys by missionaries from Moose Factory up to the railway line, west to Winnipeg by train, and down the Nelson-Echimamish-Hayes to York Factory, or variations of such trips. Federal and provincial surveyors, too, were using the railway as a jumping-off point for tours of duty in Northern Ontario.

After a spur line of the CPR reached Edmonton in 1891, a wagon trail made the connection north to Athabasca Landing and the barge and steam-boat system of transportation which the Hudson's Bay Company provided for servicing its posts on Great Slave Lake and the Mackenzie River. The northwestern rivers could now be reached by more than official travellers. Parts of Canada's far North became a mecca for adventurers, sportsmen, and scientists. Transportation arrangements could take them to a point where the real adventure could begin.

Late in the nineteenth century, northern gold made canoeists out of ordinary fortune seekers. Gold had been attracting miners and prospectors into the southern and central British Columbia interior since the days of the Cariboo in the 1850s. Discoveries in the north of the province in the Omineca district, involved the head-waters of the Peace River, while in the Cassiar district, boat traffic opened up parts of the Stikine River and spilled north to the Liard River. These were just the curtain-raiser for the Klondike madness of 1898, when thousands of otherwise sane, ordinary people were suddenly seized by gold-fever. The majority reached the Klondike by steam-boat to Skagway, climbed the Chilkoot Pass and went down the Yukon River. In those years the Yukon River was filled with water-craft of every imaginable size and shape. The remainder, still a large number, passed through Edmonton and with flotillas of small boats went down the Athabasca-Slave and Mackenzie Rivers, up tributaries of the Mackenzie to passes over the Rocky Mountains, going down tributaries of the Yukon on the other side. Some of the prospectors went up the Keele and down the Macmillan, while others went up the Peel and down the Porcupine.

Before World War I, George Douglas had reached the lower Coppermine by way of Great Bear and the Dismal Lakes. Access to northern rivers was facilitated by the construction of two more transcontinental railways, the National Transcontinental–Grand Trunk Pacific and the Canadian Northern, both of which merged with the eastern GTR in the early twenties to become the Canadian National. Both lines generally ran north of the CPR. In Central Canada, the building of the Temiskaming and Northern Ontario Railway (ONR after 1946) was at least as important. The TNOR reached Temagami and Timiskaming in 1905, the Timmins-Porcupine gold camps on the Mattagami in 1912, Cochrane near the Abitibi in 1914 and finally arrived at Moosonee on James Bay in 1932. Keewaydin Camp in Temagami sent its first "section" to the Bay, paddling to and down the Abitibi and back up the Mattagami and Nighthawk in 1911. The arrival of the railway ended forever the need for rigorous upstream paddling (usually via the Abitibi-Frederick House-Montreal Rivers route), after diverse downstream Bay trips. The Northern Alberta Railway's arrival at Waterways, by Fort McMurray, in 1920 had a similar effect for the Mackenzie River.

Always there is the search for "new frontiers," unexplored territory, remote aboriginal lands and previously unknown rivers. After the rivers of the northwest, Ungava and Labrador provided the right combination. Ungava, a harsh and unforgiving land, was only marginally a part of fur-trade territory and is still very little travelled. Leonidas Hubbard, early in this century, hoped to make his name by a first descent of the George River, in what he called "Labrador". When he died in the attempt, his wife Mina's successful exploration assured that the name of Hubbard would be forever associated with the area. William Brooks Cabot, from a patrician Boston family, explored the relatively short rivers of northern Labrador with the express purpose of making contact with the Naskapi (now called Innu) people, and over a period of twenty years he learned their language, visited their camps and travelled the rivers of Labrador and the North Shore of the St. Lawrence. The magnificent river of Central Labrador, the Churchill (also called the Grand or Hamilton) with its powerful falls, and its tributary, the Unknown River with its four sets of falls, was an area of much exploration and speculation until this complex area was mapped by Watkins and Scott in 1929.

By the 1960s, trips on the Albany, Abitibi and to a degree the Missinaibi be-

Lunchtime fishing on the Romaine River, 1980. [Stewart Coffin]

came quite numerous and consequently were so unsung that reporting them in anything approaching totality has not been possible.

Soon the Moisie and other northern St. Lawrence rivers were being run regularly and remote Ungava and northern Labrador rivers were being increasingly traversed. Indeed, following the completion of the trips of the Wild River Survey in 1974, very few mainland Arctic Rivers had not been travelled for most of their length on a canoe trip.

THE CRAFT[8]

The earliest recreational and administrative trips appear to have used traditional birch bark canoes. Usually they would be obtained locally through the native people or from the Hudson's Bay Company. Some of the early trips combined winter travel, by snowshoe and/or dog team, with summer travel, for which canoes had to be obtained locally or built on the spot by the travellers. Some of the Northern Ontario Land Surveyors in the summer of 1900 combined overland line surveys with subsequent river travel; it is unclear how some of them obtained their canoes en route. The 16-foot or 17-foot Peterborough and Peterborough-style cedar or basswood strip canoes soon tended to predominate. Reports indicate that they went almost everywhere that the paddlers went.

During the inter-war years and in the fifties, the classic canvas-covered cedar canoe came to dominate. Canvas-covered canoes built by Chestnut in New Brunswick and by Old Town and other builders in Maine had appeared even earlier and had long been used in the Atlantic region, and along with the Peterborough-Trent Valley canvas-covered models, they became the almost universal form of canoe travel on northern rivers.

In the late fifties, the unaesthetic but strong and resilient Grumman or other aluminum craft came to dominate the market for the far north. Eric Morse and his colleagues were firmly committed to this innovation. The Grumman certainly made shooting whitewater rapids less problematic; the previous possibilities of serious mishaps and the destruction of the boat were converted into relatively minor mishaps. Persuaded by Eric Morse, the HBC developed its Grumman U-Paddle[9] rental service, disbanded in 1984, between significant river and coastal posts. Some of the wood-canvas canoes, however, did continue to be used; they remained the boat-of-choice for most of the youth camp trips in the James Bay watershed at least until the mid-1970s.

By the early 1970s, the fibreglass canoe and finally the relatively indestructible ABS "rubber canoe" had made their appearances on far northern rivers. After 1974 the latter, made in many varieties and by various manufacturers (all basically American) would come to dominate the northern waterways.

The use of other craft needs to be mentioned. Between the wars, little outboard "kickers" appeared on V-stern wood-canvas and cedar strip canoes and were used to deal with short upstream hauls without great portages. They were, however, quite inappropriate for long-distance travel, being limited by the number of cans of gasoline that could be transported. A few travelled by kayak and umiak which are generically "canoes" and go back to our aboriginal heritage, in this case to the Inuit. The kayak was rarely used for distance travel before 1974, although Erwin Streisinger in the mid-sixties preferred it as a craft for river travel. It was also used, along with the umiak,[10] on the Arctic and northern British Columbia coasts. The tremendous surge in northern coastal kayaking came only after 1974 and included travel along the coasts of Greenland, the Queen Charlotte Islands and, to a lesser extent, the rivers of the High Arctic.

THE MOTIVATION

Unless one were paid handsomely to do the task, as only a few were, there were dozens of reasons not to make the effort. Hard physical work, deprivation, wet and cold weather, mosquitoes and black flies, serious and potentially dangerous isolation are only a few of the negatives. Yet, a majority of canoeists paid handsomely for the precious privilege of being able to attempt the journey and endure its hardships. For most of the people described in this account, covering roughly the hundred years between the mid-1870s and the mid-1970s, canoeing the great rivers flowing northward toward the Arctic seas has been a passion.

Experiencing heritage, broadly and metaphysically defined, was certainly important. The heritage link, not necessarily associated with the same rivers as the myths and history of fur-trade transportation, remains important. The late Harold Innis, Canada's greatest economic historian, claimed, with less than total accuracy, that Canada had been made by the fur trade and by the combined voyageur maps of the two competing fur empires.[11] By this assertion, canoes, canoeists, northern rivers and beavers put Canada together. Although many of today's recreational canoeists reside in Toronto and southwestern Ontario,[12] the heritage of the fur trade was almost non-existent in the area. Both there and in the Atlantic provinces the fur-trade routes bypassed them by going west and north from Montreal and through the Ohio valley to Minnesota and westward to the upper reaches of the Missouri. Nevertheless, northern river travel is a vital part of Canada's living heritage.

Canoeists who feel this heritage are still emotionally affected by the voyageur art of Frances Hopkins.[13] It is more than coincidental that pride of place in Canada's National Archives has been given to her paintings. Though limited to canoeing scenes south of the north-flowing rivers in this study, they have influenced the many Americans and other non-Canadians who have canoed in the North.

Important as experiencing living heritage has been for northern canoeists, there were many other reasons for them to dip their paddles in these waters. The canoe trip by itself could become a passion whether that travel was in the far North or on lakes and rivers close to home. The extended canoe trip on northern rivers was the highlight, the temporary climactic fulfilment of that core passion for the voyage by canoe.

For some the trip was undertaken to experience the landscape. These river travellers picked their desired northern route in order to see the floral beauty, the caribou, the birds of prey of the Barrens, the canyons and the mountain sheep of the western Mackenzie rivers or the shallow shores of central Canada's salt water sea which they called the Bay. For this reason they learned to canoe better in order to pass through the region and reach their destination. A few only learned to paddle on the trip itself; the canoe was primarily the means to another end.

Canoeing northern rivers involved a search for remoteness, for the essence of continuing wilderness, for the landscape of the imagination, for the platonic view of nature which exists only in the mind or in the heart. For most sensitive people engaged in that quest, there remained the light presence of native people living in harmony with that landscape and its waterways. Most non-aboriginal paddlers remained visitors. The northern rivers lie mainly outside of our national or provincial parks, or inside our recently created wilderness or river parks and are the lands and waters of old North America. Here American citizens paddle and dream in full franchise with their Canadian cousins. In the late Victorian and Edwardian years, David Hanbury and the other British northern travellers were "exploring" the remote reaches of the British Empire, following the river flow as had Franklin, Back and Simpson. Perhaps the next trip would be to the Northwest Frontier of India or to deepest Africa. More recently, for European immigrants or even for visitors from eastern and central Europe, travel on remote northern rivers takes them wistfully and atavistically back to the commonality of our diverse tribal pasts.

For Geological Surveyors, Mounties and magistrates, the canoe trip was part of the job. For those of the GSC, the trips had scientific and research implications and yet there is evidence that for many the trip was part of the pleasure of the job. Many held their positions partly so that they could experience the adventure of travel by canoe, snowshoes, dogsled and horseback. During the three summers of 1972-74 Priidu Juurand and most of the dozens of young men and women who conducted the Wild River Survey did so with zeal and passion for the adventure and not just for the employment.

Some of the early adventurers like Hanbury intended to justify the trip by writing and selling books to a broad market thereafter. Later, this could hardly be more than a byproduct for all but a few, even though the books, some of very high quality, continue to be written.[14]

For some, the long northern river voyage is part of a quest pattern, for some even a vision quest, a journey into the unknown, a challenge, an exploration, a

Early morning mist on a northern river. [Seth Gibson]

task, and then the return. The recreational traveller is not usually the first to descend the remote river, not even the first non-native. More often she or he has been part of a group, the tenth or twentieth group down the river. Still it has a quest pattern. Ultimately, as several have written, the exploration moved from place, to group, to the discovery of the inner-self and the soul. Trip records are often written or presented by people who are reluctant to admit openly this deep reflection, and yet it is there, even if disguised. More recently several have put it to paper, none better than William James, Bob Henderson and James Raffan.[15]

For many, the far northern river trip involved the mastering of white-water and other canoeing and bush lore skills. In the late 1960s and the 1970s the development of very sophisticated white-water techniques became particularly important, even though the wise admitted that the cold and remote waters of the far North were not the venue to push these skills to the limits. Far better to portage the more severe rapids which might have been attempted in the warmer, southern reaches of Canada's canoe country, even though canoe travellers of the 1970s had much better canoeing abilities than those of the 1870s.

The desire to visit the remote communities of the Dene, Cree, Innu and Inuit, to partake briefly of their culture and perhaps to purchase samples of their arts and crafts, is an additional reason for undertaking a northern trip.

By contrast, some early voyages, such as those of F.C. Selous on the Macmillan-Pelly, were in the form of big game hunting expeditions, securing trophies for oneself or for some foreign institution. In more recent decades, such behaviour would seem offensive. It finds its more recent equivalent in those who talk of "triumphing over nature," of beating the waters of the Missinaibi, or "Huit contre le Broadback". Increasingly, however, tuning one-self and the group to the natural environment and absorbing concern for the ecosystem now seem more appropriate.

The wilderness canoe trip has been extolled and promoted for its character building, for its development of cooperative and group living skills, for its training for leadership, self-reliance, sense of self worth and comradeship, even for its therapy related to physical and mental health.[16] In this context the remote northern river trip simply did this more deeply, more eloquently. Certainly many of these goals have been important to the dozen or so youth camps which organized lengthy canoe trips on north-flowing rivers, some reaching into the far north.[17] Many of these goals were also important to canoeists like Pierre Trudeau.[18]

Most northern canoeists were not antiquarians or primitivists. They did not eschew small scale technological achievements. Wistfully, most adopted the new canoe materials, reserving the cedar strip and the wood-canvas canoe for gentler or more ceremonial occasions. They wanted the latest maps; the first recreationalists frequently had hardly any reliable maps at all. The more recent canoeists used sophisticated transport for access and egress. They welcomed better food packaging, better and lighter tents, more safety equipment, improved medical kits and toward the end of the period a few took Emergency Locating Devices and "high tech" two-way radios.

Throughout the hundred-odd years under study, the northern canoe trip seemed to fulfil a need. For many, it seemed to feed what Bill Mason called a heartwarming, sensual and spiritual addiction.[19] This was an addiction which could be satisfied in one's later years, imperfectly and vicariously by gentler rivers or symposia participation, or in an armchair with memory, books, maps, slides and friends.[20]

The experiences gained on the canoe trip can be on many different levels, from the purely physical to the spiritual exploration of self which is part of the solo experience. It can be an exercise in group dynamics, from the sociability of the campfire to the tensions occasioned by living and striving in too close proximity with the group. Sometimes it is the re-creation of an historic trip, with the book or journals of an earlier journey read on the trip for comparison and identification of the landmarks described. For example, Jim McNamara and his wife, of Fairbanks, Alaska, in 1992, on an 80-day canoe trip in the Barrens, canoeing a circular route of 1000 miles without a food-drop or an airplane pick-up and paddling upstream to their starting point, re-created the experience of the early surveyors.[21]

On the northern wilderness trip, difficulties are over-shadowed by the pleasures and satisfactions. Our atavistic nature revels in being temporarily nomadic and once again part of a "hunter-gatherer" society, even if the hunt is only for fire-wood and the gathering, berries. The loaded canoe is a wonderfully silent vehicle of self-sufficiency, the basic needs of food and shelter contained in the packs, the paddle for locomotion. The North, intensifying ones feelings by the isolation, the clarity of the air, the connection with the land, the call on inner resources, the fragility and preciousness of life itself, once experienced, demands to be experienced again. One of Canada's great surveyors, Guy Blanchet, writing in his journal for his bride and looking forward to being at home with her, commented on how strange it was to think that this would be his last trip in the North.[22] That was in 1928 and Blanchet was still returning to the North twenty years later. The North would not let him go.

Rivers are the arteries of a nation and a river journey is a metaphor for life itself. From the gestation of planning and preparation, the labour of arriving at the starting point, learning the rhythm of motion, meeting the challenges along the way, to the finality of arriving at the end of the river – it is a vision of life. We may have only one journey through life, but there are scores of wonderful northern rivers to enjoy on that journey.

ENDNOTES

1. Arthur J. Ray, *Indians in the Fur Trade: their role as hunters, trappers and middlemen in the lands southwest of Hudson Bay, 1660-1870* (Toronto, 1974); Elaine Mitchell, *Fort Timiskaming and the Fur Trade* (Toronto, 1977); Daniel Francis and Toby Morantz, *Partners in Furs: a history of the fur trade in Eastern James Bay, 1600-1870* (Kingston and Montreal, 1983).

2. Note the Quebec James Bay films produced for the National Film Board by Boyce Richardson, especially his *Cree Hunters of Mistassini* (1974).

3. From George T. Marsh, "The Old Canoe", in *Scribner's Magazine*, v. 44 (October 1908), p. 447, and reprinted in the Frontispiece of the first of his eleven novels, *Toilers of the Trail*, (Philadelphia, 1921).

4. Sylvanna Grimm, "Recreational Specialization among River Users: the case of Nahanni National Park Reserve" (unpublished master's thesis, U. of Waterloo, 1987). She also found that 69% were Canadian (26% from Ontario) and 21% American. In total (619 people) 77% were canoeists, 3% Kayakers and 11% rafters. Just over three-quarters of the participants were male (pp. 63, 70 and 74).

5. Morris Zaslow, *Reading the Rocks: the story of the Geological Survey of Canada, 1842-1972* (Ottawa, 1975).

6. *Report of the Survey and Exploration of Northern Ontario, 1900* (Toronto, 1901).

7. The mimeographed Wild River Survey Reports were available at Canada Parks Service and the Canadian Heritage River System Offices in Ottawa.

8. Kenneth G. Roberts and Philip Shackleton, *The Canoe: A history of the Craft from Panama to the Arctic* (Toronto, 1983).

9. Eric Morse, *Freshwater Saga: Memoirs of a Lifetime of Wilderness Canoeing in Canada* (Toronto, 1987).

10. George Dyson, *Baidarka* (Edmonds, 1986).

11. Harold Adams Innis, *The Fur Trade in Canada* [1930] (Toronto, 1962). For criticism of the claimed geographic relationship between the fur trade and the map of modern Canada, see W. J. Eccles, "A Belated Review of Harold Adams Innis's *The Fur Trade in Canada*," in his *Essays on New France* (Toronto, 1987).

12. C.E.S. Franks, "White Water Canoeing as an aspect of Canadian Socio-Economic History" and "The Revival", in his *The Canoe and White Water* (Toronto, 1977), pp. 53-68.

13. Janet E. Clark and Robert Stacey, *Frances Anne Hopkins, 1838-1919: Canadian Scenery – Le Paysage Canadien* Thunder Bay Art Gallery, (Thunder Bay, 1990); Don Burry, *The Canoe in Art*, unpublished Ph.D thesis, U. of Alberta, Edmonton, 1993.

14. Bibliography of this volume, noting works by Peter Browning, Davidson and Rugge, G.H. Evans, Clayton Klein, Eric Morse, Judith Niemi, David Pelly, Robert Perkins, and James Raffan; also Bruce Hodgins and Margaret Hobbs, eds. *Nastawgan* (Toronto, 1985) contains information on the canoeing voyages of the following, already mentioned or alluded to in this Introduction: Thompson, the Tyrrells, Whitney, Russell, Pike, Munn, Hanbury, Pelletier, Douglas, Mina Hubbard and George Marsh.

15. William C. James, "The Quest Pattern and the Canoe Trip," in *Nastawgan*, pp. 9-23, referred to above, the original version called "The Canoe Trip as Religious Quest", in *Studies in Religion/Sciences religieuses*, 10/2 (Spring 1981), pp. 151-66; Bob Henderson, "Reflections of a Bannock Baker", in James Raffan and Bert Horwood, eds., *Canexus: the Canoe in Canadian Culture* (Toronto, 1988), pp. 83-92; and James Raffan, "Probing Canoe trips for Recreational Meaning", in *ibid.*, pp. 171-186 and *Summer North of Sixty: By Paddle and Portage Across the Barren Lands* (Toronto, 1990).

16. Leslie Kroening, "Motivations of Wilderness Canoeists" (unpublished thesis for a master's degree, U. of Alberta, 1979) noted all of these motivations and identified the single most important one as

"The desire to experience the out-of-doors intensely". She found wilderness canoe trippers to be a relatively homogeneous group, individualistic and unorganized, and a relatively small group of people in comparison to other types of recreationalists.

17. Bruce W. Hodgins and Seana Irvine, "Temagami Youth Camping, 1903-1973" in Hodgins and Bernadine Dodge, eds., *Using Wilderness: Essays on the Evolution of Youth Camping in Ontario* (Peterborough, 1992), pp. 143-56; Ruth Goldman, "Canadian Outward Bound Wilderness School and the 'Women of Courage' Program", in *ibid.*, pp. 61-68; Brian Back, *The Keewaydin Way, A Portrait, 1893-1983* (Temagami, 1983); Bert Horwood, "Doors to the Primitive", in *Canexus*, pp. 123-34; Jamie Benidickson, in "Paddling for pleasure: recreational canoeing as a Canadian way of life" in John S. Marsh and Geoffrey Wall, eds., *Recreational Land Use: Perspectives on its evolution in Canada* (Toronto, 1982), pp. 323-40, and many of his other essays and his forthcoming volume on the history of recreational canoeing in Canada.

18. P.E. Trudeau, "Exhaustion and Fulfillment: the Ascetic in a Canoe", in Borden Spears, ed., *Wilderness Canada* (Toronto, 1970) p. 4, (article also published, *en français* in 1944).

19. Bill Mason, *Path of the Paddle* (Toronto, 1980), p. 4.

20. The annual January Canoeing Symposium in Toronto organized by George Luste for the Wilderness Canoe Association, symposia without which this volume probably would not have been possible. George Luste's opening remarks for January 1993, an apologia on canoeing Northern rivers and the symposia, are printed in the WCA's *Nastawgan*, 20, 1 (Spring 1993). Also, on the whys and wherefores, note in the same issue, Willem Lange, "Romancing the Tree", the river between the Coppermine and the Hood, probably first tripped in 1991.

21. Personal communication from McNamara and a reference in the "Take Out" column of *Canoe*, May 1992.

22. Blanchet's survey journals are held by the Archives of British Columbia in Victoria.

CHAPTER ONE

JAMES BAY AND BEYOND:
THE ONTARIO CRADLE
OF THE FUR TRADE

MOOSE
MISSINAIBI–MATTAGAMI–ABITIBI

Through the James Bay Lowlands three great rivers flow north in Ontario, join in their last 80 kilometres to form the broad Moose River and empty into James Bay. All three rivers rise high in the Canadian Shield, tumble through turbulent rapids, canyons and falls, pass through the Great Clay Belt, to flow finally over low limestone ridges as they join their waters in the mighty Moose. All three rivers have been significant transportation routes to and from the vital Hudson's Bay Company port at Moose Factory on the island in the middle of the Moose river estuary.

Long before the Europeans, the Cree reached the "North Sea" from the Ottawa River, up to Lake Timiskaming and down the Abitibi; or from Lake Huron, up the Spanish or the Montreal River and down the Mattagami. The Missinaibi and the Abitibi were particularly heavily travelled, the Missinaibi rising in the height of land close to the Michipicoten which flows into Lake Superior, and the Abitibi with overland connections to Lake Timiskaming and the Ottawa River. The Mattagami, with its tributaries the Ground-hog-Ivanhoe and the Kapuskasing became much more accessible with the advent of the railways, especially the east-west National Transcontinental in 1912-14, which became part of Canadian National in 1919.

In 1932 the Temiskaming and Northern Ontario Railway, now known as the Ontario Northland Railway, began service to Moosonee, the site of the Revillon Frères post on the mainland, opposite Moose Factory. The opening of the TNOR changed the entire pattern of canoe travel to the Bay. Whereas canoe trips chronicled here between 1883 and 1931 began at small railway stops on the Canadian Pacific, or later at stops on the TNOR or the Northern Transcontinental and returned paddling and poling upstream, trips after 1932 on any of the James Bay rivers returned south on the railway from Moosonee.

MISSINAIBI

The Missinaibi, the most westerly of the three tributaries of the Moose, rises in Lake Missinaibi and flows north and northeast, joining the Mattagami to continue as the Moose River. The Missinaibi has two main tributaries, the Pivibiska and the Mattawitchewan.

1663 *The Hudson's Bay Company established Fort Moose, later named Moose Factory, near the mouth of the Moose River. Cree canoeists engaging in the fur trade travelled up and down the Missinaibi.*

1730 *Moose Fort, or Factory, was re-established by the HBC as its main port on James Bay. Increased Cree travel on the rivers followed.*

1775-76 *In the face of growing competition from the Montreal traders, the HBC sent Edward Jarvis from*

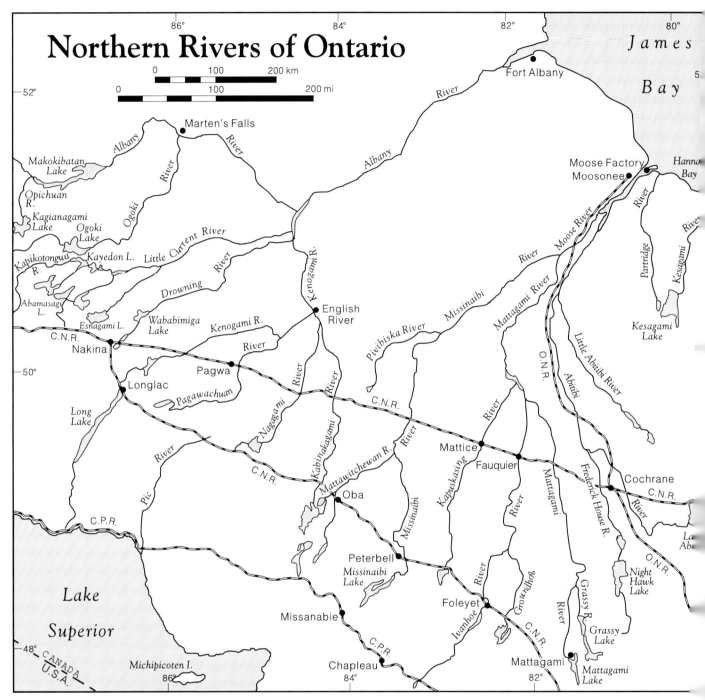

Northern Rivers of Ontario

Fort Albany to Moose Fort to reconnoitre up the Moose and Missinaibi, over the divide and down the Michipicoten to Lake Superior, visiting the Canadians there and returning north. [Mitchell, p. 23]

1777-78 To meet increased Montreal competition, the HBC sent John Thomas up the Missinaibi, past the newly established small post of Wapiscogami, later called Brunswick House, on the middle stretch of the river, and down the Michipicoten, returning to the source of the Missinaibi where he established a small trading post. [Ibid. p. 24]

1780 *Philip Turnor, HBC, from Moose Factory, travelled up the Moose and Missinaibi rivers and down the Michipicoten River to Lake Superior. He travelled along Superior to the Magpie River, canoed up that river to Wawa and Hawk lakes, then up the Hawk and Michipicoten rivers to Missinaibi Lake.*

1788 *HBC personnel, travelling upstream to the upper Missinaibi, established Micabanish, later renamed New Brunswick House in 1791 when the other posts were abandoned. [Ibid., p. 24]*

1791-1821 *Intense conflict between the two fur empires continued on upper Missinaibi waters until the merger in 1821. [Ibid., pp. 64-130]*

1822-83 *There was continuous heavy use of the Missinaibi for fur-trade travel to and from Moose Factory. [Ibid. and Baldwin]*

1880 Samuel W. Very, G.W. Hill, Nautical Almanac Office, Washington, and C.H. Rockwell, Americans on a private recreational trip on which they made magnetic, astronomic and meteorological measurements, travelled from Detroit by train to Sault Ste. Marie and steamer to Michipicoten. With six Métis, including John Boucher, Daniel Mackaye, Neil and Antoine, and using one birchbark canoe and one large HBC canoe, they went up the Michipicoten, crossed the height of land and after hiring Mungoose, a local Ojibwa, as guide, they went down the Missinaibi to Moose Factory. They returned upstream and down to Michipicoten in time to catch the steamer to Sault St. Marie. ["A canoe trip in the Hudson Bay district" – provenance unknown]

1881 John Galbraith, professor from the University of Toronto, bought a 17-foot canoe in Red Rock, took the steamer to Michipicoten, hired a Métis guide and an Indian and went up to the height of land at Missanabie. They canoed down the Missinaibi-Moose rivers to Moose Factory. The men were sent back and Galbraith hired two others to continue with him around the end of James Bay to Rupert House. Again the men were sent back, and three men, one of them named Namagoous, were hired at Rupert House for the trip up the Rupert River to Lake Mistassini. They

went upstream to Lake Nemiscau and from there up the Marten River, rejoining the Rupert before they reached Lake Mistassini. When they were at Nemiscau they caught up with the Mistassini Brigade, five large and five small canoes, thirty men and twenty women, and camped with them for a night. At Mistassini post, Namagoous and the other two Indians were sent back and Galbraith engaged two new men to take him to Lake St. John down the Chamouchouane River. Once again, at Lake St. John, he hired two new guides and proceeded up the Belle River, through lakes Kenogami and Kenogamichiche and down the Saguenay to Tadoussac. Altogether it was a journey of 1200 miles completed in seventy-seven days. [*Bulletin of the Society of Geography of Quebec*, 1885, pp. 1-12]

1883 Edward Barnes Borron – see Kenogami-Albany

1886 Edward Barnes Borron, Stipendiary Magistrate, made a circular tour of duty from Missanabie Station on the CP railway. He canoed through a series of lakes to Lake Kabinakagami, descended the Kabinakagami River, crossed over to the Pivibiska River and descended it to the Missinaibi. He then returned up the Missinaibi and Mattawitchewan and down the Oba River to Missanabie. [Zaslow, "Edward Barnes Borron", pp. 297-311 in Armstrong, F.H., ed.]

1887 A.P. Low, for the Geological Survey, with a survey crew, travelled down the Missinaibi to Moose Factory and surveyed the islands of James Bay, returning up the Moose-Missinaibi. [Cooke and Holland, p. 258]

1888 A.P. Low with a Geological Survey crew returned to James Bay by the Missinaibi on their way to an extensive expedition in Ungava. [Cooke and Holland, p. 250]

1892 Rev. J.A. Newnham, Anglican missionary, with his bride from Montreal, canoed down the Missinaibi from the railway at Missanabie in a new Peterborough canoe which Rev. Newnham had brought for their use from Moose Factory. The canoe took a lot of damage on the trip, but Mrs. Newnham found the rapids exciting. Travelling in convoy with the Newnhams were Mr. Sanders, the missionary at Brunswick House and Mary Gunter who was going to Moose Factory. [Shearwood, Chap. 6]

1892-1904 The Newnham family made an annual trip up and down the Missinaibi River, with different companions and for varying reasons. Rev. Newnham went out from Moose Factory to Winnipeg in 1893 to be consecrated bishop. Mrs. Newnham travelled up-river with their 15-month-old baby one year, and returned the following year with that child and twin babies. On this occasion she was accompanied by her sister-in-law, Sophy Newnham who wrote a little book about the experience, *The Babes in the Wood*. In 1904 the Newnhams made their last trip up the Missinaibi when he was transferred to Saskatchewan. [*Ibid.*]

1896 Ragge and Thompson – see Abitibi

1897 W.A. Charlton, MPP and a Mr. Worthington, with a crew of ten, using a 30-foot canoe, paddled the Missinaibi River from the town of Missanabie to Long Rapids, the last falls on the river. [Pain, p. 86]

1900 Alex Niven, leader, J.L. Bremner and J.M. Milne, foresters, and A.C. Burrows and E.L. Fraleck, geologists, Northern Ontario Land Survey Party #2, after examining and paddling the Kapuskasing, ascended the upper Missinaibi to Missanabie on the CP railway. [*NOLS*, pp. 52-82]

1900 Alex Baird, Northern Ontario Land Survey Party #4, starting at Missanabie on the CP railway went up the Magpie River to Lake Esnagi, crossed to Lake Kabinakagami and went down the Kabinakagami River almost to the Kenogami River. They then crossed east to the upper Missinaibi River to New Brunswick post and returned up the Missinaibi to Missanabie on the CP railway. For most of the trip the party included G.M. Stewart, Laidlaw, Miles, John McConachie and an Indian guide. [NOLS, pp. 114-38]

1901 Rev. Joseph Lofthouse, with a young clergyman, canoed down the Missinaibi to Moose Factory

from the CP railway line on his way to Rupert House. [Lofthouse, p. 182]

1902 Miss Caine, on her way to Rupert House to marry a clergyman, made the trip down the Missinaibi with a canoe brigade to Moose Factory. [Shearwood, p.198]

1902 Bishop Joseph Lofthouse of Keewatin went up the Missinaibi to the CP railway. [Lofthouse, p. 183]

1902 Owen O'Sullivan, Geological Survey, came down the coast from Churchill to Moose Factory and canoed up the Missinaibi River to Missanabie on the CP railway.

1902 Fifty Indians in twenty canoes were freighting down the Missinaibi River for Revillon Frères. Altogether the company had ninety Indians engaged in freighting on the river. [HBC Archives, A.12/FT.217/2]

1903 Robert Bell with a party from the Geological Survey went down the Missinaibi River to view the lignite deposits on the banks of the Moose River. One canoe and its load of supplies were lost in the river. [HBC Archives]

1903 Two French traders for Revillon Frères went down the Missinaibi-Moose rivers. [HBC Archives]

1903 Large numbers of Indians were involved freighting on the Missinaibi River for the HBC, for the prospecting and survey parties sent out by the Governments of Canada and Ontario and for the new railways. Revillon Frères was having trouble getting crews. [HBC Archives]

1904 Owen O'Sullivan and William Spreadborough, GSC, with two canoes, started at Missanabie and canoed down the Missinaibi River to Moose Factory. They made a survey of the coast of James Bay to Cape Henrietta Marie, on foot and using their canoes whenever possible. They returned down the coast and up the Missinaibi River. [GSC Report 1904; *Canadian Field-Naturalist*, March 1933, p. 40]]

1906 Stephen and Florence Tasker, from Philadelphia, on a private recreational trip, guided by George

Elson and Job Chapies, canoed down the Missinaibi from Missanabie to Moose Factory on the first leg of their Ungava journey. [Hoyle in Hodgins and Hobbs, ed., p.128]

1907   William Tees Curran and Horace P. Adams on a private Canadian prospecting expedition came down the Missinaibi to Moose Factory with a crew. At Moose Factory they split into two groups. One group spent two weeks exploring up the Eastmain River and returned up the Missinaibi. The other group, which included Curran, sailed north to the Nastapoka Islands and visited the mouth of the Nastapoka River, returning on the *Erik* to St. John's and Montreal. [Curran, p. 4]

1908   A.R. Horr and Adrian G. Newcomb, Cleveland, Ohio, with Indian guides Presque Petrant and William Peshabo from Bear Island, Temagami, in one large wooden canoe, left from Missanabie Station and canoed down the Missinaibi and Moose rivers to Hudson Bay. They returned up the Moose, Abitibi and Frederick House rivers, crossed over the divide to the Matachewan and Montreal rivers and continued south to Temagami. [Hodgins in Hodgins and Hobbs, ed., p. 194]

1908   Alanson Skinner, anthropologist, with two Indian guides, canoed down the Missinaibi from Missanabie to James Bay. [Skinner, Intro. p. 7]

1908   Walter Edmund Clyde Todd, M.A. Carriker Jr., with guides Will Bain and Jerry Solomon, using a 19-foot Peterborough freight canoe, canoed down the Missinaibi from Missanabie to Moose Factory and back, making an avifaunal survey for the 4th Carnegie Museum Expedition. [Todd, p. 15]

1911   W.T. Curran and H.A. Calkins, Canadian prospectors, went down the Missinaibi and up again during a six week trip. [Curran, p. 25]

1911   Camp Keewaydin: Bill Hanshaw and Maynard Ross led a boys' group down the Missinaibi River, returning up the Mattagami, over to the Nighthawk and Montreal rivers, descending them to Lake Temagami. [Back, B., p. 172]

1912   W. Tees Curran, H.A. Calkins, H.F. Strong with a crew of prospectors and Indian canoemen, in three canoes, paddled down the Missinaibi from Missanabie, on the CP railway, to Missinaibi Crossing on the Canadian Northern railway where they met the balance of the group with two shallow draft motor boats, a wagon for the portages, and the bulk of the supplies and fuel for an extensive mineral exploration of the eastern Hudson Bay coast. They returned up-river after freeze-up by sledge. [Curran, 1917]

1923   E.M. Kindle – see Abitibi

1926   John B. Semple, W.E.C. Todd, George M. Sutton and guide Paul Commanda, using a 22-foot Peterborough freight canoe fitted with an outboard motor, and with two Indians and two French-Canadians using a smaller canoe, went down the Missinaibi River from Mattice on the CN railway to Moose Factory. (The four unnamed guides returned up-river with the small canoe.) The group used canoe and motor to travel up the Hudson Bay coast to Richmond Gulf where the breaking of the main shaft of the motor forced them to travel farther north by steamer. A Revillon boat took them to Port Harrison where they changed to the *Albert Revillon*, continuing north and around the coast to Quebec. This was the 11th Carnegie Museum expedition for avifaunal research. [Todd, p. 35]

1945?   Richard and Lynn Harrington traced the historic fur-trade route from Lake Superior up the Michipicoten, across Pigeon portage to Manitowich Lake, two portages to Dog and Crooked lakes, Lake Missinaibi and down the Missinaibi River. [*Canadian Geographic*, August 1946 p. 73]

1948   Clayton Klein canoed the upper Missinaibi to the CN railway at Peterbell. [Personal communication]

1960   John K. Rugge, his son John, Lee Hunt and Harold Hand, put in at Mattice and canoed the lower Missinaibi River to Moose River Junction. [Personal communication – Jim Davidson]

1964-69 Russell Miller and friends canoed on the Missinaibi, moose hunting. In 1964 they put in at Peterbell and took out at Mattice. In the other years they put-in and took-out at Mattice, going up-river and returning downstream. [Personal communication]

1968 Camp Wanapitei: Steve Peck and Murray Rowsell led a boys' group from Peterbell down the Missinaibi to below Mattice. [Wanapitei trip report]

1968 Wendell Alexander, Mark Andcent, Philip Betcherman, Alison and Ralph Carter canoed down the upper Missinaibi River from Missanabie railway station to the station at Mattice. [Morse files, p. 13]

1968 A small group of canoeists came down the Missinaibi and Moose rivers. [*Appalachia*, December 1968, p.285]

1969 Herb Pohl canoed the Missinaibi River alone. [Personal communication]

1969 Fred Gaskin, Lyle Malcolm, Bill Law and Dave Weston canoed down the Missinaibi River from Mattice to Moosonee. [Personal communication – Gaskin]

1970 Camp Wanapitei: Ted Moores led a boys' group from Peterbell down the Missinaibi to Moose Factory. [Wanapitei trip report]

1970 John Moore, Jean Marc Lapointe, with a group of voyageurs from a boys camp, canoed from Lake Superior, up the Magpie River and down the Missinaibi to Moosonee. [Morse files, p. 13]

1970 Fred Gaskin, Rod Copeland, Sylvia Fairbank and Jamie Walmsley canoed down the Missinaibi River from Mattice to James Bay. [Personal communication – Gaskin]

1970 John Moore and Sandy ? canoed from Mattice down the Missinaibi River to Moosonee. [Morse files, p. 13]

1970 Jim Matthews, Ash Winter, Nick Best, Peter Sutherland, Bill Pearce and Charles Fairfax put in their canoes at Missanabie and canoed down the Missinaibi River to Mattice. [Personal communication – Matthews]

1971 Camp Onondaga: Andy Gallagher, Bob Howard, Wren Hughes, Jim Kilgour, Larry and Randy Russe, David Sainsbury, Dave Tate, Tor Utne and Steve Vandewater canoed from Mattice down the Missinaibi-Moose rivers to Moosonee. [Morse files, p. 18]

1971 Several other groups left Mattice five days ahead of the Camp Onondaga group to canoe the Missinaibi River. [Morse files, p. 18]

1971 The Bytown Bushwackers, Michael Berry, Keith Betteridge, John Cassells, Jon de Laurier, Ron Niblett, Ian Ritchie, Tom Skinner and Dick Walcott, canoed from Mattice down the Missinaibi-Moose rivers to Moosonee. [Morse files, p. 5]

1973 Camp Kandalore: John Fallis led a group of boys by canoe down the full length of the Missinaibi River to Moosonee.

1973 George and Linda Luste canoed from Dog Lake to Mattice. George continued solo down the Missinaibi to Moose River Crossing. [Personal communication]

1973 A Wild River Survey led by Vaha Guzelimian with Daryl Peck, Don Thomas and Robert Amos canoed from Peterbell to Moosonee down the Missinaibi-Moose rivers. [Parks Canada – files]

1974? Paul Richards, his wife Marilyn and their son Tim canoed down the Missinaibi-Moose rivers from Mattice to Moosonee in a fibreglass canoe. [*Outdoor Canada*, April 1975]

1974? Four university students canoed the Missinaibi River. [*Ibid.*]

1974 Camp Kandalore: John Fallis and Guy Delaire led a boys' group down the Missinaibi River to Moose Factory.

1974 A group from Michigan set out to canoe the Missinaibi, one 18-year old drowned in the river near Mattice. [Morse files, p. 17]

1979 *Toni and Ria Harting canoed the Missinaibi River. [Personal communication – Harting]*

Just below Hell's Gate on the Missinaibi, Toni and Ria Harting prepare to run the Long Rapids in 1979. [Toni Harting]

MATTAGAMI

The Mattagami, the central of the three great tributaries of the Moose, rises in Lake Mattagami and flows due north for half its length, veers west and then swings northeast, becoming the Moose River at its junction with the Missinaibi. The main tributaries of the Mattagami are the Kapuskasing and the Groundhog, which has its own tributary, the Ivanhoe.

1794 *John Mannall, for the HBC, ascended the Mattagami all the way to Kenogamissi Lake and established a trading post there to compete with the Canadians at Forts Timiskaming and Abitibi for trade with the Cree. The same year, Donald McKay for the Fort Timiskaming traders retaliated by crossing over from the upper Montreal River onto the headwaters of the Mattagami and establishing Matawagamingue Post on Lake Mattagami, just upstream from the HBC post. [Mitchell, p. 48]*

1795-1821 *There was intense rivalry for the Indian trade on the upper Mattagami until the merger of the two fur companies in 1821 after which the more northerly post was abandoned. [Ibid., pp. 48-130]*

1800 *Crossing over from the upper Montreal River, the North West Company traders from Fort Timiskaming established Flying Post on the upper Groundhog, a tributary west of the main river. [Ibid., p. 68]*

1822-83 *Trade travel on the Mattagami remained important.*

1875 Robert Bell, Geological Survey, canoed from Lake Huron up the Wanapitei River, crossed the height of land to the Mattagami and canoed down to Moose Factory. [Zaslow, p. 121, map p. 119]

1882 Edward Barnes Borron – see Albany River

1899 Bishop Newnham, returning from Toronto, took

the CP railway to Biscotasing where he met Rev. Sanders and they paddled together throughout the Mattagami district on lakes and rivers and canoed to Moose Factory. [Shearwood, p. 165; *NOLS*, p. 54]

1900 George Gray, J.L. Rowlett Parsons, G.E. Sylvester and DeMorest, for the Northern Ontario Land Survey, Party #3, surveyed from Metagama on the CP railway, up the Spanish River, over the height of land, down the Mattagami to Fort Mattagami (previously Matawagamingue). Returning upstream to the upper Grassy, they crossed the height of land and came down the Montreal and Lady Evelyn rivers, Lake Temagami and the Sturgeon River. [*NOLS*, pp. 83-113; Pain, p. 97]

1900 Alex Niven – see Missinaibi and Abitibi

1901 Charles Camsell, Philip Camsell and Louis Miron, surveying for the Algoma Central Railway from the railway at Biscotasing, made their way by canoe through a series of lakes and rivers over to the Groundhog River, descended it and canoed down the Mattagami River to Moose Factory. They continued along the shores of James Bay to the mouth of the Nottaway. At the end of the summer they returned up the Moose River in the company of Mackintosh Bell of the GSC, Bell going up the Mattagami and Kapuskasing rivers and Camsell up the Abitibi and Frederick House rivers back to Biscotasing. [Camsell, p. 139]

1906 Bishop Renison returned to Moose Factory down the Chapleau, Kapuskasing, Mattagami-Moose rivers. [Renison, p. 80]

1910 Robert J. Flaherty and an Englishman named Crundell, in a Chestnut canoe, went down the Groundhog and Mattagami rivers from the railway at Groundhog Crossing to Moose Factory. Flaherty continued up the coast of James and Hudson Bay in a York boat to explore for iron-ore deposits in the Nastapoka Islands for Sir William Mackenzie. His trip out was made in the winter. Robert Flaherty had travelled with his father, Robert H. Flaherty, with mining engineers and prospectors, through the hinterland of On-

tario and Quebec since he was a boy, making river trips to Hudson Bay. [Flaherty, Chap. 1]

1911 Robert J. Flaherty, exploring for minerals on behalf of Sir William Mackenzie, and with a strong personal interest in the Inuit people, canoed down the Mattagami-Moose rivers on his way to Ungava, bringing with him a motor which he fitted into the 36-foot boat, *Nastapoka* to explore the Belcher Islands. The *Nastapoka* foundered on a reef and Flaherty managed to reach Great Whale River. With Mavor, the HBC man from Great Whale River, he canoed down the Hudson Bay coast to the Fort George post, where he wintered. [*Geographical Review*, Vol. 5, #66, 1918, pp. 433-58]

1911 The Timmins-South Porcupine gold rush on the Mattagami River, and the arrival of the TNOR, made canoe access to the river much simpler.

1911 Camp Keewaydin – see Missinaibi

1911 Camp Keewaydin – see Abitibi.

1912 Walter E.C. Todd, Alfred E. Preble, Charles Barrett and Ojibwa guides Paul Commanda, Jacko Couchai and Andrew Tapp, with the 5th Carnegie Museum expedition, made an avifaunal survey starting from west of Cochrane at the National Transcontinental crossing of the Kapuskasing River and canoeing down the Kapuskasing and Mattagami rivers to Moose Factory. They spent time around the south and eastern shores of James Bay travelling as far north as Fort George in a York boat with local Indians as crew. A.E. Preble returned independently from Fort George via the islands in James Bay to Moose Factory and up the Mattagami River. On their return Todd and Barrett joined forces at Moose Factory with J.G. MacMillan, Canadian Government engineer, and his Indian guide, tracking their canoes up the Abitibi River and reaching Cochrane in November as the ice was forming and they were out of provisions. [Todd, pp. 17-20]

1912 Camp Keewaydin: Chess Kittredge led a boys' group canoeing from Temagami via the Grassy, Mattagami-Moose rivers to Moose Factory and returning up the Abitibi and Frederick House rivers to Temagami. [Back, B., p. 172]

1912 Camp Keewaydin: Rad Heermance and Jack Green led a boys' group from Temagami via the Grassy, Mattagami-Moose rivers to Moose Factory, returning up the Moose, Mattagami and Nighthawk rivers, over to the Montreal River to Temagami. [*Ibid.*]

1913 Camp Keewaydin: Brad Hall and Jack Green led a boys' group from Temagami via the Grassy, Mattagami-Moose rivers to Moose Factory, returning up the Abitibi and Frederick House rivers. [*Ibid.*]

1914 Camp Keewaydin: Jack Dixon and Jack Green led a boys' group from Temagami, down the Mattagami-Moose rivers to Moose Factory. They travelled by schooner to Charlton Island and returned up the Abitibi and Frederick House rivers. [*Ibid.*]

1914 Todd – see Rupert

1915 Camp Keewaydin: Chess Kittredge and Jack Green led a boys' group canoeing down the Kapuskasing, Mattagami-Moose rivers to Moose Factory. They travelled by schooner to Charlton Island and the Belcher Islands and returned from Moose Factory up the Abitibi and Frederick House rivers. [*Ibid.*]

1916 Robert J. Flaherty, his father, Robert H. Flaherty, Dr. E.S. Moore, geologist, and W.H. Howard, surveyor, canoed up the Moose-Mattagami and Groundhog rivers to the railway line, following R.J. Flaherty's winter of exploration in the Belcher Islands. R.H. Flaherty, Moore and Howard had joined R.J. Flaherty on the Belcher Islands, coming from Moose Factory by York boat, presumably having come down the Moose-Mattagami and Groundhog rivers earlier in the season. [Flaherty, p. 73]

1919 M.Y. Williams, on a geological trip, canoed down the Groundhog, Mattagami-Moose rivers, returning up the Abitibi and Frederick House rivers. [*Canadian Field-Naturalist*, October 1920, pp. 121-26]

1920 Camp Keewaydin: Ted Saunders and Jack Green led a boys' group canoeing down the Mattagami River to Moose Factory and returning up the Abitibi River to Island Falls on the TNOR. [Back, B., p. 172]

pre-1952 R.K. Gordon canoed on the Montreal, Matachewan and Mattagami rivers and lakes Temagami and Mattawabika. [*Beaver,* June 1953, *Queen's Quarterly*, Summer 1952 pp. 198-205]

1957 Fred Helleiner and George Toller canoed down the Ivanhoe and Groundhog rivers, putting in at Kormak on the highway, passing through Foleyet and taking out at Fauquier on Highway 11. [Personal communication – Helleiner]

1960 Austin Hoyt and Tracey Perry canoed down the Mattagami. [*Sports Illustrated*, 1963 p. 34]

1961 Camp Wanapitei: John Scott leading a boys' group, which included Ted Moores, canoed from Temagami to Gowganda and Grassy River to Timmins. Scott and Bruce Hodgins then led the trip down the Mattagami to Moose Factory. [Wanapitei trip report]

1961 Shan and Margie Walshe, on their honeymoon trip, canoed from Smooth Rock Falls, on the CN railway, down the Mattagami to Moosonee.

1963 Camp Wanapitei: Stuart Hunter led a boys' group from Temagami via Gowganda down the Grassy, Mattagami-Moose rivers to Moose Factory. [Wanapitei trip report]

1968 A group of canoeists returned from Moosonee on the railway after a trip down the Mattagami River. [*Appalachia*, December 1968, p. 286]

1973 Cliff Jacobson, Tom Helvie, Ken Saelens and Roger Grosslein canoed from near Foleyet down the Groundhog, Mattagami-Moose rivers to Moosonee. The river was in flood and the bugs were very bad. There were two other parties known to be on the river, one of them suffered a drowning and the other wrecked their canoes and walked out to the railroad through the bush. [Personal communication – Jacobson]

1974 Paul Michaelis and Jim Thompson canoed down

In a wet September camp in 1974, George Drought, his young son Richard, Bob Hill, Peter Puddicombe and Louis Jacques make supper beside the Mattagami. [Toni Harting]

the Groundhog River from Foleyet to Fauquier. [Personal communication – Michaelis]

1974 George Drought, his eight-year-old son Richard, Bob Hill, Louis Jacques, Peter Puddicombe and Toni Harting, with three canoes, two of them canvas-covered, canoed from Smooth Rock Falls, had a pre-arranged drive around the thirteen un-navigable miles of the hydro dam and continued down the Mattagami-Moose rivers to Moose River Crossing. Six miles beyond there, a badly damaged canoe ended the trip and they found their way through the bush to the railway line, returning by train. [*Outdoor Canada*, August 1975, p. 52]

ABITIBI

The Abitibi flows west from Lake Abitibi, turns sharply north and gradually swings northeastward, flowing into the Moose River midway between the junction of the Missinaibi and Mattagami and James Bay. From a canoeing standpoint, the Frederick House River, rising south of the Abitibi is the important tributary. Historically the Little Abitibi provided another route from Moose Factory to Lake Abitibi.

1686 *Pierre de Troyes, Pierre Le Moyne d'Iberville, his two brothers, St. Hélène and Maricourt with Père Antoine Silvy led a military expedition of 100 men*

following the Ottawa-Lac Temiscamingue-Lac Abitibi-Abitibi-Moose River route to the Bay where they sacked the HBC posts at Moose Factory, Fort Albany and Charles Fort, later named Rupert House. D'Iberville and four companions upset in one rapid and two of the group were drowned. Later this became one of the two main fur-trade routes from Timiskaming to the Bay, the other being up the Montreal River, across to Frederick House and down the Abitibi. [Kenyon, 1971; Gibbon, p. 37; Mitchell pp. 8-11, 22-23]

1709 *Seventy French-Canadians, with thirty Mohawk Indians from Quebec, descended the Abitibi-Moose rivers and failed in their attack on Fort Albany, which the English had retaken in 1693. [Francis and Morantz, p. 36]*

1713 *The Moose-Abitibi region returned to English control and trade on those rivers increased.*

1720 *The French, crossing over from Temiscamingue, established Fort Abitibi on Lake Abitibi but it had only an interrupted existence.*

1730 *Moose Fort was re-established and became the permanent post for trade travel, mainly by the Cree.*

1770? *Canadian fur traders out of Montreal, based at Fort Timiskaming, crossed over the divide using the upper Abitibi and nearby streams, re-established Fort*

Abitibi, gathering Cree trappers into commerce with them.

1774 *John Thomas, HBC, moved upstream from Moose Factory, with three Cree paddlers, to study the feasibility of establishing a post to compete with the "Pedlars". They ascended the North French, a lower tributary of the Moose, the Nettogami, crossing over to Lake Kesagami, and from there to the upper Turgeon waters, part of the Harricanaw system and via Rivière la Reine to Lake Abitibi. They stayed with their Canadian rivals at Fort Abitibi and returned north down the Abitibi River. [Mitchell, pp. 20-24]*

1785 *Philip Turnor, HBC, ascended the Abitibi to the Frederick House River, continuing up to Frederick House Lake where he established the post of the same name to compete with the Canadian traders at Forts Timiskaming and Abitibi. [Ibid., pp. 26-31]*

1794 *George Gladman, HBC, established Abitibi House on Lake Abitibi, continuing south to Timiskaming for a visit with the rival traders. [Ibid., pp. 42-48]*

1797 *John Thomas, HBC, travelled up the Abitibi and Frederick House rivers and met some of the Canadians in an attempt to divide the territory, the trade and the Indians. The attempt failed and rivalry grew. [Ibid., pp. 57-80]*

1804 *Three large canoes manned by Iroquois from Oka came down the upper Abitibi with supplies for the North West Company. [Francis and Morantz, p. 108]*

1804-12 *This was the peak period of bitter trade rivalry with heavy travel on the Abitibi and Frederick House rivers. [Mitchell, pp. 78-92]*

1812 *Richard Good, HBC, paddled up from Moose Factory to Lake Abitibi and arranged a partial territorial division with the Canadians whereby the former would abandon Lake Abitibi and the latter their post, Devils Island, on Frederick House Lake. [Ibid., p. 84]*

1813 *An Indian murdered the HBC trader and resident Cree at Frederick House and that post was never reopened, leaving Kenogamissi as the only inland HBC post on either the Abitibi or the Mattagami. [Mitchell, p. 84; Beaver, Spring 1973]*

1821-70 *The merger of the fur companies increased the commercial river travel down the Abitibi to Moose Factory.*

1840 *Rev. George Barnley made his way to Moose Factory by way of the Ottawa River, Lake Timiskaming and down the Abitibi River. [Boon, p. 75]*

1860 *Charles Drexler, an American naturalist sponsored by the Smithsonian Institution and with financial aid from Dr. Henry Bryant, with James Mackenzie and Indian guides, canoed from Lake Timiskaming to Lake Abitibi, down the Abitibi-Moose rivers to Moose Factory. They canoed along James Bay to Fort George, returning by the same route in the fall. [Todd, p. 9]*

1865 *Paul Fountain (16-years old) with two Cree, Monchuapiganon and Chuckochilgegan, and with Andrew Whitting and his Indian wife Chompel, canoed from the headwaters of the Ottawa River, near Lake Timiskaming to Moose Factory and back. [Fountain, p.2]*

1867 *Paul Fountain, Achil Guelle and Tom returned from their explorations on the Hayes and the Severn rivers up the Moose and Abitibi rivers to Lake Abitibi and the camp from which they had started. [Ibid., pp. 150-62]*

1872 Walter McOuat, Geological Survey, canoed from Lake Timiskaming via Lac des Quinze to Lake Abitibi. [Zaslow, p. 120]

1877 A.S. Cochrane, Geological Survey, canoed from Lake Abitibi down the Abitibi River to Moose Factory. [Zaslow, p. 119, map]

1882 Father Charles Alfred Marie Paradis and Father Nedelec, Oblates, arrived at Timiskaming by steamer from Mattawa, canoed to Lac des Quinzes, continued upstream to Lac Opesatica, crossed the divide to Fort Abitibi and returned the way they had come. [Hodgins, *Paradis*]

1882 Anglican Bishop John Horden returned to Moose Factory, canoeing up the Ottawa River to Timiskaming, over to Lake Abitibi and down the Abitibi River. [Boon, p. 135]

1884 Fathers Paradis, Proulx and Nedelec, Bishop

Father Charles Paradis and other Oblate priests made several missions from Quebec into Northern Ontario in the 1880s, travelling via the Abitibi River. [Public Archives of Ontario S13100]

Lorrain, Oblates with others canoed from Timiskaming to Lake Abitibi, down the Abitibi River to Moose Factory and continued up the coast to Fort Albany. They returned, canoeing up the Abitibi and over to Lake Timiskaming. The trip was done in a *canot de maître*, with a bowman and six paddlers. [Hodgins, *Paradis*]

1892 Rev. J.A. Newnham, Anglican, with two Indian canoemen from Moose Factory, came up the Moose and Abitibi rivers to Abitibi Lake and Lake Timiskaming, to the CP railway at Mattawa. [Shearwood, Chap. 5]

1892 Fathers F.X. Fafard and Joseph-Étienne Guinard and Brother Grégoire Lapointe, Oblates, in a large canoe with Indian canoemen, including one named Opwan, left from Ville-Marie on Lake Timiskaming, crossed to Lake Quinze and Lake Abitibi and canoed down the Abitibi-Moose rivers to Moose Factory. They sailed north to Fort Albany in an HBC boat, carrying their canoe with them. [Bouchard, *Mémoires*, pp. 37-41]

1894 Father Fafard went from Albany to Montreal, travelling by canoe up the Abitibi River. [Bouchard, *Mémoires*, p. 56]

1894 Bishop Newnham with an HBC doctor and a crew of Cree came up the Moose and Abitibi rivers to New Post on the Abitibi and returned downriver to Moose Factory. [Shearwood, p. 105]

1895 Father Guinard, with two Cree guides, went from Moosonee up the Moose-Abitibi rivers to New Post and returned downstream, continuing up the coast to Fort Albany. [Bouchard, *Mémoires*, p. 58-59]

1896 E.C. Ragge, John Thompson et al in two canoes, 15-foot and 16-foot, canoed from Lake Timiskaming, crossed through Quinze and Barrier lakes, Lonely River, Snake Creek to Lake Abitibi and down the Abitibi River to Moose Factory. They returned up the Missinaibi River to Missanabie Station. [Morse files, p. 15 from Ragge, "Log of trip by canoe to Moose Factory on James Bay in 1896"]

1900 T.B. Speight, Northern Ontario Land Survey Party #1, started at Mattawa and canoed via the Quinze River to Lake Abitibi, went down the Little Abitibi River, crossed to the Burnt Bush River, down to Hannah Bay, returning up the Abitibi River to Long Sault Rapids. [*NOLS*, 1901]

1900 Alex Niven, leading the Northern Ontario Land Survey Party #2, with at least six members in the group, canoed from Timiskaming via the Quinze to Lake Abitibi and part way down the Abitibi River. Using Jawbone Creek, he surveyed a 100 mile line at 49° 35' 30" N between the Abitibi and the Missinaibi rivers. He continued south up the Missinaibi to Missinaibi Lake and took the train to Toronto. The two geologists, A.C. Burrows and E.L. Fraleck, and one forester, James Milne, with an Indian canoeman, examined the land on either side of the river past Frederick House River, north to Driftwood Creek, where they crossed west and up the Mattagami and Ground-hog rivers to Missanabie on the CP railway. [*NOLS*, p. 52-82]

1901 Arthur Heming and his sister Kate made their way to the HBC post on Upper Lake Abitibi and travelled south to the head of Lake Timiskaming with the fur brigade, paddling their own birch-bark canoe. Heming was sponsored by *Scribner's Magazine* and Kate was the first white woman at Fort Abitibi. [*Beaver*, Summer 1967 p. 32]

1903 D'Aigneaux, his wife and child, Capt. William Berry, and a total of forty-five persons, after being shipwrecked in James Bay, off Fort George, on the *Eldorado* on a fur-trading expedition for Revillon Frères, were taken to Moose Factory by the HBC. There they embarked on a canoe trip up the Abitibi and overland to the upper Ottawa River where they took a steamboat to New Liskeard and the train to Montreal. [*Beaver*, Autumn 1968, pp. 27-31]

1905 E.A.E. Sullivan led a survey party including A.W.G. Wilson, geologist, from New Liskeard by the Quinze route to Lake Abitibi and down the Abitibi to James Bay. [Pain, p. 237]

1905 Indian Affairs, Treaty 9 – see Albany

1906 Henry Toke Munn, travelling with another prospector canoed up the Abitibi, presumably returning from a trip down the same river. [Munn, p. 140]

1907 Two University of Toronto students – see Ogoki-Albany

1908 A.R. Horr – see Missinaibi

1909 Charles Kenneth Leith, Arthur T. Leith and two others, on a private American geological expedition from the U. of Wisconsin, canoed down the Abitibi-Moose and explored the east coast of James and Hudson Bay as far north as Richmond Gulf. Two returned up-river late in the summer and the other two returned by snowshoe and dog team. [Cooke and Holland p. 321]

1910 Capt. Hans Andersen and the crew of the wrecked Danish sailing vessel *Sorine* canoed up the Moose-Abitibi to the railhead at Cochrane from Moose Factory. [Anderson, J., p. 14]

1910 Rev. Robert Renison canoed up the Abitibi from Moose Factory to Cochrane. [Renison, p. 278]

1911 George Marsh – see Albany

1911 Camp Keewaydin: Ed Ruge and George LeClaire led a boys' group canoeing down the Abitibi River to Moose Factory. They returned up the Mattagami River, crossed to Nighthawk Lake, over to the Montreal River and down to Temagami. [Back, B., p. 172]

1912 5th Carnegie Museum Expedition – see Mattagami

1912 Camp Keewaydin – see Mattagami

1912 Rev. Walton and his family, went from Fort George via Moose Factory up the Moose and Abitibi rivers en route to England. [Curran, p. 231]

1913 Camp Keewaydin – see Mattagami

1914 Camp Keewaydin – see Mattagami

1914 James Cosmo Dobree Melvill, as part of the Canadian Fisheries expedition, took the train to Cochrane and canoed down the Abitibi to Moose Factory. He investigated the eastern shore of James Bay north to Cape Jones. With A.R.M. Lower, he returned up the Moose-Mattagami to the railway. [Cooke and Holland, p. 339]

1915 Olaus J. Murie, on the 7th Carnegie Museum expedition, made a winter journey from Moose Factory along the James Bay coast to Rupert House, Eastmain and Great Whale River, continuing north to Richmond Gulf and as far as the

Nastapoka River. He examined the coastal islands as far north as Port Harrison, sailed to the Belcher Islands and continued further avifaunal surveys in James Bay until mid-October. He returned to Moose Factory and canoed up the Abitibi to the TNOR at Cochrane. [Todd, pp. 24-26]

1915 Camp Keewaydin – see Mattagami

1919 M.Y. Williams – see Mattagami

1920 Thierry Mallet of Revillon Frères, Miss A. Reynolds, schoolteacher for Moose Factory, and six canoemen, including Abraham Jeffries, Jimmy Mink and Jack Hunter, with three canoes, made the trip down the Abitibi-Moose rivers to Moose. [Revillon Archives, Mallet diary, 1920]

1923 E.M. Kindle, Geological Survey, went down the Abitibi and up the Missinaibi, ending his journey at Mattice on the CN railway. [*Geographical Review*, 1925, p. 226]

1923 John B. Semple, George M. Sutton, W.E.C. Todd, for the 10th Carnegie Expedition, with Indian guides Joe Stevens and Angus Beaucage, in a 19-foot Peterborough canoe, travelled down the Abitibi-Moose rivers from Cochrane to Moose Factory. They explored around Partridge Creek on Hannah Bay and returned up the Moose and Abitibi to Cochrane. [Todd, p. 34; Sutton, p. vi]

1928 Camp Keewaydin – see Nottaway

1930 W.E.C. Todd – see Hudson Bay Coast

1930 Camp Keewaydin – see Nottaway

1931 Camp Keewaydin – see Harricanaw.

1931 Camp Keewaydin – see Mattagami.

1931 Murray Watts – See Hudson Bay Coast

1932 Camp Keewaydin – see Albany. This was the last Keewaydin trip to paddle back upstream. The TNOR had reached Moosonee and most Bay trippers henceforth took the train south.

1933 Horace G. Richards, New Jersey State Museum, made a canoe trip down the Abitibi-Moose rivers from Matheson, to collect marine mollusks. [*Canadian Field-Naturalist*, April 1936, p. 58]

1945 Peter Randall and J.T.H. Johnson, M.D.D. with five other Army medical school students from Johns Hopkins School of Medicine, outfitted at Cochrane, took the train to Island Falls and canoed down the Abitibi to Moose Factory. They returned by train to Cochrane. [*Beaver*, June 1946, p. 34]

1954? Frank T. O'Connor led a group of Kirkland Lake Scouts down the Abitibi-Moose to Moosonee. [Personal communication – Helleiner]

1956 Fred Helleiner and Ken J. Macdonald put in at Gardiner's Ferry and canoed to Moosonee down the Abitibi-Moose rivers, doing the section from Otter Rapids to mile 115 on the ONR. [Personal communication – Helleiner]

1957 Austin Hoyt canoed down the Abitibi. [*Sports Illustrated*, August 26, 1963]

1963 George Luste made his first canoe trip, solo, down the Abitibi. [Personal communication]

1967 Camp Wanapitei: Ted Moores led a boys' group canoeing from Iroquois Falls down the Abitibi to Moose Factory. [Wanapitei trip report]

1968 Camp Kandalore: Craig MacDonald led a group of twenty-three boys on a canoe trip down the Abitibi River to Moose Factory. [Personal communication – MacDonald]

1968 Fred Sawyer, his wife Mary Jane, Henry Deleuran, Dick Shaffer, Grant Dowse and Russell Sawyer, with three canoes, drove from New York and Boston to Smooth Rock Falls and canoed down the Abitibi River to Moosonee, running or lining all the rapids. They returned on the train to Cochrane. [*Appalachia*, December 1968, p. 277]

1971 Ron Lucas and John Pisarki, brothers-in-law, canoed down the Abitibi-Moose rivers to Moosonee. [Morse files, p. 18]

1972 Bob Davis made a solo canoe trip from his home in Haliburton via Muskoka and Algonquin Park and then followed de Troye's historic route north through Timiskaming and down the Abitibi-Moose rivers to Moose Factory. [Personal communication]

1972 Nicolaas Verbeek and a friend canoed down the Abitibi River. [*Canadian Field-Naturalist*, 1974, p. 233]

PARTRIDGE

The Partridge rises near Kesagami Lake and flows north into James Bay close to the mouth of the Moose River.

1969? Terry Damm, for the Dept. of Lands and Forests, with Xavier Bird, Winisk-born Cree, "who had been my partner on several trips and projects," canoed from Kwataboahegan to the Partridge River and down to the coast. [*Canadian Geographic*, August 1971, p. 52]

KESAGAMI

The Kesagami River is about 100 kilometres long and entirely within Ontario. Its source is Kesagami Lake in the James Bay lowlands and it flows due north into Hannah Bay very close to the mouth of the Harricanaw. Since 1983, much of the Kesagami River is now a Provincial Wilderness Park and is accessible off the Portage Lake Road.

1903 J. Mackintosh Bell, for the Geological Survey, explored a good part of the Kesagami. [Reid and Grand]

1970? Terry Damm with Xavier Bird, exploring possible canoe routes for the Dept. of Lands and Forests, canoed from Kesagami Lake in a Chestnut canoe to Hannah Bay and around the Bay to Moosonee. [*Canadian Geographic*, August 1971, p. 52]

1984? Ron Reid and Janet Grand canoed the Kesagami River and wrote about it. [Reid and Grand, pp. 282-92]

1987 Camp Wanapitei: Jeff Edwards and Andrea Platt led the first of several trips by the camp down the Kesagami. [Wanapitei trip reports]

ALBANY RIVER

The traditional First Nations route from Lake Superior to James Bay was up through Lake Nipigon, then up a series of rivers and lakes into one of the tributaries or branches of the Albany and down the Albany to James Bay. Later the Albany River – or Kashechewan, to give it the Cree name – became one of the great fur-trade waterways. Fort Albany, established in 1682, near the mouth of the river was second only to Moose Factory as a transportation centre, serving all the fur-trade posts in northwestern Ontario.

The building of the three railways across northern Ontario, the Canadian Pacific in the mid-1880s, the Canadian Northern and the National Transcontinental just before World War I, was the harbinger of change in both the fur trade and its transportation system. World War I further hastened the change. While the Hudson's Bay Company was self-sufficient with regard to shipping, its rival, the French company of Revillon Frères, was left without ships to supply the Bay posts during the war. They developed a supply route from Montreal to Pagwa station by rail freight on the National Transcontinental, later part of the CN railway, with the year's supply of goods being sent down the Pagawachuan, Kenogami and Albany rivers in a flotilla of specially constructed barges which could negotiate the two smaller streams only at spring flood. After the two companies consolidated in the 1920s this route was used instead of the supply ships to the Bay. With the completion of the Temiskaming and Northern Ontario Railway to Moosonee in 1932, the railway took over the bulk of the shipping and the Albany River was again left primarily to canoeists and other sportsmen.

The main branch of the Albany River rises in Lake St. Joseph, flows northeast, then due east, turns southeast before making a final right-angle turn northeast to James Bay. Many rivers flow into it, but the two main canoeing rivers are the Ogoki and the Kenogami. The Kenogami itself has several tributaries, the Kabinakagami, the Nagagami and the sometimes navigable Drowning. Three water diversions in upstream sections have reduced the water flow in the Albany River: a dam at the beginning of the Albany River forces much of the water of Lake St. Joseph to flow west into Lac Seul; the Waboose Dam on the Ogoki River has created Ogoki Reservoir upstream from Ogoki Lake; a diversion on the upper Kenogami River sends the water of Long Lake south to Lake Superior.

Only a small percentage of canoe trips traversed the entire Albany route. The majority of trips began from the railway line at Pagwa or Calstock, or latterly from the

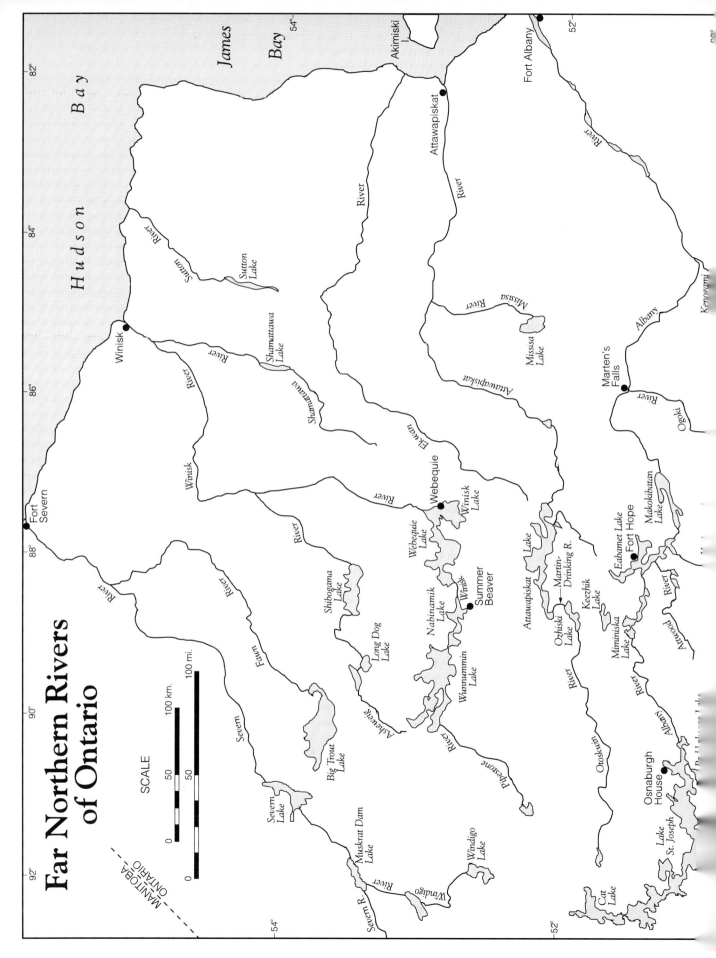

highway at Hearst, using the Pagawachuan, the Nagagami or the Kabinakagami to reach the Kenogami. A favourite starting place was at Limestone Rapids, just below Calstock, from which there are no significant rapids.

For many years until his death in 1982, Bill Anderson ran a trading post in Fort Albany, first for Revillon Frères, then for the Hudson's Bay Company and from 1951 as a free trader on Anderson Island. His guest ledger contains the signatures of the hundreds of travellers who entered his store, many of whom were canoeists. This ledger has been used as a source of information about canoe travel on the Albany. The names and dates of those who signify their canoe trip are given, as well as the names and dates of recognized canoeists. All others are combined as a total (see p. 52), and it should be noted that this total is necessarily low because not all trips registered at the Anderson store.

The trips are listed as Albany when the full river or a section of the river is canoed. Ogoki-Albany and Kenogami-Albany sections follow. Where the exact route is not known trips are listed under the Kenogami-Albany section, the more usual trip.

ALBANY

1661-62 *Radisson and Groseilliers were probably on parts of the Albany River, reaching it from Lake Superior. [North of 50° Atlas, Plate 31]*

1683 *Fort Albany was established by the Hudson's Bay Company near the mouth of the River. Increased travel on the river by the Cree followed. The post was in French hands briefly from 1686-89 and 1690-93.*

1780 *Philip Turnor, HBC, ascended the Albany River to the area of the Ogoki and others followed. [North of 50° Atlas, Plate 33]*

1852 *Bishop David Anderson, Anglican Bishop of Rupertsland, canoed from Winnipeg to Moose Factory down the Albany River. [Shearwood, p.4]*

1867 *Paul Fountain (see Severn River) completed his trip by canoeing down Perrera Creek to Lake St. Joseph, three days below Osnaburgh House and continued down the Albany River to James Bay. [Fountain, pp. 139-40]*

1871 Robert Bell, for the Geological Survey, reached Lake St. Joseph from Nipigon and canoed down the upper Albany to Ogoki, returning to Nipigon up the Ogoki River. [Zaslow, pp. 119-21]

1882 Edward Barnes Borron, Stipendiary Magistrate, Nipissing District, having started at Michipicoten, ascended the upper Missinaibi, travelled by various creeks, lakes and portages overland to the Groundhog River and canoed down the Groundhog and the Mattagami to Moose Factory. He canoed up the James Bay coast to Fort Albany, returned up the Albany River to Lake St. Joseph and crossed over to Lac Seul, 1600 miles by canoe. [Zaslow, "Edward Barnes Borron", pp. 297-311 in Armstrong, F.H., ed.]

1884 Anglican Bishop John Horden travelled up the Albany River to Marten's Falls and Osnaburgh House. [Boon p. 135; Peterson, p. 15]

1885 Thomas Fawcett, Dominion Land Surveyor, surveyed the upper Albany River. [*NOLS*, p. 176]

1886 Robert Bell, John MacMillan, Alfred P. Murray, GSC, with six voyageurs using four birchbark canoes, travelled from Sault Ste. Marie to Wabigoon on the CP railway. After a 9-mile carry to Big Sandy Lake, they crossed into Minnitaki Lake and worked their way northeast to Lake St. Joseph. They descended the Albany River to the Eabamet River which they ascended, crossing the height of land at Lake Miminiska. They could not find the Martin-Drinking River and descended the Boulder River to the Attawapiskat River below Lake Attawapiskat. MacMillan,

Robert Bell began with the Geological Survey as a schoolboy of fifteen and over the years his survey trips ranged across Northern Ontario, Quebec and as far west as Great Slave Lake. [GSC collection]

Murray and four voyageurs returned to the Albany River, ascended it and explored the upper reaches around Cat Lake. Leaving a voyageur named Nolin on an island named for him at the mouth of the Boulder River, Bell with one voyageur ascended the Attawapiskat to the lake which Bell believed was two lakes. He named the first one Attawapiskat, and the upper one, Lansdowne. They then returned downstream, picking up Nolin, and continued down the Attawapiskat to the coast of Hudson Bay. They canoed down the coast to Fort Albany, ascended the Albany and Kenogami rivers, crossed over to Long Lake and descended a river to reach the CP railway. [GSC, Robert Bell's report, 1887]

1896 Anglican Bishop Newnham, along with Archdeacon Vincent and his daughter travelled from Moose Factory to Winnipeg by going up the coast to Fort Albany and up the Albany River to Wabigoon where they were able to join the railway to Winnipeg. He travelled in a large canoe with a good crew. [Shearwood, p. 146]

1898 Three brothers, Robert, William and George Renison, in a birchbark canoe with Indian guides Michel and Thomas, travelled from their home in Nipigon, north to Fort Hope, down the Albany to the coast and along the coast to Moose Factory. [Renison, 1957]

1900 H.B. Proudfoot – see Ogoki

1903 William McInnes – see Winisk

1904 William McInnes – see Winisk

1905 Owen O'Sullivan, for the Geological Survey, canoed up the Albany River from Fort Albany to Lake St. Joseph. [Zaslow, p. 152]

1905 Indian affairs, Treaty 9 expedition travelled the full length of the Albany River from Dinorwic to Fort Albany and Moose Factory, and back to the Lake Abitibi HBC post. The members of the expedition were Duncan Campbell Scott, Samuel Stewart, D.G. MacMartin, Dr. A.G. Meindle, T.C. Rae (HBC), and Constables Parkinson and Vanasse (RWNMP). The Indian canoemen were David Sugarhead, Oombash, Simon Smallboy,

Daniel Wascowin, and Jimmy Swain. The route from Dinorwic was through Lac Seul, up the Root River to Lake St. Joseph, visiting Osnaburgh House and Fort Hope. They continued down the Albany River to Fort Albany and along the coast to Moose Factory. The return was up the Abitibi River to Abitibi Lake. [NAC, Treaty 9 Report]

1905-24 The Treaty 9 Annual Reports give details of most of the yearly trips made by the Treaty party from Dinorwic, or other stops farther east on the railway, through Lac Seul and down the Albany River to Fort Albany. It was customary for the group to make a detour up the Kenogami River to English River post and down to the Albany again. The usual return was down the coast by steamer and up the Abitibi. In 1910 one of the party went by steamer to Fort George and Great Whale River. In 1917 the party extended their travel to Attawapiskat by coastal boat and this became a regular part of the itinerary. In 1923 the return from Moose Factory was by airplane and the following year an airplane was used on the outward journey after Fort Hope. Duncan Campbell Scott made the trip twice, J.G. Ramsden, W.J. McLean and Mr. Awrey were the most frequent commissioners, accompanied by several different doctors, Meindle, Caldwell, Jacobs, Baker, Bell and Hartry. In the years in which there is no report available, the travel of the Treaty Party is reported through other sources. [NAC Treaty 9 Annual Report]

1905 W. McInnes, Geological Survey, canoed from Lac Seul up the Root River to the Albany and crossed north over the height of land to the Winisk River. [*Ottawa Naturalist*, 1906/7, p. 29]

1908 The treaty party went down the Albany River and passed through Fort Hope. [Cyril Lech – unpublished diary]

1909 The treaty party went down the Albany River. [HBC Archives]

1909 Alanson Skinner, anthropologist, with two Indian guides, canoed from Dinorwic down the full length of the Albany River to James Bay. [Skinner, p.7]

1911 George Marsh with his friend and guide, Thomas Hoar from Maine, and a "half-breed Cree named Charlie", using two Maine canoes, travelled up the Sturgeon River to Lac Seul. At Lac Seul they engaged Ojibwa guide, Wabininishib to take them up the Root River as far as Osnaburgh on Lake St. Joseph and continued down the Albany River to Fort Albany. They canoed along the coast to Moose Factory where they sold their shattered canoes and dismissed Charlie. In a new Peterborough canoe, with two Abitibi Cree, Chief Esau and Bertie, they canoed up the Abitibi River to McDougall Chute, on the National Transcontinental Railway. At Fort Albany they learned that they were the first sportsmen to descend the Albany River. Marsh claimed that 200 miles was about the limit of travel for the northern Indian into country which he does not know. [*Scribner's*, 1912, April, p.433]

Pre-WWI Two young Americans with John Wesley, Indian guide from Osnaburgh, went on an expedition across country to York Factory, came down the coast to Fort Albany and canoed up the Albany River to Osnaburgh. [North, p. 62]

1915 Capt. Rev. Robert Renison, as head of an Indian Trade Commission for the Federal Government, travelled from Lac Seul down the Albany and returned up the Abitibi to Cochrane. The group consisted of Mr. Awrey, Dept. of Indian Affairs, Dr. J.D. Caldwell, a medical student, a nurse, another student, an RCMP officer, a cook, Ole Olsen and J.D. McKenzie from HBC Fort Hope. They travelled in three large canoes with a crew of twelve Indians. [Renison, pp. 94-99]

1917 Capt. Rev. Robert Renison made a trip down the Albany from Dinorwic, through Osnaburgh, Fort Hope and Marten's Falls to Fort Albany to recruit Indians for the forestry battalions of the Canadian army for the Canadian government. He was successful in recruiting 200 Indians. [*Ibid.*, p. 100]

1927 Robert Carver North, aged twelve, from Walton, New York, went by train with his father to Cochrane, via Montreal and Ottawa. In Cochrane his father left him with Bishop John Anderson who took young Carver along on his trip with the Treaty party from Osnaburgh to Fort Albany, up the coast to Attawapiskat, returning up the Albany and the Kenogami to the railway at Pagwa. He returned home by rail, meeting his mother in Montreal, after his 72-day trip. The book *Bob North by Canoe and Portage*, was published the following year from his journal. They had travelled in various canoes with several different Indian paddlers including David Sugarhead, Eddie and Steven Papah, Zapi and his family, Gaius Wesley and Alec, Mark Goodwin and his fiancée. [North, 1928]

1935 Six Americans from Harvard and other New England colleges, Martin K. Bovey, Brewster Breeden, Donald Forbes, Winthrop Brown, Holden Gutermuth and Edward Hall, with two guides, George Carey and Joe Gagnon, travelling in two freight canoes paddled the full length of the Albany River from Chivelston Lake, through Harris and Savant lakes and Pashkokogan River to Lake St. Joseph. When they reached Fort Albany they canoed down the Bay to Moose Factory and returned south by train. [*Beaver*, March 1936, p. 40]

1936 A group of American college students were canoeing down the Albany to James Bay when forest fires drove them off the river and they had to run for Fort Hope and the safety of Eabamet Lake. [*Beaver*, December 1936]

1936 Arthur Moffatt, aged seventeen, made a solo canoe trip from Sioux Lookout down the Albany River to James Bay. [*Sports Illustrated*, March 9, 1959, p. 71]

1936 F. Duxbury and G.R. Crampton canoed to Fort Albany. [Anderson log]

1941 Edwin Mills and Jim Vanderbeck with a Chestnut canoe, landed at Keezhik Lake, canoed down the Keezhik River to Miminiska and Petawanga lakes and down the Albany River to Fort Hope. [Mills, 1985; *Beaver*, June 1942, p. 33]

1946 Harry MacLean and Bill Downie canoed the Albany River to Fort Albany. [Anderson log]

1947 John P. Kelsall and Louis Lemieux, of the Canadian Wildlife Service, canoed to Fort Albany. [Anderson log]

1948 Arthur Moffatt and his wife Carol canoed the Albany River. [Anderson log]

1950s Camp Wabun with trip leader Whitney Cannon began doing the circuit trips that are detailed in 1962, the beginning of recreational trips from the Temagami camps down the Albany River. [Personal communication – Jon Berger]

1950 When Edwin Mills was on a fishing trip on the Albany, he saw half a dozen other fishing parties while going from Washi Lake 60 miles down to Marten's Falls, as well as a party on the Little Current River and more on the Opichuan, all of them American sportsmen. [Mills, 1985]

1950 A group led by Gunnar Peterson and his wife, from Syracuse University Outing Club, including Arthur Stoner, Jay Hutchinson, Dick Boysen, Alan Knox, Paul Strauss, A. Hessel, Henry Noldan and Donald Miller canoed down the Albany to the Bay. [Anderson log]

1952 Arthur Moffatt led Skip Pessl, Bradford Sturtevant and Joe Karet on a canoe trip down the Albany River. According to *Sports Illustrated*, Moffatt led yearly trips down the Albany from 1950 to 1954. [*Sports Illustrated*, March 9, 1959, pp. 68-76; Anderson log]

1952 Gene Meyer and Bud Byers canoed down the Albany to Fort Albany. [Anderson log]

1952 Peter Spoehr, Donald Bergman, Ned Jannotta and Robert Berner from Ely, Minnesota, using two Grumman canoes, canoed through Quetico Park to Atikokan, down the English River to Sioux Lookout, across Lac Seul and Lake St. Joseph and down the Albany to Fort Albany. They went down the James Bay coast with a mission boat to Moosonee and took the train to Cochrane. The 920-mile canoe trip took one month. [Personal communication – Spoehr]

1953 Arthur Moffatt made a canoe trip down the Albany River. [*Sports Illustrated*, March 9, 1959, pp. 68-76; Anderson log]

1954 Arthur Moffatt led one of his yearly canoe trips down the Albany River. Peter Franck was on one of these trips, probably in 1954 and Fred (Skip) Pessl was on several of the Albany River trips.

For many years Bill Anderson's trading post at Fort Albany was a favourite stopping place for canoeists who had made the trip down the Albany River to the James Bay coast. Signing the log book was part of the ritual. Shown here are some entries for 1952, including those of Art Moffatt and Skip Pessl. [Anderson family]

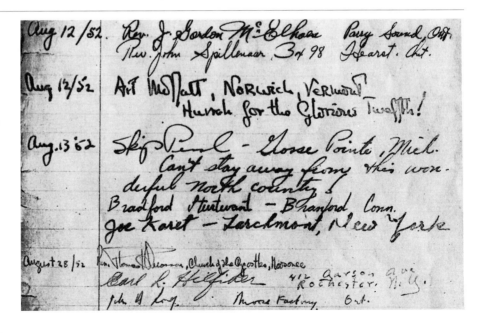

The Anderson log has gaps in its chronology in this period. [*Sports Illustrated*]

1954 John Blunt made a solo canoe trip down the Albany River from Sioux Lookout to Fort Albany. [Browning, p. 14]

1956 Lloyd Fischer and Sid Gulliver, with an Indian guide from Fort Hope, in a canoe with a motor, canoed up and down the Eabamet River, continuing down the Albany River to Fort Albany on a fishing trip. They went down the coast by HBC supply boat. On the river at the same time were two newspapermen from Illinois with a man from the Department of Tourism and another group of four men from Kitchener and Toronto with guides. [*Hamilton Spectator*, October 18, 1956; personal communication – Fischer]

1959 Robin and Victoria Fraser in a 16-foot canvas cedar-strip Peterborough canoe, starting at Sioux Lookout, canoed across Pelican Lake to Lac Seul, up the Root River and down the Albany to James Bay. [Personal communication – Robin Fraser]

1960 Maurice Renard and Bill Miller canoed from Sioux Lookout, via Lac Seul, up the Root River to Lake St. Joseph and down the Albany River to Fort Albany. [Camp Owakonze trip report 1965]

1960 Camp Wabun: Andy Smyth led and Leo Belanger guided a boys' group from Savant Lake station on the CN railway to Fort Albany. [Camp communication]

1961 Ron Cholasinski, Darrell Johnson, Ed Banfi and Noble Johnson, from Indiana, canoed the Albany River to Fort Albany. [Anderson log]

1962 Camp Wabun: Andy Smyth with Buddy Nelson as guide, and campers Jon Berger, Roland Fisch, Chris Hallowell, Monk Terry, Bill Bissell, Jerry Large and two brothers, put in at Chivelston Lake from the CN tracks east of Savant Lake Station and canoed through a series of lakes to Savant, McCrea and Pashkokogan lakes to the Albany River. They canoed down the Albany to Fort Hope on Eabamet Lake and continued down the Albany to Fort Albany. They returned by a small power-boat down the coast to Moosonee. [Personal communication – Jon Berger]

1963 Camp Keewaydin: Heberton Evans and Dave Corcoran, with Nishe Belanger as guide, led a group of campers which included Bill Walles, Charles Neill, Thompson Goldsmith, John Weeks, Ken Rafferty, William Rich and B. Archibald, down the Albany River from Savant Lake to Fort Albany. [Back, B., 1983; Anderson log]

1964 Bob and Carl Thum, Tom Bose and Bucky Walters canoed from Ely, Minnesota, to Fort Albany, 1100 miles, presumably through the boundary waters, north by a series of lakes to Sioux Lookout and down the Albany River. [Anderson log]

1965 Camp Keewaydin: Heb Evans led and Nishe Belanger guided a group of campers, including Gary Hummel, Jim Kilgore and Ben Bosher, from Savant Lake to Fort Albany. [Back, B., 1983; Anderson log]

1965 Camp Owakonze: F.B. Hubachek, Jr., with Steve Kling for the first two weeks and Don Williamson for the remainder of the trip, led campers Mark Anderson, Bill Dickinson, John Hansen, Bill Hubachek, Peter Ickes, John Sanders, Bob Stickler and Skip Welles in four 17-foot Grumman canoes, from Sioux Lookout through Hooker and Miniss lakes to Lake St. Joseph and down the Albany River to Fort Albany. They canoed along the coast to Moosonee and returned by train. [Camp Owakonze 1965 trip report]

1965 Camp Temagami: Andy Smyth led campers including Russell Morgan, Dave Whiteside, Jim Kiberd, Peter Gorman, Ian Urquhart, Graham Dare, Ted Severing, Ted Johnson, John Maron, Jay Peabody and John McNally, down the Albany River from Savant Lake to Fort Albany. [Anderson log]

1966 Robin and Victoria Fraser, Tom Wickett, Charlotte Holmes, Peter Garstang and Dick Irwin canoed from Cedar Rapids at the eastern end of Lake St. Joseph down the Albany River to Ogoki. [Personal communication – Robin Fraser]

1966 Camp Wabun: Boys' group canoed from Savant Lake to Fort Albany. [Camp communication]

1967 Ed Banfi and Frank Rafinske from Indiana canoed the Albany River. [Anderson log]

1968 Carl Thum, John Hayden and Bucky Harris, from Ohio and West Virginia, canoed the Albany River to Fort Albany. [Anderson log]

1968 Camp Wabun: Richard Neunherz led a boys' group from Savant Lake to Fort Albany. [Camp communication]

1968 Camp Wabun: Peter Spiler led a boys' group from Savant Lake to Fort Albany. One canoeist drowned on this trip. [Camp communication; Jon Berger]

1968 Camp Owakonze: John Hillner led a canoe trip down the Albany, following the 1965 route. [Camp Owakonze trip reports]

1969 Herb Miller and Graham Lamont canoed to Fort Albany. [Anderson log]

1969 Fred Gaskin and Lyle Malcolm canoed the Albany River. [Anderson log]

1970 Camp Owakonze: Don Williamson leading a group of nine campers canoed from the camp, 90 miles west of Thunder Bay, up to Sioux Lookout, across Vincent and Miniss lakes to Lake St. Joseph and down the Albany River to the mouth of the Attwood River. The level of the Attwood River was too high to complete the trip up that river as planned and they were flown out. [Camp Owakonze trip reports]

1971 Raymond Coppings led a group of eleven students from Hampshire College, Amherst, Massachusetts, down the Albany River. [Anderson log]

1971 Herb Miller and Ron Hunt canoed to Fort Albany. [Anderson log]

1971 Camp Kandalore: Craig Macdonald led a boys' group from Savant Lake to Fort Albany. They continued down the coast to Moosonee and returned by railway.

1971 Wilderness Way: Andy Smyth and Jon Berger led a coed group from Chivelston Lake across to Savant Lake, down Savant River, across Pashkokogan Lake and down the Albany River to Fort Hope. From Fort Hope they crossed by a series of lakes and rivers to Lake Attawapiskat and continued down the Attawapiskat River to James Bay. [Personal communication – Berger]

1971 Jon Berger reported meeting three other groups on the Albany before Fort Hope.

Jon Berger, having canoed the rivers of Northern Ontario and Quebec as a camper and a trip leader, introduces the next generation, his son Michael. [Kit Wallace]

1971 Camp Wabun: John Edmonds led a boys' group from Savant Lake to Fort Albany. [Camp communication]

1971 Drs. Don McLean, Al Hart, Bill Kennedy and Bob Martin canoed down the Albany from Kagiami Falls to Marten's Falls and back on a fishing trip. [Personal communication – McLean]

1972 A group of eight canoeists from Camp Minocqua, Wisconsin, which included Helen Broomell, started at Osnaburgh and canoed partway down the Albany, possibly to Ogoki. [HBC Archives – U-Paddle file]

1972 Camp Temagami: a group of campers canoed down the Albany and bought supplies at an HBC store along the way. [HBC Archives – U-Paddle file]

1972 Camp Owakonze: John Hillner and Jack Stultz led campers Mike Bray, Harry Drucker, Allan Gilbert, Peter Hosbein, Don Roose, Nick Streuli and Chris Wheeler from Sioux Lookout, down the Marchington River, through a series of lakes including Vincent and Miniss to Lake St. Joseph, down the Albany River to the mouth of the Attwood River at Gowie Bay, down-river from Fort Hope. The trip continued up the Attwood and Witchwood rivers, down a section of the Ogoki and the Caribou River to Armstrong where they returned to the camp by car. They found water-levels very low on the Albany and a large number of fly-in fishermen on both river systems. [Camp Owakonze 1972 trip report]

1972 Four high school teachers from Canton, Illinois, Bob Fidler, Marvin Robinson, Gary Taylor and Bud Lehnhausen, canoed down the Albany River to Fort Albany. [Camp Owakonze 1972 trip report; Anderson log]

1972 Camp Kandalore: Craig Macdonald and Pat Geale led a group of campers including Rob James, Ronald Groves, John Gravelle, Paul Fleet, Rob Arnup, Howard Strange, Mark Wilson, Barry Collins, Jamie Alexander, Rob Laver, Doug Edmonds, Mikhail Rockmar, Dave Harris, Pierre Bernier, Dave Winch and David Cudmore from Osnaburgh down the Albany River to Fort Albany and continued down the coast to Moosonee. [Personal communication – Macdonald; Anderson log]

1972 Thirteen Thunder Bay high school students, the Lakeview Outers, with one older guide, canoed down the Albany and up the Attwood River finishing their trip at Armstrong. [Camp Owakonze 1972 trip report]

1972 A group of young people from the western United States were canoeing down the Witchwood and Attwood rivers to continue down the Albany to Fort Albany. [*Ibid.*]

1972 Bob Davis heard that there were 600 travellers on the various Albany River routes that year. [*Outdoor Canada*, June 1974, p.47]

1973 Bob Davis made a solo canoe trip from Sioux Lookout to Moosonee, heading northwest out of Lac Seul, up to Birch Lake and by a series of lakes into Lake St. Joseph and Osnaburgh Lake. He continued down the Albany River and along the coast of Hudson Bay early in September in rough weather. [*Outdoor Canada*, June 1974, pp. 41-47; *Canoe*, May/June, 1975; Personal communication]

1973 Two Americans canoed down the Albany River with their eighteen-year-old dog. [*Outdoor Canada*, June 1974, p. 46]

1973 Richard Carlson rented canoes to canoe from Sioux Lookout to Fort Albany. [U-Paddle file, HBC Archives]

1973 Camp Keewaydin: Marshall Clunie and Will Bramen led a boys' group from Savant Lake to Fort Albany. [Back, 1983]

1973 Voyageurs North: Tom Terry and Rebecca Dinsmore led a coed group from Sioux Lookout to Fort Albany.

1973 Wild River Survey led by V. Guzelimian with D. Peck, D. Thomas and R. Amos canoed the upper Albany from Rat Portage to the mouth of the Ogoki. [Parks Canada files]

1973 Drs. Don McLean, Al Hart, Bill Kennedy and Bob Martin canoed from Fort Hope to Ogoki on the Albany River. [Personal communication – McLean]

1973 No records for this year in the Anderson log.

1974 Jeremy and Jean Schmidt, from Wyoming and Tom Schmidt from Wisconsin canoed from Sioux Lookout to Fort Albany. [Anderson log]

1974 Richard and Marjorie Carhart, their children Sarah, David and Dan, along with Jack Kaecli, Norman Strahm, Sandra Danforth and a small dog, canoed from Sioux Lookout down the Albany River, taking thirty-six days. [Anderson log]

Between the years 1938-1974, more than 100 groups who may very well have been canoeists, but who could not be positively identified as such, signed the Anderson log. That figure is in addition to the many others who could be identified as fly-in hunters, government officials and local visitors from Moosonee. The numbers seemed to be increasing from the 1960s but not in a smooth curve. From the log and from conversations with those who knew him, Bill Anderson was a man who enjoyed people. The log was kept for no other purpose than his pleasure.

OGOKI–ALBANY

"We have a rich country of timber and land … the area of this rich land is so extensive as to be beyond belief. Here we have space to build homes for the millions with great timber resources, a country teeming with fish and game, also water power to turn the wheels of a nation, and a climate that, if we take this year as a criterion, is fine as I have ever seen either in Muskoka or Parry Sound districts or even the county of Simcoe, and in proof of this our party saw no frosts until the 25th of September. When we were on James Bay we saw in a garden at Fort Albany potatoes, their tops as green as they would be in August. In this part of Ontario they grow all garden produce that we grow here where I live [Utterson, Muskoka]." J.L. Hanes, of the NOLS Survey Party #6, describing the land between the Ogoki and the Albany.

1871 Robert Bell – see Albany

1900 H.B. Proudfoot, survey leader, with James Sharp, forester, F.J. Snelgrove, geologist, and four others for the Northern Ontario Land Survey, Party #7, started at Wabinosh Bay on Lake Nipigon and canoed the lake portage route west via Smoothrock Lake to the upper Ogoki at Wabakimi Lake (which Proudfoot thought was Savant Lake) – now the heart of Wabakimi Provincial Park. They continued down the Ogoki to Kenojiwan Lake, crossed north over portages to Pashkokogan Lake and down its outlet to the Albany, making the short ascent to Lake St. Joseph and Osnaburgh House. Returning to the Ogoki at Kenojiwan, they descended the upper Ogoki, past Whitewater to Whiteclay, crossed south over the divide and down the Pitikigushi River to Lake Nipigon. [*NOLS*, pp. 173-89]

1900 J.M. Tiernman, leader, with J.L. Hanes, forester, A.H. Robinson, geologist, and five others, Northern Ontario Land Survey Party #6, started at Lake Nipigon, canoed up the Ombabika River and down the Ogoki River from the "French Channel" to the Albany River to James Bay. They continued along the coast to Moose Factory. Tiernman died of typhoid fever very soon after the trip and the enthusiastic report, quoted in the introduction to the Ogoki was written by Hanes. [*NOLS*, pp. 158-72]

1904 W.J. Wilson was surveying on the Ogoki River for the Geological Survey.

1907 Two University of Toronto students went by boat from Parry Sound to Nipigon and canoed, without guides, across Lake Nipigon, down the Ogoki and Albany rivers to Fort Albany. They continued down the coast to Moose Factory and up Abitibi River to McDougall's Chute on the TNOR.

1923 James, Lonsdale and Joseph Green from Chicago, Washington and Cincinnati, from the CN railway at Ombabika, canoed up the Ombabika River to Summit Lake, crossed over to the Ogoki River and descended it to the Albany. They returned up the Albany. Their guides were Alfred McCue, Bill Smoke and Wheatung Shamus. James Green had canoed many summers in the region west of Hudson Bay. [*Beaver*, March 1947, p.22]

1936 Martin R. Bovey led a group of five American college students including John Somes, Morrison, Hobbs, and Breeden on a circuit in the Ogoki River area. Starting from Cavell on the CN railway, they went down the Kowkash River to Abamasagi Lake, to Meta, Ara and Ogoki lakes, down the Ogoki River, up to Fort Hope and returned down part of the Ombabika route back to Abamasagi Lake and Cavell. Their guides were George Carey of Moose Factory and Duncan Nabigon of Longlac. The forest fires were so bad that summer that a train stood by at Nakina ready to evacuate the town which for days was completely surrounded by fire. [*Beaver*, December 1936]

1936 G.D. Luard came from England to meet Paul Snyder from the United States for a fishing trip on the Ogoki-Albany rivers. With two Cree guides, Ronald and Joe, and using a 25-foot canoe with a small motor and a smaller canoe, they started from somewhere along the CN railway, went upstream, crossed to the Ogoki River and to Lake Kagianagami. They descended the Opichuan River to the Albany and returned down the Albany and up the Ogoki. An American named Whitlock was fishing on the Opichuan with an Indian guide at the same time. [Luard, 1950]

1945 Edwin Mills was fishing on the Ogoki River. [Mills, 1985]

1947 Harold Hanson – see Albany-Kenogami. In the course of this trip Hanson ascended and returned down a section of the Ogoki River.

1951 Edwin Mills fished on Ogoki Lake and Ogoki River below the Waboose dam. [Mills, 1985]

1959 Camp Wabun: Andy Smyth led a boys' group canoeing a circular route which included the Ogoki River. [Camp communication]

1964 Camp Wabun: Boys' group canoed a circular route which included the Ogoki River. [Camp communication]

1965 Bill Rom, Jr., and Rudy Heath, from Minnesota, canoed from Auden to Fort Albany up the Ombabika and down the Kapikotongwa, Ogoki and Albany rivers. [Anderson log]

1965 Dr. H.A. McMurray, Jon Kelton and John Kunkle, Jr., from Pennsylvania and Ohio, canoed from Auden to Fort Albany. [Anderson log]

1967 Camp Temagami: Andy Smyth and Hugh Stewart led a group of campers from Lake Pashkokogan up Lake Joseph to Cat Lake. They crossed to the Otoskwin River, canoed down to Lansdowne House on Lake Attawapiskat and crossed by a series of lakes and rivers to Fort Hope and south to the railway at Auden. [Personal communication – Stewart]

1973 V. Guzelimian, D. Peck, D. Thomas, R. Amos for the Wild River Survey flew into Kayedon Lake, canoed down the Ogoki River to the Albany River, up the Albany to Fort Hope and Osnaburgh House and went out from there to Savant Lake and the railway at Ghost River. [Parks Canada files]

1974 Camp Keewaydin: Marshall Clunie and Jon "Skeeter" Webber led a boys' group from Lake St. Joseph to Cat Lake, across to the Otoskwin River and down to Lansdowne House on Lake Attawapiskat. They crossed by a series of lakes and rivers to Fort Hope where they joined the Albany River and descended it to the Opichuan River. They canoed up the Opichuan to Lake Kagianagami, crossed over to the Ogoki River, descended it a short distance, crossed over to Kapikotongwa, up that river and down the Ombabika River to the CN railway line at Auden. [Back, B., p. 173]

1974 Wilderness Way – see Winisk

KENOGAMI–ALBANY

1871 Robert Bell, Geological Survey, canoed from Lake Superior down the Albany River and returned up the Kenogami and Pic rivers to Lake Superior. [Zaslow, p. 121]

1883 Edward Barnes Borron, Stipendiary Magistrate, started at Nipigon House, went up to Long Lake House, crossed to the Kenogami River and continued down the Albany to Fort Albany. He went down the coast to Moose Factory and returned up the Missinaibi River to New Brunswick House and crossed to Michipicoten on Lake Superior. [Zaslow, "Edward Barnes Borron", pp. 297-311, in Armstrong, F.H., ed.]

1886 Robert Bell – see Albany

1900 Walter S. Davidson, leading the Northern Ontario Land Survey Party #5, canoed from Jackfish Station on Lake Superior to Long Lake, down the Kenogami River to the Albany and continued down the Albany to the Bay. Their mandate was to explore for 20 miles on each side of the Kenogami River and any large streams flowing into the Albany from the south. [*NOLS*, 1901; Thomson, Don, v.3, p.288]

1903 W.J. Wilson and Owen O'Sullivan, GSC, started from Montizambert (Mobert) on the CP railway with local canoemen and three canoes, crossed the height of land via White Lake and descended the Nagagami River to English River post. They surveyed several tributaries of the Kenogami, the Little Current, the Drowning and the Kabinakagami. They completed their survey up the Nagagami and returned the way they had come. [GSC Report 1903]

1904 W.J. Wilson and W.H. Collins, GSC, with two canoemen from Timiskaming, continuing the survey of the previous year, ascended the Pic River from Heron Bay on the CP railway to McKay Lake, crossed over to Pagwachuan Lake and canoed down the Pagawachuan River to the junction with the Kenogami. They then ascended the Kenogami to Long Lake, hired a guide and made their way by a series of lakes and portages to Wababimiga Lake, descending the Drowning River to the area of the previous survey. They returned up the Drowning, crossed over to the Kenogami and returned upstream to Long Lake for resupply. They completed the survey of the Little Current River and returned across the divide and down the Pic River to the railway. [GSC Report 1903]

1905 Rev. Robert Renison, with Solomon, his "Indian mentor", and Solomon's grandson, canoed in a Chestnut canoe from Fort Albany up the Albany, the Kenogami and the Nagagami to White River. [Renison, p. 71]

1914 A.R.M. Lower with Robert and Joe King as canoemen, from Hearst on the Northern Transcontinental railway, canoed down the Nagagami, Kenogami and Albany rivers to the coast. He spent the summer on the James Bay coast for the Canadian Fisheries Research Expedition and returned from Moose Factory up the Mattagami and Groundhog rivers to Fauquier on the same railway. [Lower, 1953]

1915-31 During these years, the Pagawachuan-Kenogami-Albany route was the main supply route from the new Northern Transcontinental railway to the Bay. Shallow-draft, motorized craft were used for this during the high water of the spring. [Revillon Frères Archives]

1920 Thierry Mallet with two Indians, John Wynn and Alphias Salmon, canoed up the Albany and Kenogami to Revillon Frères' English River Post and up-river to Pagwa. [Revillon Frères microfilm]

1920 M.Y. Williams, GSC, canoed from Pagwa down the Pagawachuan-Kenogami-Albany rivers to Fort Albany. [*Canadian Field-Naturalist*, May, 1921, p. 94]

1932 Camp Keewaydin: "Moose" Wilson and Art Montreuil led a boys' group from Pagwa River station down the Kenogami-Albany rivers to Fort Albany. They paddled down the coast to Moose Factory and up the Abitibi River to Island Falls on the TNOR. [Back, B., p. 169]

1943 Edwin Mills with his son and a friend, and guided by Emile Côté, went down the Drowning River from the CN railway crossing to Lake Waba-bimiga, up the Wababimiga River to Waba Lake and out to the railway at Nakina. [Mills, 1985]

1946 Harold C. Hanson, for the Illinois Natural History Survey, came down the Albany River. [Anderson log]

1947 Harold C. Hanson, for the Arctic Institute of North America, canoed from the village of Pagwa River down the Pagawachuan-Kenogami-Albany rivers to Fort Albany, studying Canada goose nesting grounds. [*Canadian Field-Naturalist*, Sept./Oct. 1949, p. 183; Anderson log]

1956 A group of canoeists came from Pagwa down the Pagwa, Kenogami and Albany rivers to Fort Albany. [Anderson log]

1961 Bill Sharp and Bob Hollies canoed the Albany River. [Personal communication – D. Grieve]

1961 Camp Wabun: Andy Smyth, with Leo Belanger as guide, and campers Jon Berger, Bill Forbes, Roland Fisch, Bob Haas, Tim Lytle, Dave True, Bill Bissell and Dave Weir made two circuits from Nakina. The first was ten days, down the Drowning River to Wababimiga River and Lake, portaging across the Squaw River and following it upstream to Nakina. The second circuit was forty days from Nakina through a series of lakes and portages, Esnagami, Abamasagi, Meta and Ara, to the Kapikotongwa River, downstream on that river and the Little Current and then upstream on the Squaw to Nakina. [Personal communication – Jon Berger]

1963 Ron Stewart, Jack Hamilton, Jack Wallwin, Jack Nixon, Jack Webb, Rollie Lesvesque, Wib Mallory and Len Roechler, all from Barrie, Ontario, using a 23-foot Rupert freight canoe, a 15-foot boiler plate steel boat, and a 14-foot Springbok aluminum boat, went from Limestone Rapids down the Kabinakagami-Kenogami-Albany rivers in late September. [Personal communication – George Drought]

1964 Morton Baker, his wife and their children Margaret, Stephen and Maria, with Dave Neegan, canoed to Fort Albany from Limestone Rapids down the Kabinakagami-Kenogami-Albany rivers. [Anderson log]

1965 Dr. Ervin Rehze and Robert Kiese, from the Max Planck Institute in Germany, canoed from Limestone Rapids to Fort Albany. [Anderson log]

1965 Alice Wendt and Erwin Streisinger from Reading, Pennsylvania, travelled down the Kabinakagami-Kenogami-Albany rivers by kayak. [Camp Owakonze 1965 trip report; Anderson log]

1967 Arthur Hopewell with his sons Keith and Jeffrey canoed from Limestone Rapids to Fort Albany. [Anderson log]

1969 Stephen Smith, John Nixon and David Scandrell, from Ontario and Chris Meadham from Australia, canoed from Hearst to Fort Albany, down the Kabinakagami-Kenogami-Albany rivers. [Anderson log]

1970 H.M. Herger and George Failey from Pennsylvania canoed down the Albany River from Limestone Rapids. [Anderson log]

1971 Camp Wanapitei: Bruce and Carol Hodgins led a coed youth group down the Nagagami-Kenogami-Albany rivers to Fort Albany and flew out to Moosonee. [Wanapitei trip report]

1972 Dave Taylor, canoeing alone, left from Chapleau and made his way to the headwaters of the Kabinakagami River, canoed down that river and the Kenogami-Albany to Fort Albany, where he spent the next two years working for Bill Anderson. [Anderson log; personal communication – Taylor]

1972 Camp Manitou: Bill and Doreen Stadwyck led a group of girls, including Kathy Willis, Anne Turner, Dorothy Mason, Jane Skurszkan, Jane Glover, Leigh Cole, Linda Trainor, Catherine Foote, Nancy Strickland, Sue Todd, Emily Noble, Anne Cole, Peggy Noble and D. Cole, from Limestone Rapids down the Albany River and along the Hudson Bay coast to Moosonee. [Anderson log]

1972 The McAllister family, Betty, Russell, Glenn, Judy, Lynn, Alec, Cynthia, Ian and Fiona, canoed from Limestone Rapids to Fort Albany. [Anderson log; U-Paddle file]

1973 Dave Taylor and his fiancée, Hélène, picked up two freight canoes with a small motor and about 1000 pounds of goods at Hearst. Towing one canoe, they made their way from Limestone Rapids to Fort Albany. [Personal communication – Taylor]

1973 Camp Wanapitei: Jamie Benidickson, Gay Wadham, and Sue Hahn leading a coed youth group, canoed down the Kabinakagami-Kenogami-Albany rivers to Fort Albany and flew out to Moosonee. [Wanapitei trip report]

1973 John Anderson in a party of four canoed down the Albany River from Limestone Rapids. [U-Paddle file, HBC Archives]

1973 Stephen Pierce canoed from Limestone Rapids to Fort Albany. [U-Paddle file, HBC Archives]

1974 Dave Taylor, Greg Laska and Dale Randall, with a canoe towing a rubber dinghy, canoed from Limestone Rapids to Fort Albany. [Personal communication – Taylor]

1974 A party of four from Toronto canoed from Lake Kabinakagami, down the Kabinakagami-Kenogami-Albany rivers in six days. [Anderson log]

1974 Brent Zobator and Robert Eddy from Thunder Bay canoed from Limestone Rapids to Fort Albany early in October. [Anderson log]

ATTAWAPISKAT

Although the Cree had long used the Attawapiskat for trade and trapping, it is unlikely that Europeans appeared on the river before 1886, despite it being a great east-west artery across what is now Northern Ontario. From 1850 the Hudson's Bay Company had an outpost on Lake Attawapiskat. It was serviced by the Fort Hope post using a route which followed a series of lakes and down the Martin-Drinking River.

The Attawapiskat has its beginnings as the Otoskwin, near Cat Lake, less than 200 kilometres east of the Manitoba border. The Otoskwin flows into Lake Attawapiskat and flows out as the Attawapiskat River. Being north of the Shield, the river descends gradually and flows in diverse channels and light rapids through limestone cliffs of stunning beauty.

1886 Robert Bell, GSC, canoed down the Attawapiskat River, having reached it from the Albany and Eabamet rivers. He descended the Attawapiskat River and continued down the coast to Fort Albany. He returned up the Albany and Kenogami rivers to Long Lake and over to Lake Superior. For complete details see Albany. [GSC, Robert Bell's Report, 1887]

1903 William McInnes – see Winisk

1904 William McInnes – see Winisk

1905 William McInnes – see Winisk

1966 George Marek, Ontario Lands and Forests, with Cameron Moonias-Gibb, Fred Sakanee-Gibb, Gordon Spafford-Gibb, flew from Lansdowne House to Nolins Island and canoed down the Attawapiskat River to James Bay.

1967 Camp Temagami: Andy Smyth and Hugh Stewart led a trip from Allenwater Bridge on the CN railway, up the Allenwater River to Kenoje Lake, up the Pallisades River to Burntrock and Greenbush lakes and across to Pashkokogan Lake. They crossed north via the Albany River to Pickle Lake and continued down the Kawinogans and Otoskwin rivers to Lansdowne House on Attawapiskat Lake. They then turned south, up the Martin-Drinking River, down the Eabamet River to Fort Hope and down to the railway at Auden, via the Albany, Opichuan, Ogoki, Kapikotongwa, Powitick and Ombabika rivers. [Personal communication – Jon Berger]

1968 Camp Temagami – see Winisk

1970 Camp Temagami: Andy Smyth led and Jon Berger guided campers Charlie Grieve, Bruce Smith, Noel Salmon and three others, from Chivelston Lake, down Savant Lake and River to Lake St. Joseph, west to Cat Lake where they worked their way on to the Otoskwin River and into Attawapiskat Lake. From there they canoed down the Attawapiskat River to James Bay, a 1200-mile trip. [Personal communication – Jon Berger]

1970 An Indian family were seen by Jon Berger travelling upstream in a heavily loaded canoe, poling up the deep, swift current of the Attawapiskat River. This was common practice. [Personal communication – Jon Berger]

1971 Robin Fraser – see Winisk

1971 Wilderness Way: Andy Smyth led and Jon Berger guided a coed group, including Julie Hutchins, Mark Barad, Luke Wilson, two other women and one man from Chivelston Lake down the Albany River to Fort Hope, up the Eabamet and down the Martin-Drinking River to Attawapiskat Lake, continuing down the Attawapiskat River to James Bay. The youngest person on the trip was twelve years old. The water on the Attawapiskat was unusually high. [Personal communication – Jon Berger]

1971 A group of canoeists turned back to Lansdowne House after being careless in the rapids on the upper Attawapiskat River. [Personal communication – Berger]

1971 An old man and a young boy were travelling up the Martin-Drinking River to go down to Fort Hope. [Personal communication – Berger]

1971 Camp Keewaydin: Heb Evans and Mike Fish led a boys' group from Savant Lake via Cat Lake, down the Otoskwin River to Lansdowne House and down the Attawapiskat River to the Bay. Mike Fish replaced Matthew Ridgway as guide after the latter was killed by a train while portaging a canoe along the railway tracks at the beginning of this trip. [Back, B., 1983]

1972 Camp Wabun: John Edmonds led a boys' group down the Otoskwin River to Lansdowne House, and down the Attawapiskat River to the Bay. [Camp communication]

1973 V. Guzelimian, D. Thomas, D. Peck and R. Amos, Wild River Survey, were flown to the mouth of the Missisa River, halfway down the Attawapiskat,

and canoed down the Attawapiskat to James Bay. [Parks Canada – files]

1974 Camp Wabun: John Edmonds led a boys' group canoeing the full length of the Otoskwin and Attawapiskat rivers to the Bay. [Camp communication]

1974 Camp Wanapitei: Marcus Bruce, Debbie Hutchins and Jamie Benidickson led a coed youth group down the Otoskwin and Attawapiskat rivers to the Bay. [Wanapitei trip report]

1974 Wilderness Way – see Winisk

1974 Steve Aho – see Winisk

1975 *Cam Salsbury and Sandy Richardson canoed down the Otoskwin River to Lansdowne House and continued down the Attawapiskat to James Bay. They met one other group starting at Otoskwin. [Wilderness Canoeist, December, 1975, p. 2]*

EKWAN

The Ekwan is a little used river which rises close to Lake Attawapiskat and due south of Winisk Lake. It flows north and then turns east to James Bay, entering a little north of the mouth of the Attawapiskat River, the mouths of both rivers being opposite Akimiski Island. It provides a safe inland passage south from the Winisk River, eliminating coastal travel.

1893 Father Joseph Guinard – see Winisk

1895 Bishop Newnham with two young Indians, John and Xavier Bird of Severn River, using a Peterborough canoe left at Fort Severn by J.B. Tyrrell, went up the Severn River, crossed a height of land to Sa-Sa-Ma-To-Wa Creek which they followed down to the Winisk River. They canoed down a section of the Winisk and by a series of overland portages reached the Ekwan which they descended to James Bay. They completed their journey along the coast to Fort Albany and Moose Factory. [Shearwood, p. 135]

1901 D.B. Dowling and W.H. Boyd, Geological Survey, having followed the Winisk River to the coast, returned up the Shamattawa, crossed the height of land to the headwaters of the Ekwan, followed it to the coast and continued down the coast to Attawapiskat. [GSC, 1902]

1962 Dave Jarden – see Winisk

WINISK

The Winisk is a long and important canoeing river which flows east, north, and finally northeast into Hudson Bay, passing through Polar Bear Provincial Park in its final kilometres. The main part of the river, from Winisk Lake, is itself a protected Wild River Provincial Park. Although there was no major fur post near its mouth, the location of the Cree village of Peawanuck, the river has long been a significant artery for Cree hunters and trappers.

From the beginning of this century, travellers have reached the Ojibwa village of Webequie on Winisk Lake by lakes and small streams from Lansdowne House on Lake Attawapiskat. More recently, canoeists have put in on the Pipestone River, a tributary of the upper Winisk, which can be reached by road from the mining community of Pickle Lake. This river route passes through the Cree community of Wunnummin on Wunnummin Lake and the Ojibwa community of Summer Beaver on Nibinamik Lake. Flying in to any of these lakes gives a variety of options to begin a canoe trip.

1893 Father Joseph-Étienne Guinard, Oblate, with Peter Kiakocic and Georges Nakotci, in a small canoe, went up the coast of James Bay from Fort Albany, ascended the Ekwan River and the Shamattawa, portaged across to the Minwenindamowi and went down the Winisk to the coast. After conducting the mission at Winisk, they were in dire need of supplies, so they canoed 200 miles up the Winisk River, crossed to Spruce Lake post, returned down the Winisk and the coast to Fort Albany. [Bouchard, *Mémoires*, pp. 48-53]

1895 Father Fafard – see Severn

1901 D.B. Dowling and W.H. Boyd, Geological Survey, canoed down the Winisk River to the coast, returned up the Shamattawa, crossing to the source of the Ekwan, following it to its mouth, then continuing down the coast to Attawapiskat.

1903 William McInnes, GSC, started from Dinorwic on the CP railway, followed Lake Minnitaki and the English River to Lac Seul, up the Root River, crossed the height of land to Lake St. Joseph and continued down the Albany River to Fort Hope. He went north to Machawaian Lake, crossed the divide to the Martin-Drinking River, following a well travelled Indian canoe route to the headwaters of the Attawapiskat River in Lake Attawapiskat. From the northeasterly bay of Attawapiskat Lake he canoed and portaged to the height of land and descended the Wabitotem River to Lake Webequie, following the Winisk River to the Hudson Bay coast. He returned upstream on the Winisk, crossing to Fort Hope as he had come, and up the Albany River to the Opichuan, ascended it, crossing to the Ogoki and Little Jackfish to reach the CP railway at Nipigon. [GSC Report 1903]

1904 William McInnes, GSC, started at Dinorwic and followed the canoe route of the previous year to Lake St. Joseph. He crossed north to the Otoskwin (Odoskwinnigemog) River and followed it down to Ozhiski Lake. He made a detour south to survey the route to Eabamet Lake, continued up the Pineimuta (north branch of the Attawapiskat) and followed it down to Lake Attawapiskat. He crossed over to Lake Webequie, explored upstream on the Winisk, returning out through Fort Hope and to the railway at Nipigon. [GSC Report 1904]

1905 William McInnes, GSC, canoed north from Fort Hope on the Albany River to Lansdowne House on Attawapiskat Lake, crossed north through Travers, Springer, Bartman, Black, Birch and Becker lakes to Webequie and explored the upper Winisk River. [GSC Report 1905]

1962 David Jarden, Eric Sailer, Jon Fairbank and Charlie Bishop with two Indian guides, flew to Lansdowne House, canoed north to Webequie and down the Winisk to the coast. They returned by canoeing along the coast to the Sutton River, ascended it, crossed to the Ekwan, followed it to the coast and down to Attawapiskat. [*Outdoor Life*, September 1963]

1964 Terk Bayly, E.S. Rogers, with Adam and Solomon Sewayanaquib, canoed from Webequie on Lake Winisk down the Winisk River to Hudson Bay. They were joined at its junction with the Asheweig River by the Hon. Kelso Roberts, Ontario minister of Lands and Forests, his son Greer and W.C. Currie, who assessed the area's potential for tourist travel and the utilization of fish and wildlife resources. [Morse files, p. 18]

1968 Camp Temagami; Andy Smyth led a boys' group down the upper Albany to Fort Hope, crossed north to Lansdowne House, north again to Webequie and down the Winisk River to the coast.

1971 Robin and Victoria Fraser, Peter Garstang, Christopher Horne, Laurie McVicar, Allerton Cushman Jr., David Watts and Lys McLaughlin canoed from Lansdowne House post on Attawapiskat Lake, northeast through lakes and streams, to Webequie post on Winisk Lake, down the Winisk River to Winisk on Hudson Bay. [Personal communication – Fraser]

1972 David Brooks, Bob Davis, Deborah Davis, Russell Roberts and Claire Haas canoed from Webequie down the Winisk River to Hudson Bay. [*American Whitewater*, 1974 or 1975; Personal communication – Brooks]

1974 Steve Aho led the Lakeview High School Outers, an Ontario Federal Youth Project from Armstrong on the CN railway, down the Caribou, Ogoki and Attwood rivers to Fort Hope, crossed north to Lansdowne House, north to Webequie and followed the Winisk River to the coast. [Lakeview trip report]

1974 Wilderness Way: Andy Smyth and Jon Berger guided a group consisting of Julie Hutchins, Lea Hutchins, Jon Brand, Bill Lawrence, Karen Krause, Dave Homolski and two others on a great circle route. The trip began from the CN tracks at Chivelston Lake and ended at the railway station at Auden, 100 miles east, on the same

railway line. They followed the established route of Savant Lake-Miniss Lake-Lake St. Joseph to Cat Lake. From Cat Lake they canoed via the upper Otoskwin and Morris rivers, over to and down the Pipestone River where many portages had to be cut through to Wunnummin Lake. There they joined the upper Winisk River to Webequie on Winisk Lake and then crossed south by a series of streams on the usual route to Attawapiskat Lake and Fort Hope on Eabamet Lake, down the Albany and up the Opichuan River to Lake Kagianagami. They portaged over to the Ogoki River, and by a series of creeks to the Kapikotongwa River, upstream to Summit Lake, across the height of land and down the Ombabika River to Auden. [Personal communication – Jon Berger]

SEVERN

The Severn is Ontario's northernmost river emptying into Hudson Bay near Fort Severn. It rises in the boreal forests of the Shield, cascades over numerous rapids and then passes quietly and broadly through a vast limestone valley of the Hudson Bay Lowlands.

The Severn rises far to the south, near the Manitoba border, in a expanse of lakes and streams. Deer Lake is the source of the main branch and it is located just north of the upper Berens, a Heritage River which flows west to Lake Winnipeg and thence to the Nelson River. The main Severn flows northeast, by Favourable Lake, past Sandy Lake and Muskrat Dam Lake where the Windigo River enters from the southwest. The Windigo River drains north from Weagamow and Windigo lakes. It is part of the old access route to the north from Lac Seul via Lake St. Joseph and Cat Lake. There is now a bush road to Windigo Lake.

On the upper waters of the Severn there are numerous Cree and Ojibwa communities of the Nishnawbe Aski who have long used the river for sustenance and travel.

Trips on the Fawn-Severn are more frequent than trips on the main Severn, and are listed separately.

1767 *William Tomison, HBC, canoed from Hudson Bay up the Severn River and down the Berens River to Lake Winnipeg. [Morse files, p. 22]*

1867   *Paul Fountain with Achil Guelle and an Indian named Tom, having wintered on a tributary of the Severn, canoed down the Severn with the spring break-up in mid-April. When they reached Fort Severn they found the coast frozen solid, so they returned up the Severn to the Owl, ascended the Owl and crossed the height of land for 20 miles to a creek flowing into the Albany, which they then followed to the coast. [Fountain, 1904]*

1886   A.P. Low and James Macoun, GSC, with several Indians and five canoes, starting from the Berens River on Lake Winnipeg, canoed up the Berens, crossed the height of land to Deer Lake, the westernmost source of the Severn and followed it all the way to the coast. They continued up the coast of Hudson Bay to York Factory. Their canoes were worn out and they could not get replacements at York Factory so they returned up the Hayes-Echimamish-Nelson to Norway House, where they obtained canoes to return down Lake Winnipeg to Winnipeg. [GSC Report 1886; Zaslow, p. 161]

1895   Bishop Newnham – see Ekwan

1895   Father Fafard, Oblate, with two Cree canoemen, went from Fort Albany up the coast of James Bay to Winisk, ascended the Winisk River, crossed north to the Severn River and followed it down to Hudson Bay, returning down the coast to Fort Albany. [Bouchard, *Mémoires*, p. 60]

1901   Anglican Bishop Newnham with Mr. Baine, HBC, made their way from York Factory to Norway House by an unmapped and unsurveyed route. They canoed up the Hayes, Gods, Shamattawa and Sturgeon rivers and crossed the height of land to the upper Severn. They ascended the Severn as far as Trout Lake, made their way across country to Gods Lake and from there down the Echimamish and up the Nelson to Norway House. [Shearwood, Chap. 21]

1901   W.J. Wilson, GSC, canoed from Lake St. Joseph via Cat Lake, up a series of lakes and streams to Windigo Lake, the headwaters of the Windigo River, a tributary of the Severn River.

1904   Charles Camsell, GSC, with his brother Frank, George Hackett, Iroquois chief, Gordon Greenshields from Montreal, Dawes, cousin of the aide-de-camp to the Governor-General, and Jimmy Cook, Ojibwa, made a survey of the full Severn River. Starting from Dinorwic they went up to Lac Seul, up the Wenasaga River to Cat Lake, where they were joined by Moses, a local Indian guide. From Cat Lake they made their way to Cedar Lake in the upper reaches of the Severn River. They followed the Windigo to the Severn River, turning back, due to a misunderstanding with their Crane Indian guide, just a few miles short of Severn Lake. [GSC Report 1904; Camsell, p. 168; Zaslow, p. 166]

1913   F.G. Stevens – see Hayes

1971   Camp Widjiwagan: Chris Bewell led Betty Gehrz, Linda Gustafson, Kitty Niemann, Judy Olsen and Katie Turnbull canoeing on the upper Severn River, starting at Lake Pikangikum and finishing at Sandy Lake. [Camp Widjiwagan Archives]

1987   *Michael Ketemer made a solo canoe trip the full length of the Severn River from Windigo Lake to Fort Severn. [Personal communication]*

FAWN–SEVERN

To the east, the Fawn River, an important tributary of the Severn, drains Big Trout Lake where a large Cree village has its own air service. The Fawn flows north through Shield country, only entering the Severn about 100 kilometres from its mouth. Canoeists sometimes access the Fawn from the upper Winisk via the Pipestone River and Wunnummin Lake. In the early years of the century the Indians at Big Trout were supplied by the Hudson's Bay post at Fort Severn and there was much canoe traffic up and down the river.

1903   William McInnes, GSC, canoed the usual route from the CP railway to Windigo Lake, worked his way northeastward by rivers and lakes to Wunnummin Lake on the upper Winisk and moving northward reached the Fawn River. He followed the Fawn down to the Severn and descended it to Fort Severn.

1912   J.B. Tyrrell, GSC, canoed from Fort Severn up the Severn and Fawn rivers to Big Trout Lake, continued up a series of streams to Round (Weagamow) Lake, Windigo Lake and south to Cat Lake, finally reaching Sioux Lookout on the CN railway.

1945   An Indian from Fort Severn canoed up the Severn and Fawn rivers and over to Pickle Lake to meet a veteran returning from the Second World War. They returned downstream together to Fort Severn. [Personal communication – Hugh Stewart]

1952   J.M. McFie, Ontario Lands and Forests, and David Ross Muir, U. of Minnesota, Ph.D. student, with two Indians from Big Trout Lake, canoed from Big Trout Lake down the Fawn and Severn rivers to Fort Severn.

Charles Camsell was born at the fur-trade post of Fort Simpson, where his father was the factor. Canoeing northern waters came naturally to Camsell and his brothers, and they had made several adventurous trips before Charles was employed by the Geological Survey in mapping parts of northern Ontario as well as large areas in the Yukon and Northwest Territories. Both a river and a portage have been named for him. He eventually rose to become Deputy Minister of Mines. The photo below shows a canoe shooting rapids on the Severn River, on the trip Camsell made in July 1904. [Camsell album, collection of Barry Penhale]

While Michael Ketemer made a lone trip on the Severn River, this solo ride down the rapids is on the Missinaibi. [Michael Ketemer]

1973   V. Guzelimian, D. Peck, D. Thomas and R. Amos, Wild River Survey, flew to Pickle Lake from Nakina. A chartered float-plane dropped them at Angling Lake, just beyond Big Trout Lake and they canoed down the Fawn and Severn to Fort Severn. [Parks Canada – files]

1978   *Hugh Stewart and Paul Rabinovitch, for Headwaters, led a group of six adults from Pickle Lake down the Pipestone River to King Lake, crossed over to Big Trout Lake and continued canoeing down the Fawn and Severn rivers to the Bay. [Personal communication – Stewart]*

1983   *George Fairfield, Mike Cadman, Earl Fairbanks and Jim Tasker, for the Ontario Breeding Bird Atlas Project of the Federation of Ontario Naturalists, using two Grumman canoes, flew from Sioux Lookout to Big Trout to the headwaters of the Fawn River. They canoed down the full length of the Fawn-Severn rivers to Hudson Bay, and on the trip the only people they saw were two Indians travelling upstream. [Nastawgan, Autumn 1983]*

CHAPTER TWO

THE LAND OF THE EASTERN CREE: QUEBEC'S JAMES BAY RIVERS

HARRICANAW

While the Harricanaw flows into James Bay in Ontario, it rises and flows mainly within Quebec except for the last 30 kilometres, and is included in the Quebec James Bay rivers.

1914   T.L. Tanton, with L. Clermont and L.I. Walker, for the Geological Survey, explored the Harricanaw. [GSC Memoir 109; Zaslow p. 319]

1915   T.L. Tanton, with G. Hanson, C.B. Dawson, and R.K. Carnochan, GSC, surveyed the Harricanaw-Turgeon Basin. [GSC, Memoir 109]

1931   Camp Keewaydin: "Moose" Wilson and Art Montreuil led a boys' group in canoeing from Lake Temagami, down the Harricanaw, along the coast to Moose Factory and returned up the Moose-Abitibi rivers to Island Falls on the TNOR. [Back, B., p. 170]

1941   Jacques and Ted Desrosiers, Guy Viau and Pierre Trudeau canoed from the Lake of Two Mountains, near Montreal, up the Ottawa River to Lake Timiskaming, up the Upper Ottawa, across the height of land to Lake Cadillac, and down the Harricanaw to James Bay crossing Hannah Bay to Moose Factory and Moosonee. They returned south by train. [Trudeau in Spears, ed.; and personal communication – Trudeau]

1946   John Atherley, Ontario, and Henry Willett, Quebec, in a 16-foot canvas-covered Chestnut canoe put in at Amos and canoed down the Harricanaw River to James Bay. They continued around Hannah Bay to Moose Factory. [Personal communication – Atherley]

1951   Camp Keewaydin: Warren Chivers and Sid Fisher leading a boys' group canoed from Lake Temagami via Lake Simard and the upper Ottawa River to Val d'Or. They travelled to Amos by road, canoed the full length of the Harricanaw to James Bay and around Hannah Bay to Moosonee. [Back, B., p. 171]

1952   Camp Keewaydin: Paul Kailey and Ken Jocko led a boys' group following the 1951 route. [*Ibid*].

1953   Camp Keewaydin: Ray Lawrence and Ken Jocko led a boys' group following the 1951 route. [*Ibid.*]

1954   Camp Keewaydin: Doug Schumann and Nishe Belanger led a boys' group following the 1951 route. One camper, Martin Engs, was drowned on this trip. [*Ibid.*, p. 154]

1956   Camp Keewaydin: Jack Mills and Nishe Belanger led a boys' group following the 1951 route. [*Ibid.*, p. 171]

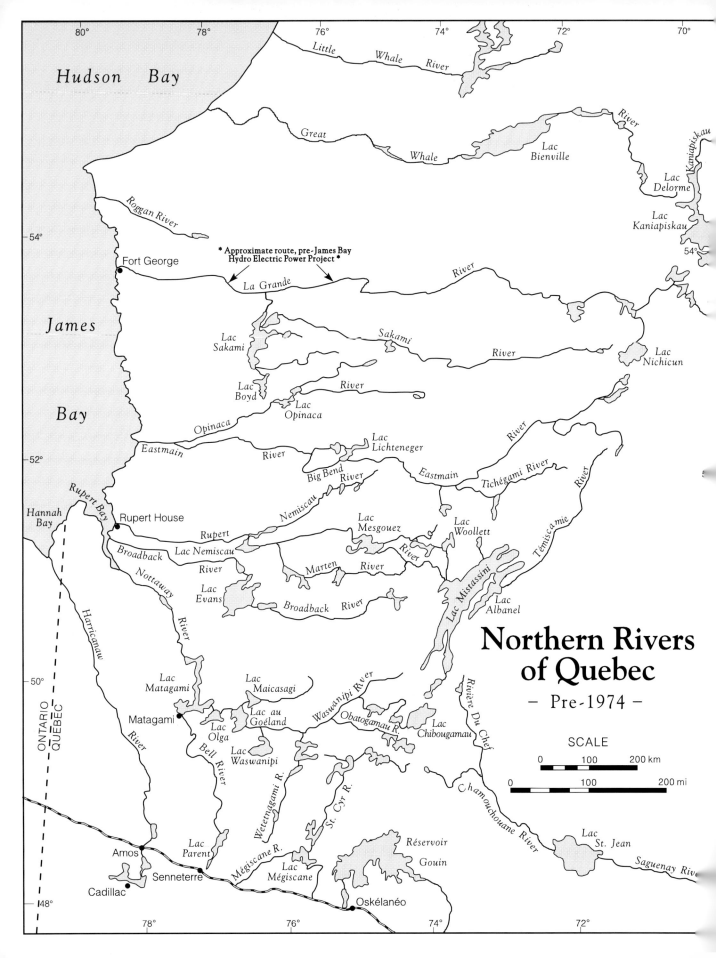

Hudson Bay

Little Whale River

Great Whale River

Lac Bienville

River

Kaniapiskau

Lac Delorme

Roggan River

54°

Lac Kaniapiskau

54°

Fort George

* Approximate route, pre-James Bay
Hydro Electric Power Project *

La Grande River

James

Lac Sakami

Sakami River

Lac Nichicun

Lac Boyd

River

Bay

Lac Opinaca

Opinaca

Eastmain River

Lac Lichteneger

River

52°

Big Bend River

Eastmain

Tichégami River

River

Rupert Bay

Nemiscau River

Lac Mesgouez

Lac Woollett

River

Témiscamie River

Hannah Bay

Rupert House

Rupert

Lac Nemiscau

Marten River

River

Lac Mistassini

Broadback

Nottaway

River

Lac Evans

Broadback River

Lac Albanel

Harricanau

**Northern Rivers
of Quebec**

– Pre-1974 –

50°

Lac Matagami

Lac Maicasagi

Waswanipi River

Rivière Du Chef

SCALE

ONTARIO
QUEBEC

Matagami

Lac au Goéland

Obatogamau R.

Lac Chibougamau

0   100   200 km

River

Lac Olga

0   100   200 mi

Bell River

Lac Waswanipi

Wetetnagami R.

St. Cyr R.

Réservoir Gouin

Lac St. Jean

Lac Parent

Chamouchouane River

Amos

Mégiscane R.

Lac Mégiscane

Saguenay River

48°

Senneterre

Cadillac

Oskélanéo

78°   76°   74°   72°

1957 Camp Keewaydin: Jim Bates and Nishe Belanger led a boys' group following the 1951 route. [*Ibid.*]

1958 Camp Keewaydin: Ron Hummel and Nishe Belanger led a boys' group following the 1951 route. [*Ibid.*]

1959 Camp Keewaydin: Peyton Conger and Nishe Belanger led a boys' group following the 1951 route. [*Ibid.*]

1960 Serge Théoret, aged sixteen, with three friends, Pierre and Jean Judd and Gabriel Ménard, all about the same age, using wood-canvas canoes they had made the previous winter, started at Lake Cadillac and canoed down the Harricanaw to James Bay, continuing around to Moosonee. They returned up the Harricanaw, taking forty-eight days. (Tragically, the following year, all but Théoret were drowned in a spring canoeing accident.) [WCA Symposium, 1994; personal communication – Théoret]

1961 Camp Keewaydin: Tom Dalglish and Nishe Belanger led a boys' group, which included Edward Lveleth, using their regular canvas-covered canoes, canoeing from Lake Temagami down the Harricanaw, as above. They were wind-bound for two days on James Bay. [Back, B., p. 172; personal communication – Lveleth]

pre-1971 An unknown canoeist was involved "in a disaster several years back." [Fenwick unpublished log]

1971 Gordon Fenwick, Jerry Hodge, Bill Johnson, John Long, Dave McDonald and Guy Saingenny canoed from Joutel down the Harricanaw to James Bay, and along Hannah Bay to Moosonee. [Morse files, p. 15]

1979 *Bernard Tremblay, Gilles Lortie, Marc Blais, Jacques Grondin, Jocelyn Roy, Danielle Vallée, Jean Brodeur, and Guy Doré canoed from Joutel down the Harricanaw River and around the bay to Moose Factory. [Personal communication – Doré]*

NOTTAWAY

The Nottaway was named for the "Nadowa", a term of abuse the Algonkian First Nations, especially the Cree, used to describe the Iroquois raiders from the south.

This river was the main invasion route of the Iroquois, coming from the St. Lawrence up the St. Maurice, across the height of land by various lakes and portages and down the Nottaway.

The Nottaway has two important tributaries, the Bell, which is really the upper Nottaway, and the Waswanipi-Chibougamau. Many of the trips which are recorded under Nottaway did not reach the Nottaway proper, and fewer reached the Bay via the Nottaway. Indeed, many travellers to Rupert House cross from the mouth of the Bell, up the Waswanipi, over to the upper Broadback, descend it until they make the "Rupert Carry" to Lake Nemiscau where they join the lower Rupert and continue down to the Bay.

1775 *John Thomas, HBC, explored for 200 miles up the Nottaway River and down again. [Francis and Morantz, p. 82]*

1793 *George Jackman, surgeon at Eastmain, having gone up the Rupert with four Rupert House people as guides, crossed over to Lac au Goéland and returned down the Nottaway. [Ibid., p. 106]*

1895 Robert Bell, for the Geological Survey, having come up the Gatineau River to Grand Lake Victoria, crossed over to the Bell River, later named for him, followed it to Lake Matagami and continued down the Nottaway River to Rupert Bay in James Bay. [Zaslow, p.170, map p. 167]

1896 Robert Bell, R.W. Brock and J. Mackintosh Bell, for the Geological Survey, explored from Lake Matagami via the Waswanipi and Chibougamau rivers to Lake Mistassini. [*Ibid.*]

1899 H. O'Sullivan, Dominion Land Survey, with his son Owen, Charbonner, and eight Indians from Point-Bleue, made the trip from Weymontachingue up the St. Maurice River, across to the Mégiscane, down the Bell and up the Waswanipi to Waswanipi. [Bouchard, *Mémoires*, pp. 104-05]

1899 Fathers Joseph-Étienne Guinard and Guéguen, Oblates, in two canoes, left the Baskatong Reserve on the Gatineau River, crossed over to the Lièvre River and went upstream on that river and the St. Maurice to the headwaters (now Gouin Reservoir), crossed to the Mégiscane following it and the Bell River down to Lake Waswanipi and went up the Waswanipi River to the village. They returned the way they had come. Father Guéguen had made this trip with Father Pierre-Marie Drouet every year from 1870-99. Father Guinard continued to make the trip every year from 1907-28. When the railway was built the trip was shortened by starting at Senneterre. [*Ibid.*, pp. 101-05]

1912   W.T. Curran in the company of an Ontario prospector travelled from Rupert House by motor boat and investigated a short distance up the Nottaway by canoe. [Curran pp. 77-83]

1912   Two survey crews set out, one from the mouth of the Nottaway, the other from Senneterre, to survey for the railway. The two parties did not get to within 100 miles of each other. Several of the Bay party were drowned and the remainder returned to Rupert House dispirited and half-starved before winter set in. [Anderson, J., p. 173]

1912   M.F. Laliberté, Quebec forestry engineer, reached Rupert House by ship, and with Indian guides explored the land between the Broadback and Nottaway rivers continuing up the Nottaway River to Lake Matagami. He returned up the Bell River to the railway. [*Bulletin de la Société de Géographie de Québec*, Jan./Fev., 1913, pp. 37-41]

1915-18   Rev. Harry Cartlidge canoed each summer from Senneterre to Waswanipi down the Bell and up the Waswanipi River. In 1917 he was accompanied by Bishop John Anderson. [Petersen, p. 77]

1918   Georges Côté was the only member of a party of four surveyors taking part in the Quebec boundary survey to escape drowning in the Mégiscane River. [Thompson, Don, v.3, p. 209]

1926   Clark Robinson, W.R. Buckminster, R.G. Harrison, J.B. Mead, and C.W. Mixter, Americans, with two canoes, explored down the Bell River from the CN railway to just above Lake Matagami and returned upstream. [*Appalachia*, December 1926, p. 518]

1929   Camp Keewaydin: "Moose" Wilson and Art Montreuil led a boys' group on a circular route

canoeing from Senneterre down the Bell River, up the Waswanipi and Wetetnagami rivers and down the Mégiscane, returning to Senneterre. [Back, B., p.170]

1930   Camp Keewaydin: "Moose" Wilson and Art Montreuil led a boys' group canoeing from Senneterre on a circular route down the Bell and up the Waswanipi rivers, as above. [*Ibid.*]

1935   Camp Keewaydin: "Hobie" Bailey and Art Montreuil, leading a boys' group, canoed from the railway at Oskélanéo over to the Chibougamau River. They descended the Chibougamau and Waswanipi rivers to Lake Matagami and went up the Bell River to Senneterre. [*Ibid.*]

1937   Camp Keewaydin: Jack Barss and Ben Parent led a boys' group in canoeing from the railway at Oskélanéo via the Oskélanéo and Obatogamau rivers, down the Chibougamau, Waswanipi and Wedding rivers, up the Bell River to Senneterre. They made their way south via Grand Lake Victoria and Lake Kipawa back to the camp in Temagami. [*Ibid.*, p. 171]

1940   Camp Keewaydin: Chief Boston and Ben Parent led a boys' group on the same route as 1937. [*Ibid.*]

1949   Camp Kapitachouane: Beginning that year, and with the exception of the years 1952 and 1955-57, under the leadership of Carl Williams, canoe trips were run from their base on Lac Choiseul just south of the CN rail line near Monet station. Before 1963, these trips followed ever-expanding circular routes using the Kekek, Eagle, Mégiscane, Wetetnagami, Opawica, au Panache, Hebert, Pascagama, Toussaint rivers, in a number of variations, all of the routes were pioneered by Carl Williams. Some of these rivers are in the Nottaway watershed, others drain south. Many of these routes continued to be used up to 1974 by a large number of Kapitachouane campers led by different trip leaders. [Personal communication – Williams]

1962   Camp Keewaydin – see Broadback and Rupert.

1963 Camp Kapitachouane: Carl Williams led sixteen campers from Lac Choiseul north across the Gouin Reservoir, and north through lakes Robert and Gabriel to Lake Chibougamau, through a series of lakes to Lake Gwillem, up the Barlow River, across the height of land to the north branch of the Chibougamau River to Miquelon on the railway line. [Personal communication – Williams]

1964 Jim Vanderlick, Austin Hoyt and Terry Townsend canoed down the Nottaway and met Heb Evans at Rupert House. [Evans, *Rupert*, p. 202]

1965 Camp Kapitachouane: Carl Williams led sixteen campers from Lac Choiseul down the southern branch of the Chibougamau River to Miquelon using a variation of the 1963 trip. [Personal communication – Williams]

1966 Camp Kapitachouane: Rod Beebe led fourteen campers from Lac Choiseul down the Chibougamau River to Miquelon. [Personal communication – Williams]

1967 Camp Kapitachouane: Rod Beebe led fifteen campers from Lac Choiseul down the Chibougamau River to Miquelon, going west from Lake Royer through a series of lakes and joining the river just south of Highway 113. [Personal communication – Williams]

1967 Camp Kapitachouane: Carl Williams led fourteen campers from Lac Choiseul down the Chibougamau River, branching off west through Lac la Ribourde, down the Maicasagi River to Lake Maicasagi and Lac au Goéland, up the Waswanipi River to Lake Waswanipi and up the O'Sullivan River to Miquelon. [Personal communication – Williams]

1967 Keewaydin Wilderness: Seth Gibson, Abby Fenn and Ted Morse, with Cree guide, Conscrit Raphael, led nine campers on an 800-kilometre trip of seven weeks duration. They started by train from Quebec City to Camp Kapitachouane on Lac Choiseul, east of Monet, canoed north up the Kekek and Eagle rivers to Keewaydin's cabin on Lake Opemisca, then continued down the Chibougamau River to Miquelon. They returned to Chibougamau by train, paddled north to Lake Mistassini, crossed to the Mistassini River and canoed down that river to Girardville where the train returned them to Quebec City. [Keewaydin, Dunmore (Vermont) report]

1968 Camp Kapitachouane: Rod Beebe led twelve campers from Lac Choiseul down the Chibougamau River to Miquelon. [Personal communication – Williams]

1968 Camp Kapitachouane: Fred Schran led ten campers from Lac Choiseul down the Chibougamau River to Miquelon using the route through Lake Royer. [Personal communication – Williams]

1968 Camp Kapitachouane: Carl Williams led sixteen campers from Chibougamau across Lac Gwillem up the Barlow, Blaiklock and Brock rivers, made an extensive circuit via Lac l'Eau Claire up to Lac Assinica, returning to West Brock River, down the Chibougamau and Waswanipi rivers and across Lac Waswanipi to Miquelon. [Personal communication – Williams]

1969 Camp Kapitachouane: Carl Williams repeated his trip of 1968 with a group of twelve canoeists. [Personal communication – Williams]

1969 Camp Kapitachouane: Rod Beebe led sixteen canoeists from Lac Choiseul down the Chibougamau River to Miquelon. [Personal communications – Williams]

1970 Camp Kapitachouane: Rod Beebe led fourteen canoeists down the Chibougamau River to Miquelon using the route through Lake Royer. [Personal communication – Williams]

1971 Camp Kapitachouane: Carl Williams led sixteen canoeists from Lac Choiseul down the Chibougamau River to Miquelon using the route through Lake Royer. [Personal communication – Williams]

1971 Camp Kapitachouane: Kevin Hagan led twelve campers from Lac Choiseul down the Chibougamau River to Miquelon.[Personal communication – Williams]

1973   Steve Braun, Howie and Dale Powell and Walt Soroka, put in at Senneterre and canoed down the Bell River, across Lake Matagami and down the Nottaway to James Bay finishing at Waskaganish. Steve Braun knew of only one other group canoeing the river in recent years, a group from Houston, Texas, which made the trip after 1973. [*Nastawgan*, Spring 1987, pp. 13-17]

1974   Camp Kapitachouane: Rod Beebe led twelve canoeists from Lac Choiseul down the Chibougamau River to Miquelon. [Personal communication – Williams]

BROADBACK

Until 1974 most trips on the Broadback cut over from below Lake Evans to the lower Rupert River via the "Rupert Carry" and Lac Nemiscau, avoiding the very heavy rapids and falls on the lower Broadback.

1914-16 H.C. Cooke, for the Geological Survey, explored the Broadback, [Zaslow, p. 319]

1962   Camp Keewaydin: Heb Evans and Nishe Belanger led a boys' group from Lake Temagami via Lake Kipawa and Grand Lake Victoria down Bell River across Matagami Lake, up a short section of the Waswanipi River, north via Goéland and Lady Beatrix lakes to the Broadback River. They continued down the Broadback, across Lake Evans and the "Rupert Carry" to Nemiscau Lake and down the Rupert River to Rupert House. [Back, B., p. 172]

1968   Keewaydin Wilderness – see Rupert

1969   Keewaydin Wilderness: Abby Fenn and Peter Potter, with Matthew Neeposh, Jr., Cree guide, led a group of campers from Mistassini post down the first section of the Rupert River south to the Broadback River, down the Broadback to Lake Maicasagi and west to Lake Matagami on a five week trip which finished at Matagami village. [Keewaydin, Dunmore (Vermont) Camp report]

1970   Camp Kapitachouane: Carl Williams led a group of twelve campers from Chibougamau up through Gwillem Lake, up the Barlow, Blaiklock, and Brock rivers north to Lac Assinica, down the Assinica and Broadback rivers to Lac Quénonisca, and by a series of lakes to Lac au Goéland, Olga and Matagami to Matagami village. [Personal communication – Williams]

1972   Camp Wanapitei: Bruce and Carol Hodgins, Marcus Bruce and Gay Wadham with a large youth group canoed from Matagami on the Bell, up the Waswanipi, over to the Broadback and down the "Rupert Carry" into Lake Nemiscau and down the Rupert to the Bay. Several of the group, led by Marcus Bruce had begun the trip on Lake Temagami. [Camp Wanapitei trip report]

1973   Camp Wanapitei: Marcus Bruce and John Clarke led an adult group, including several leaders of the "Save James Bay" Committee, in canoeing from Matagami on the Waswanipi-Broadback-Nemiscau-Rupert route. [Camp Wanapitei trip report]

1974   Camp Wanapitei: Alister Thomas and Christine Sivell – see Rupert

1974   Gérard Champigny led Maude Morin, Jean Francœur, Claude Baribeau, Yves Lafontaine, Claude Laurendeau, Raymond Pinard (filmmaker), and Bertrand Morin (soundman), with four 16-foot fibreglass canoes, flew from Chibougamau to Lac Assinica, canoed down the full length of the Broadback River, and around the bay to Rupert House. Pinard and Morin flew out from the mouth of the Broadback. [*Le Maclean*, Jan. 1975, p.16]

RUPERT

Historically the Rupert has been the most travelled of all the Quebec James Bay rivers. From the St. Lawrence, up the Saguenay to Lac St. Jean and then up the Ashuapmushuan (Chamouchouane) to Lac Mistassini, the Rupert provided the most direct route to James Bay for the First Nations and the early French explorers. Another route from Lac St. Jean went up the Peribonka and across the height of land into the Lac Mistassini watershed. In the early twentieth century canoeists reached the Rupert from the east-west National Transcontinental route of the CN railway at Oskélanéo, canoeing upriver to Lac Chibougamau and down to Lac Mistassini. Many canoeists paddled from the upper Ottawa, over the divide to the upper Bell, or more recently began on the upper Bell, continued downstream to Lac Matagami and then northwest to the Broadback, descending it part way, crossing over the historic "Rupert Carry" to Lake Nemiscau and the Rupert.

1661 Père Dablon and Sieur de Vallière ascended the Saguenay to Lac St. Jean, crossed the height of land to Lac Mistassini, and went down the Rupert River. [A.P. Low, GSC Report, 1896]

1663 The French knew that the Indians had long reached James Bay from the St. Lawrence by ascending the Saguenay River to Lac St. Jean, across the height of land to Lac Mistassini, and down the Rupert River. Guillaume Couture, Pierre Duquet and Jean Langlois, with forty-four canoes of Indians, were the first Europeans to reach Lac Nemiscau via Lac Mistassini, well down the valley of the Rupert River. [Francis and Morantz, p. 17]

1672 Father Charles Albanel, Sieur de Saint Simon and Sebastien Pennara, with sixteen Indian paddlers, came up the Saguenay from Tadoussac in 1671, wintering over in the Lac St. Jean area. In the spring they continued upstream, over the height of land and down various streams to the lower Rupert and onto the Bay where they saw an English ship, the beginning of Hudson's Bay Company fur competition. Albanel and his group returned by the same route. [Thwaites ed. covering 1671 and 1672]

1674 Father Albanel repeated his trip from the St. Lawrence to James Bay, via the lower Rupert. There he met Charles Bayley, who as HBC governor of Rupert's Land had just established Charles Fort by the mouth of the river. [Ibid.]

1679 Louis Jolliet and Père Antoine Silvy with eight coureurs des bois in birchbark canoes followed Albanel's route to the Bay and back. [Francis and Morantz, p. 27]

1685 Zacharie Jolliet canoed down to Lac Nemiscau and established a French fur post for the Compagnie du Nord.

1686 Pierre de Troyes – see Abitibi

pre-1693 The control of the lower Rupert passed back and forth between the French and the English until 1693, when it became a Hudson's Bay Company post.

1776+ The HBC established a major post, Rupert House, near the mouth of the Rupert. Brisk trade up and down the lower river followed. But the Canadian traders were active over the divide and on the Rupert down to Lac Nemiscau. [Mitchell, 1977; Francis and Morantz, pp. 101-14]

1778 James Robertson, HBC, left Eastmain House and explored up the Rupert River with two Indians. [Francis and Morantz, p. 103]

1779 James Robertson, Matthew Tate, HBC, with five canoes of Indians went up the Rupert to build a "log tent" at Mistosink Lake, and returned downstream the following year. [Ibid.]

1780 Thomas Buchan went up the Rupert River with the Indians and died inland of starvation. [Ibid.]

1790 John Clarke with eight Indian men and women was possibly the first HBC person to reach Lac Mistassini. [Ibid., p. 104]

1792 Michaux, a French botanist, travelled from Lac St. Jean to Mistassini but not down the Rupert. [Canadian Geographic, October 1948, p. 144]

1793 George Jackman, the surgeon at Eastmain House, went up the Rupert with Rupert House people as guides, crossed over to Lac au Goéland, and returned down the Nottaway. [Francis and Morantz, p. 106]

1803-06 This was the peak period of inland competition between the Hudson's Bay Company and the Montreal based fur companies. In 1804, Angus Shaw for the North West Company, descending the Eastmain, even established a post adjacent to Rupert House. Robert Folster made the NWC strong on Lac Nemiscau. After 1806 the HBC was again clearly in control of the lower Rupert. [Mitchell, 1977]

1812 James Robertson, HBC, went up the Rupert from the Bay to Mistassini.

1812 John Isbister, HBC, with two other men travelled up the Rupert River and established a post at Lac

John Galbraith, professor of engineering at the University of Toronto, makes camp at Rupert House on a summer vacation canoe trip in 1881 from Lake Superior to the St. Lawrence River via James Bay. [Galbraith family and University of Toronto Archives]

Mistassini. The post only lasted for four years. [Francis and Morantz, p. 110]

1819 *James Clouston, Patrick Flynn and Robert Chilton for the HBC went up the Rupert. Their journey is recorded in Clouston's* Journal of a Journey in the Interior of the Peninsula of New Britain.

1834 *James Killock and Robert Chilton, HBC, canoed up the Rupert and Eastmain rivers to Lac Nichicun. [Cooke, p. 144]*

1870 James Richardson, for the Geological Survey, explored the southern part of the region coming up the Chamouchouane to Lac Mistassini and returning down a series of lakes and rivers to the Gatineau and Ottawa rivers. [Zaslow, p. 120]

1871 Walter McOuat for the Geological Survey, came up the Mistassini River from Lac St. Jean to Lac Mistassini. [Zaslow, p. 120].

1881 John Galbraith – see Missinaibi

1885 A.P. Low and James Macoun for the Geological Survey, having made their way to Lac Mistassini, canoed down the Rupert River to the coast in thirteen days. [Zaslow, p. 168; *Ottawa Naturalist*, 4, April 1890. pp. 11-28]

1892 A.P. Low and A.H.D. Ross, for the Geological Survey, went up the Chamouchouane River to Lac Mistassini, canoed down the Rupert to the point at which they could portage across to the Eastmain and descended the Eastmain to the James Bay coast. They completed the journey by paddling down the coast and up the Moose River to the CP railway – a total journey of 2000 kilometres by canoe. [Cooke, p. 154]

1893   A.P. Low and D.I.V. Eaton, for the Geological Survey, went up the Chamouchouane River from Lac St. Jean to Lac Mistassini, canoed down the Rupert and portaged across to the Eastmain. They continued up the Eastmain to Lac Nichicun and Lac Kaniapiskau and down the Kaniapiskau and Koksoak rivers to Ungava Bay. From Fort Chimo on Ungava Bay they caught the Hudson's Bay Company steamer to North West River. [*Ibid.*]

1903   Bishop J.A. Newnham, paddling his own canoe, travelled up the Rupert-Marten River system from the Bay to Lac Mistassini with the HBC brigade and returned down the same route in a group of three canoes with young and inexperienced Indians and eighty-year-old Nibosh. [Shearwood, Chaps. 23,24]

1909-13?   Thierry Mallet with Indian canoemen for Revillon Frères canoed up the Chamouchouane to Lac Mistassini and down the Rupert to the coast. The exact year is unclear. [Mallet, *Plain Tales*, p. 63; Mallet's inspection report 1920, p. 41, Revillon Archives]

1912   Two naturalists from the Carnegie Institute in Pittsburgh were on the Rupert River and continued over to the Eastmain. [Curran, p. 63]

1912   Anglican Bishop John Anderson came down the Rupert with the Indian fur brigade in a large birchbark canoe, having visited the parishes from Lac St. Jean to the Bay for two months. [Curran, p. 64]

1914   Walter Edmund Clyde Todd and Olaus J. Murie, making an avifaunal survey for the 6th Carnegie expedition, with guides Paul Commanda and Jacko Couchai, in a 20-foot Peterborough canoe, travelled from Cochrane in northeastern Ontario by National Transcontinental train to Senneterre at the Bell River crossing. They canoed down the Bell to Lac Matagami, continued upstream on the Waswanipi and Broadback rivers, taking the "Rupert Carry" to Lac Nemiscau. From Nemiscau,

in the company of local Indians, they canoed down the Rupert River to the James Bay coast. From Rupert House, Paul Commanda's place was taken by William Morrison, their canoe was exchanged for a larger sailing canoe, and they continued north along the coast to Great Whale River; on their return they also visited Charlton Island and Moose Factory, the whole trip taking from May 23 to October 6. Todd returned up the Mattagami River with the guides Commanda and Couchai to Cochrane, while Murie wintered over, visiting Rupert House, Eastmain and Great Whale rivers. [Todd, pp. 20-24]

1917   Bishop John Anderson and Rev. Harry Cartlidge continued their trip from Waswanipi by canoe up the Chibougamau River, across the height of land to Lacs Waconichi and Mistassini and down the Rupert-Marten-Rupert rivers to Rupert House. [Petersen, p. 77]

1927   J.B. Mawdsley, for the Geological Survey, was on the Rupert River. [Evans, *The Rupert That Was*, p. 19]

1933   Frank R. Pentlarge and party canoed from Lac Mistassini to James Bay down the Rupert River, "a route very infrequently travelled." [*Canadian Field-Naturalist*, April 1936, p. 59]

1934   Camp Keewaydin: "Hobie" Bailey, with Art Montreuil as guide, led a group of boys in canoeing from Lake Temagami down the Rupert-Marten-Rupert route. They started from the railway at Oskélanéo, travelled upstream to lacs Chibougamau and Mistassini and down the Rupert. After reaching Rupert House they continued around the coast to Moose Factory and took the new TNOR train south from Moosonee. [Back, B., p. 170]

1939   Camp Keewaydin: Rod Cox, with Jack Decaire as guide, leading a group of boys canoed from Oskélanéo up to Lac Mistassini and down the Rupert-Marten-Rupert route to end their canoe trip at Rupert House. [*Ibid.*, p. 171]

1943   Father Ernest Lepage and Father Arthème Dutilly, botanists, canoed up the Rupert and

Marten rivers from James Bay to Lac Mistassini and south on the Chamouchouane. On the latter part of their journey they believed they were following the route of André Michaux, 1792. [Cooke, p. 169; *Arctic*, #4, 1956, p. 270]

1944-46 Dr. Jacques Rousseau and Dr. Ernest Rouleau explored the Lac Mistassini region. [*Canadian Field-Naturalist*, March-April 1949, p. 80]

1947 Edward S. Rogers and Murray Rogers, on an archaeological reconnaissance supported by the Peabody Foundation for Archaeology and the Viking Fund, began at Oskélanéo on June 8. Their route took them up the Oskélanéo River, through the Gouin Reservoir, lacs Dubois, Obatogamau, Chibougamau and Waconichi to lacs Mistassini and Albanel and the Témiscamie River, which they explored. They canoed down the Rupert River to James Bay and flew out from Rupert House. [*Beaver*, September 1948, p. 29; *Canadian Field-Naturalist*, Sept/Oct l949, p. 183]

1947? James Neilson and three others prospected on the headwaters of the Rupert in the Lac Mistassini district. They flew in, and using canoes with motors, were on the Témiscamie and Kawashkiamishka rivers, and lacs Albanel and Mistassini. [*Canadian Geographic*, October 1948, p. 144]

1948 Edward S. Rogers and Murray Rogers ascended the Tournemine River, a tributary of the Témiscamie, the inward route from Long Portage, connecting lacs Albanel and Mistassini, canoed south across lacs Obatogamau and Dubois, east through lacs Jourdain and Ducharme, the Scatsi River, and lacs Potrincourt, Buade and Normandin, conducting an archaeological investigation for the Peabody Foundation. [*Canadian Field-Naturalist*, Sept/Oct, 1949, p. 183]

1948 Camp Keewaydin: Warren Chivers, with Bruce Carswell as guide, led a group of boys from Oskélanéo to Rupert House down the Rupert-Marten-Rupert route. [Evans, *The Rupert That Was*, p. 21; Back, B., p. 171]

1955? Jack Francine from Pennsylvania, a member of the Explorers Club, who had been a fur trader

around Mistassini in 1939, set out from Quebec City to follow the 1672 route of Father Albanel. Using a 19-foot aluminum canoe with a $7^1/_2$-horsepower motor, he went down the St. Lawrence, up the Saguenay to Lac St. Jean. There he hired two Mistassini Cree guides to take him up the Chamouchouane to Lac Mistassini, and down the Rupert-Marten-Rupert route to the coast. He continued to Moose Factory in a 23-foot canoe with the two Mistassini REE and two Rupert REE. [*Beaver*, Autumn 1956, p. 42]

1955-64 Tom Dodds, chemistry professor from New Jersey, spent each summer at Nemiscau studying the Cree language. He travelled there alone in a 14-foot canoe by different routes from Lac Mistassini down the Rupert, from Senneterre down the Bell River, and finally from Waswanipi. He went out each fall by canoeing down the Rupert River. In 1964 he bought an airplane to reduce his travelling time and died in a crash. [Evans, *The Rupert that Was*, p. 161; *Beaver*, Spring 1964, p. 32]

1958 Two young men from Ottawa disappeared canoeing from Lac Mistassini down the Rupert River. [Morse files, p. 4]

1962 Camp Keewaydin: Heberton Evans, with Nishe Belanger as guide, led a group of boys down the lower Rupert River. The route from Lake Temagami took them through Kipawa, Grand Lake Victoria, down the Bell River to Lac Matagami. They crossed to Lac au Goéland via the Waswanipi River, then north through a series of lakes down a section of the Broadback River, to Lac Evans, portaged the "Rupert Carry" to Lac Nemiscau, and then down the Rupert River to Rupert House. They flew back to Camp Keewaydin. [Back, B., p. 172; Evans, *Rupert*, p. 6]

1963 D.A. Chant, E.E. Lindquist, J.E.H. Martin and W.R. Allen, for the Dept. of Agriculture Research Laboratory, canoed the Rupert to collect insects and mites to add to Canada's national collection of insects. They flew in to Lac Lecordier and canoed down the Marten-Rupert rivers to Rupert

Beginning in 1962, Heb Evans led many trips for Camp Keewaydin in Northern Ontario and Quebec, particularly on the Eastmain River where he pioneered a new route each year in the 1970s. [A.S. Barnes and Co.]

House, flying out to Moosonee. [*Beaver*, Spring 1964]

1963 Robin and Victoria Fraser, John and Betty Dashwood, Dick Irwin and Bob Chambers canoed from Lac Chibougamau to Lac Waconichi to Lac Mistassini and down the Rupert River to Rupert House. [Personal communication – Fraser]

1963 Camp Wabun: Andy Smyth led a group of boys down the Rupert-Marten-Rupert on the route from Oskélanéo to the Bay. [Evans, *Rupert*, p. 21]

1964 E.S. Rogers, with Indian guides David Blacknet and George Georgekish, canoed up the Rupert to Nemiscau and down again to Rupert House. Sponsored by the Royal Ontario Museum and the University of Toronto, he collected ethnographic specimens, photographed the area, and collected data on the Indian hunting dog. [*Beaver*, Summer 1965, p. 30]

1964 Camp Keewaydin: Heb Evans, with Indian guide Albert "Nishe" Belanger, led campers Ray Banghart, Bob Dickgeisser, Steve Blanchard, Fife Symington, George Revington, John Celantano, John Hanna and Ken Singmaster down the Rupert-Marten-Rupert from Oskélanéo to Rupert House. [Evans, *The Rupert that was*]

1964 John Lentz, and friends, Wick and Kevin, with Johnny Smallboy, Cree from Moose Factory as guide, drove from Senneterre to Chibougamau and flew to the headwaters of the Rupert. They canoed down the Rupert-Marten-Rupert route to Rupert House. [Lentz trip report; Evans, *Rupert*, p. 202]

1964 A man and his wife paddled down the Rupert alone to Nemiscau. At Nemiscau they abandoned their rock-damaged canoe and hired two Indians to take them out to Rupert House. [Evans, *Rupert*, p. 171; Lentz trip report]

1964 Surveyors from Quebec Hydro were on the Marten River. [Evans, *Rupert*, p. 138]

1965 Camp Wabun: trip took the Rupert-Marten-Rupert route to the Bay.

1965 Keewaydin Wilderness: Warren King and George Morse, with Matthew and Murray Neeposh, Cree guides, led a group of campers to James Bay up the Chibougamau and down the Rupert River to Rupert House. [Keewaydin Dunmore (Vermont) Camp report]

1966 Camp Keewaydin: Heb Evans, with Tom Lathrop as guide, led a group of campers down the Rupert-Marten-Rupert route from Oskélanéo. [Back, B., p. 172]

1966 Camp Temagami: A trip guided by Jon Berger and led by Andy Smyth, with George and Jim Kiberd, Dave Clement, Brian Wilson, Paul Wright and three others put in from the CN tracks on the Oskélanéo River, canoed across the Gouin Reservoir, crossed over the height of land through a series of lakes to lacs Chibougamau, Waconichi and Mistassini and followed the regular Rupert-Marten-Rupert River route to Rupert House. Many Indians were using the trails and the Rupert River. [Personal communication – Jon Berger]

1966 Frank Cooke, Nick Groom, Doug Howe and John Topelko canoed from Lac Mistassini down the Rupert-Marten-Rupert to Rupert House. [Morse files, p. 21]

1966 A party of canoeists was overdue at Rupert House and was searched out by Hydro workers. [Evans, *Rupert*, p. 188]

1966 Keewaydin Wilderness: Abby Fenn and Peter Potter led a group of campers up the Chibougamau and down the Rupert rivers to Rupert House. Allan Matoush was the Cree guide on the Chibougamau, and Matthew and Joseph Neeposh on the Rupert. [Keewaydin Dunmore (Vermont) Camp report]

1967 Keewaydin Wilderness: Warren King and Peter Potter, with Matthew Neeposh, Jr. as Cree guide, led a group of campers down the Rupert River to James Bay. [Keewaydin Dunmore (Vermont) Camp report]

1968 Camp Keewaydin: Heb Evans, with George Revington as guide, led a group of campers from Lac Mistassini, down a portion of the upper Rupert, up Misticawasse Creek, Neoskweskau, down Eastmain River, with a detour around Clearwater River, to Eastmain House. [Back, B., p. 172]

1968 Keewaydin Wilderness: Warren King and Jim Spiegel, with Matthew Neeposh, Jr., Cree guide, led a group of campers down the Rupert and Broadback rivers to James Bay. [Keewaydin Dunmore (Vermont) Camp report]

1968 A party of canoeists was southbound on the TNOR after canoeing the Rupert River. [*Appalachia*, December 1968, p. 286]

1970 Michel Landry led a group of six canoeists, including David Beevis, from Mistassini post down the Rupert River to Rupert House on James Bay. The Hudson's Bay post at Nemiscau had closed that summer in anticipation of the James Bay project. [Personal communication – Beevis]

1970 Camp Wabun: Skip Porter led a group of campers on a Rupert-Marten-Rupert trip to the Bay. [1970 Wabun Report]

1970 Camp Keewaydin: Heb Evans, with Dan Carpenter as guide, led campers from Lac Mistassini to Eastmain House following the Indian portage route: Lac Mesgouez, a portion of the Rupert River, Lac Nasacauso, Eastmain River, Lac Pivert, Eastmain River. [Back, B., p. 172]

1970 Keewaydin Wilderness: Abby Fenn and Peter Potter, with Charlot Gunnar as guide, led a group of campers down the Rupert River. [Keewaydin Dunmore (Vermont) Camp report]

1971 Keewaydin Wilderness: Al Chase and Dan Roby, with Charlot Gunnar as guide, led a group of

campers down the Rupert-Marten-Rupert rivers. [Keewaydin Dunmore (Vermont) Camp report]

1972 Camp Wanapitei: Bruce and Carol Hodgins, Marcus Bruce and Gay Wadham led a large trip of youths from Matagami on the Bell-Waswanipi-Broadback-Nemiscau route to the Bay. Part of the group led by Marcus Bruce had begun the trip on Lake Temagami, reaching Matagami via the Bell. At Oatmeal Falls on the lower Rupert the entire group was surprised to run into construction of the highway for the giant James Bay Hydro Project. [1972 Wanapitei Report]

1972 Skip Porter (former Wabun trip leader) soloed the Rupert-Marten-Rupert route as far as Nemiscau where he joined up with the Wanapitei group to the Bay. [*Ibid.*]

1972 Camp Kapitachouane: Carl Williams led a group of fourteen from Lac Waconichi to Lac Mistassini and down the Rupert-Marten-Rupert rivers to Rupert House. [Personal communication – Williams]

1973 Camp Wanapitei: Marcus Bruce and John Clarke led an adult group including David and Jean Glassco and several members of the Montreal-based "Save James Bay Committee" down the Matagami-Broadback-Nemiscau-Rupert route. [Wanapitei Report]

Charlot Gunnar, kneeling on the right, with his family on Lake Mistassini, before setting off on his annual guiding trip for Keewaydin Wilderness campers. [Seth Gibson]

1973 Camp Kapitachouane: Carl Williams led a group of twelve starting at Lac Waconichi into Lac Mistassini and down the Rupert, through Woollett Lake, Rupert River, Lac Mesgouez, Rupert River, Lake Nemiscau, Rupert River to Rupert House. [Personal communication – Williams]

1973 Wild River Survey Group #5 canoed from Mistassini to Rupert House on the Rupert-Marten-Rupert route. [Parks Canada files, trip report written by Max Blanchet]

1974 Camp Kandalore: Richard Heron and Fred Loosemore led a group of ten boys canoeing down the Rupert-Marten-Rupert route from Mistassini to the Bay. [1974 Kandalore Report]

1974 Camp Wanapitei: Alister Thomas and Christine Sivell led an adult trip down the Matagami-Broadback-Nemiscau-Rupert route. [Wanapitei Report]

1974 Keewaydin Wilderness: Seth Gibson and Jack Hanly, with Matthew Neeposh, Jr., Cree guide, led a group of campers from Lac Mistassini down the Rupert-Marten-Rupert rivers. [Keewaydin Dunmore (Vermont) Camp report]

1974 Duke Watson, having canoed from Lac Hecla (see Eastmain) early in the season, with G. Bogdan continued down the Rupert River from the Quebec Hydro camp, 50 miles above Nemiscau to the bay below Oatmeal Rapids. The trip was cut short here due to freezing weather and snow storms. They returned in 1975 and completed the trip to the mouth of the Rupert River and down the James Bay coast to the mouth of the Harricanaw. [Personal communication – Watson]

EASTMAIN

In the early 1700s the Indians, in groups of three or four canoes, came down the Eastmain, Fort George (now the LaGrande), Rupert and Nottaway rivers to trade at the Bay posts. By the 1780s the parties might be as large as thirty-three canoes.

1755 *French fur traders from Canada were descending the Eastmain River to within a day's travel of the coast. [Francis and Morantz, p. 98]*

A.P. Low surveyed and mapped large sections of Northern Quebec, Ungava and Labrador on canoe journeys that were of spectacular length and duration. His travels for the Geological Survey took him from Ellesmere Island to the St. Lawrence River between the years 1882 and 1906. [GSC collection]

1776 *Thomas Buchan, HBC, with two coastal Indians, George Gun and Jack Spires, explored up the Eastmain River from Eastmain House hoping to reach Lac Mistassini but they were unsuccessful. [Ibid., p. 102]*

1812 *John and Thomas Isbister, HBC, guided by six Indians, established a post at Lac Nichicun, 200 miles beyond Neoskweskau, at the headwaters of the Eastmain River. The post lasted until 1822. [Ibid., p. 110]*

1834 *James Killock – see Rupert*

1892 A.P. Low and A.H.D. Ross, for the Geological Survey, came up the Chamouchouane River to Lac Mistassini, canoed down a short section of the Rupert and crossed north to the Eastmain, descending it to the James Bay coast. They completed the journey by paddling down the coast and up the Moose and Missinaibi rivers to the CP railway, a total journey of 2000 kilometres by canoe. [Zaslow, map p. 167]

1893 A.P. Low – see Rupert

1904 Clifford Easton made a 700-mile canoe trip in Canada. John Rugge believes that this canoe trip ended with a descent of the Eastmain River. [Davidson and Rugge, *Great Heart*, p. 195; personal communication – Rugge]

1907 W.T. Curran with a Welsh miner named Jones canoed 125 miles up the Eastmain and down again. [Curran, p. 95]

1956 Fathers Arthème Dutilly and Ernest Lepage with two Indian guides, using an outboard motor on a rowboat, ascended the Fort George River for 50 miles, then detoured south to lakes Sakami and Boyd, down the Opinaca and Eastmain rivers to Eastmain post. [*Arctic*, 1956 #4, p. 270]

1960? Dave Jarden, with Mike Buckshott from Pembroke, Ontario, as guide, and two others, went upstream to Lac Mistassini and worked their way north via Wabassinon and Tichégami to the Eastmain River. They canoed down the Eastmain to James Bay. [Personal communication – Jon Berger]

1967 Camp Keewaydin: Heb Evans and George Revington led a boys' group, which included Dan Carpenter Jr., from Lac Mistassini north through Chapichinatoune and Woollett lakes north to Neoskweskau, down the Eastmain River, around the Great Bend of Eastmain River and down to Eastmain House. They lost one canoe in Basil Gorge. [Back, B., p. 155]

1968 Camp Keewaydin: Heb Evans and George Revington led a boys' group from Lac Mistassini down the Rupert River, up Misticawasse Creek to Neoskweskau and down the Eastmain River, avoiding the Big Bend by crossing to Lake Lichteneger. They continued down the Clearwater River and the Eastmain River to Eastmain House. [*Ibid.*, p. 172]

1969 Camp Keewaydin: Heb Evans and Tom McDuffie led a boys' group from Albanel Lake, up the Témiscamie River, over to and down the Tichégami River, down the Eastmain, over to Lake Lichteneger, and the Clearwater River and down the Eastmain River to Eastmain House. [*Ibid.*]

1970 Camp Keewaydin: Heb Evans and Dan Carpenter Jr. led a boys' group from Lac Mistassini through Lac Mesgouez down the Rupert River. They crossed north through Lac Nasacauso and down the Eastmain River, making a detour through Lac Pivert and then rejoining the Eastmain River they descended it to Eastmain House. [*Ibid.*, p. 172]

1970 Robert Perkins, Denny Alsop, Nick Shields, Chris White, Bill Emmons and Steve MacAusland, on a two month trip, canoed from Lac

Mistassini up to the Eastmain River and followed it down to the coast of James Bay, taking the Lac Lichteneger-Clearwater River cut-off. When one of the canoes swamped in the Ross Gorge, they lost half their food and were on short rations from there to the coast. [Perkins, *Against Straight Lines*, p. 21, 104-8]

1971 Steve MacAusland canoed from Lac Mistassini to Eastmain House on James Bay down the Eastmain River. [Personal communication]

1972 Camp Keewaydin: Heb Evans and Dan Carpenter Jr. led a boys' group from lacs Albanel and Mistassini, up the Wabassinon River, over to and down the Tichégami River, up the Eastmain, crossing over via lacs Rossignol and Gasparin to the Sakami River. They descended the Sakami River through Lac Sakami, cut south through Lac Boyd, down the Opinaca River, and down the Eastmain River to Eastmain House. Heb Evans had to re-cut most of the portages on the Opinaca and the Little Sakami, and as a result the trip was five days behind schedule. [Back, B., p, 172; Evans, *Rupert*]

1972 Wilderness Way: Andy Smyth and Jon Berger guided Julie Hutchins, Lea Hutchins, Noel Salmon, Luke Wilson, Dave Homolski and Kenny Wapner from Mistassini Post to the north branch of the Rupert, to Woollett Lake and Lac Mesgouez, up Misticawasse Creek to Tide Lake on the Eastmain. On the Eastmain they travelled downstream to the Big Bend where they cut across Lac Lichteneger and the Clearwater River, rejoining the Eastmain, passing through Basil Gorge and coming out at Eastmain Village. [Personal communication – Jon Berger]

1972 George Luste, Dick Irwin, John Bland, Canadians, John Brimm and Joel Sklar, California, and Chris Horne from New Zealand canoed from Lac Mistassini down the upper Rupert River with a crossover to the Eastmain and down to the coast. [Personal communication – Luste]

1972 Steve MacAusland canoed down the Eastmain River from Lac Mistassini to James Bay. [Personal communication]

1972 Keewaydin Wilderness: Al Chase and Dan Roby, with Matthew Neeposh, Jr., Cree guide, led a group of nine campers from Mistassini post, up Lac Mistassini, up to Lake Woollett, across the height of land to Lac Baudeau, down the Tichégami River and the Eastmain River to James Bay. [Keewaydin, Dunmore (Vermont) Camp report]

1973 Camp Keewaydin: Heb Evans and Dan Carpenter Jr. led a boys' group from lacs Albanel and Mistassini up the Wabassinon River, crossed over to and up the Tichégami River to Lac Hecla. They crossed to and descended the Eastmain River, crossed over to Lac Lichteneger and the Clearwater River, returning to the Eastmain River, then crossed to the Wabamisk River, following it down to the Little Opinaca and the Opinaca rivers, which flow into the Eastmain River before it reaches Eastmain House. [Back, B., p. 173]

1973 Wilderness Way: Andy Smyth and Jon Berger guided a coed group of twelve, including Miriam Philips, aged twelve, and Noel Salmon. The route from lacs Albanel and Mistassini followed the route of Heb Evans' 1972 trip down the Tichégami, up the Eastmain and then following the Indian route via Quentin Lake to Wolf River to the Sakami. They canoed down the Sakami to Lac Sakami, portaged to the Opinaca and ran down the Opinaca, joining the Eastmain at Basil Gorge to reach Eastmain House. This was a 51-day trip, with more than 350 portages and over 300 rapids. Most of the route is now underwater. [Personal communication – Jon Berger]

1974 Duke Watson, E. Boissey, A. Hovey and R. Watson, very early in the year, canoed from Lac Hecla down the Eastmain to Île le Veneur, crossed the height of land by a series of lakes and streams, and continued down the Rupert River to the Quebec Hydro camp, 50 miles above Nemiscau. The Eastmain was in flood, and disaster was narrowly averted when one of the canoes shot over a 10-foot drop which was encountered sooner than anticipated due to the flooded channel and the changed appearance of the river.

George Luste contemplates the logistics of getting past a fallen tree on a portage on the Eastmain in 1972. [Luste]

Duke Watson returned to Lac Hecla, and with a different group descended the Kaniapiskau River. [Personal communication – Duke Watson]

1974 Camp Keewaydin: Heb Evans and Dan Carpenter Jr. led a boys' group in canoeing from lacs Albanel and Mistassini up the Wabassinon River, crossing over to and down Tichégami River, up the Eastmain and up Kawatstakau River to Quentin Lake. They crossed over to the upper Sakami River, came down through Lac Gasparin and the Sakami River to Lac Sakami, crossed over to Old Factory River and descended it to James Bay. They continued south along the James Bay coast to Eastmain House. [Back, B., p. 173]

1974 Stephen Loring, Tom Hallenbeck, Bill Ritchie, Charles Luckmann, Mike MacDonald and one other, Americans, canoed down the Eastmain River. [Personal information – Hallenbeck]

1974 Steve MacAusland canoed from Lac Mistassini down the Eastmain River to James Bay. He ran into the first crews of the James Bay Project. [Personal communication]

1975 *Stephen Loring and Tom Hallenbeck left Mistassini post, crossed Lac Mistassini, ascended the Wabassinon River, and crossed the height of land to Lac Albanel. They descended the Tichégami River to the Eastmain where they followed the traditional Cree travel route around the Great Bend, portaging into the Clearwater River system and rejoining the Eastmain above Clousten Gorge down to Eastmain village. The purpose of the trip was to record evidence of previous land use of the region by Cree families and to search for traces of prehistoric occupations in the region. [Personal communication – Loring]*

1977 *Camp Wanapitei: Marcus Bruce and Kelly Lawson led a coed youth group, which included Shawn and Glenn Hodgins, down the full Eastmain River. This was probably the last trip before most of the river was diverted into the La Grande, as part of the James Bay Power Project.*

LA GRANDE (FORT GEORGE)

1895 A.P. Low, for the Geological Survey, spent the summer exploring the Outardes and Manicouagan rivers and came down the Fort George River to the coast. [Zaslow p. 169, map p.167]

1888 A.P. Low – see Great Whale

1956 Fathers Dutilly and Lepage – see Eastmain

ROGGAN

1888 A.P. Low – see Great Whale

1945 Fathers Dutilly and Lepage travelled the Roggan and Wiachuan rivers. [*Arctic*, 1956 #4, p. 270]

GREAT WHALE

1816 *George Atkinson, Jr., and John Stewart, HBC, explored up the Great Whale River to its source. [Davies, p. xxxix; Francis and Morantz, p. 119]*

1888 A.P. Low for the Geological Survey explored the lower courses of the Fort George, the Roggan and Great Whale rivers. [Zaslow, p. 168, map p. 166]

1899 A.P. Low and G.A. Young, GSC, after exploring the entire east coast of Hudson and James Bay, explored up the Great Whale and Little Whale rivers. [*Ibid.*, p. 170]

1979 *Sylvain Beaudry, Johanne Lagarde, Guy Garant and Lise Côté, followed three days later by Alain Chevrette, Monique Goyetche, Gilles Larose, Robert Payette, Serge Théoret and Rock Marcil, canoed from Lake Menihek, up the McPhayden River, crossed to the Kaniapiskau River, descended it, crossing to Lake Bienville, and down the Great Whale River to James Bay. This was a 1025-kilometre trip, taking 49 days. [Personal communication – Théoret]*

1979 *François Boulanger, Daniel Rémy, Geneviève Guertin, and one other, for the FQCC, canoed from Lake Kaniapiskau down the Great Whale to the Bay. [Personal communications – Serge Théoret and Mike Ketemer]*

1984 *Jon Berger and Kit Wallace made a 35-day trip from Schefferville down the Great Whale River to Hudson Bay. [Personal communication – Berger]*

1986 *Mike Ketemer made a solo trip down the Great Whale River from its headwaters to the Bay. [Personal communication]*

1989 *Serge Théoret and Pierrette Lefebvre from Québec, Claude Contant, American, and Francis Bernier, Jean Luc Libersac and Jean Lavigne from France, canoed from the Kaniapiskau reservoir, across Lake Bienville and down the Great Whale River. The Frenchmen made a film for the French TV network. [Personal communication – Théoret]*

LITTLE WHALE

1818 *George Atkinson, Jr., HBC, with a band of Indians went up the coast to Richmond Gulf, crossed to Lake Clearwater, reached the height of land near Upper Seal Lake and returned down the Little Whale River. [Davies, p. xl; Francis and Morantz, p. 119]*

1899 A.P. Low – see Great Whale

HUDSON BAY COAST

1744 *Thomas Mitchell, HBC factor at Eastmain House, with Mustapacoss and John Longland, sailed north on the sloop* Phoenix *to the Fort George and Great Whale rivers and Richmond Gulf and returned down the coast. [Francis and Morantz, p. 66]*

1749 *Capt. William Coats on the* Mary, *and Thomas Mitchell, HBC, on the sloop* Success, *sailed down the coast from Cape Digges to Richmond Gulf, completing an HBC exploration of the coast. [Ibid., p. 67]*

1830 *Nicol Finlayson and Erland Erlandson, HBC, with fifteen men travelled up the coast of James Bay from Moose Factory to Richmond Gulf, ascended the Clearwater to Seal Lake, crossed the height of land and descended the Larch and Koksoak to Ungava Bay. [Cooke, p. 143]*

pre-1847 *Rev. George Barnley settled at Moose Factory, but visited frequently up the coast to Rupert House and Fort George. [Francis and Morantz, p. 161]*

1858 *Rev. John Horden travelled from Moose Factory up the coast to the Whale rivers. [Ibid., p. 145]*

1875 Bishop John Horden canoed from Rupert House up the coast of James Bay to Fort George.

1898 Owen O'Sullivan and his father, H. O'Sullivan, GSC, using two 18-foot canoes, surveyed the east coast of James Bay from Rupert House to Eastmain. [GSC Report 1904, p. 177A]

1906 Florence and Stephen Tasker — see Koksoak

1907 W. Tees Curran — see Moose-Missinaibi

1912 W. Tees Curran and H.A. Calkins with a group which included L.C. McFarlane, engine man, explored the Hudson Bay coast from Moose Factory north to the Nastapoka River, north of Richmond Gulf. Their purpose was geological exploration and private prospecting. They travelled in a small dory, with sail, and powered by a 6-horsepower marine engine, with a kerosene converter attachment, and towing a canoe for exploration. Motorboats were almost unheard of on Hudson Bay at this time, and their arrival at each of the Hudson's Bay posts along the coast caused great excitement. They travelled without a guide, except when they were transporting Bishop Anderson from Fort George to Little Whale River. Another group led by Harold Strong with seven men, travelled north from Moose Factory in a York boat with sail. The two groups met above Great Whale River, joined forces to explore the Nastapoka Islands with a base camp on Clark Island. They explored the Nastapoka River on foot above the 125-foot falls. They returned down the coast in September, motorboat and York boat rendezvousing at Fort George and at Eastmain in stormy and difficult weather with the approach of winter. The motorboat was able to make Moose Factory in late October and Curran and Calkins walked out, up the Abitibi-Moose in December with dogs and pulling their own toboggans to Cochrane. Harold Strong with his seven-man crew had to put the York boat into winter quarters at Eastmain, and with four men to a canoe came down the coast to Rupert and around Hannah Bay to Moose Factory. [Curran, 1917]

1912 Mr. McCall, surveying for the North Railway Company, travelled from Rupert House to Moose Factory in a sponson canoe with a small sail late in October. He joined with Tees Curran to cross Hannah Bay. [Curran, p. 280]

1912 Flaherty — see Povungnituk

1915 Olaus J. Murie, on the 7th Carnegie Museum expedition, made a winter journey to the mouth of the Nastapoka River from Moose Factory. When the ice broke up, he canoed northward up the Hudson Bay coast with two Inuit guides as far north as Port Harrison (Inukjuaq). He returned south to Great Whale River, catching the HBC steamer *Inenew*. The steamer called at the Belcher Islands and went on to Charlton Island. He returned to Moose Factory by sailboat and travelled up the Abitibi River to Cochrane with the HBC mail packet. [Todd, p. 24-26]

1915 Camp Keewaydin — see Mattagami

1920 Thierry Mallet, with two Cree, Peter Thomas Cook and Scipio, in a 20-foot canoe, went up the coast from Fort George to Pte. Louis XIV and back on a private hunting trip. [Revillon Archives, Mallet diary, 1920]

1930   W.E.C. Todd with Paul Commanda travelled down to Moose Factory in winter and up the Hudson Bay coast as far as Port Harrison with local dog teams. A 19-foot Peterborough canoe with motor had been delivered there the previous year for their use. They reached Richmond Gulf with motor trouble, sailed and paddled to Great Whale River where they got a lift by steamer to Moose Factory. They travelled south with a canoe brigade up the Abitibi River to the end of steel. This was the 13th Carnegie Museum Expedition. [Todd, p. 38]

1931   Murray Watts, Mike McCart, W.B. Airth and one other, prospectors with the Cyril Knight Prospecting Company, in two 22-foot Lac Seul model canoes with 9-horsepower motors, left from Cobalt, Ontario, and canoed, probably down the Abitibi, to Moose Factory, continuing up the James and Hudson Bay coast to Cape Smith, north of Povungnituk. Each canoe was loaded with 3800 pounds, mainly gasoline for the coastal trip. The group wintered at Cape Smith, exploring inland for hundreds of miles by dog-team and canoe. [*Star Weekly*, May 22, 1937; *Canadian Mining Journal*, Feb. 1933, pp. 59-63]

1935   Reinhold L. Fricke, J. Kenneth Doutt and Mrs. Doutt were taken up by steamer from Moosonee to Great Whale River and the Twin Islands in James Bay. With an Indian guide, they paddled and sailed their canoe down the coast to Moosonee where they caught the train south. This was the 17th Carnegie Museum Expedition. [Todd, p. 42]

1938   J.K. Doutt and Dr. Arthur Twomey, on the 18th Carnegie Museum expedition, made a winter trip with inland Indians and one Inuk, Ekumiak,

from Great Whale River post up the Hudson Bay coast to Wiachuan River and inland to the Seal Lakes and back to collect specimens of fresh water seal. Then by motorboat, with George Moore as guide, cook and interpreter, they went to the Belcher Islands, where they were joined by their wives, as well as Mr. and Mrs. Lawrence Wood and Col. Paul Hunt. They continued south visiting the other islands in James Bay. [*Beaver*, June 1939, p. 44; Todd, p. 44]

1941   W.E.C. Todd and Karl Haller, with George Carey as guide, using a 21-foot freight canoe with motor and sail, travelled around the Hudson Bay coast from Moosonee to Eastmain. They continued up the coast to Old Factory by steamer because of bad weather and on to Fort George and the offshore islands. They returned to Moosonee via Strutton and Charlton Islands by steamer. This was the 20th Carnegie Museum Expedition. [Todd p. 50]

1946   Bishop and Mrs. Renison with three Indians, in a canoe with a small outboard motor, travelled up the coast from Eastmain to Old Factory River, and did the same trip in reverse another year. [Renison, p. 235]

1947   Ilmari Hustich, Finnish botanist, Ernst H. Krank, geologist, W.K.W. Baldwin, James Kucyniak and Risto Tuomikoski, botanists, canoed from Rupert House to Great Whale River collecting botanical and ecological information. [Cooke p. 169]

1950   Thomas Manning and Andrew Macpherson canoed from Moosonee up the coast of James Bay, making an ornithological survey for the National Museum between Long Point, north of Old Factory River, and Cape Jones, and returned to Moosonee. [*Canadian Field-Naturalist*, Jan./Feb., 1952, pp. 1-35; *Arctic*, Vol. 4, No. 2, 1951, p. 122-30, *Polar Record*, July 1953, p. 798]

CHAPTER THREE

HUDSON BAY COAST: MANITOBA AND KEEWATIN

HAYES
(including Echimamish and Gods Rivers)

Rising just east of the northern end of Lake Winnipeg, the Hayes River became the major historic route to the western interior, both to Red River and to the Saskatchewan, the upper Churchill and the Athabasca country beyond the divide. The English Hudson's Bay Company and the French traders aided by French naval forces struggled for control of the area at its mouth and at the adjacent mouth of the Nelson until the 1713 Treaty of Utrecht guaranteed English control.

In 1682, the Hudson's Bay Company, under Radisson and Des Groseilliers, established a small post on the narrow neck of land which separates the mouth of the Nelson from the mouth of the Hayes, called Fort Nelson. Shortly thereafter it was taken by the French and renamed Fort Bourbon. In 1684 it was again briefly English, then French, and the next year English. So from 1685 to 1694 it was in English hands. That year D'Iberville retook the post, but Fort Bourbon fell again the next year. D'Iberville returned successfully in 1697, and the French and Canadian traders and officials held control of the mouths of those two rivers until the peaceful surrender in 1714.

During these years the Europeans rarely went inland. Cree and other First Nations traders paddled down the Hayes River to the post. The exception to this pattern was the great interior trip by Henry Kelsey in 1690-92.

With the 1714 acquisition by the Hudson's Bay Company, the post became known as York Factory, and was situated on the northern bank of the Hayes. With competition from the North West Company from the 1780s, more Hudson's Bay traders travelled upstream and west to establish interior posts. In 1811-15, it was the route of the Selkirk settlers to Red River.

After the merger of the fur-trade companies in 1821, the Hayes River became a complex link in the principal fur-trade highway to the interior. The main or Lower Track went up the Hayes, continuing past Oxford Lake, crossed the short "Painted Stone Portage" to the Echimamish River, following it down to where it emptied into the upper Nelson at the top of Cross Lake. From here it was a relatively short distance upstream on the Nelson River to what became Norway House on Playgreen Lake, a narrow arm of Lake Winnipeg. Travel on only that portion of the Nelson, as a link to the Hayes, is included in this Hayes listing. A second or Middle Track left the Hayes much earlier and came up the Fox and Bigstone rivers, crossing over to the northeast end of Cross Lake and sometimes proceeding west to the Saskatchewan, avoiding Lake Winnipeg altogether.

1690-92 Henry Kelsey, HBC, with Indians travelled up the Nelson Hayes system for twenty-eight days, about 600 miles southwest, "five lakes and thirty-three car-

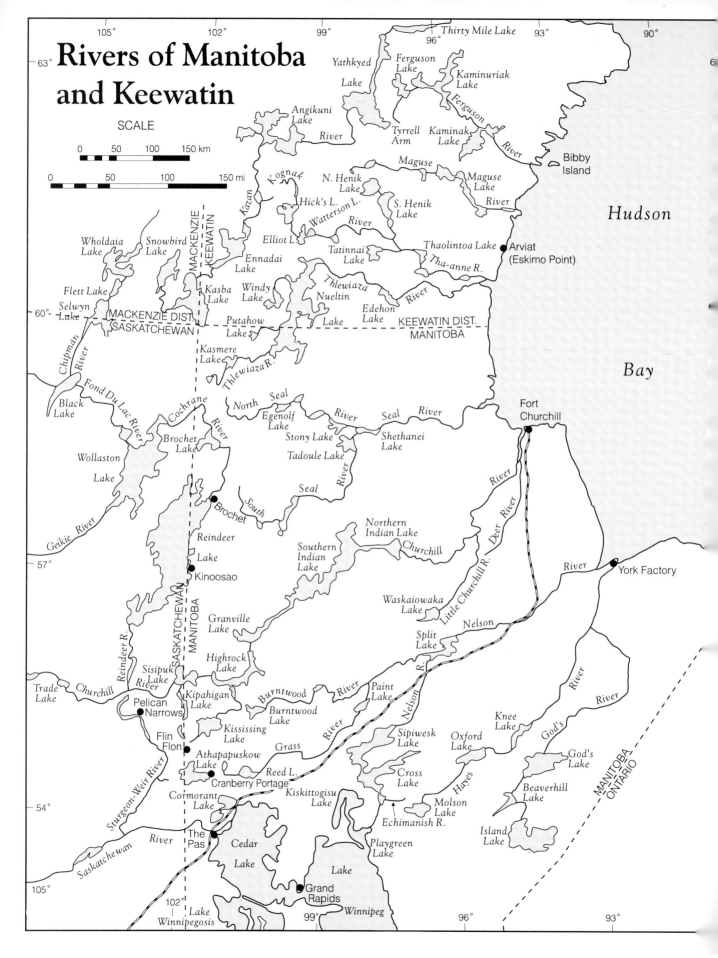

Rivers of Manitoba and Keewatin

SCALE

0   50   100   150 km

0   50   100   150 mi

Thirty Mile Lake

Yathkyed Lake

Ferguson Lake

Kaminuriak Lake

Ferguson River

Angikuni Lake

River

Tyrrell Arm

Kaminak Lake

Maguse River

Bibby Island

Kognak

N. Henik Lake

Maguse Lake

Hudson

Hick's L.

S. Henik Lake

Watterson L.

River

Kazan

Elliot L.

Tatinnai Lake

Thaolintoa Lake

Arviat (Eskimo Point)

Wholdaia Lake

Snowbird Lake

Ennadai Lake

Tha-anne R.

MACKENZIE

KEEWATIN

Kasba Lake

Windy Lake

Thlewiaza

Nueltin

River

Flett Lake

Selwyn Lake

MACKENZIE DIST. SASKATCHEWAN

Putahow Lake

Lake

Edehon Lake

KEEWATIN DIST. MANITOBA

Bay

Chipman River

Kasmere Lake

Thlewiaza R.

Fond Du Lac River

North Seal River

Fort Churchill

Black Lake

Cochrane River

Egenolf Lake

Seal River

Wollaston Lake

Brochet Lake

Stony Lake

Shethanei Lake

River

Geikie River

Brochet

Tadoule Lake

Seal

South

Deer River

York Factory

Reindeer Lake

Northern Indian Lake

Churchill

River

Kinoosao

Southern Indian Lake

Little Churchill R.

Nelson

Granville Lake

Waskaiowaka Lake

Split Lake

Reindeer R.

Highrock Lake

River

Trade Lake

Churchill

Sisipuk Lake River

Burntwood

Paint Lake

Nelson R.

God's River

Kipahigan Lake

Burntwood Lake

Pelican Narrows

Sipiwesk Lake

Oxford Lake

Knee Lake

SASKATCHEWAN MANITOBA

Kississing Lake

River

God's Lake

Flin Flon

Grass

Hayes

Beaverhill Lake

Athapapuskow Lake

Reed L.

Cross Lake

MANITOBA ONTARIO

Cranberry Portage

Kiskittogisu Lake

Molson Lake

Sturgeon-Weir River

Cormorant Lake

Echimanish R.

Island Lake

The Pas

Cedar Lake

Playgreen Lake

Saskatchewan River

Lake

Grand Rapids

Lake Winnipegosis

Winnipeg

riages to Deerings Point" which may be present day Le Pas, or farther up the Saskatchewan River. He wintered on the Plains, returned to Deerings Point in 1691 to receive a shipment of trade goods from the Governor at York Factory. In 1692 he returned down the same rivers with a large fleet of Indian canoes. [Kelsey, 1929]

1715   William Stewart, with the Chipewyan woman Thanadelthur, set out from York Factory with 150 Cree, on orders from James Knight, to find Thanadelthur's people, far to the northwest, for trade, and to improve relations between the Cree and the Chipewyans. The route is unclear and was travelled by snowshoe, on foot, and by canoe. They may have reached as far west as Lake Athabasca or Great Slave Lake, crossing or travelling on parts of the Kazan, Dubawnt, Reindeer, etc. [Beaver, 1974, pp. 40-45; Houston, To the Arctic, p. 316]

1715   According to James Knight at York Factory, 172 Indian canoes arrived at the post to trade, nearly all coming down the Hayes River. Most were Cree and Assiniboine, many Cree coming from the upper Churchill areas, even from Reindeer Lake. Many came from what is now southeastern Manitoba and areas between the Saskatchewan and Churchill rivers. There were also Bloods and Blackfoot from the west. Thirty of the 172 canoes were filled with "Mountain Indians" – Hidatsa and probably Mandans from the upper Missouri and as far west as the Rockies; there were even "Sarsi" – Sarcee from farther to the southwest. This pattern continued. [Ray, pp. 51-60]

1717   James Knight indicated that the crews of twenty-two canoes of "Mountain Indians" at the post reported that most of their compatriots had starved on the return journey in 1716, because the trip was so long and no supplies had arrived by ship for them. "It grieves me to the very heart to think how a country is ruin'd by a senseless blockhead not having thought, care nor consideration." [Ibid.]

1721   Henry Kelsey at York Factory reported large numbers of Indian canoes arriving, including for the last time, Mandans. Although a few Blackfoot continued to travel to York Factory, increasingly travel on

the Hayes River was by Cree and Assiniboines. Plains Indians preferred horse travel and traded their furs to the Cree for transport. [Ibid., pp. 60-71]

1730-54   There was a decline in the numbers of southern Indians travelling down the Hayes because of La Verendrye and French competition in the eastern prairies. [Ibid., pp. 52-55]

1754   Anthony Henday explored west from York Factory, up the Hayes with a canoeing party of Cree, and up the Saskatchewan as far as the Carrot River. He returned down-river the following year with a large fleet of canoes. [Gibbon, p. 40]

1757-71   The numbers of Cree canoes on the Hayes carrying furs to trade increased during these years. [Ray pp. 60-71]

1772-76   Matthew Cocking, for the HBC, was sent inland up the Hayes by canoe to the Saskatchewan, and all the way west to the Red Deer River to encourage more western trade contacts. [Ibid., pp. 44-45, 61]

1774-75   Samuel Hearne, for the HBC, was sent inland up the Hayes route to establish Cumberland House at the cross over between the Saskatchewan and the upper Churchill rivers. [Ibid., p. 45]

1786   David Thompson, for the HBC, ascended the Hayes River to make an extended trip southwestward to the Bow River. [Tyrrell in Thompson's Narrative p. lxxiii]

1790   David Thompson surveyed from Cumberland House to the mouth of the Saskatchewan and returned to York Factory through Playgreen Lake, up the Echimamish, and down the Hayes, through Oxford Lake, Trout River, Knee and Swampy lakes, and the Hayes. He returned upstream by the same route later that year. [Ibid, p. lxxiii]

1791   David Thompson returned to York Factory down the Hayes River route. [Ibid, p. lxxiii]

1793   David Thompson ascended the Hayes River route and continued on to an area on the North Saskatchewan. [Ibid, p. lxxv]

1811-12   Miles Macdonell, for Lord Selkirk (HBC), used the Hayes-Echimamish route for the transportation of the Scottish immigrants who would establish the

Red River colony. After wintering in York Factory, they set out up the Hayes River and reached Red River in 1812. [Cole, 1979]

1812-13   A second party set out for Red River from Scotland via York Factory and reached its destination in 1813.

1813-14   The third and largest Selkirk party was on the Hayes-Echimamish route.

1815   Robert Semple brought 100 Highlanders to Red River using the Hayes-Echimamish route. That year Lord Selkirk himself also came out to Canada.

1819   Sir John Franklin, Royal Navy, on his first northern voyage, with Dr. John Richardson, George Back, Robert Hood, John Hepburn and others, travelled from York Factory up the Hayes-Echimamish route to Cumberland House in a York boat.

1821   With the merger of the Hudson's Bay and the North West Companies, the upper Nelson-Echimamish-Hayes route to York Factory became the primary fur-trade route from the northwest interior to the British market.

1821   Peter Rindisbacher, with his family and others who had been recruited as settlers for the Red River settlement, made their way up the Hayes-Echimamish-Nelson route. Rindisbacher's drawings made en route have an important place in Canadian art history. [Dictionary of Canadian Biography Vol. 6, p. 648]

1827   David Douglas, the botanist for whom the Douglas fir was named, left Fort Vancouver with Edward Ermatinger and seven HBC employees for the overland trek east. From Rocky Mountain House they embarked in two birchbark canoes and went down the Saskatchewan, continued down the Assiniboine, etc., went north on Lake Winnipeg and down the Nelson-Hayes system to York Factory, travelling from Cumberland House in the company of George Back and Thomas Drummond from the Franklin expedition. [Douglas, D., London, 1914.

1843   Lieut. John Henry Lefroy, Royal Artillery, Bombardier William Henry, with two Iroquois canoemen, Laurent Thewhawassin and Baptiste Sateka, and Roubilliard and three other voyageurs, having travelled from Montreal with the HBC brigade, contin-

ued by "north canoe" from Fort William to Lake Winnipeg and Norway House, then down the Lower Track to York Factory. The purpose of the trip was to conduct a magnetic survey. Having completed the measurements at York Factory, they immediately returned upstream by the same route, crossed Lake Winnipeg, went up the Saskatchewan and Churchill rivers, crossed the Methye Portage, and descended the Clearwater and Athabasca rivers to winter at Fort Chipewyan. [Lefroy, 1955]

1846   Major J. Crofton led a contingent of British troops up the Hayes-Echimamish-Nelson rivers, across Lake Winnipeg and down the Red River to Lower Fort Garry. [Winnipeg Free Press, July 1967; Morse files, p. 2]

1851   Commander Pullen – see Mackenzie

1866   Paul Fountain with Indians Tom, Sam, Natanyan and Otmasquiloton, and French-Canadian voyageur Achil Guelle went from Fort Garry to Norway House and travelled up the Echimamish and down the Hill rivers. Sam and the two younger Indians returned home leaving Fountain, Guelle and Tom to winter in the area. [Fountain, 1904]

1868   Rev. Egerton Ryerson Young, Methodist, travelled from Norway House to Oxford House by birchbark canoe with Martin Papanekis and another Indian. Young made this trip on a regular basis, as well as canoe trips on the Nelson River. [Young, 1894]

1878   Robert Bell surveyed the Hayes River for the Geological Survey of Canada. [Zaslow, map p. 119]

1883   Rev. Joseph Lofthouse, Anglican missionary, to reach York Factory from Moose Factory, canoed up the Missinaibi with three Indians, crossed the height of land and went down the Michipicoten to Lake Superior. Taking a steamer to Port Arthur, a train to Winnipeg, another steamer to Norway House and a York boat down the upper Nelson, up the Echimamish and down the Hill River to Oxford House, he was ready to resume his canoe journey. With two local Indians in a birchbark canoe he completed the trip to York Factory down the Hayes River. [Lofthouse, pp. 21-29]

Rev. Joseph Lofthouse explored the coastal rivers of Keewatin and made a lengthy journey across the Barrens with James Tyrrell in addition to much regular canoe travel. [Lofthouse, *A Thousand Miles from a Post-Office*, 1922]

1885 Rev. Joseph Lofthouse, his invalid wife and six-teen month baby went from Churchill to York Factory to travel to England for medical treat-ment. The weather was bad and the ship too small so their journey was made by flat-bottomed boat with four Indians going up the Hayes, Fox, and Hill rivers to Oxford House and by birchbark canoe via the Echimamish-Nelson to Norway House. It was too late in the year for a steamer so they had to continue down Lake Win-nipeg by York boat, finally catching a steamer near Berens River. [*Ibid.*, p.81]

1888 Franklin Remington, just out of Harvard, with his classmate Bill, paddled to Selkirk, Manitoba in their Peterborough canoe and took passage on a schooner up Lake Winnipeg to Norway House. With two Indian guides they went down the up-per Nelson, crossed over to the Echimamish, and down the Hayes. [*Beaver,* December 1944]

1889 Bishop John Horden travelled from Winnipeg to York Factory down the Nelson-Echimamish-Hayes route. [Boon, p. 135]

1895 Bishop Newnham and Mr. Buckland, a layman of the Anglican church, travelled from Norway House to York Factory by the Echimamish-Hayes route in twelve days by canoe. [Shearwood, p. 110]

1898 Rev. Joseph Lofthouse, with his invalid wife, re-turned to England from Churchill by the inland route because his wife was too ill for the ocean voyage on Hudson Bay. Leaving York Factory with two canoes, two Indians, Joseph Kitchekesik, native catechist, and two native children, they travelled up the Hayes, Fox and Hill rivers to Oxford House, down the Echimamish, and up the Nelson to Norway House. Leaving his wife there, Lofthouse and the incoming minister, Mr. Chapman, with three Indians paddled down the Nelson to Split Lake. Lofthouse returned up the Nelson to Norway House and he and his wife re-sumed their journey to England via Winnipeg and New York. [Lofthouse, pp. 170-77]

1899 Bishop Newnham, Mrs. Chapman and her two children travelled from Norway House to York Factory via Oxford House, and the Hill, Fox and Hayes rivers. [*Ibid.*, p. 179]

1890s Arthur Heming, artist and writer, travelled on the rivers and lakes in the area of Gods Lake and York Factory, in the company of Indians, without giving specific details. [Heming, 1936]

1900 Edward A. Preble and his brother Alfred E. Preble, Biological Survey of the U.S. Dept. of Agriculture, made their way from Winnipeg to Norway House by canoe and steamer, and then with two Indians canoed down the established Echimamish-Hayes route to York Factory. They sailed north to Churchill where E.A. Preble con-tinued up the coast to the Thlewiaza River and Eskimo Point, and then both retraced their route to Winnipeg. [Cooke and Holland, p. 288]

1905 Owen O'Sullivan, for the Geological Survey, ca-noed from Norway House through Knee Lake down the Hayes River to York Factory. [*Ottawa Naturalist,* 1906/7, p. 31]

1908 Thierry Mallet – see Nelson

1910 The Governor-General, Earl Grey, with a total party of thirty-eight men canoed from Norway House to York Factory on the Nelson-Echimamish-Hayes Rivers. The members of the party were George Grey, cousin of Earl Grey, Major Trotter, aide-de-camp, Prof. MacNaughton, McGill University, L.S. Amery, *The Times* (of London), Prof. Brock, GSC, Dr. John McCrae,

Major Moodie, Sergeant Nicholls, Constables McDiarmid and Withers, RNWMP, special constable Collins, a cook and two men servants. They travelled in a flotilla of twelve Peterborough canoes, each paddled by two Indians, seven canoes carrying two passengers each, and five carrying baggage. The Indians were Thomas, Edward and John Mooneas, Philip Osbourne, Amos Robinson, James Sinclair, Albert Saunders, Thomas Farmer, Alex Halcrow, Frederick and John York, James Meswagen, Percy Walker and Isaac Fletcher, Jimmuck Neckaway, Thomas Menow, William Anderson, Charles Wesley, Charles Saunders, James Painter, James Vagg, James MacKay. Thomas Carson was the guide and interpreter. The Governor-General sailed on from Churchill by steamer to Ungava, Newfoundland and the Maritimes. [*Beaver*, Summer 1971 p. 14, Winter 1972 p. 48]

1911   Richard Church, New York City, with Billy Morrison, Chapleau, as cook, and Jack Robinson, Norway House, as guide, canoed from Norway House via the Nelson-Echimamish-Hayes rivers to York Factory. He returned to St. John's, Newfoundland on the HBC ship, *Beothic*, via Charlton Island in James Bay, and by ship to New York. [*New York Times*, September 10, 1911]

1911   Travelling at the same time as Richard Church were two "scrip buyers", Chester Thompson and Horace Halcrow, in two canoes with three Indians, offering the Indians cash for their treaty land. At Oxford House the group was joined by Herman Johnson, another "scrip buyer", in a large canoe with three Indian guides. [*Ibid*]

1911   Kenneth Campbell, Winnipeg dentist, and three friends, Richard Craig, Laurie Boyd, and Arthur Hogg, with Indian guides Solomon Farmer and James Fletcher, and bowmen Johnnie Robertson and Thompson MacDonald, using two canoes, made a recreational trip from Norway House on the Nelson-Echimamish-Hayes rivers to York Factory, and returned by the same route, tracking upriver. The canoes travelled for part of the trip in company with a brigade of York boats, and members of the party took turns running the rapids in the York boats. [*Beaver*, Aug./Sept 1992, p. 19]

1911   As the Campbell party were travelling up the Echimamish River they met two Indians and a boy canoeing from Gods Lake to Norway House.

1913   F.G. Stevens, Methodist missionary, with Peter Murdoch, Indian canoeman and assistant, and with Abraham Painter as guide, canoed from Norway House via the Nelson-Echimamish-Hayes rivers to Oxford House. They were accompanied for part of this route by the Indian fire patrol which was going halfway to Oxford House to meet the Oxford House patrol. They crossed over to Gods Lake, then upstream and across to Island Lake. Abraham Painter returned to Norway House, and two local men, Jacob and Jeremiah guided them east to the Severn River, including a nine mile portage. They canoed up the Severn River to Deer Lake, changed guides again and crossed over to the Berens River, descending it to Lake Winnipeg. [*Christian Guardian*, Oct. 8, 1913, pp. 9-11]

1922   T.M. Vesey with three friends (two of them surveyors named Mac), six Indians, including Beardy who had made the trip from Norway House to York Factory twenty-seven times, canoed up the Hayes River to Swampy Lake, over McNab Portage, through Knee Lake, Oxford Lake, down the Echimamish River and up the Nelson to Norway House where they caught the boat to Winnipeg. [*Outing*, December 1922, p. 99]

1922   An Indian family with three children canoed down the Hayes River from Oxford House to York Factory. [*Ibid*.]

1930   Eric Sevareid, seventeen, and Walter Port, nineteen, canoed from their home in Minneapolis to York Factory and back to the railway crossing on the Nelson River – a total of 2250 miles in an Old Town canoe. Having spent much of the summer on the early part of the trip, the season was well advanced when they reached Norway House. Without adequate maps or a guide they found their way on the Nelson-Echimamish-Hayes rivers to Gods Lake, down Gods River, and down the Hayes River to York Factory. They returned up the Nelson to the railway in the company of a group of Cree Indians. [Sevareid, *Canoeing with the Cree*; Sevareid, *Not So Wild a Dream*, pp. 13-27; *Audubon*, Sept. 1981, p. 44, describes the journey and their retracing of the route by plane]

1932   G.E. Webber with one or more companions canoed from Norway House on the Nelson-Echimamish-Hayes rivers to Oxford Lake and returned by the same route. [Morse files, p. 3]

1934   Wallace Kirkland with his son Bud, John and Gordon MacLean, Harris Barber, John Granata, Merrill May, Earl Gilbert, Will Adcock and John Stern, in four 17-foot canoes, paddled from Norway House on the Nelson-Echimamish-Hayes rivers to Gods Lake, down Gods and the Hayes rivers to York Factory. From the beginning of the Hayes River they were guided by Jim Begg, Carl Sherman and an Indian named Thomas who joined them for three days at Gods Lake gold mine. They returned up the Nelson to the Hudson Bay Railway at mile 352, and then canoed from Mile 185 across Land, Sipiwesk and Cross lakes up the Nelson to Norway House. [*Beaver*, June 1935; Stern, 1934]

1934   Ben Ferrier, with a group from Des Moines, canoed the Nelson-Gods-Hayes route. [Stern, 1934]

1941   Ben Ferrier with his wife Marion and a group of students canoed the upper Nelson, Gods, Hayes, Nelson route. Marion Ferrier claimed to be the first non-native woman down the Gods River. [Ferrier, 1956, p. 131]

1942   Leonard and Hilda Mason, American canoeists, travelled as passengers with an HBC Brigade, in seven canoes loaded with freight, up the Echimamish and down the Hayes, from Norway House to Oxford House. [*Beaver*, March 1943 p. 17]

1946   Ben Ferrier led a group from Norway House, down the upper Nelson, up the Echimamish, to Gods Lake, down Gods River and the Hayes to York Factory. They returned up the Nelson using the HB Railway from Mile 352 to Thicket Portage. The group included Marion Ferrier, stu-

dents Franklin Dunbaugh, Charles Nadler, Adlai Stevenson III, Charles Albright, Fred Hord, William Kellogg III, U. of Minnesota botanists John Olmsted and Orwin Rustad, and Art and Walt Eschbach, father and son from Iowa who came along as cooks to get experience in Canadian waters. This was Ben Ferrier's ninth time making this trip. [Ferrier; *Beaver*, June 1947, p. 18]

1946   A Mennonite missionary, two women and an eight-year-old child were making their way out to Winnipeg up the Hayes and down the Echimamish. [Ferrier, p. 29]

1949   H.J. Scoggan, N. Neufeld, J.D. Campbell, J.S. Robinson on a biological survey canoed from Norway House on the Nelson-Echimamish-Hayes rivers to York Factory. They returned up the Nelson to Limestone Rapids. [Scoggan, "Botanical investigations along the Hayes River route", *National Museum Bulletin*, 123, 1951, pp. 139-61]

1951   William Davis with various Indian guides canoed from Norway House on the Nelson-Echimamish-Hayes rivers to York Factory, doing the last 110 miles of the Hayes River alone. He returned in a party of three Indians using a "kicker" motor on the canoe, up the Nelson to the Weir River, and along the Weir to the HB Railway up to Churchill, Manitoba. He returned by train to the Weir portage, planning to canoe alone to Norway House, but 20 miles of travel proved the water too high and swift for a solo canoeist. He returned to the Weir portage and took the train to Winnipeg. [*Canadian Field-Naturalist*, Oct.-Dec., 1953, p. 148]

1955   Mr. Maurer, with two men, two women and a fourteen-year-old girl, Americans on a recreational trip, canoed from Norway House to York Factory on the upper Nelson-Echimamish-Hayes route. [Morse files, p. 3]

1956   Eric Morse, Tony Lovink, Tyler Thompson and Frank Delaute canoed from Norway House up the Echimamish, down Gods and Bayly lakes, Wolf River, Fishing Eagle and Knee lakes, up the

Hayes River to Oxford Lake, up the Carrot River, to Walker and Cross lakes, and up the Nelson River to Norway House. [Morse, *Freshwater Saga*, pp. 26-31]

1960 Bob O'Hara did a reconstruction of the 1930 Sevareid trip. [WCA Symposium, Toronto, 1991]

1961 Jay Pritchett and Mike Naughton, Americans, started at Norway House and canoed down the Nelson, up the Echimamish, crossed to the Hayes and from Oxford Lake to Gods Lake, continuing down Gods and the Hayes rivers to the Hudson Bay coast. They returned up the Nelson River to the settlement of Bird on the railway line. [Personal communication – Pritchett]

1963 Barry MacKichan, nineteen, and two others, aged fifteen and seventeen, canoed from Pine Falls up the length of Lake Winnipeg and followed the upper Nelson-Echimamish-Hayes route to Hudson Bay. They tracked and paddled 60 miles up the Nelson River to Amery where they flagged a train. [*Wilderness Camping*, Feb./Mar., 1977]

1964 Denis Coolican, Blair Fraser, Tony Lovink, Sigurd Olson, Elliot Rodger and Omond Solandt canoed from Norway House to York Factory following the upper Nelson-Echimamish-Hayes route. [Morse files, p. 2]

1964 Camp Owakonze: Steve Kling and Maurice Renard led Dan Addis, Herb Eckhouse, Hank Fox, Ray Higgins, Bill Hubachek, Frank Hussey, Mike Jackson, Herb Stern and Rick Wilson on a forty-four day, 1300-mile canoe trip using four 17-foot Grumman canoes. They began at Otter Rapids on the upper Churchill River, crossed over the Churchill-Nelson divide via Flatrock Lake and continued down the Burntwood River to Thompson, Manitoba. There they joined the HB Railway for a two-hour trip to Thicket Portage on the Nelson River. They continued paddling up the Nelson River to Cross Lake, down the Carrot River to Oxford Lake, and via Bayly to Gods Lake. F.B. Hubachek, Jr., sponsor of the trip joined them at this point before they canoed

down Gods and Hayes rivers to York Factory. Having knowledge of the Eric Morse trip coming behind, they left messages at York Factory for them. Half the group were airlifted from York Factory to Fort Nelson and tracked up the Nelson to Mile 352 on the HB Railway, but a problem with the airplane left the rest of the group stranded at York Factory. They were eventually flown to Churchill where they caught the train and met the others at Mile 352. The group were re-supplied at various Hudson's Bay posts along their route. Forest fires were serious in northern Manitoba that summer. [Camp Owakonze trip report]

1965 Camp Widjiwagan: Allan Johnson led Tom Binger, Bob Hebbel, Dick Perrin, Bruce Taylor and Jim Ude canoeing from Norway House on the Nelson-Echimamish-Hayes rivers to Hudson Bay, returning up the Nelson River to Mile 352 on the railway. [Camp Widjiwagan Archives]

1966 Camp Owakonze: Jack Stultz led a thirty-nine-day trip on a slightly shorter version of the 1964 trip. [Camp Owakonze trip reports]

1969 Camp Owakonze: John Hillner led a group on the same route as their 1966 canoe trip. [Camp Owakonze trip reports]

1973 Camp Owakonze: John Hillner and Jack Stultz led campers Mike Bray, Harry Drucker, Allan Gilbert, John Hayes, Peter Hosbein, Don Roose and Nick Streuli from Thicket Portage on the HB Railway, up the Nelson River, across Sipiwesk and Cross lakes to Norway House. They then canoed the Nelson-Echimamish-Hayes rivers, crossing over to Gods Lake and down Gods and Hayes rivers to York Factory. They canoed around to Fort Nelson and tracked up the Nelson River to Mile 352 on the HB Railway. [Camp Owakonze trip report]

1973 Bennett Redhead of Shamattawa, and other Indians, frequently canoed down the Hayes and tracked up the Nelson to Mile 352 on the railway. [Camp Owakonze trip report]

NELSON

There were three traditional routes used by the fur trade to reach York Factory from the western interior. The Lower and Middle Tracks have been described under the Hayes River. The Upper Track from York Factory was up the Nelson River to Split Lake, and then from the southwestern corner of that lake up the Grass River to the cross-over at Cranberry Portage which leads travellers either up the Sturgeon-Weir to the Churchill watershed or south to the waters of the Saskatchewan. The Burntwood River is another major tributary of the Nelson, flowing into Split Lake at the northwestern corner.

1682 *Radisson and Des Groseilliers established a post at the mouth of the Nelson River. [Francis and Morantz, p.27]*

1742 *Joseph La France, coureur de bois, travelled from Cedar Lake (Le Pas) down the Nelson River to York Factory with a fleet of 100 canoes carrying 200 Swampy Cree Indians. [Gibbon, p. 38]*

1792 *Philip Turnor, surveyor for the HBC, accompanied Indians to Chatham House on Sipiwesk Lake and returned down the Nelson River to York Factory. [*Musk-Ox, *#15, 1975, p. 34]*

1792 *David Thompson and William Cook, HBC, with two canoes, ascended the Nelson River, making a survey as they went. After Split Lake, Cook turned up the Grass River and Thompson continued to Sipiwesk Lake where he built a trading post. [Tyrrell, in* Thompson's Narrative, *p. lxxiv]*

1793 *David Thompson continued his survey in the area of Sipiwesk Lake, crossed to the Churchill River ascending it a short distance, turned back and canoed down the Burntwood and Nelson rivers to York Factory. [Ibid, p. lxxiv]*

1794 *David Thompson returned from northern Saskatchewan down the Burntwood and Nelson rivers to York Factory and after a short stay returned up the Nelson and Grass rivers to Reed Lake. [Ibid, p. lxxvii]*

1795 *David Thompson and Malcolm Ross came down the Grass and Nelson rivers to York Factory with three large and two small canoes. They left two weeks later and ascended the Nelson and the Churchill to the*

west end of Sisipuk Lake. Ross continued up the Churchill to the mouth of the Reindeer River. [Ibid, p. lxxvii]

1850s *Rev. James Evans, Methodist, had a canoe made out of sheet tin and carried a soldering iron for repair. He was stationed at Norway House and travelled thousands of miles by canoe. In attempting to cross the north by "the back route" – down the Nelson and westward by a series of lakes and rivers – with his interpreter, Hasselton, and another Indian, Evans accidentally shot the interpreter on the Nelson River and killed him. [Young, p. 145]*

1868 *Rev. Egerton Ryerson Young – see Hayes*

1879 Robert Bell, for the GSC went down the Churchill and up the Nelson. [Zaslow, p. 119]

1898 Rev. Joseph Lofthouse – see Hayes

1899 Mr. C. Chapman, Anglican missionary, completed his journey begun the previous year from Split Lake to York Factory down the Nelson River. [Lofthouse, p. 176]

1901 Harry Macfie, a Swede, and Sam Kilburn from Manchester, England, canoed down the Nelson River from Norway House up the Megaleepneebe, southeast from the Nelson, in search of gold. They panned and found some small gold nuggets, but the Indians drove them out of the area. [Macfie, 1951]

1906 William McInnes, GSC, canoed down the Nelson River to Split Lake, also exploring the Burntwood, File and Grass rivers. [GSC Memoir 30]

1908 Thierry Mallet and Raoul Thévenet, with George Elson, Métis from Missanabie, made an exploratory trip for Revillon Frères to Churchill. They canoed from Norway House with six local Indians in four canoes down the Nelson via Cross Lake to Split Lake. They continued, with four of the Norway House Indians, five from Split Lake and one extra canoe, crossing by lakes and rivers to the Deer River, a small river which joins the Churchill near its mouth. This was the route of choice by the Indians who found the Churchill too dangerous. Leaving George Elson in Churchill and concealing their identities as rival traders, they returned down the coast of Hudson Bay to York Factory with Donald McTavish in an HBC boat, and out by the Hayes-Echimamish route to Norway House. [Revillon Frères Archives]

1909 E.S. Miles, with one assistant and two Indians, for the Federal Dept. of Public Works, canoed from Norway House and surveyed the total length of the Nelson River. [Thompson, Don, v.2, p. 204]

1916 Christian Leden, Norwegian anthropologist from the University Museum in Kristiania, studying Eskimo culture west and northwest of Hudson Bay 1913-16, travelled south on the steamer *Nascopie* from Chesterfield Inlet to Port Nelson and canoed up the Nelson River to the railway. [Cooke and Holland, p. 333]

1919 Charles Bramble, with a Swampy Cree canoeman, started from Cumberland House, went up to Lake Athapapuskow, portaged into the Cranberry Lakes, crossed to the Grass River, a tributary of the Nelson, and returned to Sturgeon Landing where a steamer took them to Cumberland House. He was looking at mining prospects for the Manitoba Government. [Bramble, 1920]

1922-23 Federal Government surveyors travelled from Reindeer Lake to Thompson, Manitoba, via the Loon River, Granville, Costello, Suwanee, and Rat lakes, Rat River and Three Point Lake. Thompson is on the Burntwood River, a tributary of the Nelson River. [Morse files, p. 4]

1927 Lewis R. Freeman, professional travel writer, covered two of Canada's drainage systems in one summer. He travelled the Peace-Mackenzie system by launch and HBC transportation. Beginning in September, the Saskatchewan-Nelson system was travelled by a variety of methods: collapsible canvas boat with small outboard to Le Pas, railway to the Limestone River crossing of the Nelson, and down the Nelson in an HBC freighter canoe with Métis guide and outboard motor. [Freeman, 1928]

1930 C.H. "Marsh" Ney canoed down the Nelson River to Port Nelson (small motors on the canoe) and down the coast of Hudson Bay to the Ontario border for the Ontario-Manitoba Boundary Survey. [Thompson, Don, v.3, p.42]

1930 Eric Sevareid and Walter Port – see Hayes

1934 Wallace Kirkland – see Hayes

1956 Eric Morse – see Hayes

1962 Bob Matteson, with his sons Sumner and Rob, canoed the Grass and Nelson rivers. [Matteson – unpublished Coppermine report]

1963 Barry MacKichan – see Hayes

1964 Camp Owakonze – see Hayes

1965 Camp Widjiwagan – see Hayes

1965 Camp Owakonze – see Hayes

1966 Camp Owakonze – see Hayes

1970 Duke Watson, W. Black, J. Docter and Jas. Docter canoed from Norway House to Split Lake down the upper Nelson River. [Personal communication – Watson]

1970 Duke Watson, J. Roush, N. Roush and M. Watson canoed from Karsakuwigimak Lake down the Rat River to Threepoint Lake on the Burntwood-Nelson River system. [Personal communication – Duke Watson]

1970 Duke Watson, B. McCrory, J. Roush and Z. Siegl canoed from Thompson, Manitoba, down the Burntwood River to Split Lake and continued down the Nelson River to Hudson Bay. [Personal communication – Watson]

1970, '72 Joe Paulson, his wife and two children, canoed from Keewatin, Ontario, down the Winnipeg River, up Lake Winnipeg, down the Nelson and Burntwood rivers to Thompson, Manitoba. [Personal communication]

1971 Larry Osgood, Erwin Streisinger, Don and Maria Scott canoed and kayaked the Burntwood River. [Personal communication – Osgood]

1973 Camp Owakonze – see Hayes

1973 Bennett Redhead – see Hayes

CHURCHILL

The Churchill River, beginning close to the border of Alberta, is the most westerly of the rivers which flow into Hudson Bay. It has been described by Edward McCourt, in *Saskatchewan*, as a freakish river in that instead of gathering its main flow from subsidiary streams over a lengthy stretch of territory it springs almost full-fledged into being. As it flows east through Saskatchewan, it is the link which joins a series of sizable lakes. This part of the river was heavily travelled by both the First Nations and the fur traders, carrying traffic north up the La Loche River to the Methye Portage, or west up the Beaver River via Lac La Biche to the Athabasca River. In the east, the connection could be made at Frog Portage via the Sturgeon-Weir to Cumberland House on the Saskatchewan River. As the Churchill River flows east and north, the river continues to be a water-chain linking together a series of lakes of astonishing number and varying magnitude, including Southern and Northern Indian lakes, with many twists and turns, before it finally flows northeast and then due north into Hudson Bay.

The first European to land at the mouth of the Churchill River was Jens Munk who wintered there in 1619 and lost fifty-nine out of a crew of sixty-one to scurvy. The Hudson's Bay Company reached the mouth of the river in 1689 sailing up from York Fort, and included in the crew was Henry Kelsey. Kelsey travelled north from the Churchill River to make contact with Dogrib Indians but was unsuccessful.

The stone Prince of Wales Fort, begun in 1730 and completed during the eighteenth century, was home to at least two distinguished explorers, Samuel Hearne and David Thompson. The lower Churchill River however did not play a large part as an exploration route. Strong currents, falls and rapids made it a difficult river to ascend, and it was not a traditional Indian route. The Nelson and preferably the Hayes were the routes of choice from the Hudson Bay coast to the interior.

The very heavy usage of the upper Churchill both historically and currently, and its relative southerliness, has dictated the arbitrary decision to chronicle travel only on the lower Churchill, beginning at the entry of the Reindeer River from the north. Thus Reindeer Lake and the Cochrane River will also be included in this section. A classic account of a canoe trip on the upper Churchill River is *The Lonely Land* by Sigurd Olson.

Upper Churchill – 1955. Eric Morse, having introduced his Ottawa friends to southern Ontario canoe trips, was persuaded to organize longer, northern expeditions following recognized fur-trade routes. The loosely-constituted group, calling themselves the "Voyageurs", are setting out from Prince Albert for the trip down the upper Churchill River that resulted in Sigurd Olson's book *The Lonely Land*. Left to right: Omond Solandt, Sigurd Olson, Denis Coolican, Eric Morse, Tony Lovink and Elliot Rodger.

1770-72 Samuel Hearne made three trips west from Prince of Wales Fort finally succeeding on the third one in reaching the Coppermine River on the Arctic Ocean.

1793 Peter Fidler, a surveyor for the HBC, after exploring the Seal River returned down the Churchill River from Southern Indian Lake and surveyed the river to its mouth. [Musk-Ox, #15, 1975, p.34]

1795 David Thompson – see Nelson

1796 David Thompson, HBC, surveyed on the Churchill River east from Sisipuk Lake to the mouth of the Kississing River. He then ascended the Churchill to the mouth of the Reindeer River, hired two Chipewyans, Kozdaw and "Paddy", and explored up the Reindeer River, north up the west side of Reindeer Lake, up Paint River, across the height of land, and down into Wollaston (Manito) Lake, continued around the north end of this lake, down the Fond du Lac (Black) River, to Lake Athabasca. On the return journey up the Fond du Lac, Thompson nearly lost his life when the Indians tracking the canoe lost control and the canoe, with Thompson in it, went over a 12-foot falls. They made their way back to Fairford House at the mouth of the Reindeer River. [Thompson, David, pp. 108-20]

1797 David Thompson, now of the North West Company, canoed down the Reindeer River on his way south and west. [Tyrrell, Thompson's Narrative, p. lxxviii]

1804 David Thompson travelled north from Fort William to Cranberry Portage and continued, crossing north up Little Swan River, down the File River into Burntwood Lake and down the Churchill River to winter at Musquawegan Post. [Ibid, p. xc]

1805 David Thompson made a journey from Musquawegan Post down the Churchill River to the south end of Southern Indian Lake and back. He then returned upstream on the Churchill, circled south to Cranberry Portage, ascended the Sturgeon-Weir to Beaver Lake, crossed over Frog Portage, descended the Churchill to Reindeer River which he ascended into Reindeer Lake. He returned south to Cranberry Portage and wintered nearby at Reed Lake. [Ibid, xc]

1822 Governor Simpson, HBC, attempting to find a shorter route from Athabasca country to York Factory, travelled from York Factory up the Nelson and Burntwood rivers, across to Kississing Lake, down the Kississing and Churchill rivers, reaching Frog Portage in fifteen days. [Musk-Ox, #15, p. 35]

1880-1 A.S. Cochrane, GSC, starting at Cumberland House crossed northward by Frog Portage to Reindeer Lake, canoed up the lake and the Cochrane River, down the Fond du Lac River and along the north shore of Lake Athabasca to Fort Chipewyan. He continued south, up the Athabasca River to Fort McMurray, up the Clearwater, crossed the Methye Portage and returned down the upper Churchill to Frog Portage. [GSC Report, 1893; Tyrrell, Thompson's Narrative, p. 114]

1882 The Geological Survey came through from Lake Athabasca, down the Churchill River to Reindeer Lake. [Buchanan, p. 97]

1892,93 J.B. Tyrrell with D.B. Dowling in 1892, and with J.W. Tyrrell in 1893, GSC, surveyed an area bounded by the Churchill and Clearwater rivers, the Athabasca River, Lake Athabasca, the Fond du Lac River, Wollaston Lake, the Cochrane River and Reindeer Lake. [GSC Report, 1893; Tyrrell, Thompson's Narrative, p. 114]

1908 William McInnes, GSC, explored Southern Indian Lake and the Churchill River as far upstream as Lac LaRonge. [GSC Memoir 30]

1908 Thierry Mallet – see Nelson

1914 Capt. Angus Buchanan, with a chance companion Joe Ryan, riverman and lumberjack, collected specimens of birds for the Museum of Natural History in Ottawa. In an 18-foot Chestnut canoe, they went down the Crooked and Beaver rivers to Île à la Crosse, down the upper Churchill River, up Reindeer River and across Reindeer Lake to Brochet. Buchanan continued up the Cochrane River for 100 miles and returned down to Brochet where he built a cabin. He travelled north in the winter to hunt caribou, but came out shortly after because of the war. [Buchanan, 1920]

684 FIFTH AVENUE
NEW YORK CITY
CIRCLE 7-7343

March 17, 1937.

Dear Mr. Downes:

Thanks ever so much for your letter of March 13th
and for the snapshot, which I will put in my collection.

I envy you for being able to take the trip down the
Kazan River to Baker Lake. I believe you will not have any
difficulty in getting out of Chesterfield by the end of the
summer. In my opinion, the quickest way would be to use a
native schooner and go down the coast to Churchill, where you
will have the railway.

My memory is getting a little hazy about Kasba Lake.
As I remember, it should take one day to paddle down from White
Partridge Lake to Yath Kyed Lake, and one day to cross that lake,
and travelling fast downstream, I should say that it would take
you ten days to Baker Lake. Watch your step when you leave
Yath Kyed Lake on the Kazan River. I ran the first rapid at
the foot of the large hill but shipped a lot of water. There
are a few more rapids after that; do not run them before looking
them over closely. You should not leave Yath Kyed Lake before
the first week of July. On my trip in 1926 I found Hiqua Liqua
Lake frozen solid on the tenth of July when only a hundred miles
from Baker Lake.

I will autograph the books and return them to you as
soon as they reach me here.

Wishing you the very best of luck, I am

Yours sincerely,

Thierry Mallet.

Mr. P. G. Downes,
Belmot Hill School,
Belmont, Mass.

In 1936 P.G. Downes, New England schoolmaster, began his summer-long sojourns around Reindeer Lake, going farther north into the Barrenlands each summer. In preparation, he requested route information from Thierry Mallet, who had been down the Kazan River in 1926. Downes (above) appreciated the Chipewyan people and emulated them, travelling light and living off the land. Note the caribou leg.
[R.H. Cockburn]

1915 F.J. Alcock, Geological Survey, mapped the Lower Churchill River Region. [*Geographical Review*, 1916, pp. 433-48]

1920 Canon Matheson with his wife Eleanor, Miss Halson, Archdeacon Mackay, Louis and Robert MacGillivray, Henry Wilson and Henry Bloomfield travelled from The Pas to Lac La Ronge and back on the Churchill River by canoe. [*Saskatchewan History*, Autumn 1969, pp. 109-17]

1924 C.S. MacDonald, for the Topographical Survey, Department of the Interior, with Cree canoemen, canoed from Fort Cumberland, up the Sturgeon-Weir to Pelican Narrows, up the Reindeer River and across Reindeer Lake to Brochet, up the Cochrane River into Lake Wollaston, continuing out to Fort Chipewyan, having crossed over into the Arctic watershed. [*Canadian Geographical Journal*, January 1931, p.3]

1926 Thierry Mallet – see Kazan

1932 Charles Planinshek ("Eskimo Charlie") with his two Métis children canoed from Windy Lake across Nueltin Lake, up the Thlewiaza and down the Cochrane River, down Reindeer Lake and Reindeer River. They continued south to the Gulf of Mexico returning by an inside passage to Florida and along the Atlantic coast to New York and Montreal. [*Beaver*, Spring 1983, p. 36]

1936 P.G. Downes with Solomon Merasty, a Cree from Southend, canoed up the Reindeer River and half way up Reindeer Lake and back in an Estabrook canoe. [*Fram*, Winter 1984, p. 131]

1937 P.G. Downes with Cree Indians canoed up Reindeer River to the south end of Reindeer Lake, and continued north to Brochet in a motorized canoe with the RCMP. [Personal communication – R.H. Cockburn]

1940 P.G. Downes with Alfred Peterson, canoed from Brochet in a 17-foot Chestnut Prospector up the Cochrane River, crossed over and down the Thlewiaza to Kasmere Lake in an attempt to map the route to Kasba Lake. (*This route was followed by Hugh Stewart in 1980 on his way to the Kazan.*) [*Beaver*, 1983, p. 36]

1961 Eric Morse, Blair Fraser, Tony Lovink, Sigurd Olson, Elliot Rodger and Omond Solandt canoed from Pukatawagan, down the Churchill River. Crossing to the Rat River, they continued down that river and the Burntwood River to Thompson, Manitoba. [*Che-Mun*, Spring 1993, p. 5]

1962 Douglas Wade and family explored the Churchill River by truck and canoe as far as Twin Lakes and Button Bay. [*Canadian Field-Naturalist*, April/June 1964, p. 130]

1966 Camp Widjiwagan: Bruce Koci leading David Buetow, Al Clapp, John Perrin, John Streater and Andy Turnbull canoed from Lynn Lake, Manitoba, via small lakes and rivers to Brochet at the north end of Reindeer Lake, then south on Reindeer Lake, down Reindeer River to the Church-ill, crossing over to the Sturgeon-Weir River which they descended to The Pas. [Camp Widjiwagan Archives]

1967 Duke Watson, A. Crooks, J. Crooks, R. Crooks, J. Docter, G. Docter, A. Watson, B. Watson, E. Wyckoff and P. Wyckoff, canoed from Southend on Reindeer Lake, down the Reindeer River and the lower Churchill River to Southern Indian Lake. [Personal communication – Duke Watson]

1967 Camp Widjiwagan: Bob Gehrz leading Greg Wascenda, Dan Schrankler, Ralph Peterson, Doug Webster and John May canoed from Reindeer Lake up the Cochrane River to Wollaston Lake and down the Fond du Lac River to Lake Athabasca, finishing the trip at Fort Chipewyan. [Camp Widjiwagan Archives]

1968 Duke Watson, A. Crooks, R. Crooks, P. Evans, J. Hossack, A. Hovey, V. Josendal, B. McCrory and P. Wyckoff canoed down the lower Churchill River from the community of South Indian Lake, finishing 7 miles above the mouth of the river due to strong incoming tides. In 1973, Watson with Bart Watson returned and completed the last 8 miles of the river. [Personal communication – D. Watson]

Al Herriot, Paul Lewis and Jim Putnam are passing a bald eagle's nest on the Cochrane River, going from Wollaston Lake to Reindeer Lake, 1973. [Al Herriot]

1972 Camp Widjiwagan: Kim Koch led a group of girls, Susan Fritts, Elizabeth Webster, Sandy Stowell, Alice Wright and Wendy Youngren from Reindeer Lake down Reindeer River to the Churchill River and crossed to the Sturgeon-Weir River to finish at The Pas. [Camp Widjiwagan Archives]

1973 Al Herriot, Paul Lewis, Bruce Stewart, Bob Hollies and Jim Putnam started at Wollaston, on the southeast side of Wollaston Lake and canoed down the Cochrane River to Brochet at the north end of Reindeer Lake. [Personal communication – Al Herriot]

1974 Eric and Pamela Morse, Marius and Constance van Wijk canoed from Brochet the length of Reindeer Lake, down Reindeer River, and crossed Frog Portage to the Sturgeon-Weir River. [Morse, *Freshwater Saga*, map #3; *Che-Mun*, Spring 1993, p. 5]

1974 Three kayakers, paddling from Southern Indian Lake down the Churchill River, had an accident in Mountain Rapids, and one man was drowned. [*Canoe*, December 1976, p. 20]

1974 Andrew Jmaeff led Brian Andres, Vaughn Christensen, Bruce Dodd, Bruce Button, Neil McLeod and Tom Brothwell, all members of the Outdoor Education Club, Technical High School, Prince Albert, Saskatchewan, on a 650-mile trip from Pelican Narrows, down the lower Churchill River, making one of the last trips on this part of the river before the completion of the hydro dam at Missi Falls. [*Canoe*, December 1976, pp. 20-23]

1975 *Duke Watson led V. Josendal, G. Rose and W. Zauche from Cunning Bay, Wollaston Lake, down the Cochrane River to Brochet at the north end of Reindeer Lake. Josendal and Rose were replaced by W. Dougall and R. Watson and the group continued from Brochet to Southend on Reindeer Lake. [Personal communication – Duke Watson]*

1975 *Robin and Victoria Fraser, their daughter Kirsten, and Allerton Cushman, Jr., canoed from Wollaston post, down the Cochrane River to Brochet. [Personal communication – Robin Fraser]*

SEAL

The main or south branch of the Seal River rises north of Lynn Lake, Manitoba, and flows northeast to Hudson Bay. It is Manitoba's northernmost major river. The north branch, which rises north of Reindeer Lake, joins the main river at Shethanei Lake. From this lake to the Hudson Bay coast the Seal is designated a Heritage River.

While the Seal River was never a main route for the fur trade, it was much used by the Inuit for hunting, fishing and travel. Prehistoric artifacts are often exposed on the surface of eskers and at archaeological sites along the River and the lakes. According to F.O. Martin, ship's chandler of Churchill, Manitoba, there were a few people who started at Lynn Lake and came down the Seal River to the coast before the 1960s but their identities have not yet been established.

1770 *Samuel Hearne, on his second attempt to locate the copper fields on the northern ocean, starting from Prince of Wales Fort at Churchill followed the Seal River on foot to Shethanei Lake, then went north by Wolverine River into the Barrens. The site of Hearne's camp is marked on the Parks Canada Heritage River map. [Parks Canada – Seal River]*

1793 *Peter Fidler explored the Seal River from Fort Churchill, discovering that it rose near Southern Indian Lake which is part of the Churchill River. [Musk-Ox, #15, 1975, p. 34]*

1964 Bob Jacobsen, Bill Jennings, Jim Arnold and Tom Spence canoed from Pukatawagan down the Churchill River to Southern Indian Lake, crossed to the South Seal River and followed it to Hudson Bay. [Morse files, p. 19]

1965 Bob Jacobsen canoed (with a group?) from Pukatawagan down the Churchill River to Southern Indian Lake, continued down the South Seal River to the North Seal, which they explored. [Morse files, p. 19]

1966 Bob Jacobsen and Dave Geilen started at Tadoule Lake, canoed up the North Seal River to Blackfish and Booth lakes and up Art Moffatt Creek to Nueltin Lake. At the south end of Nueltin Lake they finished the trip at Hawkes Summit. [Morse files, p. 19]

1968 Bob and Suzy Jacobsen, Jan Freed and Guiseppi Slater explored from Hawkes Summit to the north end of Nueltin Lake, finishing the trip at Sealhole Lake. [Morse files, p. 19]

Pre-1972 An unnamed Minnesota canoeist smashed his canoe in rapids on the Seal River and had to wait nearly a month to be rescued. [Klein, *Cold Summer Wind*, p. 93]

Travel on the Seal River in the late 1970s and 1980s was somewhat more frequent with youth camp trips by Kandalore and Wanapitei in particular.

THLEWIAZA

The Thlewiaza River rises in northern Manitoba, north of Lake Brochet, flows east into the southwest corner of Nueltin Lake, reappears flowing out of the north end of that lake and continues east to Hudson Bay. Many travellers who reach the Barrens through Nueltin Lake are on the Thlewiaza River for part of its course.

1770 Samuel Hearne on his second unsuccessful attempt to reach the Coppermine River turned back at Dubawnt Lake and came down sections of the Thlewiaza and Seal rivers.

1908 C.P. Ault and C.C. Stewart, with two guides from Cumberland House, travelled to Pelican Narrows, canoed up the Reindeer River, Reindeer Lake, up the Cochrane River, over to and down the Thlewiaza to Kasmere and into Putahow Lake, then called "canoe limit". They returned the same way. [*Carnegie Institute Magnetic Land Surveys*]

1912 Ernest Oberholtzer from Minnesota, American conservationist in his early 20s, with Billy Magee (Titapeshwewitou), Ojibwa from Mine Centre, Ontario, set out from The Pas, Manitoba, to re-trace Tyrrell's 1894 Kazan route as far as Yathkyed Lake in an 18-foot Chestnut canoe. Their intention was to hire guides along the way, but this proved impossible. Their route was through Cumberland House, north up Reindeer Lake, up the Cochrane River to Kasmere and Nueltin lakes, down the Thlewiaza River to Hudson Bay. They sailed down Hudson Bay to Churchill with an Inuit family and continued by canoe along the

coast to York Factory. They travelled up the Hayes River in company of York Factory Indians to Oxford House, and down the Echimamish River to Norway House. They were too late for the last southbound steamer and had to paddle the length of Lake Winnipeg. [*Beaver*, January 1986, p. 4; Rutstrum, p. 126]

1922 Glenn Madill led a Dominion Observatory Magnetic Survey expedition by canoe to Nueltin Lake, down the Thlewiaza River and into Putahow Lake. Del Simons of Revillon Frères travelled with Madill's group. [Personal communication – R.H. Cockburn]

1924 Cecil Harris, I.H. Smith and William Varvison, trappers, explored the Nueltin Lake area. [Morse files, p. 19]

1927 W.E. "Buster" Brown, HBC, canoed down the Thlewiaza River from the north end of Nueltin Lake, making a track and compass survey of the river. Harry Ford with a motorboat picked him up and took him up the coast to Eskimo Point. [Personal communication – R.H. Cockburn]

1928 Count Ilia Tolstoy with three men and six Cumberland House Cree, for the D.M. Burden Expedition of the American Museum of Natural History, canoed up Reindeer River, Reindeer Lake, and the Cochrane River and down the Thlewiaza to Nueltin Lake in the company of Wally Laird. They continued up Nueltin Lake and the Windy River to the Revillon post at Windy Lake. The object was to film the caribou migration. They returned by dog team in winter. [*Beaver*, 1990, p. 17]

1939 P.G. Downes with John Albrecht canoed from Brochet up the Cochrane River and down the Thlewiaza to Nueltin and Windy lakes. Albrecht returned the way they had come while Downes flew out. [Downes, 1943]

1940 P.G. Downes and Alfred Peterson canoed from Brochet, on Reindeer Lake, up the Cochrane, down the Thlewiaza into Kasmere Lake and up the Little Partridge River in an attempt to reach the Kazan River. They visited "Eskimo Charlie"

Planinshek at Putahow Lake and returned downstream to Brochet. The HBC motor schooner took Downes and his canoe down Reindeer Lake and he canoed down the Reindeer River. [*Beaver*, Spring 1983, p. 36]

1947 Dr. Francis Harper and Farley Mowat, with the Canadian Wildlife Service, canoed from Nueltin Lake to Brochet, on Reindeer Lake, and returned in the company of Charles Sweder, free-trader. They then canoed down the Thlewiaza River to Hudson Bay. [*Arctic Circular*, 1948, p. 39; *Canadian Field Naturalist*, Jul./Sept, 1955, p. 93]

1948 Farley Mowat and Andrew Lawrie, with the Canadian Wildlife Service, canoed widely in the area of Nueltin and Angikuni lakes. [*Canadian Field Naturalist*, Jul./Sept., 1955, p. 93]

1954 Maurice Renard and Rich Newcom canoed from the south end of Nueltin Lake down the Thlewiaza River and along the coast to Eskimo Point (Arviat). [*Outdoor Life*, Jan. 1960, p. 37]

1963 Ernest Oberholtzer returned to Nueltin Lake. [Morse files, p. 19]

1965 Barry MacKichan and two others canoed from Reindeer Lake up the Cochrane, down the Thlewiaza to Nueltin Lake and out to the Hudson Bay coast on the same river. They canoed up the coast to Eskimo Point. [*Wilderness Camping*, Feb./Mar, 1977]

1967 Jay Pritchett and Jack West, Americans, started at the headwaters of the Geikie River and canoed down to Wollaston Lake. They continued northward down the Cochrane River, crossed to Kasmere Lake on the headwaters of the Thlewiaza and descended that river, through Nueltin Lake, to the Hudson Bay coast. They returned south down the coast to Hubbard Point. [Personal communication – Pritchett]

1968 Clayton and Darrell Klein, Bryan Beasley and Lauren Jonckheere, of Michigan, put in by plane at Snowbird Lake, canoed to Kasba Lake, portaged to the Little Partridge River which flows into the Thlewiaza, continued up that river, across the height of land, down the Cochrane to

Brochet on Reindeer Lake. [Klein, *Cold Summer Wind*, 1983]

1970 K.E. Eade, GSC, studied stratigraphy in the area of Nueltin and Edehon lakes, canoeing down the Thlewiaza River to Tatinnai Lake. [*Arctic Circular*, 1971, p. 7]

1973 Camp Widjiwagan: Paul Rusterholz leading David Anderson, Jamie Cowie, Fred Nauer, Robert Rees and Bruce Anderson canoed down the full length of the Thlewiaza River to Hudson Bay. [Camp Widjiwagan Archives]

THA-ANNE

Tha-anne is a short river running east in Keewatin, just "north of 60", and flowing into Hudson Bay south of Arviat.

1896 Rev. Joseph Lofthouse with two Indians paddled up the Hudson Bay coast from Churchill in his Peterborough canoe to the Tha-anne River. They travelled upstream to Thaolintoa Lake and up into Tha-anne Lake (now South and North Henik lakes). They were within three days travel of Yathkyed Lake when they turned back. At Thaolintoa Lake they portaged to Lake Todatara and canoed down the Fish River to Hudson Bay. This was as much an exploratory as a missionary venture. [Lofthouse, 1922]

1969 Bob Jacobsen – see Maguse

MAGUSE

This short river enters Hudson bay north of Arviat, and is sometimes reached by a difficult route from the Thlewiaza River.

1929 L.J. Weeks and D.F. Kidd, GSC, began survey work in the area of the Maguse River. [GSC Report 1932]

1932 L.J. Weeks, A.W. Derby and W.C. Gussow, GSC, ascended the Maguse River from its mouth to Kingaryualik Lake, close to the headwaters, and returned by crossing to Kaminak Lake on Ferguson River where they were picked up by airplane. [GSC Report 1932]

1935 Harold Way, Alec Stewart, Mike McCart and Sherman Oliver, geologist, mining engineer and prospectors with the Cyril Knight prospecting company, set out in June of 1934 from the Revillon post of Windy Lake on Nueltin Lake to explore the area geologically, wintering at Windy Lake. The following year, Way and Oliver trekked north to South Henik Lake, traded their 18-foot canoe for a 22-foot freighter with a small outboard, and went down the Maguse River to the coast. In their travels they made contact with, and photographed, Kakoot, the Inuit who had guided Mallet on his Kazan trip in 1926. [*Beaver*, Autumn, 1968, p. 48]

1969 Bob Jacobsen and Giuseppi Slater started at Kinasao on Reindeer Lake, canoed up the Cochrane River to Maria Lake, portaged across to the North Seal River, canoed up to Nueltin Lake, north to Sealhole Lake, up the Thetinne River to the Kognak River, continued down to the Tha-anne River where it flows into South Henik Lake, Ameto Lake and Kinga Lake to the settlement of Padlei, where they joined the Maguse River and canoed out to Eskimo Point. [Morse files, p. 19; note in cairn on Tha-anne River, supplied by George Luste]

1977 *Jay and Carolyn Pritchett, with Jim Abel as expedition doctor, led a party of twenty-four canoeists from Whitmore College, Spokane, Washington, starting at the headwaters of the Dubawnt River, canoeing downstream, along Wholdaia Lake, across to Kamilukuak Lake and eastward to Angikuni Lake. They continued downstream on the Kazan to Yathkyed Lake, crossed east to Ferguson Lake, continued south through Kaminuriak Lake, Kaminak Lake, crossed to the Maguse River and followed it to Hudson Bay. [Personal communication – Pritchett]*

FERGUSON

The Ferguson River begins in Ferguson Lake, just northeast of Yathkyed Lake, flows east through the southern part of Kaminuriak Lake and empties into Hudson Bay opposite Bibby Island.

1894 Tyrrell – see Kazan

1930 D.F. Kidd, GSC explored the Ferguson River up to Quartzite and Kaminak lakes. [GSC Report 1932]

1974 Hugh Stewart – see Kazan

1976? *Mike Kusugak, Inuit from Rankin Inlet, with Harry Towongie, Doug Harp and Tony Sloan, in two 17-foot canoes, started from Ferguson Lake, canoed down the Ferguson River, across Kaminuriak Lake, and continued down the river to the coast of Hudson Bay. Tony Sloan's place in the canoe was taken by Mike's wife, Sandy, for the second week of the trip. [Canadian Govt. – Office of Tourism]*

CHAPTER FOUR

RIVERS OF THE BARRENS: THELON AND ITS TRIBUTARIES

THELON

"The great interior plateau, which has an elevation of about 700 feet above Great Slave Lake, approaches to within a few miles of the lake and the descent is abrupt and of very rugged character. When leaving the lake, therefore, to travel north or east one is immediately confronted by this barrier. Due to the hardness of the rock the streams discharging from the interior have been unable to cut channels and tumble over the escarpment in a succession of cascades and falls.

"In the past attempts have been made at several points to ascend rivers flowing into Great Slave Lake and, though the interior lakes were reached, the journey entailed great hardships and supplies had to be cut down to absolute essentials. The Indians never use the rivers but follow portage routes taking advantage of chains of lakes. Although there are several of these, there is only one practicable for heavy loads, namely that first used by Warburton Pike in 1890 and to which his name has been applied. It unites Great Slave Lake with Artillery Lake, the first of the great lake series. The distance between them is 24 miles and includes ten small lakes. The only difficult portage is the first, by which the climb out of the valley is made by a sandy glacial spill-way. It may be said that anything that can be manhandled can be taken over the portage.

"Pike's Portage route brings you to Artillery Lake, the start of a connected series of large lakes. These wa-terways occupy a strategic position in giving access to a stretch of country appealing to the imagination in its vastness and from the mists of obscurity that veil much of it. The three great rivers of the north, Coppermine, Back's and Thelon, with over a thousand miles of inter-cepted seacoast, may be reached by short portages over the height of land, and by them bases may be estab-lished at advanced points from which the great un-known country off the waterways may be explored.

"Should the traveller be anticipating an increasing ruggedness and bleakness, as the name 'Barren Land' suggests, he would find himself much mistaken, for the rough topography of the bordering zone of the plateau gradually subsides to long low hills and wide, flat val-ley, rock exposures become increasingly rare, and the boulders, which at the edge of the plateau lie scattered in every direction, become more and more imbedded in the drift. The trees disappear, it is true, but a healthy growth of shrubbery, moss and grass replaces them. One passes from rocky broken hills with scattered and stunted trees to open rolling plains covered with a fairly abundant vegetation. The name 'Barren Lands' might better be replaced by 'Northern Plains'." [Guy Blanchet, *Canadian Field-Naturalist*, January and March, 1924]

The Thelon watershed is very extensive, encom-passing a large part of the Keewatin District, and emp-tying from Baker Lake into Chesterfield Inlet of Hud-

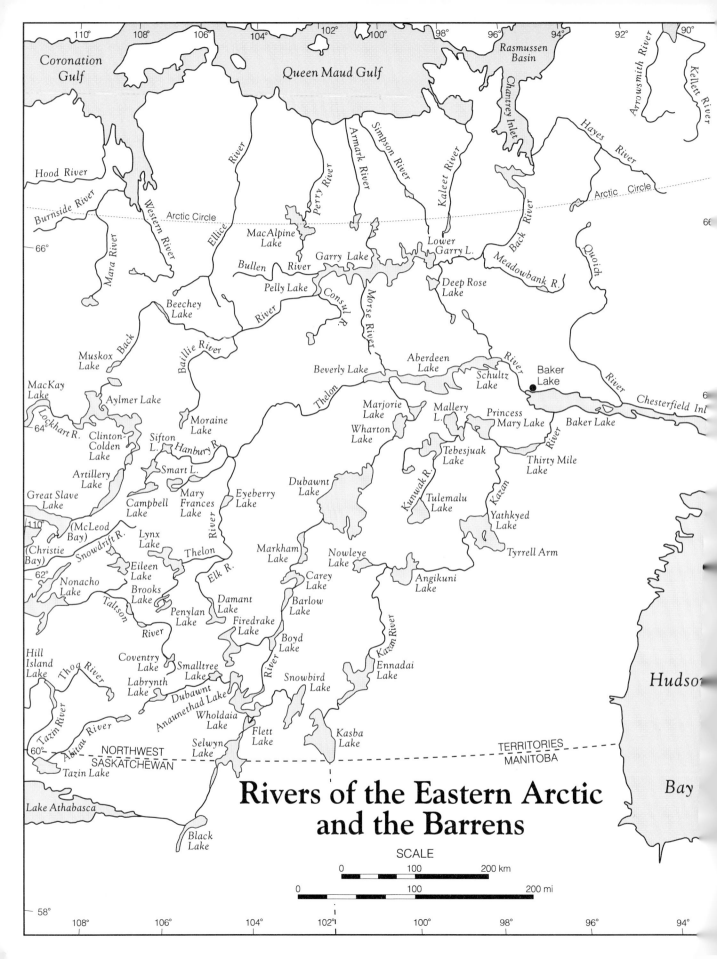

Rivers of the Eastern Arctic and the Barrens

SCALE

0   100   200 km

0   100   200 mi

son Bay. Trips on its two great north-flowing tributaries, the Dubawnt entering at Beverly Lake, and the Kazan entering at Baker Lake, are listed separately. Dubawnt trips which continued down the Thelon to Baker Lake are mentioned. The Quoich, a south-flowing tributary, flowing out of the eastern Barrens and entering Chesterfield Inlet below Baker Lake, is a river which is seldom travelled.

The Thelon trips listed here still constitute a complex mix of routes. The Hanbury and upper Thelon meet at the Forks, below Helen Falls on the Hanbury. Many trips entered the system on the Hanbury from the Artillery Lake area, crossing north and passing through Sifton Lake. Later, others came in from the south using the Elk and the upper Thelon.

1762 Moses Norton, HBC, with Capt. Christopher in the sloop Churchill *ascended Chesterfield Inlet to Baker Lake. [Tyrrell, GSC, 1901]*

1771-72 Samuel Hearne, HBC, probably crossed the Thelon on his overland trip from Churchill to the Coppermine.

1793 Captain Charles Duncan, HBC, ascended the Thelon, 30 miles above Baker Lake. [Tyrrell, GSC, 1901]

1853 John Rae, HBC, coming from Churchill ascended Chesterfield Inlet and travelled up to Baker Lake.

1893 Joseph B. Tyrrell and James W. Tyrrell took a lengthy canoe trip through the Barrens for the Geological Survey. Their entourage consisted of Michel, Pierre and Louis, Iroquois from Caughnawaga, François Maurice and James Corrigal from Île à la Crosse and John Flett from Prince Albert. From Lake Athabasca they crossed over to the Chipman River, Selwyn Lake and Wholdaia Lake and on down the Dubawnt River to its mouth at the Thelon, calling it the lower Dubawnt, past Aberdeen Lake to Baker Lake and Chesterfield Inlet – then along the coast to Churchill. [Tyrrell, 1897]

1899 David Hanbury, British explorer, sledged from Churchill to Chesterfield Inlet, then canoed up to Baker Lake, up the Thelon to the Forks and up the Hanbury (Arkil-inik). He crossed to Clinton-Colden and Artillery Lake, and continued down

James W. Tyrrell, fluent in some Eskimo dialects, eloquently described the trip he made with his brother Joseph for the Geological Survey in 1893. From Lake Athabasca, they went down the Dubawnt and Thelon rivers to Hudson Bay, where they were caught by the onset of winter and barely escaped with their lives. [Tyrrell, *Across the Sub-Arctic of Canada*, 1897]

to Fort Resolution on Great Slave Lake. [Hanbury, 1904]

1900 James W. Tyrrell, GSC, C.C. Fairchild, Ontario Land Surveyor, and Rev. Joseph Lofthouse from Fort Churchill, with Robert Bear and John Kipling, Métis from Winnipeg, Percy Acres, cook, Pierre French and Harry Monette, Iroquois canoemen, and Toura, Chipewyan canoeman, having travelled from Edmonton by dog-team to Fort Resolution and across Pike's Portage, canoed from Artillery Lake to Clinton-Colden Lake, crossed to Smart and Sifton lakes and the Hanbury River, which they named, and followed it down to the Forks of the Thelon. They continued down the Thelon to the mouth of the Dubawnt on Beverly Lake. Tyrrell returned up the Thelon and continued exploring 128 miles of the upper Thelon from the mouth of the Hanbury. Realizing that it was too far to attempt crossing to Lake Athabasca, he returned halfway down the upper Thelon and set off to walk westward across country, sending the canoe and canoemen back the way they had come. After much difficulty, Tyrrell reached the cache on Artillery Lake ahead of his canoe. Fairchild and Lofthouse with two canoes and four voyageurs continued down the Thelon to Baker Lake and Chesterfield Inlet. Lofthouse returned home down the coast of Hudson Bay while Fairchild returned up the Thelon, meeting Tyrrell at Artillery Lake. A Hudson's Bay Company boat met them at Fort

Reliance and took them across to Fort Resolution, and they continued, canoeing up the Slave River to Fort Chipewyan and waiting there for freeze-up before proceeding south by dog-team. [Tyrrell, Geological Survey Report, 1901]

1901-02 David Hanbury, and Hubert Darrell from Manitoba, with Chipewyan, Sousie Benjamin departed from Fort Resolution on July 13, travelled past Artillery Lake, Campbell Lake, the source of the Hanbury, and all the way down the Thelon to Chesterfield Inlet. They were not met by the expected ship with their supplies so they returned up the Thelon to Baker Lake to winter, making a winter trip to Meadowbank, a Back river tributary. In the spring they canoed up the Thelon to Tibielik Lake, then northwest overland to the Consul River and the Back River. They continued north down the Armark River to the Arctic Ocean, followed the coast to the Coppermine, came up to the Kendall River and crossed over to Great Bear Lake and Fort Norman, August 30, 1902. [Hanbury, 1904]

1908-09 E.A. Pelletier, M.A. Joyce, P.H. Walker and P.R. Conway, on a RNWMP patrol, left Fort Resolution on July 1, passed Artillery Lake and followed the Hanbury and Thelon rivers reaching Chesterfield Inlet on August 31. They were met by the patrol boat, *MacTavish*, but were shipwrecked and went by dog team to Churchill reaching there January 11. [Jennings, in Hodgins and Hobbs, eds., p.83]

1911-12 Harry Radford and T.G. Street, on a private American zoological expedition, left from Fort Resolution and Artillery Lake, descended the Hanbury and Thelon rivers to Chesterfield Inlet and returned upstream to winter at Schultz Lake. In early spring they crossed overland with two Inuit to Bathurst Inlet where both men were murdered by other Inuit. [*Beaver*, Spring 1972]

1917 RNWMP Inspector French, replacing W.J. Beyts who had been at Baker Lake since 1914, travelled from Baker Lake via the Thelon River, Garry and Pelly lakes to a crossing of the Back River. When he reached Bathurst Inlet, he discovered the "Radford" killers, but he also heard a story of provocation and made no arrests. On his return he rejoined the Thelon at Beverly Lake and reached Baker Lake in January 1918, having travelled 4800 miles. [*RNWMP Report of 1917-18 Bathurst Inlet Patrol*, Ottawa, 1919)

1925 John Hornby and J.C. Critchell-Bullock, on a wildlife survey for the Canadian Department of the Interior, after wintering on the Casba (now Lockhart) River, sledged their two canoes to Campbell Lake and canoed the Hanbury and Thelon rivers to Chesterfield Inlet. They took passage on a Revillon Frères boat to Port Harrison and went from there by ship to Newfoundland. [*Canadian Field-Naturalist*, 1930, May, p. 53; Whalley, *Legend*, pp. 191-244]

1926-27 John Hornby, Edgar Christian and Harold Adlard travelled from Fort Resolution via Artillery Lake and the Hanbury-Thelon rivers. They wintered in a cabin on the Thelon, past Grassy Island, and slowly died of starvation in early spring. [Whalley, *Legend*; Whalley, ed., *Death in the Barren Grounds*]

1927 Thelon Game Sanctuary was established.

1928 H.S. Wilson and K.M. Dewar, on a private geological trip, canoed the usual Hanbury-Thelon route and discovered the Hornby cabin and remains. [*Canadian Geographic* 97 (1), 1978]

1928-29 W.H.B. Hoare and Jack Knox, for the Department of the Interior, set out to establish a base to investigate the new Thelon Game Sanctuary. Hoare left Fort McMurray in February by sled travelling to Fort Smith where he picked up Knox. From there they sledged via Forts Resolution and Reliance, over Pike's Portage and Ford Lake, then by canoe (sometimes using an outboard motor), they travelled via Campbell and Smart Lake route to the middle Hanbury above Sifton Lake, not reaching their base site, Warden's Grove, on the Thelon below the Forks, until late October (the last part by sled). In late November they left by sled for Reliance to reprovision, reaching it in mid-December. During the winter they visited Snowdrift. In early March they started back to Warden's Grove reaching it in mid-April. They left by canoe for Baker Lake in mid-July. [Thomson ed., 1990]

1929 W.H.B. (Billy) Hoare canoed up the Hanbury in flood season and returned down the Hanbury-Thelon to Warden's Grove. [*Ibid*]

1929 Inspector Charles Trundle, RCMP, with R.A. Williams, E.A. Kirk, and M.E. Bobblets, using an outboard motor, canoed from Fort Reliance the usual Hanbury-Thelon route to confirm the Hornby deaths and found the Christian diary. [Whalley, *Legend*, p. 321]

1929 Hjalmar Nelson, trapper, from the Eileen Lakes, travelled alone down the Thelon in a handmade boat until he joined Hoare and Knox at Schultz Lake where all three were ice-bound for a time. They continued on to Baker Lake together. [Thomson ed., 1990]

1936 Col. Harry Snyder, American, flew into the Thelon Game Sanctuary to photograph musk-ox. [MacKinnon, "A History of the Thelon Game Sanctuary", *Musk-Ox*, Vol. 32, 1983, pp. 44-61]

1936 Billy Hoare and Dr. C.H.D. Clarke were dropped by plane here and there in the Game Sanctuary to inspect it. [Thomson, ed., 1990]

1937 Hoare and Clarke canoed from Heuss Lake to Baker Lake. [Clarke, *A Biological Investigation of the Thelon Game Sanctuary*, National Museum of Canada, Bulletin 96, 1940]

1939 Corporal Thompson arrested three Dene for hunting muskox in the Sanctuary. [MacKinnon]

1948 J.B. Bird, Mrs. Bird, W.G. Dean, and A. Laycock for the Department of Mines and Resources, along with Louis Tapatai, Inuit hunter, went from Baker Lake upstream to Beverly Lake and back in two canoes, exploring the country by canoe and on foot for the Geographic Bureau. [*Arctic Circular*, 1948 p. 84]

1948 A.W.F. Banfield and A.L. Wilk, for the Canadian Wildlife Service, canoed from Clinton-Colden Lake down a stretch of the Hanbury River. [*Arctic*, 1951, pp. 113-21]

1951 J.P. Kelsall and N.G. Perret, wildlife biologists, canoed from the Hanbury-Thelon Forks to Baker Lake. [*Arctic Circular*, Nov. 1951, p. 72, Jan. 1953, p.6]

1952-54 Two pairs of Wildlife Survey Officers led by J.P. Kelsall, and one pair of Topographical Survey Officers canoed the Hanbury-Thelon route. [MacKinnon]

1952 J.S. Tener summered in the Sanctuary studying musk-ox.

1954-55 The Geological Survey mapped the Baker Lake and the lower Thelon area using three helicopters and a ground crew of eighteen. An experienced trapper, Gus D'Aoust, helped to establish the main gas cache. [MacKinnon]

1955 George Grinnell and others of the Arthur Moffatt party – see Dubawnt

1959-60 A.H. Macpherson – see Kazan

1960-63 A.H. Macpherson and his wife, Elizabeth, were in the area of Aberdeen Lake in 1960, 1961 and 1963 studying lemmings. [*Canadian Field-Naturalist*, 1966, p. 89]

1961 Fred Riddle, a trapper, built a cabin at Warden's Grove for the Canadian Wildlife service. Meanwhile, the National Film Board, from a base camp above Hornby's cabin filmed *Edge of the Barrens*. [MacKinnon]

1962 Eric and Pamela Morse, Arch Jones and Bill Nicholls canoed from Sifton Lake down the Hanbury-Thelon route to Baker Lake; they were the first Canadian recreational canoeists to cross the Barrens. [Morse, *Freshwater Saga*, pp. 79-104]

1964 Irving Fox, Orris and Henry Herfindahl, and David Brooks, an American recreational group, canoed a similar route to that of the Morse party. [*North*, Vol. XII, # 5, 1965]

1965 George Rossback, Henry W. Briggs, Wayne Dunbar and Wm. Meier, Americans, on a photographic and botanical trip, flew from Yellowknife to the Thelon Forks, explored Helen Falls, and canoed down the Thelon to Baker Lake. [*Beaver*, Autumn 1966]

Bill Nicholls, Arch Jones and Pamela Morse enjoy the evening light beside the Hanbury River in 1962. [Eric Morse/ Pamela Morse]

1965 Robin and Victoria Fraser, John Dashwood and Ron Gaschen started at Deville Lake, just east of the Hanbury Portage, canoed down the Hanbury River and through Sifton Lake, Lac du Bois, Hoare Lake and Hanbury Lake, portaged Dickson Canyon and continued down the Thelon River to Baker Lake. [Personal communication – Robin Fraser]

1966 Bob Matteson with his two sons, Rob and Rick, and Bob Colgate, canoed from Sifton Lake down the Hanbury-Thelon rivers to Baker Lake. [Morse files, p. 8]

1967 Jack Goering and Peter Ferguson led a party of Trinity College School–Camp Onondaga boys down the Hanbury-Thelon to Chesterfield Inlet. The group consisted of Ken Biggs, David Thompson, Ian MacLaren, Bill Orr, Dan Sawyer and Robert Sculthorpe. [*Beaver*, Autumn 1968; cairn at Helen Falls]

1967 Camp Owakonze: F.B. Hubachek, Jr. and Jack Stultz led a group of boys including Bill Hubachek, John Sanders, Peter Ickes, Jonathan Bernstein and Richard Idler canoeing from Sifton Lake down the Hanbury-Thelon rivers to Baker Lake. [Cairn at Helen Falls; Camp Owakonze trip reports]

1968 Babette and John Coleman, Rochester New York, on a botanical and photographic trip, canoed the Hanbury-Thelon to Baker Lake. [Cairn at Helen Falls]

1969 Jim Boone, Bob Miller, Bill Spragge, Keith Acheson, Mike Thompson, Walter Gunn, Ash Winter and Dave Storey, Canadians, flew to Sifton Lake and canoed down the Hanbury-Thelon rivers to Baker Lake. It was the first whitewater trip for most of them and in preparation they were given two three-day weekend instructional sessions on the Petawawa River, one by Eric Morse and the other by Jack Goering. [Personal communication – Boone; cairn at Helen Falls]

1969 Charlie Wolf and Doug Best, from Alaska, started from Fort St. John with a 19-foot Grumman, canoed down the Peace River and using a borrowed motor crossed Great Slave Lake from Fort Resolution to Snowdrift. They flew from Snowdrift to Artillery Lake, where they were icebound for ten days, and canoed down the Hanbury-Thelon rivers to Baker Lake. [Cairn at Helen Falls; McGuire, p. 61, 166; personal communication – Best]

1970 Henning Harmuth and Robert Schaefer paddled from Great Slave Lake down the Hanbury and Thelon rivers to Baker Lake. [*Nastawgan*, vol. 12/4, 1985, pp. 12-13]

1970 Peter Browning and John Blunt canoed from Black Lake, Saskatchewan, crossed the Chipman Portage and continued from Selwyn Lake to Wholdaia Lake, then via Veira, Jost, Firedrake, Jarvis and Damant lakes to the Elk River. They then canoed down the Elk and Thelon rivers to Baker Lake, seeing no other people for the 70 days of the trip. [*Smithsonian Magazine*, October 1972]

1971 Brian Yorga, Ginny, Steve and Heather (10 months) Burger canoed on the upper Thelon River in connection with an archeological project. [Cairn at Helen Falls]

1971 Alex Hall and Ron Thorpe canoed the Hanbury-Thelon rivers from Sifton Lake to Baker Lake. [Personal communication – Hall]

1971 Jay Pritchett and Jack West started at Selwyn Lake and canoed north down the headwaters of the Dubawnt River, crossed to the Elk River and descended it to the Thelon, continuing down the Thelon to Baker Lake. [Personal communication – Pritchett]

1971 E.K. Dean, Tom York and Ed Winacott canoed from Yellowknife to Baker Lake, in a 17-foot Chestnut canoe. [Cairn at Helen Falls]

1971 Fred Gaskin, Lyle Malcolm, Jack Purchase and Rob Caldwell canoed the Hanbury-Thelon rivers. [Personal communication – Gaskin]

1971 Prof. A.C. Hamilton with his sons, Ian, Malcolm and Peter, from Kingston, canoed from the Hanbury portage to Baker Lake. [Cairn at Helen Falls]

1971 Camp Widjiwagan: Frank "Twinkle" Johnson led Eric Buetow, William Fox, Ted Haberman, Mike Runyon and Mark Sugden canoeing from Fort Reliance, over Pike's Portage and down the Hanbury-Thelon rivers to Baker Lake. [Camp Widjiwagan Archives; Morse, *Freshwater*, p.60]

1972 Jay Pritchett led a party of twenty-four canoeists from Whitmore College, Spokane, Washington, starting from Courageous Lake down the Snake and Lockhart rivers to Clinton-Colden Lake, crossing to the headwaters of the Hanbury River and descending it to the Thelon which they followed to Baker Lake. [Personal communication – Pritchett]

1972 Loran McDonald, Mike Hauser, Ned Therrien and Ron Haakensen canoed the Hanbury-Thelon rivers. [Cairn at Helen Falls]

Charlie Wolf's canoe rambles began when he retired in Alaska. On Beverly Lake, he is approaching Baker Lake after starting on the Peace River in 1969. [Doug Best]

1972 Lewis and Fred Vermeulen, Duncan Hepburn and Ron Lawson canoed the Hanbury-Thelon rivers. [Cairn at Helen Falls]

1972 Richard Black made a solo canoe trip down the Hanbury-Thelon rivers. [Cairn at Helen Falls]

1972 Fred Cramp, Sue Cramp, Greg Ewert and John Horricks, Wild River Survey, flew to Sifton Lake on the upper Hanbury and canoed to Baker Lake. [Parks Canada files]

1972 Rolf Esko, Arne Lindgren, Erik and Steffan Svedberg, Bengt and Kjell Windelhed, from Sweden, canoed from Carlson's Landing on the Peace River, down the Slave and Little Buffalo rivers, across Great Slave Lake, crossed Pike's Portage to Artillery Lake and continued down the Lockhart and Hanbury-Thelon rivers to Baker Lake. [Morse files, p. 9]

1972 Strickler with at least three other canoeists canoed down the Thelon River finishing at Baker Lake. [HBC Archives – U-Paddle file]

1973 Eric and Pamela Morse, Jane, Jim and Terk Bayly, and Angus Scott canoed from Campbell Lake, headwaters of the Hanbury River to Beverly Lake. [Morse, *Freshwater Saga* map # 4; *Che-Mun*, Spring 1993, p. 5]

1973 Alex Hall and Dennis Voigt – see Coppermine

1973 Frank Cooke, George Montgomery, Doug Howe, David and Gail Rees, Ulrich and Diane Kretschmar and Dick Abbott canoed from Campbell Lake down the Hanbury-Thelon rivers to Baker Lake. [D.L. Rees, "Hanbury-Thelon, 1973", unpublished, in Parks Canada files]

1973 John Lentz with Larry, Frank, Mary, Dale and Peter, put in at Lynx Lake on the headwaters of the Thelon and paddled through Eyeberry Lake and the full length of the Thelon River to Baker Lake. [Lentz – personal communication]

1973 Camp North Woods (Cleveland YMCA Camp based in Temagami): Mark Paulin, with Kip Ault and Dave Schmitz, led Norm Fulmer, Scott Fowler, Dave Freedman, Bob Cruse, and Dave Moore, some of them in their early teens, as

Alex Hall, with tundra wolf pups, has made many long, solitary trips starting in the headwaters of the Thelon River. [Lia Ruttan]

young as thirteen, from Fort Smith over Pike's Portage, across Artillery Lake and down the Hanbury-Thelon rivers to Baker Lake. [Cairn at Helen Falls]

1974 Alex Hall and Peter Griffiths canoed down the upper Taltson from Coventry Lake, crossed over to the Thelon drainage system through Penylan Lake, down an unnamed river via La Haise Lake, Howard Lake to Lynx Lake on the headwaters of the Thelon River. They continued down the Thelon River to Baker Lake. [Personal communication – Alex Hall]

1974 Clayton and Darrell Klein paddled from Damant Lake down the Elk and Thelon rivers to an arranged pick up on Aberdeen Lake. They met large caribou migrations on both the Elk and Thelon rivers. [Klein, *Cold Summer Wind*, pp. 106-49]

1974 Joe Berkeland with three others canoed down the Hanbury-Thelon rivers to Baker Lake. [Cairn at Helen Falls]

1974 Tom and Sally McGuire from Alaska started at Fort St. John and canoed down the Peace and Slave rivers, around the eastern end of Great Slave Lake to McLeod Bay, crossed Pike's Portage and canoed from Artillery Lake down the Hanbury-Thelon rivers. They were on the 84th day of their trip when they stopped at Helen Falls. [Cairn at Helen Falls]

After 1974 the number of canoe trips on the Thelon increased substantially. Your authors, Hodgins and Hoyle, were on a Wanapitei trip on the Thelon in 1981.

1980 *Chris Norment, Robert Common, John Mordhorst, Kurt Mitchell, Mike Mobley and Gary Anderson were wintering in the cabins at Warden's Grove, having canoed from the Yukon via the Nahanni, the Mackenzie and the regular route from Great Slave Lake. Their winter of solitude was disrupted when a Soviet satellite, Cosmos, fell half a day's paddle downriver from them. They were unaware of this radioactive interloper until Canadian Forces planes began landing in their area to make a search for it. Norment wrote the book,* In the North of Our Lives, *as a result of this experience.*

1980 *Jay and Carolyn Pritchett, with Jim Abel as expedition doctor, led a party of twenty-four canoeists from Whitmore College, Spokane, Washington, on an interesting variation of the Thelon route. Beginning on the headwaters of the Elk River, they descended the Elk and the Thelon to Beverly Lake, went upstream on the Dubawnt to Wharton Lake, crossed overland to Tebesjuak and Mallery lakes, continued downstream on the Kazan to Baker Lake. [Personal communication – Pritchett]*

DUBAWNT

The Dubawnt River rises in Wholdaia Lake and flows north through Dubawnt Lake, one of the largest lakes in the Barren Grounds. It empties into the Thelon River at Beverly Lake. Wholdaia Lake is just north of Selwyn Lake on the Saskatchewan-North West Territories border. The waters of Selwyn Lake flow south and west past Stony Rapids and Fond du Lac into Lake Athabasca. This was the usual access to a great wilderness river before the advent of the airplane.

1770 *Samuel Hearne reached Lake Dubawnt on his second abortive attempt to reach the Coppermine.*

1868 *Father Alphonse Gaste reached Dubawnt Lake from Reindeer Lake with Chipewyan Indians. [Eskimo, Spring-Summer, 1986]*

1893 Joseph Burr Tyrrell and James William Tyrrell, for the Geological Survey, picked up their canoes from the railway at Athabasca Landing and travelled downriver to Lake Athabasca. From Fond du Lac, with three Indians from Caughnawaga, Michel, Pierre and Louis, and two Métis from Île à la Crosse, François Maurice and James Corrigal, and John Flett, interpreter, from Prince Albert, they canoed to Black Lake, up the Chipman River to Selwyn Lake, Wholdaia Lake and down the Dubawnt River, across Dubawnt Lake, and again down the river to Aberdeen Lake, part of the Thelon River system, and down to Baker Lake and Chesterfield Inlet. Their return south was by dog-team down the coast of Hudson Bay to Churchill and Winnipeg. [Tyrrell, 1897]

1926 Guy Blanchet with a crew of three on a Dominion Land Survey trip searched for Samuel Hearne's route. Their route was from Tazin Lake, north of Lake Athabasca, up Abitau River to the height of land, across Insula and Labyrinth lakes and down the Dubawnt River. They returned via Smalltree and Wholdaia lakes to Fond du Lac. [*Beaver*, September 1949, p. 8]

1955 A party of Americans led by Arthur Moffatt, including George Grinnell, Peter Franck, Joe Lanouette, Bruce LeFavour and Skip Pessl canoed from Black Lake to Selwyn Lake and down the Dubawnt River and across Dubawnt Lake. Following an accident in the rapids entering Marjorie Lake, Moffatt died of exposure and is buried in Baker Lake. The rest of the group completed the trip down the Dubawnt and Thelon in late September. [*Sports Illustrated*, March 9, pp. 68-76, and March 16 pp. 80-88, 1959; personal communication – Grinnell; *Canoe*, July 1988, p. 18]

1958 Professor Elmer Harp of Dartmouth College made an archaeological collection at Grant Lake on the Dubawnt. [Lentz, *North*, 1970]

1962 John Blunt was a member of a geological survey crew around Black Lake in the Dubawnt watershed. [Browning, p. 8]

1964 Peter Browning and John Blunt, Americans, canoed from Black Lake, at the eastern end of Lake Athabasca, up the Chipman River route to Selwyn and Wholdaia lakes and up the Dubawnt River to Smalltree Lake. They then crossed to the headwaters of the Taltson River through a series of lakes and canoed down the Taltson for 100 miles, crossing a height of land to Eileen Lake on the upper Snowdrift River and following the Snowdrift down to Snowdrift village on Great Slave Lake. [Browning, 1989]

1966 Donald Chant, Roger Hansell, James Chillcott and Joel Weintraub flew from Stony Rapids to Wholdaia Lake and canoed down the Dubawnt, across Boyd and Carey lakes to Aberdeen Lake, collecting amphibians and reptiles. They flew back to Stony Rapids having experienced easy conditions on Dubawnt Lake. [*Arctic*, 1971, p. 233; *Canadian Field Naturalist*, Vol. 81, p. 106]

1966 A party of Princeton students canoed down the Dubawnt. [*Beaver*, Spring 1968, p.11]

1968 Two young men flew in from Stony Rapids and had to be rescued from the Dubawnt River by Lamb Airways. [Morse files, p. 10]

1968 Eric Morse – see Kazan

1968 Barry MacKichan – see Kazan

1969 John Lentz, George Luste, Dick Irwin, R. Herendeen, Keith McLaren and Mark Rubin flew to the headwaters of the Dubawnt, canoed 750 miles to Baker Lake and believed they were the first group to travel the full length of the river. [*Beaver*, Summer, 1971, p. 48; *North*, May 1970, p. 22]

1971 Jay Pritchett – see Thelon

1972 Shortly before this year a party of Minnesota canoeists were ice-bound on the Dubawnt for two weeks and ran out of food. [Klein, *Cold Summer Wind*, p.93]

1972 Camp Widjiwagan: Andy Turnbull led Kurt Bjorklund, Andy Fulton, Chris Muetze, George

Peter Scott, on Sid Lake at the beginning of the Dubawnt River, ignores the pot of gold at the end of the rainbow and searches for the Morse River (see p. 184). [Michael Peake]

Bonga and Tom Swenson canoeing from Wholdaia Lake down the Dubawnt River and Thelon River to Baker Lake. [Camp Widjiwagan Archives]

1973 Alex Hall and Dennis Voigt – see Coppermine

1974 Fred Gaskin, Jack and Susie Purchase, Steffan Svedberg, Katie Hayhurst and Gretchen Schneider canoed the Dubawnt. They retraced Tyrell's Barrenland route from Uranium City to Baker Lake. Gaskin and Hayhurst continued down Chesterfield Inlet to Hudson Bay with a party of Inuit. [*Canadian Geographic*, Dec./Jan. 1976-77, p. 46; personal communication – Hayhurst]

KAZAN

The Kazan River, known to the Inuit as the Inuit Ku, rises south of the Saskatchewan-North West Territories border, above Kasba Lake and flows north, passing through Ennadai and Yathkyed lakes, before emptying into Baker Lake on the Thelon River. The travel season on the Kazan is short because the large lakes on the Barren Grounds often remain frozen well into July. The river valley is rich in archeological remains from the past inland Inuit activity.

1868 Alphonse Gaste, a priest, paddled with Indians from Reindeer Lake up the Cochrane River and onto the Kazan. They travelled part way down to a meeting with friendly Inuit and then returned. [Eskimo, Churchill, 1986]

1894 Joseph Burr Tyrrell, GSC, and Robert Munroe Ferguson, aide to the Governor-General with a taste for adventure, set off from Brochet at the north end of Reindeer Lake with Inuit guides, travelled up the Cochrane River, across a series of lakes, over the height of land to Kasba Lake and down the Kazan River to Yathkyed Lake. From the Tyrrell Arm in the southwest corner of Yathkyed Lake they crossed another height of land to Ferguson and Kaminak lakes and continued down the Ferguson River to Hudson Bay. They returned south by dog team via Churchill, Split Lake and Lake Winnipeg. [Annual Report, GSC, vol. 9, 1896]

1922 Kaj Birket-Smith, on a Danish government expedition, travelled from Yathkyed Lake to Baker Lake. [*Beaver*, Spring 1968, p.4]

1926 Thierry Mallet, of Revillon Frères, Del Simons and two Cree, Peter Linklater and Joe Cadotte, on a private recreational trip travelled in a 19-foot canoe with outboard motor from Le Pas, Manitoba, north to Brochet on Reindeer Lake, up the Cochrane River and a series of lakes to Kasba Lake. They canoed down the Kazan, without the motor, and finding Yathkyed Lake frozen solid in mid-July were forced to turn back. Their Inuit guide was Kakoot, who had been with his father on Tyrrell's expedition. [*Beaver*, March 1950]

1930 Dr. A.E. Porsild, Chief Botanist at the National Museum, researched the area for the possibilities of domesticated reindeer pasture. [*Beaver*, Spring 1968 p.4]

1947 Francis Harper, naturalist with the Canadian Wildlife Service, was on the Kazan to study Inuit archaeological remains, animal and plant life. [*Beaver*, Spring 1968, p.4]

1959-60 A.H. Macpherson, biologist Canadian Wildlife Service, and Pequiaq, Inuit predator control officer, canoed areas of the Thelon around Aberdeen Lake and lakes near the Dubawnt River, continuing up the Kazan River to Kazan Falls, examining fox dens. [*Arctic Circular*, 1960, pp. 31-34]

1963 James Larsen, University of Wisconsin, and William N. Irving canoed from Ennadai Lake to Angikuni Lake, up a small river to Nowleye and Kamilukuak lakes and down to Dubawnt Lake. [*Canadian Field Naturalist*, 1973, p. 241]

1966 John W. Lentz, Stewart Coffin, Norman Wright and Bill Malkmus, on a private American expedition to experience the land and investigate abandoned Inuit camps, travelled by train to Lynn Lake, Manitoba, and by bush plane to Snowbird Lake. In 17-foot fibreglass and 18-foot aluminum canoes they paddled into Kasba Lake and the Kazan River System, across Ennadai and Yathkyed lakes to Baker Lake. [*Beaver*, Spring 1968, p.4]

Bill Mathers, Ernie Howard and Pat Baird line down rapids on the Kazan in 1968 on one of the Morse trips. [Eric Morse/ Pamela Morse]

1968 Eric and Pamela Morse, Angus Scott, Bill Mathers, Pat Baird, Peter Blaikie, Ernie Howard and Tom Lawson flew into Stony Rapids at the eastern end of Lake Athabasca and chartered a flight to Boyd Lake on the Dubawnt River. Their route was across Carey Lake, portage to Kamilukuak River, Kamilukuak Lake, portage to Nowleye Lake, across Angikuni and Yathkyed lakes, partially frozen, and Forde Lake where they were windbound. Here they were picked up by plane, short of their destination, Baker Lake. [Morse, *Freshwater Saga*, pp. 127-44]

1968 Barry MacKichan and Keith Roberts started at Selwyn Lake, canoed down the Dubawnt River to Dubawnt Lake, up the Kamilukuak River and down the Kazan to Baker Lake. [*Wilderness Camping*, Feb./Mar. 1977]

1970 Camp Widjiwagan: Jim Ude led Mike Frantes, Bill Johnson, Steve Johnson, Herb Tousley and Dave Wright canoeing from Ennadai Lake down the Kazan River to Baker Lake. [Camp Widjiwagan Archives]

1972 Clayton and Darrell Klein, father and son from Michigan, paddled from Hisbalia Lake on the Manitoba boundary, north into Kasba Lake and followed the regular Kazan route. They were plagued by high winds and storms, and then ice-bound on Yathkyed Lake for eight days. Eight miles above Kazan Falls they were picked up by an airplane out of Baker Lake. (*In 1976 they returned, flying into Princess Mary Lake, canoed down the Kunwak River to the Kazan at Thirty Mile Lake, completed the run down the Kazan and continued down Chesterfield Inlet to Hudson Bay.*) [Klein, *Cold Summer Wind*, pp. 47-105]

1972 Jim Arnold, Gary Heiling and four others from Minnesota flew into Snowbird Lake and canoed the Kazan to Baker Lake. [*Ibid.*, p. 87]

1973 Fred Gaskin, George Dobbie, Jack and Susie Purchase flew to Snowbird Lake and paddled the Kazan all the way to Baker Lake. [*Canadian Geographical Journal*, vol. 93/3, 1976-77, p.46; McKay, p. 120]

1973 Larry Osgood, Donald and Maria Scott, using kayaks, put in at the Northwest arm of Ennadai Lake, portaged to an unnamed stream and a string of unnamed lakes to Nowleye and Angikuni lakes, where they joined the Kazan River and descended it to Baker Lake. [Private communication to Clayton Klein from Scott; personal communication – Osgood]

1974 George Luste, John Martin, Mike Good and John Blackborrow retraced J.B. Tyrrell's 1894 route from Coop Point on Reindeer Lake, up the Cochrane River to Kasmere Lake and into Kasba Lake via the Little Partridge River. There they joined the Kazan River and continued down to Baker Lake. [*Beaver*, Spring 1975, p.40; personal communication – Luste]

1974 Hugh Stewart and Bob Davis canoed from Reindeer Lake down the upper Kazan to Yathkyed Lake. They had intended to continue down the Ferguson River following Tyrrell's 1894 route but running short of time they cut north to the Wilson River and followed it to Whale Cove on Hudson Bay. [WCA Symposium, 1991; personal communication – Stewart]

1975 *Larry Osgood, Bob Pammett, Matt Foreman and Steve Rosenmeier started from a flight into Tulemalu Lake and followed the Kunwak River through lakes Tebesjuak, Mallery and Princess Mary, joining the Kazan just above Thirty Mile Lake. They finished the trip at Baker Lake. [Personal communication – Osgood]*

1975 *Charles Doehlert, Frank King, Bob Corliss, Bill Walker, John Anderegg and Jim Wood flew into Carruthers Lake, canoed into Angikuni Lake and*

down the Kazan River to Baker Lake. [Doehlert unpublished trip report]

1977 *Jay and Carolyn Pritchett, with Jim Abel as expedition doctor, led a party of twenty-four canoeists from Whitmore College, Spokane, Washington, from the headwaters of the Dubawnt, crossing from Wholdaia to Kamilukuak Lake, down the Kazan to Yathkyed Lake, then across to Ferguson Lake, finishing their trip down the Maguse River to Hudson Bay. [Personal communication – Pritchett]*

1977 *Sandy Richardson and Don Callfas began at the south tip of Kasba Lake and canoed down the Kazan River to Baker Lake. [Personal communication – Richardson]*

1977 *Chuck and Dot Cleaver, Patty Hager, Kip Cleaver, Bob Putnam and Brad Bond started on Angikuni Lake and canoed the Kazan River. [Kazan Falls cairn]*

1977 *Kris Inwood, Cameron Hayne, Jonathan Theobald and Ken Buchan followed the Tyrrell/Luste route from Reindeer Lake down the Kazan River – 800 miles to Baker Lake. [Kazan Falls cairn]*

1980 *Jay Pritchett – see Thelon*

Some fish are bigger than others: George Luste and John Martin on the Kazan, 1974. [Luste]

Sandy Richardson spellbound by the power of the falls on the Kazan. [Richardson]

In 1982, David Pelly, John McKay, Osker von Dungern, Genevieve Ombrechune, Charles Heschal, Tony Louwman, Mike Whittier and Nancy Scott flew to Kasba Lake and paddled the full length of the Kazan to Baker Lake. John McKay published Arctic Adventure: A Kazan River Journal *the following year. Its appendices contain the names of canoeists for the years 1973-82 which were left in the cairn built by George Luste 10 kilometres above Kazan Falls. A book containing copies of the entries of names and messages left in the cairn from 1974 to 1991 has been published by David Pelly. As a result of the 1982 trip, Pelly organized and led the large international Operation Raleigh trip on the Kazan in 1988.*

QUOICH

The Quoich River rises in the land between the north-flowing Back River and Wager Bay, flows south and east into Chesterfield Inlet just east of Baker Lake.

1853 *Dr. John Rae explored for ten days up the river and named it. [Dictionary of Canadian Biography, Vol. XII]*

1979 *Bob O'Hara canoed up the Quoich River to the headwaters and down again to Chesterfield Inlet. [WCA Symposium, 26/1/91]*

1992 *Duke Watson, A. Black, H. Muller, Bob O'Hara, with J. Roush and P. Schoening for part of the trip, canoed from Lunan Lake down the northeasterly branch of the Quoich River and continued up Chesterfield Inlet to the community of Baker Lake. [Personal communication – Watson]*

CHAPTER FIVE

THE ROUTE OF THE EXPLORERS: THE MACKENZIE WATERSHED

If rivers are the blood-vessels of a country, carrying the essential stuff of life between their banks, the mighty Mackenzie is one of the main arteries. The Mackenzie was the way to the far north for Europeans ever since Alexander Mackenzie, hoping to find the Pacific Ocean in 1789, made his way down the river that was named for him. Since that time the river has seen every type of boat from skiffs made from painstaking hand-sawn boards, large and small canoes, kayaks and sailboats, to tugboats pushing a strings of barges and paddle steamers. The river, several kilometres wide in places, drains a huge area east of the Rockies, and two of the country's largest lakes, Great Slave and Great Bear.

Many of the trips on the Mackenzie are part of a longer voyage, perhaps beginning as far up the watershed as the headwaters of the Peace, or on the Clearwater which joins the Athabasca and continues down the Slave. Mackenzie's epic journey began at Fort Chipewyan on Lake Athabasca where the Peace and the Athabasca Rivers come together to become the Slave. He had reached the fort by the traditional fur-trade route from Montreal to the northwest, following the Clearwater into the Athabasca.

During the gold rush years, 1898-99, it is impossible to know the names of all the travellers on the Athabasca-Slave system. Prospectors and miners, hangers-on and adventurers were coming down the rivers in flotillas of scows and canoes, several hundred persons at a time. Most trips continued on from the Mackenzie up a tributary and over the high water-shed of the mountains of the Yukon and down the other side on the tributaries of another mighty river, the Yukon, possibly following it all the way to the Bering Sea.

Where possible, trips are filed by the principal downstream river, and the information will not be duplicated, but will be cross-referenced in each river section. Even some recreational trips on these large waterways made use of small outboard motors, and these have been included for completeness.

CLEARWATER–ATHABASCA–SLAVE

The Clearwater rises in far north-central Saskatchewan and flows south and west past the northern end of the historic Methye Portage, or Portage La Loche, into Alberta to enter the Athabasca at Fort McMurray. The Athabasca then flows north, passing Fort Chipewyan at the western end of Lake Athabasca and merging with the Peace to become the Slave which empties into Great Slave Lake.

The lower Clearwater was a vital link in historic exploration and was the fur-trade voyageur route to the Athabasca country, the Mackenzie and the Western Arctic. It had long been Chipewyan or southern Dene country; its people made and still make great use of river travel. In 1778 Peter Pond of the North West Company was the first European to cross the great

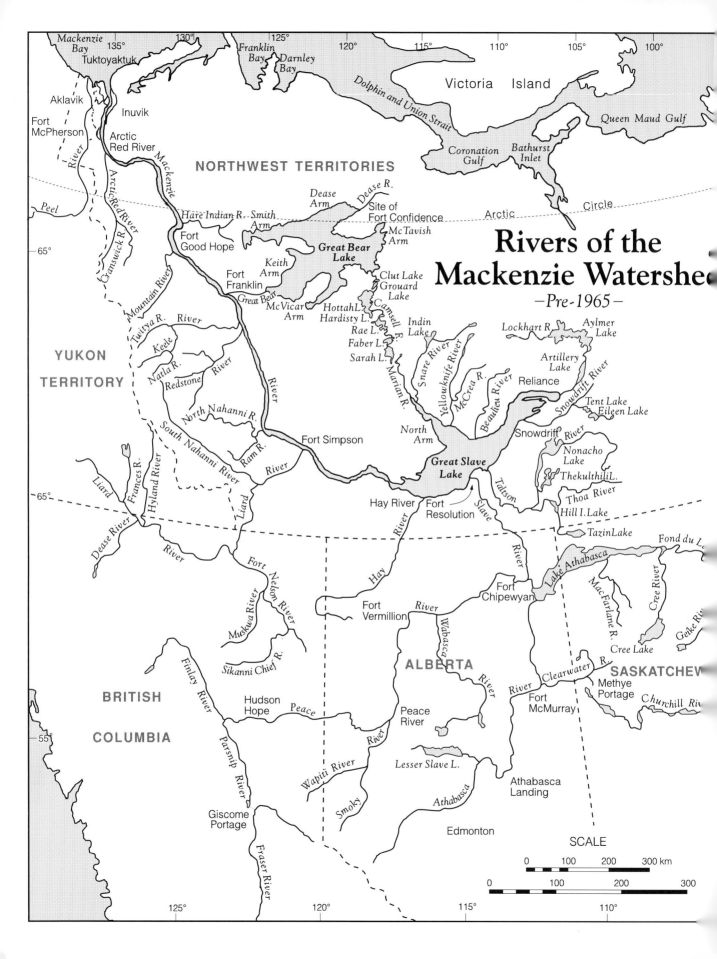

Rivers of the
Mackenzie Watershed
-Pre-1965-

Methye Portage, 21 kilometres long. It begins at the headwater of the Churchill River at Lac La Loche and continues to where the lower Clearwater leaves the Shield below Contact Rapids. Alexander Mackenzie followed nine years later, crossing it ten times between 1787 and 1794 on his trips to and from the Arctic and the Pacific.

The Portage and the Clearwater became the traditional highway for fur brigades of the North West Company and eventually for the Hudson's Bay Company. The clearing on the north end of the portage was one of the great meeting places for the wintering partners, traders and voyageurs coming in from the far east and the Bay. There were thus countless travellers on the Clearwater between 1793 and about 1872. Until 1870 it was the border crossing between Rupert's Land and the North Western Territory. In that year Fort McMurray was established at the junction with the Athabasca. Franklin, Richardson, Hood, King, Simpson and many others passed over this carry and onto the Clearwater, and many wrote about it. Obviously only a few of the famous and none of the unsung voyageurs are identified in the pre-1874 listings.

When horse-drawn cart traffic from Edmonton to Athabasca Landing on the main river became possible, especially after 1883 when steamboats appeared on the Athabasca running north from the Landing, the Clearwater route fell into relative obscurity, although the local Dene and other trappers continued to use it and the carry. In 1920, a rail line pushing north from Edmonton reached Waterways just upstream from, and now part of, Fort McMurray. For some time thereafter Waterways became the put-in point for trips, by steamboat, barge and occasionally canoe, to the Far North. We have listed such trips under the main Athabasca heading, along with those beginning at the Landing.

The beautiful upper Clearwater, rising near rugged Lloyd Lake, was rarely traversed, apart from local trappers, until 1972. Soon thereafter it could be accessed off the dead-end mining road, the Sawchuck Trail (Highway 955). The Clearwater in Saskatchewan has now become a Canadian Heritage River at the core of a broad provincial Wilderness Park.

1778 *Peter Pond, of the North West Company, was the first European to reach the Athabasca River, having come over the Methye Portage and down the Clearwater River from the Churchill River. He wintered at Lake Athabasca and established a fur base, Fort Chipewyan. [Francis, pp. 63-65]*

1787 *Alexander Mackenzie, of the North West Company, made his first of ten crossings of the Methye Portage and continued down the lower Clearwater and Athabasca to Lake Athabasca, to serve initially under Peter Pond.*

1788-90 *Alexander Mackenzie, on his fifth crossing of the Methye Portage, travelled north, past Lake Athabasca, all the way down the Mackenzie River to the Arctic Ocean in 1789, with a Chipewyan guide known as the "English Chief". He returned south and east over the carry again. [Mackenzie, 1927]*

1791-92 *Philip Turnor, Malcolm Ross and family, Peter Fidler, Hugh Leaks, Robert Garroch, Malcolm Grott and Peter Brown in two canoes crossed from La Loche to the Clearwater on a rough route west of the Methye Portage, paddled the Clearwater-Athabasca to Fort Chipewyan and returned east in the spring via the Methye. [Musk-Ox, #20, 1977, p. 34]*

1792-94 *Alexander Mackenzie, on his ninth crossing, paddled down the Clearwater-Athabasca to Fort Chipewyan and continued west to Forks Fort. In 1793 he ascended the Peace and crossed over to the Pacific and back, crossing the Methye again probably in May 1794. [Mackenzie, 1927; Francis, pp. 63-69;* Musk-Ox, #20, 1977, pp. 28-49]

1796 *David Thompson canoed from the mouth of Reindeer River, up the Churchill River, crossed over the Methye Portage and down the Clearwater-Athabasca to Lake Athabasca. He returned by the same route.*

1799 *David Thompson, of the North West Company, left Lac La Biche on horseback and reached the Pembina River where a canoe was waiting for him. He descended the Pembina to the Athabasca, surveyed upstream to Lesser Slave Lake, returned downstream on the Athabasca to the mouth of the Clearwater and continued up the Clearwater, over Methye Portage and down the upper Churchill to Île à la Crosse. [Tyrrell, in* Thompson's Narrative, *p. lxxxiv]*

1804   *David Thompson — see Peace*

1820   *Lieut. John Franklin, Royal Navy, on his first exploration, 1819-22, with Dr. John Richardson, George
Back, Robert Hood, John Hepburn, Orkney boatmen, Canadian voyageurs, two Inuit and a varying
number of Indian hunters and their wives (up to
fifty at times) crossed the Methye Portage travelling
west from York Factory, having wintered at
Cumberland House. They continued down the
Clearwater-Athabasca-Slave Rivers to Fort Providence on Great Slave Lake. From there they headed
north to the Coppermine (see Coppermine), crossing
back over the Methye Portage in 1822 (without
Hood and nine others who had died). [Franklin's*
Narratives *I; Francis, pp. 86-93; Houston, ed.* To
the Arctic by Canoe*]*

1825-27   *Franklin, on his second voyage, with Richardson,
Back, and E.N. Kendall, British seamen, a few Ca-
nadian voyageurs and Indian hunters crossed the
Methye on his way north, continuing down the Mac-
kenzie and out onto the coast. They returned in 1827.
[Franklin's* Narratives *II; Francis, pp. 95-97]*

1833   *George Back with William King and others crossed
the Methye Portage and travelled down the
Clearwater-Athabasca-Slave to Great Slave Lake to
begin their trip on the Back (Great Fish) River to
search for John Ross. (see Back River)*

1843   *Lieut. John Henry Lefroy, RA — see Hayes*

1848   *Sir John Richardson, then aged sixty, with Dr. John
Rae, Jack Fiddler and others crossed over the Methye
Portage and went down the Clearwater-Athabasca-
Slave River and down the Mackenzie River as part
of the search for the lost Franklin Expedition.*

1858   *James Hunter was the first Anglican missionary to
reach the Mackenzie River, travelling from Red
River via the Methye Portage and the Clearwater-
Athabasca-Slave Rivers to Fort Simpson. [Cooke
and Holland, p. 214]*

1858   *Henri Grollier, Oblate, was the first Catholic missionary to reach the Mackenzie River, travelling
from Île à la Crosse up the Churchill, across the
Methye, down the Clearwater-Athabasca-Slave*

*Rivers to Fort Resolution and on to Fort Simpson.
[Cooke and Holland, p. 214]*

1859   *Robert Kennicott, representing the U.S. Zoological
Survey, the Smithsonian Institution and the
Audubon Club of Chicago travelled with the HBC
canoe brigade up the Churchill, across the Methye
and down the Clearwater-Athabasca-Slave Rivers
to Fort Simpson. [Cooke and Holland p. 216]*

1862   *Rev. Robert McDonald started from Red River, canoed up the Churchill, crossed the Methye Portage
and continued down the Athabasca-Slave-Mackenzie Rivers. He then went up the Peel, over the Rat
Portage and down the Porcupine to arrive at Fort
Yukon. [Cody, p. 57]*

1865   *Rev. William Bompas, Anglican, with two Métis,
having travelled to Portage La Loche with the fur
brigade, continued canoeing west down the Clearwater and Athabasca Rivers to Fort Chipewyan as
winter was closing in. At Fort Chipewyan he was
supplied with a larger canoe with three Indian
paddlers and continued as far as possible down the
Slave River until ice filled the river. They reached
Fort Resolution on foot. [Ibid., p. 36-37]*

1867   *Rev. William Bompas travelled from Fort Resolution
up the Slave River to Fort Chipewyan. [Ibid., p. 65]*

1873   *Rev. William Bompas, with two Indians, canoed up
the Porcupine River, crossed the divide to Fort
McPherson on foot. With two other Indians and a
canoe, he made his way up the Mackenzie, across
Great Slave Lake, up the Slave and Athabasca River
to Portage La Loche. He continued to Red River by
dog-sled and on to London to be consecrated bishop.
[Ibid., p. 144]*

1874   Bishop Bompas, newly consecrated and with his
new bride, returned to the North with the HBC
brigade boats, down the Clearwater-Athabasca-
Slave-Mackenzie Rivers to Fort Simpson, Bishop
Bompas doing his share of the work on the
portages. [*Ibid.*, p. 159]

1882   Robert Bell, GSC, surveyed from Lac La Biche
down the Athabasca River, up the Clearwater River
and the Methye portage. [GSC Memoir 108]

1888   James Macoun and Thomas Fawcett, Dominion Lands Survey, explored the Athabasca from the mouth of Lesser Slave River to the junction with the Clearwater, continued upstream and crossed the Methye Portage. [Preble, p. 76]

1898   Charles Maltby, Andrew Smith, Henry Chomiere, Plenderleath McGinnis and Ebenezer McAdam, all of Montreal, reached Duck Lake, Saskatchewan, by train and La Loche by horse and wagon. With canvas folding canoes brought with them, they descended the La Loche River, the Clearwater, and the Athabasca to Smith Landing. They continued to Fort Simpson on the steamer *Wrigley*, where they bought a York boat and rowed and sailed down the Mackenzie, passing Fort McPherson. They tracked back up the Mackenzie, up the Peel and Wind Rivers to winter at the prospector camp of Wind City. [Moyles, ed., 1977]

1932   Erik Munsterhjelm and Karl (?), Swedes, crossed the Methye Portage, built a 20-foot canoe and went down the Clearwater and Athabasca Rivers at spring break-up. They went along Lake Athabasca to Fond du Lac, up to Stony Rapids and up the Porcupine River into the headwaters of the Dubawnt where they trapped for two winters. [Munsterhjelm, 1953]

1936   Sheldon Taylor and Geoffrey Pope, started from New York City following the voyageur route west, crossed the Methye Portage and went down the Clearwater, Athabasca and Slave Rivers to Fort Smith where they spent the winter before resuming their journey to Nome, Alaska. [Steber, 1987]

1938   P.G. Downes, with two Chipewyans, Nigorri Tous-les-Jours and William Janvier, canoed from Île à la Crosse up the Churchill, across the Methye Portage and down the Clearwater to Waterways. He continued alone in a 13-foot canoe, bought for twenty-five dollars at Fort McMurray, down the Athabasca and Slave Rivers to Fitzgerald. He travelled on by launch to Great Slave and Great Bear lakes. [*Beaver*, Spring 1983, p. 36]

1950   Emmerson Scott and Raymond Driessen, from Michigan, canoed from the Great Lakes to Aklavik, crossing the Methye Portage and canoeing down the Clearwater-Athabasca-Slave and Mackenzie Rivers. [*New York Times*, Sept. 7, 1950, p. 37]

1958   Eric Morse, Elliot Rodger, Maj-Gen Rockingham and Art Maybee canoed from Île à la Crosse up the Aubichon Arm, crossed the Methye Portage and canoed down the Clearwater to Waterways. They flew out. [Morse, *Freshwater Saga*, pp. 32-34]

1958   Camp Widjiwagan: Dewey Cedarblade leading Julian Andersen, Andy Driscoll, Lee Boerbon, Jack Weston and John Wilke canoed from Fort McMurray, up the Clearwater River, across Methye Portage and down the upper Churchill River to Lac La Ronge. [Camp Widjiwagan Archives]

1971   Verlen Kruger and Clint Waddel, Americans, paddled from Montreal to the Bering Sea using the fur-trade routes. Their trip took them across the Methye Portage, down the Clearwater, Athabasca, Slave, MacKenzie, up the Rat and down the Porcupine and Yukon in one canoeing season. [Klein, *One Incredible Journey*]

1971   Duke Watson with a group of twelve canoeists canoed two sections of the upper Athabasca River. Between 1971 and 1979, Watson, with a variety of companions, traced the route from the headwaters of the Athabasca River, up the Clearwater, across the Methye Portage, and down the Churchill to its confluence with the Reindeer. His travels were mainly by canoe, but where necessary, on foot or on skis. This linked up with trips done by Watson between 1969 and 1985 to complete a retracing of the fur-trade route from York Factory to the mouth of the Columbia River on the Pacific Ocean. [Personal communication – Watson]

1972   Priidu Juurand led a Wild River Survey crew of David McClung, Bill Pisco and Malcolm McIntyre down the full length of the Clearwater River from Lloyd Lake to Fort McMurray. [Personal communication – Juurand]

1973   Betty and Jim Wentzler, their son Jack, and Jim's brother Joseph Wentzler canoed the Clearwater River from Lloyd Lake to Fort McMurray. [Personal communication – Jim Wentzler]

ATHABASCA–SLAVE

The Athabasca River rises high in the Rocky Mountains above Jasper, flows east and north, picking up the waters of Lesser Slave Lake from the Lesser Slave River, twists through a tortuous route until it passes through the town of Athabasca, once called Athabasca Landing. It then settles on a straight northerly course, with one sharp bend to the east where the Clearwater River enters at Fort McMurray, before flowing on into Lake Athabasca. Just below Fort Chipewyan, on the northwest side of the lake, the Peace River enters and merges with the Athabasca to form one mighty river rushing north to empty into Great Slave Lake. An interesting phenomenon occurs at the confluence of the two rivers during the spring run-off when the heavy flow of the Peace causes the waters of the Athabasca to back up and appear to be running upstream.

Athabasca Landing was a fur post for the Hudson's Bay Company from 1848 until 1883 when the railway reached Edmonton, 150 kilometres to the south, and it became the distribution centre for the north. Horse-drawn wagons made regular trips between Edmonton and the Landing on the stage road which was sometimes little better than a quagmire. Water transport began at the Landing where a flotilla of specially-built scows, each about 50 feet long, rowed by long oars and guided by a 40-foot steering sweep, carried both freight and passengers. Of the 90 miles of rapids on the Athabasca, some were run with the scows full, others required delicate manoeuvres and the scows ran empty. From Fort Chipewyan, the Hudson's Bay Company operated one steamer down the Slave to the long wagon road portage before Fort Smith, while another steamer at Fort Smith took the cargo and passengers onward to the mouth of the Slave, across Great Slave Lake and down the Mackenzie.

Before 1883 all trips down the Athabasca-Slave were made by paddle-power alone. After that date many travellers, even some recreational travellers took advantage of the transport system to avoid the hazards of the Athabasca-Slave and the big waters of Great Slave Lake before dipping their paddles. For the trips which are chronicled here, when it is certain that canoes were used descending the Athabasca-Slave, the fact is mentioned.

In addition, the Fond du Lac River which flows into Lake Athabasca from Wollaston Lake is part of the Athabasca system and is included under this listing. Wollaston Lake is unique in that it is drained by two equally large rivers, one flowing to Hudson Bay via the Churchill River, and the other to the Arctic Ocean. The MacFarlane and Cree Rivers which flow from the area of Cree Lake north into the southeastern end of Lake Athabasca are also part of the system.

1802   *David Thompson, North West Company, returning from Fort William, crossed overland from the Saskatchewan River to the Athabasca River, descended it, canoed up the Lesser Slave River and Lesser Slave Lake and reached the "Forks of the Peace River", now the town of Peace River. [Tyrrell, in* Thompson's Narrative, *p. lxxxvii]*

1804   *David Thompson surveyed the Athabasca River from its mouth upstream to the Clearwater River. [GSC Memoir 108]*

1810   *David Thompson explored a portion of the upper Athabasca River. [GSC Memoir 108]*

1812   *David Thompson, returning from the Columbia River, crossed Athabasca Pass with a brigade of six canoes, descended the Athabasca River to the La Biche River, ascended it to Lac La Biche, crossed over to the Beaver River and descended it to the upper Churchill, continuing east to Montreal. This was David Thompson's last canoe journey in the north and the west. [Tyrrell, in* Thompson's Narrative, *ci]*

1817   *Ross Cox, North West Company, left Astoria at the mouth of the Columbia River, travelled upstream to cross over the Rocky Mountains to the Athabasca, descended it to the point where he could cross over to the upper Churchill and continued east to Montreal. [Cox, 1957]*

1889   Edouard de Sainville – see Mackenzie

1889   Warburton Pike came down the Athabasca-Slave on his way to the Barrens on a hunting expedition. [Pike, *Barren Ground*]

1889-90 R.G. McConnell, coming from the south, explored and surveyed the Athabasca and part of the Peace River for the Geological Survey. [Zaslow, map p. 158]

1891 H. Somers Somerset and Hungerford Pollen, British sportsmen inspired by reading Warburton Pike, travelled from Edmonton down the Athabasca to Lake Athabasca, up the Peace, and across the Rockies to Fort McLeod. [Somerset, 1895]

1893 J.B. Tyrrell and J.W. Tyrrell in three canoes with six crewmen, descended the Athabasca River and surveyed the north shore of Lake Athabasca. [Thompson, Don, v. 2, p. 289]

1893 Frank Russell, University of Iowa, and Dr. Mackay, HBC factor in charge of the Athabasca district, travelling by HBC transportation, shot the rapids of the Slave River from Smith's Landing to Fort Smith. Russell later descended the Slave River and ascended the Salt River looking for avifaunal specimens. [Russell, pp. 61-65]

1894 Henry Toke Munn and Walter Gordon-Cumming, on a private hunting expedition, travelled from Athabasca Landing by scow and steamer down the Athabasca and Slave Rivers to the foot of Pelican Rapids, canoeing the 200 miles to Fort Resolution, at the mouth of the Slave. At Fort Resolution they hired a birchbark canoe, with Métis guide Moise Mandeville and a Yellowknife Indian named Charles, canoed to the eastern end of Great Slave Lake and by a series of lakes and portages reached Artillery Lake. They cached the canoe, hunted musk-ox unsuccessfully on foot in the Barren Lands and returned to Fort Resolution. Munn returned to the Barren Lands in the fall with eight Indians, including Chief Henri and interpreter Michel Mandeville, in two canoes and took part in a winter hunt. Gordon-Cumming returned south the way they had come. [Munn, 1932]

1897 Thomas Gillis – see Keele and Macmillan

1897 C.J. "Buffalo" Jones descended the Athabasca-Slave Rivers on his way to the Barren Grounds to attempt to secure live muskox. [Preble, p. 81]

1898 E.J. Corp – see Keele

1898 George Mitchell – see Peel

1898 Anderson and his partner, with nine other men in three boats, ran the rapids on the Athabasca River to Fort Smith heading for the Klondike. [Moyles, ed., 1977]

1898 R.H.S. Cresswell, Tallman, Skynner, C.D. Mills, D.J. McAuliffe, Ed Ingraham, and A.D. Stewart (the former mayor of Hamilton, who later died of scurvy on the trip), all from Hamilton, descended the Athabasca River to Fort Smith on the way to the Klondike. [Moyles, ed., 1977]

1899 The Treaty #8 commissioners travelled on the Athabasca and Peace Rivers in two scows and a York boat throughout the summer and autumn. The group, headed by the Hon. David Laird, included the Hon. James Ross, J.A. McKenna, Father Lacombe, Harrison Young, J.W. Martin, H.A. Conroy, Dr. West, with Bishop Grouard as a guest of the Commission, Pierre d'Eschambault as interpreter and Henry McKay as camp manager. There was also a Métis Scrip Commission consisting of Major Walker, J.A. Côté, J.F. Prudhomme and Charles Mair. The RNWMP was represented by Snyder, Anderson, Fitzgerald, McClelland, McLaren, Lett, Burman, Lelonde, Burke, Vernon and Kerr. It was a party of fifty with only thirteen available trackers so that the members of the RNWMP were pressed into service. The steersman was Pierre Cyr who had been with Richardson on his last journey in the North, and with Rae at Repulse Bay in 1853. Peokus, a Blackfoot was also a member of the crew. The whole group left Athabasca Landing and tracked up the Athabasca to Lesser Slave Lake. There they split into three groups. Ross and McKenna went up the Peace to Fort Dunvegan and down again, returning downstream to Athabacsa Landing. David Laird went down the Peace River to Vermilion, visited Lake Athabasca and Fond du Lac, went down the Athabasca-Slave to Fort Smith and returned up the Slave-Athabasca to Fort McMurray. The Scrip Commissioners crossed from Lesser Slave to the Peace River by wagon, floated down the Peace River, ran the rapids in a York boat, reached Fort Chipewyan, returned up the Athabasca in a steamer to Fort McMurray and tracked up the Athabasca to Athabasca Landing with a side-trip by canoe up the Pelican River to Wabasca. Auger Cardinal was their canoeman. [Mair, 1908]

1899 Among those travelling down the Athabasca at the same time as Mair were a priest and his companion canoeing in the area of Lesser Slave Lake and a survey crew from the Rocky Mountains in a York boat. [*Ibid.*, p.37]

1900 J.A. MacRae of the Indian Office met with the Indians at Fort St. John, Sturgeon Lake, Hay River and Fort Resolution, having travelled on the Athabasca-Peace-Athabasca-Slave Rivers. [*Ibid.*, p. 66]

1901 Edward Alexander Preble and his brother Alfred E. Preble, for the U.S. Dept. of Agriculture, Bureau of Biological Survey, starting from Edmonton, canoed from the Landing down the Athabasca to Fort Chipewyan and down the Slave to Fort Resolution. A.E. Preble surveyed around the shores of Great Slave Lake, while E.A. Preble crossed Great Slave Lake to Fort Rae on the North Arm of the lake. Both men returned by steamer to Grand Rapid on the Athabasca and canoed up to Athabasca Landing. [Preble, 1908]

1902 Charles Camsell and Duncan McKay, a schoolmate, working for the Geological Survey, starting from Athabasca Landing in a Peterborough canoe, paddled down the Athabasca and Slave Rivers to Fort Smith. By canoeing up the Salt, the Little Buffalo and the Jackfish Rivers they reached the Peace and continued upstream to the Central Canada railway at Peace River Crossing. The most exciting part of the trip was the run down the Athabasca to Fort McMurray – 90 miles in a day and a half. [Camsell, p. 148]

1903 E.A. Preble, A.E. Preble and Merritt Cary, starting from Edmonton, canoed from Athabasca Landing to Fort Resolution on Great Slave Lake. A.E. Preble and Cary continued along Great Slave Lake to Hay River and Fort Providence,

down the Mackenzie to the mouth of the North Nahanni River and on to Fort Wrigley, returning up the Mackenzie by the steamer, *Wrigley*. [Preble, 1908]

1903 E.A. Preble, with James Mackinlay, crossed Great Slave Lake to Fort Rae, engaged two Fort Rae Indians as guides and canoed along a chain of lakes and rivers, Lake St. Croix, Lake Marian, Grandin River, to Great Bear Lake. They continued along the shore line of Great Bear Lake, down Great Bear River and up the Mackenzie River. Winter caught them near the mouth of the North Nahanni River and they abandoned the canoe, reaching Fort Simpson, where they wintered, on foot. [*Ibid.*]

1907 Ernest Thompson Seton and E.A. Preble, on a private naturalists' expedition, using a Peterborough canoe, went from Athabasca Landing to Fort McMurray. There they bought a 30-foot boat with oars, hired William Loutit as guide and continued down the Athabasca in the company of a RNWMP patrol under the command of Major Jarvis. The river was in flood and they could float down without effort until they reached Lake Athabasca. There the flood on the Peace River had reversed the flow on the Rocher River which connects Lake Athabasca with the

Edward A. Preble, in the stern, and Ernest Thompson Seton setting off from Athabasca Landing on a trip to the Barrenlands in 1907. Preble had travelled in the north extensively for the U.S. Biological Survey, but for Seton it was a unique experience. [Seton, *The Arctic Prairie*, 1911]

Peace. At Fort Smith they explored the small rivers of the area and eventually canoed down the Little Buffalo to Great Slave Lake. A hired York boat took them to the east end of Great Slave Lake and they continued up Pike's Portage to Artillery Lake, Clinton-Colden and Aylmer lakes. They returned up-river on the Slave, tracking the canoe until above Fort Smith they found a tugboat going south. [Seton, 1911]

1911 Footner – see Hay

1911 Robert Service travelled from Athabasca Landing to Fort McPherson on the HBC boats, having canoed the first part of the trip with George and Lionel Douglas, August Sandberg and an Indian guide named Henry. [Service, p. 408]

1913 John Alden Mason for the Geological Survey on an anthropological reconnaissance, having reached Fort Resolution from the south by scow and steamer, returned too late for the southbound steamer and canoed up the Slave and Athabasca Rivers to Athabasca Landing, leaving Fort Resolution on September 16. [Cooke and Holland, p. 331]

1914 Camsell – see Taltson River

1919 E.M. Kindle and T.O. Bosworth, GSC, canoed from Waterways, down the Athabasca-Slave Rivers, the entire length of Mackenzie Valley and parts of Great Bear, Root, North Nahanni and Liard Rivers. [GSC Summary Report, 1920 B]

1920 E.M. Kindle and T.O. Bosworth, GSC, continued their exploration of the Mackenzie Valley by canoe. [GSC Summary Report, 1920 B]

1920 Hugh Kindersley, son of the Governor of the HBC, with Capt. T.P. O'Kelly, a member of their fur-trade staff, canoed from Athabasca Landing down the Athabasca, Slave, Mackenzie Rivers, up the Rat and down the Porcupine to Fort Yukon where they boarded a steamer for Skagway and Vancouver. Without an Indian guide, this was a recreational trip for Kindersley, while O'Kelly conducted a little business en route. [Beaver, First issue, October 1920, p. 14]

1920 Francis Harper, Hamilton Laing and Alden Loring, for the U.S. Biological Survey, having travelled from Edmonton to the end of steel, near Fort McMurray, canoed down the Athabasca River to Lake Athabasca, continuing east on the lake to Poplar Point and the MacFarlane River. They retraced their route in October. [Canadian Field-Naturalist, March 1931, p. 68]

1921 Michael Mason – see Rat-Porcupine in the Yukon

1922 Michael Mason and Dave McRae, having arrived at Fort Smith in winter from the north, travelled back to Fort McPherson down the Mackenzie River, in a home-made canoe with a sail, and continued over the Rat Portage and down the Bell and Porcupine Rivers. [Mason, p. 214]

1923 G.S. Hume, GSC, with a survey party, canoed from Waterways down the Athabasca and Slave Rivers and continued down the Mackenzie River to Great Bear River. [GSC Summary Report, 1923 B]

1924 J.C. Critchell-Bullock, with two assistants, canoed from Waterways to Fort Smith. Three tons of supplies were waiting for them there and were transported to Fort Reliance in a power-driven scow. They were joined at Fort Reliance by John Hornby and four other men. Guy Blanchet, Topographical Survey, with W. Macdonald having just completed an exploration of the lake system north of Great Slave Lake transported the group, with five canoes and provisions to the foot of Pike's Portage. [Canadian Field-Naturalist, 1930, May, p. 53]

1924 C.S. MacDonald, Topographical Survey of the Department of the Interior, completed a 1000-mile canoe trip by canoeing from Wollaston Lake down the Fond du Lac River and Lake Athabasca to Fort Chipewyan. The trip had started at The Pas by steamer, and continued from Fort Cumberland by canoe. [Canadian Geographical Journal, January 1931, p.3]

1930 Dick and Stan Turner canoed from Waterways down the Athabasca and Slave Rivers, along Great Slave Lake, down the Mackenzie and up the Liard to Fort Liard to spend the winter trap-

This was the method of portage between Fort Smith and Fitzgerald in 1928. [George Douglas/Kathy Hooke]

ping. The winter has stretched out to a lifetime and they are still there. [Turner, 1975]

1930? Raymond, Marion and Max Diesel, three brothers from Lac La Biche, Alberta, using a Chestnut Prospector with a "kicker", travelled from Lac La Biche down the Athabasca, Slave, and Mackenzie Rivers, up Great Bear River to Great Bear Lake where they spent the next three years trapping, exploring and prospecting. [Personal communication – Ray Chipeniuk]

1932 Fred Peet and Olaf Slaatten in a 21-foot freight canoe with an outboard motor travelled from Fort McMurray down the Athabasca-Slave Rivers, across Great Slave Lake, which was partially covered with ice, up the Marian and down the Camsell Rivers to Great Bear Lake. [Watt, p. 183]

1932 J. Dewey Soper did ornithological work by boat and canoe in the Slave River delta. [Canadian Field-Naturalist, April-June, 1957, p. 74].

1935 Ben Ferrier with a companion canoed from Athabasca Landing to Fort Yukon, sailing their canoe most of the way to the Mackenzie Delta. This was the third part of Ferrier's retracing of Alexander Mackenzie's travels from Montreal to the Arctic and Pacific Oceans. [Explorers Journal, September 1967]

1945-51 J. Dewey Soper was in the Slave River delta doing ornithological work by boat and canoe. [Canadian Field-Naturalist, April-June, 1957, p. 74]

1957 Eric Morse, Denis Coolican, Sigurd Olson, Elliot Rodger, Omond Solandt and Tyler Thompson canoed north from Southend on Reindeer Lake, crossing over to Wollaston Lake via Swan Lake and Blondeau River, to descend the Fond du Lac River to Stony Rapids. [Che-Mun, Spring 1993, p. 5]

pre-1959 Jennings Carlisle, with a 14-foot canoe, went from Athabasca Landing, down the Athabasca to Fort McMurray, continued down the Athabasca-Slave, along Great Slave Lake and down the Mackenzie to Aklavik. [Field and Stream, November 1959, p. 46]

1961 Peter Allen, Eddy Jackman, Hugh and Peter Gordon, Winton Noble, Canadian university students, shipped their 17-foot aluminum canoes to Hay River and canoed from Hay River to Fort Providence and down the Mackenzie to Fort Simpson. There they switched to a 27-foot river scow and using a motor went up the Liard and the South Nahanni through the First and Second Canyons. After Hell's Gate they shattered their last spare propeller and had to turn back. At Fort Simpson they returned to their canoes, continued down the Mackenzie River to Fort Good Hope, were flown to Hay River, and drove back to Toronto. [Canadian Geographic, November 1967, p. 168]

1964 Robin and Victoria Fraser, Charlotte Holmes,

Tom Wickett, Ronald Gaschen and Dick Irwin starting from Kinasao, crossed Reindeer Lake, and canoeing via Swan Lake, Blondeau River, Middle Lake to Wollaston Lake, went down the Fond du Lac River and a series of lakes to Stony Rapids on Lake Athabasca. [Personal communication – Robin Fraser]

1964 A Navy survival expert with a writer from the *National Geographic* went down the Athabasca into Lake Athabasca in a dangerously overloaded 16-foot canoe. The naval man left the expedition at this point and the writer continued alone, capsizing in the Slave River and losing much of his equipment. [Helmericks, p. 273]

1967 Camp Widjiwagan: Bob Gehrz led Greg Wascenda, Dan Schrankler, Ralph Peterson, Doug Webster and John May from Reindeer Lake down the Fond du Lac River to Lake Athabasca, finishing the trip at Fort Chipewyan. [Camp Widjiwagan Archives]

1968 R.C. Quittenton, with three others (Peter, Derek and Chip) canoed from Athabasca to Fort McMurray down the Athabasca River. [Morse files, p. 15]

1968 Camp Widjiwagan: Joe Prouse led Bill Bierman, Tom Campbell, Brian Bunce, Kelly Davis and Reed Doerr canoeing from Jasper, Alberta, down the Athabasca River to Fort McMurray. [Camp Widjiwagan Archives]

1969 Tom Green, Mat Opack, Bill Steger and Tom McGuire, in Klepper kayaks, starting from Jasper, went down the Athabasca and Slave Rivers, along Great Slave Lake, and down the Mackenzie River to Inuvik. They continued the trip by flying to Summit Lake and paddling down the Porcupine River to Fort Yukon. Steger and McGuire continued down the Yukon River to Galena, Alaska. [McGuire (no relation), p. 83, 126]

1971 Duke Watson – see Taltson

1972 A Wild River Survey crew of Priidu Juurand, David McClung, Bill Pisco and Malcolm McIntyre canoed the Fond du Lac River into Lake Athabasca. [Personal communication – Juurand]

1973 Camp Widjiwagan: Katie Knopke led Mary DeBuhr, Keelin Kane, Wendy Friedlander, Sally Stockwell and Karen Gustafson canoeing down the Fond du Lac River to Lake Athabasca. [Camp Widjiwagan Archives]

1974 Robert Mead – see Mackenzie

CREE AND MACFARLANE

These two relatively small rivers in northern Saskatchewan flow north into the Mackenzie watershed, and because of difficulty of access there have been only a few recently recorded trips. The Cree flows out of Cree Lake into Black Lake at Stony Rapids. The MacFarlane, roughly parallel to the Cree, flows into the southeastern corner of Lake Athabasca.

CREE

1985 *Bob Dannert, Polar Arctic Expeditions, Reb Bowman, Steve Bany and Kurt Melancon believed that they were the first group to canoe this river recreationally. [Personal communication – Dannert]*

1990 *Cliff Jacobson, Tom and Jack Schwinghamer, George and Jeff Loban and Walt Hirschey were told that they were the second group to canoe this river. [Personal communication – Jacobson]*

MACFARLANE

1920 Francis Harper – see Athabasca-Slave

1990 *Bob Dannert, Steve and Lynda Bany, and Jim Schulz, began on the Snare River and canoed down the MacFarlane River to Lake Athabasca. [Personal communication – Dannert]*

1991 *Dave Bober, Roger Devine, Daryl Sexsmith and Bill Jeffery flew into Lisgar Lake and canoed down the MacFarlane River to Lake Athabasca. [Nastawgan, Autumn 1993, pp. 1-7]*

PEACE–SLAVE

The beginnings of the Peace River are high in the Rocky Mountains of northern British Columbia. Brawling mountain streams with Indian names such as Omineca, Ingenika, Kechika, Kwadacha tumble into the Finlay which follows a straight course south. From Summit Lake, the Pack and the Crooked Rivers flow into the Parsnip, which itself flows due north. The Finlay and the Parsnip meet head-on at Finlay Forks and the combined force of water finds a gap in the mountains. The resultant river, flowing east, is the Peace which begins as a river of size and substance. For most of its length the Peace lives up to its name with minor exceptions such as near the beginning, the Parle Pas Rapids which give no warning sound, and the almost impassable 12-mile Rocky Mountain Canyon before Hudson Hope.

From Summit Lake, at the headwaters of the Parsnip River, the Giscome Portage, near Prince George, crosses over to the great bend of the Fraser River. This was an area of great activity early in the century as surveyors, prospectors, miners, and adventurers made their way over the network of waterways.

In 1965 the face of the upper Peace River changed forever with the building of the W.A.C. Bennett Dam above Hudson Hope. The valleys of the Finlay, Parsnip and upper Peace Rivers were flooded to form Williston Lake.

The Peace River rolls east from Hudson Hope to Peace River Crossing where it is crossed by the railway. Railways came early to Peace River country as independent short lines were built north from Edmonton to service the developing agricultural lands. At Peace River Crossing the river flows north to Fort Vermilion, then bends due east again through Vermilion Chutes, merging with the Athabasca to form the Slave River just below Lake Athabasca.

"The Peace River like every great river possesses a strong individuality. It has its own look, its own characteristic forms and color effects. In the 600 miles from the [Hudson] Hope to Vermilion the character of the banks changes only in degree; the bordering hills very gradually scale down from 1000 feet to one hundred. These hills are the feature of the river. They are not really hills for the country is flat on top and it is a kind of gigantic trough in the prairie that the river has dug for itself. But hills they appear from the river, of an infinite variety in contour and color. On the northerly side where the sun beats directly they are for the most part covered with grass; on the other side, timbered. It is the steep grassy hills in the late afternoons with the sun gilding the high places, and casting rich shadows athwart the hollows, that remains in our minds as the most characteristic impression of the Peace." [Footner, *New Rivers of the North*, New York, Doran, 1912]

1792 *Alexander Mackenzie canoed up the Peace River from Fort Chipewyan to the forks of the Peace and the Smoky, above Fort Vermilion, and wintered there before his epic journey to the Pacific.*

1793 *Alexander Mackenzie set out from the forks of the Peace and Smoky Rivers with Alexander Mackay, Joseph Landry, Charles Ducette, François Beaulieux, Baptiste Brisson, François Courtois, Jacques Beauchamp and two Indians as hunters and interpreters. In a 25-foot birchbark canoe, so light that it could be carried by two men, they travelled up-river to the source, crossed the Peace River Pass and eventually reached the Pacific. They returned over the same route and down the Peace to Fort Chipewyan. Mackenzie left for the east the following year. [Mackenzie, 1927]*

1804 *David Thompson, North West Company, with his wife and two children canoed from Peace River down to Lake Athabasca, continued up the Athabasca and Clearwater Rivers, crossed the Methye Portage to the upper Churchill, arriving eventually at Fort William. [Tyrrell,* Thompson's Narrative, *p. lxxxviii]*

1805 *Simon Fraser of the North West Company led a party of twenty men up the Peace River and established a fur-trade post at Rocky Mountain Portage. [Fraser, 1960]*

1806 *Simon Fraser, with John Stuart, La Malice, Bazile, Menard, LaLonde, La Garde, St. Pierre, Saucier (replaced by Blais at Ft. McLeod), Wananshish, Gagnon and Gervais Rivard followed the beginning of Alexander Mackenzie's western route from Rocky Mountain Portage up the Peace, Parsnip and Pack Rivers to three small lakes and a creek, down the MacGregor to the Fraser. They continued down a short section of the Fraser and up the Nechako to Stuart Lake where they established Fort St. James. This was the preliminary to the famous exploration of the Fraser River undertaken in 1808. [Ibid.]*

1824 *Samuel Black, HBC, with Donald Manson, clerk; voyageurs, Joseph La Guarde, Antoine Perreault,*

Joseph Cournoyer, J. Tarrangeau, J. M. Bouché and Louis Ossin, (the latter two deserted early in the trip), La Prise, Chipewyan interpreter, and his wife who both deserted later, explored up the Peace and the Finlay to its headwaters at Lake Thutade by canoe. They cached the canoe and continued on foot into the surrounding mountains, reaching the headwaters of the Stikine River. [Rich, 1955]

1844 *Lt. John Henry Lefroy, RA, and Bombardier Henry, who had travelled from Fort Chipewyan to Fort Simpson by dog team, down the Mackenzie by HBC boat to Fort Good Hope and back to Great Slave Lake, recovered their canoe, and with Louis, Iroquois bowman, and their voyageurs they canoed up the Slave and Peace Rivers to Fort Dunvegan. They returned to Edmonton by horseback and by the southern fur-trade rivers to Montreal. [Lefroy, 1955]*

1868 *Rev. William Bompas, Anglican, travelled from Fort Vermilion down the Peace and Slave Rivers, along Great Slave Lake and down the Mackenzie River to Fort Simpson. [Cody, p. 79]*

1870 *Rev. William Bompas canoed up the Mackenzie, Slave and Peace Rivers to Fort Vermilion. [Ibid., p. 123-24]*

1871 *Rev. William Bompas canoed down the Peace River to Fort Chipewyan and returned up the Peace as far as Rocky Mountain Portage to the head-waters of the river. [Ibid., p. 130]*

1872-73 *Arthur Harper, Frederick Hart, George Finch, Andrew Kansellar and Samuel Wilkinson built a boat and went down the Peace River to the Mountain Rapids where they crossed over Mountain Portage to Halfway River. They exchanged their boat with the CPR survey engineers, took their dug-out cottonwood canoes up the Halfway River and made the cross-over into the next watershed in winter, camping until spring. They built more dug-out canoes and in spring went down the Sikanni Chief and Fort Nelson rivers to the Liard where they met McQuesten, Mayo and James McKnipp. McQuesten exchanged his large boat for Harper's dugouts. Wilkinson went alone up the Liard. Harper and his other three men went down the Liard and Mackenzie, up the Peel and Rat, and down the Porcupine to*

the Yukon River, prospecting all the way. McQuesten, Mayo, McKnipp and Nicholson arrived at Fort Yukon a few days later. [Ogilvie, pp. 88-95]

1873 *Capt. W. F. Butler ascended the Peace River and went up the Finlay to the Omineca. [Butler, 1874]*

1875 Alfred R.C. Selwyn, Arthur Webster and John Macoun, for the Geological Survey, after travelling with a train of pack horses into northern British Columbia, canoed from the confluence of the Finlay and Parsnip Rivers down the Peace River to the mouth of the Smoky, at "The Forks", in a collapsible canoe. Macoun with W.F. King, HBC, in a small cottonwood dugout continued down the Peace River. Below Fort Vermilion the dugout capsized in a rapid and they lost most of their outfit, saving Macoun's specimen box. With difficulty they made the last 200 miles to Fort Chipewyan. [Zaslow, p. 108; Waiser, p. 29]

1877 Bishop Bompas in a canoe with several Indians started from Dunvegan and went up the Peace and Parsnip Rivers in October. They reached Fort McLeod, continued on through Babine Lake, went down the Skeena River to the Pacific coast and along the coast by canoe to Metlakahtla. [Cody, p. 191-95]

1878 Bishop Bompas returned up the Skeena and down the Parsnip and Peace Rivers in the early spring. [*Ibid.*, pp. 199-200]

1879 George M. Dawson and R.G. McConnell, GSC, explored through northern British Columbia and the Peace River district, travelling down three tributaries of the Peace River – the Pine, the Wapiti, and the Smoky. Dawson went overland to the Athabasca River and descended it to Athabasca Landing. McConnell explored the north shore of Lesser Slave Lake and descended the Athabasca River from Athabasca Landing to the La Biche River. [GSC Memoir 108]

1881 Bishop Bompas canoed down the Peace and Slave Rivers, along Great Slave Lake and down the Mackenzie to Fort McPherson. He then worked his way back up the Mackenzie to Fort Simpson and up the Liard to the Fort Nelson River, returning downstream to Fort Norman at freeze-up, having a narrow escape crossing the Mackenzie. [Cody, p. 204-14]

1884 William Ogilvie, for the Dept. of the Interior, made a survey on the Peace River. [GSC Memoir 108]

1889-90 R.G. McConnell – see Athabasca-Slave

1891 William Ogilvie – see Mackenzie

1893 R.G. McConnell, for the Geological Survey, came down the Parsnip to the Finlay, explored the Omineca and ascended the Finlay to its source, the Fishing Lakes, above the Long Canyon. [Zaslow, p. 162, map p. 158]

1895 Father A.G. Morice, Oblate, guided and paddled by two Indians, Duncan Paquette and Rovert, left Lake Takla in a dugout canoe and went up the Driftwood River to Bear Lake, where they were joined by Karta, a Sikanni chief, and Thomas. The five men with two dogs climbed the height of land, 6000 feet, and descended to the head waters of the Omineca River, the Indians and the dogs carrying the loads and also carrying Father Morice across torrents. Morice sounded and measured lakes, naming each lake and river. They made their way overland, rafting down streams to Fort Grahame on the Finlay, continuing down the Finlay and up the Parsnip to Fort McLeod, before returning across country on horseback to Fort St. James. [Mulhall, pp. 104-08]

1897 J.D. Moodie, RNWMP, searching for information on the best route to the Yukon goldfields from Edmonton, canoed from Lesser Slave Lake, up the Peace and Finlay to Fort Grahame. [Cooke and Holland, p. 276]

1898 Four Americans – see Liard

1898 A group of English prospectors, the "Helpman party", descended the Peace River from Peace River Crossing to Smith's Portage and wintered at Fort Resolution on Great Slave Lake. Jeffries and Hall Wright, Capt. Hall and Mr. Simpson prospected northeastern Great Slave Lake. Also prospecting at that end of Great Slave Lake was a Chicago group, Yukon Valley Prospecting-Min-

ing, led by W.J. McLean, ex-HBC, and originally intending to go to Dawson. Wollums, one of the organizers, built boats at Peace River Crossing and they descended the Peace River. [Mair, p. 107]

1898 Jack Grose and party, heading for the Klondike, started by an overland route, came down the Peace River from Peace River Crossing and continued down the Slave and Mackenzie, eventually going up the Peel and Wind. [Moyles, ed., 1977]

1899 The steamer *Grahame* carried 120 Klondikers returning to the United States, including one woman. Sixty were still down the Mackenzie hoping to get out before winter. [Mair, p. 118]

1899 Two Klondikers returned down the Peace-Athabasca by canoe. Five more Klondikers returned down the Peace River. A York boat loaded with Americans came down the Peace River from the Klondike. Tryon and Blackford, two prospectors, canoed down the Peace River from the mining camp at Poker Flats in northern British Columbia. Four Americans from Wyoming were returning from the Klondike by raft down the Peace River [*Ibid.*, pp. 42, 46, 82, 86]

1899 Treaty #8 Commission – see Athabasca-Slave

1899 Father A.G. Morice with four Indian canoemen went to Fort McLeod via the Fraser River and Giscome Portage and down the Crooked River to the Parsnip. [Mulhall, p. 144]

1900 J.A. MacRae – see Athabasca-Slave

1903 Hugh Campbell, geologist, Bob Smith, land surveyor, Mr. Davies, civil engineer and leader of the group, and John S. Leitch, assistant surveyor, looking for coal in Peace River Canyon, came up the Peace River from Peace River Crossing with horses to the Canyon where they camped to do their prospecting. When it came time to leave they built a 30-foot by 15-foot raft, double layered, and rode down the river through the canyon to Hudson Hope. They were thought to be the only men to run the length of the Peace River Canyon. [*Beaver*, Spring 1963, p. 26]

1907 Capt. Sir Cecil Denny, RNWMP, alone in a 20-foot dug-out canoe, came down the Finlay from

Fort Grahame and down the Peace River, sweeping through the Parle Pas Rapids. He left the canoe at Rocky Mountain Canyon, walked the 12 miles to Hudson Hope where he built a raft and drifted on down the Peace River to Peace River Crossing. Denny was part of a RNWMP detachment cutting a pack horse trail for an all-Canadian route to the Klondike. The river trip was his holiday at the end of the summer. *The Law Marches West*, published posthumously, is the story of his career. [*Beaver*, March 1943 p. 10]

1909 Lincoln Ellsworth, son of a wealthy American family, with a prospector, made their way up the Skeena River from Prince Rupert and crossed the height of land to the headwaters of the Peace River. They spent some time prospecting and hunting at the headwaters, traded with a Sikanni Indian for a cottonwood dug-out and canoed down the Peace River to a town (possibly Peace River Crossing) where they could obtain horses. They rode on to Edmonton. [Ellsworth, pp. 74-82]

1911 Footner – see Hay River

1911 A party of surveyors canoed down the Peace River as far as Fort St. John where they were picked up by steamboat. [Footner, p. 142]

1911 Hugh Savage, a Vancouver reporter, canoed up the Fraser, lost his outfit in a fire at Prince George, continued down the Parsnip-Peace on a barge with a surveyor's contractor who was delivering supplies to the surveyors in Rocky Mountain Canyon. The barge carried, as well as the contractor, Bower, a cook, Indian Bob, and an adventurer who had been rafting down the Fraser with four others to Prince George. [*Ibid.*, p. 89] (This is included to show the kind of traffic on these rivers in this period.)

1912 Frederick K. Vreeland went from Hudson Hope on the Peace River to north of Laurier Pass by pack-horse for the U.S. Biological Survey.

1913-14 F.C. Swannell, George Copley, James Alexander and a Chinese cook, Nip Ah Yuen, for the Geological Survey, in a hand-made dug-out canoe, came down the Pack and Parsnip Rivers and

went up the Finlay to the Ingenika. They explored up the Ingenika and continued up the Finlay to explore the head waters. They returned down the Finlay and Peace to Peace River Crossing – 1200 miles by dug-out canoe. [*Beaver*, Spring 1956, p. 32]

1915 Charles Camsell was surveying on the Omineca-Finlay for the Geological Survey. [Zaslow, p. 319]

1916 Charles Camsell surveyed on the Peace, Slave and Salt Rivers for the Geological Survey. [*Ibid.*]

1916 Paul Leland Haworth, a New York history professor, with Joe Lavoie as guide, in a Chestnut sponson canoe, went up the Fraser to Giscome Portage, across to Summit Lake and down the Crooked and Parsnip Rivers to Finlay Forks. They continued up the Finlay, explored the Quadacha and the upper Finlay, mainly on foot, and then came down the Finlay and the Peace to Hudson Hope. Haworth continued to Peace River Crossing by launch. While searching out the "last wilderness", he cheerfully predicted the arrival of the railway and civilization. A self-styled naturalist, he shot indiscriminately at anything and everything, fortunately without great success. [Haworth, 1917]

1921 M.Y. Williams, Dr. G.S. Hume and E.J. Whittaker, GSC, with ten men, built a 50-foot scow at Peace River Crossing, and using two outboard motors, and piloted by Joe LaFleur from Fort Vermilion came down the Peace River from Peace River Crossing and continued down the Athabasca and Slave Rivers. At Fort Smith, they were joined by members of the Topographical Survey, and on Great Slave Lake, by a party led by Guy Blanchet, making a flotilla of five scows and sixty men. Williams with A.H. Bell explored the Mackenzie around the mouth of the Liard. Hume continued down the Mackenzie to 50 miles below Fort Norman. Whittaker's group split off at Fort Providence to explore the Mackenzie River valley. [GSC Summary Report, 1921 B; *Canadian Field-Naturalist*, 1922, April, p. 61]

1921 Will Ogilvie – see Mackenzie

1924 John Hornby with four men came down the Peace River from Peace River Crossing and joined Critchell-Bullock at Fort Reliance on Great Slave Lake. [*Canadian Field-Naturalist*, May 1930, p. 53]

1925 Herb Porter drowned on the Finlay River and is buried at Finlay Forks. [Johnston, p. 175]

1926 Judge Robertson, his son Jack, Fred Fraser, and Pete Wilson came from Summit Lake down the Crooked, Pack, Parsnip and Peace Rivers to Hudson Hope in a boat with a small motor. [*Ibid.*, p. 163]

1927 Lukin Johnston, Judge Robertson and his son Seymour, in a 28-foot flat-bottomed boat with a "kicker" motor, came from Summit Lake down the Crooked, Pack and Parsnip Rivers to Finlay Forks. This was Judge Robertson's twelfth trip over these waters. They continued down the Peace to Rocky Mountain Portage, crossing it by wagon to Hudson Hope. At Hudson Hope they sold the boat and went on down the Peace to Fort St. John by motor scow. [Johnston, 1929]

1927 Joe Armishaw, the road superintendent from Rolla, travelled up the Peace to Finlay Forks, and up the Finlay and the Black Canyon to Manson Creek. Ernie Burden and Jim McIntosh, prospectors and surveyors were travelling south down the Ingenika, Finlay and Parsnip Rivers. [*Ibid.*, pp. 182, 173]

1928 Fenley Hunter, with Albert Dease and George Ball, in a 20-foot canoe with a small motor, came down the Peace River from Peace River Crossing to Lake Athabasca, continued down the Slave River, along Great Slave Lake, and down the Mackenzie River to Fort Simpson. They continued up the Liard to the Nahanni. [NAC – Hunter's journal]

1930 Tony Onraet and Charlie Hansen, in two homemade canoes and hauling a skiff, left from Dunvegan and canoed down the Peace and Slave Rivers. They lost most of their outfit when the skiff caught in a "sweeper" on the Slave. They were joined by two men who were travelling by raft, John (?), and Harry Jebb who had lost his canoe and outfit coming down the Wapiti and Smoky Rivers. Onraet and Hansen continued across Great Slave Lake and down the Mackenzie to Great Bear Lake. Many people were on the Mackenzie River heading for the uranium strike on Great Bear Lake. Onraet crossed Great Bear Lake as crew on a fishing boat, but returned to Fort Norman to trap and trade there. [Onraet, 1944]

1932 Bishop Renison, his wife Elizabeth, with their sons Robert and George, made a holiday camping trip down the Peace River from the town of Peace River through Fort Vermilion to Vermilion Chutes in an 18-foot flat-bottom punt with a 3-horsepower motor and oars. From the Chutes they travelled on the HBC post boat with motor and two Indian guides to Fort Chipewyan and up the Athabasca on the HBC boat *Distributor* to Fort McMurray. [Renison, pp. 143-49]

1932 Joe Gerhart, his wife and two men, prospectors, rode two gas-engined scows down the Peace-Slave-Mackenzie Rivers, up the Great Bear River and across Great Bear Lake to Cameron Bay. [Watt, p. 194]

1939? Arthur P. Woollacott, FRGS, with a canoeman, paddled from Summit Lake down the Crooked River to Fort McLeod, down the Parsnip to Finlay Junction and continued down the Peace River to Peace River Crossing, with a 14-mile portage by wagon around the canyon. [*Beaver*, March 1940 p. 43]

1939? A prospector from Fort Simpson ascended the Liard and Fort Nelson Rivers, abandoned his canoe and hiked across the Rockies, descended the Quadacha in an improvised moose-hide boat to Fort Grahame, where he obtained a boat to go to Peace River Crossing, and out to New York. [*Beaver*, March 1940 p. 43]

pre-1945 Dr. Froelich Rainey of the American Museum of Natural History came down the Peace River from Hudson Hope to search out prehistoric Indian remains. [*Beaver*, September 1945, p. 48, picture only]

1946 Peter Burtt started from Victoria and canoed north up the British Columbia coast to Bella

Coola. He crossed the coastal mountains on horseback, canoed down the Nechako River to Prince George, portaged to Summit Lake and canoed down the Crooked, Pack, Parsnip and Peace Rivers. Making his way across through Lesser Slave Lake and south to Edmonton, he stowed his gear for the winter. The following July he continued canoeing the fur-trade route to Ottawa, took the train to Montreal, canoed up the Richelieu River, down Lake Champlain and the Hudson River to New York City. The *New York Times* carried a photograph of him portaging his canoe through the lobby of the Hotel Pennsylvania! [*New York Times*, Nov. 26, 1947, p. 25]

1949 Raymond M. Patterson, canoeing alone, followed the trail of Sir William Butler and R.G. McConnell in their exploration of the Black Canyon of the Omineca. He continued down the Finlay and Peace to the highway. [Patterson, *Finlay's River*]

1955 R.M. Patterson and his wife Marigold, put their canoe into Trout Lake from the highway near Prince George and canoed down the Pack, Parsnip and Peace Rivers to Peace River Crossing on the Alaska highway. [*Beaver*, Winter 1956, p. 14]

1956 Ben and Marion Ferrier, Col. Gilbert Parker and Dr. Ed Little canoed up the Peace and Parsnip Rivers to Summit Lake. From Summit Lake, Ben Ferrier travelled with Frank Buchanan and Henry Wrestle down the Bad (James Creek), Herrick, McGregor, and Fraser Rivers with one canoe. Ferrier walked the portage trail of West Road River and canoed the Bella Coola River to reach Mackenzie's Rock on the Pacific coast. This represented the fourth section of Ferrier's undertaking to follow Mackenzie's journeys. [*Explorers Journal*, September 1967]

1960 Ben Ferrier, Gilbert Parker and three younger men canoed down the Peace River to Lake Athabasca. [Morse files, p. 22]

1961 Camp Widjiwagan: Russ Williams led Gary Clements, Bud and Tat Knopke, Dave Lundberg and Dave Pontham from the headwaters on the

Camp Widjiwagan: Dave Lundberg, Bud and Tat Knopke, Russ Williams, Gary Clements and Dave Pontham are off on their 800-mile trip down the Peace River in 1961. [Camp Widjiwagan archives]

Finlay River down the Peace River on an 800-mile trip. [Camp Widjiwagan Archives]

1964 Two young American men in two kayaks with small auxiliary motors came from Summit Lake down the Parsnip and Peace Rivers, down the Slave, along Great Slave Lake, and down the Mackenzie, up the Peel and Rat Rivers and down the Porcupine and Yukon, finishing in Alaska before the end of the summer. [Helmericks, p. 273]

1964 Constance Helmericks, with her daughters Jean, fourteen, and Ann, twelve, from California, in a 20-foot Chestnut canoe with a 9-horsepower motor, put in at Taylor, near Dawson Creek, and went down the flooding Peace River, stopping at most communities and settlements. At Fort Vermilion, Ann was stricken with appendicitis, operated on, and required further surgery in Edmonton. When she recovered she was flown to Yellowknife to be looked after by friends, while her mother and sister continued down the Peace to Lake Athabasca and down the Slave to below Fort Smith. There they put their canoe on the last barge of the year and travelled in it across Great Slave Lake to Yellowknife. [Helmericks, 1968]

1964 Three Germans canoed down the Peace and Slave Rivers and finished at Fort Smith. In a separate trip, two young Germans came down the Peace and Slave Rivers in a canoe, capsized in the rapids near Fort Smith and one of them was drowned. [*Ibid.*, p. 27]

1965   Palmer Lewis, Seattle, with a Canadian guide, Art van Somer, spent two weeks exploring Finlay Forks, the Black Canyon of the Omineca, Fort Grahame, and Deserters' Canyon before this area was flooded by the building of the W.A.C. Bennett Dam. Lewis went back to see the change in 1971. [*Beaver*, Autumn, p. 36]

1965   Dr. Paul and Nancy Luxford, Chuck and Lucille Flavelle, Stewart and Meg Cline, in three Grumman canoes started north of Prince George, canoed down the Pack, Parsnip and Peace Rivers. At Hudson Hope the crew who were building the Peace River dam took them around the 21-mile portage by truck and they continued down the Peace to Fort St. John. Their provisions were augmented by potatoes grown by trappers who lived along the river, and by fishing. They believed that their canoe trip was the last one down the Peace River before the dam was completed. [Personal communication – Luxford]

1968   Ray Chipeniuk and Les Eliuk canoed from the headwaters of the Wabasca River, in northern Alberta, to where it enters the Peace River just above Vermilion Chutes. In 300 kilometres they saw nobody, and found Cree spruce bark canoes decaying on the river-bank. [Personal communication – Chipeniuk]

1969   Charlie Wolf – see Thelon

1969   Emile Gautreau, from New Brunswick, a forest pathologist with the Dept. of Fisheries and Forests, was on a regular trip down the Peace River when his canoe capsized in the Boyer Rapids just shortly before Charlie Wolf and Doug Best arrived on the scene. They rescued him and continued down the Peace River together to Peace Point, Gautreau giving Wolf and Best a lift past the portages to Fort Smith in his camper truck. [Personal communication – Best]

1974   Robert Mead – see Mackenzie

1974   Tom McGuire – see Thelon

MACKENZIE

While the watershed of the Mackenzie extends over a huge area encompassing the northeast corner of British Columbia, much of Alberta, part of northern Saskatchewan, nearly half of the land mass of the Northwest Territories, and part of northern Yukon, the Mackenzie River itself rises in Great Slave Lake and flows west and northwest, broad, strong and single-minded until it reaches the confused and many-channelled delta, where it empties into the Arctic Ocean. Several kilometres wide in places near its source, the Mackenzie flows along at a steady 5 miles an hour. As it flows north the Mackenzie Mountains rise on the western side, the river narrows and cuts through the Upper and Lower Ramparts. Apart from one dangerous and well-publicized rapid, the Sans Sault, between Norman Wells and Fort Good Hope, the greatest hazard comes from the sudden violent squalls which can whip up huge and destructive waves on the wide body of water.

1789   *Alexander Mackenzie of the North West Company set out from Fort Chipewyan in a birchbark canoe with a crew of four Canadians, including Joseph Landry and Charles Ducette, two of them attended by their wives, a German, an Indian known as the "English Chief", his two wives in a small canoe, and two young Indians (followers of the Chief) in another small canoe. The "English Chief" was one of the followers of the chief, Matonabbee, who con-*

A modern version of the portage: Emile Gautreau, in gratitude to Charlie Wolf and Doug Best for rescuing him after his capsize on the Peace River in 1969, transported them to Fort Smith to continue on to the Thelon and Baker Lake. [Best]

ducted Samuel Hearne to the Coppermine. The Indians served as interpreters and hunters. Other Indians were sometimes persuaded, sometimes coerced, to travel with the expedition as local guides as the party advanced into unknown territory. They reached the Arctic Ocean on July 12, and returned up-river the way they had come, tracking the canoes much of the way. [Mackenzie, 1927]

1825-27 Sir John Franklin, RN, with Dr. John Richardson, British seamen, a few Canadian voyageurs, Indian hunters and two Inuit interpreters descended the Mackenzie in two boats to Great Bear Lake where they built Fort Franklin near the egress of Great Bear River and spent the winter. Franklin and Kendall descended the Mackenzie River to its mouth and returned to Fort Franklin. In the spring of 1826, using four mahogany long boats, they embarked for the Arctic Ocean. Richardson and Kendall went east as far as the Coppermine River to map the coast. Richardson then returned south. Franklin and Back, exploring west, discovered and named Herschel Island. They returned up-river to Great Bear Lake where they wintered, returning up the Mackenzie in 1827, when Franklin discovered and named the Peel River. [Coates and Morrison, p. 118; Francis, p. 95-97; Karamanski, p. 158]

1825 Peter Warren Dease, as part of the Franklin expedition, having wintered at Great Slave Lake, descended the Mackenzie River to Great Bear Lake. [Preble, p. 59]

1837 Thomas Simpson and Peter Warren Dease descended the Mackenzie River to the Arctic coast and explored it between Return Reef and Point Barrow. They returned up-river to winter on Great Bear Lake at Fort Confidence, near the mouth of the Dease River. They discovered and named the Colville River. [Karamanski, p. 159]

1848 Sir John Richardson and Dr. John Rae, accompanied by Jack Fiddler and others, descended the Mackenzie River and examined the coast to the Coppermine River in a search for Franklin's lost expedition. [Story, p. 293]

1849 Lt. William Pullen, as part of the Royal Navy's search for the Franklin expedition, with fourteen officers and men, in two 27-foot whale-boats and an umiak, explored the Arctic coast eastward from Point Barrow to the Mackenzie Delta. As they turned up the Mackenzie River, Mr. Hooper, five men and one boat stopped at Fort McPherson. The umiak was broken up and the skins saved for moccasins. Lt. Pullen and the remaining men continued tracking the whale boat up-river to Fort Good Hope, where it was exchanged for an HBC York boat, and with the help of four HBC men they reached Fort Simpson. [Pullen, 1979]

1850 Commander William Pullen, having gone up the Mackenzie with his men on his way back to England, received, along with notice of a promotion, an urgent message from the Admiralty to return down the Mackenzie and search the coastline east of the Mackenzie delta. Using the whale boat, a York boat, and an inflatable rubber boat called a Halkett boat, which had been used by Richardson and Rae on the Coppermine River, the party, augmented by three HBC servants, Neil McLeod, William Hepburne and Jerome St. George, and two Hare Indian guides, one of whom had accompanied Dease and Simpson, descended the Mackenzie, explored the coastline as far as Cape Bathurst and returned upstream to Fort Simpson. [Ibid.]

1851 Commander Pullen and his men, using the York boat, went up the Mackenzie, along Great Slave Lake and joining with the HBC brigades travelled the usual fur-trade route across to York Factory. [Ibid.]

1860 Robert Kennicott, having wintered in Fort Simpson, continued down the Mackenzie River to Fort McPherson. [Cooke and Holland, p. 216]

1861 Rev. W.W. Kirkby, with two Indians, canoed down the Mackenzie River from Fort Simpson to Point Separation on the Mackenzie delta. [Hind, v.2, p. 163]

1866 Rev. William Bompas travelled down the Mackenzie from Fort Simpson to Fort Norman, returning up-river to Fort Simpson with Robert McDonald, who had come up the Porcupine and down the Rat and Peel. [Cody, p. 57-58]

1869 William Bompas — see Porcupine

1872 William Bompas — see Hay

1873 William Bompas – see Clearwater

1876 Rev. Robert McDonald – see Porcupine

1889 Edouard de Sainville, on a private French expedition, hired an Indian and Métis crew and travelled down the Athabasca, Slave and Mackenzie Rivers from Athabasca Landing to Fort McPherson. He spent at least five years around the Mackenzie delta. He also surveyed the Peel River up to Wind River and the upper course of the Porcupine. [Cooke and Holland, p. 261]

1891 William Ogilvie, Department of the Interior, canoed down the Mackenzie to the Liard, up the Liard, Fort Nelson and Sikanni Chief Rivers, crossed the watershed to the Peace River and continued down the Peace to Fort St. John. [Thompson, Don, v.2, p. 150]

1892 Rev. Isaac Stringer, Anglican, with Jimmy Barber, Indian, and Kenneth Stewart, Métis, canoed from Fort McPherson down the Mackenzie to Point Separation on the Mackenzie delta. He began his missionary work at Kittigazuit (Aklavik) with George Greenland as interpreter and returned up-river after ten days to Fort McPherson. [Peake, p. 18]

1892 Comte de Sainville and Joe Hodgson, HBC, with an Indian and George Greenland, an Inuit, canoed from Fort McPherson down the Mackenzie to the mouth of the delta to explore. They returned up-river with Kenneth Stewart, leaving George Greenland to act as interpreter for Rev. Stringer. [*Ibid.*]

pre-1894 An American woman returning from a scientific journey down the Mackenzie, left behind a barrel of alcohol containing specimens of fish at one of the Hudson's Bay posts with interesting results. [Munn p. 54]

1894 Frank Russell, University of Iowa, canoed alone in a Slavey birchbark canoe from Fort Good Hope down the Mackenzie to Fort McPherson. At Fort McPherson he joined with Comte de Sainville and they canoed to Herschel Island. Russell canoed in a 14-foot Louchoux birchbark canoe, and de Sainville, with two Louchoux, Vusso and Tothin, in a large canvas canoe. Both

men returned to San Francisco by whaling ship. [Russell, pp. 134-50]

1894 Rev. Isaac Stringer, with two Indians, Peter Tsul and Enoch Moses, canoed down the Peel and Mackenzie Rivers from Fort McPherson to Kittigazuit (Aklavik) in the Mackenzie delta. They returned up-river in the fall in a whale-boat donated by the whaling captains at Herschel Island. [Peake, p. 30]

1898 Rev. Stringer with his wife Sadie set off from Fort McPherson for Herschel Island by whale-boat, taking with them George Mitchell, a prospector who had been up the Wind and Peel Rivers and who wished to return home to Montreal from Herschel Island. [*Ibid.*, p. 64]

1898 Andrew Stone – see Liard

1898 After mid-summer and throughout the following winter, Fort McPherson was one of the busiest spots north of Edmonton. In that year some 500 Klondikers descended on the post. [MacGregor, p. 150]

1900 James Mackintosh Bell, for the Geological Survey, with two canoemen, Charlie Bunn and Louis Tremblay started at Fort Resolution, crossed Great Slave Lake with dogs pulling a heavy canoe on the ice. They travelled from Fort Providence to Fort Simpson on the *Wrigley* then canoed down the Mackenzie to Fort Norman. At Fort Norman they were joined by Charles Camsell and Johnny Sanderson. Together they canoed up the Great Bear River and along the north shore of Great Bear Lake, explored up the Dease River and walked overland to the Kendall and the Coppermine. At the Coppermine, Bell and Camsell turned back while the other men lagged behind because of a blizzard and shortage of food. On their return to camp, Bunn did not appear and could not be found before it was time for the party to begin their return to the south. From Conjuror Bay on the southeast corner of Great Bear Lake, they proceeded up the Camsell River – a tortuous course of lakes and rivers. They finally stumbled on a camp of Dogrib Indians who gave them lavish hospitality and two young men to guide them up the Camsell, across the height of land to the Marian River which they followed down to Fort Rae. They crossed Great Slave Lake to Fort Resolution, Camsell and Bell continuing up the Slave River to Fort Chipewyan and by dog team to Edmonton. Miraculously, Charlie Bunn fell in with a band of Hare Indians and returned with them to Great Bear Lake and down Great Bear River to Fort Norman. [Bell, Chap. 2]

1904 In the summer of 1904, E.A. Preble, having wintered in Fort Simpson, canoed down the Mackenzie to Fort McPherson and returned up-river on the steamer *Wrigley*. [Preble, 1908]

1921 Will Ogilvie, William Dyer, geologist, and Rex Henderson, on a private expedition to prospect for oil, travelled from Peace River Crossing, down the Peace, Athabasca, Slave and Mackenzie Rivers to Fort Norman in a 16-foot disappearing propeller boat and a 15-foot Peterborough canoe. They returned up-river by steamer. Ogilvie published his reminiscences privately in *Way, Way Down North*, in 1990. [*Peterborough Examiner*, December 4, 1990]

1921-22 A.H. "Joe" Miller, travelling by barge, wagon train, pack horse and on foot, with two tons of provisions and equipment, made two trips to the lower reaches of the Mackenzie River to make a gravity survey in cooperation with the Geological Survey. [Thompson, Don, v.3, p. 226]

1922 M.Y. Williams – see Liard

1922-23 Magnetic data was collected along the Peace, Athabasca, Slave and Mackenzie Rivers by the Topographical Survey Branch of the Dept. of the Interior. [Thompson, Don, v.3, p.224]

1929 Amos Burg – see Porcupine

1932-35 A.E. Porsild, based in Aklavik, travelled extensively by canoe in the Mackenzie delta during the summers. [*Canadian Field-Naturalist*, Jan./Feb. 1945, p. 4]

1932 Earl Harcourt and Billy Graham – see Liard

1933 Dick and Vera Turner, newly married at Hay River, travelled from Fort Providence to Fort

Simpson in a small hand-made wooden boat with a 3-horsepower motor. [Turner, p. 102]

1937 Sheldon Taylor and Geoffrey Pope, having wintered in Fort Smith, completed their New York to Nome trip, canoeing along Great Slave Lake, down the Mackenzie, up the Peel and Rat, down the Porcupine and Yukon to the Alaska coast and around the coast to Nome. [Steber, 1987]

1938 Alden C. Hayes, Dick Hayes, Tom Cain, Joe Maloney, Doug Osborne and Wes Bliss, American university students, mainly of anthropology. Only the Hayes brothers were experienced in canoes. Beginning at Conroy Landing on the Sikanni Chief River they made a 2500-mile journey by canoe using one 16-foot and two 19-foot Peterborough canoes with one outboard motor. They canoed down the Fort Nelson and Liard and Mackenzie Rivers to Aklavik where they sold their motor and one canoe. They continued up the Mackenzie, Peel and Rat and down the Porcupine to Old Crow where they hitched a ride to Circle City on the Yukon River in a motorized scow. [Hayes, 1989]

1957 George Appell, anthropologist, with his wife Laura, using a 17-foot Peterborough canoe started from Hay River on Great Slave Lake intending to go all the way down the Mackenzie to make an ethnological survey of some of the Indian tribes living along the river. They went as far as Fort Simpson where their plans changed, and they returned up-river by barge. [*Appalachia*, June 1958, p. 37]

1957 Henning Harmuth and Anne Harmuth-Hoene, with a folding canoe, reached Hay River by bus and canoed down the Mackenzie, up the Peel and Rat, down the Bell and Porcupine to Fort Yukon. They returned by steamer up the Yukon. [*Nastawgan*, Winter 1984, pp. 1-4]

pre-1959 Jennings Carlisle – see Athabasca-Slave

1960 Hugh Donald Lockhart Gordon and two others canoed the Athabasca, Slave and Mackenzie Rivers. The canoe capsized in the Sans Sault Rapids on August 10, and Hugh Gordon was drowned. [Nickerson, p. 116]

1960 Camp Widjiwagan: Ned Therrien led Bruce Christiansen, Steve Lissick, Allan Johnson, Frank Metcalf and Tom Whyatt in canoeing from the shores of Great Slave Lake down the Mackenzie River to the Arctic Ocean. [Camp Widjiwagan Archives]

1963 Carmichael and Judy Sumner with John Higginson, on a private American recreational trip, travelled down the Mackenzie from Hay River to Tuktoyaktuk in a 19-foot skiff with a 10-horsepower motor and a sail. They included a side trip up and down the Great Bear River. Recreational travellers on the Mackenzie were still rare enough that the barges watched out for them, and the HBC posts provided hospitality. [*Beaver*, Spring 1965, p. 26]

1963 Jean Poirel and Maurice Saraillon kayaked down the Mackenzie to Tuktoyaktuk. [Poirel, p. 18]

1963 Two Germans went down the Mackenzie and up the Rat River. One disappeared and the other was driven mad by mosquitoes. [*Ibid.*, p. 79]

1963-66 Luther Duc Meyer from California made annual trips down the length of the Mackenzie. In 1963 he travelled by kayak finishing at Tuktoyaktuk while in 1964 he made the trip by motorboat with his young grandson. The following year, at age seventy, after kayaking down the river he had a scow built at Inuvik with an 18-horsepower motor to go up-river. He swamped at Ramparts sustaining injuries and had to be flown out. Undaunted he returned and made a solo kayak trip in 1966. [Nickerson, p. 146]

1964 Two young Americans – see Peace

1965 Constance Helmericks, and daughters Jean and Ann, continued the trip started the year before on the Peace River in their 20-foot Chestnut canoe with small motor, going from Yellowknife along the north shore of Great Slave Lake and down the Mackenzie to Inuvik. [Helmericks, 1968]

1965 An Australian in a 16-foot canoe with a motor travelled down the Mackenzie to the coast and back again. [*Ibid.*, p. 430]

1966 Thomy and Virginia Nilsson, Canadians, paddled and sailed an HBC rental canoe from Fort Providence to Inuvik. [*Ibid.*, p. 187]

1966 Paul and Andy Fisher from England met three Canadians, George Day, Rod Copeland and Rob Caldwell, working in the mines in Yellowknife. They combined forces, bought two freight canoes and paddled and sailed from Yellowknife to Inuvik. [*Ibid.*, pp. 105, 153]

1966 The Nickerson family from California, Richard and Elinor, and their sons Devon, nineteen, Lincoln, twelve, and Brian, ten, in three kayaks, travelled down the Mackenzie from Fort Providence to Inuvik. [*Ibid.*, 1967]

1966 Don Ross – see Liard

1969 Keith McCrory led a canoe trip of boys from the Christian Science Brigade down the Mackenzie River. [HBC Archives – U-Paddle]

1970 Fred Gaskin and Lyle Malcolm canoed from Fort Providence to Inuvik down the Mackenzie River. [Personal communication – Gaskin]

1971 Mark Riddell and a Czechoslovakian, who met at Hay River while working as firefighters, bought an inexpensive canoe and paddled down the Mackenzie River to Norman Wells. [Personal communication – Riddell]

1972 James Martineau canoed from Fort Wrigley down the Mackenzie River to Norman Wells. [HBC Archives – U-Paddle file]

1973 Duke Watson, V. Josendal, H. Muller, P. Sharpe and P. Sharpe, Jr. canoed from Fort Norman to Arctic Red River. (see Great Bear) [Personal communication – Watson]

1974 Robert Douglas Mead and his son Jim, following Alexander Mackenzie's route, and using a 17-foot Old Town canoe, paddled from Fort McMurray down the Athabasca-Slave Rivers and along Great Slave Lake to Hay River. They were taken by truck to Fort Providence, and canoed down the Mackenzie River and the east channel of the delta to Whitefish Station. [Mead, 1976]

CHAPTER SIX

THE RIVER OF MANY WATERS: WESTERN TRIBUTARIES OF THE MACKENZIE

The western side of the Mackenzie is flanked by mountains. The Mackenzie Mountains, with their highest peak, Mt. Sir James MacBrien, on the South Nahanni River, are the source of the western tributaries of the Mackenzie. The Mackenzie Mountains are slightly to the east of the Rocky Mountain chain. The valley between the Mackenzie Mountains and the Selwyn Mountains, an extension of the Rockies, defines the boundary between the Northwest Territories and the Yukon. The mountainous nature of the whole area west of the Mackenzie River defines the nature of the tributaries of the Mackenzie.

The Liard is one of the largest of the tributaries, rising in the Yukon, and touching northern British Columbia in a swing southward before it turns northeast to empty into the Mackenzie. The main boundary-defining tributaries are the North Nahanni, the Redstone, the Keele, and the Arctic Red rivers. There are two other important tributaries: the Peel River flows out of the Ogilvie Mountains deep in the Yukon through the valley which separates the Selwyn and Richardson Mountains; and the Rat, a very short river, flows out of the Richardson Mountains and is important because it gives access to McDougall Pass, the lowest pass in the whole mountain chain.

LIARD

The Liard being the most southerly as well as the largest of all these rivers has a significant place in fur-trade history. It also has a tributary which is more important to canoeists than the Liard itself, namely the South Nahanni (frequently called just "Nahanni"). Its other major tributaries provided transportation links: the Dease, flowing from the southwest, is on the route to or from the Pacific via the Stikine and was heavily used during the Cassiar and Klondike gold rushes; the Frances, flowing in from the north, was the old route to the Pelly River, an important tributary of the Yukon River; the Fort Nelson, flowing from the southeast is part of the system of small rivers which lead eventually to the Peace River.

About 1823, Fort Liard was established as a Hudson's Bay Post about 180 kilometres up the lower section of the Liard River, above the mouth of the South Nahanni. To confuse matters, the Company later built Lower Post on the upper Liard at the mouth of the Dease River. The intention was to extend the trade routes into the unexplored hinterland of the southern Yukon. The Liard River has canyons, the Little Canyon and the Grand Canyon, and it has Hell's Gate, the Devil's Portage around the Devil's Gorge and Mountain Portage, names which explain the respect and trepidation with which the voyageurs approached the river, known by Robert Campbell as the "River of Malediction". The difficulties of travelling the Liard curtailed the fur-trade activities, and other than Fort Liard and Lower Post, other posts using the river were soon abandoned.

The Alaska Highway, built in 1942, crosses the Liard in northern British Columbia and again near Watson Lake. Watson Lake was for a time the base for flying in to the headwaters of the South Nahanni.

1824 Murdoch McPherson, HBC, travelled the mid-Liard basin up as far as the Beaver River. [Coates and Morrison, p. 19]

1831 John McLeod, HBC, travelled from Fort Simpson, up the Mackenzie, Liard and Frances rivers to Lake Simpson. [Ibid.]

1834 John McLeod, HBC, ascended the Dease to Dease Lake and portaged across into the Stikine watershed to the Tuya River. [Ibid.]

1836 Robert Campbell, HBC, ascended the river and built a post at Dease Lake. In 1837 he spent the winter at a fur-trading outpost known as Fort Halkett at the junction of the Smith and Liard rivers. Fort Halkett was abandoned in 1865. [Wright, A., 1976]

1838 While travelling the Liard River, Robert Campbell named it the Bell River for John Bell, not realizing it was the same river which had been explored by John McLeod four years earlier. The name did not stick. [Coutts, p. 159]

1840 Robert Campbell, HBC, from Fort Halkett on the Lower Liard ascended the river to Frances Lake which he named for Lady Simpson. He continued up Finlayson River to Finlayson's Lake and crossed the height of land to the Pelly River. [Burpee, 1926]

1859 Robert Kennicott, naturalist from the Smithsonian Institution, made a trip up the Liard River to Fort Liard from Fort Simpson. [Preble, p. 70]

1872 Henry Thibert and Mr. McCulloch first reached Dease Lake from the Stikine River and discovered gold near Fort Halkett on the Liard. Other miners joined them on McDame Creek, a tributary of the Dease River, from the Stikine, the Cariboo and the Omineca. [Pike, Through the Subarctic Forest, p. 57]

1872 Jack McQuesten – see Bell-Porcupine

1872 Arthur Harper, Frederick Hart and others left the Omineca gold diggings, went down the Liard and Mackenzie rivers, up the Peel and Rat and down the Bell-Porcupine, reaching Fort Yukon in 1873. [Coutts, p. 121]

1873 Robert Hyland was the first man to ascend the Hyland River, having come up the Liard. The Indians were believed to be afraid to go up the Hyland. [Ibid., p. 134]

1874 John Sayyea and three companions came from Dease Lake up the Liard River to Sayyea Creek, a tributary of the Upper Liard, and discovered gold. [*Ibid.*, p. 232]

1878 Emil Fortune Stanilas Joseph Petitot, Oblate missionary, came to Great Slave Lake in 1862 and made missionary journeys between 1862-78, exploring the area between the Mackenzie and the Liard rivers. In 1878 he discovered a tributary of the Liard which was named the Petitot in his honour. [Petitot, 1875]

1887 George Mercer Dawson, R.G. McConnell and J. McEvoy, Canadian Government Yukon exploration and the Geological Survey, came up the Stikine and Dease rivers to the Liard. Dawson and McEvoy with L. Lewis and D. Johnson from Victoria, two Tshimsian and three Tlinkit Indians continued up the Liard and Frances rivers to Frances Lake and portaged across the height of land to the upper Pelly River. The Indians returned to the coast, and the four men built a canvas canoe and descended the Pelly to the confluence with the Lewes (upper Yukon). There they built a wooden boat and ascended the Lewes to

R.G. McConnell's gruelling trip down the Liard was just part of a 4000-mile circular journey beginning on the Stikine in 1887 and finishing at Skagway a year later. [GSC collection]

its source. They came out across the Chilkoot Pass and down the Lynn Canal to the coast. [Dawson, 1987]

1887   McConnell, with Louis Trepanier and John McLeod, built a wooden boat and travelled down the Liard from the mouth of the Dease River to the Devil's Portage. Their wooden boat was too heavy to portage so McConnell constructed a canvas covered boat from a shaped piece of canvas brought from Ottawa for just such a purpose and continued down the Liard with one Indian to Fort Liard. At the fort he exchanged the canvas boat for a birchbark canoe and reached Fort Simpson. He continued up the Mackenzie to Fort Providence, visited the Slave, Salt and Hay rivers and wintered at Fort Rae. [*Beaver*, December 1948]

1891   William Ogilvie – see Mackenzie

1892   Warburton Pike with Reed and Charles Gladman explored up the Hyland River, a tributary of the Liard, and returned down-river seeing no other travellers. The Indians considered the river unlucky and preferred to pack their loads through the woods. [Pike, *Through the Subarctic Forest*, p. 81]

1892   A Californian mining expert went up the Liard and Hyland rivers from the Lower Post on the Liard to look at a quartz ledge and returned downstream two weeks later. [*Ibid.* p. 82]

1892   Henry Thibert and a boat-load of prospectors were going up the Dease River to the Liard after a summer's work. [*Ibid.*, p. 57]

1897   Charles and Fred Camsell, on an abortive route to the Klondike, with D.W. Wright and A.M. Pelly, British Columbia game-hunters, and Dan Carey, a miner from the Peace River area, with his son Willie, went up the Liard by scow with a crew of Indians and continued up to Frances Lake where they wintered. The Careys and Pelly left. The Camsells and Wright built a boat and came down the Frances and Liard rivers to the Lower Post and went up the Dease River to Dease Lake. There they worked for Warburton Pike's company, the Casca Trading Co., at

Laketon on Dease Lake through the winter of 1898-99. They came out by dog-team down the Stikine River to Wrangell. [Camsell, p. 59]

1898   J.D. Moodie, RNWMP, searching for information on the best route to the Yukon goldfields from Edmonton, continued from Fort Grahame (see Peace) up the Liard to Frances Lake and down the Pelly to Fort Selkirk on the Yukon River. [Cooke and Holland, p. 276]

1898   Frank Watson from England arrived on the Upper Liard having come from Edmonton. He stayed in the area, prospecting and trapping on the upper Liard and its tributaries and living at Watson Lake which was named for him. With the building of the Alaska Highway in 1941, he found the area too crowded and moved to another lake north of Watson Lake. [Coutts, p. 280]

1898   Andrew Jackson Stone, from the American Museum of Natural History, collecting bird and mammal specimens, came from Wrangell, up the Stikine to Dease Lake and down the Dease and the Liard to the mouth of the "Black" River. He explored up that river and during the winter moved his outfit by dog-team down the Liard to a navigable point past the canyons. Deserted by his helpers, he constructed a 24-foot canvas boat and launched it on the Liard River, below Hell's Gate Canyon just after spring break-up. Travelling alone to Fort Liard, and then with the help of local Indians, he continued down to Nahanni Butte. After exploring in the Nahanni Range on foot, he continued down the Liard to Fort Simpson and down the Mackenzie to Fort McPherson, which he used as a base for exploration in the mountains and on the Arctic coast, from Herschel Island to Cape Lyon. [*Everybody's Magazine*, Dec. 1900, pp. 535-44; *Bulletin. American Museum of Natural History*, Vol. XIII, pp. 31-62]

1898   Four Americans from Wyoming travelled from Fort St. John, down the Pine and Fort Nelson rivers and up the Liard River to reach the Klondike. They returned down the Peace River by raft in 1899. [Mair, p. 86]

1899 Charles and Fred Camsell, in an 18-foot canoe, with Johnny Sanderson, an Indian, and his wife, came from Dease Lake down the Dease and Liard rivers to the Mackenzie. [Camsell, pp. 70, 105]

1919 E.J. Whittaker with a party, from the Geological Survey, tracked up the Liard from Fort Simpson. The Liard was in flood with water levels higher than had been seen before. The trip lasted six weeks. [*Canadian Field-Naturalist*, 1921, Jan., p. 7]

1922 Dr. G.S. Hume explored the Liard River for the Geological Survey. [*Canadian Field-Naturalist*, Feb. 1933 p. 23]

1922 M.Y. Williams, Dr. G.S. Hume, and party, travelled by gas boat and scow up the Peace River, by pack train 150 miles from Taylor Flats to the headwaters of the Sikanni Chief, canoed down that river and the Fort Nelson River to the Liard. Williams and his party continued down the Liard and Mackenzie and up the Great Bear to the foot of Mt. Charles, a canoe journey of 900 miles. They returned by gas boat and steamer. [*Canadian Field-Naturalist*, Feb. 1933, p. 23]

1923 Fenley Hunter, probably with Albert Dease, in a 20-foot canoe with a small motor went up the upper Liard River and the Frances River to Frances Lake. [NAC – Hunter's journal]

1925 Tom Smith, a trapper, with his teen-aged daughter Jenny ran the Liard River on a raft with their winter's furs. Tom Smith was drowned in Devil's Canyon, but Jenny survived and reached Fort Liard with the help of local Indians. [Camsell, p. 70; Turner, p. 23]

1925 A Swede in a 32-foot cottonwood dug-out frequently came down the Frances and Liard to the Lower Post. He was a prospector, known only as "The Swede", who lived in the area between 1900 and 1930 and was known for his beautifully built dug-out canoe. [Money, p. 80; Coutts, p. 256]

1925-27 Anton Money and Amos Godfrey, in two weeks, cut the trees, whip-sawed the lumber, built a 28-foot boat and named it *Come What May*. Using oars and poles, they came down the

Dease River from Dease Lake to Lower Post and poled up the Liard and the Frances rivers to Frances Lake. On Frances River they passed the cabin of a white trapper named Watson for whom Watson Lake is named. They found gold and silver but left after the summer, running down the Frances and Liard to Lower Post with an empty boat. Money later returned and lived on Frances Lake with his wife for several years. On their first visit they found a cache left by a previous traveller at the mouth of the Finlayson River, either by the Camsell group in 1898 or by Dr. G.M. Dawson in 1887. Money believed that apart from HBC employees only twenty-two non-natives had ever come up the Liard to Lower Post. [Money, p.80]

pre-1928 Stainer swamped and Cpl. Churchill, RCMP, lost his boat in the Rapids of the Drowned on the Liard River. [NAC – Fenley Hunter journal]

1928 Starke and Stevens came down the Liard River, from Devil's Portage on the upper river to Fort Simpson using a power scow, and went up the Nahanni. [Patterson, *Dangerous River*, 1989 ed. p. 87]

1932 Earl Harcourt and Billy Graham, University of Alberta students, paddled a 16-foot canoe from the headwaters of the Fort Nelson River, down that river, the Liard and Mackenzie rivers, up Great Bear River and across Great Bear Lake to the mining boom area of Conjuror Bay. [Watt, p. 192]

1938 Alden Hayes – see Mackenzie

1948 R.M. Patterson, having come up the Stikine by river-boat, the *Hazel B*, had his 14-foot canoe and outfit portaged from Telegraph Creek to Dease Lake. He canoed alone down the lake, the Dease River and a short section of the Liard to the Lower Post. [Patterson, *Trail to the Interior*, Macmillan, 1966]

1954 R.M. Patterson, with his cousin Christopher, in a 20-foot Chestnut canoe with a 5-horsepower motor, flew to Fort Nelson, paddled down the Fort Nelson River to Nelson Forks and went upstream on the Liard to Hell's Gate, tracking the canoe when necessary. They canoed down the Liard to Nahanni Butte. [*Beaver*, Spring 1955, p. 20]

1960 Peter Gordon left the ill-fated group which included his brother (see Mackenzie), and canoed alone up a section of the Liard River. [Personal communication – Pamela Morse]

1965 Dr. E. T. Tozer from the Geological Survey of Canada, and Dr. N. J. Silberling, from the U.S. Geological Survey, travelled on the Liard River. [*Canadian Geographic*, August 1976, p.4]

1966 Don Ross from Alaska, using a Folboat, kayaked alone down the Fort Nelson and lower Liard rivers, motored up the South Nahanni to Virginia Falls with others before continuing down the Mackenzie to Inuvik. Along the way, he made an excursion by barge into Great Bear Lake. He then flew to Summit Lake and kayaked down the Bell-Porcupine rivers to Fort Yukon, where he flew north to Arctic Village and canoed down the Chandular River in Alaska. [Personal communication]

1968 Charlie Wolf, from Alaska, starting from the Alaska Highway at Fort Nelson, in a 13-foot Grumman, canoed down the Muskwa and Fort Nelson rivers, down the lower Liard and Mackenzie, returning up the Rat and down the Porcupine to Fort Yukon. It was the third time he had made this trip and on this occasion he was accompanied by Elmar and Brigitte Engel in kayaks. [McGuire, p.25, Klein, *Passion for Wilderness*, p. 37]

1970 Ferdi Wenger, Doug and Harvey Fraser, Adolf Teufele, Leland Bradford and Jeff Harbottle, Canadians, Dale Hambelton, American, and Frank from Switzerland, in hand-built canoes, canoed down the Liard from Watson Lake to Fort Simpson on the Mackenzie River, avoiding the Grand Canyon but canoeing through the Little Canyon. [*B.C. Outdoors*, August, October, 1972]

1971 John Jennings and Patrick Saul canoed from Dease Lake to the Lower Post on the Liard. [Personal communication – Jennings]

1971? Klaus Streckmann – see Nahanni

Following his trip down the Back River in 1969, Duke Watson went north by icebreaker from Resolute to Ellesmere Island, where this picture was taken. From the 1950s to the present, Watson has travelled thousands of miles across northern Canada mainly by canoe, from the tip of Labrador to the Yukon and beyond. His canoe journeys, including one on the Liard in 1977, are recorded in ten of the chapters of this book. [Watson]

1972 Ferdi Wenger, Harvey Fraser, Adolf Teufele, Leland Bradford, Mike Stein and Jim McConkey, all from British Columbia, portaged across the Devil's Portage, canoed most of the Grand Canyon and down the river to Fort Liard where they were flown out. [*B.C. Outdoors*, 1973]

1973 Harry Collins led a Wild River Survey crew consisting of Roger Beardmore, David McClung and Steve Stesco down the Frances and Liard rivers, from Frances Lake to Fort Liard. [Parks Canada files]

1973 Harry Collins led a Wild River Survey crew of Roger Beardmore, David McClung and Steve Stesco from the bridge crossing of Yukon highway #10 down the Hyland River, a tributary of the Liard, to the bridge crossing of the Alaska Highway. [Parks Canada files]

1974 Ferdi Wenger and Harvey Fraser, canoeing instructors with Canoe Sport British Columbia, guided two men from San Francisco down the Liard from Watson Lake to Fort Liard. The two guides began the trip with Jim Fornelli and Mel Gardner who did a preliminary run to cut the portage trails. In the Grand Canyon they used the technique of fastening the two canoes in catamaran style to safeguard against the whirlpools. [*Canadian Geographic*, August 1976, p. 4]

1976 *Duke Watson, A. Black, F. Black, J. Ketcham, S. Ketcham, W. Ketcham, D. Wheeler and L. Wheeler canoed from Dease Lake down the Dease River to Lower Post on the Liard. [Personal communication – Watson]*

1977 *Duke Watson, A. Hovey, V. Josendal and H. Muller canoed from Lower Post through the canyons of the Liard to Fort Nelson. Watson continued down the Liard and Mackenzie to Fort Norman at the confluence with Great Bear River with G. Rose, W. Zauche and H. Zogg. [Personal communication – Watson]*

1988 *Dave Harrison, Brian, Andy, and Chris put their canoes in off the Nahanni Range Road and canoed down the Hyland River to the Alaska Highway just before the river enters the Liard. The river was swollen with the rains which fell throughout the trip, making the canyon more dangerous than usual. [Canoe, July 1989, p. 28]*

SOUTH NAHANNI

Of all the northern wild rivers, the South Nahanni is unique as a source of mystery and legend. The watershed has been the scene of mysterious deaths and disappearances of adventurers, trappers and prospectors whose stories are told and re-told in each book on the Nahanni. But beside those who died on the Nahanni are the trappers, traders and prospectors who chose to live on the river and became legends in their own right: Charlie Yohin, Diamond C, Albert Faille, Jack LaFlair, Ole Lindberg, Gus Kraus, Poole Field and Dick Turner. Some of the features of the river were named for these early adventurers: Mary River for Mary Lafferty, Lafferty's Riffle for Jonas Lafferty, May Creek for May Mattson, McLeod Creek for Frank and Willy McLeod, Starke's Rock for one of the British pair, Starke and Stevens who were on the Nahanni at the same time as R.M. Patterson and Gordon Matthews. Patterson's book *Dangerous River* chronicles the adventures of many of these legendary figures. For many people it remains the quintessential book of the Nahanni.

The Nahanni's physical features are as impressive as its legends. Best known are Virginia Falls (known by the Dene as Naili Cho) and the canyons whose walls rise as much as 4000 feet above the water. For much of the summer the Nahanni is a swift, turbid, yet placid river, but prolonged rains can cause it to rise at the rate of several feet per hour, making rapids such as the Figure-of-Eight Rapids truly dangerous. In flood, whole trees thrash in the current or are swept downstream. Hot springs are fairly common in the watershed and over millennia some have built spectacular tufa mounds. Some are salty, others are teeming with aquatic plants which attract unusual numbers of animals.

Unlike most of Canada, much of the Nahanni watershed escaped glaciation for most or all of the last ice age. This gave running water time to carve the canyons as well as the most spectacular northern karst landscape in the world, where water slowly but relentlessly dissolved limestone north of the First Canyon creating a network of disappearing streams, underground rivers, sinkholes, rock arches and vast cave systems. Some caves contain animal skeletons, notably those of Dall sheep, while others are draped in stalactites and stalagmites. The traveller who takes time to hike up and away from the river will see the most varied set of geophysical features in Canada, not to mention an incredibly beautiful landscape.

1805 *The North West Company built "Old Fort 1805" on the Liard River just above the entrance of the Nahanni River. This post was very short lived. [Cook and Holland, p. 128]*

1823-24 *John M. McLeod and A.R. McLeod from the Hudson's Bay Post at Fort Simpson made two ex-*

Making a leap into Rabbit Kettle hot springs, after a short hike up from the Nahanni River. [John Jennings]

ploratory trips up into the lower mountainous "Nahanny Lands" and persuaded some of the Nahanni Indians to accompany them back to the Fort. Governor Simpson planned an HBC outpost by Nahanni Butte at the mouth of the river. [Patterson, Dangerous River, p.206; Beaver, Summer 1961, p.40]

1904 Willie, Frank and Charlie McLeod, sons of Murdock McLeod, HBC factor at Fort Liard, had been told of the existence of gold up the Flat River, the longest tributary of the South Nahanni. They approached the area from the west coast coming up the Stikine River along Dease Lake to the Liard River, over the Macmillan Mountains and into the upper Flat River country, where they found Cassiar Indians with sluice boxes and gold nuggets. After panning without great success, they made a crude boat out of the sluice boxes and started a run down the Flat River to the Nahanni but swamped in the Flat River Canyon, lost their gold and everything but their rifle. They finally made it safely down the lower Nahanni and up the Liard to Fort Liard in another homemade boat with moose-hide tracking lines. [Patterson, Dangerous River, pp. 9-11]

1905 Willie and Frank McLeod, with a Scottish engineer named Weir or Wilkinson, returned to the Nahanni to search for gold and were never seen again. [Ibid.]

1908 Charlie McLeod started upstream in a search for his brothers, found their camp in the valley between the Lower (or First) and the Second Canyon, their bones scattered and their heads missing. This valley, henceforth, became known as Deadmen's Valley and the mystery of the death of the McLeod brothers grew and multiplied with each telling. [Ibid. pp. 8-14]

1910-12? Jorgenson and Poole Field had a trading post on the Ross River in the Yukon, just over the divide (the Macmillan Pass) from the source of the South Nahanni. Jorgenson walked across the divide to look for the McLeod mine and built a cabin near the mouth of the Flat River. Two years

later he sent for Poole Field, with a map and a message that he had struck it rich. Field arrived to find the cabin burned and Jorgenson's bleached skeleton lying between the cabin and the river. [Ibid., p.16]

1921 Four prospectors from the Yukon, Langdon, Rae, Brown and Smith travelled down the Flat and Nahanni rivers on their way out. [Ibid., p.20]

1927+ Albert Faille went up the Nahanni, using an 18-foot Chestnut canoe with a 3½-horsepower motor. He wintered on the Nahanni and the upper Flat River. This pattern continued for many years, Faille coming out in the spring to trade his furs and buy supplies.

1927 R.M. Patterson, travelling alone in a 16-foot Chestnut canoe, explored up the Liard and the Nahanni, working his way up through the canyons to the base of what was soon to be named Virginia Falls. [Ibid., p.17; Turner, p.263]

1928-29 R.M. Patterson and Gordon Matthews, with three canoes loaded with gear, four dogs and a "kicker" motor, which died just above the Splits, went up the Nahanni and built a cabin on the south side of the river in Deadmen's Valley above Meilleur Creek. They had come down the Fort Nelson and Liard rivers. They wintered there and explored up the Nahanni and up the Flat River and the different creeks which feed into the Nahanni, coming out the following spring. [Ibid.]

1928 Fenley Hunter, FRGS, of Flushing, New York, with George Ball and Indian canoeman Albert Dease, (a descendent of Peter Warren Dease) poled, dragged, motored and lined a 20-foot canoe with a 2½-horsepower motor up the Nahanni to the Falls. Hunter measured and charted the Falls, and later requested permission to name the Falls for his infant daughter Virginia, Ottawa giving approval two years later. [Bill Hoyt, 1991 from research in the NAC] They took twenty-four days to go up 122 miles, and fourteen hours to come down. Hunter's original plan to cross from the Nahanni to the Gravel (Keele) River and descend it in a skin boat had to be abandoned because of the lateness of the season. The Hunter party camped several times with Patterson and Matthews. [*Beaver*, September 1944, p.30; Hunter's journal is held on micro-film in the NAC]

1928-29 Greathouse, Southland and Quinlan, trappers, prospectors and adventurers wintered in a cabin on the Nahanni near the Splits and hunted up the Meilleur River in the spring. [Patterson, *Dangerous River* pp. 211-13]

1928-29 Carl Aarhuis and Ole Loe, trappers, had a cabin up the Jackfish River. [*Ibid.*, p. 211]

1928-29 Starke and Stevens, prospectors, trappers and adventurers, with a power scow, came down the Liard from the Devil's Portage to Fort Simpson, and then up the Nahanni and the Flat rivers. They wintered over and came out in the spring with Patterson and Matthews. [*Ibid.*, p. 87, p. 259]

1928 Dropped by plane, Charlie McLeod guided three prospectors, Wrigley, Grizzly Simmonds and one other, down the Flat and lower Nahanni rivers in sectional canoes. [*Ibid.*, p. 146]

1929 Gilroy, Hay and Hall, prospectors from Fort Nelson, went up the Nahanni in flood, through the first two canyons and headed overland toward the Flat River. Angus Hall, travelling light, went ahead and was never seen again. Gilroy and Hay met four prospectors, Hill, Cochrane and two unnamed, who had come up-river by boat; all six then travelled down the Nahanni together. [*Ibid.*, p. 18]

1931 Phil Powers went up the Nahanni to the Flat River to trap and failed to appear in the spring of 1933. His charred remains were found inside his burned-out cabin. [Patterson, *Dangerous River*, p. 21; Turner, p. 161]

1934 Dick Turner, Ole Loe, and Bill Epler, in a 28-foot river boat with two small "kickers", went up the Nahanni, the Flat and some of the creeks feeding into the Flat, searching for gold. They joined forces with Albert Faille who was coming down from his winter trapping and canoed down in Faillie's canoe. [Turner, pp. 112-25]

1935 A.E. Cameron and P.S. Warren, for the Geological Survey, made a reconnaissance up the South Nahanni for 80 miles, as far as The Gate above Second Canyon, looking at the geology of the area. This was the first geological investigation on the Nahanni. [*Canadian Field-Naturalist*, Feb. 1938, p. 15]

1935 Harry Snyder, Canadian industrialist, his daughter Dorothy, George Goodwin, from the American Museum of Natural History, and S.J. Sackett from Chicago, on an 11-week expedition explored Nahanni country north and east from Fort Reliance, using pack trains, river boats and dog teams (to carry packs in the mountains). [*Canadian Geographic*, October 1937, p.169]

1936 Bill Epler and Joe Mulholland, trappers from the area, flew into Rabbit Kettle Lake, well equipped and prepared to build a canoe to go down the river in the spring. They were never seen again. [Turner, p. 163]

1937 Jim Ross led a quasi-scientific expedition, financed by Harry Snyder, a director of Eldorado at Great Bear Lake, accompanied by Mrs. Ida Snyder, Fred Lambert, geographer and scientist, George Goodwin, naturalist, Col. A.J. McNab, U.S. Army retired, with a crew consisting of Carl Stein, Ted Boynton, and Joe Callao. They travelled by river boat from Fort Smith, down the Slave, Great Slave Lake, Mackenzie and up the Liard and Nahanni to a base camp at Britnell (now Glacier) Lake. From here they hunted, climbed in the Snyder Mountains (name now changed) and collected scientific data using a collapsible canoe. They also flew from Fort Smith into the Nahanni Canyons. While on this expedition Harry Snyder arranged to meet the Governor-General, Lord Tweedsmuir, at Great Bear Lake. [*Canadian Geographic*, October 1937, p. 169]

1948+ Dick Turner took a group of American tourists up to the Falls in his power boat. [Turner, pp. 255-63]

1948+ Albert Faille was living in Fort Simpson and still making his annual trek up the Nahanni, portaging his packs up over Virginia Falls and prospecting on the upper river. [Patterson, *Dangerous River*]

1949 A man named Shebbach, having come through the mountains from the Alaska Highway to trap at the mouth of Caribou Creek on the Flat River, died of starvation when his partner, who was to bring supplies in by river, never arrived. [*Ibid.*, p. 13]

1950 Dave R. Kington, John C. Martin, and Charles Yderstad, making a geological reconnaissance, were flown from Watson Lake to the Nahanni at the junction with Broken Skull Creek and using a rubber boat they descended the Nahanni to Virginia Falls. [*Polar Record*, July 1953, p. 798, excerpted from *Bulletin of the American Assoc. of Petroleum Geologists*, Vol. 35, No. 11, 1951, p. 2409-26]

1951 Curtis Smith, of St. Albans, Vermont, leading a party which included R.M. Patterson and Frank Wood, travelled down from Fort Nelson and up to Virginia Falls by power boat carrying with them two canoes. They canoed from the Falls down to the Flat River and Nahanni Butte. [*Beaver*, June 1952]

1952 Harry Snyder with Dr. Harry Jennings, on a private Canadian expedition, flew into Glacier Lake and using it as a base made excursions on parts of the Nahanni, checking caribou specimens for the Federal Government. [Personal communication – John Jennings]

1952+ Dick Turner was now making several trips a year to the Falls by power boat. [Turner, 1975]

1959 Austin Hoyt in a kayak, with two friends in a canoe, re-traced Patterson's 1927 trip up to the Falls and returned down the river to Nahanni Butte. They became ill with trichinosis from eating under-cooked bear meat and required hospitalization at Fort Simpson. [*Sports Illustrated, 1963*]

1959 Two persons left a marker near Rabbit Kettle. [Lentz unpublished trip report]

1962 Albert Faille starred in a National Film Board film, portraying his life of travelling up and down the Nahanni, portaging the Falls.

1961 Peter Allen – see Mackenzie River

1963 Capt. Berry and a party from the Princess Patricia regiment of the Royal Canadian Army explored the Nahanni. [Poirel, p.28]

1963 Wolfgang Manheke, Fritz Weisman and Manfred Wutrick, on a private Swiss expedition, drowned when their aluminum canoe crashed on a rock in the canyon below the Falls. [*Ibid.*, p. 13]

1964 Jean Poirel, Bertrand Bordet and Claude Bernadin from France, with Roger Rochat from Montreal, claimed to be the first group to travel the full river. From a plane based at Watson Lake they parachuted into the area of the Moose Ponds near Mt. Wilson. With one inflatable boat ("marsouin" or "porpoise") they made their way down the Nahanni, three on foot and one handling the boat. At the end of the Rock Garden, they divided their equipment and food into two equal parts, inflated two dinghies and deflated the porpoise and set off down the river. The two groups became separated because of heavy rain and flooding. One group was camped at Virginia Falls for five days before the other group arrived. At the Falls they met Albert Faille who advised portaging the canyon below the falls. After some discussion the three Frenchmen chose to run the canyon in the two dinghies and the porpoise, leaving Rochat to portage. Their run with the inflatable boats bouncing from wall to wall of the canyon took eighteen minutes. Rochat walked for four and one half hours. They descended the rest of the river with two riding in the porpoise. [Poirel, 1980] (John Brucher and Don Turner, local residents, reported that Poirel and his party had started their trip near Brokenskull Creek - Lentz trip report.)

1964 E.B. Owen and P.M. Youngman, for the Geological Survey, were at the confluence of the Flat and South Nahanni rivers. [*Canadian Field-Naturalist*, 1974, p. 489]

1965 John Lentz, David Jarden, Dix Leeson and Johnny Smallboy, a Cree from Moose Factory, having had a cache of food flown to Rabbit Kettle Lake, flew from Watson Lake into the headwaters of the Nahanni with one aluminum and one canvas-covered Chestnut canoe. After running part of the canyon below Virginia Falls they took a lift with Brucher and Turner in their 32-foot scow to below the Figure Eight Rapids and then continued by canoe to Fort Simpson. [Lentz trip report; *Beaver*, Spring 1968, p. 4]

1965 Five Americans on a collecting expedition were taken up to the Falls by scow. Hunters were also being taken up-river to hunt above the Falls in the newly established Mackenzie Preserve. [Lentz trip report]

1965 Albert Faille was hoping to get above the Falls. [Lentz trip report]

1966 Bill Addison with his wife Wendy, using a 15-foot Peterborough canoe, travelled the Nahanni on their honeymoon. They flew to Glacier Lake, portaged out to the Nahanni and canoed to Virginia Falls. With an overloaded canoe and no spraycovers they took a lift from the Falls down to Gus Kraus's cabin and continued from there by canoe. [Personal communication]

1966 Don Turner and John Brucher were on the Nahanni River at the same time as the Addisons. [*Canadian Field-Naturalist*, 1974, p. 488]

1966 Don Ross – see Liard

1970 Prime Minister Pierre Elliot Trudeau and party flew to Virginia Falls and went down to Nahanni Butte by motorboat. [Personal communication – Trudeau]

1970-73 Jean Poirel, Jean Marion, Claudie Jubert and four others went up the Nahanni beginning at Fort Nelson, travelling in two inflatable boats with large motors. They set up a base camp at the lower canyon. Between 1971-73 Poirel made two more speleological expeditions, discovered and named more than 150 caves, including the cave containing the skeletons of Dall sheep from 2500 years ago. [Poirel, pp. 205-22]

1970 George Scotter and Norman Simmons, for the Canadian Wildlife Service, conducted ecological research in the Flat River region of the Nahanni, meeting Jean Poirel there. [*Canadian Field-Naturalist*, 1974 p. 489]

1971 Hugh Stewart and Richard Grant canoed the Nahanni. ["Excerpts from Logs of a Trip down the Nahanni River – Summer 1971", *Copperfield*, 1974]

1971 George Luste, John Bland, John Brimm, Dick Irwin, Trevor Kinmond and Jim Prentice, flew from Sheldon Lake on the Ross River and canoed from the Moose Ponds down the Nahanni in one Grumman and two cedarstrip canoes. It was a dry summer and the smoke from forest-fires was in the air. At a campsite in Deadmen Valley, the group camped with Hugh Stewart and Richard Grant, who had preceded them down the Nahanni. Firefighters arrived by plane and with helicopters. Trevor Kinmond was flown out due to an infection. George Luste and Jim Prentice continued down the Nahanni to Nahanni Butte, and the other three members stayed on to work as firefighters, canoeing out to Fort Simpson later in the season. [Personal communication – Luste]

1971? Klaus Streckmann with several companions from Germany started from Tungsten to go down the Little Nahanni. The companions were not prepared for the difficulties of the river so Streckmann went down alone by kayak. The others portaged 20 miles across country for eight days and met Streckmann near Moore's hot springs, below the mouth of the Little Nahanni. They continued together down the South Nahanni, Liard, Mackenzie, up the Rat and down the Bell and Porcupine arriving at Fort Yukon after three months of travel. [Personal communication – Keith Morton]

1971 Sir Ranulph Twistleton Wykeham-Fiennes, Joseph Skibinski, Jack McConnell and Stanley Cribbett, all members of the Scots Greys regiment, Bryn Campbell, *Observer* photographer, Richard Robinson and Paul Berriff from the BBC film unit, and Ben Usher, Royal National Lifeboat Institute, started on the Fort Nelson River in flood, rowing or paddling two 16-foot

RFDs and one 13-foot C-Craft inflatable boats with 40-horsepower motors, down the Fort Nelson and the Liard rivers to Nahanni Butte. There they rented a 32-foot river scow for the film crew and made their way up to Virginia Falls. They returned down-river to Nahanni Butte where the photographer and film crew flew out. The four Scots Greys returned upstream to Fort Nelson. [Fiennes, 1973]

1971 Stirling Pickering and two companions were on the Nahanni River. [*Canadian Field-Naturalist*, 1974, p. 488]

1971 George Scotter, Canadian Wildlife Service, visited one of the caves near First Canyon on the Nahanni River. [*Ibid.*, 1974, p. 489]

1972 Drake and Anna Hocking, Henrietta Bolgar, Ed Daniel and Hans Baer, in two fibreglass canoes, 16-foot and 17-foot, drove to Tungsten, NWT, and canoed from Flat Lake down the Little Nahanni. On this river they saw the remains of two home-made fibreglass canoes, but no other signs of human usage. At the confluence with the South Nahanni they smashed one canoe but managed to repair it using spruce gum, tape, twine, wire, spruce roots, etc. They completed the run down the South Nahanni to Nahanni Butte with several swamps and spills. [Trip report – unpublished]

1972 George Scotter, Canadian Wildlife Service returned to the caves near the First Canyon of the Nahanni River. [*Canadian Field-Naturalist*, 1974, p. 489]

1972 The Nahanni was declared a National Park Reserve.

1972 John Jennings, Ramsay Derry, Biff Matthews and Patrick Saul flew into the Moose Ponds and canoed the full river to Nahanni Butte. [Personal communication – Jennings]

1972 Don Ross, setting out alone by kayak from the headwaters of the South Nahanni, joined forces with Don Maynard and one other canoeist and paddled down to Nahanni Butte. [Personal communication – Ross]

1972 Derek Ford and Gordon Brook, McMaster University, explored the caves of the Nahanni. [*Canadian Geographic*, June 1974, p. 36]

1973 E.C. Ted Abbott, from Quebec, and five others (John, Ken, Den, Mike and Robin) flew into Rabbit Kettle Lake from Watson Lake and paddled the Nahanni to the Butte and the Liard to Fort Simpson. At Fort Simpson they visited with

The South Nahanni River was declared a National Park Reserve in 1972. Recreational canoeing on the river had barely begun by that year. With only a few trips recorded in the 1960s, the trip made by John Jennings and Biff Matthews in 1972 from the headwaters near Mount Wilson, known as the Moose Ponds, down the river to Nahanni Butte is among the earliest. [John Jennings]

Albert Faille (who died in late December 1973) at his cabin; Dick Turner was also present. [Abbott, "Nahanni Summer", 1973 – unpublished]

1973   Rod Dunfie, Lynne Allen, Dave Robinson, Keith Morton, Don Beckett and his daughter Diane, using one cedar strip/canvas canoe, two kayaks, and one closed fibreglass canoe, flew from Sheldon Lake on the Ross River to the Moose Ponds and canoed down the Nahanni and Liard rivers to Fort Simpson. [Personal communication – Don Beckett]

1973   Gordon Bradshaw and Guy Nevin of Clinton Creek, Yukon, kayaked the Nahanni, meeting the Abbott party at Virginia Falls. ["Nahanni Summer", 1973]

1973   Four members of the Northwest Voyageur Canoe Club of Edmonton, possibly including Fred Vermeulen, canoed the Nahanni, meeting the Abbott party at Virginia Falls, as did a couple from West Germany. ["Nahanni Summer", 1973]

1973?   Carl Norbeck, Fredrick Wooding, Kenneth Palmer, Michael Wooding and Dr. Fred Sparling, with a professional rafter from Utah, rafted from Rabbit Kettle to Nahanni Butte. [*Canadian Geographic*, September 1974]

pre-1974   Marc H. Wermager canoed up the Ross, crossed over Macmillan Pass and canoed down the South Nahanni. [Morse files, p. 22]

1974   Poirel guided the Karst group from McMaster. [Poirel, 1980]

1974   Sandy Richardson, Roger Smith, Alan Brailsford and Cam Salsbury, of the Toronto-based and recently formed Wilderness Canoe Association, flew from Fort Simpson into a lake on the upper Ross River, hauled over to the Moose Ponds and paddled the Nahanni to the Butte and the Liard to Fort Simpson. [Nahanni Wilderness trip report – unpublished]

1974   Henry Homonick, Stu Hunt, Ron Niblett, Ian Ritchie, Tom Skinner, J. Swabey, J.R. Turner and T. Turner, known as the "Bytown Bushwackers", canoed the Nahanni River. [Morse files, p. 5]

1974   Jim and Alison Prentice, Dick and Mary Kirby canoed from the Moose Ponds down the Nahanni to Nahanni Butte, and continued down the Liard to Fort Simpson. They visited Glacier Lake, the hot springs, the caves and experienced very high water. [Personal communication – Prentice]

The spectacular scenery, including the mountains, Virginia Falls and the deep canyons below the Falls, has attracted large numbers of canoeists to the South Nahanni each year. Don Beckett and his daughter Diane were among those on the Nahanni in 1973. [Keith Morton]

1974 Lawrence Gregoire, Robbert Hartog, John Bell, Ed Brook, Bart Brophy, Evan Monkman, Bill Moore and Eric Mundinger, from Ontario, canoed down the South Nahanni. [*Beaverdam*, June 1975; personal communication – George Drought]

1974 Tim Kotcheff and Craig Oliver canoed the Nahanni River. [*Imperial Oil Review*, 1975; Morse files, p. 15]

1974 A team of biologists working on plans for the national park encountered Kotcheff and Oliver at Virginia Falls. [Morse files, p. 15]

1975 *Mary Lou and John Roder reached the source of the Nahanni via the Macmillan-Willow Creek-Ross River route and canoed down to Nahanni Butte. [Canadian Geographic, Feb./Mar., 1977, pp. 64-67]*

That same year, for Camp Wanapitei, Marcus Bruce and Mary Ann Haney led a co-ed youth trip, on which Malcolm Thomas was a participant, down the Nahanni from the Moose Ponds. Shortly after, both Trailhead/Black Feather and North West Expeditions, as licensed operators, were leading several trips each year on the Nahanni. Overall, the number of trips on the river multiplied more than tenfold.

1978 *Malcolm Thomas, leading a trip for Camp Wanapitei, disappeared without trace from the cliffs below Virginia Falls. [Wanapitei trip report]*

1985 *Debbie Ladouceur and David Salayka made a late winter-early spring journey from Ross River with snowshoes, hauling their canoe to the headwaters of the South Nahanni. They canoed down the River to Nahanni Butte. [Nastawgan, Winter 1985]*

While most groups flew in to the Moose Ponds, some chose to cross a watershed to reach the river. The top photo shows Sandy Richardson (stern) and Alan Brailsford. In the second photo, Richardson, Roger Smith, Cam Salsbury and Brailsford stand in front of the massive rock known as "The Gate", the entrance to the Third Canyon, having reached the Nahanni from the upper reaches of the Ross River in 1974. [Richardson]

NORTH NAHANNI

The North Nahanni is a much shorter river than the South Nahanni, and unlike the South Nahanni which is a tributary of the Liard, it flows directly into the Mackenzie midway between Fort Simpson and Wrigley. The valley of the North Nahanni is scarcely more than a quarter of a mile wide with mountains on either side which rise precipitously to over 700 metres.

1921 Dr. G. S. Hume and J.B. Mawdsley explored up the North Nahanni and the Root rivers for about 60 miles for the Geological Survey. [GSC Summary Report, 1921 B; *Canadian Field-Naturalist*, Feb. 1938 p. 15]

1922 Hume ascended the North Nahanni for 70 miles to where the mountains formed a barrier to progress. [*Canadian Geographic*, 1936]

1988 *Pat and Rosemarie Keough, their young daughter Rebekka Dawn, Ben Sharp and Damir Chytil, canoed a section of the Ram River, a tributary of the North Nahanni. Having explored both the Ram and the North Nahanni by helicopter, they began at Round Rock Creek below the 1000-foot walls of Scimitar Canyon and followed the Ram to its confluence with the North Nahanni, only a few miles before it reaches the Mackenzie. The trip is recorded on a film,* The Nahanni and Rebekka Dawn, *which has been shown on CBC-TV. They report that both the Ram and the North Nahanni are extremely difficult and dangerous, beginning as shallow, braided rivers where the depth can vary as much as 40 feet seasonally or with rainfall. Where the rivers break through the Ram Plateau, they have carved deep, sheer canyons, with sharp turns and drops over waterfalls before they broaden out in the Mackenzie lowlands. The only previous travellers on some sections of the Ram are believed to be a few German kayakers. In 1994, Mike and Nina Fischesser, with three others, in inflatable kayaks, descended the Ram, doing Twisted Canyon by helicopter. [Personal communication – Rosemarie Keough]*

SOUTH REDSTONE

The Redstone River has two branches, the North and the South, the South being the longer. It enters the Mackenzie just a few kilometres south of the mouth of the Keele River.

1923 W.A. Kelly, with J.O.G. Sanderson, W.N. McDonald and J.L. Lafond, GSC, found it impossible to ascend the Redstone River by canoe, but with a local trapper, W. Haywood, made an overland survey trip into the headwaters in the mountains. [GSC Summary Report, 1923 B]

1972 Ian Donaldson, Roger Beardmore, Bill Pisco and John Roder, Wild River Survey, landed at the Little Dal Lakes, portaged to the South Redstone River and canoed down to the Mackenzie and down-river to Norman Wells. [Parks Canada files]

KEELE

The Keele River begins at Christie Pass, about 2210 metres, and enters the Mackenzie between Wrigley and Fort Norman. It was the cross-over route to reach the South Macmillan in the Yukon. It has two notable tributaries, the Natla and the Twitya. The Keele was originally called the Gravel River and its name was changed to honour a distinguished member of the Geological Survey. It was reputed to be the boat route of the Indians from the mountains to the Mackenzie River.

1843 *Adam McBeath, HBC, with four Indians and an engagé named LaRocque canoed and tracked up the Keele, or Gravel as it was called, to the headwaters where they were abandoned by their Indian guides in the mountains. [Coates and Morrison, p. 22]*

1897 Thomas Duncan Gillis, a Nova Scotian, returned to the Yukon, travelling from Edmonton down the Athabasca-Slave-Mackenzie, up the Keele River and across the divide, coming down the Macmillan. [Coutts, p. 229]

1898 E.J. Corp, Jack Phillips, Dr. Dillabough Jr., Chas Krugg, Vic McFarland and Alf Willis were part of the Klondike gold-rush from Hamilton, Ontario. They built a flat-bottomed scow and hired a guide, Billy Clark, to go down the Athabasca from Athabasca Landing, continued down the Slave, along Great Slave Lake and down the Mackenzie to the Keele River. Joined by another group from Hamilton and five Norwegians from Fort Norman, they went up the Keele as far as possible before ice formed. Altogether thirty men and two women crossed the divide that winter and a total of no more than seventy-five people used this route during the gold-rush. On the other side of the divide they built another boat and went down the Stewart and McQuesten rivers. [*Arctic Circular*, 1958 p. 35]

1907-08 Joseph Keele, Robert Riddell and J.M. Christie, GSC, canoed up the Pelly River and the Ross River to its source. They crossed the height of land (Christie Pass) in winter to the headwaters of the Keele, built two boats and descended the Keele to the Mackenzie when the river opened. [GSC Memoir 284]

1931? Marion and Max Diesel, using a Chestnut Prospector with a "kicker", travelled from Great Bear Lake, up the Mackenzie and up the Keele River for 75 miles, explored in the Mackenzie Mountains and returned to Great Bear Lake, where they trapped and prospected. [Personal communication – Ray Chipeniuk]

1972 Ian Donaldson, Roger Beardmore, Bill Pisco and John Roder, Wild River Survey, put their canoe in at O'Grady Lake by float plane and canoed down the Natla and Keele and down the Mackenzie to Norman Wells. [Parks Canada files]

1975 *Don Ross and Francis Mayuer, using Klepper kayaks, descended the Natla-Keele rivers to the Mackenzie. [Personal communication – Ross]*

1976 *Four canoeists, including Dick Abbott, in two Grumman canoes, preceded the Beckett party down the Natla-Keele rivers. [Personal communication – Beckett]*

1976 *Don Beckett, Lynne Allen, Brian Symms and Bruce Fisher, with two Grumman canoes, flew from Ross River on the Canol Road to O'Grady Lake and after a week of hiking in the mountains canoed down the Natla, Keele and Mackenzie rivers to Fort Norman. [Personal communication – Beckett]*

1976 *Wally Schaber led a group down the Natla-Keele rivers. [Personal communication – Schaber]*

MOUNTAIN

The Mountain River flows swiftly down from the headwaters at 2668 metres and enters the Mackenzie near the San Sault Rapids.

1972 Ian Donaldson led a Wild River Survey crew of Roger Beardmore, Bill Pisco, and John Roder down the Mountain River starting at Palmer's Lake, several miles north of the river, and finishing at the Mackenzie River. [Parks Canada – files]

1984 *Chris Larkin, English naturalist, artist, photographer, having wintered near the headwaters of the Mountain River, started down the river by canoe in the spring when the river was in flood. At the "Third Canyon" he capsized and lost everything except his lifejacket and matches. After ten days of hunger and torment by mosquitoes, having walked 80 miles, he met a group of Indians who helped him to reach Fort Good Hope. [Personal communication – John Blunt]*

1986 *Wally Schaber, Bill and Paul Mason, Louise Gaulin, Judy Seaman and Chris Harris made a canoe trip down the Mountain River. [Personal communication – Wendy Grater]*

1986 *Wendy Grater led the first of Trailhead/Black Feather's annual trips on the Mountain River. [Personal communication – Grater] Arctic Edge, Whitehorse, also runs trips on the Mountain. [Arctic Edge 1994 brochure]*

1989 *About seventeen persons descended the Mountain River according to the RCMP at Fort Good Hope. [Personal communication – Blunt]*

1990 *Richard Hagg leading a group of twelve from Lakefield College canoed down the Mountain River in June and saw no other canoeists. [Personal communication – Hagg]*

1990 *John Blunt made a solo canoe trip down the Mountain River and met one other party on the river. [Personal communication – Blunt]*

1990 *Dr. Bruce Daly and seven others, with four canoes, canoed down the Mountain River. [Personal communication – Blunt]*

1992 *Richard Hagg and Kirsten Franklin led a group of twelve from Lakefield College canoeing down the*

Mountain River. Three other groups were on the river one week after their departure. [Personal communication – Hagg]

1993 *John Blunt made a solo canoe trip down the Mountain River. [Personal communication – Blunt]*

1993 *There were two Wanapitei trips down the Mountain River. Shawn Hodgins led an adult trip; Andrea Hodgins and Michael Craig led a co-ed youth group which had started from the Canol Road in the Yukon. [Wanapitei trip reports]*

ARCTIC RED

The Arctic Red River rises on the eastern side of the mountain peak which towers above Bonnet Plume Lake. It flows north, closely following the border of the Northwest Territories and enters the Mackenzie River at the village of Arctic Red River.

1960 W.E.S. Henock, Geographical Branch, Dept. of Mines and Technical Surveys, and Stephen Blasko, University of Western Ontario, with Antoine Andre, Loucheux, as guide and cook, ascended the Mackenzie from Aklavik by the Hudson Bay Channel, canoeing up the Arctic Red River as far as Cranswick River, about 100 miles, and also explored up the Sainville River, a tributary. [*Arctic Circular*, 1961, pp. 52-58]

pre-1975 Marc H. Wermager canoed up the Stewart River to its source, crossed over and went down the full length of the Arctic Red. [Morse files, p. 22]

PEEL

The Peel River, almost entirely within the Yukon Territory, rises high in the Ogilvie Mountains, east of the valley of the Yukon River. It flows due east until just before it crosses the eastern border of the Yukon when it turns north and empties into the Mackenzie River, just behind a large island in that river. The Hudson's Bay Company established an important fur-trade post, Fort McPherson, a few kilometres up from the mouth of the river, around 1840, and for many years it was the company's most northerly post. Later it was the last port of call for the steamboats which came down the river from Fort Smith and in 1903 a vital Royal North West Mounted Police post was established there. Fort

McPherson is mentioned as a stopping place for many travellers in the far North, Stefansson and Robert Service to name just two. In 1898, 500 gold-seekers bound for the Klondike passed through Fort McPherson. With the completion of the Dempster Highway in the late 1970s it is now possible to drive from the Yukon to Fort McPherson.

The Peel River has many important tributaries: the Ogilvie, which is really the beginning of the Peel River; the Blackstone; the Hart; the Wind, the route of choice for about 200 men heading for the Klondike; the Bonnet Plume, possibly named for Loucheux guide, Andrew Bonnet Plume; and the Snake, parallel to the Yukon border for much of its route. Camsell, writing for the Geological Survey in 1919, calls the Bonnet Plume an unexplored river.

1826 *Sir John Franklin noted and named the Peel River for the British Prime Minister, Sir Robert Peel, when returning up the Mackenzie from his second Arctic expedition. The Loucheux Dene had been using it for centuries.*

1840-41 *Alexander Kennedy Isbister, HBC, explored farther up the Peel River. [Coutts, p. 209]*

1900 Two prospectors, travelling east, crossed the divide at the head of Chandindu River in the Ogilvie Mountains and descended the whole length of the Peel River to Fort McPherson on a raft. They were the first non-natives to make the trip and thought they were on the Stewart River, discovering their whereabouts only when they reached Fort McPherson. [GSC Memoir 284]

1931 Albert Johnson, the "Mad Trapper of Rat River", rafted down the Peel River from the direction of Dawson, bought a canoe in Fort McPherson, and paddled down the Peel and 15 miles up the Rat River where he built a cabin. [Anderson, F., 1982]

1958 W.E.S. Henock, Geographical Branch, Dept. of Mines and Technical Surveys, and Donald Brown, University of Western Ontario, with Angus Firth from Fort MacPherson, in a 22-foot canoe with outboard motor, travelled up the Peel to the confluence with the Caribou River, studying physical and human geography. [*Arctic Circular*, 1960, pp. 9-15]

OGILVIE–PEEL

1971 Wild River Survey with Dave Wilford and three others canoed down the Ogilvie from Ogilvie River bridge and down the Peel and Mackenzie to Inuvik. [Parks Canada files]

1983 *Jim and Pam Boyde, Ted Curtis and Brian Brooke put their canoes in on the Ogilvie River from the Dempster Highway, crossed over the divide to the Mines River and continued down the Porcupine and Yukon rivers. [Personal communication – Jim Boyde to researcher Hayhurst]*

1986? *Dave and Judy Harrison, their son Dave and his friend Jason, with two adult friends and four other teen-agers canoed the Ogilvie-Peel rivers, putting in at the Dempster Highway and taking out at Fort McPherson. [Canoe, August 1987, pp. 15-17]*

BLACKSTONE–PEEL

1969 James Gregg and Lloyd Hummert, from California, put their canoe into the Blackstone River where it crossed a newly constructed section of the Dempster Highway and canoed down that river and the Peel to Fort McPherson. [Unpublished trip report – Parks Canada files]

1979 *Jim Boyde, Dean Hull, Bill Parry, Ann Bogden, John Hatchard and Tynka Braaksma, from the Yukon, canoed down the Blackstone and Peel rivers, continued up the Rat and down the Little Bell-Bell-Porcupine-Yukon rivers to the railway bridge of the Prudhoe Bay-Valdez line. [Personal communication – Jim Boyde to researcher Hayhurst]*

1981 *Jim Greenacre, Penny Clarke, Graham Barnett, Tony Bird, Mark and Graeme Riddell canoed down the Blackstone and Peel rivers to Fort McPherson. They saw very few signs of previous travel on the Blackstone. [Wilderness Canoeist, Autumn 1981, pp. 8-10]*

1982 *Camp Wanapitei: Hugh Glassco and Ben Wolfe led a coed youth group down the Blackstone-Peel rivers from the Dempster Highway to Fort McPherson. John Jennings and Nicola Jarvis, who were married immediately after the trip, led an adult group on the same route. [Wanapitei files; personal communications – Jennings]*

HART–PEEL

1983? *Craig and Bruce Lincoln, Dan Brizee and Barry Hutten put their canoes in at McQuesten Lake, lined up the Beaver River, crossed over the divide to the headwaters of the Hart River, descended it to the Peel River and finished the 40-day trip at Fort McPherson. [Alaska, September 1984, p. 24]*

WIND–PEEL

pre-1885 Alexander MacDonald, a prospector exploring alone, ascended the Stewart, McQuesten and Beaver rivers, crossed the Bonnet Plume Pass and descended the Wind and Peel rivers. It is believed that he was the first European to follow this complete route. [Coutts, p. 181]

1898 George Mitchell, with two friends Jack and Cecil, from Toronto, left for the Yukon goldfields via Edmonton. They travelled by scow from Athabasca Landing to Lake Athabasca with Pierre Ecureuil as guide through the Slave Rapids. Many others were travelling at the same time. The HBC steamer towed the flotilla of thirty to forty boats along Great Slave Lake to the Mackenzie River where they continued down-river to Fort MacPherson. A collection of fifty boats (about 200 men) poled and tracked up the Peel River with Andrew Bonnet Plume as guide, using a copy of de Sainville's map. Cutting their boats

Nicola Jarvis Jennings cooking breakfast beside the Peel River, which had risen several feet during the night and was approaching the fireplace, 1982. [John Jennings]

down in size to make them more manoeuvrable in the rapids, they proceeded as far as possible up the Wind River and made a winter camp, "Wind City". Mitchell mapped the Wind, the Little Wind and other tributaries of the Peel, exploring and prospecting the area. Three-quarters of the men were affected by scurvy and about 10 per cent died. Mitchell broke his knee cap and was taken to the Loucheux camp. The knee was operated on and set by two Indian women in the lodge and it healed perfectly. In the spring Mitchell returned down the Wind and Peel to Fort MacPherson with the Indians. The surviving Klondikers crossed over the divide and went down the Stewart River to the Yukon. [Graham, 1935]

1898   Charles Maltby and group – see Clearwater

1898   Some of the Klondikers going up the Peel and Wind rivers to winter at Wind City were Fred Dench, Dick Feltham, "Doc" Waterman, Chas Conklin, Chas Vogelsand, Jack Grover, Dave Mulholland, Fred Payzant, Ralph Crichton, McQuaide, Hetu, Joe Millette, Dr. Brown, Judge Morse, MacKinnon, Moran, Harris, Kendrick, Peacock, Barclay, Dave Hopkins, Frank Sennet, Joe White, Chas Mills, Charles Hall, Pat Curran, Merrit, Patterson, Coatsworth, Craigie, Francis Segard, Rennsalar, Bob Onslow, Johnson, Jean Lanonette, Doc Conley, Ben W., Bennett, the Peck brothers, Dad Like, Doc Sloan, M.E. Putnam, George Dalgleish, McGruder, the Imisk, Idaho, Hendricks, "Enterprise" parties. The Loucheux guide who is most often mentioned is named Andrew – probably Andrew Bonnet Plume. Casualties were J. Bouret and Tim Orchard, drowned; Doc Mason, Billy Guch and the Bowman brothers, died of scurvy. [Moyles, ed., 1977]

1905   Charles Camsell, GSC, with Fred Camsell, Jack Deslauriers, Louis Cardinal, F. Heron, Percy Nash and an Indian to help with the upstream work, using three canoes, reached Frazer Falls on the Stewart River by steamer. They went upstream on the Stewart River, up the Beaver River,

portaging their load 15½ miles across the divide at Braine Pass and canoed down the Wind and Peel rivers to Fort MacPherson. They continued down the Mackenzie to the delta and returned up the Mackenzie, Peel and Rat and down the Porcupine and Yukon. Frank Williams, who prospected and trapped in the district, assisted Camsell in his exploration of the Wind and Peel rivers. [Camsell, p. 179; GSC Memoir 284; Coutts, p. 288]

1980   *Jim and Pam Boyde, Yukon, canoed from McCluskey Lake down the Wind and Peel rivers to Fort McPherson. [Personal communication – Jim Boyde to Hayhurst]*

1987   *Tom and Lisa Hallenbeck from Maine, Jed Good and Bill Bruck from Texas, canoed down the Wind and Peel rivers, putting in at a small lake near the Wind River and canoeing down to Fort McPherson. [Personal communication – Tom Hallenbeck]*

BONNET PLUME–PEEL

1893   Comte Edouard de Sainville, who spent the years 1889-94 in the area and around the Mackenzie delta, made a trip with two Indians and one canoe up the Peel River to the junction with the Bonnet Plume. Leaving the canoe at the mouth of the river, they followed the Bonnet Plume upstream along the riverbank for 25 miles, crossed to the Wind River, walked downstream and back to the canoe, returning downstream. He produced a detailed map of the area and was the first European to travel any distance up the Bonnet Plume. [GSC Memoir 284; Graham, p. 106; *Fram*, Summer 1984, p. 540-50]

1972   Duke Watson, M. Sheeran, A. Zob and M. Watson, in C-2 canoes, paddled down the headwater tributary from Source Lake, down the Bonnet Plume River and portaged across to Fairchild Lake. [Personal communication – Duke Watson]

1973   A Wild River Survey crew canoed from the north east end of Bonnet Plume Lake down the Bonnet Plume and Peel rivers to Fort McPherson. [Parks Canada files]

1979 *Don Ross and Francis Mayuer, from Alaska, using fibreglass kayaks paddled down the Bonnet Plume River. [Personal communication – Ross]*

1981? *Bruce Lincoln canoed down the Bonnet Plume River. [*Alaska, *September 1984, p.25]*

1982 *Jim and Pam Boyde, Ted Curtis and Lauren Cherkezoff canoed from Bonnet Plume Lake down the Bonnet Plume and Peel rivers to Fort McPherson. [Personal communication – Jim Boyde to researcher Hayhurst]*

1984 *Ted Johnson, Robert Fowler, John Godfrey, Eddie Goldenberg, Tim Kotcheff, John Macfarlane, Craig Oliver and Peter Stollery, the Arctic and Rideau Canoe Club, put in at Bonnet Plume Lake and canoed down the Bonnet Plume and Peel rivers to the confluence with the Trail River. The group was picked up by pre-arrangement by Neil Collin of Fort MacPherson with a motorized scow. [Personal communication – Johnson]*

1984? *Bill Hoyt led a group down the Bonnet Plume, making a video which was later shown on television.*

1985 *Bill and Keefer Irwin, Dave Gavett and Peter Ord flew from Mayo to the headwaters of the Bonnet Plume River, on the NWT/Yukon Divide, about 15 miles south of Bonnet Plume Lake. After Dave and Peter had climbed some glaciers, the group lined their canoes to Bonnet Plume Lake and canoed down to the Fort McPherson/Peel River ferry crossing. Peter and Dave paddled on through the Mackenzie Delta to Tuktoyaktuk, while the Irwins hitchhiked back down the Dempster Highway to Mayo. [Personal communication – Keefer Irwin]*

1985 *Ned Franks, Peter Milliken, Shawn Hodgins, Saundra Raymond, Bob and Helene Edwards, flew in to Bonnet Plume Lake, with three Old Town canoes, paddled down the Bonnet Plume and the Peel. Neil Collin, a Loucheux Indian, towed the canoes down the last slow 110 kilometres to Fort McPherson. En route down the Bonnet Plume they passed a group of four, including Kiefer and Bill, from the Mad River Canoe Company. [Franks, in Raffan, ed.,* Wild Waters, *p. 98; personal communication – Shawn Hodgins]*

SNAKE–PEEL

1839 *John Bell, HBC, explored up the Peel River for 180 miles and up the Snake. The following year he built Fort McPherson. [Kamaranski, p. 165]*

———————

1980 *Hector and Ann Mackenzie, David Cosco, Dorothy Pollit and one other, from the Yukon, canoed a quick and challenging Snake River in surprising flash flood conditions. [Personal communication – Hector Mackenzie to researcher Hayhurst]*

1981 *Hector Mackenzie led a group which included John Bayly on a canoe trip down the Snake and Peel rivers. [Boden and Boden, eds. p. 216]*

1984 *Thomas Hallenbeck and Martin Brown guided an American named Sandy, with his family, in canoeing down the Snake and Peel rivers. [Klein,* Passion for Wilderness, *p. 244, 259-60]*

1986 *Tom Hallenbeck began leading regular canoe trips for Sunrise County Canoe Expeditions down the Snake River, with about twelve people on each trip. [Personal communication – Hallenbeck]*

1990 *Bill and Keefer Irwin with Stearnie and Dodie Stearns flew to Duo Lake, portaged over a couple of ridges to the Snake River and canoed down to the Trail/Peel River confluence. Dave Loeks, of Arctic Edge, was leading a trip on the river at the same time. The two groups completed the trip by sharing a motorboat to Fort McPherson. [Personal communication – Keefer Irwin]*

RAT

The Rat River is a very short river, which actually flows into the Peel River near its mouth. It would not be mentioned except that it is the route to McDougall Pass, which at 1441 metres, is the lowest pass in the overall Rocky Mountain chain. Most trips involving the Rat River describe an ordeal of up-river lining and poling in icy water to reach Summit Lake at the top of the pass. Therefore most Rat River trips are included in the Yukon-Porcupine section. On many occasions no attempt was made to use the Rat River and a backpacking "portage route", taking about seven days, was used instead. However, there are actually two downstream canoe trips recorded on the Rat River.

1965 An American team of canoeists lost their canoes in the canyon coming down the Rat River and walked for five days before attracting the attention of a passing aircraft. [*Arctic Circular*, 1968, p. 48]

1967 Dr. Rob Shepherd and Dr. Yves Langlois started at Summit Lake, portaged a half mile into the pond near Long and Ogilvie lakes, floated the canoe in the small creek to Twin Lakes. They took three days to *descend* the Rat River. They had a dump in the canyon, 30 miles below Summit Lake, where they had assistance from another canoe party in rescuing most of their gear. They continued down the Peel and Mackenzie, via the Husky Channel, to Aklavik. [*Arctic Circular*, 1968, pp. 47-49]

CHAPTER SEVEN

EVEN THE LAKES CONTRIBUTE: EASTERN TRIBUTARIES OF THE MACKENZIE

The tributaries on the eastern side of the Mackenzie, with its generally lower terrain, are the Hare Indian and the Great Bear rivers. The Great Bear, only 150 kilometres long has an extensive history of canoe travel being the connecting link between the Mackenzie River and Great Bear Lake. Great Bear Lake itself has many rivers draining into it some of which will be dealt with in this section. Great Slave Lake as the primary source of the Mackenzie is fed by many rivers, large and small.

HARE INDIAN

The Hare Indian River, a small river with several branches, rises north and west of the Smith Arm of Great Bear Lake. It flows west into the Mackenzie at Fort Good Hope and provides a route to the Arctic coast via the Anderson or the Horton rivers which avoids the Mackenzie delta.

1857 *Roderick MacFarlane, HBC, with four Indians and one Métis, from Fort Good Hope, having canoed to the mouth of the river later named the Anderson, returned upstream following the main branch, crossed over through Gassend, Niwelin and Colville lakes to the Hare Indian River and descended it to Fort Good Hope. [Cooke and Holland, p. 213]*

1972 Ian Donaldson led the Wild River Survey crew of Roger Beardmore, Bill Pisco and John Roder from the Smith Arm of Great Bear Lake portaging to the Hare Indian River and following it to the Mackenzie River. [Parks Canada files]

GREAT BEAR

The Great Bear River, a mere 150 kilometres long, may take five days to ascend with loaded boats, and be descended in one day, so swift and powerful is the current. The ice-cold, clear water of Great Bear River flows from Great Bear Lake, one of the largest and deepest bodies of water in Canada outside of the Great Lakes. Many rivers drain into Great Bear Lake, most of them small and relatively unimportant to canoeists. There are two that are significant to this story for different reasons and they will be included in this section. The Camsell, in the south, connects a series of lakes which forms the route to Great Slave Lake and is canoed in summer. From the 1960s, an ice road was used on this route in winter during the years of heavy mining activity on Great Bear Lake. The Dease River on the northeast arm of the Lake is a small stream flowing from the area below the Dismal Lakes and it is included because it was used historically as a major route to the lower Coppermine.

Activity on Great Bear Lake became frenzied in the early 1930s with the discovery of uranium and the opening of the Eldorado Mine at Port Radium on the eastern shores of the Lake in Echo Bay. There was a rush of prospectors arriving from different directions and by different means. The uranium mine closed in

1959 but five years later Echo Bay Mines Limited began extracting high-grade silver ore at the same location.

1825-27 *Franklin ascended and descended the Great Bear River several times on his second expedition to the Arctic and wintered at Fort Franklin on Great Bear Lake near the egress of the river. [Francis, pp. 95-97]*

1827 *Dr. John Richardson with Edward Nicholas Kendall, part of the second Franklin expedition, returned up the Coppermine and the Kendall rivers to the Dismal Lakes, crossed over and descended the Dease River to Great Bear Lake. [Ibid]*

1837-39 *Thomas Simpson and Peter Warren Dease, HBC, returned to Fort Confidence in Dease Bay on Great Bear Lake from exploring the Arctic coast of Alaska as far as Point Barrow. The fort had been built for them during the time of their exploration. After wintering there they ascended the Dease, crossed over to and descended the Coppermine, exploring east to Turnagain Point. They returned up the Coppermine and down the Dease to winter again at Fort Confidence. In 1839 they returned to the Arctic coast in a milder spring and reached Chantrey Inlet, thus completing the survey from Point Barrow to the Boothia Peninsula. They returned late in the season up the Coppermine-Dease route to Fort Confidence and struck out overland to the Mackenzie and Great Slave Lake. [Ibid., pp. 118-20]*

1848-51 *Dr. John Richardson – see Coppermine*

1857 *Richardson – see Coppermine*

1900 J. Mackintosh Bell and Camsell – see Coppermine

1902 David Hanbury, returning from his epic journey from the Thelon River, ascended the lower Coppermine to the Kendall River, crossed over and descended the Dease River to Great Bear Lake. [Hanbury, 1904]

1903 Preble – see Athabasca-Slave

1909 John Hornby, Cosmo Melvill, James Mackinlay and Peter McCallum, with Tato and three other Indians, including Tato's mother who could remember Sir John Richardson wintering at Fort Confidence in 1848 and who would act as guide, left their base camp on the Dease River near Great Bear Lake in March and crossed overland to the Coppermine around the Big Bend. They hunted on the east side of the river and Melvill went downstream to opposite the Kendall. They returned to their base in May. [Whalley, *Legend*]

1910 V. Stefansson – see Coppermine

1911-12 George and Lionel Douglas with August Sandberg, on a private prospecting expedition, from a cabin they built on Great Bear Lake at the mouth of the Dease River, explored by canoe up the Dease River to the Dismal Lakes and down the Kendall River to the Coppermine in 1911. In 1912, George and Lionel Douglas descended the Coppermine to the sea and returned to Great Bear Lake. [Douglas, G., 1914; Mallory, 1989]

1913 Fathers Rouvière and LeRoux – see Coppermine

1915 Inspector Denny La Nauze, RNWMP, having come from Edmonton by HBC steamer to track down the murderers of Fathers Rouvière and LeRoux, with D'Arcy Arden guiding the party, ascended the Great Bear River by York boat and canoe and crossed Great Bear Lake to Dease Bay where they established winter quarters. In the early spring the police patrol travelled north along the Coppermine River, caching the canoe along the way. [*Geographical Journal*, 1918, p. 316]

1915 J. J. O'Neill – see Coppermine

1916 K.G. Chipman – see Coppermine

1922 M.Y. Williams – see Liard

1925 W.H.B. "Billy" Hoare – see Coppermine

1929 Geoffrey Gilbert – see Coppermine

1932 Fred Peet and Olaf Slaatten, in a 21-foot freight canoe with an outboard motor, travelled from Fort McMurray, down the Athabasca-Slave rivers, across Great Slave Lake, still partially covered with ice, continued up the north arm of the lake, up the Marian River and down the Camsell to Great Bear Lake to prospect in the mining boom of that year. They had carried a ton of supplies over fifty-one portages. [Watt, p. 183]

1932   Earl Harcourt and Billy Graham, University of Alberta students, paddled a 16-foot canoe from the headwaters of the Fort Nelson River down that river, down the Liard and the Mackenzie, up the Great Bear River and across Great Bear Lake to the mining boom area of Conjuror Bay. [*Ibid.*, p. 192]

1930-33   Raymond, Max and Marion Diesel, three brothers from Lac La Biche, Alberta, spent three years trapping, exploring and prospecting in Great Bear country. Their trips to and from the area appear in the appropriate sections. [Personal communication – Ray Chipcniuk]

1934   F. Jolliffe and D.F. Kidd, for the Geological Survey, explored the Marian-Camsell route. [Zaslow, p. 363]

1936   Robert Clutter and friends canoed from Rae up the Marian River to Sarah Lake, down the Camsell River to Great Bear Lake and down Great Bear River to the Mackenzie. [Morse files, p. 5]

1959   Eric Morse, Sigurd Olson, Tyler Thompson, Elliot Rodger, Omond Solandt, Denis Coolican, Blair Fraser and Harry Fast flew to Sarah Lake and canoed down the Camsell River to Great Bear Lake. They were transported across Great Bear Lake by the Eldorado Mining and Refining Company and canoed down Great Bear River and down the Mackenzie to Norman Wells, flying out from there. [Morse, *Freshwater Saga*, p. 37]

1965   A woman anthropologist, with an Indian guide, canoed down the Great Bear River. [Helmericks, p. 462]

1966   Graham Bromley and Ian Calder, from Yellowknife, canoed from Fort Rae up the Marian and down the Camsell River to Great Bear Lake. [*Polar Record*, September 1968, p. 361]

1966   Don Ross – see Liard

1966   Robert Frisch (pseud. Bob Skovbo) travelling alone by kayak, set off from Fort Rae up the Marian River. His kayak capsized and sank in Mazenod Lake and he was marooned on an island for two weeks. He was rescued by a canoeing party which took him down the Camsell River to Great Bear Lake. [*Natural History*, June 1970]

1969?   Robert Frisch and Paul von Baich with others canoed from Fort Rae up the Marian River and down the Camsell River and Rae Lakes to Great Bear Lake. [*Ibid.*, p. 56]

1971   Wally Eamer – see Coppermine

1973   Duke Watson canoed alone from the mouth of the Sloan River to Port Radium. *In 1978, with J. Sharpe, P. Sharpe and H. Zogg, he canoed from Fort Franklin to Port Radium, making an eleven mile portage across Grizzly Bear Peninsula.* [Personal communication – Watson]

1973   Duke Watson, A. Hovey, V. Josendal, H. Muller, P. Sharpe and P. Sharpe, Jr. canoed from Fort Franklin down Great Bear River and the Mackenzie to Norman Wells where Hovey left the group. They continued down the Mackenzie to Arctic Red River where they were joined by W. Dougall, who replaced Josendal and Muller. They ascended the Peel and the connecting overflow channel to Husky Channel, descended Husky Channel to the confluence with the Rat and made their way up the Rat, wading, dragging and lining the canoes. At Summit Lake the Sharpes were replaced by L. Dougall, E. Jenkins, W. Jenkins, J. Ketcham, S. Ketcham and M. Watson for the descent of the Bell and Porcupine rivers to Old Crow and Fort Yukon. [Personal communication – Watson]

1975   *Camp Widjiwagan: Jim Ahrens led Jim Barnett, Louis Bolster, Tom Frantes, David Jones and David Ostergren canoeing from Great Slave Lake up the Marian and down the Camsell rivers to Great Bear Lake. [Camp Widjiwagan Archives]*

RIVERS FLOWING INTO GREAT SLAVE LAKE

The list of tributaries of the Mackenzie includes the rivers that flow into Great Slave Lake. Apart from the Slave, which appears under the principal listing of the Mackenzie, the main travelled rivers are: the Marian, the Snare and the Yellowknife, flowing into the North Arm; the Beaulieu, flowing from the north; the Lockhart, flowing into McLeod Bay from the north; the Snowdrift flowing into Christie Bay from the east; and the Taltson-Tazin-Thoa and the Hay, flowing from the south. Trips on any of the three rivers flowing into the North Arm are usually part of a longer trip. They are cross-referenced with the primary reference being on the major downstream river. The Hoarfrost, a small river, flowing into McLeod Bay from Walmsley Lake, was the route followed by Capt. George Back to reach Artillery Lake in 1833.

MARIAN

The Marian, a very short river, connects by a chain of lakes with the Camsell, flowing into Great Bear Lake, and is part of an important route between these two large bodies of water. More frequently canoeists go up the Marian and down the Camsell.

1900 J. Mackintosh Bell, for the Geological Survey, returning from an extensive exploration of the Great Bear-Coppermine-Kendall area, returned late in the season up the Camsell River and was guided by Dogrib Indians through a series of lakes and down the Marian River. This is the first recorded use of this route. [Bell, Chap. 2]

1932 Fred Peet – see Great Bear

1931-32 D.F. Kidd, F. Jolliffe, J.Y. Smith and S.E. Malouf, GSC, examined the shore-lines of all lakes adjacent to the canoe route between Rae and Great Bear Lake. [GSC Memoir 187]

1934 D.F. Kidd, GSC, completed the reconnaissance mapping, extending south from the Camsell River to where the exploration had stopped in 1932. [GSC Memoir 187]

1936 Clutter – see Great Bear

1966 Robert Frisch – see Great Bear

1966 Graham Bromley – see Great Bear

1969? Robert Frisch – see Great Bear

1971 Wally Eamer and Mr. Sprout, two Canadian university students from Ottawa, went up the Yellowknife River through Singing, Snare, Jolly and Courageous lakes, down a short section of the Coppermine River, crossed to the Hook River and continued down the Sloan River to Great Bear Lake. They returned along the shore

of Great Bear Lake, up the Camsell River and down the Marian River. [Morse files, p. 4]

1975 *Camp Widjiwagan – see Great Bear*

SNARE

The Snare River has its beginnings in the area of small lakes north of Great Slave Lake, over a short divide from Jolly Lake. It flows briefly north to Winter Lake and then southwest through Indin and a series of lakes to enter the North Arm of Great Slave Lake at Rae. There is a dam on the lower Snare.

1912 David Wheeler – see Coppermine

1934 D.F. Kidd, GSC, mapped the southwest part of the Snare River area. [GSC Memoir 187]

1935 F. Jolliffe, GSC, made a reconnaissance survey of most of the Snare River area. [GSC Memoir 235]

1938 C.S. Lord, with R.W. Ashley, J.C. Scott, F.G. Smith, M.S. Stanton and J. Woolfenden, GSC, mapped the southern end of the Snare River area. [GSC Memoir 235]

1938 John Carroll, topographical surveyor for the Dept. of Mines and Natural Resources, searched in the area of Winter Lake and found the site of Franklin's Fort Enterprise. [Morse files, p. 11]

1939 F.G. Smith, with J.D. Allan, J.M. Browning, G.C. Camsell, A.F. Killin, K.W.B. Moodie and C.I. Robertson, GSC, mapped the northeast quarter of the Snare River area. [GSC Memoir 235]

1964 Eric and Pamela Morse, Angus Scott and Terk Bayly flew from Yellowknife into Aylmer Lake. They canoed up the Lockhart River to MacKay Lake, up the Snake River to Courageous Lake and Jolly Lake, across the height of land to the source of the Snare River. The Snare River swells out to a series of lakes including Winter Lake, the site of Franklin's Fort Enterprise, Roundrock and Snare lakes. They portaged around the Snare River Canyon, reached Indin Lake and continued down the river to Big Spruce Lake, the headpond behind the Snare dam. By a chain of small lakes and fifteen portages they reached Slemon Lake where an RCMP boat took them out to Rae. [Morse, *Freshwater Saga*, pp. 105-26]

1964 At Indin Lake below the canyon the Morse party met two brothers from Toronto who had been coming to the area since 1941 as prospectors. [*Ibid*, p.119]

1964 Two young Americans chartered in to Indin Lake with a canoe and small motor, lost both canoe and gear and were rescued after several days, being spotted by a passing airplane. [*Ibid*, p. 121]

1965 Dexter Davidson – see Coppermine

1970 Tim Losey and five others made an archaeological expedition to Franklin's Fort Enterprise on Winter Lake, near the headwaters of the Snare River. [*Arctic Circular*, 1971, pp. 111-17]

1971? David Repp – see Coppermine

1972 Fred Cramp leading a Wild River Survey crew of Sue Cramp, Greg Ewert and John Horricks which was flown into Winter Lake canoed down the Snare to the dam site 16 kilometres below Big Spruce Lake. It was early in the season, the water levels were high and there was still ice in the lakes. Under the right conditions they believed that they could have gone all the way to Rae. [Parks Canada files]

1973 A. C. Hamilton – see Coppermine

1974 A.C. Hamilton, professor at Queen's University, with his sons, Ian, Malcolm and Peter, followed the Morse route. [Morse, *Freshwater Saga*, p. 114]

1984 *Camp Wanapitei: Shawn Hodgins and Jennifer Wolfe led a youth trip from Rae up the full length of the Snare, using the small lake portage route from Slemon to Big Spruce Lake. They crossed over from Winter Lake to the Coppermine watershed and canoed down to the Arctic Ocean. [Wanapitei – trip report]*

YELLOWKNIFE

The headwaters of the Yellowknife are close to Jolly and Courageous lakes in the headwater area of both the Hanbury and the Coppermine rivers. It empties into Great Slave Lake in Yellowknife Bay.

1820 *Lieut. John Franklin and party went up the Yellowknife River to Winter Lake where they built Fort Enterprise, wintering there on the way to explore the Arctic Ocean from the mouth of the Coppermine River.*

1893 Frank Russell, on a private expedition from the University of Iowa, with an Indian boy, Andrew Leviolette as interpreter and camp helper, in two small birchbark canoes, went up the Yellowknife River to Prospect Lake and down again. With a group of Indians he crossed Great Slave Lake to Fort Resolution. [Russell, pp. 71-78]

1932 C.H. Stockwell – see Coppermine

1970 Angus Scott, John Davis, John Bayly, Jack Matthews, Jack Goering and John "Hoop" Birkett, as part of the centennial celebration of the Northwest Territories and also the 150th anniversary of Sir John Franklin's first Arctic Expedition, combined with another group to retrace Franklin's complete route from Yellowknife to the mouth of the Coppermine. The trip was organized by Eric Morse who, at the last moment, was unable to participate. Both groups landed at Lac de Gras, near Obstruction Rapids. They paddled together to Point Lake, then at Franklin Bay the group named above turned south and with many portages crossed south to Winter Lake on the Snare and over to the headwaters of the Yellowknife River, following it to Yellowknife. [Morse, *Freshwater Saga*, p. 145; personal communication – Jack Matthews]

1971 Wally Eamer – see Marian

1973 Bill Gilbert with five friends went up the Yellowknife River to the Carp Lakes and back. [Pamela Morse p. 17]

1973 An American group successfully retraced Franklin's route up the Yellowknife River to Winter Lake, across to and down the Coppermine. [*Canadian Boating*, April 1977, p. 6]

1974 Mike Ecker – see Coppermine

1976 *Fred Gaskin, Jack Purchase, Jim Lochead and Ted Goddard, using Old Town ABS canoes, went up the Yellowknife River and following Franklin's portage route through a chain of nine lakes and up Winter River crossed the height of land to Point Lake. Here*

A group commemorating in 1970 the 150th anniversary of Franklin's first Arctic expedition: standing, Arthur Adamson, Jim Bayly, Jack Matthews, "Hoop" Birkett, Jack Goering, Angus Scott, Peter Blaikie, Terk Bayly, Scott Griffin; seated, John Davis, Bill Mathers and John Bayly. They landed at Lac de Gras, half went north down the Coppermine, and half went south down the Yellowknife River. [Pamela Morse].

they were joined by Rob Caldwell and Matt Ardron and they continued the trip down the Coppermine River. [Canadian Boating, *April 1977, p. 4; Lochead unpublished trip report*]

BEAULIEU

The Beaulieu River flows into Great Slave Lake on the angle of land between the North Arm and McLeod Bay. It was probably named for the Beaulieu clan of Yellowknife Indians who supplied guides and canoemen to many explorers and sportsmen including Alexander Mackenzie, Warburton Pike, Ernest Thompson Seton and Guy Blanchet.

1771 Samuel Hearne with Matonabbee and his entourage followed the Beaulieu River from MacKay Lake down to Great Slave Lake. [Sean Peake – unpublished manuscript]

1974 John and Cristine Bayly, Dietrich and Katherine Brand, began at Spencer Lake, canoed down the Beaulieu River, crossed to the Cameron River through Hearne and Harding lakes and continued down the Cameron to Reid Lake, close to the city of Yellowknife. [Morse files, p. 15]

1976 John Bayly, Michael Hartley and Dietrich Brand with his two young sons, Tiemo and Henrich, from Yellowknife, flew to Hearne Lake and paddled down the Beaulieu River to Beaulieu Bay on Great Slave Lake, completing their "exploration" of the Beaulieu River begun in 1974. [Personal communication – Bayly]

LOCKHART

"The Lockhart River is a powerful river constrained to flow through a narrow, unyielding, rocky valley and making a big drop in a comparatively short distance. The drop is distributed in four large falls and almost innumerable rapids and cascades which keep its course broken by white water. Parry Falls are the most striking. They had been estimated by Back to be 400 feet high and the most spectacular he had seen in his travels in many parts of the world. Actually they have a drop of about 100 feet and they justify their reputed wildness." [Guy Blanchet, *Canadian Field-Naturalist*, December 1924]

The Lockhart River, or Ah-hel-dessy, described by Sir George Back as this "small but abominable river", begins in Lockhart Lake and connects a series of very large lakes, MacKay, Aylmer, Clinton-Colden and Artillery, circling east and south before plunging over the escarpment into Great Slave Lake at the eastern tip of McLeod Bay.

The portage route, bypassing the steepest terrain, from Great Slave Lake up onto the traditional hunting grounds of the Dene people begins with a gradual 5-kilometre climb followed by a 40-kilometre chain of small lakes. It was named for Warburton Pike, who travelled it in 1889.

Some canoeists begin their Hanbury-Thelon trip from Fort Reliance at the eastern end of Great Slave Lake so their trips are cross-referenced in this section.

1833   *George Back, returning from Clinton-Colden and Artillery lakes, with Maufelly as steersman and De Charlôit as canoeman, descended the Lockhart River until it became impossible to navigate. [Back, G., reprint 1970]*

1834   *George Back, returning from his exploration of the Back River, descended the Lockhart River to Anderson's Falls. [Ibid.]*

1890   Warburton Pike – see Back

1899   David Hanbury – see Thelon

1900   James Tyrrell – see Thelon

1901-02   David Hanbury – see Thelon

1907   Ernest Thompson Seton – see Athabasca-Slave

1908-09   E.A. Pelletier – see Thelon

1923   Guy Blanchet with Sousi Beaulieu, grandson of the Beaulieu who accompanied Alexander Mackenzie and son of King Beaulieu, guide to Warburton Pike, and Black Basile, Yellowknife, explored the headwaters of the Coppermine and Back rivers by canoe. From Fort Resolution, they travelled up Pike's Portage to Artillery, Clinton-Colden and Aylmer lakes, up the Lockhart River to MacKay Lake, following eskers and caribou migrations to the source lakes of the Back and Coppermine rivers. [Blanchet, *Beaver*, Autumn 1964]

1924   Critchell-Bullock – see Athabasca-Slave

1926-27   John Hornby – see Thelon

1928   H.S. Wilson – see Thelon

1929   Inspector Charles Trundle – see Thelon

King Beaulieu, scion of the Beaulieu tribe, who guided Warburton Pike in 1890, and whose family members provided canoemen from the time of Alexander Mackenzie to the recent past. [Pike, *The Barren Ground of Northern Canada*, 1892]

1964   James A. Larsen and Prof. John Thomson, University of Wisconsin, with Noel Drybone of Fort Reliance and Henry Catholique of Snowdrift, canoed for many weeks from Great Slave Lake, crossing over Pike's Portage to Artillery, Clinton-Colden and Aylmer Lake and to the headwaters of the Back River, studying the vegetation. [*Canadian Field-Naturalist*, 1971, p. 147]

1965   Ron Hill and Gerry Wherley – see Back

1967   Earl and Shirley Mosberg, Brian and Merle Underhill, and Jane Showacre, with a Grumman, a 16-foot Kidder and a kayak, canoed from Camsell Lake through MacKay Lake, down the Lockhart River to Aylmer Lake. Here they were confronted by heavy pack-ice. They found a route out from a south bay of Aylmer Lake, up a river and through a chain of lakes into Lac de Charlôit. Another chain of small lakes and many portages led them into Artillery Lake and finally over Pike's Portage to Fort Reliance. [*Appalachia*, June 1968, p. 103]

1969   Charlie Wolf – see Thelon

1970   Henning Harmuth – see Thelon

1971   E.K. Dean – see Thelon

1971   Eric and Pamela Morse, Ed Levinson and Rob Shepherd started from Campbell Lake, the source of the Hanbury River, canoed into Smart Lake, crossed over Hanbury Portage and went down the Lockhart River to Artillery Lake and down Pike's Portage to Fort Reliance on Great Slave Lake. The Morses continued paddling west on Great Slave Lake but because of forest fires crossed to Snowdrift and flew out from there. [Morse, *Freshwater Saga*, p. 60]

1971 Camp Widjiwagan – see Thelon

1972 Rolf Esko – see Thelon

1972 Duke Watson, with A. Hovey, V. Josendal and H. Muller canoed from Aylmer Lake down the Lockhart River and portaged Pike's Portage to Great Slave Lake, hiking in to Parry Falls. [U-Paddle file, HBC Archives; personal communication – Watson]

1973 Alex Hall – see Coppermine

1973 Richard Cranne – see Back

1986 *George Luste, his son Tait, Dick Irwin and Walter Lohaza canoed from Wollaston Lake to Black Lake, and by way of Selwyn, Flett, Firedrake, Damant, Lynx and Whitefish lakes to Artillery Lake. They continued down the Lockhart River, avoiding Pike's Portage, to Fort Reliance on Great Slave Lake. [Nastawgan, Summer 1987]*

SNOWDRIFT

The headwaters of the Snowdrift River are close to the headwaters of the Thelon, an area that was a favourite hunting ground of the Caribou-Eater band of the Chipewyans described in Helge Ingstad's *Land of Feast and Famine.*

1925 Guy Blanchet with four men, a 19-foot canvas canoe and a folding canoe, left Fitzgerald and surveyed up the Dog and Taltson rivers, up Nonacho Lake and Gray Lake, crossed over the height of land to Lake Eileen and canoed down the Snowdrift River to Great Slave Lake. [*Beaver*, June 1950, p. 34]

1927 Helge Ingstad, a Norwegian who spent four years trapping alone and with the Caribou-Eater Indians on the Barrens in the area of the headwaters of the Thelon and the Snowdrift rivers, went up the Snowdrift with a Canadian named Fred and canoed down through the rapids. [Ingstad, 1933]

1960 Pat Brown – see Coppermine

1964 Peter Browning and John Blunt, canoed from

Black Lake, up the Chipman River and through a chain of lakes to Wholdaia Lake, up the Dubawnt River to Smalltree Lake, to the headwaters of the Taltson River. They canoed down the Taltson River 100 miles, crossed the height of land to Eileen Lake, followed the Eileen River to the upper Snowdrift River coming down the Snowdrift to Snowdrift village. This was a 600-mile canoe trip from northern Saskatchewan to Great Slave Lake. [Browning, 1989]

1971 Duke Watson – see Taltson

1975 *Alex Hall – see Taltson*

1979 *Maureen Crowe and Lois Little [Personal communication – John Bayly]*

TALTSON–TAZIN–THOA

The Taltson River rises far to the east of Great Slave Lake in the area of the headwaters of the Elk and Dubawnt rivers. It flows west and then turns south through Nonacho Lake, joins with the Tazin, which rises in Tazin Lake just north of Lake Athabasca, and the two rivers flow into Great Slave Lake on a course that is parallel to that of the Slave River. The Thoa rises close to the headwaters of the Dubawnt and flows into the Tazin before it meets the Taltson.

1771,2 *Samuel Hearne followed parts of the Thoa River en route to the Coppermine River and again on his return. [Personal communication – Alex Hall]*

1914 Charles Camsell and A.J.C. Nettell, GSC, Francis Harper, naturalist from the Brooklyn Museum, canoemen Stan McMillan, Baptiste Forcie and three Ojibwa from Sault Ste. Marie, John Souliere, George Greensky, Joe Nolan, in three Peterborough canoes, came from Athabasca Landing down the Athabasca River to Lake Athabasca. They crossed the height of land into Tazin Lake, now known as the Camsell Portage, and canoed down the Tazin and Taltson rivers. Their return was up the Slave and Athabasca rivers to Athabasca Landing. [Camsell, p. 220; GSC Memoir 84]

1925 Guy Blanchet – see Snowdrift

1929 Two canoes carrying prospectors, Stan, Howells, John and two others, came down the Athabasca and Slave rivers pulled by a skiff from Waterways to Fort Resolution and went up the Taltson. [*National Geographic*, August 1931, p. 127]

pre-1964 A neatly stacked wood-pile found by Peter Browning was the sign of an earlier camp by non-natives. [Browning, p. 90]

pre-1964 Peter Browning reported evidence of earlier non-native use of a portage between the Taltson River and Eileen Lake. [Browning p. 117]

1964 Peter Browning – see Snowdrift

1971 Daylen Bayes, his wife and two children canoed the lower part of the Taltson. [Morse, *Freshwater Saga*, p. 152]

1971 Duke Watson began this trip on Cunning Bay, Wollaston Lake and finished it at Fort Reliance with several different groups of canoeists. With G. Bogdan and B. Watson he descended the Fond du Lac River to Black Lake, Saskatchewan. From Black Lake, with H. Muller, H. Williams and H. Zogg, he ascended the Chipman River and reached Ingalls Lake by a series of portages, in the headwaters of the Dubawnt and Taltson watersheds. From Ingalls Lake he crossed to McArthur Lake on the Taltson River with T. Barrett, A. Crooks and B. McCrory. With K. Carpenter, A. Hovey and V. Josendal, he continued down the Taltson, crossed to the Eileen, (where R. Crooks replaced K. Carpenter) and continued crossing to the Snowdrift and by a series of small lakes and streams to Harry Lake, part of Pike's Portage, finishing at Fort Reliance. The whole trip involved 111 portages, only twenty at the beginning were over established trails, the rest were unmarked and through bush or tundra. [Personal communication – Watson]

1972 Eric and Pamela Morse, John Bayly, John Davis, Jim Matthews and Angus Scott, flew to Uranium City, Saskatchewan and chartered a plane to take them to Dymond Lake. They followed the Taltson River down to Twin Gorges dam and flew out from there to Fort Smith. [Morse, *Freshwater Saga*, p. 150]

1972 Daylen and Randy Bayes, brothers from Seattle, with a canvas-covered Chestnut canoe, flew in and travelled down the Taltson River. [*Ibid.*, p. 152]

1972 Robert Bromley and W. Salo, Game Management Division of the NWT Government, flew in and canoed down the Taltson while conducting research on muskrat habitat. [*Canadian Field-Naturalist*, 1973 p. 301]

1974 Alex Hall made a solo canoe trip down the Tazin and Taltson rivers in late May, early June. [Personal communication – Alex Hall]

1974 Alex Hall – see Thelon

1975 *Alex Hall started at Nonacho Lake and canoed up the Taltson River to above Gray Lake, crossed the old Indian portage to Eileen Lake, ascended Sled Creek to Sled Lake and crossed north to Lynx Lake, the headwater of the Thelon River. He continued down the Thelon River, crossed north to the Mary Frances River, canoed up the Mary Frances to Mary Frances Lake, crossed over to Campbell Lake, went down the Hanbury River to Smart Lake, crossed over the "Hanbury Portage" to Clinton-Colden Lake and down the Lockhart to Artillery Lake, came down Pike's Portage and around the end of Great Slave Lake by an inland water route to the village of Snowdrift. [Personal communication – Hall]*

1975 *Alex Hall, Philip Carter, Cliff Train and Mike West canoed down the Taltson River from Dymond Lake to Gray Lake. Hall and Train crossed over the portage to Eileen Lake and continued down the Eileen River to a point near the Snowdrift River. Hall soloed the last 10 miles of the Eileen and down the Snowdrift River to Siltaza Lake, flying out to Yellowknife. [Personal communication – Hall]*

1976 *Alex Hall made a solo canoe trip on the Thoa River and believed that he was the first to do so since the Indians used the river. [Personal communication – Hall]*

1978 *Camp Widjiwagan: Judy Meier led Karen Bergstrom, Jane Bixby, Alison Gray, Bev Lyle and Michele McGrath canoeing from MacArthur Lake down the Taltson River to Tsu Lake. [Camp Widjiwagan Archives]*

HAY

The Hay River, rising deep in Peace River country, has a different character to the other rivers which tumble off the high central plateau. It flows smoothly for most of its length, dropping over two falls, Alexandra and Louise, as it approaches Great Slave Lake.

1872   *Bishop Bompas, Anglican, descended the Hay River, discovered and named Alexandra Falls but did not mention the second falls farther down the river. He continued along Great Slave Lake and down the Mackenzie River to Fort McPherson, wintering in that area.* [Cody, p. 133-38; Footner, p. 158]

1887   R.G. McConnell, GSC, surveyed the Hay River from its mouth up to the falls. [Footner, p. 190] McConnell had reached Fort Simpson from the Dease and Liard rivers, and would winter at Fort Providence. He travelled to Fort Smith by steamer and explored up the Slave, Salt and Hay rivers with two Indians in a birchbark canoe. [GSC 1891]

1898   Three men bound for the Klondike descended the Hay River. [Footner, p. 158]

1911   Hulbert Footner and Auville Eager, possibly journalists from Edmonton, were among the first non-natives to travel down the Hay River and view the two great waterfalls. Their canoe journey began at Tête Jaune Cache on the headwaters of the Fraser, upstream and across the Giscome Portage to Summit Lake, then down the Crooked, the Parsnip and the Peace rivers to Fort Vermilion. A five-day portage with Indians and horses took them with their collapsible canoe across to the Hay River. At the Hay River they found a long narrow dug-out canoe, sent their collapsible canoe back with the Indians, and used the dug-out to descend the Hay River to the falls. After a day spent photographing both sets of falls they returned up-river in the dug-out, walked back across the portage to Fort Vermilion in time to catch a steamboat up the Peace River to Peace River Crossing. They crossed by wagon to Grouard on Lesser Slave Lake and canoed down the Athabasca to Athabasca Landing where they found a train on the almost completed railway to Edmonton. [Footner, 1912] In January of that year Footner and C.A. Edgar had been canoeing in the Florida Everglades. [*Outing*, August, 1911, pp. 515-24]

1917   A.E. Cameron, GSC, made a traverse of the Hay River to its mouth. [GSC Sum. Rep, 1921 B]

A rare picture of Pamela Morse, who was with Eric on all of his later canoe trips. The Taltson River had many good runnable rapids as well as frequent sightings of wildlife in 1972. In the foreground is John Bayly. [Angus Scott/Pamela Morse]

CHAPTER EIGHT

THE DESTINATION IS NORTH: THE WESTERN ARCTIC

*The rivers that flow into the Arctic Ocean
apart from the Mackenzie*

FIRTH

The Firth River rises in Alaska, and flows down through the British Mountains in the Yukon Territory emptying into the Arctic Ocean through a delta opposite Herschel Island. From the Firth it is possible to cross the height of land and connect with the Old Crow River which flows into the Porcupine River.

1914   J.J. O'Neill and J.R. Cox of the Geological Survey made a geological traverse up the Firth River as part of the Canadian Arctic Expedition. [Zaslow, p. 323]

1956   E.F. Cashman and R.E. Leech investigated insect fauna in connection with the National Museum from a base camp on the Firth River. [*Arctic Circular*, 1957, p. 12]

1956, '58   Richard MacNeish, Gordon Lowther and a local Inuk, Alex Irish, explored the Firth River archaeologically, by hiking and crossing and re-crossing the river. [*Arctic Circular*, 1959 p. 27]

1972   A Wild River Survey crew, Roger Beardmore, Ian Donaldson, William Pisco and John Roder, were dropped by float-plane into Margaret Lake and canoed 72 miles of the Firth River to the Arctic Ocean. [Parks Canada files]

1976   *Don Ross from Alaska, travelling alone in a fibreglass kayak, made a trip down the Firth River. A Canadian party in canoes was on the river but*

abandoned the trip because of the difficulties. [Personal communication]

1981   *Jim Lavalley led a rafting group consisting of Richard Harrington, Bob Donnelly and Pat Weatherhead down the Firth. For ten years he had cherished his dream of the Firth after having encountered some canoeists who had attempted to run the wild river ... "too fierce, the canyons were impassable". [Canadian Geographic, August 1983, p. 18]*

1983   *Jim Boyde, from the Yukon, in a Zodiac with oars, made the trip from Margaret Lake down the Firth to Herschel Island. [Personal communication – Boyde to researcher Hayhurst]*

1990s   *Dave Loeks of Arctic Edge from Whitehorse now runs an annual rafting trip on the Firth.*

J.J. O'Neill was a member of the Geological Survey group which was attached to the Canadian Arctic Expedition, organized in 1913 and led by Stefansson. O'Neill surveyed the parts of the Arctic coastline and many of the rivers draining into the Arctic Ocean. [National Museums of Canada]

ANDERSON

The Anderson River rises in the hills north of Great Bear Lake, flows north, bends due west and then settles on a course due north. It is a rather lengthy river east of the Mackenzie delta, the final north-flowing section demarking the eastern boundary of the Reindeer Grazing Reserve. Its headwaters are close to the headwaters of the Hare Indian River which flows into the Mackenzie at Fort Good Hope. It has two tributaries, the Iroquois and the Carnwath which make it accessible from Fort Good Hope through a series of lakes. Another route from Colville Lake through Niwelin and Gassend lakes follows a small stream which some canoeists have called the Ross.

1857 *Roderick MacFarlane, HBC, with four Indians and one Métis, from Fort Good Hope, canoed through Loon, Rorey and Carcajou lakes, down the Iroquois River into the Carnwath River and then down the river which was later named the Anderson to its mouth. They returned up the Anderson, following the main branch, to Gassend, Niwelin and Colville lakes, went overland to the Hare Indian River and descended it to Fort Good Hope. [Cooke and Holland, p. 213]*

pre-1861 *Mr. C.F. Anderson was on Anderson's River.*

1865 *Father Emil Petitot, Oblate, travelled to Fort Anderson from Fort Good Hope, explored the Anderson River to its mouth with a party of Inuit and returned up-river.*

1955 Dr. J.R. Mackay and J. Stathers, Geographical Branch, Dept. of Mines and Technical Surveys, made a motor canoe journey of ten days up the Anderson River and down again. [*Canadian Field-Naturalist*, Apr./June, 1959, p. 93]

1963 A party of three, using two kayaks, had an accident on the Ross River, wrecking one of the kayaks. [Klein, *Passion for Wilderness*, p. 165]

1976 *Bern Brown, priest at Colville Lake, and his wife Margaret, canoed down the Ross and Anderson rivers. [Ibid., p. 156]*

1978 *Larry Osgood flew in from Colville Lake, with Bern Brown as the pilot, to a bend in the river at approximately 67° 30' and made a solo trip by kayak down the Anderson to the mouth of the river. He was flown out to Inuvik. [Personal communication]*

1981 *Mick Smuk, with a man and a woman, Minnesotans, with two kayaks, went down the Ross and Anderson rivers. [Klein, Passion for Wilderness, p. 153]*

1982 *Camp Widjiwagan: Nina Koch leading Laura DeWitte, Sara Hobbie, Jeanne Francis, Mary Linders and Renee Luehrs canoed down the Ross and Anderson rivers to the Arctic Ocean, returning up the Eskimo Lakes to Inuvik. [Camp Widjiwagan Archives]*

1985 *Clayton, Darrell and Deborah Klein canoed down the Ross and Anderson rivers from Colville Lake. [Klein, Passion for Wilderness, pp. 139-96]*

1985 *Camp Widjiwagan Voyageurs: Maude Patnode leading Kim Benson, Kris Stone, Karen Pick, Jennifer Cowger and Tara Fahey canoed down the Ross and Anderson rivers from Colville Lake and returned through the Eskimo Lakes finishing at Sitidgi Lake near Inuvik. [Ibid, p. 178-81]*

HORTON

The Horton River rises in the hills north of the Dease Arm of Great Bear Lake and flows into Franklin Bay on the other side of the peninsula from the Anderson River. Its course follows approximately the western edge of the tree line and curves through low sandy banks.

1867-68 *Father Emil Petitot, Oblate, followed the Hare Indian River to its source from Fort Good Hope, then travelling north by Belot, Colville and Niwelin lakes to the Anderson River, crossed it and explored the middle courses of the Horton and Hornaday rivers. He continued exploring in this region until 1872.*

1974 Larry Osgood with a kayak, Don and Maria Scott in a canoe, flew into Horton Lake and descended the Horton River to Franklin Bay. The bay was full of ice and they made their way through it for four days before abandoning boats and all but emergency gear. They started walking out to Paulatuk and were sighted by chance and picked up later in the day by a helicopter from an

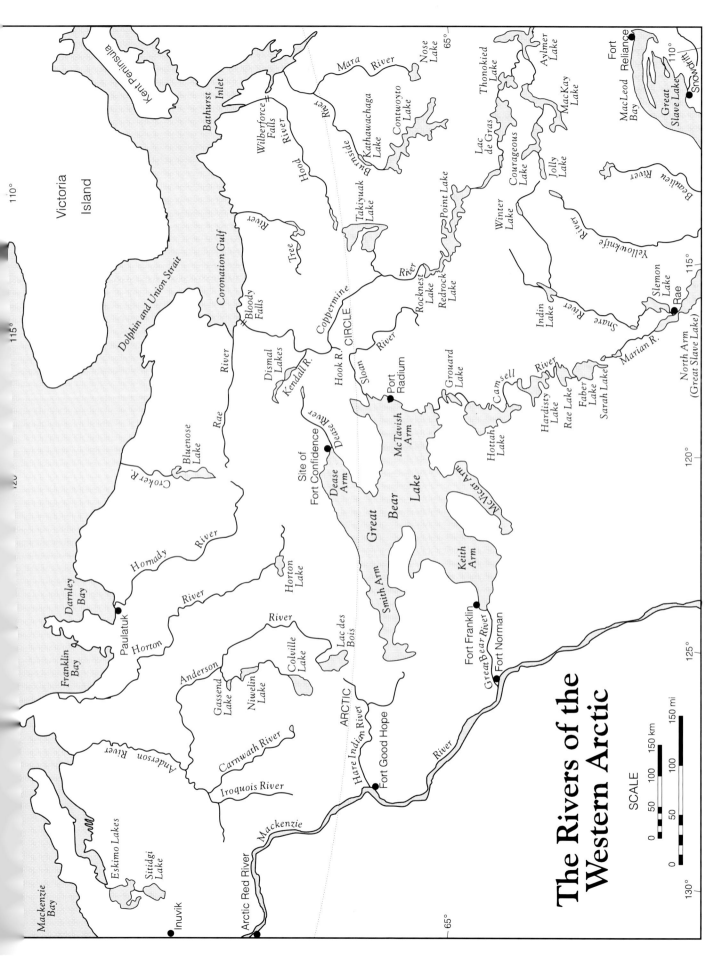

The Rivers of the Western Arctic

SCALE

0   50   100   150 km

0   50   100   150 mi

Atlantic-Richfield experimental oil drill in the Smoking Hills. The helicopter retrieved their abandoned gear and flew them to Inuvik. [Personal communication – Osgood]

1987 Bill Hoyt, Peter Raymont, Eric Poggenpohl, Roger Vaughan, Steve Lunsford, Bill Fleming, Jim Magavern, and Fred Seidl, an American and Canadian group, with four Grumman canoes, canoed from Horton Lake down the Horton River for 300 miles, finishing a few days short of the their goal, the Arctic Ocean. [Canoe, July 1988, p. 75; American Whitewater*, March/April 1988, p. 40]*

1987 A group of six men and women canoed down the Horton River from Horton Lake to Franklin Bay. [WCA Symposium, 1991]

HORNADAY

The Hornaday River flows parallel to the Horton and enters the Arctic Ocean at Darnley Bay at the small Inuit community of Paulatuk.

1867-68 Father Emil Petitot – see Horton

1915 J.J. O'Neill and K.G. Chipman, Geological Survey members of the Canadian Arctic Expedition went up the Hornaday River. [*Geographical Review*, October 1917, p. 241]

1977 Larry Osgood, Maria Scott, Steve Kahn and Chuck Rollins, using kayaks, were flown in to an unnamed lake northeast of the Hornaday, the source of the major tributary of the river and canoed down the Hornaday River to Paulatuk where they got a scheduled flight to Inuvik. Osgood felt that kayaks were the only possible craft because of the heavy rapids in the 30-mile canyon and below La Ronciere Falls. [Personal communication – Osgood]

CROKER

The Croker is a very short river which flows from Bluenose Lake due north to the Arctic Ocean, entering at the west end of Dolphin and Union Strait.

1916 Kenneth Chipman, GSC, surveyed the Croker River in March for 30 miles from its mouth. [*Canadian Geographic*, January 1974, p.8]

RAE

The Rae River flows out of the Melville Hills into Coronation Gulf, very close to the mouth of the Coppermine River.

1915 John R. Cox of the Geological Survey, attached to the Canadian Arctic Expedition, surveyed the Rae River. [Thompson, Don, v.2, p. 301]

1970 J.A. Donaldson, Geological Survey, studied the sedimentary rocks along the Rae River, as well as the Richardson, the Asiak and lower part of the Coppermine. [*Arctic Circular* XXI #1, p. 8, 1971]

COPPERMINE

The historic Coppermine River is one of the most popular of Arctic canoeing rivers. Used for millennia in the lower reaches by the Inuit, once called by others the Copper Eskimo, and by the Dene on the upper river, the river was first seen in 1771 by a European, Samuel Hearne, on his epic overland journey from Fort Prince of Wales at the mouth of the Churchill River.

The Coppermine rises at Lac de Gras in the centre of the Barrens, swings northwest to lengthy Point Lake, passes through a forested area and winds northward through huge rock outcroppings and great clay banks all the way to Coronation Gulf. Historically the Coppermine was reached by laborious upstream or winter travel from Great Slave Lake, up the Snare, Yellowknife or other rivers, usually passing through Winter Lake and finally crossing the height of land. The lower river was often reached by crossing the ridges from Great Bear Lake, up the Dease, over to the Dismal Lakes and down the Kendall, a tributary of the Coppermine. Recently, most canoeists fly into the mid-river lakes from Yellowknife.

1771 Samuel Hearne, HBC, with Matonabbee and his entourage, reached the Coppermine River, 30 miles from its mouth, on his search for copper. Hearne travelled with a group of Chipewyan Indians overland from Prince of Wales Fort at Churchill on Hudson Bay, having left in December 1770. Hearne reached the western part of the Arctic Ocean in July, the first European to do so. At "Bloody Falls", the Chipewyans set upon an encampment of Inuit and massacred them. He returned overland via Great Slave Lake reaching his base in June 1772. [Hearne, 1911]

Many people choose to follow the route of an early explorer, using his journal as a guide in addition to their own maps. In 1979 George Luste, Sandy Richardson, Paul Skinner and Fritz Brace set out from Lac-Disant, north of Great Slave Lake, to follow Samuel Hearne's route to the Coppermine River. Bloody Falls, near the mouth of the Coppermine and named for the massacre Hearne's companions inflicted on the unsuspecting Inuit camped there, is the background of the picture. [Richardson]

1820-21   Lieutenant John Franklin, Dr. John Richardson, midshipmen Robert Hood, George Back and John Hepburn, with other naval men, Métis voyageurs and Indians, leaving York Factory in 1819 reached Great Slave Lake via the upper Churchill, the Clearwater, Athabasca and Slave rivers. They briefly visited the upper Coppermine River at Point Lake, in September 1820, guided from Fort Providence by Akaitcho. From Fort Providence they canoed up the Yellowknife River and crossed over to Winter Lake where they built Fort Enterprise. In 1821 they descended the Coppermine River to its mouth and travelled eastward along the coast to Point Turnagain which they reached in July. They then travelled westward along the coast, ascended the Hood River, crossed overland in late autumn to the Burnside and then to the Coppermine at Obstruction Falls above Point Lake. Hood was murdered by Michel, one of the Iroquois, and others died of starvation and exposure before the tattered group reached Fort Providence in December 1821. [Houston, ed., To the Arctic by Canoe*; Houston, ed.,* Arctic Ordeal*]*

1827   Dr. John Richardson with Edward Kendall, on the second Franklin RN Expedition, descended the Mackenzie River and travelled east along the coast.

*They returned up the Coppermine and Kendall to the Dismal Lakes and down the Dease River to Great Bear Lake. [*Dictionary of Canadian Biography, *vol. 9]*

1838-39   Thomas Simpson and Peter Warren Dease, HBC, left Fort Confidence on Great Bear Lake, canoed up the Dease River to the Dismal Lakes and down the Kendall to the lower Coppermine, exploring the coastal areas. They returned upstream late in the year with difficulty. The following year the trip was repeated and they travelled westward along the coast as far as Boothia. [Simpson, 1845]

*1848-51   Dr. John Richardson, until 1849, and Dr. John Rae, making the trip twice, left from Fort Confidence on Great Bear Lake and travelled the Dease-Kendall-Coppermine route to the coast in separate searches for Sir John Franklin who had disappeared in 1847. [*Dictionary of Canadian Biography, *vol. 9]*

1864-72   Emil Petitot, Oblate, explored the region bounded by the Coppermine River, the Rocky Mountains, Great Slave Lake and the Arctic Ocean. [Petitot, 1875]

1894   Frank Russell snowshoed northeast from Fort Rae with hired Indians, crossing the Coppermine and returning. [Hobbs, in Hodgins and Hobbs, p.57]

George Douglas's love of canoeing did not end with his Coppermine trip in 1911. For easy transportation on his Hudson car, he had a collapsible canoe, shown at Lakefield in 1932. [George Douglas collection/Kathy Hooke].

1895   Caspar Whitney, with hired Indians, snowshoed from Fort Resolution across Great Slave Lake northward across the Coppermine River and returned. [*Ibid.*]

1900   J. Mackintosh Bell and Charles Camsell, Geological Survey, touched the Coppermine River on a trip from Great Bear Lake via the Dease River, Dismal Lakes and Kendall River. [Bell, 1931]

1902   David Hanbury – see Thelon

1909   John Hornby – see Great Bear

1910   V. Stefansson travelled up the Coppermine and over the Kendall-Dismal Lakes route to Great Bear Lake in late spring, meeting Hornby and Melvill there. [Whalley, *Legend*]

1911   George Douglas – see Great Bear

1912   George and Lionel Douglas descended the Coppermine to the sea and returned to Great Bear Lake. [Douglas, 1914; Mallory, 1989; Grant in Hodgins and Hobbs, p.99]

1912   David Wheeler on a private expedition from Rae Lake canoed up the Snare River to Winter Lake and from there onto the Coppermine River. [*Nastawgan*, vol. 16/3, 1989, pp. 1-3]

1913   Fathers J.B. Rouvière and G. LeRoux frequented the lower Coppermine from Great Bear Lake. They were murdered by their Inuit guides, Sinisiak and Uluksuk, near Bloody Falls in November. [Whalley, *Legend*]

1915   J.J. O'Neill and J.R. Cox, Geological Survey and attached to the Canadian Arctic Expedition, ascended the lower Coppermine and crossed over to Great Bear Lake via the Kendall and Dease rivers on a winter trip. [*Geographical Review*, October 1917, p. 241]

1916   K.G. Chipman, of the Geological Survey and the Canadian Arctic Expedition, with D'Arcy Arden, trekked across country from the mouth of the Coppermine River to the Mackenzie, via Great Bear Lake, continuing south to the Peace River settlement. They left in April and arrived in August. [Thompson, Don, vol. 2, p. 301]

1923 Guy Blanchet – see Lockhart

1925 W.H.B. "Billy" Hoare travelled by dog sled up the Coppermine and Kendall rivers, the Dismal Lakes and over to Great Bear Lake and the Mackenzie River. [Thomson, ed., 1990]

1929 Geoffrey Gilbert with three companions, prospectors, entering the river at a point near the mouth of the Kendall River canoed down the last 70 miles of the Coppermine to the Arctic Ocean. They made a sketch map. [Jack Goering's 1966 unpublished trip notes; Morse files, p. 5]

1932 C.H. Stockwell, H.S. Hicks, O.R. Wray and Bill Odjick, GSC, ascended the Yellowknife River from Yellowknife, crossed over the height of land via Winter Lake and explored the Coppermine around Point Lake, returning down the Barnston River toward the east end of Great Slave Lake. This was one of the last extensive trips by canoe for the Geological Survey. [*Canadian Geographic*, September 1934; Zaslow, pp. 362-63; *Musk-Ox*, #26, 27, 1980]

1945-46 "Exercise Muskox" was a winter manoeuvre by the Canadian Army using tracked snow vehicles from Churchill via Baker Lake to Cambridge Bay, south on the lower Coppermine and over to the Mackenzie, Norman Wells and eventually to Edmonton.

1960 Pat Brown, Dave Grout, Chuck Eddy, Bill Kemp, Bill Hughes and Tim Heinley on a private recreational sixty-five-day trip beginning at Uranium City, canoed to the Coppermine River from the Snowdrift River and down the Coppermine to its mouth. [*North*, March/April, 1962]

1962 Richard Martin and -? Miller canoed the Coppermine. [Morse files, p. 5, from Jack Goering]

1965 Dexter Davidson led a forty-one-day trip down the Coppermine River starting from Fort Rae up the Snare River. [Morse files, p. 5, from Jack Goering]

1966 Eric and Pamela Morse, Bill and Tom Mathers, Angus Scott, Pierre Trudeau, Arch Jones and Jack Goering were flown into Lac de Gras, paddled down through Point Lake and the full length of the Coppermine River. [Morse, *Freshwater Saga*, p. 74, map 5]

1966 Alice Wendt and Erwin Streisinger, Americans, on a recreational Coppermine trip by kayak, flew into Rocknest Lake, capsized in Sandstone Rapids where they were rescued and joined the Morse trip. [Morse 1966 unpublished trip report]

1970 Dave Buetow, Bruce Koci, Jim Novotny and John Streater, on a private expedition from Minnesota, canoed down the Coppermine in two wood-canvas canoes. They took a side trip up the Kendall to visit the Dismal Lakes. [*Beaver*, Summer 1978]

1970 Two associated groups made a commemorative retracing of Franklin's route. Jim and Terk Bayly, Scott Griffin, Peter Blaikie, Bill Mathers and Arthur Adamson flew into Lac de Gras and canoed down the Coppermine to its mouth. For details of the second group, see Yellowknife River. The double expedition, organized by Eric Morse, was sponsored by the NWT Government. [Pamela Morse, WCA Symposium, 26/1/1991; Eric Morse, *Freshwater Saga*, p. 146]

1970 Keith McColl was encountered at Bloody Falls by the group retracing Franklin's route. [Morse files, p. 12]

1970 Robin and Victoria Fraser, Dick Irwin, Christopher Horne, Allerton Cushman, Jr. and David Watts canoed from Lac de Gras down the Coppermine River to Coppermine Village, including a paddle up the Kendall River and a hike to the Dismal Lakes. [Personal communication – Robin Fraser; Matteson unpublished trip report]

1970 Bob Matteson, his son Sumner, John Lentz and Bob O'Hara, flew into Lac de Gras and paddled from the headwaters of the Coppermine to Coppermine Village. Bob O'Hara remained in Coppermine for two weeks in the hope of going on a seal hunt, while the other three were flown out. [Matteson unpublished trip report]

Pierre Trudeau and Angus Scott run a set of rapids below Lac de Gras on their way to the Coppermine River in 1966. [Eric Morse/ Pamela Morse]

1971? David Repp with four companions, in two aluminum canoes, left from Rae, paddled up the Snare River to Winter Lake, crossed the height of land, reaching Point Lake and canoed down the Coppermine. [*Beaver*, Summer 1972]

1971 Ken Hall, Keith Dunker, Grant McNabb, Keith Thompson, Charles Doehlert, Bob Corliss, John Anderegg and Bob Bird, Canadians and Americans, put their canoes in at Rawalpindi Lake and canoed to Coppermine Village. [Unpublished trip report filed at Parks Canada]

1971 Wally Eamer and -? Sprout, university students from Ottawa, canoed down part of the Coppermine in a circuit which began with the ascent of the Yellowknife River to Singing, Snare, Jolly and Courageous lakes, down the Coppermine River, up the Hook River, and down the Sloan to Great Bear Lake, up the Camsell and down the Marian rivers to return to Yellowknife. [Morse files, p. 4]

1971 Frank Cooke and others made a trip down the Coppermine River with a leaky canoe. [U-Paddle file, HBC Archives]

1972 Donald and Maria Scott, Erwin Streisinger and Larry Osgood put in at Redrock Lake and canoed down the Coppermine. Donald Scott thought they were the only group on the river that year. [Personal communication from Scott to Clayton Klein; also Osgood]

1972 David and Carol Jones paddled downstream to Rocky Defile Rapids where they were drowned. There is a cairn and plaque in their memory on the riverbank.

1972 Fred and Sue Cramp, Greg Ewert and John Horricks, Wild River Survey, put in their canoes at Point Lake and canoed to Coppermine Village. [*Outdoor Canada*, March and June, 1976]

1972 Duke Watson with A. Hovey, H. Muller, and M. Sheeran canoed from Courageous Lake, up the Lockhart River, crossed over from Starfish Lake to Point Lake. Hovey and Muller were replaced by R. Crooks, J. Docter, J. Roush and E. Wyckoff and the group continued down the Coppermine

Maria Scott, Erwin Streisinger, member of the Explorers Club, Larry Osgood, novelist, and Don Scott, all kayakers with wide experience on northern rivers, pause on a hillside overlooking the Dismal Lakes, during their trip down the Coppermine in 1972. [Osgood]

to the Big Bend, ascending the Hook River, crossing over via the Kamut and Jaciar lakes and down the Sloan River to Great Bear Lake where they were picked up by plane, 40 miles from Port Radium. [U-Paddle file, HBC Archives; personal communication – Watson]

1973 Alex Hall and Dennis Voigt flew to an unnamed lake 50 miles north of Lake Athabasca, canoed down a short section of the Dubawnt through a series of lakes, down the Elk and upper Thelon rivers, up the Mary Frances, down a short section of the Hanbury, up the Lockhart River from Clinton-Colden Lake to Courageous Lake, over to the Coppermine downstream from Lac de Gras and down the Coppermine River to the Arctic Ocean. [*Beaver*, Summer 1976]

1973 A.C. Hamilton with his sons Ian, Malcolm and Peter started at Jolly Lake, canoed up the Snare River to Courageous and Desteffany lakes and down the Coppermine River. [Morse files, p. 12]

1973 Jay Pritchett led a group of twenty-three students including Natalie Ho, from Whitmore College, Spokane, Washington, on the "Second Expedition" which started at Courageous Lake, crossed to Lac de Gras and canoed down the Coppermine River to the Arctic Ocean. [*Seventeen*, August 1974, p. 112; personal communication – Pritchett]

1973 An American group successfully retraced Franklin's route up the Yellowknife River, across the height of land at Winter Lake and down the Coppermine River. [*Canadian Boating*, April 1977, p. 6]

1973 Henning Harmuth and others made a trip down the Coppermine River. [HBC Archives – U-Paddle file]

1974 Bill Grant, Mike Kestle, Bob and John Miller, Don Sproule and Arthur Westgarth canoed from MacKay Lake through Thonokied Lake to Lac de Gras and down the Coppermine River to Point Lake. They produced "Some observations on Arctic summer weather to aid canoe trippers." [Morse files, p. 15 and p. 17]

1974 Robert Dannert, Neil von Bush, Bob Dedrick and Dr. Guy R. Honold, from Minneapolis, ca-

noed the Coppermine River early in July when the water level was very high. Guy Honold was drowned on July 15 in Rocky Defile Rapid. The three survivors continued down-river to Coppermine Village. [Personal communication – Matthews; personal communication – Dannert]

1974 Jim Matthews, Terry Guest, Don Arthurs, Bill Pearce, Peter Jarvis and John Davis canoed from Lake Providence, above Obstruction Rapids, down the Coppermine to the Arctic Ocean. Just below Rocky Defile Rapid they found the body of the drowned canoeist, Honold, from the group which had preceded them by two weeks. [Personal communication – Matthews]

1974 Mike Ecker, Tom Hinan, Dave Simmons, Mark Smith, Rick Thompson and Dick Tupper started at Prosperous Lake, canoed up the Yellowknife River, worked their way over to Point Lake and canoed down the Coppermine River to the Arctic Ocean. [Morse files, p. 22; *Outdoor Life*, ??]

1974 Camp Widjiwagan: Phil Bratnober led Brad Cochrane, Doug Haberman, Paul Homuth, Marty Leitze and Dave Peebles on a 700-mile canoe trip which ended by descending the Coppermine River to the Arctic Ocean. [Camp Widjiwagan Archives]

1979 *Bruce and Carol Hodgins led an adult Wanapitei trip from Redrock Lake down the Coppermine to Coppermine Village. [Wanapitei trip report]*

1979 *George Luste, Sandy Richardson, Paul Skinner and Fritz Brace started at Lac Sans-Disant, north of Great Slave Lake, and made their way down the Coppermine. [Personal communication – Luste]*

HOOD

The Hood is named for Midshipman Robert Hood, one of the men assigned to the Franklin expedition because of his combination of artistic ability and navigational skills.

"For the first time since our Hood River trip began, we didn't have to break camp. We had two days in our schedule to enjoy the spectacular scenery around Wilberforce Falls, rain or no. The day before we had all

Barrenland travel can present many different faces. The empty curving sand beaches along the Coppermine River, covered with a pattern of caribou tracks, are a picture more idyllic than a travel brochure for the Carribean. On the other hand, the brief summer may be even briefer than expected. On this trip, which began early in July, Sandy Richardson and his party encountered ice on MacKay Lake and had to drag the canoes across the broad expanse until they reached open water. [Richardson]

agreed, despite overcast light, this fifty-metre falls and four-kilometre canyon was the most spectacular sight we had ever seen, better even than Virginia Falls on the Nahanni." [Bill Mason, concerning his 1983 trip, "Hood: In Franklin's Wake", in Raffan, ed., *Wild Waters*, p. 82]

1821 *John Franklin, Dr. John Richardson, midshipmen Robert Hood and George Back, John Hepburn with other naval men etc. ascended the Hood to above Wilberforce Falls and crossed overland to the Burnside, crossing it by canoe. The canoe abandoned, they continued their trek across the Barrens to Fort Enterprise on Winter Lake. They were stopped at Obstruction Rapids on the Coppermine where a cockleshell craft of painted canvas was constructed to take them across. The approaching winter and starvation dogged their path. Robert Hood was murdered by Iroquois hunter, Michel, before the remnants of the group reached Fort Enterprise.* [Houston, ed., To the Arctic by Canoe, 1974]

1976 *Jay and Carolyn Pritchett led a party of twenty-four canoeists from Whitmore College, Spokane, Washington, from Lac de Gras down the Coppermine River to Point Lake. They went upstream to Itchen Lake, crossed the height of land to Takiyuak Lake and made what is thought to be the first recreational descent of the Hood River.* [Personal communication – Alex Hall; personal communication – Pritchett]

1979 *A Canadian group attempting to canoe the Hood River was stopped by ice in Takiyuak Lake.* [Canoe, June 1983 p. 46]

1980 *Ted Johnson, Robert Duemling, John Godfrey, John Gow, Tim Kotcheff, Craig Oliver, David Silcox and Peter Stollery put in at the headwaters and canoed down the Hood River to the Arctic Ocean, seeing much wildlife on the way.* [Personal communication – Johnson]

1982 *Cliff Jacobson, Bob and Dave Dannert, Reb Bowman, Kent Swanson and Marc Hebert flew in to Point Lake and canoed down the Coppermine River and via a series of lakes and small streams, including Rocking Horse Lake, to Takiyuak Lake and*

down the Hood River to Bathurst Inlet. [Canoe, June 1983, p. 46; personal communication – Bob Dannert; Jacobson, Campsite Memories, pp. 89-99]

1983 *John Lentz, Todd Buchanan, Charles Bond, Bob Sands, John Schultz and Joe Lederle flew in to a lake at the height of land, canoed to Takiyuak Lake and portaged to the headwaters of the Hood River. Using ABS canoes they descended the Hood River to the Arctic Ocean and flew out to Yellowknife.* [National Geographic, January 1986; Explorers Journal, September 1986]

1983 *Bill Mason, Wally Schaber, Bruce Cockburn, Gilles Lebreque, Alan Whatmough and Gilles Couet canoed from Takiyuak Lake down the Hood River. Some of the group ran the rapids in the canyon below Wilberforce Falls.* [Raffan, Wild Waters]

1992 *This trip is included because it was unique. While there have been a few honeymoon canoe trips, this is the only recorded wedding. It took place at the top of Wilberforce Falls during a canoe trip which began at the entrance to the Hood River. The trip was led by the groom, Cliff Jacobson. The bride, Sue Harings, wore an ermine-trimmed, white satin gown and green "Wellies", and was attended by Brad Bjorklund. The marriage was performed by specially commissioned Charlie LeFevere. Best man was Biff Kummer, and tuxedo T-shirts were provided by Dr. Jerry Noller. Four other trip members and two Canadian geologists were the guests.* [Jacobson, Campsite Memories, pp. 1-11]

BURNSIDE

Rising in long and complex Contwoyto Lake, the Burnside River runs parallel to the Hood River, emptying into the head of Bathurst Inlet. It has an important tributary, the Mara.

1821 *John Franklin – see Hood*

1975 *Jay and Carolyn Pritchett of Alaska led a party of twenty-four canoeists from Whitmore College, Spokane, from Lac de Gras, north on Lac de Sauvage and Contwoyto Lake and made what is believed to be the first recreational descent of the*

The wedding of Cliff Jacobson and Sue Harings, above Wilberforce Falls, in 1992. Underneath that beautiful wedding gown, the bride was wearing green "Wellies". [Jacobson]

Burnside River. [Personal communication – Alex Hall; personal communication – Pritchett]

1976 *Alex Hall made a solo canoe trip down the Burnside River. He started from Lac de Gras, the headwaters of the Coppermine River, canoed to Lake Providence, went up an unnamed river for about 60 miles, crossed the height of land to Contwoyto Lake and thence down the Burnside River. [Beaver, Spring 1980]*

1979 *John Turner, his wife Geills, and their children Elizabeth, fifteen, Michael, thirteen, and David, eleven, Bob Engle and two seventeen-year-old students, Donald Konantz and Fraser Norrie, flew to Kathawachaga Lake and canoed down the Burnside River to Bathurst Inlet. [*Toronto Life*, August 1981; Jacobson,* Canoeing Wild rivers *p. 253]*

1980 *James Raffan, Gail Simmons, Catherine Laing, Norm Frost, John Fallis and Lorraine McDonald flew into Munn Lake, paddled and portaged to Aylmer Lake, crossed it, portaged down a dry stretch of the Back River, portaged and paddled through small lakes to Contwoyto Lake. Behind schedule because of weather, they flew from the weather station on Conwoyto Lake to the outlet of the lake and canoed down the Burnside River to Bathurst Inlet. [Raffan,* Summer North of Sixty]*

1980 *A professor and five students from Dartmouth College, New Hampshire canoed down the Burnside River. [ibid. p. 201]*

1981 *Raffan – see Mara*

1981 *Abel – see Mara*

1983 *Ted Johnson, John Godfrey, John Gow, Tim Kotcheff, John Macfarlane, Craig Oliver, David Silcox and Peter Stollery put in at Kathawachaga Lake and descended the Burnside River to Bathurst Inlet. [Personal communication – Johnson]*

MARA

1981 *Jim Raffan, Pat Geale, John Fallis and Lorraine McDonald made what they believed was the first canoe descent of the Mara River, putting in at Nose Lake and canoeing down to Bathurst Inlet. [Personal communication – Raffan]*

1981 *Jim Abel led a group from Whitmore College down the Mara River. They had put in at Eskimo Point (Arviat) on Hudson Bay and crossed the Barrens by a series of lakes and rivers, including the Kazan and part of the upper Back. [Personal communication – Raffan]*

1987 *Charles Hodgson and five others canoed down the Mara and Burnside rivers to Bathurst Inlet. [Paddler, Fall 1988, p. 14-17]*

1989 *George Drought, Barbara Burton, Karen Beeswanger and Dieter Keck entered the Mara River just below Nose Lake and canoed down the Mara and the Burnside rivers to Bathurst Inlet. [Personal communication – Drought]*

QUEEN MAUD GULF AND EAST: RIVERS FLOWING INTO THE ARCTIC OCEAN

WESTERN

The Western River rises in the hills south of Bathurst Inlet and flows due east before turning sharply northwest to empty into the narrow southern bay of Bathurst Inlet.

1986 Jay and Carolyn Pritchett started on the Thonokied River, crossed via Glowworm and Tarpon lakes to the Contwoyto River and followed it to the Back River, descending it to Beechey Lake. They turned up a small stream, crossed over to the Western River and followed it to Bathurst Inlet. [Personal communication – Pritchett]

1987 Jay and Carolyn Pritchett started on the headwaters of the Western River, canoed down to the bend where they crossed east to the Ellice River. They continued down the Ellice to approximately 66°, turned upstream on an unnamed tributary, crossed north, then west, then south to the headwaters of the Hiukitat River and followed it to Bathurst Inlet. [Personal communication – Pritchett]

ELLICE

The Ellice River rises close to the Back River, midway between Beechey and Pelly lakes and flows into the Arctic Ocean at Queen Maud Gulf.

1972 John Lentz, Bob Schaefer, Bob Goulding and Lewis B., having canoed from the headwaters of the Baillie River, continued down the Back River

for part of one day. They continued up an unnamed creek for three days of up-hill struggle, portaged across the height of land to the headwaters of the Ellice River and followed it to the waters of Queen Maud Gulf. [Unpublished trip report – John Lentz]

1978? Erwin Streisinger, Don Scott, Lisa Wurm and Anna Gerenday in two folding kayaks and one canoe paddled from the headwaters of the Ellice River to the Arctic Ocean. [Explorers Journal, June 1980]

1979 Jay Pritchett – see Baillie River

1986 Robert Dannert, his son David, Reb Bowman, Marc Hebert, Steve Bany and Kurt Melancon, from Minnesota, put in at Glowworm Lake, canoed down the Icy River into the Back River to below Beechey cascades. They portaged north 5 miles to a small lake, crossed over through a series of lakes to the west branch of the Ellice River and followed it to the Arctic Ocean. [Personal communication – Dannert]

1987 Jay Pritchett – see Western

PERRY

The Perry River is a short and silty river which rises in MacAlpine Lake and flows due north through the centre of Queen Maud Gulf Bird Sanctuary. Thomas Simpson mapped the coastal area at the mouth of the

"Arctic circle" at the head-waters of the Perry River shows the Arctic Barrens expedition members clasping hands to celebrate their arrival in the Arctic in 1988. The members are Kurt Wise in plaid mackinaw jacket, and clockwise, Chris Barker, Dick Winslow, Dave Cannon, Peter Mitchell, Tim Demers, Cheryl Heiner, Sam Woo, Michele Dickson, Herb Van Winkelen, Peter Franck, Tom Turner, Tom Benander, Mike Taylor, Laura Nault, Dave Massell and Laurie Gullion. [Jim Abel]

river in 1839 and David Hanbury explored the area in the winter of 1902. As late as 1940 C.D.H. Clarke stated that the area of the Barrens drained by the Back River is the least known of the Arctic mainland.

1940   Angus Gavin and E. Donovan, HBC, with four Inuit, ascended the Perry River by canoe to search for the nesting grounds of Ross's goose. [*Canadian Field-Naturalist*, Dec. 1940, p. 127; *Beaver*, Dec. 1940; *Polar Record*, January 1941, p. 364]

1941   Angus Gavin explored up the Perry River by canoe. [Hanson, p. 7]

1949   Peter Scott, ornithologist son of "Scott of the Antarctic", Paul Queneau, American organizer of the expedition and Harold Hanson, zoologist from the Illinois Natural History survey, were based at the Perry River from the beginning of June until the end of July to study the nesting grounds of the Ross's goose, which was thought to be facing extinction. They also investigated the "tule" or whitefront goose. In addition they carried out mapping, photography, zoological and meteorological studies of a small area of the Perry River. Their equipment included a 12-foot Grumman canoe in which they travelled up and down a short length of the Perry and a tributary in their search for the nesting grounds. At the end of July they were joined by Jim Bell, a pilot

from Sudbury, Ontario, for two weeks of aerial exploration. [Scott, Peter, 1951; Hanson, 1956]

1988   *Jim Abel, Laurie Gullion and Dave Massell led an Arctic Barrens Expedition group which included Dick Winslow, Peter Franck, Tim Demers, Tom Benander, Herb Van Winkelen, Sam Woo, Cheryl Heiner, Kurt Wise, Mike Taylor, Dave Cannon, Peter Mitchell, Chris Barker, Tom Turner, Michele Dickson and Laura Nault, down the Perry River. They flew to Lockhart Lake, canoed through ice to MacKay, Aylmer, Clinton-Colden lakes, crossed over the height of land to Moraine Lake, canoed down the Baillie and Back rivers to Pelly Lake, continued up the Bullen River, crossed over to MacAlpine Lake, and descended the Perry River to the Arctic Ocean. [Up-here, July/August 1989, p. 28; unpublished manuscript – Winslow]*

1992   *Jay and Carolyn Pritchett, from Alaska, started on a tributary of the Thelon River, proceeded down the Thelon past Ursus Island, went up an unnamed stream and crossed over to the Consul River, following it down to the Back River. They canoed down the Back a short distance, went upstream on the Bullen River, crossed over to the MacAlpine River, followed it down to MacAlpine Lake and continued down the Perry River to Queen Maud Gulf. [Personal communication – Pritchett]*

ARMARK

The Armark rises in Armark Lake near the north arm of Garry Lake on the Back River and flows due north into Queen Maud Gulf.

1901-02 David Hanbury – see Thelon

1990 *Jay and Carolyn Pritchett, having started on the headwaters of the Hanbury River, canoed down the Hanbury and Thelon to the west end of Beverly Lake. They went upstream on an unnamed river, crossed overland to the headwaters of another unnamed river and went down north into Upper Garry Lake. They crossed Garry Lake and continued up the north arm of the lake, went upstream and crossed to the headwaters of the Armark River and followed it to Queen Maud Gulf. [Personal communication – Pritchett]*

SIMPSON

The Simpson is a cloudy, silted river which rises close to the lower end of the Garry Lakes on the Back River and flows northwest through the Queen Maud Gulf Bird Sanctuary, emptying into the Arctic Ocean in a delta at Johnson Point.

1988 *Jay and Carolyn Pritchett had intended to descend the Simpson River but the water levels were too low. (Their trip started at Lynx Lake, continued down the upper Thelon River, crossed to the Dubawnt River at Sid Lake and continued down the Dubawnt to the west end of Beverly Lake.) [Unpublished manuscript – Winslow; personal communication – Pritchett]*

1989 *Jay and Carolyn Pritchett descended the Baillie and Back rivers past Buliard Lake, crossed the height of land to the headwaters of the Simpson River and followed it to Queen Maud Gulf. [Personal communication – Pritchett]*

1992 *Bob Dannert, his son David, Steve and Lynda Bany, Kurt Melancon and Pete Memmer, from Minnesota, flew into Consul Lake, canoed down the Consul River to the Back River, leaving it beyond the Garry Lakes. They turned north on a small river, ascended it to its source, portaged a kilometre across to the Simpson River and followed it to the Arctic Ocean. Water levels were high. There were many Inuit sites on the lower portion of the Simpson River. [Personal communication – Dannert]*

KALEET

The Kaleet River rises close to the lower end of Garry Lake on the Back River. It flows due north into Sherman Basin, a body of water almost land-locked by the Adelaide Peninsula. It forms the eastern boundary of the Queen Maud Gulf Bird Sanctuary.

1957 Tom Manning, Andrew Macpherson and his wife were on the Adelaide Peninsula collecting birds and mammals for the National Museum. In a 22-

Laurie Nault and Mike Taylor, part of the Arctic Barrens expedition in 1988, plunge down an unnnamed rapid on the Perry River. This trip began on Lockhart Lake, crossed the large Barrens lakes, descended the Baillie and a section of the Back, before crossing the final height of land to reach the Arctic Ocean. [Dick Winslow]

Bob Dannert from Minnesota, has led many trips for Polar Arctic Expeditions, including his rare descent of the Simpson River in 1992. [Dannert]

foot canoe they travelled from Barrow Inlet to Gladman and Falcon Inlets and into Sherman Basin, where they ascended the Kaleet River for 15 miles and returned downstream, canoeing back to King William Island. [*Arctic Circular*, 1958, p. 24]

1986 *Jim Abel, Dave Massell and Laurie Gullion led an Arctic Barrens Expedition which included Sam Woo, Dave Cannon, Peter Mitchel and Michele Dickson to the Kaleet River. They canoed down the Hanbury and Thelon rivers to Schultz Lake, crossed by unnamed streams to the Back River. After a day's travel on the Back they went up a shallow stream and portaged to an upland lake which led eventually to the Kaleet River. The water in the river was very low and silty, and after two days on the Kaleet the expedition was flown out. [Unpublished manuscript – Dick Winslow; personal communication – Gullion]*

BACK

Of Canada's long Arctic rivers, the Back River is the most remote. Rising in the western Barrens, it flows for hundreds of kilometres northeasterly through the large Pelly and Garry lakes, turns north passing through Franklin Lake before flowing into Chantrey Inlet in the Eastern Arctic, where there is no Inuit settlement only a fishing camp. The Back has three notable tributaries, the Baillie, the Morse and the Meadowbank. There are no recorded trips on the Meadowbank, which flows into the Back just before it turns to the north. It was, however, a traditional Inuit winter route over to Baker Lake.

1833 *Capt. George Back, with Maufelly as guide, De Charlôit as bowman, Malley, servant, Louison, interpreter, using a birchbark canoe, ascended the Hoarfrost River up to Lake Walmsley, portaged*

across to and ascended the Lockhart River, crossed Clinton-Colden and skirted Aylmer Lake, crossed the height of land to Sussex Lake and saw the beginnings of the river they were seeking – the Thleweechodezeth or Great Fish – later named the Back River. They returned as they had gone, caching the canoe at the outlet of Artillery Lake and portaging back to Fort Reliance. [Back, G. reprinted 1970]

1834 *Capt. George Back, RN, with Richard King, surgeon, James McKay, steersman, George Sinclair and Charles McKenzie, bowmen, Peter Taylor, James Spence, John Ross, William Malley and Hugh Carron made a private trip subsidized by the British Government and the HBC. They used a 30-foot boat of planking which was built during the spring on the Lockhart River near the beginning of Artillery Lake. The trip was originally mounted to search for Sir John Ross, missing off the Arctic coast, but having learned that Ross had been found they chose to do further exploration. They set out from Fort Reliance at the east end of Great Slave Lake, ascended the Lockhart system, reached the headwaters of the Great Fish River and descended it to Chantrey Inlet and Montreal Island. They explored some coastline and returned upstream and over to Great Slave Lake. [Back, G., reprinted 1970; Richard King, 1836]*

1855 *James Anderson, chief factor HBC and James Green Stewart in a party of ten which included Jack Fiddler, were sent down the Great Fish (Back) River in two canoes to search for Kraus of the Franklin expedition, reached Montreal Island and returned. [Journal of Royal Geographic Society, vol. 27, London, 1857; journal reprinted in* Canadian Field-Naturalist *beginning in Vol. 54, May 1940, p. 63, and continuing into Vol. 55]*

1890 Warburton Pike, on a private hunting expedition with James Mackinlay, HBC from Fort Resolution, Murdo Mackay, HBC post servant, Moise Mandeville, Métis, Pierre Lockhart, Yellowknife Indian, and David, an Inuk from Peel River, canoed across Great Slave Lake. At Fond du Lac they were joined by several members of the Beaulieu family, Capot Blanc, Saltatha, Syene, Marlo and Carquoss, who with their wives, children and dogs, considerably slowed their progress. They travelled by way of Lac de Mort, Wolverine, Camsell, and MacKay lakes. Crossing by the Lockhart River to Aylmer Lake, they descended the Back River to Lake Beechey. They returned via Aylmer, Clinton-Colden and Artillery lakes and by the portage which became known as Pike's Portage back to Great Slave Lake. [Pike, *The Barren Ground of Northern Canada*; James Mackinlay's diary, *Arctic Circular*, 1957, p. 35; *Ottawa Naturalist*, 1893/4, p. 85]

1907 Ernest Thompson Seton and E.A. Preble travelled north from Great Slave Lake to Aylmer Lake on the Back River to photograph musk-ox. [Seton, 1911]

1948 A.W.F. Banfield and A.L. Wilk, Canadian Wildlife Service, canoed from Clinton-Colden Lake down a section of the Back River. [*Arctic*, 1951, pp. 113-21]

1950 Father Joseph Buliard built a tiny hut on an island in Garry Lake (Back River), and served the Inuit in that area from 1950 until his unexplained death, either by drowning or lost in a blizzard, in October 1956. His travel from Baker Lake and down to the Perry River was by airplane and dog team but in 1954 he acquired a canvas-covered canoe with a small outboard motor, which he used on the Back River. [Klein, *Cold Summer Wind*, pp. 204-22; *Eskimo*, Churchill, various issues, 1978-83]

1953 Robert and James Wilkie, Dr. W. J. Breckenridge (leader), John Jarosz, Dr. Lou Larson, R.T. Congdon, H.L. Gunderson and Spence Taylor on an expedition financed by the Wilkie Foundation and the University of Minnesota flew from Churchill to Baker Lake and from there to camp on the Back River, near the Meadowbank River, to carry out biological and geological studies. Most of the work was done within 8 miles of the base camp. Breckenridge and Taylor flew to Lake Macdougall and travelled downstream to base camp, 85 miles by canoe with a small motor. [*Beaver*, spring and summer 1955; *Canadian Field-Naturalist*, Jan./Mar., 1955 p. 1]

1955 John Tener, Canadian Wildlife Service, and Lloyd Beebe, from Sequim, Washington, flew to Beechey Lake and canoed down the Back to the Baillie River. They canoed 10 miles up the Baillie River and returned downstream on the Baillie and Back rivers to Pelly Lake, flying out from there. [*Canadian Field-Naturalist*, July/Sept, 1956, p. 138]

1960 R.G. Blackadar, Geological Survey, with Dr. Heywood, J.L. Blanchard, two students and two cooks, carried out a geological survey and mapping of the Back River by helicopter and airplane. They examined the cairn left by Thomas Simpson at Cape Britannia in 1838. No Franklin relics were found (see below 1962 "Beacon Six"). [*Arctic Circular*, 1961, pp. 35-36]

1962 John Lentz, Kit Gregg, Austin Hoyt and Tracey Perry were dropped at Sandhill Bay on Aylmer Lake and canoed the full length of the Back River to Chantrey Inlet on the Arctic Ocean. They collected meteorological data and made animal counts for the Canadian government. [*Sports Illustrated*, August 26, 1963, pp. 34-41; *Explorers Journal*, March 1965]

1962 Robert Cundy, David Gordon-Dean, Robin Challis and Russell Polden descended the river in three two-man British naval kayaks, from Beechey Lake to Cape Britannia on Chantrey Inlet. One kayak was wrecked in rapids at the outlet of Macdougall Lake. To reach Britannia Cape the two remaining kayaks were fastened together and an outboard motor was used to take them from the Inuit fishing camp at the head of Chantrey Inlet. They were picked up at the Cape by a pre-arranged charter plane. The purpose of the trip was to find "Beacon Six", the cairn built by Thomas Simpson in 1838, in the hope of finding a message left by the Franklin expedition. When they reached the cairn there was a note from the recent Canadian geological expedition, led by Blackadar, to say that they had searched the cairn and found nothing (see 1960). [Cundy, 1970]

1965 Ron Hill and Gerry Wherley, from Minnesota, flew in a chartered plane from International Falls, Minnesota, to Great Slave Lake, canoed up the Lockhart River, and down the Back River to Chantrey Inlet, where they were picked up by pre-arranged charter, after a 57-day trip. [Personal communication – Duke Watson]

1967 Graham Peter Bromley and Ian David Calder, after twenty-seven days of canoeing down the Back River, drowned in the rapids 130 kilometres above the Chantrey Inlet estuary. Robert Bromley, sixteen years old, was rescued ten days later by an air search party. [*Polar Record*, September 1968, p. 361]

1969 Duke Watson, A. Crooks, J. Crooks, P. Evans, A. Watson, B. Watson, R. Watson, E. Wyckoff and P. Wyckoff canoed from Sussex Lake down the Back River to upper Garry Lake, continuing a trip which began for Duke Watson, A. Crooks and others on Jolly Lake. Duke Watson and his group were flown out to Seattle for eleven days. Watson then returned with A. Hovey, V. Josendal and P. Phillips and continued down the Back River to a point just above the Sandhill Rapids. Watson returned to the river in 1970 and with Hovey, Josendal and E. Wyckoff canoed to the outlet of Franklin Lake, and later with C. Clark, S. McIntyre and R. Watson to Chantrey Inlet and into Cockburn Bay. [Personal communication – Watson]

1972 Fred Gaskin, George Dobbie, Lyle Malcolm and Jack Purchase canoed from Sussex Lake, the headwaters of the Back River, the full length of the river to Chantrey Inlet. [*Weekend Magazine*, July 21, 1973]

1972 John Lentz – see Baillie

1972 A group of Barren Land voyageurs did a thirty-day photographic trip on the Back River, setting off from the northwest arm of Great Slave Lake. [John Bayly – unpublished trip report of the Taltson]

1973 Richard Cranne, Paul Roberts, Paul Keller and Jerry Hudson, American university students, with two 17-foot canoes, canoed from Yellowknife, along the north shore of Great Slave Lake, up Pike's Portage, to Artillery Lake, up the Lockhart River to Clinton-Colden and Aylmer lakes, crossed the height of land to Sussex Lake and canoed down the Back River to Chantrey Inlet, a journey of 1660 kilometres in fifty-six days. [*Polar Record*, January 1975, p. 388]

1973? Bob O'Hara canoed the full length of the Back River. [WCA Symposium 26/1/1991]

1974 The RCMP flew a rescue search for an older man and his girlfriend lost somewhere on the Back River. [Personal communication – Jim Matthews]

1974 Jay Pritchett led a party of twenty-four canoeists from Whitmore College, Spokane, down the Back River from Muskox Lake to Chantrey Inlet. [Personal communication – Pritchett]

1975 *Dave and Judy Harrison, Jack and Susy Wadsworth, and Bob and Gayle Greenhill, using a Grumman, a C2, and a Mad River, put in at Beechey Lake and canoed to Chantrey Inlet. At Escape Rapids, the Grumman canoe broached on a rock and was twisted beyond the possibility of salvage. The group left behind all non-essential gear and completed the trip in two canoes. [Canoe, Jan./Feb. 1976, pp. 14-46]*

1976 *Rob Perkins and Bernie Peyton hiked up Pike's Portage from Fort Reliance. Their 17-foot, wood and canvas Old Town canoe and the bulk of their supplies had been dropped for them at Artillery Lake. They canoed up the Lockhart River to Aylmer Lake, crossed over to the headwaters of the Back River and followed it down to Chantrey Inlet. [Outdoor Life, August 1977; Harvard Magazine, July/August 1977, p. 37]*

1977 *Bob Dannert, Neil von Bush, Jim Hoel and Orv Voxland, from Minnesota, canoed down the Back River past the Garry Lakes, portaged into the north*

Carolyn and Jay Pritchett above Bathurst Inlet where they have ended first descents of several Arctic rivers, the Hood, Burnside and Western. [Pritchett].

end of Deep Rose Lake and ascended an unnamed river. They crossed the height of land, portaging east through a chain of lakes, descended a small unnamed river south into the northwest corner of Schultz Lake and continued down the Thelon to Baker Lake. [Personal communication – Dannert]

1977 *Frank, Dave, Don, Keith, Tom and Eckhart made a trip down the Back River ahead of the Pelly group. [Pelly,* Expedition, *p. 95]*

1977 *David and Brian Pelly, Thomas Mawhinney and Peter Dion flew to MacKay Lake, canoed down a short stretch of the Lockhart River to Aylmer Lake, crossed over to Sussex Lake, the headwaters of the Back River and followed it to Pelly Lake. On Pelly Lake they erected a cairn and placed on it a plaque honouring an ancestor of the Pellys', a former governor of the Hudson's Bay Company. [Pelly,* Expedition*]*

1988 *Rob Perkins made a solo trip on the Back River. [Perkins,* Into the Great Solitude, *1991]*

BAILLIE

The Baillie River flows generally northeast and enters the Back River between Beechey Lake and Pelly Lake.

1955 John Tener – see Back

1972 John Lentz, Bob Schaefer, Bob Goulding and Lewis B. flew from Yellowknife to the headwaters of one branch of the Baillie River above Healy Lake and canoed down the Baillie to the Back River. They continued the trip, working their way up a creek from the Back River and crossing the height of land to the headwaters of the Ellice River which they followed to the Arctic Ocean. [Unpublished trip report – John Lentz]

1974 Erwin Streisinger and a field biologist colleague, Kay, kayaked down the Baillie River to the confluence with the Back River. They were picked up by pre-arrangement on the Back River. [*Explorers Journal*, Spring, 1992]

1979 *Jay and Carolyn Pritchett, with Jim Abel as expedition doctor, led a party of twenty-four canoeists from Whitmore College, Spokane, which started just north of Whitefish Lake, on the headwaters of the Hanbury River. They canoed down the Hanbury, cut north-*

Rob Perkins, in his wooden canoe, *Loon,* shoots the Hawk Rapids on the Back River. Perkins was on one of his solo trips on the Back, which resulted in his book *Into the Great Solitude,* when he encountered the group which was heading for the Perry River in 1988. [Dick Winslow]

ward at Musk-ox Hill to the headwaters of the Baillie River and followed it down to the Back River. After a few miles on the Back River they turned north up an unnamed stream and crossed to the headwaters of the Ellice River, following it down to Queen Maud Gulf. [Personal communication – Pritchett]

1985 *Alex Hall, of Canoe Arctic Inc., guided a group of eight canoeists down the Baillie and Back rivers from near Moraine Lake to the McKinley River junction on the Back River. [Personal communication – Hall]*

1985 *Jay and Carolyn Pritchett started at Campbell Lake, crossed to the headwaters of the Baillie River and canoed down the Baillie and Back rivers to Lower Macdougall Lake. They turned upstream to Deep Rose Lake, continued upstream on a small unnamed river, crossed the height of land and picked up a small river which took them down to the eastern arm of Schultz Lake. They continued down the Thelon River to Baker Lake. [Personal communication – Pritchett]*

1988 *Jim Abel – see Perry*

1990 *Erwin Streisinger, Patrick Bellinger and Gail Ferris, in three kayaks, flew to the headwaters of the Baillie River and paddled down to the confluence with the Back River, being picked up 20 miles down the Back River. [*Explorers Journal, *Spring, 1992]*

Muskox grazing beside the Morse River, watched by members of the Hide-Away Canoe Club. Muskox will browse quietly, like cows in a pasture, until becoming aware of a foreign presence, whereupon they snort steam from their nostrils and dash off with astonishing speed. Anyone facing a muskox which is standing its ground should retreat when the animal rubs its nose on its fore-leg – a signal for attack. [Michael Peake]

MORSE

The Morse River was named for Eric Morse while he was still alive, an unusual honour which recognized his tremendous contribution to northern recreational canoe travel. It rises just north of Beverly Lake, an expansion of the Thelon River, and flows due north, entering the Back River in a bay of Garry Lake.

1985 *Michael, Sean and Geoffrey Peake, and Peter Scott, using Old Town Trippers, started at Selwyn Lake and canoed down the Dubawnt River, crossing Wholdaia Lake, to Carey Lake. They crossed by a series of lakes and portages to the upper Thelon River and continued down the Thelon to the confluence with the Hanbury where they were joined by two other members of the Hide-Away Canoe Club, Bill King and Peter Brewster. They continued down the Thelon to Beverly Lake, tracked up a small stream, crossed the height of land and canoed down, and named, the Morse River, continuing down the Back River to Chantrey Inlet. [Che-Mun, Outfits 42,43, Autumn and Winter 1985]*

HAYES

The Hayes River flows into Chantrey Inlet very close to the mouth of the Back River. It flows generally northwest, having begun close to the end of Wager Bay and in its last few kilometres it makes a right-angled turn to the southwest.

1980 *Duke Watson, A. Black, J. Roush and A. Zob canoed from Lake 823+, the headwaters of the Hayes River, down the river to its confluence with the Back River near Chantrey Inlet. While this is known as an Inuit winter route, the Inuit in Baker Lake knew of no summer travel on it. [Personal communication – Watson]*

1988 *Erwin Streisinger, flew from Hall Beach and alone, by kayak, started down the Hayes River. In a 5-mile stretch of rapids the kayak struck a rock and was destroyed beyond repair. Streisinger got ashore and spent several days before being picked up by the plane from Hall Beach. This river was thought to be previously unexplored. [Explorers Journal, March 1990]*

KELLETT AND ARROWSMITH

The Kellett and Arrowsmith rivers are two short rivers which follow parallel courses and flow into Pelly Bay, an arm of the Gulf of Boothia.

1956 Andrew Macpherson of the National Research Council and McGill University, with Dr. W.F. Black of the Arctic Institute, and an Inuk, Alexis, carried out ornithological research in Pelly Bay, exploring by canoe up the Kellett and Arrowsmith rivers. [*Arctic Circular*, 1958, p. 12]

CHAPTER TEN

IN SEARCH OF GOLD:
THE YUKON AND
NORTHERN BRITISH
COLUMBIA

THE HISTORIC YUKON

"This Yukon River is unique among rivers in that it rises within 15 miles of tidal waters in the Dyea Inlet of the Pacific coast, whence it flows in a northwesterly direction nearly 1000 miles, just crossing the Arctic circle, where it turns southwest through the middle of Alaska, and then flows more than 1200 miles until it reaches the ocean within sight of which it rose; for we may properly call Bering Sea a part of the Pacific Ocean. This grand stream is also surprising in the length of navigation way it gives in proportion to its length, for less than fifteen miles north from where its tiniest streamlets trickle from the summit of Dyea Pass lies beautiful Lake Bennett, whose head is the beginning of steamboat navigation on this noble stream....

"From the head of Bennett to Bering Sea is about 2500 miles by the course of the river, and all this length, with the exception of three and a half miles at the canyon and rapids is navigable, thus all its length, except the first fifteen steep miles down the slope of its source and the three and a half at the canyon is navigable. Can this be said of any other river in the world?" [William Ogilvie, from *Early Days on the Yukon*, 1913]

The Yukon River has seen every manner of floating vessel on it, being the waterway which carried miners, prospectors and hopefuls to the gold-fields beginning in the 1880s and rising to a crescendo during the Klondike madness of 1898. It is a river with such a

strong current that trips on it are almost always made downstream, often drifting with the current. Returns upstream were made on the paddlewheel boats which made regular runs up and down the river after 1898. The upper section of the Yukon was called the Lewes and it was several years before the survey crews realized that it was all one river.

For millennia, the Yukon Valley rivers have, in parts, been canoed by a diversity of First Nations: the Loucheux, now called the Gwich'in, on the Bell-Porcupine; the Han in the central area; and the Tutchone in the south, on the Pelly and the Macmillan.

The Russians explored the Yukon from its mouth on the Bering Sea, I. S. Lukeen of the Russian Trading Company coming up as far as Fort Yukon in 1863. Before that they had stayed close to the coastal area. The Hudson's Bay Company was established at Fort Yukon deep inside Russian territory in 1847 and actively traded throughout what is now the Yukon Territory. In 1867 the United States purchased Alaska from the Russians and Fort Yukon was abandoned for Rampart House, a short distance up the Porcupine River. Later still the post was moved further up the Porcupine to New Rampart House, and when that was closed the post was located at Old Crow.

The history of canoe travel in the Yukon is not as clear-cut as in other parts of northern Canada. In the years following the gold rush of 1898, those miners and

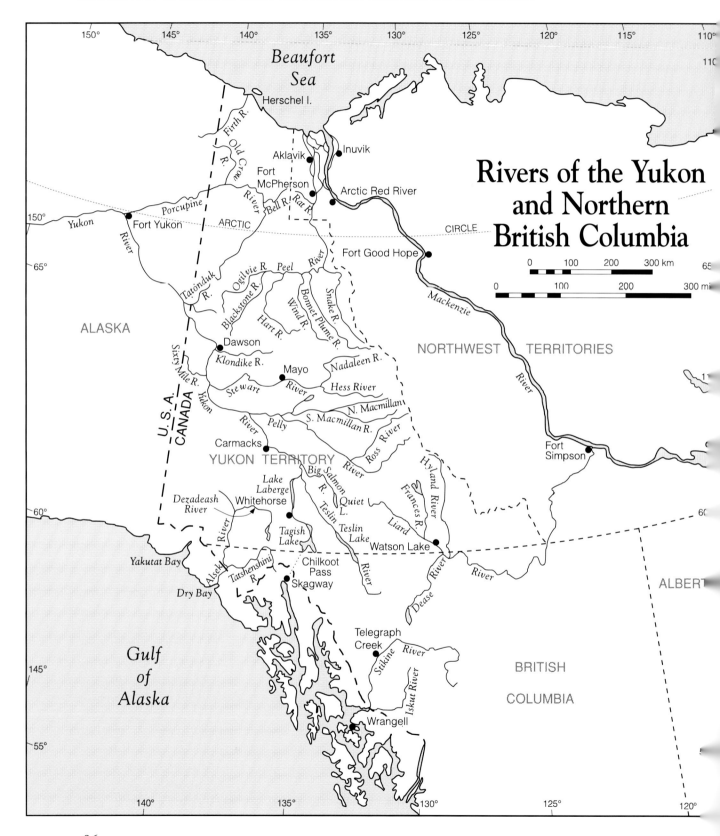

Rivers of the Yukon
and Northern
British Columbia

prospectors who had chosen to stay in the country moved out along the tributaries of the Yukon, built cabins and lived by hunting, trapping and panning for gold. While there was continuous travel on these rivers, it is largely unrecorded because to those who did it, canoeing was just part of their regular way of life. Beginning quite early, small steamboats were used on many of the lower reaches of the larger tributaries to provide transportation as far as navigation would permit. This pattern of life continued until the outbreak of the Second World War brought social change throughout the territory. Many of the cabins and homesteads in the back-country were abandoned as men joined the armed forces. The building of the Alaska Highway during the war, and to a lesser extent, the Canol Pipeline, brought further changes to the nature of travel.

The building of roads made some of the rivers more accessible to canoeists, but recreational canoeists did not begin to make their appearance until the 1970s and the Yukon people did not consider trips on the rivers which were their highways as anything worth recording.

While it may appear that there are gaps in the research on the Yukon, communication with several of the well-known canoeists, guides and outfitters, and also a qualified researcher working on our behalf in Whitehorse, have confirmed these findings.

Among the tributaries, the Porcupine River rising in the Richardson Mountains at the lowest pass of the ranges, is a long and especially important one because it was a major link in fur-trade travel between the forts in the Yukon and on the Mackenzie River, as well as being one of the principal routes for the Klondikers. The other canoeing rivers are the Klondike, North and South Macmillan, Pelly, Stewart, Sixty Mile, Ross, Tatonduk, Teslin and Big Salmon.

Because early Hudson's Bay Company exploration of the Yukon valley used a variety of approaches to and exits from the Yukon River and its tributaries, it is simpler to give the chronology of their explorations between the years 1839 and 1852 in a separate section. Travel, concentrated on the main Yukon River, including the Lewes or upper Yukon, begins immediately after that section, followed by each of the principal tributaries.

HUDSON'S BAY COMPANY EXPLORATION IN THE YUKON

1839 John Bell, from HBC Fort Good Hope, on the Mackenzie River, ascended the Rat River, crossed over to the Bell, later named for him and returned to the Mackenzie River.

1840 Robert Campbell, HBC, with Hoole, his interpreter and two Indians, Lapie and Ketza, journeyed up the Liard to Frances Lake, which he named, and up the Finlayson River, crossing the divide at what became Campbell Creek. There he saw a large river flowing northwest and named it the Pelly for the Governor of the Hudson's Bay Company. He built a raft and floated downstream for a few miles. [*Canadian Geographic*, April 1945, p. 200]

1842 The Hudson's Bay Company constructed Fort Pelly Banks, 31 miles above Hoole Canyon on the upper Pelly River. It burned in 1849 and was abandoned in 1850.

1842 John Bell crossed the Richardson Mountains from Fort McPherson, went up the Rat River and descended the Bell River and the Porcupine for 100 miles, with two voyageurs, Wilson and Boucher, a Rat Indian guide and an Indian interpreter. They built a raft for the downstream trip which they used until they found Indian hunting canoes. The Indian guide deserted at the Porcupine River and the group returned to Fort McPherson. [Karamanski, p. 205; Coates and Morrison, p. 21]

1843 Robert Campbell returned to the Pelly with Hoole, two French-Canadians and three Indians from Fort Pelly Banks, built canoes and descended the river to the confluence with another large river which he named the Lewes. Having also seen the mouths of two other rivers, he named them the Ross and the Macmillan and returned to Frances Lake. [*Canadian Geographic*, April 1945; Sheldon, p. 251; the diary of Robert Campbell's exploration of the Pelly River was printed by the *Manitoba Free Press* in 1885]

1845 John Bell explored the Porcupine River to its mouth with two engagés and two Indians, in birchbark canoes which they constructed at Summit Lake, the height of land. They returned upriver. [Karamanski, p. 222]

1846   Lapierre House, a half-way trading post, was built on the Bell River. [Coates and Morrison, p. 22]

1847   Alexander Hunter Murray, with his wife Anne, went over the mountains from Fort McPherson to Lapierre House in the early spring. Murray settled his wife there with an Indian woman and went back to Fort McPherson. He returned in June with Manuel and Tarshee and they set off from Lapierre House with trading goods in a river boat, down the Porcupine to the Yukon where he built a trading post, Fort Yukon. Murray returned up the Porcupine to Lapierre House in 1848 and found that his wife had given birth to their first child. [Murray, 1910]

1848   Robert Campbell went down the Pelly to its confluence with the Lewes, or Yukon, and built Fort Selkirk. [Coates and Morrison, p. 24]

1851   Robert Campbell continued his exploration of the Yukon down to Fort Yukon where he met Alexander Murray. Campbell and Murray ascended the Porcupine to Lapierre House, crossed the Richardson Mountains to Fort McPherson and went up the Mackenzie to Fort Simpson, thereby completing a circle, Campbell having originally gone up the Liard to his post from Fort Simpson. [Karamanski, p. 266]

1852   Robert Campbell descended the Yukon and went up the Porcupine, down the Rat and Peel and up the Mackenzie to Fort Simpson. Fort Selkirk, at the confluence of the Yukon and Pelly rivers, was attacked by Chilkoots and abandoned. Campbell continued out by snow-shoe to Minnesota and then to London to try unsuccessfully to persuade the Committee of the Hudson's Bay Company to rebuild the fort. [Karamanski, p. 270; Coates and Morrison, p. 25]

YUKON

1835-38   *Russians under Glasunoff explored up the Yukon from the coast to the mouth of the Pelly which they called Kwikhpak. [Dawson]*

1850s   *Rev. Robert McDonald travelled up and down the Yukon and Porcupine rivers with headquarters at Fort Yukon, working among the Indians. He died at Fort MacPherson in 1910. [Ogilvie, p. 85]*

1866   *Mr. Byrnes from British Columbia crossed the Tahko Pass to one of the sources of the Yukon River and reached the lakes close to the site of Fort Selkirk, nearly 450 miles. [Schwatka, p. 117]*

1867   *Frank Ketchum, Saint John, New Brunswick, and Michael Labarge, Montreal, employed by the Western Union Telegraph Company, ascended the Yukon River from Fort Yukon to the mouth of the Lewes River, i.e. the confluence with the Pelly, and returned downstream. [Dawson, p. 142B]*

1869   *The first river steamer, named* Yukon, *was launched on the lower Yukon River.*

1869   *Captain Raymond surveyed the lower Yukon and established the fact that Fort Yukon was on American territory. The Americans evicted the Hudson's Bay Company from Fort Yukon, having purchased Alaska from the Russians in 1867. The Hudson's Bay Company removed their fort a short distance up the Porcupine River to Rampart House, not realizing that it was still just over the border in American territory. [Schwatka, p. 279; Wright, A., 1976]*

1873   *Rev. William Bompas, Anglican, travelled to the upper Yukon River during the summer and returned downstream to Fort Yukon, continuing up the Porcupine, Mackenzie, Slave and Athabasca, on his way out to London to be consecrated bishop. [Cody, p. 141]*

1878   George Holt, private gold prospector, was the first non-native to enter the Yukon from the Pacific coast. He crossed either the Chilkoot or the White Pass to the upper Yukon or Lewes River, followed it down to Marsh Lake and to the confluence with the Teslin River. He returned to the coast by the same route. [Cooke and Holland, p. 243]

1880 Edward Bean led a prospecting party of twenty-five men, which included R. Steel and George Langtry from Sitka, to Lake Lindeman where they built boats and descended the Yukon to Teslin River. They ascended the Teslin and returned they way they had come. [Dawson, p. 179B]

1880 Johnny Mackenzie and "Slim Jim" Wynn came down the Yukon from Lake Lindeman to prospect. [*Ibid.*, p. 180B]

1881 George Langtry, P. McGlinchy and two others descended the Yukon to the Big Salmon and ascended it for 200 miles. [*Ibid.*]

1881 A party of Arizona prospectors went down the Yukon and 200 miles up the Stewart. [Ogilvie, p. 106]

1882 Joseph Ladue and William Moore, private gold prospectors, crossed the Chilkoot Pass and descended the Yukon River to Fort Reliance, just below present-day Dawson. [Cooke and Holland, p. 248]

1882 Two prospecting parties descended the upper Yukon and ascended the Pelly to Hoole Canyon, some going beyond the canyon. [Dawson, p. 180B]

pre-1883 Another party on a prospecting tour, including a young lawyer from the Eastern United States, drifted down the upper Yukon River to Fort Selkirk and ascended the Pelly. [Schwatka, p. 179]

1883 Richard Poplin, Charles McConkey, Benjamin Beach and C. Marks went down the Yukon and up the Stewart to the McQuesten, prospecting as they went. [Ogilvie, p. 108]

1883 Lieut. Frederick Schwatka, Dr. George F. Wilson, surgeon, Charles A. Homan, topographer and photographer, Sergeant Charles A. Gloster, artist, Corporal Shircliff, Private Roth all of the U.S. Army Engineers, and J.B. McIntosh, miner with Alaskan experience came up the Inland Passage by steamer, hired a large number of Indians to pack them across the Chilkoot Pass and travelled the full length of the Yukon River. They built a large raft, 16 feet by 42 feet, double thickness, with two elevated decks and a steering sweep at the bow or the stern, launched it on Lake Bennett, towing a canoe for emergencies or exploration. After travelling 1303 miles by raft, they abandoned it at a trading post just beyond the mouth of the Tanana River in Alaska and completed the journey on a schooner. The expedition was the result of the American army's need to find out more about Alaska in case it should be called upon to defend the territory. Schwatka grandly named all the geographical features along the route, especially in the Yukon, for American and European dignitaries and scientists, ignoring the local or Indian names. Not all of the names have stuck. [Schwatka, 1894; *Century Magazine*, May – October, 1885, pp. 738, 819, 970; Coates and Morrison, p. 63]

1884 Michael Hess came over the Chilkoot Pass and down the Yukon River, prospecting many of its tributaries. [Coutts, p. 126]

1884 Poplin, McConkey, Beach and Marks were again up the Stewart River, returning up the Yukon in the fall going out over Dyea Pass. [Ogilvie, p. 108]

1885 George Carmack, California, with seven miners crossed the Chilkoot Pass and went down the Yukon River to the Stewart River. [Coutts, p. 48]

1885 Poplin returned with Peter Wybourg, Francis Morphet and Jeremiah Bertrand, descending the Yukon River and going up the Stewart where they had great success. [Ogilvie, p. 108]

1885 Willis Everette, ethnologist, was sent down the Yukon River by the U.S. Army as a civilian scout, following the route of Frederick Schwatka. He spent a month at the mouth of the White River, south of Dawson, and wintered farther down the Yukon River in Alaska. [Wickersham, p. 104; Sherwood, p. 103]

1887 William Ogilvie, Dominion Land Surveyor with the Dept. of the Interior, with Capt. William Moore and a crew, using two canoes and a boat which they built at Lake Bennett, surveyed for the Alaska-Yukon boundary. They canocd the Yukon River "making a reasonably accurate topographical survey of 640 miles of the river" and wintered on Fortymile River. George Carmack, Skookum Jim Mason and Tagish Charlie had helped to pack supplies over the Pass for the surveyors. One hundred or more miners were wintering in the territory that year. [Ogilvie, p. 53 and 133]

1887   Dawson and McEvoy – see Stikine

1889   Prof. Israel C. Russell, United States Geological Survey, came up the Yukon by steamer from St. Michael, Alaska, on the Bering Strait to Fort Selkirk and continued up the upper Yukon with a group of miners, poling and towing an open boat that they had built. Crossing the Chilkoot Pass in late autumn weather, they reached Dyea. Russell, with one Indian, canoed down the Lynn Canal to Juneau. [*Journal of the Am. Geo. Soc. of New York*, 1895, Vol. 27, No. 2, pp. 143-60]

1889   Arthur Harper, with his family, travelled up the Yukon River on the steamer with Prof. Russell to Fort Selkirk where he established a trading post. [*Ibid.* p. 153]

1891   Lieut. Frederick Schwatka, Charles Willard Hayes and a prospector, Mark Russell, having come from Juneau up the Taku River in a 2-ton dugout canoe, with seven Indians as boatmen and packers, crossed to the Teslin River. The three men, using two collapsible canvas canoes, continued down the Teslin and Yukon rivers to the site of Fort Selkirk. The party then struck out overland to the southwest, with prospector, Frank Bowker and eight Indians, over the great interior plateau toward the St. Elias Mountains. When they reached Copper Creek, the original three men continued, hiking down the valley of the White River. With Nicolai, the chief of the Copper River Indians, they continued down to the coast in a large skin boat, manned by ten Indians. [*National Geographic*, May, 1892, p. 117-62]

1893   Frederick Funston, making a botanical collection for the U.S. Department of Agriculture, with McConnell, a Canadian prospector, Thompson, a miner from Idaho, and Mattern, a German miner, crossed the Chilkoot Pass, travelled down lakes Lindeman and Tagish which were still frozen. On Lake Marsh, McConnell, Funston and Mattern built an 18-foot flat-bottomed skiff from green timber (Thompson having joined another group of miners) and travelled down the Yukon River to the mouth of Fortymile River. The following year, Funston continued down the Yukon River alone in the same boat all the way to the coast of Alaska. [*Scribner's Magazine*, July-December, 1896, pp. 572-85]

1893   Warburton Pike, Smith (ex-HBC manager from Lower Post), and two Red River Métis cousins, Archie and Alick Flett, left Lower Post on the Liard in winter and moved their outfit up the Liard and Frances rivers to Frances Lake. A local Indian, Secatz, travelled with them as guide and interpreter as far as the Pelly River and another Indian, Narchilla, joined them as a guide at Frances Lake. With dogs and sleighs they hauled the canoe up the ice to Yus-ez-uh and then to Lake McPherson. They followed Narchilla Creek up to the height of land and named it, found and named Ptarmigan Creek where they waited for the ice to break up. The Indian guides turned back and Pike and his companions paddled the last few miles of Ptarmigan Creek to the Pelly Lakes. They explored north and east, considered crossing to the Mackenzie but an accident to a rifle decided their course down the Pelly, Yukon and Kuskokwim rivers to the Bering Sea. They returned south by schooner and ship down the Pacific coast. [Pike, *Through the Sub-Arctic Forest*, 1896]

1895   William Ogilvie came over Dyea Pass, again with Skookum Jim Mason and Tagish Charlie as his packers, and canoed down the Yukon to the boundary where he had wintered previously, repeating his survey. His plan to return up-river after the spring break-up changed when he was asked to stay as Commissioner of the International Boundary Commission. The mandate of the Commission collapsed, winter closed the river to travel, so in 1897 he travelled up the Yukon to Fort Selkirk and out by steamer through St. Michael, Alaska. [Ogilvie, p. 152]

1896 There were about 500 miners along the Yukon River in the area of Forty Mile, some wintering in the territory, others travelling out up the river.

1897 Hazard Wells, Frank Walthers, John Duffy, S.W. Foote and George Fulk, American prospectors, travelled down the Yukon River in a 26-foot hand-built boat. [Wells, 1984]

1897 J.H.E. Secretan, with five men, and two Peterborough canoes, came up from Victoria by ship, crossed the Chilkoot Pass, and waited at Lake Lindeman for break-up. They built a 26-foot boat at Lake Bennett in which they sailed, rowed and drifted down to Dawson. Secretan continued down the Yukon by steamer to St. Michael the same year. [Secretan, 1898]

1897-98 The Klondike gold-rush brought thousands down the Yukon in every sort of conveyance.

1898 Henry Toke Munn, acting for the British-America Corporation, undertook to pilot the staff of the Bank of British North America to Dawson. The group consisted of David Doig, Finlayson, Stow, and "Fred", carrying $225,000 of the bank's money. They canoed from Lake Bennett to Dawson in three canoes. Munn continued down the Yukon River alone in a 16-foot canoe with $5000 cash to St. Michael (80 miles from the mouth of the river) to buy cord-wood and returned up-river in the company's steamer. [Munn, pp. 81-114]

1899 Bishop Bompas travelled up the Yukon River to lakes Bennett and Atlin, visiting Indian camps along the way, and returned down river to Forty Mile. [Cody, p. 287]

1899 G.M. Skirving, RNWMP, travelled down the Yukon and up the Porcupine by canoe and steamer to Old Crow in search of three gold-seekers lost on the way to the Klondike. At Old Crow he hired a dog team, pushed on up the Bell River and over the mountains to Fort McPherson. He returned to Dawson on foot. [Cooke and Holland, p. 285]

Joseph Keele, a topographer with the Geological Survey, made a remarkable exploration in 1907-08 across the mountains from the Yukon to the Mackenzie. For this the Keele River was named in his honour. [GSC collection]

1900s Hudson Stuck, Episcopal Bishop of Alaska, came over the White Pass by rail with his 32-foot motor launch *Pelican* and travelled the length of the Yukon River. [Stuck, 1917]

1904 Stratford Tollemache, with a partner, went down the Yukon River by rowboat to the Hootalinqua and continued alone to Fort Selkirk at the confluence with the Pelly River. [Tollemache, 1912]

1907 A joint U.S.-Canadian survey party was working along the banks of the Yukon River for the Alaska-Yukon boundary survey. [Thompson, Don, v. 2, p. 197]

1907-08 Joseph Keele, for the Geological Survey, assisted by Charles Wilson, travelled from the Yukon up the Pelly and Ross, investigated the areas drained by those rivers, crossed over Christie Pass and travelled down the Gravel, now named Keele, to the Mackenzie. [*Ibid.*, p. 92]

1926 Harold A. Innis and W.K. Gibb, in an 18-foot Yukon river boat with oars, using the spare oar as a rudder in the current, travelled down the Yukon from Whitehorse to Circle, Alaska. They also rigged up a sail, travelled 12 hours and about 60 miles a day. They travelled out from Circle on the steamer up-river and crossed to Skagway. [*Canadian Geographic*, March 1934, p. 123]

1926 Pierre Berton with his parents, Francis and Laura, and sister travelled the Yukon River between Dawson and Skagway. [Berton, 1973]

1929 Amos Burg and Fred Hill, in an 18-foot canvas-covered spruce-ribbed canoe, decked at the bow, paddled north from Juneau to Skagway. They took the train over White Pass and launched their canoe on Lake Bennett, canoeing down the Yukon River to Russian Mission where the canoe was wrecked (empty) in a raging storm, about 150 miles short of the coast. [*National Geographic*, July 1930, pp. 85-126]

1932 Francis George Berton travelled alone down the Yukon from Whitehorse to Dawson in his hand-built motorboat, the *Bluenose*. [Berton, p. 87]

1950 Charlie Wolf from Fairbanks, Alaska, travelled by bus to Whitehorse and alone, in a 13-foot Grumman, made the first of many trips down the Yukon River, canoeing on this occasion from Whitehorse to Circle, Alaska. [McGuire, p. xiii, p. 35]

1963 Bob Allensworth and Ed Ferrell, using a 17-foot aluminum canoe with a 3-horsepower motor, put in at Lake Bennett and followed the trail of '98 down the Yukon River as far as Circle, Alaska. [*Beaver*, Autumn 1964, p. 48]

1970 A joint American-Canadian expedition, led by Alan Innes-Taylor, Yukon Government and well known local river-boat captain and guide, made a September canoe trip from Lake Laberge down the Yukon River to Fortymile River. The group included H.K. Eidsvik, Bruce Harvey and Tatro, of Canadian Parks and Wildlife Service, Ben Gale and Bob Howe of U.S. National Parks, Burt Silcock, Alaska Bureau of Land Management, J. Deagan, Alaskan Government, Carl Malvihill, Skagway Historical Society, and Gary McLaughlin, Yukon Government. [Parks Canada files]

1970 Charlie Wolf and Tom McGuire, from Fairbanks, Alaska, got a lift by truck to Whitehorse. Lake Laberge was not yet clear of ice and on the advice of Alan Innes-Taylor they put their 17-foot Grumman into the Teslin River at Johnson's Crossing. They canoed down the Teslin and Yukon rivers, following the Yukon to Holy Cross in Alaska. There they flew to the Kuskokwim River

and followed it from Aniak to Bethel. This was one of Wolf's many trips down the Yukon River but the first time that he had gone beyond Tanana, Alaska. Wolf celebrated his seventieth birthday in Bethel and planned to continue making long northern canoe trips. In a letter to Eric Morse he described every conceivable type of transportation in use on the Yukon River. [McGuire, 1977; Morse files, p. 12]

1970 Arvo Koppel and five other McGill University students built a raft at Johnson's Crossing on the Teslin River and floated down the Teslin and Yukon rivers, planning to go as far as Tanana. They had a small rubber raft with them as well. [McGuire, p. 77]

1970 Tom Green and Mat Opack, from Minnesota, in Klepper kayaks, started at Whitehorse and travelled down the Yukon River, planning to go the full length of the river. [*Ibid.*, p. 83]

1972 Eugene Cantin, using a Klepper folding kayak, made a solo trip from Lake Bennett to Tanana, Alaska, 1200 miles down the Yukon River. [Cantin, 1973]

1972 Pierre and Janet Berton, their children, Penny, Pamela, Patsie, Peter, Paul, Peggy and Perri, nephew Berton Woodward, Robert Holmes, with crew Skip Burns, his wife Cheri, Scotty Jeffers and Ross Miller, using three motorized inflatable boats and a freight canoe, drifted down the Yukon River from Lake Bennett to Dawson. Berton recreated his father's 1898 Klondike journey, as well as his own childhood trips on the river. [Berton, 1973]

1972 A family from New Jersey, including three young children, canoed down the Teslin (sic) and Yukon rivers. [*Ibid.* pp. 103-04] – see Harrison – Pelly]

1972 A lone canoeist, having left his party in Whitehorse, was travelling down the Yukon River. [*Ibid.*, p. 105]

1972 Keith Tryck, Bob Clark, Paul Crews, Jr. and Jerry Wallace, having come over the Chilkoot Pass in the early spring, went up the Homan (King) River and cut logs to build a 37-foot by 22-foot raft, which they launched on Lake Bennett. Carrying a canoe on the raft, they poled and sailed down the Yukon River to Dawson, reaching it late in August. They returned the following summer and continued down the Yukon to Ruby, Alaska, where they built a cabin from the logs of the raft, staying until it was possible to complete the trip to the coast by dog-team with an Alaskan Inuit. They made a video of the journey for *National Geographic.* [Tryck, 1980]

BELL–PORCUPINE

The Porcupine River rises high in the Nahoni Range of the Ogilvie Mountains and describes a semicircle in its course, first flowing northeast, then due north and finally due west into the Yukon River. The upper reaches of the Porcupine, before its confluence with the Bell River, were seldom travelled. The route universally used is from Summit Lake, down the Little Bell, Bell and Porcupine rivers to Fort Yukon on the Yukon River.

1860-62 *Robert Kennicott of the Smithsonian Institution, having wintered in Fort Simpson, travelled down the Mackenzie, up the Peel and Rat and down the Bell-Porcupine to Fort Yukon where he spent the winter. He travelled back and forth on the Rat-Porcupine system between Fort McPherson and Fort Yukon until 1862 collecting flora and fauna. [Coates and Morrison, p. 34]*

1862 *Rev. William Kirkby, with two Indians, travelled the Peel-Rat-Porcupine to Fort Yukon. He stayed seven days and returned by the same route to Fort McPherson. [Cody, p. 55-56]*

1862-63 *Oblate priests travelled the Rat-Bell-Porcupine route to Fort Yukon and returned. [Wright, A., 1976]*

1866 *Rev. Robert McDonald canoed up the Porcupine-Bell, down the Rat-Peel rivers and down the Mackenzie to Fort Simpson. [Cody, p. 57-58]*

1869 *Rev. William Bompas canoed the Mackenzie-Peel-Rat-Bell-Porcupine route to Fort Yukon. He returned up the Porcupine River and down the Rat to Fort McPherson and spent the winter in the Mackenzie delta among the Inuit. [Cody, p. 107]*

1872 *Arthur "Cariboo" Harper with Frederick Hart and others left the Omineca goldfields in northern Brit-*

ish Columbia, canoed down the Liard and Mackenzie rivers, went on the Peel-Rat-Porcupine route, reaching Fort Yukon in 1873. [Coutts, p. 121]

1872 *Oblate priests travelled the Rat-Bell-Porcupine route to Fort Yukon and returned.*

1873 *Leroy Napoleon "Jack" McQuesten and Alfred Mayo had met Harper and Hart while wintering at the mouth of the Fort Nelson River on the Liard. The two groups split up in 1872 to travel separately. In 1873 McQuesten and Mayo went down the Liard and Mackenzie, took the Peel-Rat-Porcupine route to Fort Yukon, reaching it just before Harper and Hart arrived. [Ibid., p. 174]*

1876 Rev. Robert McDonald travelled up the Porcupine and Bell and down the Peel and Mackenzie to Fort Simpson for the Anglican Synod, returning to the Yukon by the same route. [Cody, p. 180]

1888 R.G. McConnell, GSC, having wintered at Fort Providence, (see Liard) travelled to Fort McPherson by dog-sled and canoe, went down the Bell-Porcupine route to Fort Yukon, up the Yukon and Lewes rivers, across the Chilkoot Pass and out by steamer. At Fort McPherson McConnell met William Ogilvie who was making the circuit in the opposite direction. [GSC Memoir 284; Zaslow, p. 160, map p. 158]

1888 William Ogilvie, having wintered at Fortymile River, (see Yukon) went up the Porcupine River and continued up the Mackenzie and Slave rivers, surveying them for the Dept. of the Interior. He went out to the railway at Edmonton – a canoe journey of 2500 miles. [Ogilvie, p. 141]

1888 F. F. Sparks, a member of William Ogilvie's party, travelling from Fortymile River to Fort McPherson found the source of the Porcupine to be a small hot-spring. [Coutts, p. 213]

1889 Prof. Israel Russell, with a group from the U.S. Coast and Geodetic Survey, ascended the Porcupine River by steamer for ten days to a point just west of the Alaska-Yukon border. This was the first steamer to ascend the Porcupine River. The survey crew remained behind while Prof. Russell returned down river and continued up the Yukon

River. [*Journal of the Am. Geo. Soc. of New York*, 1895, Vol. 27, pp. 143-60]

1891 The Hudson's Bay Company built New Rampart House in Yukon Territory and abandoned the original Rampart house which was just inside American territory. [Wright, 1976]

1892 Bishop Bompas, having wintered at Rampart House, canoed down the Porcupine River and met Mrs. Bompas, coming up the Yukon River by steamer from St. Michael. They continued together up the Yukon to Forty Mile. [Cody, p. 260]

1892 Rev. G.C. Wallis and Mrs. Wallis went up the Porcupine River to Rampart House. [*Ibid.*, p. 263]

1897 Daniel Cadzow, a Scot, left Edmonton for the Klondike by the Athabasca-Slave-Mackenzie-Peel-Rat-Porcupine rivers. He reached the Klondike in 1899. [Coutts, p. 41]

1898 "Buffalo" Jones, with John Rea as guide, after wintering in the Barrens, descended the Mackenzie River, went up the Peel to Fort McPherson, crossed the divide and descended the Porcupine and the Yukon to the sea. [Preble, p. 81]

1898-99 After midsummer and throughout the following winter some 500 Klondikers descended on Fort McPherson. We can assume that all of them made the trip over the Rat River portage and down the Bell-Porcupine. [MacGregor, p. 150]

1899 Andrew Jackson Stone, from the American Museum of Natural History, having wintered at Fort McPherson, (see Liard) continued his collection of bird and mammal specimens down the Porcupine and down the Yukon to St Michael, boarding a steamer there for Seattle. [*Bulletin. American Museum of Natural History*, Vol. XIII, pp. 31-62]

1905 Charles Camsell, for the Geological Survey, with Fred Camsell, Jack Deslauriers, Louis Cardinal, F. Heron and Percy Nash, with three canoes, having completed their survey up the Stewart and Beaver rivers, crossed the divide and descended the Wind and Peel rivers to Fort MacPherson. They continued down the Mackenzie to the delta, returning upstream to Fort McPherson, travelled the Peel-Rat-Bell-Porcupine-Yukon rivers. [Camsell, p. 179; Coutts, p. 288]

1906 Elihu Stewart, Canadian Government superintendent of forestry who had been studying timber in the Mackenzie basin, concluded his tour of duty with a recreational trip. He had brought a Peterborough canoe with him on the steamers from Edmonton. At Fort McPherson he chose to leave the canoe and portage the 80 miles with five Loucheux Indians, Charlie Fox and his wife, John Tizzard and his son Jacob, and John Quatlot, the leader, and their dogs. The Indians, from Old Crow, accomplished the portage in less than five days. A nervous Stewart went down the Bell and Porcupine in a narrow, decked birchbark canoe with John Quatlot, who did not permit him to paddle the heavily loaded and tippy canoe. Quatlot and Jacob Tizzard took him down the river to Rampart House, where he engaged a Métis and his son with a rowboat to take him to Fort Yukon. His return up the Yukon was by steamer. [Stewart, 1913]

1906 V. Stefansson was a fellow-passenger with Elihu Stewart travelling north on the steamer *Wrigley*. He accompanied Stewart on the first few miles of the Rat portage and helped him set up his first camp and returned to Fort McPherson waiting to go north. While there he received the news that the Arctic explorers Leffingwell, Mikkelson and Storkerson were safe and was anxious to telegraph the news to the outside before the false story of their deaths reached the world via the HBC steamer *Wrigley* at Athabasca Landing. He walked from Fort McPherson over the portage route, built a raft, 20 feet by 10 feet, carrying a fireplace of stones so that he could travel without stopping, and rafted down the Bell and Porcupine rivers to Eagle City, Alaska, to reach the telegraph line. [Stefansson, pp. 205-40]

1906 A group of non-native men with an Indian guide were headed for the upper Porcupine River to spend the autumn and winter trapping. A young man whose father was important in the city and port of Montreal was on the upper Porcupine preparing to spend the winter. [Stewart, pp. 144, 146]

1909 Bishop I.O. Stringer and Rev. Charles F. Johnson, using a Peterborough canoe, and with guides Enoch Moses and Joseph Vittrekwa and lay missionary, W.H. Fry, with a small canvas canoe, to accompany them to the head of the Rat River, set out from Fort McPherson on September 1, down the Peel and up the Rat rivers. After a few days Enoch Moses was taken ill and Bishop Stringer with Joseph Vittrekwa returned with him to Fort McPherson, losing more than a week in doing so. With ice forming and a shortage of provisions they reached the divide on September 20. Stringer and Johnson continued down the Bell River but were stopped by ice before they reached the Porcupine. They cached the canoe and their non-essential equipment and without snowshoes struck out across the mountains for Fort McPherson. After twenty-four days of hardship and near starvation they reached the Peel River and were taken to Fort McPherson by Indians. The Bishop made the journey over the Rat-Porcupine a month later with Indians by dog sled, recovering the cached canoe. Johnson went later still with the police patrol. [Peake, pp. 118-26; *Maclean's*, July 9, 1955]

1910 Hudson Stuck in the *Pelican*, a 32-foot motor launch, went to the Ramparts, halfway up the Porcupine River, 70 miles below Old Crow and returned down the river. [Stuck, pp. 221-47]

1911 Robert Service, having come from Edmonton by canoe and steamer (see Athabasca) reached Fort McPherson. He had bought a birchbark canoe at Fort Resolution and being unable to find a guide to take him up over the Rat Portage, he joined up with a Scottish trader, McTosh, his wife and a trapper named Jake Skilly. Along with two Indians they laboured up the Rat River with McTosh's heavy scow loaded with trade goods and furs. When they reached the top of the pass, Service struck out on his own and canoed down the Bell and Porcupine, joined later by Skilly who

had had a falling out with McTosh and who was also suffering severely from nicotine deprivation. At the trading post at Ramparts they could not land because of an outbreak of smallpox. They continued down the Porcupine until they met a stern-wheeler and took passage to Dawson up the Yukon. [Service, 1945]

1917 Archdeacon Hudson Stuck and Bishop Stringer travelled up the Porcupine in Stuck's mission launch the *Pelican*. [Peake, p. 138]

1921 Michael Mason, Harry Anthony, Jim, Fred, and the "Old Man", having been prospecting for oil during the winter along the Mackenzie opposite Norman Wells, built a 28-foot scow at Fort Norman and rowed and drifted down to the beginning of the Mackenzie Delta. They rowed up the Peel to Fort McPherson, portaged over the Rat Portage using dogs and the help of Andrew, an Indian from Fort McPherson. At the Bell River they built a boat and went down the Bell-Porcupine rivers to Fort Yukon. [Mason, 1924]

1921 Lokke, Hester and Burnell made the trip from Fort McPherson over the Rat portage and down Bell-Porcupine rivers at the same time as the Mason group. [*Ibid.*, p. 206]

1922 Michael Mason and Dave McRae, in a homemade canoe with a sail, travelled down the Mackenzie from Fort Smith to Fort McPherson, portaged over the Rat Portage, built a canvas boat on the Bell River during a heavy snow storm and canoed down the Bell-Porcupine rivers to Old Crow. [*Ibid.*, p. 214]

1924 Bishop and Mrs. Stringer travelled down the Yukon to Fort Yukon on the launch *Hazel B* and then up the Porcupine on a smaller launch, the *Kemath*, taking supplies to the various missions up to the head of navigation, 15 miles below Lapierre House, at the confluence of the Bell and Eagle rivers. With three Indians and six packing dogs and an elderly Indian, William Blindgoose, too old to make the trip alone, they hiked nine days over the Rat Portage to Fort McPherson. Mrs. Stringer was thought to be the first non-native woman to make this trip. [Peake, p. 140]

1926 Clara Coltman Rogers (later Lady Vyvyan) and Gwen Dorrien Smith from England reached Fort McPherson on the HBC steamers. Neither of them had ever canoed, and they expected to be able to go across the entire Rat-Porcupine system with guides. At Fort McPherson they were informed that Lapierre House, where they planned to obtain guides for the down-river trip, had been closed two years before. They hired two Loucheux Indians, Lazarus Sittichili and Jimmy Koe, to take them up the Rat River and the two women canoed alone down the Bell and Porcupine to Old Crow where another guide was available to take them on to Fort Yukon. On the river boat up the Yukon they travelled in company with Harold Innis. [Vyvyan, 1961; *Canadian Geographic*, Jan. 1931, p. 48; Hoyle in Hodgins and Hobbs, eds. p. 130]

1928 Fenley Hunter, with Albert Dease and George Ball, having come from Fort Simpson on the HBC boat *Distributor*, reached Fort McPherson on September 13. They abandoned the canoe which had brought them from Peace River Crossing and up the Nahanni, hired two Loucheux Indians, Andrew Tshoe and Edward Snowshoe with five packing dogs and went over the Rat River trail to Lapierre House, George Ball carrying the outboard motor. On September 21 they started from Lapierre House in a 12-foot canoe and went down the Bell and Porcupine rivers to Salmon Cache, the canoe icing up on the Bell River. There they got an 18-foot Chestnut canoe and continued on to Fort Yukon, the Porcupine River freezing up behind them. They had travelled 3000 miles in ninety days. [NAC – Hunter's journal]

1929 Amos Burg and Dr. George Rebec travelled from Waterways, down the Athabasca-Slave, in a flotilla of three canoes pulled by a skiff (see Taltson), running some of the rapids in the Slave River. At Fort Resolution, Amos Burg canoed alone along Great Slave Lake to Hay River. Dr. Rebec went by launch and at Hay River the launch took both men and canoe to Fort Providence. They canoed down the Mackenzie to Fort Norman where Dr. Rebec left to return by HBC steamer. Amos Burg joined by Hans, a trapper, using a dory with a motor trailing two canoes, continued down-river to Arctic Red River, Burg going on to Fort McPherson. There he sold his canoe, hired a Loucheux guide, Abraham for the hike up to the height of land at Lapierre House, where he inflated a 10-pound rubber boat and continued his trip down the Bell and Porcupine rivers to Old Crow. From Old Crow he continued on to Fort Yukon as a passenger in an Indian motor scow. [*National Geographic*, August 1931, p. 127]

1927 Shields and Chase crossed by canoe from the Mackenzie via the Porcupine River to Fort Yukon. [Bendy, 1936]

1931 Albert Johnson, who became known as the "Mad Trapper of Rat River", rafted down the Peel River from deep inside the Yukon Territory, bought a large canoe at Fort McPherson and poled and paddled his way up the Rat River for 15 miles. [Anderson, F., 1982]

1933? Raymond, Marion and Max Diesel, brothers from Lac La Biche, Alberta, using a Chestnut Prospector with a "kicker", returned home from Point Separation in the Mackenzie Delta, up the Mackenzie, Peel-Rat-Little Bell-Bell-Porcupine route to Fort Yukon. There they took the steamboat to Dawson City and went out by train. [Personal communication – Ray Chipeniuk]

1935 Ben Ferrier with a companion, having canoed down the Athabasca-Slave-Mackenzie, went up the Rat River and canoed down the Porcupine River to Fort Yukon. [*Explorers Journal*, September 1967]

1936 W. R. Bendy and his wife Sylvia, with Indian guide Paul Koe and his twelve-year-old son Fred as far as Summit Lake, came from South America to travel down the Bell-Porcupine system to Fort Yukon by canoe. [Bendy, *The Rat River and McDougall's Pass*, 1936 – photostat held in the library of Northern Affairs, Ottawa]

1936 Two men from Ontario, T.J. Wood and "Duke" Duxberry, canoed the Bell-Porcupine rivers, having first come down the Athabasca and Mackenzie rivers. [Bendy]

1936 Four college students from Chicago with a professor went up the Rat River. The professor drowned, or died of other causes. The students abandoned the trip and took the body down to Aklavik, passing the Bendys on the way. [Bendy]

1938 Alden Hayes – see Mackenzie

1939 Dr. B.F. Ederer from Minnesota went from Aklavik to Fort Yukon up the Peel, Husky Channel and followed the Rat-Little Bell-Bell-Porcupine route in a canoe with a small motor. [*Beaver*, September 1941, p. 19]

1940 Dr. B.F. Ederer repeated the trip from Aklavik to Fort Yukon as a guide to two young Americans, Bob and Jerry, who were selling Bibles and Home Doctor books in the north. [*Ibid.*]

1940 Elkin Morris and his wife went with Indian guides from Fort McPherson to Summit Lake and canoed on to Alaska. [*Ibid.*]

1952 Otto W. Geist, palaeontologist from the University of Alaska, sponsored by the Explorers Club, explored the Old Crow River basin in a river boat with two Indians. [Parks Canada files]

1953 Otto Geist went up the Porcupine with Victor Peterson in a river boat with six Indians from Fort Yukon, Moses Lord, Donald, Steve and Gordon Frost, Abraham Thomas, and Lazarus Charlie, and explored the cave at the foot of a 3272-foot mountain. [Parks Canada files]

1957 Anne E. Harmuth-Hoene and Henning F. Harmuth canoed from Hay River, down the Mackenzie River, and followed the Peel-Rat-Bell-Porcupine route, continuing upstream on the Yukon to Fort Reliance, just below the confluence with the Klondike River. [*Nastawgan*, Autumn 1984, p. 1-4]

1958 Alan Cooke canoed from Aklavik up the Mackenzie to Fort McPherson and followed the Peel-Rat-Porcupine route to Fort Yukon. [Morse files, p. 1]

1965 Eric and Pamela Morse, Terk Bayly, Bill Sheppard, Jack Goering and David Woods, using three Grumman canoes, canoed from Fort McPherson

The hard work on the Rat is rewarded on the Porcupine in 1965. Jack Goering, Eric Morse (using the communal razor) and Bill Shepperd enjoy a floating lunch. [Pamela Morse]

on the Peel-Rat-Little Bell-Bell-Porcupine route to Old Crow. To make up for the time lost on the upstream section they hired a motorboat to take them down as far as Rampart House and canoed on to Fort Yukon. [Morse, *Freshwater Saga*, p. 159]

1966 Don Ross – see Liard

1966 Richard Harrington went up the Porcupine River from Fort Yukon by power boat to Old Crow to begin anthropological and archaeological research on the Old Crow River. He was joined soon after by William Irvine and in 1967 by Richard Morlan.

1968 Charlie Wolf, in a 13-foot Grumman, with Elmar and Brigitte Engel in kayaks, began at Fort Nelson, and travelled down the Muskwa, Fort Nelson, Liard, and Mackenzie rivers, and followed the Peel-Rat-Porcupine route to Fort Yukon. This was Charlie Wolf's third time making the trip from Fort Nelson to Fort Yukon. On one trip up the Rat he travelled with William Vittrekwa, his Indian "brother" from Fort McPherson. [McGuire, p. xii, 9, 25, 55, 142; Klein, *Passion for Wilderness*, p. 37]

1968 Bob Matteson and his sons, Rob and Sumner, using one canoe went from Fort McPherson on the Peel-Rat-Little Bell-Bell-Porcupine rivers to Fort Yukon. [Matteson unpublished trip report]

There is no easy way to ascend the Rat River. Jack Goering, Bill Sheppard, David Woods and Terk Bayly, wading in the icy mountain run-off, drag one of the canoes against the swift current in 1965. Head-nets, even in midstream, attest to the ferocity of the mosquitoes. [Eric Morse/Pamela Morse]

1969 Tom Green, Mat Opack, Bill Steger and Tom McGuire, all from Minnesota, paddling Klepper kayaks, started at Jasper, Alberta, and followed the Athabasca-Slave-Mackenzie rivers to Inuvik. They flew to Summit Lake and kayaked down the Bell-Porcupine rivers to Fort Yukon, Steger and McGuire continuing down the Yukon River to Galena, Alaska. [McGuire (no relation), p. 83 and 126]

1970 James W. Scott and Wayne Boden, from the U.S. Bureau of the Interior in Alaska, chartered a plane to take them from Dawson to the mouth of the Bell River and canoed down to Fort Yukon. [Parks Canada files]

1971 Priidu Juurand, led a Wild River Survey crew of David McClung, Bill Pisco and Malcolm McIntyre from Summit Lake down the Bell-Porcupine to Fort Yukon. [Parks Canada files]

1971 Verlen Kruger – see Clearwater-Athabasca-Slave

1971? Klaus Streckmann – see Nahanni

1973 Duke Watson, having started on Great Bear Lake with other canoeists, continued down the Bell-Porcupine with W. Dougall, L. Dougall, E. Jenkins, W. Jenkins, J. Ketcham, S. Ketcham and M. Watson. [Personal communication – Watson]

1950-77 Charlie Wolf of Fairbanks, Alaska, in a 13-foot aluminum canoe travelled the Fort McPherson-Mackenzie-Peel-Little Bell-Bell-Porcupine-Fort Yukon route on a regular basis. [*North/Nord*, May/June, 1977 p. 2]

1980 *Jim Boyde and Mark Ostopkowicz, from the Yukon, canoed down the Eagle River, a tributary of the Bell, and continued down the Bell-Porcupine to Old Crow. [Personal communication – Boyde to researcher Hayhurst]*

1983 *Bruce and Carol Hodgins led a Wanapitei adult trip*

198

Nearing the summit of McDougall Pass, the current and the depth of the Rat River diminish and the canoe can be poled. [Pamela Morse]

from Summit Lake down the Bell-Porcupine rivers to Old Crow. [Personal communication – Hodgins]

TATONDUK

The Tatonduk River is a small river with several branches which flows into the Yukon just below the village of Eagle in Alaska. The main branches rise high in the Ogilvie Mountains across the divide from the headwaters of the Porcupine River, while the smaller southern branch rises across the divide from the feeder streams of the Ogilvie River.

1888 William Ogilvie, Dominion Land Surveyor, was the first non-native known to traverse this stream when he and his party travelled its length in the spring on their way from Forty Mile to Fort McPherson. [Coutts, p. 262]

1969 Two men went up-river for 80 miles and down again and submitted a trip report to Parks Canada without names or many details. [Parks Canada files]

pre-1981 Robert Frisch and Paul von Baich explored the Tatonduk Valley on foot and using a home-made wooden raft. [Natural History, August 1982, p. 65]

1988 Steve Read and Hank Harrison canoed down the Yukon River from Whitehorse, went up the Tatonduk, crossed the height of land and down the Miner River to the Porcupine. [Nastawgan, Summer 1989]

KLONDIKE

By Yukon standards the Klondike is a relatively short and insignificant river, flowing out of the south side of the Wernecke Mountains into the Yukon River at Dawson. Its importance is entirely due to its tiny tributary, Bonanza Creek, where the first big gold strike touched off the Klondike gold-rush.

Carol and Bruce Hodgins in 1983 standing beside historic Lapierre House, a once-important fur-trade post abandoned early in this century, situated at the confluence of the Bell and Porcupine Rivers. [Hodgins]

pre-1896 The mouth of the Klondike was the site of a seasonal fish camp of the Han First Nation People of the Yukon river valley. The name is thought to come from the Han word for "Hammer Water", a reference to the action of hammering in the posts for fish traps. [Coutts]

1896 George Carmack, Skookum Jim Mason and Tagish Charlie made the first big gold strike on Bonanza Creek, a tributary of the Klondike River, giving the signal for the Klondike gold-rush of 1898. [*Ibid.*]

1896 Robert Henderson, Nova Scotia, was on Bonanza Creek, as well as David McKay who was elected Mining Recorder by the twenty-five men on the creek at the time. [*Ibid.*]

1897-1905 Bonanza Creek was heavily mined and a number of reports were made of finding earlier workings. [*Ibid.*]

1906-52 Gold mining companies began dredge mining of the lower Klondike valley in 1906. Over the next forty years, between the river mouth and Hunker Creek, 12 kilometres, the dredges churned through the valley moving the river course from the south to the north side of the valley. [Green, *The Gold Hustlers*, p. 305]

1971 A Wild River Survey crew put their canoes in from the Dempster Highway on the North Klondike River and continued down the Klondike River to Dawson. [Parks Canada files]

SIXTY MILE

Sixty Mile River is a very short river connected historically with the gold-rush. It rises on the Alaska-Yukon border and flows south into the left bank of the Yukon River south of Dawson.

1876 Arthur Harper explored and named this river. [Coutts, p. 242]

1894 Joseph Ladue, New York, explored the Sixty Mile River. [*Ibid.*, p. 152]

1901 R.G. McConnell and Joseph Keele, GSC, with two canoemen from Sault Ste. Marie, using a Peterborough canoe, descended the Yukon River from the mouth of the Big Salmon and made a track survey of the Sixty Mile River. [GSC Memoirs 123, 284]

1971 Tom Wallace led a Wild River Survey crew of Roger Beardmore, Steve Paul and Harry Collins from Glacier Creek on the highway down the Sixty Mile and the Yukon rivers to Dawson. [Parks Canada files]

STEWART

The headwaters of the Stewart River are close to those of the Bonnet Plume, on the Yukon-Northwest Territories border. The Nadaleen and the Beaver rivers flowing into it from the north, close to its source, were used as the route by Klondikers from the Peel and Wind rivers during the gold-rush. The Hess River, a tributary which flows in on the south side of the Stewart, rises close to a tributary of the Keele. The Stewart flows generally west, and is joined by the McQuesten not long before it reaches the Yukon River at the town of Stewart River.

1849 *James G. Stewart, HBC clerk, travelling in the winter crossed this stream on the ice, and Robert Campbell named the river for him. [Coutts, p.251]*

1881 A party of Arizona prospectors went down the Yukon and 200 miles up the Stewart. [Ogilvie, p. 106]

1883 Richard Poplin, Charles McConkey, Benjamin Beach and C. Marks, private gold prospectors, followed the Stewart River up to the McQuesten River. They returned down the Stewart and up the Yukon the following year. [*Ibid.*, p. 108]

1885 Jack McQuesten, trader and prospector, went up the Stewart and McQuesten rivers. [Coutts, p. 175]

1885 Frank Moffatt found an abundant source of gold on a bar of the Stewart River. "Slim Jim" Wynn found a rich bar 100 miles up the Stewart. [*Ibid.*, p. 251]

1885 George Carmack – see Yukon

1885 Poplin, Wybourg, Morphet and Bertrand – see Yukon

1885 Thomas and George Boswell from Peterborough, Ontario, were the first miners up the Nadaleen River, a tributary of the Stewart. [Coutts, p. 193]

1885 Michael Hess prospected up the Hess River, a tributary of the Stewart. [*Ibid.*, p. 126]

1886 Franklin and Henry Madison prospected up the Stewart and McQuesten, then downstream to the Fortymile and up the Fortymile to the Yukon-Alaska Border. [Ogilvie, p. 111]

1886 Two brothers named Day were up the Stewart River. [*Ibid.*]

1886 Five men from Seattle were prospecting up the Stewart. There was a mining camp at the confluence of the Stewart and Yukon – the only one in the Territory. Eighteen or twenty miners wintered there in the winter of 1886-87. [*Ibid.*, p. 38]

1886 There were about 100 men on the Stewart. [*Ibid.*, p. 108]

1887 Alexander MacDonald, prospector from New Brunswick, ascended the Mayo River to Mayo Lake and continued up creeks to prospect in the Gustavus Mountains. He crossed to the McQuesten River, built a raft and floated down the McQuesten and Stewart rivers. [GSC Memoir 284]

1898 J.J. McArthur, for the Dominion Topographical Survey, mapped the upper portion of the Stewart River to the mouth of the Hess River. [GSC Memoir 284]

1898 Ernest Scroggie and H. LeDuke, Quebec, J.G. Stephens, North Dakota, with six other prospectors travelled up the Stewart River and up Scroggie Creek. [Coutts, p. 235]

1898 George Mitchell – see Peel

1899 Charles Maltby, with a group of prospectors from Montreal (see Clearwater, and Peel) moved up from Wind City, up the Little Wind and the Bear, climbed over the pass, built boats of whip-sawn timber caulked with spruce gum and also used folding canvas boats to descend the Stewart and Yukon rivers to Dawson. [Moyles, ed., 1977]

1899 Frank Braine and Jack Garnett, Englishmen, with three Indians, descended the Stewart River in a skin boat. Peacock, Barclay, Geltham, Payzant and Crichton, having come over the pass from the Wind-Peel rivers, lost their boat and their goods in an ice-jam. White, Sennett, Joe Millette and Judge Morse continued down the Stewart River from the Wind-Peel. [*Ibid.*]

1899 E.J. Corp and a group of prospectors from Hamilton (see Keele), having crossed the pass from the Keele River in winter, built a boat and went down the Stewart and McQuesten rivers. About seventy-five people came across on this route during the gold-rush. [*Arctic Circular*, 1958 p. 35]

1900 R.G. McConnell and J.F.E. Johnson, GSC, ascended the Stewart River to Frazer Falls and returned down-river, continuing down the Yukon to below Cliff Creek. [GSC Memoir 284]

1905 Joseph Keele, GSC, assisted by George Ortell and two other miners, went by steamer from Dawson up the Stewart River to Frazer Falls where they began their exploration by canoe, continuing up the Stewart River and its tributaries, the Hess, the Lansing, the Beaver and the Rackla. [GSC Memoir 284]

1905 Charles Camsell – see Bell-Porcupine

1922-23 It was believed that miners on upper reaches of the Beaver River built boats and came down the Beaver and Stewart rivers. [Bond, p. 172]

1947 James Bond, an American big game trophy hunter, with Louis Brown and Norman Mervyn as guides, made his way with horses from Mayo into the headwaters area of the Wind and Bonnet Plume rivers, an area undisturbed since the miners abandoned it in 1923 and where Brown ran a solitary trap-line. At the end of the fifty-day hunt, the trophies were too much for the horses to carry back through the muskeg of the low ground. The guides built a 10-foot moose-hide boat and Bond and Mervyn came down Carpenter Creek, Beaver and Stewart rivers to Mayo Crossing on the Stewart River in the heavily-laden boat, while Brown returned to Mayo with the horses. [Bond, 1948; *Beaver*, Winter 1959, p. 44]

1954-80 Monty Alford, hydrologist for the Water Survey of Canada, with crews, travelled by powered craft up the lower reaches of the Stewart River on a regular basis to record water levels at hydrology stations. [Personal communication to researcher Katie Hayhurst]

1971 Ian Donaldson, David Wilford, Jean de Grosbois and one other member of a Wild River Survey crew canoed down the Stewart River from Stewart Crossing and down the Yukon to Dawson. [Parks Canada files]

pre-1974 Wermager – see Arctic Red

1987 *Jim and Pam Boyde, Neil and Travis Davies, Jim and Jeff Carmichel, Bruce Thomson and Mike McGinnes canoed from McQuesten Lake down the Beaver and Stewart rivers to Mayo. [Personal communication – Boyde to researcher Hayhurst]*

1987 *Jim and Pam Boyde, Ted Curtis, Andy Davis, Ray Masnok and Ray (?) canoed from Porter Creek down the Hess and Stewart rivers to Mayo. [Personal communication – Boyde to Hayhurst]*

1992 *Bill and Keefer Irwin with Stearnie and Dodie Stearns flew to Misty Lake, lined down a narrow overgrown feeder stream to the Stewart River and*

canoed down the Stewart to Mayo. [Personal communication – Keefer Irwin]

PELLY

The Pelly River rises in the Selwyn Mountains close to the Yukon border with the Northwest Territories. Its beginning streams merge in the Pelly Lakes and after a short curve south it settles firmly on a northwesterly direction, gathering strength from its tributaries, the Ross and the Macmillan, and flowing into the Yukon River somewhat beyond Pelly Crossing on the Klondike Highway. Because the headwaters of the Pelly are close to streams flowing into Frances Lake which connects with the Liard River, the Pelly was part of the earliest explorations by the Hudson's Bay Company.

1882 Two prospecting parties ascended the Pelly to Hoole Canyon, some going beyond the canyon. [Dawson, p. 180B]

1884 There was a little mining on the Pelly River. [*Ibid.*, p. 181B]

1887 G.M. Dawson and J. McEvoy, GSC, with L. Lewis and D. Johnson from Victoria, two Tshimsian and three Tlinkit Indians, came up the Stikine, portaged from Telegraph Creek to Dease Lake and canoed down the Dease River to the Liard. They continued up the Liard and Frances rivers to Frances Lake and crossed the height of land to the Pelly River. The Indians returned to the coast and the four men built a canvas canoe and descended the Pelly to the Lewes (Yukon). There they built a wooden boat and ascended the Lewes to the headwaters, crossed the Chilkoot Pass and went down the Lynn Canal to the coast. [Dawson, reprint, 1987; Zaslow, p. 159, map p. 158]

1889 Arthur Harper re-established Fort Selkirk at the mouth of the Pelly River as an independent trading post.

1892 Bishop Bompas established an Anglican mission at Fort Selkirk.

1893 Warburton Pike – see Yukon

1898 J.D. Moodie, RNWMP, seeking information on the best route to the Yukon gold-fields from Edmonton, continued the journey begun the year

George Dawson, in spite of a deformed spine giving him the height of a schoolboy, and lungs so weak that his life was endangered by even a common cold, was an untiring geologist, botanist, zoologist and ethnologist for the Geological Survey. He did important work in the rugged terrain of northern British Columbia and the Yukon. [Anne V. Byers]

before (see Peace) by canoeing up the Liard to Frances Lake and down the Pelly to Fort Selkirk on the Yukon River. [Cooke and Holland, p. 276]

1898 Robert Riddell was the first non-native to explore and trap on the headwaters of the Pelly, Ross and Gravel (Keele) rivers. [Coutts, p. 222]

1898 Olivier LaRose came into the Yukon with the Klondikers and travelled up the Pelly to prospect and trade. [*Ibid.*, p. 225]

1899-1905 With Fort Selkirk as the temporary headquarters of the Yukon Field Force, there was considerable prospecting up the Pelly and Macmillan rivers.

1900 Dell Charles VanGorder and Ira Van Bibber reached the Yukon about the turn of the century and prospected and trapped up the Pelly River. [*Ibid.*, p. 274]

1902 R.G. McConnell and Joseph Keele, for the Geological Survey, went up the Pelly to the Macmillan. The party divided, one exploring the South Macmillan and Riddell, and the other the North Macmillan to the headwaters. They returned down-river to Fort Selkirk. [Cooke and Holland p. 293]

1903-04 Stratford Tollemache, with two French-Canadians, came up the Yukon by steamer from Dawson to the mouth of the Pelly River. They built a boat, and using oars, they rowed, poled and hauled it up the Pelly River, built a cabin and trapped. They returned down-river in the spring to Fort Selkirk. [Tollemache, 1912]

1905 Gilmore and Elsie Starr prospected up the Pelly River as far as Starr Creek. [Coutts, p. 247]

1905 Charles Sheldon – see Ross

1906 F.C. Selous – see Macmillan

1907 Joseph Keele, Robert Riddell, and J.M. Christie, for the Geological Survey, went down the Yukon to Fort Selkirk and surveyed up the Pelly and Ross rivers. They were assisted by a miner, Robert Henderson, who was in the employ of the Yukon government. They wintered at the head of the Ross River, built a cabin and two boats and in the spring they went down the Gravel, now named Keele, to the Mackenzie. [GSC Memoir 284; Thompson, Don, v.3, p. 92]

1930s The paddle-wheeler, *Yukon Rose*, annually brought supplies to Old Ross village up the Yukon and Pelly rivers. [Katie Hayhurst]

1947 Indian Agent Meek came down the Pelly River from the headwaters. [Bond, p. 117]

1952-80 Monty Alford, hydrologist for the Water Survey of Canada, drove to Pelly Crossing and travelled the Pelly River by power boat. No recreational paddlers were met on the river. [Personal communication to researcher Katie Hayhurst]

1969 Hal and Jean Bennett – see South Macmillan

1970 Bob Sharp, Martyn Williams, Roger McDonnell, Harry Atkinson, Hans Algotsson and Ernie Lennie spent much of the summer training on the Pelly River to win the honour of representing the Yukon in the 28-day NWT Centennial Canoe Race. [Personal communication – Bob Sharp to Katie Hayhurst]

1972 The Harrison family from New Jersey, David and his wife Judy, and their children, Nancy, Juli, and Dave Jr. ranging in age from thirteen down to eight, using two 17-foot aluminum canoes, started from the community of Ross River and canoed down the Pelly and Yukon rivers to Dawson. [*Canoe*, Jan./Feb. 1974, pp. 14-21]

MACMILLAN

The Macmillan River has two significant branches, the North and the South, which join halfway to the confluence with the Pelly River near Pelly Crossing on the Klondike Highway. The South Macmillan rises close to Christie Pass, the headwaters of the Keele River, and can be reached now from the Canol Road. The North Macmillan rises close to the Hess River.

1843 Robert Campbell saw the mouth of the Macmillan River as he came down the Pelly. [Sheldon, p. 88]

1897 Thomas Duncan Gillis, prospector from Nova Scotia, came to the Yukon via the Edmonton Trail, up the Keele River and over Christie Pass. He built a raft and went down the South Macmillan River thinking it was the Stewart, discovered gold in Russell Creek and continued down the Pelly and Yukon to Dawson. [Coutts, p. 111; Armstrong, N., pp. 205-06]

1902 R.G. McConnell and Joseph Keele, GSC, with two canoemen from Sault Ste Marie, using two Peterborough canoes, started from Whitehorse, descended the Yukon River to the Pelly and ascended it to the Macmillan. On the Macmillan, McConnell explored up the North fork to a few miles above Cache Creek, continuing up that stream to the head, while Keele ascended the South fork for 50 miles. [GSC Memoir 284; Zaslow, p. 224]

1904 Frederick Courtney Selous, British explorer and sportsman, Charles Sheldon, American zoologist, with guides Louis Cardinal and Coghlan, went up the North Macmillan River. Carl Rungius, American wildlife artist, Wilfrid Osgood, U.S. Biological Survey, with Charles Gage as guide, went up Russell Creek. Judge Dugas and D.A. Cameron, sportsmen from Dawson, J.A. Patterson, Edmonton, with two French-Canadian guides and Bob Hunter, a Klondiker, went up the South Macmillan. Starting late in August, all three parties travelled together by steamer up the Pelly and Macmillan rivers to just below the Forks of the Macmillan where the three groups split off with canoes. This was essentially a trophy-hunting and collecting trip. Sheldon's interest was in mountain sheep and many of his specimens found their way into American museums. Near the end of September all three groups canoed down the Macmillan and Pelly rivers to Fort Selkirk as ice was forming on the river. [Sheldon, Chaps. 5-9; Selous, 1909]

1905 Stratford Tollemache, having gone up the Pelly and 100 miles up the Macmillan by steamer the previous year, wintered on the Macmillan and came downstream by boat in the spring to Fort Selkirk. [Tollemache, 1912]

1905 George French, Landale and Jackson, who had gone up the Pelly and South Macmillan rivers to Russell Creek, by steamer and horseback, to assist Nevill Armstrong in building his cabin, returned downstream by canoe late in the year and had a very bad trip. [Armstrong, N., 1936]

1906 Nevill A.D. Armstrong, his wife Marian, G.H. Leith and his wife, C. Pomeroy and John Barr, having come up the Pelly and South Macmillan rivers the previous year by steamer and horseback to Russell Creek, returned downstream in two canoes. Nevill Armstrong was game warden on the Macmillan River and until 1914 he spent most summers on Russell Creek searching for gold. [Armstrong, N., 1936; Coutts, p. 9]

1906 F.C. Selous, with canoemen Charles Coghlan, and Roderick Thomas who had previously crossed the Barrens with J.B. Tyrrell, using a 20-foot canoe, canoed from Whitehorse down the Yukon to Fort Selkirk, up the Pelly and Macmillan taking the south fork and up a section of the Riddell River. This was a trophy-hunting expedition. They returned down-river to Fort Selkirk and took a steamer up to Whitehorse. [Selous, Chaps. 8, 9]

1942-44 The Canol pipeline was constructed from Johnsons Crossing on the Teslin River straight across the mountains to Norman Wells on the Mackenzie River. The attendant road which survived into the post-war years in the Yukon Territory changed the pattern of river travel, providing access to the upper reaches of the South Macmillan.

1969 Hal and Jean Bennett and Vern Coats, from California, flew from Whitehorse to a small lake off the Canol Road, near mile 337.5, and in two-seater folding kayaks paddled down the South Macmillan, Pelly and Yukon to Dawson. [Unpublished trip report in Parks Canada files]

1971 A Wild River Survey crew, Harry Collins, Roger Beardmore, Tom Wallace and Steve Stesco, canoed from above Russell Creek off the Canol Road to Pelly Crossing. [Parks Canada files]

1976 *Jim and Pam Boyde, Dave Sakamoto, Carol Tasell, Sam McCall and Jim Berta canoed from the first Macmillan bridge on the Canol Road down the South Macmillan, Pelly and Yukon rivers to Dawson. [Personal communication – Jim Boyde to researcher Hayhurst]*

1984 *Bill and Keefer Irwin, Jim and Kay Henry with their children, Dana and Carrie, Rick Kolstad and Deb Peters put their canoes in off the Canol Road and canoed down the South Macmillan and Pelly rivers to Pelly Crossing. [Personal communication – Keefer Irwin]*

1984 *Jim and Pam Boyde, Mark Ostopkowicz, Andy Davis, Bill Parry and Debbie Witala canoed from the upper South Macmillan up the small tributary descending from Summit Lake, crossed to the upper*

Ross River and continued down the Ross, Pelly and Yukon rivers to Dawson. [Personal communication – Jim Boyde to Hayhurst]

ROSS

The Ross River, a tributary of the Pelly River, rises close to Christie Pass near the headwaters of the South Nahanni and has been used as a route to reach that river. The Ross enters the Pelly at Ross River, a community at the crossroads of the Canol Road and the Robert Campbell Highway.

1900 Prevost, French-Canadian, was probably the first non-native to travel the Ross River. Prevost Canyon was named for him. [Coutts, p. 214]

1901 Cassat and Dumas, French-Canadian trappers, ascended the Ross River to just above Prevost Canyon. [Sheldon, p. 251]

1902 Lewis and a partner ascended the Ross River a short distance and returned while two other trappers ascended farther. Cassat and Dumas ascended the east branch and up the Prevost River at the same time as a Russian went up to the first lake. [*Ibid.*]

1903 Lewis and his partner trapped at Lewis Lake, LaCroix and Prevost trapped on the Prevost River. [*Ibid.*]

1904-05 A trapper wintered at Lewis Lake. According to Lewis, these were the only non-natives who had ascended the Ross River. [*Ibid.*]

1905 Charles Sheldon, American zoologist, with Tom Jefferies, French-Canadian guide, a 21-foot Strickland canoe and a horse, went up the Pelly River by steamer to Nahanni House at the confluence with the Ross River. With his horse he explored the Pelly mountains and up the Lapie River. Leaving the horse at Nahanni House, they ascended the Ross River by canoe to Lake Sheldon and explored Mt. Sheldon and Mt. Riddell hunting for sheep. They canoed down the Ross and Pelly rivers, exploring the Rose and Glenlyon Mountains, and continued down-river to Fort Selkirk. They believed they were the first non-natives above Lake Lewis. [*Ibid.*, Chaps. 16-19]

1907 Charles Wilson assisted Joseph Keele, GSC, in mapping the headwaters of the Ross River. He had come into this area at the beginning of the gold-rush. [Coutts, p. 288]

1930s The paddle-wheeler *Yukon Rose* annually brought supplies to Old Ross village by way of the Pelly and Yukon rivers. [Katie Hayhurst]

1952-80 Monty Alford, hydrologist for the Water Survey of Canada, flew several times a year to the community of Ross River, travelling up the river 4 miles each time by power-boat. [Personal communication with researcher Katie Hayhurst]

1971 Priidu Juurand led a Wild River Survey crew of David McClung, Bill Pisco and Malcolm McIntyre from an air-drop on John Lake down the Ross and Pelly rivers to Fort Selkirk. [Parks Canada files]

1974 Sandy Richardson – see South Nahanni

pre-1975 Marc Wermager – see South Nahanni

BIG SALMON

The Big Salmon River rises in Quiet Lake in the Big Salmon Range of the Pelly Mountains and flows north and northwest to enter the Yukon River at Carmacks.

1881 George Langtry, Patrick McGlinchy and two other prospectors from Juneau, Alaska, ascended this river for 200 miles, the first non-natives to explore the Big Salmon River. [Coutts, p. 23]

1887 John McCormack, from New Brunswick, Hoffman and three other prospectors explored up the Big Salmon River as far as Quiet Lake. [*Ibid.*, p. 24]

1887-93 George Carmack, from California, Skookum Jim Mason, his sister Kate and Tagish Charlie, Tagish Indians, prospected up the Big Salmon River. [*Ibid.*, p. 48]

1898 R.G. McConnell, GSC, with two Indians from Lake Timiskaming, using a Peterborough canoe and a canvas boat, crossed the Chilkoot Pass and went down the Yukon River to the mouth of the Big Salmon River as soon as the ice broke. They ascended the Big Salmon to Quiet Lake and ex-

plored the North and South Forks and the valleys in between. They returned down the Big Salmon and the Yukon to Dawson. [GSC Memoir 284]

1901 A prospector named Meany found gold on Summit Creek, a tributary of the Big Salmon. [Coutts, p. 255]

1950s Bill Hayes travelled the Big Salmon area as telegraph operator of the Yukon Telegraph Line. [Personal communication – Monty Alford with researcher Hayhurst]

1954-80 Monty Alford, hydrologist for the Water Survey of Canada, regularly travelled the lower 15 miles of the Big Salmon by river boat usually with George Shorty and Alex van Bibber. [*Ibid.*]

1963 Ross Mavis, Don Graham, Ralph DeCoste, Gerry Kubiski, Roy Perrin and Des Duncan canoed 285 miles from Quiet Lake down the Big Salmon and Yukon to Carmacks. [Hayhurst from Sept. 1963 Newsletter]

1971 A Wild River Survey crew, Harry Collins, Roger Beardmore, Steve Stesco and Tom Wallace, canoed from Quiet Lake off the Canol Road down the Big Salmon to the Yukon River. [Parks Canada files]

TESLIN

The Teslin or Hootalinqua River rises in Teslin Lake on the Yukon border with British Columbia and flows northwest to enter the Yukon River just below Lake Laberge. It is reached from Johnsons Crossing on the Alaska Highway and provides an access to the Yukon River, by-passing the Five-finger Rapids.

1897 St. Cyr, for the Dominion Lands Branch, travelled the length of the Teslin River. [GSC Memoir 284]

1898 R.G. McConnell, GSC, with two Indians from Lake Timiskaming, explored the Teslin River and Teslin Lake. [GSC Memoir 284]

1920-70s Taylor and Drury, merchants, ran supply boats up the Teslin from the Yukon River as far as Johnsons Crossing and Teslin. [Personal communication – Ellen Davignon to researcher Katie Hayhurst]

1920s A fox farm used boats to transport their furs down the Teslin and up the Yukon to White-horse. [Personal communication – Ida McCormick to Hayhurst]

pre-1940s Bill Cooms from Mayo prospected and mined on the Teslin River. [Hayhurst]

ALSEK–TATSHENSHINI

The Alsek and the Tatshenshini are spectacular rivers which rise in the mountains, the Alsek in the southwestern Yukon, the Tatshenshini in the northwestern corner of British Columbia. The Tatshenshini flows north into Yukon territory, makes a hairpin bend and then flows parallel to the course of the Alsek due south through a narrow pass in the St. Elias Range. The Alsek passes through aptly named "Turnback Canyon", where calving glaciers add icebergs to the turbulent waters. Below the canyon, the two rivers meet and continue as the Alsek, emptying into the Pacific at Dry Bay, Alaska. The volume of their combined waters entering the Pacific Ocean is exceeded only by that of the much longer Columbia River, hundreds of miles to the south.

ALSEK

1961 Clem Rawert and John Dawson, from Alaska, in a double Klepper kayak, started at the headwaters and made what is possibly the first river trip down the Alsek to Turnback Canyon, portaged across the glacier, and continued to Dry Bay. They tried to paddle to Yakutat, but weather forced them back to Dry Bay, where they were eventually picked up by a fishing tender. [*Appalachia*, Dec. 1972, pp. 13-22; Dr. Andrew Embick, unpublished manuscript]

1966 Mike Hoover, filmmaker, and Gary Francis, using an Avon Redshank raft with canoe paddles, paddled down the Alsek River to Turnback Canyon and hiked out to the Alaska Highway. [Dr. Embick, unpublished manuscript]

1967 Graham Stephenson, Russell Rasmussen, Donna Dauner Rasmussen and fifteen-year-old Chris Marr, using a 12-foot raft with an outboard motor, put in at Haines Junction, descended the Alsek to Turnback Canyon, portaged the glacier, flipped below the canyon losing considerable gear and food and reached Dry Bay after twenty-eight days. [*Ibid.*]

1970 Clem Rawert led Dee Crouch, Bill Evans, June Weinstock, Vivian Mendenhall and Richard Tero, using Klepper folding kayaks and one fibreglass kayak, from Haines Junction down the Dezadeash and the Alsek to Turnback Canyon. They portaged 10 miles across the Tweedsmuir Glacier and completed the run to Dry Bay on the Alaskan coast. [*Appalachia*, Dec. 1972, pp. 13-22; *Alaska*, March 1971, p. 37]

1971 Walt Blackadar, from Idaho, alone in a Mithril Vector kayak, started from Haines Junction and kayaked down the Alsek all the way to Dry Bay, including Turnback Canyon. In his journal he emphasized that the Canyon is unpaddleable and should not be attempted. [*Sports Illustrated*, Aug. 14, 1972, pp. 42-50; *American Whitewater*, Nov./Dec. 1986, pp. 21-24]

1971 Gary Anderson and his father landed their floatplane on the Alsek River near its confluence with the Tatshenshini. The plane capsized and was swept away carrying the older Anderson who was never found. Gary Anderson was picked up after thirty-eight days, having survived on roots. [Dr. Embick, unpublished manuscript]

1974 Dee Crouch and Richard Tero in single Kleppers and Klaus Streckmann in a 17-foot fibreglass kayak paddled down the Alsek River to Turnback Canyon. They planned to portage the Tweedsmuir glacier, but finding the glacier too broken up, they abandoned their boats and hiked out five days to the highway at Dalton Post. Streckmann filmed the trip on 8mm film, including aerial footage made during the recovery of the kayaks. [Personal communication – Keith Morton; Embick – unpublished manuscript]

1978 *Klaus Streckmann, Dr. Kay Swanson, Bob Bleile, Steve Zack and Bev Evers, in whitewater kayaks, started on the Jarvis River, continued down the Kaskawulsh and the Alsek to the entrance to*

Turnback Canyon where they built a memorial to Dr. Walt Blackadar. Blackadar had died in a kayaking accident in Idaho. They lined their boats up the Alsek to Range Creek, crossed over a low pass and paddled down Detour Creek to the Tatshenshini and followed it down to the Alsek and Dry Bay. [Dr. Embick -unpublished manuscript]

1979 *Roland Goerger, from Germany, with a partner, made a trip by kayak from Dezadeash down the Alsek to Range Creek, up and over to Detour Creek, down the Tatshenshini and Alsek rivers. [Ibid.]*

1980 *Klaus Streckmann, Jack Schick, Kluane Park naturalist, Larry Nichols, Ralph Smith, Michael Jones, Joe Martin, Mark Linen, Sally Nichols and two others, using three kayaks and rafts, travelled down the Alsek to Turnback Canyon and made the portage by prearranged helicopter. [Ibid.]*

1980 *Rob Lesser, Bo Shelby, John Wasson, Don Banducci and Kathy Blau, in Perception Mirage kayaks, making the trip down the Alsek late in August ran Turnback Canyon. Kathy Blau hiked across the glacier and Lesser made a second solo run in her kayak. [Dr. Embick – unpublished manuscript; personal communication – Lesser]*

TATSHENSHINI

1890 E. J. Glave, an African explorer, with Jack Dalton and an Indian guide named Shank, in a 20-foot cottonwood dugout canoe, canoed from Neskatahin down the Tatshenshini and the Alsek to the Pacific. They returned the following year with packhorses. Dalton returned in 1894 and established a trading post and the Dalton trail. [*Arctic Circular*, XXIV #1, p. 1, 1976; *Alaska Journal*, Summer 1973, pp. 180-88]

1973 Walt Blackadar and Dr. Kay Swanson kayaked down the Tatshenshini River. [Personal communication – Dick Tero]

1975 *Hector MacKenzie, Alan Dennis and Martyn Williams spent a long day exploring from near the source of the Tatshenshini down to Dalton Post. [Personal communication – MacKenzie to Hayhurst]*

1976 *Walt Blackadar, his son Bobby and others made a*

kayak trip down the Tatshenshini. This was the same year that commercial river rafters made their first trip down the river. [Personal communication – Dick Tero]

1993 *Keith Morton and his wife, three other couples and two men canoed the Tatshenshini in five canoes. There were two other canoe trips on the river, one of them consisting of two persons with two canoes. [Personal communication – Morton]*

1993 *There were 1200 visitors on the Tatshenshini. [Neil Hartling on CBC "Morningside", April 12, 1994]*

STIKINE

The Stikine River flows west in British Columbia from the Cassiar Mountains into Frederick Sound, an arm of the Pacific Ocean, at Wrangell, Alaska. The access to the river mouth was controlled by the Russians until after the Alaska purchase in 1867, although the Hudson's Bay Company had established a fort on Wrangell Island in 1840. In 1866 the HBC built a post at the mouth of the Anuk River inside British territory. The limited access from the coast plus the wild nature of the river kept early exploration to a minimum. While the fur trade had a tenuous toe-hold at the mouth of the river during the Russian period, the Hudson's Bay Company reached the headwaters at the same time as they were pushing into the Yukon. The impetus for exploration of the Stikine came from miners and prospectors heading for the Cassiar and the Omineca goldfields and also from the attempt of Western Union Telegraph to cross the mountains and create a link between the hemispheres. The laying of the first trans-Atlantic cable finished this initiative.

The river has two canyons; the smaller one, between Glenora and Telegraph Creek, is navigable on the upstream or downstream, but the larger canyon, higher up the river is considered almost impassable. Beginning in 1862 when traffic was heavy on the Stikine, steamers ran a regular schedule from tide-water to Telegraph Creek where a mule-train portaged across to Dease Lake along the valley of the Tanzilla River, a distance of 70 miles. The portage route is now a road for vehicles.

The watershed of the Stikine includes the Spatsizi, the Tanzilla, the Tuya and the Tahltan. The Iskut rises close to the Stikine and flows out to the Pacific in a roughly parallel course. While the Stikine is not a "north-flowing" river, it is included because it is a great northern river analogous to those which flow into the north shore of the lower St. Lawrence River.

1824   Samuel Black, HBC, was the first non-native to reach the headwaters of the Stikine and Metsentan Lake, having come up the Finlay River and crossed the divide. [Patterson, Trail to the Interior, p. 53]

1833   Peter Skene Ogden, HBC, explored up the first 50 miles of the Stikine River by ship with plans to build a trading post upstream. This prompted the Russians to prohibit the HBC from entering the Stikine and trading with the natives. [Ibid, p. 75,76; Cline, p. 111]

1834   J. McLeod, HBC, reached the Upper Stikine near Dease Lake from the Mackenzie and the Liard. [Dawson, p. 62B]

1838   Robert Campbell, HBC, with one Métis and two Indians, established a trading post on Dease Lake and explored to the Stikine River. The trading post was abandoned the following year. [Ibid., p. 84B]

1861   Two miners, Alexandre "Buck" Choquette and Carpenter, found placer gold on the bars of the Stikine. [Ibid., p. 62B]

1862(3)   Russians under naval Lt. Perelshin ascended the Stikine in a ship's boat from the coast to just above the Little Canyon. W.P. Blake was a member of the group. A seaman named Sergiev was drowned while lining up a rapid. [Dawson, p. 62B; Patterson, Trail, p. 85]

1866   Major Pope explored the Stikine for the Western Union Telegraph. [Dawson, p. 62B]

1867   M.W. Byrnes, Vital Lafleur, W. McNeill and P.J. Leach explored most of the tributaries of the Stikine for the Western Union Telegraph. [Ibid.]

1867   P.J. Leach, Western Union exploration survey, traversed the Iskut River and came down the Stikine. [Ibid., p. 50B]

pre-1873 Robert Hyland was one of the first men in the rush to the Stikine River and the Cassiar gold-fields. [Coutts, p. 134]

1873   The Stikine River became the route to the Cassiar gold-fields. [Dawson, p. 46B]

1873   Miners Henry Thibert and McCullough, having come down the Mackenzie and up the Liard and Dease in 1871, wintered at Fort Halkett, discovered gold in the Cassiar region and met miners on the Stikine in the autumn of 1873. [Ibid., p. 63B]

1875   G.B. Wright made a sketch map of the Stikine River, Dease Lake and Dease River for the British Columbia Department of Mines. [Ibid., p. 47B]

1877   Joseph Hunter, civil engineer from Victoria, was appointed by the federal government to make a partial survey of the Stikine River for the Yukon-Alaska boundary survey. [Thompson, Don, v.2, p. 147]

1878   W.H. Bell made a trip up the Stikine River by steamer to Glenora and described the glaciers and the canyons. Indians were making their way up the river by canoe. [Scribner's Monthly, 1879, pp. 805-15]

1879   John Muir, the noted naturalist-conservationist, was on the Stikine, probably hiking, as reported in the San Francisco Bulletin. [Dawson, p. 51B]

1887   G.M. Dawson, R.G. McConnell and J. McEvoy, Geological Survey, arrived at Wrangell by steamer. Dawson and McEvoy continued by steamer up the Stikine to Telegraph Creek and by pack horses to Dease Lake. McConnell, with L. Lewis and D. Johnson from Victoria, two Tshimsian and three Tlinkit Indian men and one Indian woman, surveyed the Stikine River in canoes. They joined Dawson at Dease Lake where the party built three boats. Dawson and McEvoy, with Lewis and Johnson and the five coastal Indians ascended the Liard and Frances rivers to Frances Lake and portaged to the Upper Pelly River. The Indians returned to the coast and the four surveyors built a canvas canoe and descended the Pelly to the confluence with the Yukon River. There they built a wooden boat, went up the Yukon (then called the Lewes) and crossed Chilkoot Pass. Dawson and McEvoy rendezvoused with William Ogilvie, Dominion Land

Survey, at the mouth of the Pelly River, Ogilvie continuing down the Yukon. McConnell, with two men and one boat, made his survey down the Liard River. [Dawson, reprint 1987]

1892   Warburton Pike, Charles Gladman and Reed with an 18-foot Peterborough canoe, poled and paddled up the Stikine, up the Little Canyon to Telegraph Creek where a 35-mule pack-train took them across to Dease Lake. At Dease Lake they put the canoe on a little steamer to the Dease River where they canoed down to the Lower Post on the Liard in the company of an Indian in his own canoe. [Pike, *Through the Sub-Arctic Forest*]

1892   A large saltwater canoe with a load of coast Indians, led by Tomyot, and including women, babies and one white man, a pioneer of the Cassiar diggings, was ascending the Little Canyon of the Stikine at the same time as Warburton Pike.

post-1893   Warburton Pike, with a sea-going canoe was going upstream above Glenora when he met another canoe coming downstream containing three white men and an Indian steersman. Five minutes after the canoe had passed it capsized in a rapid and two men were drowned.

1896   Andrew J. Stone, for the American Museum of Natural History, made a trip from Fort Wrangell,

Alaska, to the headwaters of the Stikine River. In the Cassiar Mountains he discovered a genus of mountain sheep which was given the Latin name *Ovis stonei*. [*Bulletin. American Museum of Natural History*, Vol. IX, 1897, pp. 111-14]

1897   Andrew Stone ascended the Stikine River to the head of navigation at Telegraph Creek (presumably by steamer) and after an expedition in the Cheonnee Mountains, crossed the divide to Dease Lake, explored in the Cassiar Mountains and descended Dease Lake and Dease River by open boat to the Liard. [*Ibid.*, Vol. XIII, pp. 31-62]

1898   Hundreds of Klondikers came up the Stikine on the ice or by river steamer to Glenora (just below Telegraph Creek) to make the difficult trek to Teslin Lake and the Yukon. Mackenzie and Mann started to build a railway up the Stikine, to be named the Cassiar Central. [Patterson, *Trail*, pp. 29, 99]

1898   Francis George Berton, Harry Francis and other Klondikers hauled their boat up the Stikine on the ice along the edge of the river from Wrangell to Glenora. The high cost of hiring packers forced them to turn back. They bought a Peterborough canoe and returned down the lower Stikine, continuing north up the coast by steamer

Looking up the Pelly River, 1887, possibly George Dawson in the bow of the canoe. [NAC – PA37560]

With its headwaters high up in the Spatizi Plateau between the Omineca and the Skeena Mountains, the Stikine River flows through spectacular scenery, circling past 2500-metre Mt. McNamara and Mt. Will before it plunges down through the Grand Canyon. [Sandy Richardson]

to make their trip in over the Chilkoot Pass. [Berton, p. 17]

1898 O'Brien, from Nova Scotia, with an Indian, tracking and poling a canoe up the Stikine was killed instantly by a rock which crashed down from the steep bank. [Patterson, *Trail*, p. 29]

1926 F. A. Kerr, GSC, began work on the Stikine River. [GSC Memoir 246]

1927-28 F. A. Kerr, GSC, continued up the Stikine River as far as Telegraph Creek, ascending the tributaries to the limits of easy accessibility. [GSC Memoir 246]

1948 R.M. Patterson took his canoe on the steamer up the Stikine to Telegraph Creek, was taken across the portage route by truck to Dease Lake, and canoed the length of Dease Lake and down Dease River to the Lower Post on the Liard. [Patterson, *Trail to the Interior*]

1973 Roger Beardmore, Harry Collins, Dave McClung and Steve Stesco, for the Wild River Survey, canoed from Tuaton Lake, the headwater of the Stikine, to Stewart-Cassion bridge and from Telegraph Creek to the Alaska Boundary. [Parks Canada files]

1975 *Duke Watson, A. Black, S. Black, J. Docter, M. Docter, L. Dougall, W. Dougall, E. Jenkins, J. Ketcham, S. Ketcham and M. Watson canoed from Telegraph Creek down the Stikine River to Wrangell, Alaska. Duke Watson, alone, returned to Telegraph Creek and hiked the Tahltan portage route to Dease Lake. [Personal communication – Duke Watson]*

1980 *Rafters were on the Stikine, led by Tom Buri. [Parks Canada files]*

1981 *Rob Lesser, John Wasson, Don Banducci, Lars Holbek and Rick Fernald, expert kayakers from the American Northwest, with helicopter support, were filmed kayaking through the Grand Canyon of the Stikine by a camera crew from the ABC television program "American Sportsmen". Two-thirds of the way through, the camera crew felt they had enough footage and the kayakers were lifted out to finish the film at the Tanzilla Narrows. Rob Lesser and John Wasson continued down the Stikine to Wrangell on the coast. [Personal communication – Lesser]*

1982 *A canoeist drowned in the lower section of the canyon of the Stikine. [Parks Canada files]*

1982 *Tom Parkin ran a solo canoe down part of the Stikine. [Parks Canada files]*

1984 *George Luste, Dick Irwin, Sandy Richardson and Syd Kreitzman canoed from Happy Lake headwaters of the Stikine to the Grand Canyon, took the trail road which is the portage route to Telegraph Creek and canoed to Wrangell, Alaska. [Personal communication – George Luste]*

1985 *Rob Lesser, Lars Holbek and Bob McDougall, kayakers from Idaho, along with a raft manned by seven experienced paddlers from California and Roland Jonas from Calgary using a Zodiac, with helicopter support and a Canadian film crew, went all the way through the Grand Canyon of the Stikine, portaging about four times around some of the major rapids. The resulting film is entitled "Hell and High Water". The kayakers continued down the Stikine to Wrangell. [Personal communication – Lesser]*

1989 *Rob Lesser, Bob McDougall and Doug Ammons, with three kayaks, put in at the Cassiar Highway,*

on the Stikine. At the first major rapid, Entry Falls, they had an accident, lost a kayak and hiked out. [Personal communication – Lesser]

1990 *Rob Lesser, Tom Schibig and Doug Ammons, with kayaks, made the first self-supported trip through the Grand Canyon of the Stikine from the Cassiar Highway to Telegraph Creek taking three days. [Personal communication – Lesser]*

1990 *Bryan Tooley, Hayden Glatte and Phil DeReimer, kayakers from Oregon, ran the Grand Canyon of the Stikine, following a couple of days behind the group led by Rob Lesser. [Personal communication – Lesser]*

1991 *Larry Hodgins led a trip down the Stikine River for York University. They were transported around the canyons. [Personal communication – Larry Hodgins]*

1992 *Ken Madsen and Jody Schick, from the Yukon, started in canoes at the headwaters of the Stikine in the heart of the Spatsizi Plateau Wilderness Park. When they reached the beginning of the Grand Canyon of the Stikine at the Stewart-Cassiar Highway, weather conditions had swelled the river to spring run-off proportions and their trip ended there. [Canadian Geographic, May/June 1994, pp. 24-37]*

1993 *Ken Madsen and Jody Schick returned to the Stikine, putting their kayaks in at the point they had finished the previous year, and became the first Canadians to make an unsupported run through the Grand Canyon. At Telegraph Creek, Schick returned to the Yukon and Madsen, in a sea kayak, continued solo down the river to Wrangell, Alaska. [Ibid.]*

CHAPTER ELEVEN

THE FROZEN LAND: UNGAVA

The name "Ungava" refers to the peninsula of Ungava as well as Ungava Bay, and for this purpose the southern boundary is the diagonal line made by following the Clearwater and the Larch rivers from Richmond Gulf to the bottom of Ungava Bay. The rivers which flow into Hudson Bay from the Ungava Peninsula, as well as those which flow into Ungava Bay from northern Quebec, are all grouped in this section.

The canoeable rivers in Ungava are the Clearwater (à l'Eau Claire), which flows out of Clearwater Lake and into Richmond Gulf; the Kogaluk; the Povungnituk; the Payne (Arnaud), which has two large branches, North and South; the Leaf (aux Feuilles), a long river rising in Lake Minto and flowing into Ungava Bay; the Koksoak, which has two important tributaries, the Larch (aux Mélèzes) and the Kaniapiskau (Caniapiscau), which has its own tributary, the Swampy Bay; the Whale (la Baleine) with its important branch, the Wheeler; the George, which rises in Labrador but flows mainly through Ungava; and the Korok. Ungava trips are long and usually involve crossing the peninsula, or at the very least, crossing watersheds, going up one river system and down another. Trips will have their main entry on the river of descent and a note of cross-reference on the river of ascent. Modern trips mainly avoid the upstream work by flying to the headwaters of the chosen river.

The Hudson's Bay post near the mouth of the Koksoak, Fort Chimo, is now known by its Inuit name of Kuujjuaq. Since most of the recorded trips took place before this change, the name Fort Chimo has been retained. Similarly, English names and spellings of the rivers are used throughout.

CLEARWATER

The Clearwater River flows from Clearwater Lake into Richmond Gulf.

1827 *Hendry – see Koksoak*

1830 *Finlayson – see Koksoak*

1884 Peck – see Koksoak

1896 Low – see Koksoak

1906 Tasker – see Koksoak

1912 Omarolluk, Wetunik and an eight-year-old boy, who had been with Robert Flaherty on the trips across Ungava, returned to Great Whale River by canoe, up the Koksoak and Larch rivers and down the Clearwater River. [Flaherty, 1924]

1944 Lepage – see Koksoak

1978 *Beebe – see Larch*

1979 *Jim Davidson and John Rugge canoed down the Clearwater River. [Personal communication – Davidson]*

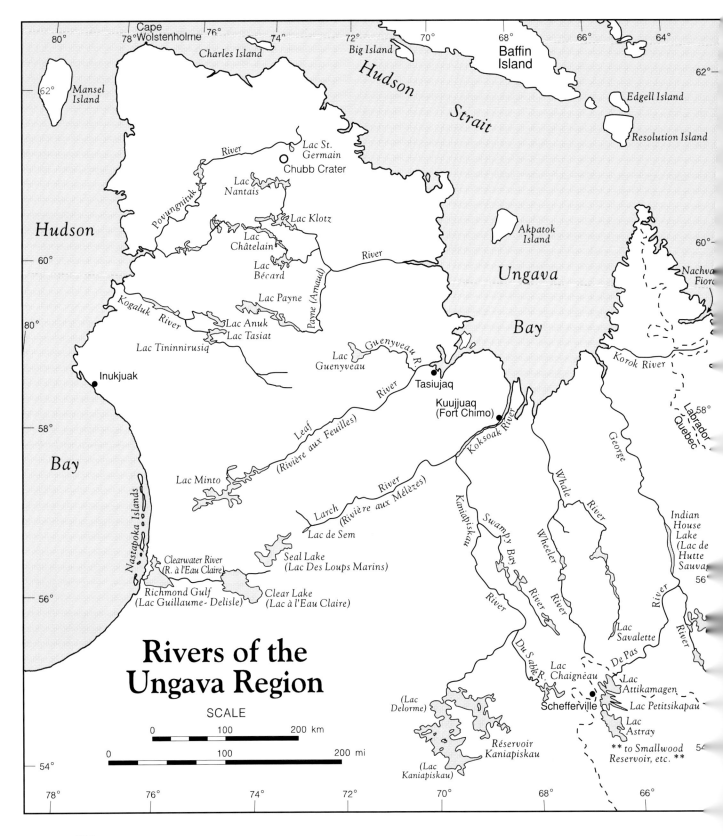

Rivers of the Ungava Region

SCALE

0   100   200 km

0   100   200 mi

1987 *Jim Raffan led a small group, for* National Geographic, *down the Clearwater River from Seal Lake.* [Personal communication – Raffan; Enchanted River, *1988]*

KOGALUK

The Kogaluk River flows out of the northern Ungava plateau through a series of lakes and enters Hudson Bay south of the community of Povungnituk. There is also a Kogaluk River in Labrador.

1945 W.E.C. Todd and Kenneth Doutt, with Paul Commanda as guide, flew from Moosonee by stages to Povungnituk in the very early spring. When the ice broke in July they explored up the Kogaluk River with three Eskimo guides in two canoes with outboard motors to just below the fifth falls, about 25 miles. Bad weather forced their return downstream. They returned down the coast on the *Nascopie*. This was the 22nd Carnegie Museum Expedition. [Todd, p. 52]

1948 Rousseau – see Payne

POVUNGNITUK

The Povungnituk is a remote, lengthy and steep river which rises just inland from the coast of Hudson Strait and crosses almost the whole of the northern tip of Ungava, flowing west and then southwest to enter Hudson Bay at the Inuit village of Povungnituk. In its upper reaches it passes close to the Chubb (or Ungava) Crater, formed by the collision of a meteor.

1912 Robert J. Flaherty with three Inuit, Omarolluk and Wetunik and, for the first half of the journey, Nero, made a sled journey from Great Whale River north to Richmond Gulf and across Ungava to Fort Chimo. Flaherty, with four Fort Chimo Inuit, Nuckey, Nawri, Ahegeek and Ambrose sailed north on a sloop, the *Walrus*, to Payne Bay. Using a 25-foot Peterborough canoe, the "man-killer", they ascended the north branch of the Payne River, crossed the height of land and canoed down what they thought was the Povungnituk to the Hudson Bay coast. They continued by canoe up the coast to the HBC post at Cape Wolstenholme where Flaherty took the HBC boat south into Hudson Bay, and the Inuit re-

turned to Ungava Bay. [Flaherty, 1924, Part III; *Geographical Review*, July/December 1918, pp. 116-31; *Bulletin de la Société de Géographie de Québec*, 1919, pp. 20-23, 139-41]

1950-51 Dr. Meen, geologist, with a party which was sponsored in 1950 by the *Globe and Mail* and in 1951 by the *National Geographic*, explored the Ungava Crater. While the Ungava Crater is within a short hiking distance of the upper Povungnituk River, the two groups which explored the crater in 1950-51 and later, in 1957, reached the crater by airplane. [Schrag, p.4]

1957 The Ungava Crater was explored by Science Search, financed by Montreal and Toronto businessmen, and a gravimetric-magnetometer survey was made by Radar Exploration of Toronto. The group which was led by Jack Tyson, included Johnny Thompson and Hans Varva, Rex Schrag, *Globe and Mail* reporter, two Inuit from Fort Chimo, Norman Gordon and Tommy Saunders and two filmmakers, Robin Hardy and Chris Slager. [*Ibid.*, p.6]

1978 *A group took four weeks to reach the crater from the headwaters of the Povungnituk because of low water.* [Che-Mun, *Autumn 1988]*

1988 *Michael and Geoffrey Peake, Peter Scott and Peter Brewster of the Hide-Away Canoe Club, following Flaherty's trail, flew to Raglan Lake near the headwaters of the Povungnituk River with two Old Town Trippers. They descended the river to Lake St. Germaine, where they hiked 3 miles to the crater. They portaged south eventually reaching Nantais Lake, went down the tumultuous Arpalirtuq River to Klotz Lake and followed an unnamed river to the village of Povungnituk using Flaherty's description. They concluded that the river he descended was not the Povungnituk but the more southerly river which joins the Povungnituk near its mouth.* [Che-Mun, *Summer and Autumn 1988]*

PAYNE

The Payne River with its several branches provides the eastern drainage for many of the large lakes in northern Ungava. The northern branch rises just south of the

Portaging a canoe through the inhospitable lunar landscape of northern Ungava, not far from the meteor-caused Ungava Crater, is a slow, careful procedure. One of the members of the Hide-Away Canoe Club, having negotiated the portage, overlooks the wild, brawling Povungnituk River, on a trip in 1988 that attempted to follow in the footsteps of the filmmaker Robert Flaherty. [Michael Peake]

Chubb Crater and flows southeast, a central branch rises in Lake Bécard in the centre of northern Ungava and flows due east and the southerly branch rises in Payne Lake and flows north. They all come together to flow into Payne Bay, an arm of Ungava Bay.

1912   Flaherty – see Povungnituk

1948   Dr. Jacques Rousseau, Edgar Aubert de la Rue, geologist, Pierre Gadbois, geographer, and Jean Michéa, ethnologist and archaeologist, with four Montagnais guides, flew to Povungnituk, ascended the Kogaluk River to Lake Tasiat,

portaged to Payne Lake and descended the Payne river to Payne Bay. They continued to Fort Chimo by boat and flew back to Montreal. [*Arctic*, Autumn 1948, pp. 133-35; Cooke, p. 167]

LEAF
The Leaf River rises in Lake Minto, a large lake north of Clearwater Lake, not far from the shores of Hudson Bay, and it flows northeast in a straight course across most of the central Ungava peninsula, entering Ungava Bay at the Inuit community of Tasiujaq on Leaf Bay.

1898 A.P. Low, for the Geological Survey, on a winter journey, explored inland from White Whale Point to Lake Minto and the first 40 miles of the Leaf River. The starving condition of his dogs forced him to retreat to the sea coast. [*Geographical Review*, July/Dec., p. 116]

1912 Robert Flaherty, starting from Great Whale River, made a winter trip with Inuit and dog-teams up the coast to Richmond Gulf, inland to Lake Minto and followed the Leaf River to its mouth on Ungava Bay. [*Geographical Review*, July/December, pp. 116-32]

1976 *Bob Davis, travelling alone, canoed from Kuujjuaq down the Koksoak River, around Ungava Bay to Leaf Bay. He ascended the Leaf River a short distance and crossed northwest by various lakes intending to connect with the Payne River. He was wind-bound on the large lakes and could not progress further so he returned down the Guenyveau River and the Leaf River, flying out from Tasiujaq. [*Che-Mun *files]

1979 *Jean Claude Dufresne, Jacques Dufresne, Luc Farmer and Christian Viau started at Inukjuaq and canoed upstream, crossed the height of land to Minto Lake and canoed down the Leaf River to Ungava Bay. [FQCC files]*

1986 *Martin Brown, Bob Barnes and Randy Cross, Americans, canoed down the Leaf River for about 200 miles to Ungava Bay. [Personal communication – Tom Hallenbeck]*

1988 *Tom Hallenbeck, for Sunrise County Canoe Expeditions, began guiding trips down the Leaf River, putting in about 200 miles upstream from Ungava Bay. [Personal communication – Tom Hallenbeck]*

KOKSOAK

Like the Moose River in Ontario, the Koksoak in Ungava is a relatively short, broad, tidal river into which flow two major rivers, the Larch and the Kaniapiskau. The river begins at the confluence of the two tributaries and flows north into the southern end of Ungava Bay. The important Inuit community of Kuujjuaq, originally the Hudson's Bay post of Fort Chimo, is situated about 50 kilometres from the mouth of the river.

LARCH–KOKSOAK

The Larch (Rivière aux Mélèzes) rises in central Ungava near Seal Lake, flows northeast and was part of the route from Richmond Gulf to Fort Chimo.

1828 *Dr. William Hendry, medical officer, with George Atkinson and four Indian canoemen, Oskutch, Maccapathscau, Nooquattamaugan and Jetchin, in two canoes, exploring for the HBC, went up the Clearwater and down the Larch and Koksoak. When the Indians saw signs of the Eskimo they were reluctant to go farther. They returned by the same route. [Davies, p. 69; Cooke, p. 143] A.P. Low, in his GSC report of 1896 misread* Mendry *for* Hendry *in the Hudson's Bay journals and the mistake is perpetuated by others.*

1830 *Nicol Finlayson and Erland Erlandson, HBC, with a crew of eleven, in three canoes, travelled from Moose Factory up the James Bay coast to Richmond Gulf, ascended the Clearwater River to Seal Lake, crossed the height of land and went down the Larch and Koksoak to Ungava Bay, establishing the post at Fort Chimo. [Davies, p. 100; Cooke, p. 143]*

1884 Edmund James Peck, Anglican missionary, with four Indians canoed from Little Whale River up the coast to Richmond Gulf, up the Clearwater, across Seal Lake and down the Larch and Koksoak rivers to Fort Chimo. He caught the HBC steamer at Fort Chimo. [Cooke, p. 149]

1896 A.P. Low, William Spreadborough and G.A. Young, GSC, from the railway at Missanabie canoed down the Missinaibi-Moose to Moose Factory. They travelled by fishing boat to Richmond Gulf, up the Clearwater to Clearwater Lake, crossed to Seal Lake and continued down the Larch-Koksoak rivers to Fort Chimo, where they caught the HBC steamer *Erik* to Quebec. [GSC Report, 1896; Zaslow, p. 170, map p. 167; Cooke, p. 156]

1906 Stephen and Florence Tasker from Philadelphia, on a private recreational trip, with George Elson and Job Chapies as guides, having canoed from Missanabie down the Missinaibi River to Moose Factory took passage on the HBC boat, *Inenew*, to Great Whale River. They canoed up the coast of Hudson Bay into Richmond Gulf, up the Clearwater River, Clearwater and Seal lakes, across the height of land and down the Larch and Koksoak rivers to Fort Chimo where they caught the HBC boat south. [*Field and Stream*, Feb. and March, 1908, p. 943; Hoyle, in Hodgins and Hobbs, eds. p. 128]

1912 Omarolluk – see Clearwater

1944 Fathers Ernest Lepage and Arthème Dutilly, botanists, canoed from Richmond Gulf up the Clearwater, across the height of land and down the Larch and Koksoak rivers to Fort Chimo. [Cooke, p. 169]

1957 Geoffrey Power, University of Waterloo, travelled the length of the Koksoak River and a short distance up the two tributaries, Larch and Kaniapiskau, doing research on salmon. [*Canadian Field-Naturalist*, Oct./Dec. 1961, p. 221]

1978 *Rod Beebe, III, Doug Williams, Bruce McPherson, Tom Addicks, Porter Turnbull and Chris Kenoyer started at Great Whale (Kuuijuaraapik), canoed up the Hudson Bay coast, passed through the "gullet" into Richmond Gulf, went up the Wiachouan River, north through the portage lake route used by A.P. Low to the Clearwater River, ascending it to Clearwater Lake, up "Noonish River", portaged to Lower Seal Lake, up "Buzzard Brook" and portaged to Lac de Sem the headwater of the Larch River. They descended the Larch River into the Koksoak River and down to Fort Chimo (Kuujjuaq). They saw no evidence of people between Richmond Gulf and the Koksoak River except for a few ancient tent rings. They believed they were the first group to navigate this route without native guides. [Personal communication – Beebe]*

1985 *Jacques Rene, Marc Laliberté, and Paul Gagnon put in at the mouth of Richmond Gulf, canoed up the Clearwater River to Clearwater Lake, crossed the height of land and canoed down the Larch to Kuujjuaq. [FQCC files]*

KANIAPISKAU–KOKSOAK

The Kaniapiskau rises in the lakes north of the divide between southern and northern Quebec, close to the Labrador border, and flows generally north. The Kaniapiskau itself has two tributaries used by canoeists: the du Sable, a small river which rises near Schefferville; and the Swampy Bay, a much longer river which rises on the Labrador border across the divide from Lake Petitsikapau and flows into the Kaniapiskau 100 kilometres from its confluence with the Koksoak. The waters of the upper Kaniapiskau, from Lake Kaniapiskau, have been diverted into the upper La Grande in connection with the first phase of the James Bay Project.

1820 *James Clouston, HBC, having come from Rupert House by way of the Rupert and Eastmain, wintered at Nichicun. In the spring, with Robert Chilton, Patrick Flynn and four Indians, they travelled overland to Lake Kaniapiskau, built bark canoes and started down the Kaniapiskau River. They canoed about 50 miles of this river, detoured inland by lakes and a river they called the Smooth Rock, crossed Lake Kenogamissi and rejoined the Kaniapiskau 40 miles above the point where the Larch flows into it, continuing down to the Koksoak. They turned back almost 100 miles from Ungava Bay and returned by Lake Kenogamissi, Clearwater Lake and Richmond Gulf, down the coast to Rupert House. [Davies, pp. xliv-xlvii; Lentz,* Explorers Journal, *1970]*

1832 *Erland Erlandson, with eight men, one small and two large canoes, left Fort Chimo and proceeded up the Koksoak River, continuing up the Kaniapiskau to near the entry of the Swampy Bay River. It was Erlandson's intention to continue up the Swampy Bay but the Indian guide refused to go on, so South River post was built on the Kaniapiskau. Erlandson wintered there and returned down-river in the spring. [Davies, p. 199]*

1834 *Erland Erlandson returned down the Kaniapiskau from his overland trip to North West River. [Ibid., p. lxviii]*

1893 A.P. Low and D.I.V. Eaton, GSC, having started from Lac St. Jean, came up the Chamouchouane to Lac Mistassini and crossed to the Eastmain, following it up to its source. They crossed the height of land to Lake Nichicun, portaged to the Kaniapiskau and followed it down to the Koksoak and Ungava Bay. At Fort Chimo they took passage on the HBC steamer to Rigolet. [GSC Report, 1896; Zaslow, p. 168, map p. 167; Cooke p. 154]

1914-15 R.B. D'Aigle, prospector, was the first to stake mining claims in the District of Ungava, in the watershed region of the Labrador hinterland. [Thompson, Don, v.3, p. 207]

1916-17 R.B. D'Aigle was prospecting in the interior of Labrador and met W.E.C. Todd with the 8th Carnegie Museum Expedition near the Swampy Bay River. [Todd, p. 30]

1917 Walter Edmond Clyde Todd, Olaus J. Murie, Alfred Marshall, with the 8th Carnegie Museum expedition, made an avifaunal survey on the Kaniapiskau River. They began at Sept Îles, canoed up the Ste. Marguerite River, portaged to the Pekans River, crossed the height of land to Chibogamo Lake, down Ashuanipi River to Menihek Lake, portaged via Petitsikapau Lake to the Swampy Bay River and descended it and the Kaniapiskau River to Fort Chimo. Their return was on the *Nascopie* to Montreal. [Todd, pp. 26-31]

1918 R.B. D'Aigle, Mackenzie and Mann Co., took a party of prospectors up the Moisie River, across the height of land and down the Swampy Bay, Kaniapiskau and Koksoak rivers to Fort Chimo. [Cooke, p. 163]

1957 Geoffrey Power – see Larch-Koksoak

1959 Comtois, d'Artois, Forbes, Pelletier, J.M. Rockingham, and J.R. Rockingham canoed from Knob Lake down the Kaniapiskau River, planning to go down the Koksoak. This was an army exercise under the General Officer Commanding Quebec command (Gen. J.M. Rockingham). The trip had to be terminated at Lac Otelnuk because the death of Premier Maurice Duplessis required Gen. Rockingham's return to Quebec City. [Morse files, p. 3]

pre-1967 Two young men starting on a canoe trip from a fishing camp on the upper Kaniapiskau were

drowned in the rapids less than an hour after starting. [*Explorers Journal*, Dec. 1970, p. 218]

1967 John Lentz, Bob Maguire, Carl Lohmann, Tracey Perry and Sandy Witherell, Americans, and Johnny Smallboy, a Cree from Moose Factory, flew in from Sept-Îles and Labrador City, using one canvas-covered Chestnut canoe and two aluminum ones started from Lac Sevestre, made a complete descent of the Kaniapiskau and then down the Koksoak to Fort Chimo. They had deposited a food cache at Eaton Canyon. [*Ibid.*]

1973 Robin and Victoria Fraser, Dick Irwin, Christopher Horne, John Bland and Stuart Kinmond canoed from the headwaters of the Kaniapiskau and down the Koksoak River to Ungava Bay. [Personal communication – Robin Fraser]

1974 A crew, sponsored by Parks Canada, consisting of Paul Montminy, leader, Pierre Deshaies, photographer, Daniel Joln, David and Lester Sharnberg and Claude Potvin, from Schefferville, canoed down the Howells, Goodwood, Kaniapiskau and Koksoak rivers to Fort Chimo, 312 miles in twenty-five days. [Parks Canada files]

1974 Duke Watson, C. Bristol, R. Norton, Bob O'Hara and E. Schindler started at Lac Hecla, part of the headwaters of the Eastmain River, crossed lakes and small streams to Lake Nichicun, crossed into

Victoria Fraser, flanked by John Bland, Stuart Kinmond, her husband Robin, Dick Irwin and Chris Horne in 1973, with the Kaniapiskau River in the background, has canoed many of Canada's northern rivers. [Robin Fraser]

the Fort George River watershed and crossed to Lake Kaniapiskau. A short distance down the Kaniapiskau, Schindler left the group, and W. Horgan and V. Josendal joined it. They continued down the Kaniapiskau and Koksoak rivers to Fort Chimo. [Personal communication – Watson]

1975 Bob Davis made a solo trip down the Kaniapiskau and Koksoak rivers. [Che-Mun files]

1976 John Fallis, Larry Biemann, Norman Frost, Jim Blair, Roger Partridge and Fred Loosemore, started from Sandy Lake, south and east of Lake Kaniapiskau and canoed down the Kaniapiskau and Koksoak rivers to Fort Chimo. [Wilderness Canoeist, December 1976, p. 1; personal communication – Fallis]

1976 Luc Farmer, Jean-Claude Dufresne, Normand Ponton, Christian Viau travelled to Labrador City by train and then by road to Mount Wright. They canoed up the Pekans River to Lac Goupil, through Lake Opisoteo to Lake Kaniapiskau and Lake Delorme and descended the Kaniapiskau River to Fort Chimo. [North/Nord, Sept./Oct., 1977, p. 36]

1977 Camp Widjiwagan: Eric Buetow led David Kunin, Mark Niemann, David Page, Geoff Seltzer and John Wartman canoeing down the Kaniapiskau River on a 550-mile trip to Ungava Bay. [Camp Widjiwagan Archives]

1978 A canoeist was drowned in the gorge at Granite Falls on the Kaniapiskau River. [Cruiser, January 1980, p. 2]

1979 Hubert Yockey, Tom Proctor, Tim Zecha and George Rines, Americans, with three decked Berrigan canoes, flew in to Lac Vincennes, the headwaters of the du Sable River, and canoed down that river, the Kaniapiskau and the Koksoak to Fort Chimo. [Ibid., p. 1]

1980 Yockey, Ed Gertler, Terry Zecha and Mark Holthaus repeated the trip of the previous year, the last on the Kaniapiskau before it was dammed and the waters of Lac Kaniapiskau diverted to the La Grande and the James Bay Hydroelectric Project. [Cruiser, January 1981, p. 2]

1980 Gilles Lortie, Guy Fournier, Jacques Grondin, Jean Brodeur, Danielle Vallée, and Guy Doré started at Schefferville and canoed by a series of lakes and the Pijor River to the Kaniapiskau River, continuing downstream to Cambrien Lake, 210 kilometres. [Personal communication – Doré]

1982 Hubert Yockey, Terry Zecha, Mark Holthaus, Joel Snyder and Joe Astroski, in decked canoes, a C-1 and two C-2s, put in at the headwaters of the Swampy Bay River and followed it to the confluence of the Kaniapiskau, continuing down that river and the Koksoak to Fort Chimo. [Explorers Journal, Winter 1990]

WHALE

The Whale River rises in Lac Savallette in the northeastern corner of northern Quebec and flows north to the southern tip of Ungava Bay. It has a significant tributary, the Wheeler, which rises in the same area and follows a parallel course to enter the Whale about 150 kilometres before the mouth of the river.

1834 Erland Erlandson, with four Naskapi Indians, left Fort Chimo in the spring, hauling canoes, went up the Whale River to Lac Savalette, including a portage of 37 miles around the canyon to Lac Ninawawe, on a trip that finished at North West River. [Davies, p. lxvii; Explorers Journal, September 1984]

1960 Geoffrey Power and G.M. Telford were on the lower reaches of the Whale River doing research on salmon. [Canadian Field-Naturalist, Oct./Dec. p. 221]

1981 Hubert Yockey, Chuck Rollins, Tom McCloud, Curt and Denise Gellerman, and Bobby Pitts, with a kayak, a C-1, a C-2 and a 17-foot Grumman, flew from Schefferville to the headwaters of the Whale River, Lac Savalette, and paddled the full length of the Whale River, the kayak running most of the rapids. They finished the trip by canoeing around the coast and into the Koksoak River to Fort Chimo. The FQCC believed that this was the first descent of the full river. [Explorers Journal, Sept. 1984; American Whitewater, July/August, 1986, pp. 18-22]

1983 Mike Ketemer and Madelaine Sauvé canoed down the Wheeler and Whale rivers to Ungava Bay. [Personal communication – Ketemer]

1989 Seana Irvine and Andrea Hodgins led a Wanapitei co-ed youth group on the same route as 1983. [Wanapitei trip report]

GEORGE

The George River rises just north of the Labrador border in northeastern Quebec and flows due north to enter the eastern side of Ungava Bay at George River, or Kangiqsualujjuaq. The River was first made famous by the Hubbard-Wallace story and the headland at the River estuary is named Point Hubbard. Before the Churchill Falls dam was built in Labrador, Lake Michikamau was the access to the George River. A tributary, the De Pas, accessible from Schefferville, is now frequently used to reach the George.

1811 B. Kohlmeister and G. Kmoch, Moravian missionaries, in an Eskimo shallop, went from Okak around Cape Chidley into Ungava Bay and were the first Europeans to enter the George River and the Koksoak River. [Davies, p. xxxvi; Hind, v. 2, p. 141]

1839 Some Europeans ascended the George River to communicate with the Naskapi Indians. [Hind, v. 2, p. 141]

1905 Mina Benson Hubbard, guided by George Elson, with Joseph Iserhoff and Job Chapies all from Missanabie, and Gilbert Blake of North West River, canoed from North West River in Labrador, up the Naskaupi to Lake Michikamau and down the George River to the HBC post. After a six-week delay the HBC boat arrived and they sailed south to Quebec. [Hubbard, 1909; Davidson and Rugge, *Great Heart*, 1988]

1905 Dillon Wallace and Clifford Easton, having canoed from North West River up the Naskaupi and following the Indian portage trail to Lake Michikamau with three other men, continued alone down the George River to the HBC post. They went on up the coast by sail-boat, and when that was frozen in, on foot to Fort Chimo. After freeze-up they returned down the coast by dog-team to Quebec. [Wallace, *The Long Labrador Trail*; Blossom, ed., pp. 349-65]

Clifford Easton (stern) and Dillon Wallace on Lake Michikamau, setting their course for the George River, were hoping to make the first descent of the river. [Wallace, *The Long Labrador Trail*, 1907]

In the photo at left, George Elson, noted guide, takes his ease in camp approaching the George River. The trip he is leading for Mina Hubbard is already ahead of the Wallace trip. The unspoken rivalry between the two continued for decades. [Hubbard, *A Woman's Way through Unknown Labrador*, 1909]

1910 H. Hesketh Prichard – see Fraser (Labrador)

1910 W.B. Cabot – see Kogaluk (Labrador)

1928 Herman J. Koehler – see Kogaluk (Labrador)

1931 J.B. Racicot, a prospector for the Cyril Knight Company, ascended the George River to its source and returned down-river to Fort Chimo. [Cooke, p. 163]

1931 Herman Koehler and Fred Cornell, Americans, with Jim Martin, local guide from Cartwright, went by ship to Fort Chimo with plans to travel up the George River by canoe and return across the height of land, down the Notakwanon to Hopedale. Cornell's body was found by Naskapi east of Indian House Lake, with a canoe paddle nearby. An American group was mapping the northern Labrador coast by aerial survey and the Indians led a flight into the Interior to retrieve the body in 1932. Koehler's body was found in 1938 about 3 miles from where Cornell's body lay. No trace of Jim Martin was ever found. [Forbes, p. 129; Henderson, *Nastawgan*, Autumn 1993, pp. 11-15]

1947 Dr. Jacques Rousseau, director of the Montreal Botanical Gardens, with four Montagnais guides, flew to Lake Hubbard, north of Lake Michikamau, the source of the George River, and canoed to Ungava Bay. [*Arctic Circular*, January 1948, p. 7; Cooke, p. 169]

1948 Duncan Hodgson, Canadian Wildlife Service, with Rene Richard, Inuit guide, Bob May, HBC, and eight Inuit hunters, went up the George River from George River post for 60 miles, in three canoes with 8-horsepower motors, and down again, investigating caribou. Bob May had

travelled extensively on the George. [*Canadian Field-Naturalist*, March-April, 1950 p. 60; *Arctic Circular*, 1948, p. 78]

1954 A.W.F. Banfield was at Indian House Lake on the George River doing ornithological research. [Todd, p. 117]

1967 Stewart Coffin, Don Barr, Bob Hatton, Kerck Kelsey, Don Peach and John Sharp, reached Schefferville by train, were flown to just below Cabot Lake and canoed down the George River to George River settlement. [Personal communication; Morse files, p. 19]

1967 Hormuth and Caruso canoed down the George ahead of the Coffin party. They used plastic Clorox bottles on their canoes as outrigging. A news clipping in the Long Island (New York) Press, July 13, 1969 has a photo showing this

From a hill-top climbed by Mina Hubbard in 1905, Don Barr, Bob Hatton, Kerck Kelsey, Don Sharp and John Sharp overlook the headwaters of the George River in 1967. [Stewart Coffin]

arrangement. [Communication from Stewart Coffin]

1969 Brigitte and Elmar Engel, journalists from Germany, using two kayaks paddled down the St. Lawrence River from Montreal to Sept Îles, flew to Schefferville and then to Jamin Lake, the headwater of the De Pas River, with the intention of kayaking the De Pas and the George rivers. On the second day on the De Pas one of the kayaks was wrecked on a rock and they lost most of their food and some gear. They continued down the De Pas, one person kayaking and one walking, until they were rescued by an observant bush pilot. [*Outdoor Canada*, October 1974, p. 16; Klein, *Passion for Wilderness*, pp. 24-50]

1973 Gilles Samson, Pierre Perreault, Serge-André Crète, José Mailhot, and a few others, conducted an archaeological exploration on the George River, travelling in two motorized canoes. [Personal communication – Samson]

pre-1974 Don Pruden, a Cree with Canadian Dept. of Northern Affairs, "made one of the half-dozen recorded canoe trips down the George." Starting by dog-team from Schefferville, he continued down the George River by canoe after break-up. [*Outdoor Canada*, October 1974, p. 19]

1974 Bob Davis, on a solo trip, starting from Schefferville, canoed down the George River, along the Ungava coast, and up into the mouth of the Koksoak River, finishing at Fort Chimo. [Personal communication]

1974 Gilles Samson, Martyne Michaud and Léonard St. Onge surveyed the shores of a section of the George River for archaeological sites from a motorized canoe. [Personal communication – Samson]

1975 *Brian McColl, Sid Magee, Ron Hirsch, Peter Norwood, Carol Conche and Joan Brown put in their canoes at Lake Griffith and canoed down the De Pas and George rivers to just north of Indian House Lake. They were flown out. [Personal communication – McColl]*

1976 *George Luste, Yu Jin Pak, John Hatton, Cameron Hayne and Richard Mably travelled by train to Schefferville. They put in their canoes at Astray Lake, canoed up 100 kilometres, crossed the height of land and continued down the De Pas and George rivers to Ungava Bay. Four wildlife biologists from Montreal made the complete trip at the same time. [Wilderness Canoeist, September 1976]*

1979 *Howard Meyer, Jake, Egan and David, with two aluminum canoes, travelled by train to Schefferville, flew to the De Pas River and canoed down the De Pas and the George to tide-water. In his trip report Meyer mentions that six men from Boston, doing the same trip, had smashed a Mad River canoe in the De Pas, but patched it up well enough to travel. Twelve people with six canoes had wrecked all six canoes on the first 6 miles of the De Pas. [Che-Mun files – Meyer unpublished trip report]*

1979 *Stephen Loring – see Kogaluk (Labrador)*

KOROK

A short river by Ungava standards, the Korok flows west out of the Torngat Mountains on the border of Labrador and enters Ungava Bay just north of the mouth of the George River.

1951 Dr. Jacques Rousseau explored Adloylik Fiord on Ungava Bay, the Korok River, part of the Torngat Mountains and the New Quebec, or Ungava, Crater.

1975 *Duke Watson and A. Hovey started at Ramah Bay, ascended the Stecker River, portaged 14 miles through the Torngat Mountains to a height of 1400 feet and canoed down the Korok River. From the lower Korok they made a traverse by a series of lakes and portages across to the George River, finishing at the community of George River. [Personal communication – Watson]*

1976 *Bob Davis, travelling alone, went up the Labrador coast by boat from Nain to Saglek Fiord with an Inuit family. He hiked up Nachvak Brook and crossed over to the Korok River, hiking and rafting down that river in a 5-pound raft which he had carried in his pack. Davis continued to George River and flew to Fort Chimo where his canoe had been shipped. He paddled down the Koksoak River,*

Members of the Smithsonian Torngat Archaeological Project in 1978, Charles Luckmann, William Ritchie, Stephen Loring and Tom Hallenbeck at Nachvak Fiord lunch out of the wind in a Thule Eskimo semi-subterranean structure; the raven "Detroit" perches on the entranceway lintel.
They are about to go up the Palmer River and cross to the Korok. [Stephen Loring]

around Ungava Bay to Leaf Bay, went up the Leaf River and crossed northwest by various lakes. He was windbound there, so returned down the Guenyveau River and down the Leaf River. He flew back to George River. [Che-Mun files – Davis letter to Nick Nickels]

1978 Stephen Loring, Thomas Hallenbeck, Charles Luckmann and William B. Ritchie, conducting archaeological, ethnohistorical and palaeoecological research, made the first canoe traverse of the old HBC winter route, described by Dillon Wallace in The Long Labrador Trail. From Nachvak Fiord, they ascended the Palmer River to its source, crossed over to the upper Korok River and ascended it to near its source and canoed down the Korok to Ungava Bay. [Personal communication – Loring]

1979 Robert Perkins flew to Nachvak Fiord with his 14.5-foot canoe, ascended the Palmer River in the Torngat Mountains, crossed over to the Korok and descended it to an Inuit cabin at the mouth of the river. This was a solo trip until the last ten days, when he was joined by pre-arrangement by a photographer, Richard Feldman. [Perkins, Against Straight Lines]

1981 Rod Beebe III, Doug Williams, Gordie Whitbeck and Russ Miller travelled from Nain up the coast of Labrador with an Inuk, Paul Nochasak. They canoed up Nachvak Fiord to Ramah Bay, went up the Stecker River, crossed through a gap in the Torngat Mountains to the headwaters of the Korok and descended it to Ungava Bay, continuing around to George River settlement. They saw a great variety of wildlife, as well as ancient Inuit sites. [Personal communication – Beebe; Canoe, April 1982]

CHAPTER TWELVE

THE LAND GOD
GAVE TO CAIN:
LABRADOR

As the saying goes, "God made the world in six days, and on the seventh, sailed inshore and hurled rocks at Labrador." Labrador, Newfoundland's mainland territory, is a high rocky plateau sloping eastward whose boundary is defined by watersheds. The rivers of Labrador flow east into the Atlantic Ocean. The First Nations people who lived by hunting caribou and travelled in these river valleys were the Naskapi, now known by their preferred name the Innu, in the northern interior and the Montagnais to the south.

The border which separates Labrador from Quebec's Ungava Peninsula was in dispute until the decision made by the British Privy Council in 1927, the territory having been claimed by both Quebec and Newfoundland. From Cape Chidley in the north, the boundary line meanders due south almost until it reaches Lake Michikamau, where it takes a wide swing to the west to accommodate an area of large lakes and rivers on the high central plateau, all of which drain east into either the Churchill or the Naskaupi River. The countless small lakes of the central plateau, labyrinth of islands, channels and bays, created an area whose drainage systems were for a long time a mystery to explorers and trappers alike. The mystery has now disappeared under water.

After 1968 the face of Labrador changed forever with the building of the mammoth Churchill Falls power project. This involved the damming of Labrador's

mightiest river, the Grand, sometimes known as the Hamilton, and in 1965 named by Premier J.R. Smallwood, the Churchill, in honour of Sir Winston Churchill. Michikamau and many of the other large lakes have since disappeared under the waters of the Smallwood Reservoir. Since most of the events recorded here took place before the Churchill Falls were harnessed to hydroelectric turbines, the river will be referred to as the Grand, or sometimes the Hamilton.

In comparison to the Grand, the other Labrador rivers are smaller but all are fast-flowing and full of rapids, coursing down from the height of land to the rocky, fiord-like coastline. Some of the rivers, such as the Fraser, the Kogaluk, the Notakwanon, the Ugjoktok and the Kanairiktok have been used by canoeists to reach across the height of land to the George River. These were not affected by the damming of Churchill Falls.

GRAND OR HAMILTON
(CHURCHILL)

The headwaters of the Grand River were the large lakes of the high central plateau, the major one being Astray Lake near present-day Schefferville. The river is also fed by the Ashuanipi which rises in Ashuanipi Lake in the southwest corner of Labrador, flows north to Astray Lake and on some maps is shown continuing southeast into Sandgirt Lake.

"Slowly and calmly the Hamilton River flows along

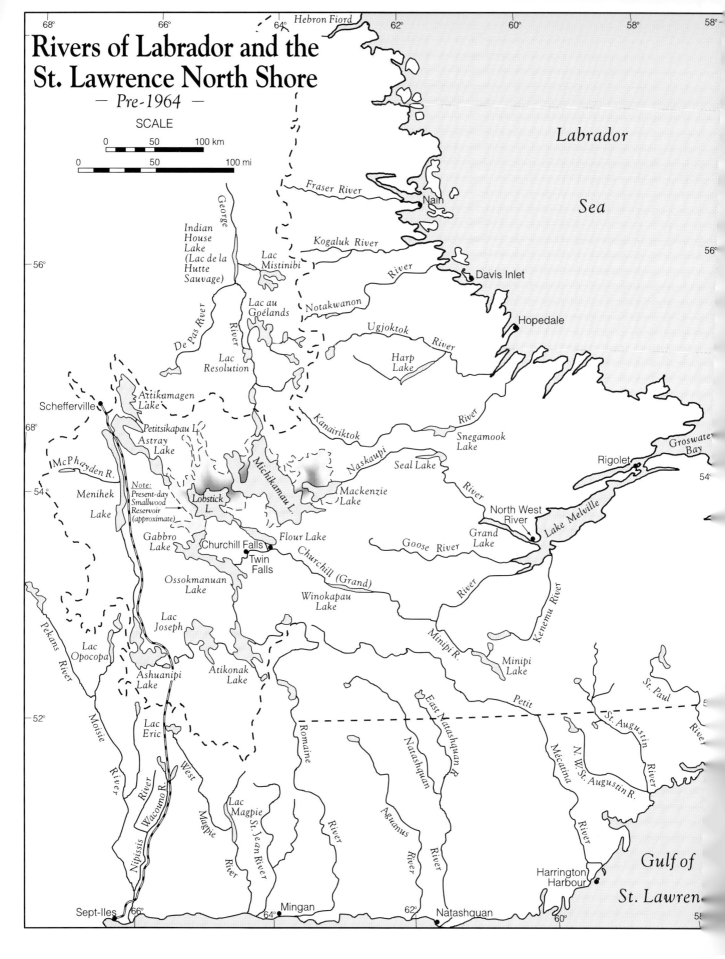

Rivers of Labrador and the St. Lawrence North Shore
— Pre-1964 —

SCALE

0   50   100 km

0   50   100 mi

Hebron Fiord

Labrador

Sea

Fraser River

Nain

George River

Indian House Lake (Lac de la Hutte Sauvage)

Kogaluk River

Lac Mistinibi

Davis Inlet

River

De Pas River

Lac au Goélands

Notakwanon

Hopedale

Lac Resolution

Ugjoktok

River

Harp Lake

Attikamagen Lake

Scheffeville

Kanairiktok

River

Snegamook Lake

Groswater Bay

Petitsikapau L.

Astray Lake

Naskaupi

Seal Lake

Rigolet

McPhayden R.

Michikamau L.

Mackenzie Lake

River

Menihek Lake

Note: Present-day Smallwood Reservoir (approximate)

Lobstick L.

North West River

Lake Melville

Grand Lake

Gabbro Lake

Churchill Falls

Flour Lake

Goose River

Twin Falls

Churchill (Grand)

River

Kenemu River

Ossokmanuan Lake

Winokapau Lake

Lac Joseph

Minipi R.

Minipi Lake

Pekans River

Lac Opocopa

Atikonak Lake

Ashuanipi Lake

St. Paul

East Natashquan R.

Petit

St. Augustin

Lac Eric

Moisie

River

Wacouno R.

West

Romaine

Natashquan

Aguanus River

River

Mécatina

N.W. St. Augustin R.

River

Nipissis River

Magpie

Lac Magpie

St. Jean River

River

River

Harrington Harbour

Sept-Iles

Mingan

Natashquan

Gulf of

St. Lawrence

through the labyrinth of lakes down to Sandgirt Lake, Flour Lake and finally Jacopie Lake at about 1600 feet above sea level. After issuing from this last, the river continues to flow comparatively calmly till about four miles from the neck of Grand Falls. One mile before it takes its leap, the river is still a noble stream, 400 yards wide, but already accelerating in speed. Suddenly the water begins to rush along in a strong current with plumes of spray and reaches the threshold of the fall above Grand Falls in four small cataracts. Reaching this point, the entire column of fleecy water is compressed within rocky banks not more than fifty yards apart. At the grand leap the heavy mass of water plunges with a deafening roar over the northern wall of Bowdoin Canyon quite vertically from the dizzy height of 316 feet into the pool below." [Henry Bryant, in *Bulletin of the Geographical Society of Philadelphia*, Vol. 1, 1894, pp. 37-84.]

Continuing east the river widens into 50-kilometre Lake Winokapau, then flows on as a river, emptying into Lake Melville, a saltwater arm of the sea, at Goose Bay. The only community historically associated with the Grand River is North West River, located farther east on Lake Melville where the Naskaupi River enters at the end of Grand Lake, an expansion of the Naskaupi.

The Unknown River which flows into the Grand River just below Grand Falls had four impressive sets of falls of its own. The river splits into two branches with two sets of falls on each branch. Twin Falls and Yale Falls are the two lower sets of falls. The waterfalls, each with a drop of about 30 metres and split on the brink by a large rock, were very similar, and they were a source of much exploration, although the visits to the falls were mainly on foot and not by canoe. Like Grand Falls they too have been dammed, and can no longer be seen.

1834 *Erland Erlandson, HBC, was the first European to cross Labrador. Travelling with five Naskapi from Fort Chimo (Kuujjuaq), on Ungava Bay, he canoed up the Whale River, crossed over to Lake Petitsikapau and probably followed an Indian route along the Naskaupi River to Hamilton Inlet, then called Esquimaux Bay and returned by the same route. [McLean, 1932]*

pre-1839 *David Dixon – or Dickson – a trader visited Grand Falls. [Cabot, p. 8]*

1839 *John McLean, HBC, with ten men, including Erland Erlandson, travelled up the George River to Petitsikapau, then to a HBC post named Fort Nascopie and canoed with Naskapi down the Grand River to the falls. The falls effectively blocked the trade route to the coast so he turned back and retraced his route to Fort Chimo, leaving Erlandson to set up a post at Indian House Lake on the George River. [Davies, ed. Introduction]*

1840 *McLean, coming from Fort Chimo, joined Erlandson on the George River and they travelled by canoe to Hamilton Inlet, making their way past the falls. [Ibid.]*

1840 *W.H.A. Davies ascended the Grand River to explore it with Indians and was ten days upstream when they caused a severe forest fire. [Hind, v.I. p. 206]*

1841 *McLean explored the Indian portage route around Grand Falls and reached Hamilton Inlet. [McLean, 1932]*

1842 *McLean again reached Hamilton Inlet by canoe. [Cooke, p. 146]*

1859 *Kennedy, HBC, persuaded an Iroquois, who did not share the Labrador Indians' dread of the falls, to take him there but he left no written account. [Cilley, p.30] (Elliott Merrick names the HBC employee, Joseph McPherson, and the Iroquois, Louis-over-the-fire. [Merrick, p. 232])*

1866 *Père Louis Babel, Oblate, canoed north from the St. Lawrence with two Indians, Xavier Maskuaro and Jean-Marie, up the St. Jean and Romaine Rivers until he reached Grand River at Lake Winokapau. He went down-river to Hamilton Inlet where he caught HBC transportation back to Mingan. [Tremblay, ed. 1977]*

1868 *Père Louis Babel, with two Indians, travelled up the Grand River to Petitsikapau and returned to the St. Lawrence down the Pakamesha and the Moisie Rivers to Sept Îles. [Ibid.]*

1870 *Père Louis Babel came up the St. Jean and Romaine Rivers to Petitsikapau and returned down the Moisie. [Ibid.]*

1875, '76? Father Lacasse travelled with Naskapi Indians from North West River to Chimo, following the portage route around the Naskaupi River to Lake Michikamau. This was most likely a winter trip. [Cabot, p. 8]

1887 Pierre Gaspé, a Micmac from the Gaspé, reached North West River by canoeing up the St. Jean and Ninipi rivers and down the Grand River. [Holme in *Royal Geographical Soc. Proc.*, Apr. 1888, p. 191]

1887 Randle F. Holme, Oxford University, on a private expedition with two local men as guides, went up the Grand River 140 miles by boat to Lake Winokapau and had to turn back 50 miles below the falls. [*Ibid.*, pp. 189-205; *Century Magazine*, September 1892]

1891 Austin Cary, Dennis M. Cole, W. R. Smith and Young were part of a private scientific expedition from Bowdoin College, Rockland, Maine, led by Prof. Leslie Lee of the biology department. While Lee led other members of the expedition on coastal and inland exploration, the four men set off up the Grand River in two 15-foot cedar boats, with oars and a paddle. They rowed and tracked through the fast current to Lake Winokapau. Because of an injury to Young's hand, he and Smith turned back and returned to North West River. Cary and Cole rowed to the end of the lake, cached their canoe and most of their provisions and hiked up-river for two days, saw and named Bowdoin Canyon and viewed the falls. Returning to their cache, they discovered a fire which had consumed their boat and part of their provisions. They made their way out by walking and rafting where possible, 300 miles in seventeen days. [Cilley, 1891; *J. of the Am. Geo. Soc. of New York*, 1892, v. 24, pp. 1-17]

1891 Henry G. Bryant and Prof. Arthur Kenaston, Americans, with local guides John Montague and Geoffrey Ban, an Inuk from Okak, in a river boat, towing a canoe, went up the Grand River to Grand Falls and canoed down. [*Century Magazine*, September 1892; *Bulletin of the Geographical Society of Philadelphia*, 1 No. 2, 1894, pp. 37-84]

1894 A.P. Low and D.I.V. Eaton, Geological Survey, explored the upper Hamilton River above the falls, the headwater lakes of Petitsikapau, Michikamau, Sandgirt and the Ashuanipi River. (They undertook this survey even though Labrador was not then part of Canada; this border would long be under dispute.) They then canoed up the Atikonak River to Ossokmanuan Lake, crossed the height of land and descended the Romaine River. [Cooke, p. 155]

1917 R.B. D'Aigle, prospector, travelled up the Hamilton River to Lake Petitsikapau. [*Ibid.*, p. 163]

1921 J.G. Thomas, from California, travelled up-river from North West River with a band of Montagnais on their way to the St. Lawrence. Leaving them he joined trappers, Arch Goudie, Philomena and Dan Michelin from North West River and canoed up the Grand River to the mouth of the Unknown River. They cached their canoes and hiked in to Twin Falls (which he named), realizing from the column of mist that there was a companion waterfall which they could not reach or see on the north branch of the river. He claimed to be the first outsider to see these falls. [*Geographical Journal*, July 1925, p. 79; *Beaver*, Autumn 1965, p. 30, Merrick, *True North*, pp. 194-95]

1925 Judge William J. Malone of Connecticut made a trip up the Grand River to the Falls. [Personal communication – Beekman Pool]

1925 Varick Frissell and another Yale student, James Hellier, with local trappers John and Robert Michelin and a Canadian gold prospector, Eugene Fournier, who joined the party en route, ascended the Grand River to the Falls. Frissell and John Michelin hiked into the valley of Ossokmanuan Lake and found the Unknown River and falls, split by a rock, which they named Yale Falls. They could not see the mist of Twin Falls on the south branch of the river. [*Geographical Journal*, March 1927, pp. 332-40; *Beaver*, Autumn 1965 p. 30]

1928 Howard Taylor, Dr. J.D. Kernan, Philip V. Rogers, his brother Ralph, Americans, with guides Wally Chambers from Mingan and Philippe Colombe from Loretteville, in two canvas canoes, ascended the St. Jean and the upper part of the Romaine River, crossed over into the Atikonak system to Ossokmanuan Lake, descended the Unknown River to a pair of 100-foot falls which were above the Twin and Yale Falls, a fact that was not discovered by Thomas or Frissell. [*Beaver,* Autumn 1965, p. 30]

1928 H.G. Watkins, J.M. Scott, Cambridge University, and L.A.D. Leslie, with Robert Michelin as local guide, started on a trip up the Grand River planning to go to the headwaters, but they were forced to return to North West River short of the Falls when their guide cut his foot with an axe. They were sponsored by the Royal Geographical Society. [Scott, J., Chap. 1]

1929 Gino Watkins, James Scott, with Robert Michelin as guide, made a winter sledge journey up the Grand River with a dog team to the mouth of the Unknown River, travelled up this river, reached the upper falls, now named Scott Falls and Thomas Falls and followed the river bank down to Yale Falls, establishing for the first time that there were upper and lower falls. They also surveyed and mapped all of the falls. [*Ibid.*, Chap. 7]

1930 Elliott Merrick, American, and Kay Austin, Australian, both employed at the Grenfell Mission in North West River, paddled and poled up the Grand River with John Michelin, as their guide, and in the company of local trappers Alvin and Robert Michelin, Arch, Fred, Harvey, Cecil and Victor Goudie, Ralph Blake, Russell Groves, Gordon Pottle and Henry Baikie, joining in the fall trapping above the falls. They visited Grand Falls and saw Twin Falls and Yale Falls, Kay being the first white woman to see Twin Falls, and snow-shoed out in winter. Merrick with Henry Blake went back to the trapping ground on Lake Winokapau in the winter of 1931 and came down-river by sled and canoe. [Merrick, 1989]

1930 Lincoln Ellsworth and Beekman Pool, Americans, with two Indian guides in two 18-foot canvas canoes, went up the Moisie and down the Grand River. Starting at Sept-Îles, they followed

the traditional Montagnais route, up the Moisie and Nipissis Rivers, up a series of three steep portages to Lake Kakatiak and up to Lake Nipissis. They crossed over to the northeast branch of the Moisie and continued up to Lake Caopacho, from which they crossed over the height of land. A few days later they reached Lake Ashuanipi and the waters of the Grand River, continuing on across Lake Menihek. The route was not well known to the guides and much time was spent scouting for the route and the portages around Grand Falls. They reached North West River after six weeks and sixty-nine portages. [Personal communication – Pool]

1939 W.E.C. Todd, Kenneth Doutt and Mrs. Doutt travelled from North West River by motor boat to the mouth of the Grand River where they began their trip with a 21-foot freight canoe and a smaller canoe, and with guides John Michelin, Cecil Blake, and Leslie Michelin. They used a small outboard motor to go up-river, as well as poles, paddles and tracking to reach Sandgirt Lake above Grand Falls. They returned down-river, taking only nine days to cover what had taken a month going up. This was the 19th Carnegie Expedition for avifaunal research. [Todd, p. 47]

1947 G.H. Desbarats, Newfoundland Dept. of Natural Resources, John Maher, surveyor, Roland Powell, trapper, Roy Myers, engineering student, with two canoes and with John Blake and Rank Hope, North West River trappers as guides, canoed up-river from Grand Falls to Sandgirt Lake and down to the Falls. They were surveying for the possibility of a hydroelectric power project. [*Canadian Geographic*, November 1948, p. 214]

1950 Andrew Brown and Ralph Gray in Grumman canoes, with guides John and Leslie Michelin from North West River, on a recreational trip, went from Schefferville, to Astray Lake, down the Ashuanipi River to Sandgirt Lake, upstream on the Atikonak, to Gabbro and Ossokmanuan Lakes, down Unknown River, explored the four sets of falls, returned upstream to Ossokmanuan

Lake and Gabbro Lake, canoed to Grand Falls and down the Grand River to North West River. [*National Geographic*, July 1951, p. 65]

1967 Robin and Victoria Fraser, Dick Irwin and Allerton (Jay) Cushman Jr. canoed from Astray Lake down the Ashuanipi River to the Grand River. The river was not yet dammed but there was heavy construction. They walked to and photographed the Grand Falls and then took the 26-mile portage through a chain of lakes around the falls and the canyon, the traditional portage route – now all under water. They were trucked over the last bit because construction had wiped out the route. They descended the Grand River to Happy Valley. [Personal communication – Robin Fraser]

1968 Dick Irwin – see Naskaupi

1968 George and Linda Luste canoed from Menihek Lake, just south of Schefferville to Goose Bay

down the Grand River, just before the dam was completed. [Personal communication]

1973 Betty and Jim Wentzler, their son Jack and his schoolmate, took the train north from Sept Îles and got off at Oreway on Lac Ashuanipi. They canoed into Lac Eau Claire, Lac Joseph, Petit Lac Joseph, Kepimits Lake and finished their trip in Atikonak Lake. [Personal communication]

FRASER

The Fraser River flows down from the height of land into Tikkoatokak Bay just beside Nain in northern Labrador.

1910 H. Hesketh Prichard, G.M. Gathorne-Hardy, their guide, Robert Porter from Newfoundland, and Boaz Obed, an Inuit from Nain, with two canoes, went inland from Nain and ascended the Fraser River. After eight days Obed deserted after being refused higher wages. The remaining three cached one canoe and continued up-river. Porter

---

GRAND FALLS BOTTLE REGISTER

It is not uncommon that those who stop at a conspicuous landmark like to leave a record of their visit. Mackenzie wrote his name with red ochre mixed with grease on a rock on the Pacific coast, Hearne incised his name into the rock at Churchill. Travellers in this century, knowing that they are not in the vanguard, build cairns in which to leave their names on slips of paper in waterproof containers. In 1891 at Grand Falls, Cary and Cole, put their names inside a bottle to mark their visit and subsequent visitors added their names. The following is a selection:

1894 A.P. Low and survey party (winter sledge trip)

1908 Sidney Delano, New York, Fred Reed, Alma, New Brunswick

1908 H.G. Bryant, C.A. Kenaston, John Montague (guide)

1913 Miss Laurie Coates, Calgary (Grenfell mission)

1922 R.W. Armitage, England, Gilbert Blake (guide)

1925 W.J. Malone, J.W. McCarthy, S.J., D.J. Munce

1928 W.B. Averill, Old Town, Maine, Edward Michelin (guide)

1930 E.T. Merrick, Kate Austin, John Michelin (guide)

1931 Charles J. Hubbard and party

1946 Barbara Munday, Nora Groves, Russell Groves, John Blake

1961 The bottle was removed for safekeeping and was one of Joseph R. Smallwood's most prized possessions.

In 1930 Elliott Merrick said the bottle contained more than fifty names, twenty of whom were a prospecting party in 1929.

[*Canadian Geographic*, November 1948, p. 221; March 1963, p. 76; Gwyn, *Smallwood*, McClelland and Stewart, 1968]

The Grand River had already been reduced by the dam-building at the Falls, when Dick Irwin, Stewart Coffin, Robin Fraser, Peter Garstang and John Dashwood stopped beside it for lunch in 1968. [Coffin]

portaged the canoe up 1500 feet out of the river valley onto the Labrador Plateau and they continued west through a chain of lakes and ponds until they were forced to cache the second canoe and proceed on foot for about ten days to reach the George River at Indian House Lake. They spent twelve days on the George River while Prichard recovered from a sprained ankle and returned by the same route, taking only two days to canoe down the Fraser. [Prichard, 1911]

1986 *Pat Lewtas and Barbara Kitowski, a nurse from Nain, went up the Fraser River to the headwaters, portaged and pond-hopped to the headwaters of the Kingurutik River, north of the Fraser and followed it down to Nain. [Personal communication – Lewtas]*

1987 *Herb Pohl, travelling by coastal steamer, was stopped by ice at Davis Inlet. In company with the canoes of George Luste's group, he canoed to Nain along the coast and alone explored up the valley of the Fraser River. [Nastawgan, Winter 1988]*

KOGALUK

The Kogaluk River flows into Voisey Bay, south of Nain. It has a small tributary, the Mistasin, which flows out of Lake Mistasin.

1903-10 William Brooks Cabot spent months of each summer exploring this area in order to make contact with the Naskapi Indians. The Hudson's Bay Company had strict rules against permitting outsiders to travel into the interior of Labrador and their traders also did not travel there. [Cabot, p. 99-101]

1904 Cabot with Robert Walcott, from Boston, and a young Inuk from the orphanage in Nain, using a wood and canvas canoe that weighed 141 pounds, went as far as the forks of the Mistasin River. [*Ibid.*, Chap. 6]

1905 Cabot with Lewis Quackenbush, New York, using a birchbark canoe, reached Lake Mistinibi. With three Naskapi, Ostinitsu, Pah-kuun-noh and Nah-payo, they travelled up to the height of land and looked down on the waters of the

In one of the few images of William Brooks Cabot that has survived, he is wearing a painted Naskapi caribou-skin coat that the owner, HBC agent Cotter, refused to sell. The picture is taken at the Davis Inlet post in 1903 while Cabot waited for the Naskapi (Innu) to come in from their hunting grounds. [William Brooks Cabot collection, National Anthropological Archives, Smithsonian Institution]

George River. Ostinitsu met Mrs. Hubbard and her party at Indian House Lake a few days later. [*Ibid.*, Chap. 7]

1906 Cabot, with Richard Winter, part-Inuit aged fifteen, went up the Kogaluk to Mistinibi, met the Naskapi Indians and was a guest in their camp. [*Ibid.*, Chap. 8]

1910 Cabot, with Scoville Clarke, Dr. George P. Howe and D.G. McMillan, went up the Kogaluk with one 15-foot canoe, two paddling and two walking, to Lake Mistinibi. They crossed over the height of land to the Naskapi camp on the George River, spent a night there and returned the same way, exploring Lake Mistasin in a side trip. [Cabot, Chap. 9; Allen, E., Chap. 9]

1928 Herman J. Koehler and his son Hans from the United States, having gone by coastal boat to Hopedale, engaged John Michelin from North West River as guide. They proceeded up the coast to Voisey Bay, canoed and portaged up Frank's Brook, the first stream north of the Kogaluk River, crossed the height of land and reached Indian House Lake on the George River. They returned the way they had come. [Scott, J., p. 90 places the "Kohlers" on the Kanairiktok and the

Grand Rivers; Henderson, *Nastawgan*, Autumn 1993, pp. 11-15]

1979 *Stephen Loring, American anthropologist, with his brother Eric, and Maine guide Tom Hallenbeck, using one canoe, started from Schefferville, portaged across the divide to the headwaters of the De Pas River, followed it down to the George River, continuing down the George to Indian House Lake. They followed the route pioneered by William Cabot which entailed a long portage to Lake Mistinibi, pond-hopped across the Labrador plateau to the Kogaluk River and descended it to the sea. They continued along the coast to Zoar Bay for a mid-October rendezvous with Inuit hunters from Nain. [Appalachia, Winter 1986-87, pp. 60-73]*

1982 *Herb Pohl and Ken Ellison, from the train to Schefferville, using two canoes, reached Lake Attikamagen, canoed down the De Pas and the George Rivers to Indian House Lake, crossed over the height of land to Cabot Lake and canoed down the Kogaluk River to Nain. [Nastawgan, Autumn 1982, pp. 1-4]*

NOTAKWANON

Rising close to the divide between Labrador and Quebec, the Notakwanon River affords another possible cross-over route from the George River of the Ungava watershed to the Labrador Sea. It flows into the Atlantic Ocean between Voisey Bay and Davis Inlet.

1906 William Cabot produced a map of the Notakwanon but did not travel on it.

1931 Herman Koehler – see George

1975 *Harry Collins with a Wild River Survey crew canoed down the Notakwanon. [Personal communication – Jim Davidson]*

1976 *Jim Davidson, John Rugge, Brad Prozeller, Pat Strohmeyer, Jess Grunblatt and Dave Peach, flew into the headwaters of the Notakwanon and canoed to the ocean and along the coast to the spit across the bay from Davis Inlet. [Canoe, March/April, 1977, p.23-27; personal communication – Davidson]*

1984 *Herb Pohl, travelling alone, reached Schefferville by train, put his canoe in at Lake Attikamagen and made his way down the De Pas to the George River. He then canoed up the George, crossed the height of land by a series of lakes and an unnamed river. A spark from a smudge fire burned the bow of the canoe but with resin and duct tape he repaired it sufficiently that he could continue down the Notakwanon, finishing his journey at Davis Inlet.* [Nastawgan, *Summer and Autumn 1985*]

1985 *George Luste, Sandy Richardson, Walter Lohaza and Dan Selig started at Iron Arm, canoed down the De Pas River to the George River, went up the George, crossed over the height of land and canoed down the Notakwanon River to Davis Inlet. [Personal communication – Luste]*

1986 *Mark Riddell, Caroline Tennent, Paul Barsevskis, Faith Hughes, Simon Rivers-Moore and Suzanne Sweetman put their canoes in at Lake Attikamagen from Schefferville, canoed down the De Pas, made a 5-mile portage to a tributary of the George River, continued up a short section of the George, crossed over to White Gull Lake and descended the south branch to the main Notakwanon, finishing their trip at Davis Inlet. [Personal communication – Tennent]*

1990 *Shawn and Eric Hodgins, Jeff Edelstan, Ken Gangbar and Rob and Jennifer Cepella, in a Camp*

At the WCA Symposium on Labrador in 1990, Herb Pohl, Jim Greenacre and Rob Perkins had a chance to discuss their various Labrador experiences on the Kogaluk, the Notakwanon and the Ugjoktok. [Michael Peake]

Bob Davis, on the Ugtoktok River in 1982, makes a portage in style, using a tump to support the wannigan with packs balanced on top. [Stewart Coffin]

Wanapitei-related trip, canoed down the De Pas to the George River and just upstream from the forks crossed over via Lac Leif and Lac Machautt to the north branch of the Notakwanon, continuing down the main river to Davis Inlet. Liz McCarney and Margo Hodgins were on the first half of the trip. [Personal communication – Shawn Hodgins]

UGJOKTOK

The Ugjoktok River, with streams flowing in from Harp Lake and Mistinippi Lake, flows into a fiord at Ugjoktok Bay just south of Hopedale.

1972 Wild River Survey, Gerry Fassett, leader, with Harry Collins, Tom Perry and Steve Stesco, flew in, and canoed down 100 miles, including a 16-mile trip into Harp Lake. [Parks Canada files]

1976 *Stephen Loring and Tom Hallenbeck, after finishing a summer of working in Labrador for the*

The rivers of Labrador descend from the high central Labrador Plateau, creating sections of wild water. Bob Davis lines a canoe past one of these rapids on the lower Ugjoktok in 1982. [Stewart Coffin]

Smithsonian Institution, started at Hopedale and canoed up the Ugjoktok – or Adlatok – River to Harp Lake, taking about three weeks on the upstream trip. They returned downstream to Hopedale. [Personal communication – Hallenbeck]

1982   *Stewart Coffin, Dick Irwin, Bob Davis and Bill Miller reached Schefferville by train, put in their canoes at Lake Attikamagen, canoed down the De Pas, upstream on the George River, crossed the height of land and canoed down the Ugjoktok. [Morse files, p. 17; Nastawgan, Summer 1985; personal communication – Coffin]*

1986   *Herb Pohl and Jim Greenacre, with two canoes, took the train to Schefferville and flew to Bonaventure Lake, the headwaters of the George River. They canoed down the George to Resolution Lake, crossed over the height of land by a series of lakes and canoed down the Ugjoktok, coming out on the north channel at Hopedale. They caught the coastal boat at Hopedale. [Nastawgan, Autumn 1987]*

KANAIRIKTOK

The Kanairiktok rises in the central plateau, has several small tributaries and flows into Kanairiktok Bay, just south of Ugjoktok Bay.

1928   Koehler – see Grand River

1928-29   Gino Watkins and J.M. Scott, with guide Robert Michelin, sledged up Grand Lake, followed the Indian portage trail up the Naskaupi, along Lake Nipishish to Lake Snegamook and down the Kanairiktok River to Hopedale. They returned by the same route. [Scott, J., Chaps. 5,6]

1972   Wild River Survey, Gerry Fassett, leader, with Harry Collins, Tom Perry and Steve Stesco, flew in and canoed down the Kanairiktok River to Hopedale. [Parks Canada files]

1985   *Karl and Peter Schimek canoed down the De Pas to the George River, went upstream to the headwaters of the George, crossed over the height of land and canoed down the Kanairiktok River to the coast. [Nastawgan, Summer 1985]*

NASKAUPI

After the Grand, the Naskaupi is the largest river in Labrador. It rises in the central plateau close to Lake Michikamau, flows east to Seal Lake where it turns southeast to empty into Grand Lake, an arm of Lake Melville. It is a river of strong rapids and the Indians traditionally used a portage route connecting many small lakes to bypass the lower part of the river to Seal Lake, continuing on a similar portage route on the upper Naskaupi.

Flowing into Grand Lake close to the mouth of the Naskaupi are Susan Brook and the Beaver River, both of which are part of the tragic story of Leonidas Hubbard.

1903   Leonidas Hubbard, Dillon Wallace, with George Elson from Missanabie as guide, using an 18-foot Old Town, canoed from North West River up Grand Lake and up Susan Brook thinking they were on the Naskaupi. They continued up the Beaver River and portaged to several lakes, including a 40-mile portage, which brought them within sight of Lake Michikamau. They were wind-bound for nearly a week and had to return by the same route because of the lateness of the season. Hubbard died on Susan Brook and Wallace and Elson barely escaped with their lives, returning to North West River. [Hubbard, 1909; Davidson and Rugge, *Great Heart*]

1905   Mina Hubbard, with George Elson, Joseph Iserhoff, Job Chapies, all of Missanabie, and Gilbert Blake of North West River, canoed up the Naskaupi from North West River and down the George River to the mouth, making their return on the HBC steamer. [*Ibid.*; Hoyle in Hodgins and Hobbs, ed., Nastawgan, and in Raffan, ed. *Cannexus*]

1905   Dillon Wallace with Clifford Easton, George Richards, Leigh Stanton and Peter Stevens, an Ojibwa from Minnesota, canoed up the Naskaupi following the Indian portage route to Lake Michikimau. Duncan McLean of North West River went along on the first part of the up-river trip as a carrier. Richards, Stanton and Stevens returned down the Naskaupi while Wallace and Easton continued down the George River. [Wallace, *The Long Labrador Trail*; Hoyle in *Cannexus*]

1921   William Brooks Cabot accompanied several Indian families over the old Innu (Naskapi) trail to Lake Michikamau. Beginning at Grand Lake they ascended the Naskaupi River to the mouth of the Red Wine River where the Innu trail leaves the Naskaupi valley to avoid the long stretch of rapids and falls below Seal Lake. Beyond Seal Lake the trail cuts northeasterly over to the Crooked River drainage. Cabot returned to North West River when the Innu families he was travelling with reached the area around Pocket Knife Lake. [Personal communication – Stephen Loring]

1968   Dick Irwin, Stewart Coffin, Robin Fraser, Peter Garstang and John Dashwood began at Astray Lake and canoed down the Ashuanipi River system to the Grand River to see Grand Falls. The rapids above the falls were already lacking water because of the dyking connected with the Churchill Falls dam. They took the portage route and ascended the Portage River to Lake Michi-

On one of the last possible trips on the Naskaupi, Robin Fraser loads the canoe at a bend in the upper river, 1968. [Stewart Coffin]

The prominent North West River Michelin family of trappers provided guides for many Labrador river expeditions. Robert Michelin leads the Cambridge University team of Watkins and Scott up the swift and shallow Kenemu. [Scott, *The Land that God gave to Cain*, 1933]

kamau, crossed the lake to the Naskaupi River, through Mackenzie, Fremont and Marie Lakes and down the Naskaupi with difficulty. After Seal Lake they took the portage route through small streams and lakes and reentered the Naskaupi above Grand Lake, continuing to North West River. This was probably the last trip down the Naskaupi before the Churchill Dam diminished the flow of the river and changed the topography. [WCA Symposium on Labrador, Toronto, Jan. 27, 1990; personal communication – Fraser]

1972 Wild River Survey, leader Gerry Fassett, Harry Collins, Tom Perry, Steve Stesco, did an aerial reconnaissance of the Naskaupi River. [Parks Canada files]

GOOSE

The Goose River lies between the Beaver River and the Grand River and flows into Lake Melville at Goose Bay.

1972 Wild River Survey, leader Gerry Fassett, Harry Collins, Tom Perry, Steve Stesco, flew in and canoed down the Goose River to Goose Bay. [Parks Canada files]

KENEMU

The Kenemu is the exception to east-flowing rivers in Labrador. It is a short river, very shallow in the upper part, and full of rapids as it drops down through the Mealy Mountains. It flows north into Lake Melville opposite the town of North West River.

1928 H.G. Watkins, J.M. Scott, L.A.D. Leslie, with two local guides Robert Michelin and Doug Best, with two canoes, went up the Kenemu River to its source near the Mealy Mountains, crossed over to the Traverspine River, a shallow, rapid river which required much wading and portaging until they came to rapids they could run just before it enters the Grand River. [Scott, J., Chap. 3]

1988 *Rod Beebe III with five others put in at the headwaters of the Kenemu and canoed down to North West River. They noted that in one 10-mile stretch of rapids the river dropped 350 feet. [Personal communication – Beebe]*

CHAPTER THIRTEEN

SOME NORTHERN WATERS FLOW SOUTH: RIVERS DRAINING INTO THE LOWER ST. LAWRENCE

"From a narrow foreland, which in places may be submerged under the sea, a fringe of rounded hills rises to many hundred feet, sometimes to 2000 feet. These hills are merely remains of the dissected edge of an upland plateau of which the border falls rather abruptly into the River and Gulf of St. Lawrence. The plateau has been cut deeply into by a series of river valleys descending in a southeasterly direction from the plateau level to the shore of the gulf." [Vaino Tanner, *Newfoundland-Labrador*, 1944]

The major rivers that drain the high Labrador plateau are the St. Paul, St. Augustin, Petit Mécatina, Natashquan, Aguanus, Romaine, St. Jean, Magpie, and Moisie. Those most used by canoeists for recreation and by explorers have been the Moisie, including its tributary the Pekans, and the Romaine. For centuries the Montagnais and the Naskapi used some of these river and portage routes travelling out to the coast from the interior.

In the nineteenth century the names of two local men are prominent in the annals of the North Shore and its rivers. Napoleon Comeau lived at Godbout and was the guardian of the Godbout River, ranging over the whole North Shore area guiding, trapping, hunting and fishing. His book *Life and Sport on the North Shore* was familiar to such well-known northern canoeists as P.G. Downes. He guided many fishing parties of prominent Canadians and Americans on the Moisie and other rivers, but only on the lower reaches. Count Henry de Puyjalon, while not a native to the North Shore, made it his home. According to his biographer, Damase Potvin, in 1880-81 he made a geological exploration of the North Shore from Watheeshoo to Blanc Sablon in a small canoe with sixteen-year-old Jules LeFrançois as companion for part of the time. In 1897 he made an inventory of the rivers and streams, ninety-five in all, looking at the salmon fishing, and as a result of this he recommended conservation laws. He was named inspector general of fishing and hunting in the region.

ST. PAUL

The St. Paul River enters the St. Lawrence just west of Blanc-Sablon, which is on the Quebec-Labrador border.

1889 H.H. Robertson, provincial land surveyor, explored some distance up the St. Paul River. [Report, Crown Lands Commission, 1890]

1892 T. Simard, land surveyor, with two canoemen, went up the St. Paul River to its source and returned down stream. [Report, Crown Lands Commission, 1893]

1913 William Brooks Cabot made a trip on the St. Paul River. [Cabot, p. 311-13]

1916 William Brooks Cabot, with two Montagnais Indians, Sylvester Marks and Winipa, went up the St. Paul (Eskimo) River to the height of land and returned the same way to the coast. [*Ibid.*, Chap. 12]

1920 William Brooks Cabot, travelling with Sylvester Marks and a party of five or six Montagnais families, ascended the St. Paul River to the lake and bog country at its source. They crossed the plateau, portaging from pond to pond and picked up the headwaters of the Paradise River which they descended to Cartwright Bay. [Personal communication – Stephen Loring]

ST. AUGUSTIN

There are two branches of this river, St. Augustin and St. Augustin Nord-Ouest, which meet at the mouth at the village of St. Augustin. The St. Augustin is the longer branch and has its rise higher up on the Labrador plateau.

1890 J.G. Alwyn Creighton on a private Canadian expedition attempting to reach Grand Falls, Labrador, ascended and descended the St. Augustin but was prevented from attaining his goal by forest fires. [Cooke and Holland, p. 262]

1900 J.-E. Girard, land surveyor, explored 27 miles up the northwest branch of the St. Augustin River. The exploration of both branches was continued in winter by E.H.N. Piton. [Report, Ministry of Lands, Mines and Fisheries, 1903, 04]

1912 Henry G. Bryant and Russell W. Porter, with two canoemen from Newfoundland, and two Montagnais who were to guide the group up to the height of land, in two 18-foot canoes, began poling and portaging upstream on the St. Augustin River. The Montagnais abandoned the trip above the first falls but the group continued upstream to Lynx Lake, where they could discern the Indian route across to Lake Melville. They returned downstream. [*Geographical Journal*, 1913, p. 340]

1917 William Brooks Cabot with John Ashini and a party of Naskapi canoed up the St. Augustin River for about 50 miles and returned downstream to the coast. [Personal communication – Stephen Loring]

1926? Herman J. Koehler made a trip on the St. Augustin River. [*Nastawgan*, Autumn 1993, pp. 11-15]

PETIT MÉCATINA

The Little Mecatina rises in Labrador, not far from Lake Atikonak, flows generally east until it crosses the border into Quebec and flows south as the Petit Mécatina into the St. Lawrence at Harrington Harbour, or Tête à la Baleine. The river drops through a 15-mile gorge with a canyon which is very difficult for canoes to navigate.

1888 John Neilson, provincial surveyor, with his three sons and a Montagnais guide, explored about 100 miles up the Petit Mécatina River. [Report, Commission of Crown Lands, 1890]

1937 John Stainer, C.C. Cholmondeley, F. J. Connell and G.F. Hanson ascended and descended the Petit Mécatina, exploring the land and tributary rivers, the Etamamiou and Wabosagoma, making a collection of birds, insects, flowers and soil specimens for the British Museum, Kew Gardens, and the Soil Science Laboratory at Oxford. [*Geographical Journal*, 1938, p. 153]

1972 Wild River Survey, led by Gerry Fassett, with Harry Collins, Tom Perry and Steve Stesco, were flown in to the river and canoed down to the North Shore. [Parks Canada files]

1977 *Serge Théoret, Alain Chevrette, Guy Garant, Sylvain Beaudry, Jean Lauzon and Jean Masson started from the railway at Oreway, canoed Lac à l'Eau Claire and à l'Eau Claire River to lakes Joseph and Atikonak, aux Pêcheurs River and upstream a short distance on the Romaine River to reach the Petit Mécatina River. To reach the Gulf of St. Lawrence down the Petit Mécatina, the group had canoed 800 kilometres in forty days. [FQCC files; personal communication – Théoret]*

1983 *Serge Théoret, Alain Chevrette with Americans, Bill Coursey, Doug Silsbee, David Price and Michael Vorteck flew in to the headwaters and canoed down the Petit Mécatina to Harrington Harbour. [FQCC files;* Canoe, *Feb./March, 1985, pp. 46-52]*

1985   *Hugh Stewart, Bob Davis, Stewart Hamilton and Guy Sayor were flown into the headwaters and canoed down the Petit Mécatina to the Gulf of St. Lawrence. [Personal communication – Stewart]*

1986   *Jean Doyen and five others from France started down the Petit Mécatina but were totally unprepared for the river and used ELT to be airlifted out. [FQCC files]*

1990   *Rod Beebe, III, Peter Bradshaw, Pete Coe and Len Carpenter put in at the headwaters of the Petit Mécatina and canoed to the fishing village of Tête à la Baleine on the St. Lawrence River. [Personal communication – Beebe]*

NATASHQUAN

The Natashquan River rises in Labrador south of the headwaters of the Petit Mécatina and flows generally south to the village of Natashquan on the St. Lawrence River. The river has two long branches, Natashquan Est, and Mistanipisipou, as well as several other streams joining in, giving the river five distinct forks. It was a principal artery for the Montagnais, who spent the winter months hunting on the Labrador plateau and returned to the coast in the spring. The 1908 census places seventy-six Montagnais as residents of the village of Natashquan.

1912   Dr. Charles Townsend and E.G. Parrot, with two French-Canadian fishermen, Edward and Charlie, in two 16-foot Indian canoes, ascended the Natashquan River for 80 miles and returned downstream. [*Bulletin of the Geographical Society of Philadelphia*, 1913, Jan.-Oct., pp. 170-82; *Bulletin de la Société de Géographie de Québec*, 1913, Sept./Oct. pp. 276-84]

1972   Wild River Survey, led by Gerry Fassett, with Harry Collins, Tom Perry and Steve Stesco, were flown in to Masquamanaga Fork and canoed the 240 miles to Pointe-Parent on the St. Lawrence in eight days. [Parks Canada files]

1982   *Bob Davis and Stephanie Hunt, for Headwaters, led an adult group, John Foster, Mike Dieder, Glen*

Carter and Dean Dix, from mile 286 on the rail line, down the Natashquan River to the Gulf of St. Lawrence. [Personal communication – Hugh Stewart]

AGUANUS

The Aguanus River rises in two branches just south of the Labrador border and flows south to the Gulf of St. Lawrence parallel to and a few kilometres west of the Natashquan.

1889   T. Simard, Provincial surveyor, surveyed 75 miles of the Aguanus River. [Report, Commission of Crown Lands, 1891]

1890   Pierre Gosselin, surveyor, explored 115 miles up the Aguanus River from its mouth. [Report, Commission of Crown Lands, 1891]

1945-75   Arthur Chevery trapped and canoed up and down the Aguanus River from the mouth to the headwaters. [Personal communication – Guy Doré]

1985   *Serge Théoret and Alain Chevrette, with Michel Lacroix, and Americans, Bill Coursey, Joel Cox and Dave Gale, flew in to a small unnamed lake at the headwaters of the Aguanus River and canoed down to the Gulf of St. Lawrence. [Personal communication – Théoret]*

1985   *Guy Doré led Bernard Goutier, Marcel Tousignant and Fernand Hudon in C2 canoes from the lake 20 kilometres above Lac Aguanus down the Aguanus River to Aguanish village on the Gulf of St. Lawrence. [Personal communication – Raymond Boyer and Doré]*

1987   *Hugh and Collette Glassco, Eric Hodgins, Isabel St. Martin, France Bildeau, Alex MacIntosh, Jean-François Proulx and Cecile Laplante flew into the source lake and repeated the 1985 Doré route. [Personal communication – Eric Hodgins]*

1989   *Wick Walker, Tom McEwen, Bob Gedekoh, Mike Bush and Doug Gordon flew to the headwaters of the Aguanus River and canoed to the Gulf of St. Lawrence using five decked C1 canoes, running some of the Class V rapids in the canyons. [*Canoe, *May 1990, p. 21]*

The rivers flowing into the North Shore of the St. Lawrence provide challenges and scenery in equal measure. Ralph Clim and Russ Binning line the rapids on the upper Romaine in 1980. [Stewart Coffin]

ROMAINE

The headwaters of the Romaine River are close to Lake Atikonak in the Quebec-Labrador border area. It flows due south, with a sharp bend to the west before entering the St. Lawrence at the village of Havre St. Pierre.

1866 *Père Louis Babel, Oblate, with Xavier Maskuaro and a young Montagnais named Jean-Marie, from Mingan, went up the St. Jean River, crossed to the Romaine to reach Lake Winokapau and continued down the Grand River in Labrador, returning to Mingan by coastal steamer. [Tremblay, ed. 1977]*

1867 *Père Louis Babel, having reached North West River in Labrador by steamer, canoed up to the lakes Winokapau and Petitsikapau and down the Romaine and St. Jean rivers. [Ibid.]*

1870 *Père Louis Babel went up the St. Jean and Romaine to Lake Petitsikapau and returned down the Moisie. [Ibid.]*

1894 A.P. Low and D.I.V. Eaton, GSC, completed a very long journey which had begun the previous

year on the Missinaibi. After transporting their equipment by sledge up the Grand River past the falls and exploring the lakes which are the headwaters of the Grand River, they canoed south by the Atikonak, the Romaine and the St. Jean. [GSC Report, 1896; Zaslow, p. 169, map 167]

1928 Howard Taylor, Dr. J.D. Kernan, Philip Rogers and his brother Ralph, Americans, with guides Wally Chambers from Mingan and Philippe Colombe from Loretteville, in two canvas canoes, ascended the St. Jean and the upper part of the Romaine rivers, crossed over to Atikonak Lake, went down the Atikonak River to Ossokmanuan Lake and down the Unknown River to the upper pair of 100-foot falls. They returned the way they had come. [Watkins, *Geographical Journal*, Feb. 1930, pp. 97-109; *Beaver*, Autumn 1965, p. 30]

1930 Mathieu Mestokosho – see St. Jean

1941 J.A. Retty, geologist, made a survey of the lower 100 miles of the Romaine River. [Cooke, p. 164]

On the lower Romaine only a portage will do – Russ Binning and Ralph Clim portage around a series of falls and rapids, 1980. [Stewart Coffin]

1945 Jacques Claveau finished the survey of the Romaine River for the Labrador Exploration and Mining Company and also surveyed some of its tributaries. [*Ibid.*]

1972 Wild River Survey led by Jean de Grosbois, with Ronald Jean, Daniel Larocque and Claude Thérriault, entered the Romaine River by float plane at Mile 80, 2 miles south of Rivière l'Abbé Huard and canoed to the Gulf of St. Lawrence at Mingan. [Parks Canada files; FQCC files]

1980 *Stewart Coffin, Dick Irwin, Ralph Clim, Jim Sindelar, Russ Binning and Brian Farrell, using two Old Town Trippers and one Mad River Explorer, took the train to Oreway, ascended a small stream out of Atikonak Lake, crossed the height of land to the headwaters of the Romaine River and ran the full length of the river, including the canyons, to tide water, with care. They saw almost no signs of use of the river. [Appalachia, June 1981, p. 57]*

1981 *Jean Trudelle led a group down the Romaine from*

Rivière l'Abbé Huard to the Gulf at the village of Mingan. [FQCC files]

1983 *Raymond Boyer led Réjean Michaud, André Béland, Diane Belzile, Jacques Forget and Claude Santerre, in three 16-foot canoes, down the full length of the Romaine River, putting in from the railway at Oreway, portaging to Lac à l'eau Claire and taking out at the Gulf of St. Lawrence. [FQCC files; personal communication – Boyer]*

1984 *Guy Doré, Gaston Dionne, Fernand Hudon and Marcel Tousignant put in at the south end of Brulé Lake and canoed down the Romaine River to Havre St. Pierre. [Personal communication – Doré]*

1987 *Bob Davis and Karl Hartwick took the train to Oreway and canoed from the headwaters of the Romaine to the Gulf of St. Lawrence. The only evidence of previous travel was a green canoe wrapped around a rock on the upper reaches of the river. Traditionally the Montagnais bypassed the canyon of the Romaine by coming down the Little Romaine and crossing over to the St. Jean. [Nastawgan, Spring 1988]*

1987   *Mark Riddell and Caroline Tennent canoed down the Romaine River from Love Lake to the Gulf of St. Lawrence. [Personal communication – Tennent]*

1989   *Pat Lewtas, canoeing alone, went up the St. Jean River, crossed to the Romaine River, using the A.P. Low portage route and returned down the Romaine River to the highway, just a mile or two before the Gulf of St. Lawrence. Many of the portage trails were overgrown, and it was a tough but beautiful trip. [Personal communication]*

ST. JEAN

The St. Jean River is a short river, entirely in Quebec, flowing into the St. Lawrence near Mingan. The headwaters of the eastern branch are close to the upper Romaine and the St. Jean provided an up-river route to the upper Romaine that was easier than upstream from the mouth of the Romaine. It was part of the traditional route for the Montagnais travelling from Mingan on the coast to their hunting grounds, which ranged from Lake Atikonak east to North West River in the Labrador interior.

1866   *Père Louis Babel – see Romaine*

1867   *Père Louis Babel – see Romaine*

1870   *Père Louis Babel – see Romaine*

1887   Pierre Gaspé – see Grand (Labrador)

1894   A.P. Low – see Romaine

1928   Howard Taylor – see Romaine

1930   Mathieu Mestokosho, with members of seven families, including Sylvestre Napish, Paul Pawstuck, Zacharie Mestokosho, Damien Sylvestre, Peter Pietasho, Bastien Thomas, Paul Nolin, Bastien Basile and many others, returned from their winter hunt in the region of Lake Winokapau to the place where their canoes had been cached the previous fall and followed the traditional route to Lake Brûlé down the Romaine and by many portages to the St. Jean River and the coast at Mingan. [Bouchard, *Chroniques*, pp. 30-52]

1983   *Marc Moisnard and Alain Rastoin, using the 1866 map of Père Babel, canoed from the Gulf of St. Lawrence to Ungava Bay, starting up the St. Jean River.*

With a view of the river, Guy Doré and Guy Fournier hang their cooking pot over the campfire after a day spent descending the St. Jean in 1984. In the second photo Guy Doré, in the bow, and Gilles Lortie ride through haystacks down a wild stretch of the Moisie. [Doré]

They canoed a total of 2500 kilometres and made a film "Sur les traces du Père Babel". [FQCC files]

1983   *Guy Doré led Gilles Lortie, Guy Fournier, Marcel Tousignant, Gaston Dionne and Fernand Hudon down the St. Jean River from St. Jean Lake to Route 138 on the Gulf of St. Lawrence. [FQCC files; personal communication – Doré]*

1989   *Lewtas – see Romaine*

MAGPIE

The Magpie River lies within Quebec and has two branches, Magpie Ouest being the longer branch. It enters the St. Lawrence at the village of Magpie.

1890   T. Simard, surveyor, went up the Magpie River to Lake Magpie, about 34 miles from the mouth of the river. [Report, Commission of Crown Lands, 1892]

1945-50 D.A. Livingston using air reconnaissance and canoes explored the valley of the Moisie, Nipissis, Wacouno and Magpie rivers to find the route for the Quebec North Shore and Labrador Railway to Schefferville. [Thompson, Don, v.3 p. 278-80]

1972 Jean Smith led a canoeing group down the Magpie River from Eric on the railway line to Magpie Lake. [FQCC files]

1978 *Tim Elledge, Wayne Hockmeyer, Alan Haley and Jay Wilson, Americans, with three kayaks and a 400-pound rubber raft ran a trip down the west branch of the Magpie River in October. They were totally unprepared for both the terrain and the season and they had several escapes from near-drowning. They reached a hunter's cabin on Magpie Lake and were picked up by plane.* [River Runner, *July/ August 1984, pp. 24-29*]

1979 *Tim Elledge, Charley Walbridge, Walt Nowak, Elliot Malamud, Tom Neal, Peter Ord and Ron Dann with kayaks, Rick Hoddenot and Dana Roberts manning a 30-foot rubber support raft flew in to the west branch of the Magpie River in September and took out on Magpie Lake. The rubber raft was extremely difficult to portage.* [Ibid.; *personal communication – Walbridge*]

1981 *Raymond Boyer, for the FQCC, led Carl Cassivi, Gilles Briand and André Cusson, using 16-foot solo canoes, down the Magpie River, putting in at Eric from the railway and taking out on the Gulf of St. Lawrence. They did not have topographical maps and many of the portages were blocked by fallen trees or were non-existent. The trip took them three weeks. Boyer labelled the Magpie a very difficult river, almost uncanoeable above Lake Magpie.*

The Magpie River has its own special problems. The canoe is being tracked down the west branch of the river in 1984. [Stewart Coffin]

[*Nastawgan, Spring 1986, pp. 1-4; FQCC files; personal communication – Boyer*]

1983 *Charley Duffy, Paul Kiefner, Mark Kiefner, John Arnett and Hubert P. Yockey, with five kayaks, made a trip down the west branch of the Magpie River. Also on the trip were Bruce Lyman and Greg Kalmbach with a 15-foot raft to provide support for the group. The steep, rocky river proved to be very difficult for the raft and they lost some of their equipment. They flew in from Sept-Îles to Lac Pierre and took out at Magpie Lake, 30 miles before the Gulf of St. Lawrence.* [*Cruiser, January 1984;* Explorers Journal, *September 1984*]

1984 *Stewart Coffin, his wife Jane and daughter Tammis, Sara Biewen, Garrett and Alexandra Conover, Russ Ottey and Larry Wesson canoed down the west branch of the Magpie River, up the River Vital and down the Wacouno to Sept-Îles.* [*Personal communication – Stewart Coffin*]

1984 *Raymond Boyer, in a 16-foot R3 solo canoe, led Daniel Malo, Charles Léger, Debby Jesson, Grégoire Bergeron, Mike Vincent and Nil Gagné, travelling in an inflatable raft with a 10-horsepower motor for calm sections of the river, from Eric on the railway line down to the mouth of the Magpie River.* [*Personal communication – Boyer*]

1984 *Eric Bailley canoed the Magpie River.* [*Nastawgan, Spring 1986, pp. 1-4*]

1985 *Paul Barsevskis, Igor Devreeze, Joanne Hale, Mark Riddell, Simon Rivers-Moore and Trudy van Dinter reached Lake Eric by train and canoed down the west branch of the Magpie River. They canoed beyond Magpie Lake but ran short of time and portaged out to the railway line. A federal Member of Parliament, his son and four other young men started at the same time, lost a canoe in the rapids and were airlifted out. Five kayakers from Pennsylvania were on the river as well.* [Ibid.]

1985 *Bob Gedekoh, Mike Bush, Jess Gonzales, Dean Smith and John Boulger, from Pennsylvania, in kayaks, flew in to the west branch of the Magpie and paddled out to the Gulf of St. Lawrence, hav-*ing run all but eleven of the most difficult chutes. [*Paddler, Summer 1989, pp. 20-24*]

1987 *Guy Doré, Fernand Hudon, Bernard Goutier, Claude Dionne, André St. Pierre and Gaston Dionne, put in at Eric and canoed down the Magpie River to Route 138 on the Gulf of St. Lawrence.* [*Personal communication – Doré*]

1988 *Shawn Hodgins, Mark Hodnett, Jeff Edwards and Nick Purdon, on a Wanapitei staff trip, canoed from Lake Eric down the Magpie River to the Gulf.* [*Personal communication – Hodgins*]

MOISIE

"The longest river tributary to the Gulf is the Moisie, which sweeps round the spur of the table-land on which the Ashwanipi takes its rise, and after a course of probably exceeding 250 miles, with a fall of more than 2200 feet from its headwaters to its mouth at the sea, eighteen miles east of Seven Islands.... For centuries the Moisie has been one of the leading lines of communication from the interior to the coast – the old, well-worn portage routes testify to the antiquity of the route." [Hind, *Explorations in the Interior of the Labrador Peninsula*, 1863]

The Moisie River rising in Lac Opocopa, close to the Labrador border, and descending 400 kilometres of swift currents, rapids and falls to the Gulf of St. Lawrence, is by far the most popular remote south-flowing, but truly northern, river. Yet, when James Davidson and John Rugge began their investigation of travelling such a route, they were warned by Quebec authorities that the Moisie was virtually impassable and should not be attempted. They were not deterred, canoed it successfully in 1972 and wrote their book *The Complete Wilderness Paddler* based on their trip. It remains a very challenging river, suitable only for the experienced. Sometimes called the "Nahanni of the East", the topography of the Moisie is awe-inspiring, the ridges and cliffs of the valley being very high.

While the ascent of the river is very difficult, it was the traditional route for the Montagnais from the coast to their winter hunting grounds which they had used for centuries. Several early European travellers reached the river from the Labrador side. The opening of the Quebec North Shore and Labrador Railway from Sept-

Îles to Schefferville in the late 1960s changed conditions both for the Montagnais, who now use the railway to ascend into the high Labrador plateau, and for canoeists. It was now possible to reach the source area of the Moisie by train 30 kilometres from Labrador City, just inside the Labrador border; others would reach the river from the Pekans River, a demanding tributary whose headwaters can be reached by road also from Labrador City. Another tributary is the Nipissis which flows into the Moisie about 30 kilometres from its mouth. The railway goes north through the valley of the Nipissis and then the valley of the Wacouno, a tributary of the Nipissis.

1853   *Halsey Chatsworth, Canadian trapper, allegedly canoed 200 miles up the Moisie. [Rugge and Davidson, p. 34; Davidson is suspicious of this reference and recommends independent confirmation – personal communication]*

1861   *Henry Youle Hind, his artist brother William Hind, J. F. Gaudet and Edward Cayley, surveyors with the Crown Lands Department of the Canadian government, five French-Canadian voyageurs, (Ignace, Joseph and Laronde and two unnamed), and two Indian guides, Pierre, an Abenakis, and Louis, a Montagnais, using three birchbark canoes, a Malecite, a Micmac and an 18-foot Ottawa, struggled upstream on the Moisie and the Nipissis for nearly a month following a chart constructed by seven Montagnais at the request of Père Arnaud. At the forks below the gorge a Naskapi, Michel, was persuaded to join the party as guide. They followed the ancient Montagnais portage up the Cold-Water (Nipissis) River to Lake Nipissis and continued north up a river, which they thought was the east branch of the Moisie, to the dividing ridge below the watershed of the Ashuanipi River. They turned downstream on July 2, and running most of the rapids, reached the mouth of the Moisie in six days. [Hind, 1863; Literary and Historical Society of Quebec Transactions, 1(1), 1863, pp. 75-92]*

1861   *Domenique, a Montagnais chief, his wife and four children, and Michel, a Naskapi, were coming down the Moisie from Ashuanipi Lake in a birch bark canoe as the Hind party went up on the main branch*

of the river. Four canoes were reported to be coming down the east branch of the river. [Hind, p. 78]

1868   *Père Louis Babel from North West River travelled up to his mission at Petitsikapau and returned to the St. Lawrence down the Moisie. [Tremblay, ed., 1977]*

1870   *Père Louis Babel – see Romaine*

1888   C.E. Forgues, surveyor, explored up the Moisie River from the foot of the first major rapids, continuing up the northeast branch and up 7 miles of the Nipissis River. C.C. Duberger surveyed the northwest branch of the Moisie and Gédéon Gagnon the northeast branch. [Report, Commission of Crown Lands, 1891]

1914   R.B. D'Aigle, prospecting for gold with a party of Montagnais, went up the Moisie to the height of land. D'Aigle continued with one man to Wabush Lake and returned down-river to Sept-Îles. [Cooke, p. 163]

1915-16   R.B. D'Aigle returned to the Wabush area possibly by the same route, up the Moisie River and down again. [*Ibid.*]

1917   W.E.C. Todd, Olaus J. Murie and Alfred Marshall, with three guides, Paul Commanda, Joseph Odjick and Moses Odjick, plus two local guides, Philip St. Onge and Charles Vollant, using three Peterborough freight canoes, went up the St. Marguerite River from Sept-Îles, over the Grand Portage (which took two weeks) and up to the Labrador Plateau. They crossed a chain of lakes to a branch of the Moisie and continued upstream to Shabogamo Lake, one of the headwaters of the Hamilton River. Because progress was slow, they cached one canoe and all non-essential equipment. They crossed the height of land in view of White Mountain, the highest point in Labrador, canoed down the Ashuanipi River into Menihek, Astray and Petitsikapau lakes. On Petitsikapau they found the site of the HBC Fort Nascopie, abandoned in 1873. After a confusing series of lakes and some travel on Swampy Bay River, they reached Fort Mckenzie and were joined by two Indian guides. They paddled to the

Kaniapiskau, canoed downstream and down the Koksoak to Fort Chimo. They returned south on the *Nascopie*, and believed they had made the first south-to-north traverse of the Labrador peninsula. This was the 8th Carnegie Museum Expedition. [Todd, pp. 26-31]

1918 R.B. D'Aigle, for Mackenzie and Mann Company, took a party up the Moisie River, across the height of land and down the Swampy Bay and Koksoak rivers to Fort Chimo. [Cooke, p. 163]

1918 James and Maud Watt, HBC, with Indians Ostinetso, his wife and two children, Alexandre Nist, and Petabino, left Fort McKenzie on the Kaniapiskau River on snowshoes, hauling a canoe to Fort Nascopie on the headwaters of the Moisie River. They canoed down the Moisie to the St. Lawrence. [*Beaver*, March 1943, p. 46]

1930 Lincoln Ellsworth and Beekman Pool, with a French-Canadian guide and two Montagnais, in two 18-foot canvas canoes, followed the traditional route up the Moisie and Nipissis rivers to Lake Kakatiak and up to Lake Nipissis. They continued up the "Deuxième Branch N.E. de la Rivière Moisie" – the Nipissis – to Lake Caopacho, crossing the height of land to Lake Ashuanipi and the waters of the Grand River and descended it to North West River. [Personal communication – Pool; Ellsworth, pp. 237-40]

1946 Nat Porter and Jeff Torney, from Maine, with two foldboats, drove to the end of the road at Baie Comeau, took the ferry to Sept-Îles and flew in to Lake Nipissis. They took a portage route for one day into the Joseph River, descended it for two days, portaged around the falls into the Moisie River, descended it in three days to what are now known as the Railroad Trestle Rapids and were transported around them by buckboard. [Personal communication – Stewart Coffin, who had interviewed both men]

1947 Nat Porter and his bride, Ruth, from Maine, spent their honeymoon descending the Moisie River in a two-man folding canoe. They flew in to Ashuanipi Lake near the end of July and fol-

lowed the old Indian route down to Sept-Îles. The blackflies were very bad and it is said that Ruth Porter was never quite the same after the trip. Nat Porter built a log cabin in Northern Quebec, accessible only by plane, and spent twenty summers there alone with his dog. [Personal communication – Stewart Coffin, including letter from Nat Porter]

1950 Roméo Régis, then aged nineteen, with about 100 Montagnais in family groups, in twenty 18- or 19-foot canoes, made the traditional trip north into their hunting grounds for the last time before the opening of the railway. Their route was up the Moisie to the Nipissis, up the Kakatiak to Lake Kakatiak and then a long portage to rejoin the Nipissis River at Lake Nipissis. The portages continued via small lakes and rivers, Mistamoué, Matinipi, and Caopacho. At Lake Caopacho they crossed over to Rivière aux Esquimaux which flows north to Lake Ashuanipi. The families split off in all directions for their winter hunting and

John Rugge and Jim Davidson pose to demonstrate the essentials in camping garb. [Drawing by Gordon Allen]

trapping ground, some of them leaving before they reached Ashuanipi. While the trip north had taken about two months with pauses to fish, smoke salmon and hunt, the return down-river in the spring was accomplished in a week or less. [*La revue d'histoire de la Côte-Nord*, Mai 1992, pp. 18-22] *In 1991, Gaétan Talbot, Raymond Boyer, authors, and others followed the traditional Montagnais route.*

1967 Bob Hatton and Stewart Coffin, returning south from Schefferville following their canoe trip down the George River, got off the train at Waco Mile 101 and canoed down the Wacouno, Nipissis and Moisie rivers without maps and with sketchy provisions. [*Che-Mun*, Autumn 1984, p. 6; *Appalachia*, date unknown]

1972 Jean de Grosbois led a Wild River Survey crew of Ronald Jean, Daniel Larocque and Claude Therriault down the Moisie River, entering at the Pekans River by plane and canoeing to Moisie Village. [Parks Canada files]

1972 James West Davidson, John Rugge, Dave Peach and Joe Hardy, in 17-foot Grumman canoes, started from the railway at Oreway on Lake Ashuanipi while there was still ice on the lake and canoed the full length of the Moisie River. [Davidson and Rugge, *Complete Wilderness Paddler*]

1972 Henry Franklin, Dick Johnson, Toby Vaughan, Kal Kallerman, Mark LaRoche, Chip Joseph Jr., Al Dearnley and Tony Brown, Americans, left the railway at Mile 21 and canoed from Lac De Mille, across Menistouc and Opocopa lakes and down the Moisie River to the Gulf of St. Lawrence. From Felix Lake to below the falls they blazed a portage trail and the carry took them two and a half days. [*Canoe*, October 1976, pp. 20-23]

1973 James West Davidson, Peter Davidson, Art Shoutis, Terry Pell, Brad Prozeller and Ron Turbayne canoed the Moisie River later in the season. [Personal communication – Jim Davidson]

1973 A scrap of paper in French from a Montreal source found at a campsite by Davidson led him to believe that they had been preceded by a French-Canadian group.

1973 Mike Brailsford, Tom Hiscott, Sandy Richardson, Al Brailsford, Bill Johnson and Gord Fenwick started from Little Wabash Lake wading upstream through rapids, over the watershed to Lac

At the end of the day, precipitous portages and wild rapids, sore muscles and wet gear are forgotten in the comforting glow of the campfire. Stewart Coffin, Dick Irwin, Bob Davis and John Brohan (standing) relax and anticipate another day on the magnificent Moisie in 1978. [Coffin]

Carheil and down the Moisie and along to Sept-Îles. [Unpublished trip report at Parks Canada]

1973 A group of six men and four women started the trip at Ross Bay Junction and went down the Moisie via Lac Felix. [Brailsford trip report]

1973 Two friends of the ten canoeists were canoeing down the Moisie at the same time. "The river is now travelled by the Canoe and Kayak Club and other groups as well." [*Ibid.*]

1975 *John Fallis, Leslie MacIntyre, Pat and Kate Geale, Rob MacKerracher and Jane Monahan put in at Lake Carheil and canoed down the Pekans and Moisie rivers to the Gulf of St. Lawrence. [*Wilderness Canoeist, December 1975; personal communication – Fallis]*

1978 *Stewart Coffin, Dick Irwin, Bob Davis and John Brohan made a trip down the Moisie. [Personal communication – Coffin]*

1978 *Guy Fournier, Jean Roy, Josianne Roy, Jocelyn Roy, Jacques Corriveau, Guy Doré, Bernard Tremblay, and Alain Desrauleau put in by float plane at the 52nd parallel and canoed down the Moisie to the confluence with the Nipissis River at the railway. [Personal communication – Doré]*

1979 *Herb Pohl made a solo canoe trip down the Moisie from Lac De Mille. [*Wilderness Canoeist, Spring 1980, pp. 15-18]*

1979 *Dave Winch and Luc Farmer, from Montreal, canoed down the Moisie at the same time as Herb Pohl. Another group of three canoes were also heading for the Moisie. [Ibid.]*

1979 *Raymond Boyer led Alain Doiron, Martine Lavoie, Donald Gonthier, Maryse Vaillancourt, Marcel Leblanc, Marie-Jeanne Murphy, Denis Couillard, Louis Desroches and Louis Ouellet, in five 16-foot canoes, from Lac De Mille near Labrador City to*

Stewart Coffin shoots through a narrow gap on the Moisie River. [Coffin]

the Gulf of St. Lawrence. [Personal communication – Boyer]*

1980 *Joe Griffith and Bruce Schnapp, canoeing the Moisie River, made a dramatic rescue using more than 175 feet of rope to reach two canoeists, Marc Gauthier and Norbert Giacalone, stranded overnight on rocks at the lip of a waterfall below Rim Canyon. [*Appalachia, *June 1992, pp. 121-23; personal communication – Théoret]*

CHAPTER FOURTEEN

THE LAST CANOEING FRONTIER: RIVERS OF THE ARCTIC ISLANDS AND MELVILLE PENINSULA

As recreational canoeing increases in popularity and canoeists search for more remote and unexplored rivers, the last frontier remaining is that of the Arctic Islands. Melville Peninsula has been included in this section since it is geographically closer to the Arctic Islands than to the Central Arctic mainland.

Originally the choice of 1974 as the cut-off date for this history of northern river travel was predicated on the popularity of recreational canoe travel exploding in the 1970s coincidental with the end of the Wild River Survey. Although there were some institutional trips by canoe, using small outboard motors, recorded in the vicinity of the Arctic Islands beginning in the 1950s, the exploration of rivers of the High Arctic really began after 1974 and therefore demanded a chapter of its own. The adventurous nature of some canoeists dictated the search for a new frontier, so it is not surprising that the rivers trips included in this section are generally thought to be first descents, although in the case of the Kuujjua and Soper rivers there are several descents. With the exception of the Isortoq River flowing from the ice cap on north Baffin Island, the rivers are described as relatively gentle. The high adventure comes from their remoteness, their inaccessibility in the case of accident and the extra danger from the more extreme climate of the high latitudes.

The rivers themselves are not always identified on maps, other than on specialized topographical maps, demonstrating further their remoteness.

BAFFIN ISLAND

SOPER

The Soper flows out of south Baffin Island through a rich valley west of the Meta Incognita Peninsula entering Pleasant Inlet of Hudson Strait just west of Lake Harbour. For centuries the Inuit of the Lake Harbour area used the valley for hunting and fishing and as a winter travel route. In 1992 the Soper was designated under the Canadian Heritage Rivers System.

1931   Dewey Soper, a biologist with the federal Department of the Interior working on Baffin Island, with Moosa and Mutuse, Inuit from Lake Harbour, in an 18-foot freighter canoe with an outboard motor, surveyed up the Koukdjuak (Kuujjuaq) River, later named the Soper River, from Lake Harbour as far as the entry of the Cascade River. They walked to the Mount Joy area and returned downstream. [Soper, p. 99; *Geographical Review*, 1936, pp. 426-38]

1950s   Akavak from Lake Harbour was travelling up and down the lower Soper to the mouth of the Livingstone River by freight canoe with a "kicker"; others followed.

1983 *Brent Boddy, Terry Gray and Goo Arnaguq were flown into the central portion of the Soper River by the mouth of the Cascade and kayaked to Lake Harbour. [Personal communication – Jane Cooper]*

1988 *Derek Cutler with a Lake Harbour Inuk paddled up to the mouth of the Cascade and down again. [Personal communication – Jane Cooper]*

1989 *Brent Boddy, Jane Cooper, Michelle Phillips, Katherine Trumper, Keith Irving, Geoff Hodgins, Patti Bowles and two Joneses repeated the 1983 route. [Personal communication – Cooper and Hodgins]*

1990 *Martin Brown of Sunrise County Canoe Expeditions flew into the upper river by Mount Joy with an American group and paddled to Lake Harbour. Brown continues to run several expeditions each year on the Soper River, as does Matty McNair of North Winds. [Sunrise County and North Winds brochures]*

SYLVIA GRINNELL

The Sylvia Grinnell rises in Sylvia Grinnell Lake in central south Baffin, flowing southeastward into Frobisher Bay.

1973 John Verby, Bruce Koci and Dave Buetow, Americans, using an 18-foot Chestnut canoe, set out from Pangnirtung with Inuit guide Norman Komotaok who took them across Cumberland Sound to Nettilling Fiord. They came up the Amadjuak River to Amadjuak Lake, crossed the height of land to Sylvia Grinnell Lake and canoed down the Sylvia Grinnell River to Frobisher Bay. [*Beaver*, Autumn 1974, p. 32]

1982 *Brent Boddy, Nigel Foster, Peter Birell, Goo Arnaguq, and Olie Manson flew into Sylvia Grinnell Lake and paddled their kayaks down to Iqaluit. [Personal communication – Jane Cooper]*

1983 *Brent Boddy, Jane Cooper, Rene Wissink, Warren Boddy, Ron Pombrey, Beth Beattie and Matthew Harvey repeated the 1982 trip. [Personal communication – Jane Cooper]*

AMADJUAK

The Amadjuak flows out of the northern bay of Amadjuak Lake and makes its way east and north into Nettilling Fiord.

1973 John Verby – see Sylvia Grinnell

ARMSHOW

The Armshow rises in the centre of the Meta Incognita Peninsula, flows northwest and then makes a hairpin turn to the southeast, emptying into the head of Frobisher Bay.

1984 *Brent Boddy and Rene Wissink flew into the upper reaches of the Armshow and kayaked to the mouth. This was a very hard trip and probably a first descent. [Personal communication – Jane Cooper]*

McKEAND

The McKeand is one of the longer rivers on Baffin Island. It flows northwest from the south central highlands of Hall Peninsula, turns north and empties into Cumberland Sound.

1985 *Brent Boddy, Jane Cooper, Rene Wissink, Bruce and Terry Rigby, Matthew Harvey, Shawn Thomas, Dick Abbot, Beth Beattie and Janice Rhanar made what they believe to be the first descent of the McKeand by canoe and kayak. Flown in, they paddled down the river for two weeks to the mouth. [Personal communication – Cooper]*

ISORTOQ

The Isortoq rises high in the Barnes Ice Cap in north central Baffin and flows south to Foxe Basin.

1987 *Ted Johnson, Tim Kotcheff, John Macfarlane, Craig Oliver, David Silcox and Peter Stollery attempted to make the first descent of the Isortoq River. The trip was cut short above Isortoq Lake following the loss of a canoe and provisions in a lining accident. [Personal communication – Johnson]*

1988 *Joe Egersagi, John Godfrey, Tim Kotcheff and Peter Stollery completed the descent of the Isortoq River, putting their canoes in above Isortoq Lake and completing the run to Foxe Basin. [Personal communication – Johnson]*

Members of the Arctic and Rideau Canoe Club lining down the Isortoq River in 1988. [John Godfrey]

Peter Stollery, Tim Kotcheff, Joe Egersagi and John Godfrey posing beside the river, and camped in glorious Arctic surroundings. [Godfrey]

RAVN

The Ravn River rises high in the northeast coastal mountains of Baffin, flows southwest into Angajurjua-luk Lake, continues west and then turns southeast as the link between a series of sizable lakes, including Quartz and Erichsen, before emptying into Steensby Inlet.

1956 Dr. R.G. Blackadar and J. Pirrit, for the Geological Survey, with a 17-foot canoe and a 3-horsepower motor, investigated the Ravn River at the head of Steensby Inlet at the northern end of Foxe Basin on Baffin Island. [*Arctic Circular*, 1956, p. 55]

BAFFIN ISLAND FIORDS

1977 *Erwin Streisinger and Anna Gerenday explored some Baffin Island fiords by kayak. [*Explorers Journal, *June 1980, p. 86]*

BANKS ISLAND

THOMSEN

The Thomsen rises close to Prince of Wales Strait and flows due north through Banks Island Bird Sanctuary No. 2 to empty into McLure Strait.

1952 Thomas Manning and Andrew MacPherson attempted to circumnavigate Banks Island in a 22-foot freighter canoe with a small outboard motor. They explored the south, west and north coastlines of the island, examining it for harbours for the Defence Research Board's motor vessel, collecting specimens of birds and mammals and looking at the remains of Thule houses. They covered 400 miles by canoe before they were forced to cache their canoe for the winter at the mouth of the Thomsen River. A fishing boat took them to Tuktoyaktuk. [*Arctic*, October 1953, pp. 171-97; *Arctic Circular*, March-May, 1953]

1953 Thomas Manning with Capt. I.M. Sparrow returned to Banks Island, crossed the island from south to north by dog team and retrieved the cached canoe at Thomsen River. They completed the exploration of the north coast and continued down Prince of Wales Strait to Holman on Vic-

toria Island, where they were picked up by plane. [*Arctic*, January 1956, p. 3]

1985 *John Godfrey, Dennis Harvey, Ted Johnson, Tim Kotcheff, Craig Oliver and Peter Stollery made what they believed to be the first descent of the Thomsen River on Banks Island. The river has a gentle flow through a picturesque, wide valley, with few rapids. [Personal communication – Johnson; WCA Symposium 1993]*

VICTORIA ISLAND

1971 T. Isono, Y. Miyaki, and K. Nakaniwa, from Tokai University Canadian Arctic Research Expedition, set out from the mainland to canoe to Victoria Island. Their canoe was found near Cambridge Bay two months later and they were presumed drowned. [*Polar Record*, September 1972, p. 411]

KUUJJUA

The Kuujjua rises in the Shaler Mountains and flows generally west through Diamond Jenness Peninsula to empty into Minto Inlet.

1980 *Larry Osgood, Maria Scott, Tom Daniel and Dorothy Poole, from an unnamed lake at the source of the river, kayaked down the Kuujjua River on Victoria Island to the mouth of the river at Minto Inlet. Inuit, hunting seals in the inlet, gave them a lift in power boats to Holman Island. [Personal communication – Osgood]*

1985 *John Lentz, John Ross, Stark Biddle, David Gilinsky, Bob Schaefer and Victor Gilinsky were dropped close to the headwaters of the Kuujjua River in the Shaler Mountains and canoed down to Minto Inlet. They were met, by pre-arrangement, by an Inuit and his two sons who took them by motorboat to Holman Island. [*Explorers Journal, *March 1986. p. 32; *Canoe, *June 1986, p. 24]*

1986 *Tom Anderson and seven others made a naturalists' trip down the Kuujjua River. [WCA Symposium, Toronto, 1993]*

The tents of the Arctic and Rideau Canoe Club on a spectacular curve of the Thomsen River in 1985. This is a river without portages, which allowed the group to camp in style with lawn chairs, barbecue, ice cream preserved in dry ice, and a selection of wines. [Godfrey]

Warmly dressed, Ted Johnson and Dennis Harvey proceed down the Thomsen River. [Godfrey]

NANOOK

The Nanook has its beginnings in central Victoria Island, flows east to Namaycush Lake and then due north to Hadley Bay.

1992 *Ed and Julia Struzik, Brian Milne, Dawn Goss, Peter and Jim, all Canadians, with Americans, Dave and Bob, flew from Cambridge Bay to the centre of Victoria Island and canoed down the Nanook River to Hadley Bay, encountering ice, rapids and a canyon in the final miles of the river.* [Equinox, *August 1993, pp. 35-45*]

ELLESMERE ISLAND

1956 Dr. R. Thorsteinsson and Dr. E.T. Tozer, Geological Survey team, with Amagualik and Jebbedi, canoed from Eureka, on the west side of Ellesmere Island, down Eureka Sound, between Axel Heiberg and Ellesmere, to Bay Fiord in a 22-foot freighter canoe with a 10-horsepower motor, and back. [*Arctic Circular*, 1956, p. 57]

RUGGLES

The Ruggles is possibly the most northerly navigable river and also one of the shortest rivers in the Arctic Islands. It flows from Lake Hazen east into Lady Franklin Bay, Hall Basin, at the north end of Ellesmere Island.

1992 Bill Fox, John Godfrey, Eddie Goldenberg, Ross Howard, Ted Johnson, Tim Kotcheff, Craig Oliver and Peter Stollery made the first descent of the Ruggles River, on northern Ellesmere Island, putting in at Lake Hazen and taking out at Chandler Fiord. This is believed to be the most northerly navigable river in the world. The flow depends on melt rate of glaciers and the river has good Grade II rapids for most of is length with no ledges. There are permanent ice walls on both banks for the last 12 miles and occasional ice bridges across the river. [Personal communication – Johnson; Destinations, June 1993, p. 32]

MELVILLE PENINSULA

KINGORA

The Kingora River, in northern Melville Peninsula, rises in the Prince Albert Hills and flows due east into Hall Lake.

1957 V.W. Sim and Donald Bissett, for the Geological Survey, used a collapsible canoe to cross and explore the Kingora River in the Melville Peninsula. [Arctic Circular, 1958, p. 27]

AJUQATALIK

The Ajuqatalik River, in the centre of Melville Peninsula, rises in the Prince Albert Hills on the western side of Melville, and flows north, then east and finally due north into Roche Bay.

1990 John Godfrey, Eddie Goldenberg, Ted Johnson, Tim Kotcheff, John Macfarlane, Craig Oliver, Peter Stollery and Bill Williams made the first descent of Ajuqatalik River on the Melville Peninsula. They put in at Ajuqatalik Lake and followed one of the most northerly navigable rivers in mainland Canada to the river mouth on Foxe Basin. [Personal communication – Johnson]

ARCTIC COAST

1972 John Bockstoce, M.R. Astor, J.M. Jackson, E.D. Kingik, R.J. Lane-Fox, C.A. Mitchell and R.O. Tevuk, American and British, travelled from Nome, Alaska, to Cape Bathurst in the Northwest Territories, by traditional walrus-skin umiak, with an outboard motor. The 9.6-metre umiak was built in Nome in 1971 under the joint supervision of John Bockstoce and D. Milligrock of Little Diomede Island. Weather, sea and ice conditions prevented them from their objective of navigating a portion of the Northwest Passage. [Polar Record, January 1973, p. 581]

1973 Colin Irwin, an Englishman on a private expedition, followed the route of Knud Rasmussen from Repulse Bay to Point Barrow, Alaska. He travelled with dogs and with three different Inuit companions and completed the journey by canoeing, with a motor, from Tuktoyaktuk to Point Barrow. [National Geographic, Vol. 145, #3, p. 295]

1992 Wendy Grater, for Trailhead/Black Feather, after leading several trips along the Greenland coast since 1986, led a two-week kayak trip from Grise Fiord east along the Ellesmere Island coast, and then one week along the coast of Devon Island. [Personal communication – Grater]

BIBLIOGRAPHY
of Printed Sources

BOOKS

Allen, Everett S. *Arctic Odyssey: The Life of Rear Admiral Donald B. Macmillan.* N.Y., Dodd, Mead, 1962.

Anderson, Frank. *The Death of Albert Johnson.* Frontier Books, Surrey, B.C., 1982.

Anderson, James. *The Fur Trader's Story.* Toronto, Ryerson, 1961.

Armstrong, F.H., H.A. Stevenson and J.D. Wilson, eds. *Aspects of Nineteenth Century Ontario.* Toronto, University of Toronto Press, 1974.

Armstrong, Nevill A.D. *Yukon's Yesterdays.* London, John Long, 1936.

Baldwin, Douglas. *The Fur Trade in the Moose-Missinaibi Valley, 1770-1917.* Toronto, MCR, 1975.

Back, Brian. *The Keewaydin Way: a portrait, 1893-1983.* Keewaydin Camp, Temagami, 1983.

Back, George. *Narrative of the Arctic Land Expedition to the Mouth of the Great Fish River.* London, Geo. Murray, 1836. Reprint.

Bell, James Mackintosh. *Far Places.* Toronto, Macmillan, 1931.

Berton, Pierre. *Drifting Home.* Toronto, M&S, 1973.

Blossom, Frederick A., ed. *Told at the Explorers Club: True Tales of Modern Exploration.* New York, Albert & Charles Boni, Inc., 1931

Boden, Jurgen & Elke Boden, eds. *Canada North of Sixty.* Toronto, M&S, 1991.

Bond, James H. *From out of the Yukon.* Portland, Oregon, Binfords & Mort, 1948.

Boon, T.C.B. *The Anglican Church from the Bay to the Rockies.* Toronto, Ryerson, 1962.

Bouchard, Serge. *Chroniques de chasse d'un Montagnais de Mingan, Mathieu Mestokosho.* Québec, Ministère des Affaires culturelles, 1977.

Bouchard, Serge. *Mémoires d'un simple missionnaire, le père Joseph-Étienne Guinard, o.m.i..* Québec, Ministère des Affaires culturelles, 1980.

Bramble, Charles A. *Land of the Lobstick: the log of a canoe journey in The Pas District of Northern Manitoba.* Prov. of Man., 1920.

Browning, Peter. *The Last Wilderness.* California, Great West Books, 1989.

Buchanan, Capt. Angus. *Wild life in Canada.* Toronto, McClelland, Goodchild and Stewart, 1920.

Burpee, Lawrence. *On the Old Athabaska Trail.* Toronto, Ryerson, 1926.

Burry, Donald. *The Canoe in Canadian Art.* unpublished Ph.D dissertation, U. of Alberta, Edmonton, 1993.

Butler, William. *The Wild Northland.* London, Dawson, 1874.

Cabot, William. *Labrador.* Boston, Small, Maynard and Co., 1920.

Camsell, Charles. *Son of the North.* Toronto, Ryerson, 1954.

Cantin, Eugene. *Yukon Summer.* San Francisco, Chronicle, 1973.

Choque, Charles, o.m.i. *Joseph Buliard: Fisher of Men.* Churchill, Man., R.C.Episcopal Corp., 1987.

Cilley, Jonathan. *Bowdoin Boys in Labrador.* Rockland, Maine Pub. Co., 1891.

Cline, Gloria. *Peter Skene Ogden and the Hudson's Bay Company.* Norman, U. of Oklahoma P., 1974

Coates, K. and W. Morrison. *Land of the Midnight Sun.* Edmonton, Hurtig, 1988.

Cody, Hiram. *An Apostle in the North: Memoirs of the Rt. Rev. William Carpenter Bompas.* Toronto, Musson, 1908.

Cole, Jean. *Exile in the Wilderness: The Life of Chief Factor Archibald McDonald, 1790-1853.* Toronto, B&M, 1979.

Comeau, Napoleon. *Life and Sport on the North Shore.* Quebec, Telegraph Printing Co., 1954, copyright 1909.

Cooke, Alan. in *Le Nouveau-Québec.* Paris, Mouton et Co., 1964

Cooke, A. and C. Holland. *The Exploration of Northern Canada: 500 to 1920,* Toronto, Arctic History Press, 1978.

Coutts, Robert. *Yukon Places and Names.* Sidney, B.C., Gray's Pub., 1980.

Cox, Ross. *The Columbia.* Norman, U. of Oklahoma P., 1957.

Cundy, Robert. *Beacon Six.* London, Eyre and Spottiswode, 1936.

Curran, T. and H. Calkins. *In Canada's Wonderful Northland,* New York, Putnam, 1917.

Davidson, J.W. and J. Rugge. *The Complete Wilderness Paddler.* New York, Knopf, 1978.

Davidson, J.W. and J. Rugge. *Great Heart: The History of a Labrador Adventure.* New York, Viking, 1988.

Davies, K.G. *Northern Quebec and Labrador Journals and Correspondence, 1819-35.* London, Hudson's Bay Record Soc., 1963.

Dawson, George. *Report on an exploration in the Yukon District, N.W.T., and adjacent northern portion of B.C., 1887.* Whitehorse, Yukon Hist.& Museum Assoc., 1987 reprint.

Douglas, David. *Journal kept by David Douglas during his travels in North America, 1822-7.* London, 1914.

Douglas, George. *Lands Forlorn.* New York, Putnam, 1914.

Downes, Prentice. *Sleeping Island.* New York, Coward-McCann, 1943.

Dyson, George. *Baidarka.* Edmonds, Alaska, NWP Co., 1986.

Ellsworth, Lincoln. *Beyond Horizons.* New York, Doubleday Doran, 1938.

Evans, G.H. *Canoeing Wilderness Waters.* New York, Barnes, 1974.

Evans, G.H. *The Rupert That Was.* Cobalt, Highway Bookshop, 1978.

Ferrier, Marion. *God's River Country.* Englewood Cliffs, P-H, 1956.

Fiennes, Sir Ranulph. *The Headless Valley.* London, H&S, 1973.

Flaherty, Robert. *My Eskimo Friends.* New York, Doubleday, 1924.

Footner, Hulbert. *New Rivers of the North.* New York, Doran, 1912.

Forbes, Alexander. *Northernmost Labrador mapped from the air.* Am. Geo. Soc., Pub #22, 1938.

Fountain, Paul. *The Great North-West and the Great Lake Region of North America.* London, Longmans, 1904.

Francis, D. and T. Morantz. *Partners in Furs.* Montreal, McGill-Queen's, 1983.

Francis, Daniel. *Discovery of the North: the Exploration of Canada's Arctic.* Edmonton, Hurtig, 1986.

Franklin, John. *Narrative of a Journey to the Shores of the Polar Sea in the Years 1819, 20, 21 and 22.* London, John Murray, 1823: Hurtig 1969.

Franklin, John. *Narrative of a Second Expedition to the Shores of the Polar Sea in the Years 1825, 1826 and 1827.* London, John Murray, 1828.

Fraser, Simon. *The Journals of Simon Fraser.* ed. Kaye Lamb. Toronto, Macmillan, 1960.

Freeman, Lewis. *The Nearing North.* N.Y., Dodd Mead, 1928

Gapen, Dan. *Fishing Rivers of the Far North.* Becker, Minn., Whitewater Pub. Inc., 1983.

Garnier, Louis. *Dog sled to airplane: a history of the St. Lawrence North Shore.* Quebec, 1949

Gibbon, J.M. *Romance of the Canadian Canoe.* Toronto, Ryerson, 1951.

Glover, R. ed. *David Thompson's Narrative 1784-1812.* Toronto, Champlain Society, 1962.

Graham, Angus. *The Golden Grindstone: The Adventures of George Mitchell.* Toronto, Oxford U. P., 1935.

Green, Lewis. *The Gold Hustlers.* Anchorage, Alaska Northwest Pub. Co., 1977

Halpenny, Francess, ed. *Dictionary of Canadian Biography.* Toronto, UTP, 1966-1989.

Hanbury, David. *Sport and Travel in the Northland of Canada.* London, Arnold, 1904.

Hanson, Harold, P. Queneau, and Peter Scott. *The Geography, Birds, and Mammals of the Perry River Region.* Arctic Instit. of North America, 1956.

Harper, Francis. *The Friendly Montagnais and Their Neighbors in the Ungava Peninsula.* Lawrence, U. of Kansas P., 1964.

Haworth, Paul. *On the Head Waters of Peace River.* New York, Scribner's, 1917.

Hayes, Alden. *Down North to the Sea: 2000 miles by canoe.* Pruett Pub., Boulder, Colorado, 1989.

Hearne, Samuel. *A Journey from Prince of Wales Fort in Hudson's Bay to the Northern Ocean in the years 1769, 1770, 1771 and 1772.* Toronto, Champlain Soc., 1911.

Helmericks, Constance. *Down the Wild River North.* Boston, Little Brown, 1968.

Heming, Arthur. *The Drama of the Forests.* Toronto, Doubleday, 1936.

Hind, Henry Y. *Explorations in the interior of the Labrador Peninsula.* 2 v., London, Longman, 1863.

Hodgins, B.W. *Paradis of Temagami.* Cobalt Highway Bookshop, 1976.

Hodgins, B.W. and M. Hobbs, eds. *Nastawgan.* Toronto, Betelgeuse, 1985.

Hodgins, B.W. and Jamie Benidickson. *The Temagami Experience*. Toronto, UTP, 1989.

Houston, C. Stuart., ed. *To the Arctic by Canoe, 1819-1821: The Journal and Paintings of Robert Hood, Midshipman with Franklin*. Montreal, McGill-Queen's, 1974.

Houston, C. Stuart., ed. *Arctic Ordeal: The Journal of John Richardson, Surgeon-Naturalist with Franklin, 1820-1822*. Montreal, McGill-Queen's, 1985.

Houston, James. *Running West*. Toronto, M&S, 1989.

Hubbard, Mina. *A Woman's Way through Unknown Labrador*. New York, 1909.

Iglauer, Edith. *Denison's Ice Road*. Toronto, Clarke Irwin, 1974.

Ingstad, Helge. *The Land of Feast and Famine*. New York, Knopf, 1933.

Jacobson, Cliff. *Canoeing Wild Rivers*. Merrillville, Ind. ICS Books, 1984.

Jacobson, Cliff. *Campsite Memories*. Merrillville, Ind. ICS Books, 1994.

Johnston, Lukin. *Beyond the Rockies*. London, Dent, 1929.

Karamanski, Theodore. *Fur Trade and Exploration: opening the Far Northwest, 1821-1852*. Vancouver, UBC, 1983.

Kelsey, Henry. *The Kelsey Papers*. eds. Arthur Doughty and Chester Martin. Ottawa, Public Archives, 1929.

Kenyon, W.A. and J.R. Turnbull. *The Battle for James Bay, 1686*. Toronto, Macmillan, 1971.

King, Richard. *Narrative of a journey to the shores of the Arctic Ocean in 1833, 1834, 1835 under the command of Capt. Back, R.N.* 2 v., London 1836.

Klein, Clayton. *Cold Summer Wind*. Fowlerville, Mich., Wilderness Adventure Books, 1983.

Klein, Clayton and Verlen Kruger. *One Incredible Journey*. Fowlerville, Mich., Wilderness House, 1985.

Klein, Clayton, ed. *A Passion for Wilderness*. Fowlerville, Mich., Wilderness Adventure Books, 1986.

Lefroy, John H. *In Search of the Magnetic North*. ed. G. Stanley, Toronto, Macmillan, 1955.

Lofthouse, Joseph. *A Thousand Miles from a Post Office*. London, S.P.C.K., 1922.

Lower, A.R.M. *Unconventional Voyages*. Toronto, Ryerson, 1953.

Luard, G.D. *Fishing Adventures in Canada and the U.S.*. London, Faber and Faber, 1950.

Macfie, Harry, with H. Westerlund. *Wasa-wasa*. (trans. from Swedish), New York, Norton, 1951.

MacGregor, J.G. *The Klondike Rush through Edmonton*. Toronto, McClelland and Stewart, 1970.

Mackenzie, Alexander, Sir. *Voyages from Montreal on the river St. Lawrence, through the continent of North America to the Frozen and Pacific Oceans, in the years 1789 and 1793*. ed. J. Garvin. Toronto, Radisson Series, 1927.

MacKinnon, A. "A History of the Thelon Game Sanctuary", *Musk-Ox*, Vol.32, 1983, pp. 44-61.

Madsen, Ken, and Graham Wilson. *Rivers of the Yukon*. Whitehorse, Primrose Pub., 1989.

Mair, Charles. *Through the Mackenzie Basin*. London, Simpkin and Co., 1908.

Malaher, Gerald. *The North I Love*. Winnipeg, Hyperion Press, 1984.

Mallet, Thierry. *Plain Tales of the North*. New York, Revillon Frères, 1925.

Mallet, Thierry. *Glimpses of the Barren Lands*. New York, Revillon Frères, 1930.

Mallory, Enid. *Coppermine*. Peterborough, Broadview, 1989.

Mason, Michael. *The Arctic Forests*. London, Hodder & Stoughton, 1924.

McClellan, Catherine. *Part of the Land, Part of the Water: A History of the Yukon Indians*. Vancouver, Douglas & McIntyre, 1989.

McDonald, T.H., ed. *Exploring the Northwest Territory: Sir Alexander Mackenzie's Journal, 1789*. Norman, U. Oklahoma P., 1966.

McGuire, Thomas. *99 Days on the Yukon: an account of what was seen and heard in the company of Charles A. Wolf, Gentleman Canoeist*. Anchorage, Alaska Northwest Pub. Co., 1977.

McKay, John. *Arctic Adventure: A Kazan River Journal*. Toronto, Betelgeuse, 1983.

McLean, John. *John McLean's notes of a twenty-five years' service in the Hudson's Bay territory*. Toronto, Champlain Soc., 1932. v.19

Mead, Robert. *Ultimate North*. Garden City, Doubleday, 1976.

Merrick, Elliott. *True North*. Lincoln, U. of Nebraska, 1989

Mills, Edwin. *Paddle, Pack and Speckled Trout*, Banff, 1985.

Mitchell, Elaine. *Fort Timiskaming and the Fur Trade*. Toronto, 1977.

Money, Anton. *This Was the North*. Toronto, General Pub., 1975.

Moore, Joanne Ronan. *Nahanni Trailhead*. Ottawa, Deneau & Greenberg, 1980.

Morse, Eric. *Fur Trade Canoe Routes of Canada/ Then and Now*. Ottawa, Queen's Printer, 1968.

Morse, Eric. *Freshwater Saga*. Toronto, University of Toronto Press, 1987.

Moss, John. *Enduring Dreams: An Exploration of Arctic Landscape*. Toronto, Anansi, 1994.

Moyles, R.G., ed. *From Duck Lake to Dawson City: The Diary of Eben McAdam's Journey to the Klondike, 1898-1899*. Saskatoon, Western Producer Prairie Books, 1977.

Mulhall, David. *Will to Power: The Missionary Career of Father Morice*. Vancouver, UBC Press, 1986.

Munn, Henry. *Prairie Trails and Arctic Byways*. London, Hurst and Blackett, 1932.

Munsterhjelm, Erik. *The Wind and the Caribou*. Toronto, Macmillan, 1953.

Murray, Alexander. *Journal of the Yukon, 1847-48.* Ottawa, Govt. printing bureau, 1910.

Nickerson, Elinor. *Kayaks to the Arctic.* Berkeley, Howell-North, 1967.

Niemi, Judith and Barbara Wieser, eds. *Rivers Running Free: Stories of Adventurous Women.* Minneapolis, Bergamot, 1987.

Norment, Christopher. *In the North of Our Lives.* Maine, Down East Books, 1989.

North, Robert. *Bob North by Canoe and Portage.* New York, Putnam, 1928.

Ogilvie, William. *Early days on the Yukon.* New York, Lane, 1913.

Onraet, Tony. *Sixty Below.* Toronto, Jonathan Cape, 1944.

Ontario, RCNE. *North of 50°: An Atlas of Far Northern Ontario.* Toronto, 1985.

Ontario. *Record of the Survey of Exploration of Northern Ontario, 1900 (NOLS).* Toronto, Queen's Park, 1901.

Pain, S. *The Way North.* Toronto, Ryerson, 1966.

Patterson, R.M. *Dangerous River.* Toronto, Stoddart, 1989, reprint.

Patterson, R.M. *Finlay's River.* Toronto, Macmillan, 1968.

Patterson, R.M. *Trail to the Interior.* Toronto, Macmillan, 1966.

Peake, Frank. *The Bishop Who Ate His Boots: A Biography of Isaac O. Stringer.* Toronto, Anglican Church of Canada, 1966.

Pecher, Kamil. *Lonely Voyage.* Saskatoon, Western Prairie Producer Books, 1978.

Pelly, David. *Expedition: An Arctic Journey through History on George Back's River.* Toronto, Betelgeuse, 1981.

Pelly, David. *Kazan.* Yukon, Outcrop, 1992.

Perkins, Robert. *Against Straight Lines: alone in Labrador.* Boston, Little Brown, 1983.

Perkins, Robert. *Into the Great Solitude: An Arctic Journey.* New York, Holt, 1991.

Petersen, Olive. *The Land of Moosoneek.* Toronto, Bryant, 1974.

Petitot, Emil. *Géographie de l'Athabaskaw-Mackenzie et des grands lacs du bassin arctique.* Paris, 1875.

Pike, Warburton. *The Barren Ground of Northern Canada.* London, Arnold, 1892.

Pike, Warburton. *Through the Subarctic Forest.* London, Edward Arnold, 1896.

Poirel, Jean. *Nahanni.* Montreal, Alain Stanké, 1980.

Potvin, Damase. *Puyjalon: le solitaire de l'Ile à la Chasse.* Quebec, 1938.

Preble, E.A. *North American Fauna.* Bulletin No. 27, U.S. Dept. of Agriculture, 1908.

Prichard, Hesketh. *Through Trackless Labrador.* London, Heinemann, 1911.

Provencher, Paul. *Provencher, Last of the Coureurs de Bois.* Toronto, Burns and MacEachern, 1976.

Pullen, Hugh F. *The Pullen Expedition.* Toronto, Arctic History Press, 1979.

Raffan, James, ed. *Wild Waters.* Toronto, Key Porter, 1986.

Raffan, J. and B. Horwood, eds. *Canexus.* Toronto, Betelgeuse, 1988.

Raffan, James. *Summer North of Sixty: By Paddle and Portage across the Barren Lands.* Toronto, Key Porter, 1990.

Ray, A.J. *Indians and the Fur Trade.* Toronto, University of Toronto Press, 1974

Reid, R. and J. Grand. *Canoeing Ontario's Rivers.* Vancouver, Douglas and McIntyre, 1985.

Renison, Robert. *One day at a time.* Toronto, Kingswood House, 1957.

Rich, E.E., ed. *A Journal of a voyage from Rocky Mountain Portage in Peace River to the Sources of Finlays Branch and North West Ward in Summer 1824.* London, Hudson's Bay Record Soc., 1955.

Ross, Hugh Mackay. *The Manager's Tale.* Winnipeg, Watson & Dwyer, 1989.

Ruggles, Richard I. *A Country So Interesting.* Montreal, McGill-Queen's, 1991.

Russell, Frank. *Explorations in the Far North.* Iowa City, U. of Iowa P., 1898.

Rutstrum, Calvin. *North American Canoe Country.* New York, Macmillan, 1972.

Satterfield, Archie. *Yukon River Trail Guide.* Harrisburg, Pa., Stackpole Books, 1975.

Schrag, Rex. *Crater country.* Toronto, Ryerson, 1958.

Schwatka, Frederick. *A summer in Alaska.* St. Louis, J.W.Henry, 1894.

Scott, Peter. *Wild Geese and Eskimos: A Journal of the Perry River Expedition of 1949.* London, Country Life Ltd., 1951.

Scott, James. *The Land that God Gave to Cain.* London, Chatto and Windus, 1933.

Secretan, J.H.E. *To Klondyke and Back.* London, Hurst and Blackett, 1898.

Selous, F.C. *Recent Hunting Trips in North America.* London, Witherby and Co., 1909.

Service, Robert. *Ploughman of the Moon.* New York, Dodd Mead, 1945.

Seton, Ernest T. *The Arctic Prairies.* New York, Harper, 1911.

Sevareid, Eric. *Canoeing with the Cree.* St Paul, Minn. Hist. Soc., 1968.

Sevareid, Eric. *Not so Wild a Dream.* N.Y., Knopf, 1947.

Shearwood, Mrs. F.P. *By Water and the Word, a transcription of the Diary of the Rt. Rev. J.A. Newnham.* Toronto, Macmillan, 1943.

Sheldon, Charles. *The Wilderness of the Upper Yukon.* New York, Scribners, 1913.

Sherwood, Morgan. *Exploration of Alaska, 1865-1900.* New Haven, Yale U.P., 1965.

Simpson, Thomas. *Narrative of the discoveries on the north coast of America effected by the officers of the Hudson's Bay Company, 1836-39.* London, Richard Bentley, 1845

Skinner, Alanson. *The Eastern Cree and Northern Saulteaux,* New York, American Museum of Natural History, Anthropological papers, Vol. 9, 1912.

Soper, J. Dewey. *Canadian Arctic Recollections: Baffin Island, 1923-31.* Saskatoon, U. of Sask., Mawdsley Memoir 4, 1981

Somerset, Somers. *Land of the Muskeg.* London, Heinemann, 1895.

Spears, Borden, ed. *Wilderness Canada.* Toronto, Clarke Irwin, 1970.

Steber, Rick. *New York to Nome, the Northwest passage by canoe from the recollections of Shell Taylor.* New York, Pocket Books, 1987.

Stefansson, Vilhjalmur. *Hunters of the Great North.* New York, Harcourt Brace, 1922.

Stern, John. *To Hudson's Bay by Paddle and Portage.* Privately printed, 1934.

Stewart, Elihu. *Down the Mackenzie and up the Yukon in 1906.* London, John Lane, 1913.

Story, Norah., ed. *Oxford Companion to History and Literature.* Toronto, Oxford Univ. Press, 1967.

Stuck, Hudson. *Voyages on the Yukon and its Tributaries,* New York, Scribners, 1917.

Sutton, George. *High Arctic.* Don Mills, Fitzhenry and Whiteside, 1971.

Talbot, Frederick. *The New Garden of Canada.* London, Cassell, 1911.

Tanner, Vaino. *Outlines of the Geography, Life and Customs of Newfoundland-Labrador,* Acta Geographica 8, No. l, Helsinki, 1944.

Thompson, David. *David Thompson's Narrative, 1784- 1812.* ed. R. Glover. Toronto, Champlain Society, 1962.

Thompson, Don. *Men and Meridians.* vols. 2,3, Ottawa, Queen's Printer, 1966-69.

Thomson, Sheila, ed. *Journal of a Barrenlander: W.H.B. Hoare, 1928-29,* Ottawa, 1990.

Thwaites, R.G., ed. *Jesuit Relations and Allied Documents.* Cleveland, Burrows, 1897.

Todd, W.E.C. *Birds of the Labrador Peninsula.* Toronto, University of Toronto Press, 1963.

Tollemache, The Hon. Stratford. *Reminiscences of the Yukon.* Toronto, Wm. Briggs, 1912.

Tremblay, Hugette, ed. *Journal des voyages de Louis Babel, 1866-1868.* Montreal, U. du Québec P., 1977.

Tryck, Keith. *Yukon Passage.* Toronto, Fitzhenry and Whiteside, 1980.

Turner, Dick. *Nahanni.* Saanichton, B.C., Hancock House, 1975.

Tyrrell, James W. *Across the Sub-Arctic of Canada,* Toronto, 1897

Van Kirk, Sylvia. *"Many Tender Ties": Women in Fur Trade Society, 1670-1870.* Winnipeg, Watson and Dwyer, 1981.

Vyvyan, C. C. *Arctic Adventure.* London, 1961.

Waiser, William. *The Field Naturalist: John Macoun, the Geological Survey and Natural Science.* Toronto, UTP, 1989.

Wallace, Dillon. *The long Labrador trail.* New York, Outing, 1907.

Wallace, Dillon. *The lure of Labrador.* St. John's, Breakwater Books, 1977, reprint.

Watt, Frederick. *Great Bear: A Journey Remembered.* Yellowknife, Outcrop, 1980.

Watters, Reginald. *Checklist of Canadian Literature.* Toronto, University of Toronto Press, 1959.

Wells, E. Hazard, Randall M. Dodd, ed. *Magnificence and Misery: a firsthand account of the 1897 Klondike Gold Rush.* N.Y., Doubleday, 1984

Whalley, George. *Death in the barren ground.* Ottawa, Oberon, 1980.

Whalley, George. *The Legend of John Hornby.* Toronto, Macmillan, 1962.

Wickersham, James. *Old Yukon.* Washington, Washington Law Book Co., 1938.

Wright, Allen. *Prelude to Bonanza: the Discovery and Exploration of the Yukon.* Whitehorse, Arctic Star, 1976.

Wright, Richard T., and Rochelle Wright. *Canoe Routes - Yukon.* Surrey, B.C., Antonson Pub., 1977.

Young, Rev. Egerton. *By Canoe and Dog Train among the Cree and Salteaux Indians.* London, Charles Kelly, 1894.

Zaslow, M. "Edward Barnes Borron, 1820-1915: Northern pioneer and public servant extraordinary", in *Aspects of Nineteenth-Century Ontario: Essays Presented to James J. Talmon,* F.H. Armstrong, H.A. Stevenson, J.D. Wilson, eds. Toronto, UTP, 1974.

Zaslow, M. *Reading the Rocks.* Toronto, Macmillan, 1975.

JOURNALS AND MAGAZINES

Arctic. By index, from the beginning to 1980

Arctic Circular. Complete.

Beaver. From 1920 to the present.

Canadian Field-Naturalist. Up to vol. 88.

Canadian Heritage River Systems. Reports.

Canadian Geographer. By index.

Canadian Geographic. Vol. 1 to the present.

Canoe. by index

Che-Mun. Outfit 1 to the present.

Explorers Journal. Relevant issues from the archivist.

Geography. By index.

Nastawgan. Previously *Beaverdam* and *Wilderness Camping.* Toronto, WCA, vol. 1 to the present.

National Geographic. 1888-1988, by index.

New York Times Indexes. 1914 - 1974.

Ottawa Naturalist. Complete.

Outdoor Canada. Relevant issues from the editor.

Outing. Vols. 37-81.

Wild River Survey Reports. 1973-74.

and selected issues of *Alaska, Alaska Journal, American Whitewater, Appalachia, Audubon, B.C. Outdoors, Bulletin of the American Association of Petroleum Geologists, Bulletin of the American Museum of Natural History, Bulletin of the Geograpical Society of Philadelphia, Bulletin of the Society of Geography of Quebec, Canadian Boating, Canadian Magazine, Canadian Mining Journal, Canadian Wildlife Service, Carnegie Institute Magnetic Land Surveys, Century Magazine, Christian Guardian, Copperfield, Cruiser, Destinations, Equinox, Eskimo, Everybody's Magazine, Field and Stream, Fram, Geographical Journal, Geographical Review, Good Housekeeping, Hamilton Spectator, Harvard Magazine. Imperial Oil Review, Journal of the Royal Geographic Society, Kanawa Magazine, Literary and Historical Society of Quebec Transactions, Manitoba Free Press, Maclean's, le Maclean's, Musk-Ox, National Museum Bulletins, 96; 123, Natural History, North/Nord, Outdoor Life, Paddler, Peterborough Examiner, Polar Record, Queen's Quarterly, La Revue d'histoire de la Cote-Nord, River Runner, Royal Geographical Society Proceedings, San Francisco Bulletin, Saskatchewan History, Scribners, Seventeen, Smithsonian Magazine, Sports Illustrated, Star Weekly, Toronto Life, Up-here, Weekend Magazine, Winnipeg Free Press.*

ARCHIVES OR FILES CONSULTED

Che-Mun

Eric Morse – personal files, compiled by Pamela Morse

Fédération Québecoise du Canot-Camping

Hudson's Bay Company

National Archives of Canada

Parks Canada

Revillon Frères

CAMP REPORTS

Kandalore

Kapitachouane

Keewaydin

Keewaydin – Vermont

Owakonze

Wabun

Wanapitei

Widjiwagan

INDEX TO PEOPLE

Abbot, Dick, 250
Abbott, Dick, 106, 149
Abbott, E.C."Ted", 145
Abel, Dr. Jim, 98, 107, 111, 176, 178, 180, 184
Acheson, Keith, 104
Acres, Percy, 101
Adams, Horace P., 33
Adamson, Arthur, 171
Adcock, Will, 87
Addicks, Tom, 218
Addis, Dan, 88
Addison, Bill and Wendy, 144
Adlard, Harold, 102
Aho, Steve, 57, 59
Ahrens, Jim, 157
Airth, W.B., 80
Albanel, Father Charles, 69
Albrecht, John, 96
Albright, Charles, 87
Alcock, F.J., 93
Alexander, James, 127
Alexander, Jamie, 51
Alexander, Wendell, 34
Algotsson, Hans, 204
Allan, J.D., 158
Allen, Lynne, 146, 149
Allen, Peter, 122, 143
Allen, W.R., 72
Allensworth, Bob, 192
Alsop, Denny, 76
Ammons, Doug, 212
Amos, Robert, 34, 51, 53, 57, 62
Andcent, Mark, 34
Anderegg, John, 111, 172
Andersen, Capt. Hans, 41
Andersen, Julian, 117
Anderson, Bill, 45, 52, 55
Anderson, Bishop David, 45
Anderson, Bishop John, 47, 66, 71
Anderson, C.F., 166
Anderson, David and Bruce, 97

Anderson, James, 180
Anderson, John, 56
Anderson, Mark, 49
Anderson, Tom, 252
Andre, Antoine, 150
Andres, Brian, 95
Appell, George and Laura, 133
Archibald, B., 49
Arden, D'Arcy, 156, 170
Ardron, Matt, 160
Armstrong, Nevill A.D., 204
Arnaguq, Goo, 250
Arnett, John, 244
Arnold, Jim, 95, 111
Arnup, Rob, 51
Arthurs, Don, 173
Ashini, John, 238
Ashley, R.W., 158
Astroski, Joe, 220
Atherley, John, 63
Atkinson, George, Jr., 78
Atkinson, Harry, 204
Aubert de la Rue, Edgar, 216
Ault, C.P., 96
Ault, Kip, 106
Awrey, Mr., 46, 47
Babel, Père Louis, 227, 240, 242, 245
Back, George, 84, 116, 131, 169, 175, 180
Baer, Hans, 145
Baich, Paul von, 157, 199
Bailey, "Hobie", 66, 71
Bailley, Eric, 244
Bain, Will, 33
Baird, Alex, 32
Baird, Pat, 110
Baker, Dr., 46
Baker, Morton, 55
Baldwin, W.K.W., 80
Ball, George, 128, 141, 196
Banducci, Don, 208, 211
Banfi, Ed, 49, 50
Banfield, A.W.F., 103, 181, 222
Banghart, Ray, 73

Bany, Lynda, 123, 179
Bany, Steve, 123, 177, 179
Barad, Mark, 57
Barber, Harris, 87
Barber, Jimmy, 132
Baribeau, Claude, 68
Barker, Chris, 178
Barnes, Bob, 217
Barnett, Graham, 151
Barnett, Jim, 157
Barnley, Rev. George, 39, 79
Barr, Don, 222
Barrett, Charles, 36
Barrett, T., 163
Barsevskis, Paul, 233, 244
Barss, Jack, 66
Bates, Jim, 65
Bayes, Daylen, 163
Bayes, Randy, 163
Bayly, Cristine, 160
Bayly, Jane, 106
Bayly, Jim, 106, 171
Bayly, John, 153, 159, 160, 163
Bayly, Terk, 59, 106, 158, 171, 197
Beach, Benjamin, 189
Bear, Robert, 101
Beardmore, Roger, 139, 148, 149, 155, 165, 200, 205, 206, 211
Beasley, Bryan, 97
Beattie, Beth, 250
Beaucage, Angus, 42
Beauchamp, Jacques, 124
Beaudry, Sylvain, 78, 238
Beaulieu, family, 180
Beaulieu, Sousi, 161
Beaulieux, François, 124
Beckett, Diane, 146
Beckett, Don, 146, 149
Beebe, Lloyd, 181
Beebe, Rod, III, 67, 68, 213, 218, 224, 236, 239
Beeswanger, Karen, 176
Beevis, David, 74

Begg, Jim, 87
Béland, Andre, 241
Belanger, Leo, 49, 55
Belanger, Nishe, 49, 63, 65, 68, 72, 73
Bell, A.H., 127
Bell, Dr., 46
Bell, J. Mackintosh, 36, 43, 65, 132, 156, 158, 170
Bell, John, 147, 153, 187
Bell, Robert, 32, 35, 45, 52, 54, 56, 65, 84, 89, 116
Bellinger, Patrick, 184
Belzile, Diane, 241
Benander, Tom, 178
Bendy, W.R. and Sylvia, 196
Benidickson, Jamie, 56, 57
Benjamin, Sousie, 102
Bennett, Hal and Jean, 204, 205
Benson, Kim, 166
Berger, Jon, 49, 50, 55-57, 59, 73, 76, 78
Bergman, Donald, 48
Bergstrom, Karen, 163
Berkeland, Joe, 106
Bernadin, Claude, 143
Berner, Robert, 48
Bernier, Francis, 78
Bernier, Pierre, 51
Bernstein, Jonathan, 104
Berry, Capt., 143
Berry, Michael, 34
Berta, Jim, 205
Berton, Francis, 191, 210
Berton, Janet, 192
Berton, Laura, 191
Berton, Pierre, 191, 192
Best, Doug, 105, 130
Best, Nick, 34
Betcherman, Philip, 34
Betteridge, Keith, 34
Bewell, Chris, 60
Biddle, Stark, 252
Biemann, Larry, 220

Bierman, Bill, 123
Biewen, Sara, 244
Biggs, Ken, 104
Bildeau, France, 239
Binger, Tom, 88
Binning, Russ, 241
Bird, Bob, 172
Bird, J.B., 103
Bird, John, 57
Bird, Tony, 151
Bird, Xavier, 43, 57
Birell, Peter, 250
Birket-Smith, Kaj, 109
Birkett, John, 159
Bishop, Charlie, 58
Bissell, Bill, 49, 55
Bissett, Donald, 254
Bixby, Jane, 163
Bjorklund, Brad, 175
Bjorklund, Kurt, 108
Black, A., 112, 140, 184, 211
Black, Dr. W.F., 184
Black, F., 140
Black, H., 112
Black, Richard, 106
Black, S., 211
Black, Samuel, 124, 209
Black, W., 90
Blackadar, Bobby, 208
Blackadar, Dr. R.G., 181, 252
Blackadar, Walt, 207
Blackborrow, John, 111
Blacknet, David, 73
Blaikie, Peter, 110, 171
Blair, Jim, 220
Blais, Marc, 65
Blake, Gilbert, 221, 235
Blake, John, 229
Blake, Ralph, 229
Blanchard, J.L., 181
Blanchard, Steve, 73
Blanchet, Guy, 26, 107, 121, 127, 161, 162, 171
Bland, John, 76, 144, 219
Blasko, Stephen, 150
Blau, Kathy, 208
Bleile, Bob, 207
Bliss, Wes, 133
Blunt, John, 49, 105, 108, 149, 150, 162
Bobblets, M.E., 103
Bober, Dave, 123
Bockstoce, John, 254
Boddy, Brent, 250
Boddy, Warren, 250
Boden, Wayne, 198

Boerbon, Lee, 117
Bogdan, G., 75, 163
Bogden, Ann, 151
Boissey, E., 77
Bolgar, Henrietta, 145
Bolster, Louis, 157
Bompas, Bishop William, 116, 125, 164, 188, 191, 193, 194, 202
Bond, Brad, 111
Bond, Charles, 175
Bond, James, 202
Bonga, George, 109
Boone, Jim, 104
Bordet, Bertrand, 143
Borron, Edward, 31, 35, 45, 54
Bose, Tom, 49
Bosher, Ben, 49
Boston, Chief, 66
Bosworth, T.O., 121
Boucher, John, 31
Boulger, John, 244
Boulanger, François, 78
Bovey, Martin, 47, 53
Bowles, Patti, 250
Bowman, Reb, 123, 175, 177
Boyd, Laurie, 86
Boyd, W.H., 57, 58
Boyde, Jim, 151-153, 165, 198, 202, 205
Boyde, Pam, 151-153, 202, 205
Boyer, Raymond, 241, 243, 244, 247, 248
Boysen, Dick, 48
Braaksma, Tynka, 151
Brace, Fritz, 173
Bradford, Leland, 139
Bradshaw, Gordon, 146
Brailsford, Alan, 146, 247
Brailsford, Mike, 247
Bramble, Charles, 90
Bramen, Will, 51
Brand, Dietrich, 160
Brand, Jon, 59
Brand, Katherine, 160
Bratnober, Phil, 173
Braun, Steve, 68
Bray, Mike, 51, 88
Breckenridge, Dr. W.J., 181
Breeden, Brewster, 47, 53
Bremner, J.L., 32
Brewster, Peter, 184, 215
Briand, Gilles, 243
Briggs, Henry W., 103
Brimm, John, 76, 144
Brisson, Baptiste, 124

Bristol, C., 219
Brizee, Dan, 151
Brock, R.W., 65, 85
Brodeur, Jean, 65, 220
Brohan, John, 248
Bromley, Graham, 157, 158, 182
Bromley, Robert, 163, 182
Brook, Ed, 147
Brooke, Brian, 151
Brooks, David, 59, 103
Broomell, Helen, 51
Brophy, Bart, 147
Brothwell, Tom, 95
Brown, Andrew, 229
Brown, Bern, 166
Brown, Donald, 150
Brown, Joan, 223
Brown, Louis, 202
Brown, Martin, 153, 217, 250
Brown, Pat, 162, 171
Brown, Tony, 247
Brown, W.E."Buster", 96
Brown, Winthrop, 47
Browning, J.M., 158
Browning, Peter, 105, 108, 162, 163
Bruce, Marcus, 57, 68, 74, 78, 147
Brucher, John, 144
Bruck, Bill, 152
Bryant, Henry, 39, 228, 238
Buchan, Ken, 111
Buchan, Thomas, 69, 75
Buchanan, Capt. Angus, 92
Buchanan, Frank, 129
Buchanan, Todd, 175
Buckminster, W.R., 66
Buckshott, Mike, 76
Buetow, Dave, 94, 171, 250
Buetow, Eric, 105, 220
Buliard, Father Joseph, 181
Bunce, Brian, 123
Bunn, Charlie, 132
Burg, Amos, 133, 192, 196
Burger, Ginny, 105
Burger, Steve, 105
Burns, Skip and Cheri, 192
Burrows, A.C., 32, 41
Burton, Barbara, 176
Burtt, Peter, 128
Bush, Mike, 239, 244
Bush, Neil von, 173, 182
Butler, Capt. William, 125
Button, Bruce, 95
Byers, Bud, 48

Byrnes, M.W., 209
Cabot, William, 20, 221, 231, 232, 235, 237, 238
Cadman, Mike, 62
Cadotte, Joe, 109
Cadzow, Daniel, 194
Cain, Tom, 133
Calder, Ian, 157, 182
Caldwell, Dr. J.D., 46, 47
Caldwell, Rob, 105, 134, 160
Calkins, H.A., 33, 79
Callfas, Don, 111
Cameron, A.E., 142, 164
Campbell, Hugh, 126
Campbell, J.D., 87
Campbell, Kenneth, 86
Campbell, Robert, 136, 187, 188, 204, 209
Campbell, Tom, 123
Camsell, Charles, 36, 60, 120, 121, 127, 132, 137, 138, 152, 156, 162, 170, 194, 201
Camsell, Frank, 60
Camsell, Fred, 137, 138, 152, 194
Camsell, G.C., 158
Camsell, Philip, 36
Cannon, Dave, 178, 180
Cannon, Whitney, 48
Cantin, Eugene, 192
Cardinal, Louis, 152, 194, 204
Carey, George, 47, 80
Carhart, Richard and Marjorie, 52
Carlisle, Jennings, 122, 133
Carlson, Richard, 51
Carmack, George, 189, 200, 201, 206
Carmichel, Jim and Jeff, 202
Carnochan, R.K., 63
Carpenter, Dan, 74, 76, 77
Carpenter, K., 163
Carpenter, Len, 239
Carriker, M.A., 33
Carroll, John, 158
Carron, Carron, 180
Carson, Thomas, 86
Carswell, Bruce, 72
Carter, Alison and Ralph, 34
Carter, Glen, 239
Carter, Philip, 163
Cartlidge, Rev. Harry, 66, 71
Cary, Austin, 228
Cary, Merritt, 120
Cassells, John, 34
Cassivi, Carl, 243

Cayley, Edward, 245
Cedarblade, Dewey, 117
Celantano, John, 73
Cepella, Rob and Jennifer, 233
Challis, Robin, 181
Chambers, Bob, 73
Chambers, Wally, 228, 240
Champigny, Gérard, 68
Chant, Donald, 72, 108
Chapies, Job, 33, 217, 221, 235
Chapman, C., 85, 89
Charlie, Tagish, 190, 200, 206
Charlôit, De, 161
Charlton, W.A., 32
Chase, Al, 74, 77
Cherkezoff, Lauren, 153
Chevery, Arthur, 239
Chevrette, Alain, 78, 238, 239
Chillcott, James, 108
Chilton, Robert, 70, 218
Chipeniuk, Ray, 130
Chipman, K.G., 156, 168, 170
Chivers, Warren, 63, 72
Cholasinski, Ron, 49
Cholmondeley, C.C., 238
Christensen, Vaughn, 95
Christian, Edgar, 102
Christiansen, Bruce, 134
Christie, J.M., 149, 203
Church, Richard, 86
Churchill, Cpl., 138
Chytil, Damir, 148
Clapp, Al, 94
Clark, Bob, 192
Clark, C., 182
Clarke, Dr. C.H.D., 103
Clarke, John, 68, 69, 74
Clarke, Penny, 151
Clarke, Scoville, 232
Claveau, Jacques, 241
Cleaver, Chuck and Dot, 111
Cleaver, Kip, 111
Clement, Dave, 73
Clements, Gary, 129
Clermont, L., 63
Clim, Ralph, 241
Cline, Stewart and Meg, 130
Clouston, James, 70, 218
Clunie, Marshall, 51, 53
Clutter, Robert, 157, 158
Coats, Vern, 205
Cochrane, A.S., 39, 92
Cochrane, Brad, 173
Cockburn, Bruce, 175
Cocking, Matthew, 83
Coe, Pete, 239

Coffin, Jane, 244
Coffin, Stewart, 109, 222, 234, 235, 241, 244, 247, 248
Coffin, Tammis, 244
Coghlan, Charles, 204
Cole, Anne, D. and Leigh, 55
Cole, Dennis, 228
Coleman, Babette and John, 104
Colgate, Bob, 104
Collins, Barry, 51
Collins, Harry, 139, 200, 205, 206, 211, 232-234, 236, 238, 239
Collins, W.H., 54
Colombe, Philippe, 228, 240
Commanda, Paul, 33, 36, 71, 80, 215, 245
Conche, Carol, 223
Congdon, R.T., 181
Conger, Peyton, 65
Connell, F.J., 238
Conover, Garrett and Alexandra, 244
Contant, Claude, 78
Conway, P.R., 102
Cook, Jimmy, 60
Cook, William, 89
Cooke, Alan, 197
Cooke, Frank, 73, 106, 172
Cooke, H.C., 68
Coolican, Denis, 88, 122, 157
Cooper, Jane, 250
Copeland, Rod, 34, 134
Copley, George, 127
Coppings, Raymond, 50
Corcoran, Dave, 49
Corliss, Bob, 111, 172
Corp, E.J., 119, 148, 201
Corrigal, James, 101, 107
Corriveau, Jacques, 248
Cosco, David, 153
Côté, Emile, 55
Côté, Georges, 66
Côté, Lise, 78
Couchai, Jacko, 36, 71
Couet, Gilles, 175
Couillard, Denis, 248
Coursey, Bill, 238, 239
Courtois, François, 124
Cowger, Jennifer, 166
Cowie, Jamie, 97
Cox, J.R., 165, 168, 170
Cox, Joel, 239
Cox, Rod, 71
Cox, Ross, 118

Craig, Michael, 150
Craig, Richard, 86
Cramp, Fred and Sue, 106, 159, 172
Crampton, G.R., 47
Cranne, Richard, 162, 182
Creighton, J.G.Alwyn, 238
Crews, Paul, Jr., 192
Cribbett, Stanley, 144
Critchell-Bullock, J.C., 102, 121, 128, 161
Crofton, Major J., 84
Crooks, A., 94, 163, 182
Crooks, J., 94, 182
Crooks, R., 94, 163, 172
Cross, Randy, 217
Crouch, Dee, 207
Cruse, Bob, 106
Cudmore, David, 51
Cundy, Robert, 181
Curran, W. Tees, 33, 66, 75, 79
Currie, W.C., 59
Curtis, Ted, 151, 153, 202
Cushman, Allerton, 59, 95, 171, 230
Cusson, Andre, 243
Cyr, Pierre, 119
D'Aigle, R.B., 219, 228, 245
D'Iberville, Pierre Le Moyne, 38
Dablon, Père, 69
Dalglish, Tom, 65
Dalton, Jack, 208
Daly, Dr. Bruce, 149
Damm, Terry, 43
Danforth, Sandra, 52
Daniel, Ed, 145
Daniel, Tom, 252
Dann, Ron, 243
Dannert, Bob, 123, 173, 175, 177, 179, 182
Dannert, Dave, 175, 177, 179
Dare, Graham, 49
Darrell, Hubert, 102
Dashwood, Betty, 73
Dashwood, John, 73, 104, 235
Dauner, Donna, 207
Davidson, Dexter, 159, 171
Davidson, Jim, 213, 232, 247
Davidson, Peter, 247
Davidson, Walter S., 54
Davies, Neil and Travis, 202
Davies, W.H.A., 227
Davis, Andy, 202, 205
Davis, Bob, 42, 51, 59, 111, 217, 220, 223, 234, 239, 241, 248

Davis, Deborah, 59
Davis, John, 159, 163, 173
Davis, Kelly, 123
Davis, William, 87
Dawson, C.B., 63
Dawson, George M., 125, 136, 190, 202, 209
Dawson, John, 207
Day, George, 134
Dean, E.K., 105, 161
Dean, W.G., 103
Dearnley, Al, 247
Dease, Albert, 128, 138, 141, 196
Dease, Peter Warren, 131, 169
DeBuhr, Mary, 123
Decaire, Jack, 71
DeCoste, Ralph, 206
Dedrick, Bob, 173
Delaire, Guy, 34
Delaute, Frank, 87
Deleuran, Henry, 42
Demers, Tim, 178
Dennis, Alan, 208
Denny, Capt. Sir Cecil, 126
Derby, A.W., 97
DeReimer, Phil, 212
Derry, Ramsay, 145
Desbarats, G.H., 229
Deshaies, Pierre, 219
Deslauriers, Jack, 152, 194
Desrauleau, Alain, 248
Desroches, Louis, 248
Desrosiers, Jacques and Ted, 63
Devine, Roger, 123
Devreeze, Igor, 244
Dewar, K.M., 102
DeWitte, Laura, 166
Dickgeisser, Bob, 73
Dickinson, Bill, 49
Dickson, Michele, 178, 180
Dieder, Mike, 239
Diesel, Marion, 122, 149, 157, 196
Diesel, Max, 122, 149, 157, 196
Diesel, Raymond, 122, 157, 196
Dinsmore, Rebecca, 51
Dinter, Trudy van, 244
Dion, Peter, 183
Dionne, Claude, 244
Dionne, Gaston, 241, 242, 244
Dix, Dean, 239
Dixon, Jack, 37
Dobbie, George, 111, 182

Docter, G., 94
Docter, J., 90, 94, 172, 211
Docter, Jas., 90
Docter, M., 211
Dodd, Bruce, 95
Dodds, Tom, 72
Doehlert, Charles, 111, 172
Doerr, Reed, 123
Doiron, Alain, 248
Donaldson, Ian, 148, 149, 155, 165, 202
Donaldson, J.A., 168
Doré, Guy, 65, 220, 239, 241, 242, 244, 248
Dougall, L., 157, 198, 211
Dougall, W., 95, 157, 198, 211
Douglas, David, 84
Douglas, George, 20, 121, 156, 170
Douglas, Lionel, 121, 156, 170
Doutt, Kenneth, 80, 215, 229
Dowling, D.B., 57, 58, 92
Downes, P.G., 93, 96, 117
Downie, Bill, 48
Dowse, Grant, 42
Drexler, Charles, 39
Driessen, Raymond, 117
Driscoll, Andy, 117
Drought, George, 38, 176
Drought, Richard, 38
Drucker, Harry, 51, 88
Drummond, Thomas, 84
Drybone, Noel, 161
Duberger, C.C., 245
Ducette, Charles, 124, 130
Duemling, Robert, 175
Duffy, Charley, 244
Dufresne, Jacques, 217
Dufresne, Jean Claude, 217, 220
Dunbar, Wayne, 103
Dunbaugh, Franklin, 87
Duncan, Des, 206
Dunfie, Rod, 146
Dungern, Osker von, 112
Dunker, Keith, 172
Dutilly, Father Arthème, 71, 75, 78, 218
Duxberry, "Duke", 196
Duxbury, F., 47
Dyer, William, 133
Eade, K.E., 97
Eager, Auville, 164
Eamer, Wally, 157-159, 172
Easton, Clifford, 75, 221, 235
Eaton, D.I.V., 71, 218, 228, 240

Ecker, Mike, 159, 173
Eckhouse, Herb, 88
Eddy, Chuck, 171
Eddy, Robert, 56
Edelstan, Jeff, 233
Ederer, Dr. B.F., 197
Edmonds, Doug, 51
Edmonds, John, 51, 57
Edwards, Bob and Helene, 153
Edwards, Jeff, 43, 244
Egersagi, Joe, 250
Eliuk, Les, 130
Elledge, Tim, 243
Ellison, Ken, 232
Ellsworth, Lincoln, 127, 229, 246
Elson, George, 33, 89, 217, 221, 235
Emmons, Bill, 76
Engel, Elmar and Brigitte, 139, 197, 223
Engle, Bob, 176
English Chief 130
Epler, Bill, 142
Erlandson, Erland, 79, 217, 218
Eschbach, Art and Walt, 87
Esko, Rolf, 106, 162
Evans, Bill, 207
Evans, Heberton, 49, 57, 68, 72-74, 76, 77
Evans, P., 94, 182
Evans, Rev. James, 89
Everette, Willis, 189
Evers, Bev, 207
Ewert, Greg, 106, 159, 172
Fafard, Father F.X., 40, 58, 60
Fahey, Tara, 166
Failey, George, 55
Faille, Albert, 141-144, 146
Fairbank, Jon, 58
Fairbank, Sylvia, 34
Fairbanks, Earl, 62
Fairchild, C.C., 101
Fairfax, Charles, 34
Fairfield, George, 62
Fallis, John, 34, 176, 220, 248
Farmer, Luc, 217, 220, 248
Farmer, Solomon, 86
Farrell, Brian, 241
Fassett, Gerry, 233, 234, 236, 238, 239
Fawcett, Thomas, 45, 117
Fenn, Abby, 67, 68, 73, 74
Fenwick, Gordon, 65, 247
Ferguson, Peter, 104

Ferguson, R.M., 109
Ferrell, Ed, 192
Ferrier, Ben, 87, 122, 129, 196
Ferrier, Marion, 87, 129
Ferris, Gail, 184
Fiddler, Jack, 116, 131, 180
Fidler, Bob, 51
Fidler, Peter, 92, 95, 115
Field, Poole, 141
Finch, George, 125
Finlayson, Nicol, 79, 213, 217
Firth, Angus, 150
Fisch, Roland, 49, 55
Fischer, Lloyd, 49
Fischesser, Mike and Nina, 148
Fish, Mike, 57
Fisher, Bruce, 149
Fisher, Paul and Andy, 134
Fisher, Sid, 63
Flaherty, Robert J., 36, 37, 79, 215-217
Flaherty, Robert H., 36, 37
Flavelle, Chuck and Lucille, 130
Fleet, Paul, 51
Fleming, Bill, 168
Fletcher, James, 86
Flett, John, 101, 107
Flynn, Patrick, 70, 218
Folster, Robert, 69
Foote, Catherine, 55
Footner, Hulbert, 121, 127, 164
Forbes, Bill, 55
Forbes, Donald, 47
Forcie, Baptiste, 162
Foreman, Matt, 111
Forget, Jacques, 241
Forgues, C.E., 245
Foster, John, 239
Foster, Nigel, 250
Fountain, Paul, 39, 45, 60, 84
Fournier, Guy, 220, 242, 248
Fowler, Robert, 153
Fowler, Scott, 106
Fox, Bill, 254
Fox, Hank, 88
Fox, Irving, 103
Fox, William, 105
Fraleck, E.L., 32, 41
Francine, Jack, 72
Francis, Gary, 207
Francis, Jeanne, 166
Franck, Peter, 48, 107, 178
Francoeur, Jean, 68
Franklin, Henry, 247

Franklin, Kirsten, 149
Franklin, Sir John, 24, 84, 116, 131, 150, 156, 169, 175
Franks, Ned, 153
Frantes, Mike, 110
Frantes, Tom, 157
Fraser, Blair, 88, 94, 157
Fraser, Doug, 139
Fraser, Harvey, 139
Fraser, Kirsten, 95
Fraser, Robin, 49, 57, 59, 73, 95, 104, 122, 171, 219, 230, 235
Fraser, Simon, 124
Fraser, Victoria, 49, 59, 73, 95, 104, 122, 171, 219, 230
Freed, Jan, 96
Freedman, Dave, 106
Freeman, Lewis R., 90
French, Inspector, 102
French, Pierre, 101
Fricke, Reinhold, 80
Friedlander, Wendy, 123
Frisch, Robert, 157, 158, 199
Frissell, Varick, 228
Fritts, Susan, 95
Frost, Norman, 176, 220
Fry, W.H., 195
Fulmer, Norm, 106
Fulton, Andy, 108
Funston, Frederick, 190
Gadbois, Pierre, 216
Gage, Charles, 204
Gagnon, Gedeon, 245
Gagnon, Joe, 47
Gagnon, Paul, 218
Galbraith, John, 31, 70
Gale, Dave, 239
Gallagher, Andy, 34
Gangbar, Ken, 233
Garant, Guy, 78, 238
Garstang, Peter, 49, 59, 235
Gaschen, Ronald, 104, 123
Gaskin, Fred, 34, 50, 105, 109, 111, 134, 159, 182
Gaspé, Pierre, 228, 242
Gaste, Father Alphonse, 107, 109
Gathorne-Hardy, G.M., 230
Gaudet, J.F., 245
Gaulin, Louise, 149
Gauthier, Marc, 248
Gautreau, Emile, 130
Gavett, Dave, 153
Gavin, Angus, 178
Geale, Kate, 248

Geale, Pat, 51, 176, 248
Gedekoh, Bob, 239, 244
Gehrz, Betty, 60
Gehrz, Bob, 94, 123
Geilen, Geilen, 95
Geist, Otto, 197
Gellerman, Kurt and Denise, 220
Georgekish, George, 73
Gerenday, Anna, 177, 252
Gertler, Ed, 220
Giacalone, Norbert, 248
Gibb, W.K., 191
Gibson, Seth, 67, 75
Gilbert, Allan, 51, 88
Gilbert, Bill, 159
Gilbert, Earl, 87
Gilbert, Geoffrey, 156, 171
Gilinsky, David and Victor, 252
Gillis, Thomas, 119, 148, 204
Girard, E., 238
Gladman, Charles, 137, 210
Gladman, George, 39
Glassco, Collette, 239
Glassco, David, 74
Glassco, Hugh, 151, 239
Glassco, Jean, 74
Glatte, Hayden, 212
Glave, E.J., 208
Glover, Jane, 55
Goddard, Ted, 159
Godfrey, Amos, 138
Godfrey, John, 153, 175, 176, 250-254
Goerger, Roland, 208
Goering, Jack, 104, 159, 171, 197
Goldenberg, Eddie, 153, 254
Goldsmith, Thompson, 49
Gonthier, Donald, 248
Gonzales, Jess, 244
Good, Jed, 152
Good, Mike, 111
Good, Richard, 39
Goodwin, George, 142
Goodwin, Mark, 47
Gordon, Doug, 239
Gordon, Hugh, 122, 133
Gordon, Peter, 122, 139
Gordon, R.K., 37
Gordon-Cumming, Walter, 119
Gordon-Dean, David, 181
Gorman, Peter, 49
Goss, Dawn, 253

Gosselin, Pierre, 239
Goudie, Arch, 228, 229
Goulding, Bob, 177, 183
Goutier, Bernard, 239, 244
Gow, John, 175, 176
Goyetche, Monique, 78
Graham, Billy, 133, 138, 157
Graham, Don, 206
Granata, John, 87
Grand, Janet, 43
Grant, Bill, 173
Grant, Richard, 144
Grater, Wendy, 149, 254
Gravelle, John, 51
Gray, Alison, 163
Gray, George, 36
Gray, Ralph, 229
Gray, Terry, 250
Green, Jack, 37
Green, James, 180
Green, James (Chicago), 52
Green, Lonsdale and Joseph, 52
Green, Tom, 123, 192, 198
Greenacre, Jim, 151, 234
Greenhill, Bob and Gayle, 182
Greenland, George, 132
Greenshields, Gordon, 60
Greensky, George, 162
Gregg, James, 151
Gregg, Kit, 181
Gregoire, Lawrence, 147
Grey, Governor-General, Earl, 85
Grieve, Charlie, 56
Griffin, Scott, 171
Griffith, Joe, 248
Griffiths, Peter, 106
Grimm, Sylvana, 17
Grinnell, George, 103, 107
Grollier, Henri, 116
Grondin, Jacques, 65, 220
Groom, Nick, 73
Grosbois, Jean de, 202, 241, 247
Groseilliers, Medard Chouart Des, 45, 89
Grosslein, Roger, 37
Grout, Dave, 171
Groves, Ronald, 51
Grunblatt, Jess, 232
Guelle, Achil, 39, 60, 84
Guertin, Geneviève, 78
Guest, Terry, 173
Guinard, Father J-E, 40, 57, 58, 65
Gullion, Laurie, 178, 180

Gulliver, Sid, 49
Gunderson, H.L., 181
Gunn, Walter, 104
Gunnar, Charlot, 74
Gunter, Mary, 32
Gussow, W.C., 97
Gustafson, Karen, 123
Gustafson, Linda, 60
Gutermuth, Holden, 47
Guzelimian, Vaha, 34, 51, 53, 57, 62
Haakensen, Ron, 105
Haas, Bob, 55
Haas, Claire, 59
Haberman, Doug, 173
Haberman, Ted, 105
Hackett, George, 60
Hagan, Kevin, 67
Hager, Patty, 111
Hagg, Richard, 149
Hahn, Sue, 56
Hale, Joanne, 244
Haley, Alan, 243
Hall, Alex, 105, 106, 109, 162, 163, 173, 176, 184
Hall, Brad, 37
Hall, Edward, 47
Hall, Ken, 172
Hallenbeck, Lisa, 152
Hallenbeck, Tom, 77, 152, 153, 217, 224, 232, 233
Haller, Karl, 80
Hallowell, Chris, 49
Hambelton, Dale, 139
Hamilton, A.C., Ian, Malcolm and Peter, 105, 159, 173
Hamilton, Jack, 55
Hamilton, Stewart, 239
Hanbury, David, 17, 24, 101, 102, 156, 161, 170
Hand, Harold, 33
Hanes, J.L., 52
Haney, Mary Ann, 147
Hanly, Jack, 75
Hanna, John, 73
Hansell, Roger, 108
Hansen, Charlie, 128
Hansen, John, 49
Hanshaw, Bill, 33, 36
Hanson, G., 63
Hanson, G.F., 238
Hanson, Harold, 53, 55, 178
Harbottle, Jeff, 139
Harcourt, Earl, 133, 138, 157
Hardy, Joe, 247
Harings, Sue, 175

Harmuth, Henning, 105, 133, 161, 173, 197
Harmuth-Hoene, Anne, 133, 197
Harp, Doug, 98
Harp, Prof. Elmer, 107
Harper, Arthur, 125, 136, 190, 193, 200, 202
Harper, Francis, 97, 109, 121, 123, 162
Harrington, Lynn, 33
Harrington, Richard, 33, 165, 197
Harris, Bucky, 50
Harris, Chris, 149
Harris, Dave, 51
Harrison, Dave, 140, 151, 182, 204
Harrison, Hank, 199
Harrison, Judy, 151, 182, 204
Harrison, R.G., 66
Hart, Dr. Al, 51, 52
Hart, Frederick, 125, 136, 193
Harting, Ria, 34
Harting, Toni, 34, 38
Hartley, Michael, 160
Hartog, Robbert, 147
Hartry, Dr., 46
Hartwick, Karl, 241
Harvey, Dennis, 252
Harvey, Matthew, 250
Hatchard, John, 151
Hatton, Bob, 222, 247
Hatton, John, 223
Hauser, Mike, 105
Haworth, Paul Leland, 127
Hayden, John, 50
Hayes, Alden, 133, 138, 197
Hayes, Charles Willard, 190
Hayes, Dick, 133
Hayes, John, 88
Hayhurst, Katie, 109
Hayne, Cameron, 111, 223
Hearne, Samuel, 83, 92, 95, 96, 101, 107, 168
Heath, Rudy, 53
Hebbel, Bob, 88
Hebert, Marc, 175, 177
Heermance, Rad, 37
Heiling, Gary, 111
Heiner, Cheryl, 178
Heinley, Tim, 171
Helleiner, Fred, 37, 42
Hellier, James, 228
Helmericks, Constance, Jean and Ann, 129, 134

Helvie, Tom, 37
Heming, Arthur, 41, 85
Heming, Kate, 41
Henday, Anthony, 83
Henderson, Rex, 133
Henderson, Robert, 25
Henderson, Robert (Yukon), 200, 203
Hendry, Dr. William, 213, 217
Henock, W.E.S., 150
Henry, Bombardier William, 84, 125
Henry, Jim and Kay, 205
Hepburn, Duncan, 106
Hepburn, John, 84, 116, 169, 175
Herendeen, R., 108
Herfindahl, Orris and Henry, 103
Herger, H.M., 55
Heron, F., 152, 194
Heron, Richard, 75
Herriot, Al, 95
Heschal, Charles, 112
Hess, Michael, 189, 201
Hessel, A., 48
Heywood, Dr., 181
Hicks, H.S., 171
Higgins, Ray, 88
Higginson, John, 134
Hill, Bob, 38
Hill, Fred, 192
Hill, G.W., 31
Hill, Ron, 161, 181
Hillner, John, 50, 51, 88
Hinan, Tom, 173
Hind, Henry Youle, 245
Hind, William, 245
Hirsch, Ron, 223
Hirschey, Walt, 123
Hiscott, Tom, 247
Ho, Natalie, 173
Hoar, Thomas, 47
Hoare, W.H.B., 102, 103, 156, 171
Hobbie, Sara, 166
Hocking, Drake and Anna, 145
Hockmeyer, Wayne, 243
Hodge, Jerry, 65
Hodgins, Andrea, 150, 221
Hodgins, Bruce, 37, 55, 68, 74, 173, 198
Hodgins, Carol, 55, 68, 74, 173, 198
Hodgins, Eric, 233, 239

Hodgins, Geoff, 250
Hodgins, Glenn, 78
Hodgins, Larry, 212
Hodgins, Margo, 233
Hodgins, Shawn, 78, 150, 153, 159, 233, 244
Hodgson, Charles, 176
Hodnett, Mark, 244
Hoel, Jim, 182
Hogg, Arthur, 86
Holbek, Lars, 211, 212
Hollies, Bob, 55, 95
Holme, Randle, 228
Holmes, Charlotte, 49, 122
Holthaus, Mark, 220
Homan, Charles A., 189
Homolski, Dave, 59, 76
Homonick, Henry, 146
Homuth, Paul, 173
Honold, Dr. Guy, 173
Hood, Robert, 84, 116, 169, 175
Hoover, Mike, 207
Hope, Rank, 229
Hopewell, Arthur, Keith and Jeffrey, 55
Hopkins, Frances, 23
Hord, Fred, 87
Horden, Bishop John, 39, 45, 79, 85
Horgan, W., 220
Hornby, John, 102, 121, 128, 156, 161, 170
Horne, Christopher, 59, 76, 171, 219
Horr, A.R., 33, 41
Horricks, John, 106, 159, 172
Hosbein, Peter, 51, 88
Hossack, J., 94
Hovey, A., 77, 94, 140, 157, 162, 163, 172, 182, 223
Howard, Bob, 34
Howard, Ernie, 110
Howard, Ross, 254
Howard, W.H., 37
Howe, Doug, 73, 106
Howe, Dr. George, 232
Hoyt, Austin, 37, 42, 67, 143, 181
Hoyt, Bill, 141, 153, 168
Hubachek, Bill, 49, 88, 104
Hubachek, F.B., Jr., 49, 88, 104
Hubbard, Leonidas, 20, 235
Hubbard, Mina, 20, 221, 235
Hudon, Fernand, 239, 241, 242, 244

Hudson, Jerry, 182
Hughes, Bill, 171
Hughes, Faith, 233
Hughes, Wren, 34
Hull, Dean, 151
Hume, Dr. G.S., 121, 127, 138, 148
Hummel, Gary, 49
Hummel, Ron, 65
Hummert, Lloyd, 151
Hunt, Lee, 33
Hunt, Ron, 50
Hunt, Stephanie, 239
Hunt, Stu, 146
Hunter, Fenley, 128, 138, 141, 196
Hunter, Jack, 42
Hunter, Joseph, 209
Hunter, Rev. James, 116
Hunter, Stuart, 37
Hussey, Frank, 88
Hustich, Ilmari, 80
Hutchins, Debbie, 57
Hutchins, Julie, 57, 59, 76
Hutchins, Lea, 59, 76
Hutchinson, Jay, 48
Hutten, Barry, 151
Hyland, Robert, 136, 209
Ickes, Peter, 49, 104
Idler, Richard, 104
Ingstad, Helge, 162
Innes-Taylor, Alan, 192
Innis, Harold, 23, 191
Inwood, Kris, 111
Irvine, Seana, 221
Irving, Keith, 250
Irwin, Bill and Keefer, 153, 202, 205
Irwin, Colin, 254
Irwin, Dick, 49, 73, 76, 108, 123, 144, 162, 171, 212, 219, 230, 234, 235, 241, 248
Isbister, Alexander K., 150
Isbister, John, 69, 75
Isbister, Thomas, 75
Iserhoff, Joseph, 221, 235
Jackman, Eddy, 122
Jackman, George, 65, 69
Jackson, Mike, 88
Jacobs, Dr., 46
Jacobsen, Bob, 95-97, 98
Jacobsen, Suzy, 96
Jacobson, Cliff, 37, 123, 175
Jacques, Louis, 38
James, Rob, 51
James, William, 24

Jannotta, Ned, 48
Janvier, William, 117
Jarden, Dave, 58, 76, 143
Jarosz, John, 181
Jarvis, Edward, 29
Jarvis, Nicola, 151
Jarvis, Peter, 173
Jean, Ronald, 241, 247
Jeffery, Bill, 123
Jeffries, Abraham, 42
Jenkins, E., 157, 198, 211
Jenkins, J., 198
Jenkins, W., 157, 198
Jennings, Bill, 95
Jennings, Dr. Harry, 143
Jennings, John, 139, 145, 151
Jim, Kiberd, 49
Jmaeff, Andrew, 95
Jocko, Ken, 63
Joel, Snyder, 220
Johnson, Albert, 150, 196
Johnson, Allan, 88, 134
Johnson, Bill, 65, 110, 247
Johnson, D., 136, 202, 209
Johnson, Darrell, 49
Johnson, Dick, 247
Johnson, Frank, 105
Johnson, J.F.E., 201
Johnson, J.T.H., M.D.D., 42
Johnson, Noble, 49
Johnson, Steve, 110
Johnson, Ted, 153, 175, 176, 250-254
Johnston, Lukin, 128
Jolliet, Louis, 69
Jolliffe, F., 157, 158
Joln, Daniel, 219
Jonckheere, Lauren, 97
Jones, Arch, 103, 171
Jones, C.J."Buffalo", 119, 194
Jones, David, 157
Jones, David and Carol, 172
Jones, Michael, 208
Josendal, V., 94, 134, 140, 157, 162, 163, 182, 220
Joseph, Chip, 247
Joyce, M.A., 102
Jubert, Claudie, 144
Judd, Pierre and Jean, 65
Juurand, Priidu, 24, 117, 123, 198, 206
Kaecli, Jack, 52
Kahn, Steve, 168
Kailey, Paul, 63
Kallerman, Kal, 247
Kane, Keelin, 123

Kansellar, Andrew, 125
Karet, Joe, 48
Keck, Dieter, 176
Keele, Joseph, 149, 191, 200, 201, 203, 204, 206
Keller, Paul, 182
Kellogg, William, III, 87
Kelly, W.A., 148
Kelsall, John P., 48, 103
Kelsey, Henry, 81
Kelsey, Kerck, 222
Kelton, Jon, 53
Kemp, Bill, 171
Kenaston, Prof. Arthur, 228
Kendall, Nicholas, 116, 131, 169
Kennedy, Dr. Bill, 51, 52
Kennicott, Robert, 116, 131, 136, 193
Kenoyer, Chris, 218
Keough, Pat and Rosemarie, 148
Kernan, Dr. J.D., 228, 240
Kerr, F.A., 211
Kestle, Mike, 173
Ketcham, J., 140, 157, 198, 211
Ketcham, S., 140, 157, 198, 211
Ketcham, W., 140
Ketchum, Frank, 188
Ketemer, Michael, 60, 78, 221
Kiberd, George and Jim, 73
Kidd, D.F., 97, 98, 157, 158
Kiefner, Mark, 244
Kiefner, Paul, 244
Kiese, Robert, 55
Kilburn, Sam, 89
Kilgore, Jim, 49
Kilgour, Jim, 34
Killin, A.F., 158
Killock, James, 70, 75
Kindersley, Hugh, 121
Kindle, E.M., 33, 42, 121
King, Bill, 184
King, Frank, 111
King, Joe, 54
King, Richard, 180
King, Warren, 73, 74
King, William, 116
Kington, Dave, 143
Kinmond, Stuart, 219
Kinmond, Trevor, 144
Kipling, John, 101
Kirby, Dick and Mary, 146
Kirk, E.A., 103
Kirkby, Rev. William, 131, 193
Kirkland, Bud, 87

Kirkland, Wallace, 87, 90
Kitowski, Barbara, 231
Kittredge, Chess, 36, 37
Kjell, Windelhed, 106
Klein, Clayton, 33, 97, 106, 110, 166
Klein, Darrell, 97, 106, 110, 166
Klein, Deborah, 166
Kling, Steve, 49, 88
Kmoch, G., 221
Knopke, Bud and Tat, 129
Knopke, Katie, 123
Knox, Alan, 48
Knox, Jack 102, 103
Koch, Kim, 95
Koch, Nina, 166
Koci, Bruce, 94, 171, 250
Koe, Jimmy, 196
Koe, Paul, 196
Koehler, Herman, 221, 232, 234, 238
Kohlmeister, B., 221
Kolstad, Rick, 205
Konantz, Donald, 176
Koppel, Arvo, 192
Kotcheff, Tim, 147, 153, 175, 176, 250-254
Krank, Ernst, 80
Krause, Karen, 59
Kreitzman, Syd, 212
Kretschmar, Ulrich and Diane, 106
Kruger, Verlen, 117, 198
Kubiski, Gerry, 206
Kucyniak, James, 80
Kummer, Biff, 175
Kunin, David, 220
Kunkle, John, Jr.,, 53
Kusugak, Mike, 98
Labarge, Michael, 188
Lacroix, Michel, 239
Ladouceur, Debbie, 147
Ladue, Joseph, 189, 200
Lafleur, Vital, 209
Lafond, J.L., 148
Lafontaine, Yves, 68
LaFrance, Joseph, 89
Lagarde, Johanne, 78
Laing, Catherine, 176
Laing, Hamilton, 121
Laird, Hon. David, 119
Laliberté, M.F., 66
Laliberté, Marc, 218
Lambert, Fred, 142
Lamont, Graham, 50

LaNauze, Inspector Denny, 156
Landry, Joseph, 124, 130
Landry, Michel, 74
Langlois, Dr. Yves, 154
Langtry, George, 189, 206
Lanouette, Joe, 107
Laplante, Cecile, 239
Lapointe, Brother Gregoire, 40
Lapointe, Jean Marc, 34
Large, Jerry, 49
Larkin, Chris, 149
LaRoche, Mark, 247
Larocque, Daniel, 241, 247
Larose, Gilles, 78
Larsen, James, 109, 161
Larson, Dr. Lou, 181
Laska, Greg, 56
Lathrop, Tom, 73
Laurendeau, Claude, 68
Laurier, Jon de, 34
Lauzon, Jean, 238
Laver, Rob, 51
Lavigne, Jean, 78
Lavoie, Joe, 127
Lavoie, Martine, 248
Law, Bill, 34
Lawrence, Bill, 59
Lawrence, Ray, 63
Lawrie, Andrew, 97
Lawson, Kelly, 78
Lawson, Ron, 106
Lawson, Tom, 110
Laycock, A., 103
Leach, P.J., 209
Leblanc, Marcel, 248
Lebreque, Gilles, 175
LeClaire, George, 41
Leden, Christian, 90
Lederle, Joe, 175
Leeson, Dix, 143
LeFavour, Bruce, 107
Lefebvre, Pierrette, 78
LeFevere, Charlie, 175
Lefroy, Lieut. John Henry, 84, 116, 125
Lehnhausen, Bud, 51
Leitch, John S., 126
Leith, Charles and Arthur, 41
Leitze, Marty, 173
Lemieux, Louis, 48
Lennie, Ernie, 204
Lentz, John, 73, 106, 108, 109, 143, 171, 175, 177, 181-183, 219, 252

Lepage, Father Ernest, 71, 75, 78, 213, 218
LeRoux, Father G., 170
Leslie, L.A.D., 229, 236
Lesser, Rob, 208, 211, 212
Lesvesque, Rollie, 55
Levinson, Ed, 161
Lewis, L., 136, 202, 209
Lewis, Palmer, 130
Lewis, Paul, 95
Lewtas, Pat, 231, 242
Libersac, Jean Luc, 78
Lincoln, Bruce, 151, 153
Lincoln, Craig, 151
Linders, Mary, 166
Lindgren, Arne, 106
Lindquist, E.E., 72
Linen, Mark, 208
Linklater, Peter, 109
Lissick, Steve, 134
Little, Dr. Ed, 129
Loban, George and Jeff, 123
Lochead, Jim, 159
Loe, Ole, 142
Loeks, Dave, 153, 165
Lofthouse, Rev. Joseph, 32, 84, 85, 89, 97, 101
Lohaza, Walter, 162, 233
Lohmann, Carl, 219
Long, John, 65
Loosemore, Fred, 75, 220
Lord, C.S., 158
Loring, Alden, 121
Loring, Eric, 232
Loring, Stephen, 77, 223, 224, 232, 233
Lorrain, Bishop, 40
Lortie, Gilles, 65, 220, 242
Louwman, Tony, 112
Lovink, Tony, 87, 88, 94
Low, A.P., 31, 60, 70, 75, 78, 213, 217, 218, 228, 240, 242
Lower, A.R.M., 41, 54
Lucas, Ron, 42
Luckmann, Charles, 77, 224
Luehrs, Renee, 166
Lundberg, Dave, 129
Lunsford, Steve, 168
Luste, George, 34, 42, 76, 108, 111, 144, 162, 173, 212, 223, 230, 233
Luste, Linda, 34, 230
Luste, Tait, 162
Luxford, Dr. Paul and Nancy,, 130

Lveleth, Edward, 65
Lyle, Bev, 163
Lytle, Tim, 55
McAllister, Betty and Russell and family, 56
McArthur, J.J., 201
MacAusland, Steve, 76, 77
McBeath, Adam, 148
McCall, Sam, 205
McCallum, Peter, 156
McCarney, Liz, 233
McCart, Mike, 80, 98
McCloud, Tom, 220
McClung, David, 117, 123, 139, 198, 206, 211
McColl, Brian, 223
McColl, Keith, 171
McConachie, John, 32
McConkey, Charles, 189
McConkey, Jim, 139
McConnell, Jack, 144
McConnell, R.G., 119, 125, 126, 136, 137, 164, 193, 200, 201, 203, 204, 206, 209
McCrory, B., 90, 94, 163
McCrory, Keith, 134
McCue, Alfred, 53
MacDonald, Alexander, 151, 201
MacDonald, C.S., 93, 121
MacDonald, Craig, 42, 50, 51
McDonald, Dave, 65
MacDonald, Ken J., 42
McDonald, Loran, 105
McDonald, Lorraine, 176
MacDonald, Mike, 77
McDonald, Rev. Robert, 116, 132, 188, 193
MacDonald, Thompson, 86
MacDonald, W., 121
McDonald, W.N., 148
McDonnell, Roger, 204
McDougall, Bob, 212
McDuffie, Tom, 76
McEvoy, J., 136, 190, 202, 209
McEwen, Tom, 239
Macfarlane, John, 153, 176, 250, 254
Macfarlane, Roderick, 155, 166
Macfie, Harry, 89
McFie, J.M., 61
McGinnes, Mike, 202
McGrath, Michele, 163
McGuire, Sally, 107
McGuire, Tom, 107, 130, 192
McGuire, Tom (Minnesota), 123, 198

McInnes, William, 46, 56, 58, 60, 89, 92
MacIntosh, Alex, 239
MacIntyre, Leslie, 248
McIntyre, Malcolm, 117, 123, 198, 206
McIntyre, S., 182
Mackay, Alexander, 124
McKay, Donald, 35
Mackay, Dr. J.R., 166
McKay, Duncan, 120
McKay, James, 180
Mackay, Murdo, 180
Mackaye, Daniel, 31
Mackenzie, Alexander, 115, 124, 130
Mackenzie, Ann, 153
McKenzie, Charles, 180
Mackenzie, Hector, 153, 208
Mackenzie, James, 39
Mackenzie, Sir William, 36
MacKerracher, Rob, 248
MacKichan, Barry, 88, 90, 97, 108, 110
Mackinlay, James, 120, 156, 180
MacLaren, Ian, 104
McLaren, Keith, 108
McLaughlin, Lys, 59
McLean, Dr. Don, 51, 52
MacLean, Harry, 48
McLean, John, 227
MacLean, John and Gordon, 87
McLean, W.J., 46
McLeod, A.R., 140
McLeod, Charlie, 141, 142
McLeod, Frank and Willie, 141
McLeod, J., 209
McLeod, John, 136, 137, 140
McLeod, Neil, 95
MacMartin, D.G., 46
McMillan, D.G., 232
MacMillan, J.G., 36
MacMillan, John, 45
McMillan, Stan, 162
McMurray, Dr. H.A., 53
McNabb, Grant, 172
McNally, John, 49
McNamara, James, 26
McNeill, W., 209
McOuat, Walter, 39, 70
Macpherson, Andrew, 80, 103, 109, 179, 184, 252
McPherson, Bruce, 218
Macpherson, Elizabeth, 103
McPherson, Murdoch, 136

McQuesten, Jack, 136, 193, 201
McRae, Dave, 121, 195
MacRae, J.A., 120, 126
McVicar, Laurie, 59
Mably, Richard, 223
Macoun, James, 60, 70, 117
Macoun, John, 125
Madill, Glenn, 96
Madsen, Ken, 212
Magavern, Jim, 168
Magee, Billy, 96
Magee, Sid, 223
Maguire, Bob, 219
Maher, John, 229
Mair, Charles, 119
Malamud, Elliot, 243
Malcolm, Lyle, 34, 50, 105, 134, 182
Malkmus, Bill, 109
Mallet, Thierry, 42, 54, 71, 79, 85, 89, 92, 93, 109
Malley, William, 180
Mallory, Wib, 55
Malone, Judge William, 228
Maloney, Joe, 133
Malouf, S.E., 158
Maltby, Charles, 117, 152, 201
Mandeville, Moise, 119, 180
Manheke, Wolfgang, 143
Mannall, John, 35
Manning, Thomas, 80, 179, 252
Manson, Donald, 124
Manson, Olie, 250
Marcil, Rock, 78
Marek, George, 56
Marion, Jean, 144
Marks, C., 189
Marks, Sylvester, 238
Maron, John, 49
Marr, Chris, 207
Marsh, George, 41, 47
Marshall, Alfred, 219, 245
Martin, Dr. Bob, 51, 52
Martin, J.E.H., 72
Martin, Joe, 208
Martin, John, 111
Martin, John C., 143
Martin, Richard, 171
Martineau, James, 134
Maskuaro, Xavier, 227, 240
Masnok, Ray, 202
Mason, Bill, 26, 149, 175
Mason, Dorothy, 55
Mason, John Alden, 121

Mason, Leonard and Hilda, 87
Mason, Michael, 121, 195
Mason, Paul, 149
Mason, Skookum Jim, 190, 200, 206
Massell, Dave, 178, 180
Masson, Jean, 238
Mathers, Bill, 110, 171
Mathers, Tom, 171
Matonabbee 168,
Matoush, Allan, 73
Matteson, Bob, 90, 104, 171, 197
Matteson, Rick, 104
Matteson, Rob, 90, 104, 197
Matteson, Sumner, 90, 171, 197
Matthews, Biff, 145
Matthews, Gordon, 141
Matthews, Jack, 159
Matthews, Jim, 34, 163, 173
Maufelly 161, 180,
Maurice, François, 101, 107
Mavis, Ross, 206
Mawdsley, J.B., 71, 148
Mawhinney, Thomas, 183
May, Bob, 222
May, John, 94, 123
May, Merrill, 87
Maybee, Art, 117
Mayo, Alfred, 193
Mayuer, Francis, 149, 153
Mead, Jim, 134
Mead, Robert, 123, 130, 134
Meadham, Chris, 55
Meier, Judy, 163
Meier, William, 103
Meindle, Dr. A.G., 46
Melancon, Kurt, 123, 177, 179
Melvill, Cosmo, 41, 156
Memmer, Pete, 179
Ménard, Gabriel, 65
Mendenhall, Vivian, 207
Merasty, Solomon, 93
Merrick, Elliott and Kay Austin, 229
Mervyn, Norman, 202
Mestokosho, Mathieu, 240, 242
Metcalf, Frank, 134
Meyer, Duc, 134
Meyer, Gene, 48
Meyer, Howard, 223
Michaelis, Paul, 37
Michaux, André, 69, 72

Michéa, Jean, 216
Michelin, John, 228, 229, 232
Michelin, Leslie, 229
Michelin, Robert, 228, 229, 234, 236
Miles, E.S., 90
Miller, Bill, 49, 234
Miller, Bob, 104, 173
Miller, Donald, 48
Miller, Herb, 50
Miller, John, 173
Miller, Russ, 224
Miller, Russell, 34
Milliken, Peter, 153
Mills, Edwin, 47, 48, 53, 55
Mills, Jack, 63
Milne, Brian, 253
Milne, J.M., 32
Milne, James, 41
Mink, Jimmy, 42
Miron, Louis, 36
Mitchell, George, 119, 132, 151, 201
Mitchell, Peter, 178, 180
Mitchell, Thomas, 79
Mixter, C.M., 66
Moffatt, Arthur, 47, 48, 103, 107
Moffatt, Carol, 48
Moisnard, Marc, 242
Monahan, Jane, 248
Monette, Harry, 101
Money, Anton, 138
Monkman, Evan, 147
Montgomery, George, 106
Montminy, Paul, 219
Montreuil, Art, 54, 63, 66, 71
Moodie, J.D., 86, 126, 137, 202
Moodie, K.W.B., 158
Moonias-Gibb, Cameron, 56
Moore, Bill, 147
Moore, Capt. William, 189
Moore, Dave, 106
Moore, E.S., 37
Moore, John, 34
Moores, Ted, 34, 37, 42
Morgan, Russell, 49
Morice, Father A.G., 126
Morin, Bertrand, 68
Morin, Maude, 68
Morris, Elkin, 197
Morrison, Billy, 86
Morse, Eric, 15, 22, 87, 90, 94, 95, 103, 106, 108, 110, 117, 122, 157, 158, 161, 163, 171, 197

Morse, George, 73
Morse, Pamela, 15, 95, 103, 106, 110, 158, 161, 163, 171, 197
Morse, Ted, 67
Morton, Keith, 146, 208
Mosberg, Earl and Shirley, 161
Moses, Enoch, 195
Mowat, Farley, 97
Muetze, Chris, 108
Muir, David Ross, 61
Muir, John, 209
Mulholland, Joe, 142
Muller, H., 112, 134, 140, 157, 162, 163, 172
Mundinger, Eric, 147
Munn, Henry Toke, 17, 41, 119, 191
Munsterhjelm, Erik, 117
Murdoch, Peter, 86
Murie, Olaus, 41, 71, 79, 219, 245
Murphy, Marie-Jeanne, 248
Murray, Alexander Hunter, 188
Murray, Alfred P., 45
Myers, Roy, 229
Nadler, Charles, 87
Nakotci, Georges, 58
Nash, Percy, 152, 194
Nauer, Fred, 97
Naughton, Mike, 88
Nault, Laura, 178
Neal, Tom, 243
Nedelec, Father, 39
Neegan, Dave, 55
Neeposh, Matthew, Jr., 68, 73-75, 77
Neeposh, Murray, 73
Neill, Charles, 49
Neilson, John, 238
Nelson, Buddy, 49
Nelson, Hjalmar, 103
Nettell, A.J.C., 162
Neufeld, N., 87
Neunherz, Richard, 50
Nevin, Guy, 146
Newcom, Rich, 97
Newcomb, Adrian G., 33
Newnham, Bishop John, 31, 35, 40, 46, 57, 60, 71, 85
Newnham, Mrs., 31
Newnham, Sophy, 32
Ney, C.H. "Marsh", 90
Niblett, Ron, 34, 146
Nicholls, Bill, 103
Nichols, Larry, 208

Nichols, Sally, 208
Nickerson, Richard and Elinor, 134
Niemann, Kitty, 60
Niemann, Mark, 220
Nigorri, Tous-les-Jours, 117
Nilsson, Thomy and Virginia, 134
Niven, Alex, 32, 36, 41
Nixon, Jack, 55
Nixon, John, 55
Noble, Emily and Peggy, 55
Noble, Winton, 122
Nolan, Joe, 162
Noldan, Henry, 48
Noller, Dr. Jerry, 175
Norrie, Fraser, 176
North, Robert, 47
Norton, Moses, 101
Norton, R., 219
Norwood, Peter, 223
Novotny, Jim, 171
Nowak, Walt, 243
O'Connor, Frank T., 42
O'Hara, Bob, 88, 112, 171, 182, 219
O'Neill, J.J., 156, 165, 168, 170
O'Sullivan, H., 65, 79
O'Sullivan, Owen, 32, 46, 54, 65, 79, 85
Oberholtzer, Ernest, 96, 97
Odjick, Bill, 171
Odjick, Joseph and Moses, 245
Ogden, Peter Skene, 209
Ogilvie, Will, 127, 133
Ogilvie, William, 126, 132, 137, 189, 190, 193, 199, 209
Oliver, Craig, 147, 153, 175, 176, 250-254
Oliver, Sherman, 98
Olmsted, John, 87
Olsen, Judy, 60
Olson, Sigurd, 15, 88, 94, 122, 157
Ombrechune, Genevieve, 112
Onraet, Tony, 128
Opack, Mat, 123, 192, 198
Ord, Peter, 153, 243
Orr, Bill, 104
Ortell, George, 201
Osborne, Doug, 133
Osgood, Larry, 90, 111, 166, 168, 172, 252
Osgood, Wilfrid, 204
Ostergren, David, 157
Ostopkowicz, Mark, 198, 205

Ottey, Russ, 244
Ouellet, Louis, 248
Owen, E.B., 143
Page, David, 220
Painter, Abraham, 86
Pak, Yu Jin, 223
Pammett, Bob, 111
Papah, Eddie and Steven, 47
Papanekis, Martin, 84
Paradis, Father Charles, 39
Parent, Ben, 66
Parker, Col. Gilbert, 129
Parkin, Tom, 212
Parkinson, Constable, 46
Parrot, E.G., 239
Parry, Ann, 151
Parry, Bill, 205
Parsons, J.L. Rowlett, 36
Partridge, Roger, 220
Patnode, Maude, 166
Patterson, Marigold, 129
Patterson, Raymond, 129, 138, 141, 143, 211
Paul, Steve, 200
Paulin, Mark, 106
Paulson, Joe, 90
Payette, Robert, 78
Peabody, Jay, 49
Peach, Dave, 232, 247
Peach, Don, 222
Peake, Geoffrey, 184, 215
Peake, Michael, 184, 215
Peake, Sean, 184
Pearce, Bill, 34, 173
Peck, Daryl, 34, 51, 53, 57, 62
Peck, Rev. E.J., 213, 217
Peck, Steve, 34
Peebles, Dave, 173
Peet, Fred, 122, 156, 158
Pell, Terry, 247
Pelletier, E.A., 102, 161
Pelly, A.M., 137
Pelly, Brian, 183
Pelly, David, 112, 183
Pennara, Sebastien, 69
Pentlarge, Frank R., 71
Perkins, Robert, 76, 182, 224
Perret, N.G., 103
Perrin, Dick, 88
Perrin, John, 94
Perrin, Roy, 206
Perry, Tom, 233, 234, 236, 238, 239
Perry, Tracey, 37, 181, 219
Peshabo, William, 33
Pessl, Skip, 48, 107

Peters, Deb, 205
Peterson, Alfred, 94, 96
Peterson, Gunnar, 48
Peterson, Ralph, 94, 123
Petitot, Father Emil, 136, 166, 168, 169
Petrant, Presque, 33
Peyton, Bernie, 182
Philips, Miriam, 77
Phillips, Michelle, 250
Phillips, P., 182
Pick, Karen, 166
Pierce, Stephen, 56
Pike, Warburton, 118, 137, 161, 180, 190, 202, 210
Pinard, Raymond, 68
Pirrit, J., 252
Pisarki, John, 42
Pisco, Bill, 117, 123, 148, 149, 155, 165, 198, 206
Pitts, Bobby, 220
Planinshek, Charles, 93
Platt, Andrea, 43
Poggenpohl, Eric, 168
Pohl, Herb, 34, 231, 232, 234, 248
Poirel, Jean, 134, 143, 144, 146
Polden, Russell, 181
Pollen, Hungerford, 119
Pollit, Dorothy, 153
Pombrey, Ron, 250
Pond, Peter, 115
Pontham, Dave, 129
Ponton, Normand, 220
Pool, Beekman, 229, 246
Poole, Dorothy, 252
Pope, Geoffrey, 117, 133
Poplin, Richard, 189, 201
Porsild, A.E., 109, 133
Port, Walter, 86, 90
Porter, Nat, 246
Porter, Robert, 230
Porter, Russell W., 238
Porter, Ruth, 246
Porter, Skip, 74
Potter, Peter, 68, 73, 74
Potvin, Claude, 219
Powell, Howie and Dale, 68
Powell, Roland, 229
Power, Geoffrey, 218-220
Preble, Alfred E., 17, 36, 85, 120
Preble, Edward A., 17, 85, 120, 133, 156, 181
Prentice, Alison, 146
Prentice, Jim, 144, 146

Price, David, 238
Prichard, Hesketh, 221, 230
Pritchett, Carolyn, 98, 107, 111, 175, 177-179, 184
Pritchett, Jay, 88, 97, 98, 105, 107, 108, 111, 173, 175, 177-179, 182, 184
Proctor, Tom, 220
Proudfoot, H.B., 46, 52
Proulx, Father, 39
Proulx, Jean-François, 239
Prouse, Joe, 123
Prozeller, Brad, 232, 247
Pruden, Don, 223
Puddicombe, Peter, 38
Pullen, Commander William, 84, 131
Purchase, Jack, 105, 109, 111, 159, 182
Purchase, Susie, 109, 111
Purdon, Nick, 244
Putnam, Bob, 111
Putnam, Jim, 95
Quackenbush, Lewis, 231
Quatlot, John, 194
Queneau, Paul, 178
Quittenton, R.C., 123
Rabinovitch, Paul, 62
Racicot, J.B., 221
Radford, Harry, 102
Radisson, Pierre-Esprit, 45, 89
Rae, Dr. John, 101, 112, 116, 131, 169
Rae, T.C., 46
Raffan, James, 25, 176, 215
Rafferty, Ken, 49
Rafinske, Frank, 50
Ragge, E.C., 32, 40
Rainey, Dr. Froelich, 128
Ramsden, J.G., 46
Randall, Dale, 56
Randall, Peter, 42
Raphael, Conscrit, 67
Rasmussen, Russell, 207
Rastoin, Alain, 242
Rawert, Clem, 207
Raymond, Saundra, 153
Raymont, Peter, 168
Rea, John, 194
Read, Steve, 199
Rebec, Dr. George, 196
Redhead, Bennett, 88, 90
Rees, David and Gail, 106
Rees, Robert, 97
Rehze, Dr. Ervin, 55
Reid, Ron, 43

Réjean, Michaud, 241
Remington, Franklin, 85
Rémy, Daniel, 78
Renard, Maurice, 49, 88, 97
Rene, Jacques, 218
Renison, Bishop Robert, 36, 41, 46, 47, 54, 80, 128
Renison, Elizabeth, 80, 128
Renison, George, 46
Renison, William, 46
Repp, David, 159, 172
Retty, J.A., 240
Revington, George, 73, 74, 76
Reynolds, Miss A., 42
Rhanar, Janice, 250
Rich, William, 49
Richards, George, 235
Richards, Horace G., 42
Richards, Paul and Marilyn, 34
Richardson, Dr. John, 84, 116, 131, 169, 175
Richardson, James, 70
Richardson, Sandy, 57, 111, 146, 173, 206, 212, 233, 247
Rick, Wilson, 88
Riddell, Graeme, 151
Riddell, Mark, 134, 151, 233, 242, 244
Riddell, Robert, 149, 203
Ridgway, Matthew, 57
Rigby, Bruce and Terry, 250
Rines, George, 220
Ritchie, Ian, 34, 146
Ritchie, William, 77, 224
Rivers-Moore, Simon, 233, 244
Roberts, Greer, 59
Roberts, Hon. Kelso, 59
Roberts, Keith, 110
Roberts, Paul, 182
Roberts, Russell, 59
Robertson, C.I., 158
Robertson, H.H., 237
Robertson, James, 69
Robertson, Johnnie, 86
Robertson, Judge, 128
Robinson, A.H., 52
Robinson, Clark, 66
Robinson, Dave, 146
Robinson, J.S., 87
Robinson, Jack, 86
Robinson, Marvin, 51
Roby, Dan, 74, 77
Rochat, Roger, 143
Rockingham, Maj-Gen J.M., 117, 219

Rockmar, Mikhail, 51
Rockwell, C.H., 31
Roder, John, 147-149, 155, 165
Roder, Mary Lou, 147
Rodger, Elliot, 88, 94, 117, 122, 157
Roechler, Len, 55
Rogers, Clara Coltman, 196
Rogers, Edward S., 59, 72, 73
Rogers, Murray, 72
Rogers, Philip, 228, 240
Rogers, Ralph, 228, 240
Rollins, Chuck, 168, 220
Rom, Bill, Jr., 53
Roose, Don, 51, 88
Rose, G., 95, 140
Rosenmeier, Steve, 111
Ross, A.H.D., 70, 75
Ross, Don, 134, 139, 144, 145, 149, 153, 157, 165, 197
Ross, Hon. James, 119
Ross, Jim, 142
Ross, John, 180, 252
Ross, Malcolm, 89, 115
Ross, Maynard, 33, 36
Rossback, George, 103
Rouleau, Ernest, 72
Roush, J., 90, 112, 172, 184
Roush, N., 90
Rousseau, Jacques, 72, 215, 216, 222, 223
Rouvière, Father J., 170
Rowsell, Murray, 34
Roy, Jean, 248
Roy, Jocelyn, 65, 248
Roy, Josianne, 248
Rubin, Mark, 108
Ruge, Ed, 41
Rugge, John, 33, 213, 232, 247
Rugge, John K., Sr., 33
Rungius, Carl, 204
Runyon, Mike, 105
Russe, Larry and Randy, 34
Russell, Frank, 119, 132, 159, 169
Russell, Prof. Israel, 190, 193
Rustad, Orwin, 87
Rusterholz, Paul, 97
Sackett, S.J., 142
Saelens, Ken, 37
Sailer, Eric, 58
Saingenny, Guy, 65
Sainsbury, David, 34
Saint Simon, Sieur de, 69
Sainville, Comte Edouard de, 118, 132, 152

Sakamoto, Dave, 205
Sakanee-Gibb, Fred, 56
Salayka, David, 147
Salmon, Alphias, 54
Salmon, Noel, 56, 76
Salo, W., 163
Salsbury, Cam, 57, 146
Samson, Gilles, 223
Sandberg, August, 121, 156
Sanders, John, 49, 104
Sanders, Rev., 32, 36
Sanderson, J.O.G., 148
Sanderson, Johnny, 132, 138
Sands, Bob, 175
Santerre, Claude, 241
Saraillon, Maurice, 134
Sateka, Baptiste, 84
Saul, Patrick, 139, 145
Saunders, Ted, 37
Sauvé, Madelaine, 221
Sawyer, Dan, 104
Sawyer, Fred and Mary Jane,
    42
Sawyer, Russell, 42
Sayor, Guy, 239
Sayyea, John, 136
Scandrell, David, 55
Schaber, Wally, 149, 175
Schaefer, Bob, 105, 177, 183, 252
Schibig, Tom, 212
Schick, Jack, 208
Schick, Jody, 212
Schimek, Karl and Peter, 234
Schindler, E., 219
Schmidt, Jeremy and Jean, 52
Schmidt, Tom, 52
Schmitz, Dave, 106
Schnapp, Bruce, 248
Schneider, Gretchen, 109
Schoening, P., 112
Schran, Fred, 67
Schrankler, Dan, 94, 123
Schultz, John, 175
Schulz, Jim, 123
Schumann, Doug, 63
Schwatka, Frederick, 189, 190
Schwinghamer, Tom and
    Jack, 123
Scoggan, H.J., 87
Scott, Angus, 106, 110, 158,
    159, 163, 171
Scott, Don, 90, 111, 166, 172,
    177
Scott, Duncan Campbell, 46
Scott, Emmerson, 117
Scott, J.C., 158

Scott, J.M., 229, 234, 236
Scott, James, 198
Scott, John, 37
Scott, Maria, 90, 111, 166, 168,
    172, 252
Scott, Nancy, 112
Scott, Peter, 184, 215
Scott, Peter (British), 178
Scotter, George, 144, 145
Scroggie, Ernest, 201
Sculthorpe, Robert, 104
Seaman, Judy, 149
Secretan, J.H.E., 191
Seidl, Fred, 168
Selig, Dan, 233
Selous, F.C., 25, 203, 204
Seltzer, Geoff, 220
Selwyn, Alfred, 125
Semple, John B., 33, 42
Service, Robert, 121, 195
Seton, Ernest Thompson, 17,
    120, 161, 181
Sevareid, Eric, 86, 90
Severing, Ted, 49
Sewayanaquib, Adam and
    Solomon, 59
Sexsmith, Daryl, 123
Shaffer, Dick, 42
Shamus, Wheatung, 53
Sharnberg, David and Lester,
    219
Sharp, Ben, 148
Sharp, Bill, 55
Sharp, Bob, 204
Sharp, James, 52
Sharp, John, 222
Sharpe, J., 157
Sharpe, P., 134, 157
Sharpe, P., Jr., 134, 157
Shaw, Angus, 69
Sheeran, M., 152, 172
Shelby, Bo, 208
Sheldon, Charles, 203-205
Shepherd, Dr. Rob, 154, 161
Sheppard, Bill, 197
Sherman, Carl, 87
Shields, Nick, 76
Shoutis, Art, 247
Showacre, Jane, 161
Siegl, Z., 90
Silcox, David, 175, 176, 250
Silsbee, Doug, 238
Silvy, Père Antoine, 38, 69
Sim, V.W., 254
Simard, T., 237, 239, 242
Simmons, Dave, 173

Simmons, Gail, 176
Simmons, Norman, 144
Simons, Del, 96, 109
Simpson, Governor George,
    24, 92
Simpson, Thomas, 131, 169
Sinclair, George, 180
Sindelar, Jim, 241
Singmaster, Ken, 73
Sittichili, Lazarus, 196
Sivell, Christine, 68, 75
Skinner, Alanson, 33, 46
Skinner, Paul, 173
Skinner, Tom, 34, 146
Skirving, G.M., 191
Sklar, Joel, 76
Skurszkan, Jane, 55
Slaatten, Olaf, 122, 156
Slater, Guiseppi, 96, 98
Sloan, Tony, 98
Smallboy, Johnny, 73, 143, 219
Smallboy, Simon, 46
Smith, Bob, 126
Smith, Bruce, 56
Smith, Curtis, 143
Smith, Dean, 244
Smith, F.G., 158
Smith, Gwen Dorrien, 196
Smith, Jean, 243
Smith, Mark, 173
Smith, Ralph, 208
Smith, Roger, 146
Smith, Stephen, 55
Smoke, Bill, 53
Smuk, Mick, 166
Smyth, Andy, 49, 50, 53, 55-
    57, 59, 73, 76
Snelgrove, F.J., 52
Snyder, Col. Harry, 103, 142,
    143
Snyder, Ida, 142
Snyder, Paul, 53
Solandt, Omond, 88, 94, 122,
    157
Solomon, Jerry, 33
Somer, Art van, 130
Somerset, H. Somers, 119
Somes, John, 53
Soper, Dewey, 122, 249
Soroka, Walt, 68
Souliere, John, 162
Spafford-Gibb, Gordon, 56
Sparks, F.F., 193
Sparrow, Capt. I.M., 252
Speight, T.B., 40
Spence, James, 180

Spence, Tom, 95
Spiegel, Jim, 74
Spiler, Peter, 50
Spoehr, Peter, 48
Spragge, Bill, 104
Spreadborough, William, 32,
    217
Sproule, Don, 173
St.Cyr 206,
St. Martin, Isabel, 239
St. Onge, Philip, 245
St. Pierre, André, 244
Stadwyck, Bill and Doreen, 55
Stainer, John, 138, 238
Stanton, Leigh, 235
Stanton, M.S., 158
Starke and Stevens, 138, 142
Stathers, J., 166
Stearns, Stearnie and Dodie,
    153, 202
Stefansson, V., 156, 170, 194
Steger, Bill, 123, 198
Stein, Mike, 139
Stephenson, Graham, 207
Stern, Herb, 88
Stern, John, 87
Stesco, Steve, 139, 205, 206,
    211, 233, 234, 236, 238, 239
Stevens, F.G., 60, 86
Stevens, Joc, 42
Stevens, Peter, 235
Stevenson, Adlai, III, 87
Stewart, Alec, 98
Stewart, Bruce, 95
Stewart, C.C., 96
Stewart, Elihu, 194
Stewart, G.M., 32
Stewart, Hugh, 53, 56, 62, 94,
    98, 111, 144, 239
Stewart, John, 78
Stewart, Kenneth, 132
Stewart, Ron, 55
Stewart, Samuel, 46
Stewart, William, 83
Stickler, Bob, 49
Stockwell, C.H., 159, 171
Stockwell, Sally, 123
Stollery, Peter, 153, 175, 176,
    250-254
Stone, Andrew, 132, 137, 194,
    210
Stone, Kris, 166
Stoner, Arthur, 48
Storey, Dave, 104
Stowell, Sandy, 95
Strahm, Norman, 52

Strange, Howard, 51
Strauss, Paul, 48
Streater, John, 94, 171
Streckmann, Klaus, 139, 144, 198, 207, 208
Street, T.G., 102
Streisinger, Erwin, 22, 55, 90, 171, 172, 177, 183, 184, 252
Streuli, Nick, 51, 88
Strickland, Nancy, 55
Stringer, Bishop Isaac, 132, 195
Strohmeyer, Pat, 232
Strong, Harold, 33, 79
Struzik, Ed and Julia, 253
Stuart, John, 124
Stuck, Bishop Hudson, 191, 195
Stultz, Jack, 51, 88, 104
Sturtevant, Bradford, 48
Sugarhead, David, 46, 47
Sugden, Mark, 105
Sullivan, E.A.E., 41
Sumner, Carmichael and Judy, 134
Sutherland, Peter, 34
Sutton, George M., 33, 42
Svedberg, Erik, 106
Svedberg, Steffan, 106, 109
Swabey, J., 146
Swain, Jimmy, 46
Swannell, F.C., 127
Swanson, Dr. Kay, 207, 208
Swanson, Kent, 175
Sweetman, Suzanne, 233
Swenson, Tom, 109
Sylvester, G.E., 36
Symington, Fife, 73
Symms, Brian, 149
Tanton, T.L., 63
Tapatai, Louis, 103
Tapp, Andrew, 36
Tasell, Carol, 205
Tasker, Jim, 62
Tasker, Stephen and Florence, 32, 79, 213, 217
Tate, Dave, 34
Tate, Matthew, 69
Taylor, Bruce, 88
Taylor, Dave, 55, 56
Taylor, Gary, 51
Taylor, Howard, 228, 240, 242
Taylor, Mike, 178
Taylor, Peter, 180
Taylor, Sheldon, 117, 133
Taylor, Spence, 181
Tener, John, 103, 181

Tennent, Caroline, 233, 242
Tero, Richard, 207
Terry, Monk, 49
Terry, Tom, 51
Teufele, Adolf, 139
Thanadelthur 83
Theobald, Jonathan, 111
Théoret, Serge, 65, 78, 238, 239
Thérriault, Claude, 241, 247
Therrien, Ned, 105, 134
Thévenet, Raoul, 89
Thewhawassin, Laurent, 84
Thibert, Henry, 136, 137, 209
Thomas, Alister, 68, 75
Thomas, Daryl, 57
Thomas, Don, 34, 51, 53, 62
Thomas, J.G., 228
Thomas, John, 30, 39, 65
Thomas, Malcolm, 147
Thomas, Roderick, 204
Thomas, Shawn, 250
Thompson, David, 83, 89, 92, 115, 118, 124
Thompson, David (Toronto), 104
Thompson, Jim, 37
Thompson, John, 32, 40
Thompson, Keith, 172
Thompson, Mike, 104
Thompson, Rick, 173
Thompson, Tyler, 87, 122, 157
Thomson, Bruce, 202
Thomson, Prof. John, 161
Thorpe, Ron, 105
Thorsteinsson, Dr. R., 253
Thum, Bob, 49
Thum, Carl, 49, 50
Tiernman, J.M., 52
Todd, Sue, 55
Todd, Walter E.C., 33, 36, 42, 71, 80, 215, 219, 229, 245
Tollemache, Stratford, 191, 203, 204
Toller, George, 37
Tolstoy, Count Ilia, 96
Tomison, William, 59
Tooley, Bryan, 212
Topelko, John, 73
Torney, Jeff, 246
Tousignant, Marcel, 239, 241, 242
Tousley, Herb, 110
Townsend, Dr. Charles, 239
Townsend, Terry, 67
Towongie, Harry, 98

Tozer, Dr. E.T., 139, 253
Train, Cliff, 163
Trainor, Linda, 55
Tremblay, Bernard, 65, 248
Tremblay, Louis, 132
Trepanier, Louis, 137
Troyes, Pierre de, 38, 69
Trudeau, Pierre, 25, 63, 144, 171
Trudelle, Jean, 241
True, Dave, 55
Trumper, Katherine, 250
Trundle, Inspector Charles, 103, 161
Tryck, Keith, 192
Tuomikoski, Risto, 80
Tupper, Dick, 173
Turbayne, Ron, 247
Turnbull, Andy, 94, 108
Turnbull, Katie, 60
Turnbull, Porter, 218
Turner, Anne, 55
Turner, Dick, 121, 133, 142, 143, 146
Turner, Don, 144
Turner, J.R., 146
Turner, John and Geills, 176
Turner, T., 146
Turner, Tom, 178
Turnor, Philip, 31, 39, 45, 89, 115
Twomey, Arthur, 80
Tyrrell, James W., 92, 98, 101, 107, 119, 161
Tyrrell, Joseph B., 61, 92, 101, 107, 109, 119
Ude, Jim, 88, 110
Underhill, Brian and Merle, 161
Urquhart, Ian, 49
Utne, Tor, 34
Vaillancourt, Maryse, 248
Vallée, Danielle, 65, 220
Vallière, Sieur de, 69
Vanasse, Constable, 46
Vanderbeck, Jim, 47
Vanderlick, Jim, 67
Vandewater, Steve, 34
Vaughan, Roger, 168
Vaughan, Toby, 247
Verbeek, Nicolaas, 43
Verby, John, 250
Vermeulen, Fred, 106, 146
Vermeulen, Lewis, 106
Very, Samuel, 31
Vesey, T.M., 86

Viau, Christian, 217, 220
Viau, Guy, 63
Vincent, Archdeacon, 46
Vittrekwa, Joseph, 195
Voigt, Dennis, 106, 109, 173
Vollant, Charles, 245
Vorteck, Michael, 238
Voxland, Orv, 182
Vreeland, Frederick K., 127
Waddel, Clint, 117
Wade, Douglas, 94
Wadham, Gay, 56, 68, 74
Wadsworth, Jack and Susy, 182
Walbridge, Charley, 243
Walcott, Dick, 34
Walcott, Robert, 231
Walker, Bill, 111
Walker, L.I., 63
Walker, P.H., 102
Walker, Wick, 239
Wallace, Dillon, 221, 235
Wallace, Jerry, 192
Wallace, Kit, 78
Wallace, Tom, 200, 205, 206
Walles, Bill, 49
Wallis, Rev. G.C., 194
Wallwin, Jack, 55
Walmsley, Jamie, 34
Walshe, Shan and Margie, 37
Walters, Bucky, 49
Walton, Rev., 41
Wapner, Kenny, 76
Wartman, John, 220
Wascenda, Greg, 94, 123
Wascowin, Daniel, 46
Wasson, John, 208, 211
Watkins, Gino, 229, 234, 236
Watson, A., 94, 182
Watson, B., 94, 163, 182
Watson, Duke, 75, 77, 90, 94, 112, 117, 123, 134, 140, 152, 157, 162, 163, 172, 182, 184, 198, 211, 219, 223
Watson, Frank, 137
Watson, M., 90, 152, 157, 198, 211
Watson, R., 77, 95, 182
Watt, James and Maud, 246
Watts, David, 59, 171
Watts, Murray, 42, 80
Way, Harold, 98
Webb, Jack, 55
Webber, G.E., 87
Webber, Jon, 53
Webster, Arthur, 125

Webster, Doug, 94, 123
Webster, Elizabeth, 95
Weeks, John, 49
Weeks, L.J., 97
Weinstock, June, 207
Weintraub, Joel, 108
Weir, Dave, 55
Weisman, Fritz, 143
Welles, Skip, 49
Wells, Hazard, 191
Wendt, Alice, 55, 171
Wenger, Ferdi, 139
Wentzler, Betty, Jim and Jack, 118, 230
Wentzler, Joseph, 118
Wermager, Marc, 146, 150, 202, 206
Wesley, Gaius, 47
Wesley, John, 47
Wesson, Larry, 244
West, Jack, 97, 105
West, Mike, 163
Westgarth, Arthur, 173
Weston, Dave, 34
Weston, Jack, 117
Whatmough, Alan, 175
Wheeler, Chris, 51
Wheeler, D. and L., 140
Wheeler, David, 158, 170
Wherley, Gerry, 161, 181

Whitbeck, Gordie, 224
White, Chris, 76
Whiteside, Dave, 49
Whitney, Caspar, 170
Whittaker, E.J., 127, 138
Whittier, Mike, 112
Whitting, Andrew, 39
Whyatt, Tom, 134
Wickett, Tom, 49, 123
Wijk, Constance and Marius van, 95
Wilford, Dave, 151, 202
Wilk, A.L., 103, 181
Wilke, John, 117
Wilkie, Robert and James, 181
Wilkinson, Samuel, 125
Willett, Henry, 63
Williams, Bill, 254
Williams, Carl, 66-68, 74, 75
Williams, Doug, 218, 224
Williams, M.Y., 37, 42, 54, 127, 133, 138, 156
Williams, Martyn, 204, 208
Williams, R.A., 103
Williams, Russ, 129
Williamson, Don, 49, 50
Willis, Kathy, 55
Wilson, "Moose", 54, 63, 66
Wilson, A.W.G., 41
Wilson, Brian, 73

Wilson, Charles, 191, 206
Wilson, Dr. George, 189
Wilson, H.S., 102, 161
Wilson, Jay, 243
Wilson, Luke, 57, 76
Wilson, Mark, 51
Wilson, W.J., 52, 54, 60
Winacott, Ed, 105
Winch, Dave, 51, 248
Windelhed, Bengt, 106
Winkelen, Herb Van, 178
Winslow, Dick, 178
Winter, Ash, 34, 104
Winter, Richard, 232
Wise, Kurt, 178
Wissink, Rene, 250
Witala, Debbie, 205
Witherell, Sandy, 219
Wolf, Charlie, 105, 130, 139, 161, 192, 197, 198
Wolfe, Ben, 151
Wolfe, Jennifer, 159
Woo, Sam, 178, 180
Wood, Frank, 143
Wood, Jim, 111
Wood, T.J., 196
Woods, David, 197
Woolfenden, J., 158
Woollacott, Arthur P., 128
Wray, O.R., 171

Wrestle, Henry, 129
Wright, Alice, 95
Wright, D.W., 137
Wright, Dave, 110
Wright, G.B., 209
Wright, Norman, 109
Wright, Paul, 73
Wurm, Lisa, 177
Wutrick, Manfred, 143
Wyckoff, E., 94, 172, 182
Wyckoff, P., 94, 182
Wykeham-Feinnes, Ranulph, 144
Wynn, John, 54
Yderstad, Charles, 143
Yockey, Hubert, 220, 244
Yorga, Brian and Ginny, 105
York, Tom, 105
Young, G.A., 78, 217
Young, Rev. Egerton Ryerson, 84, 89
Youngman, P.M., 143
Youngren, Wendy, 95
Zack, Steve, 207
Zauche, W., 95, 140
Zecha, Terry, 220
Zecha, Tim, 220
Zob, A., 152, 184
Zobator, Brent, 56
Zogg, H., 140, 157, 163

INDEX TO LAKES AND RIVERS

Abamasagi Lake, 53, 55
Aberdeen Lake, 101, 103, 106, 107, 109
Abitibi Lake, 38-41, 46
Abitibi River, 33, 36-43, 47, 54, 63, 80
Aguanus River, 237, 239
Albanel Lake, 72, 76, 77
Albany River, 43, 45-59
Alsek River, 207
Anderson River, 166
Angikuni Lake, 97, 98, 109, 111
Arctic Red River, 135, 150
Armark River, 102, 179
Artillery Lake, 101, 102, 106, 107, 119, 121, 160-163, 180, 182
Asheweig River, 59
Ashuanipi Lake, 225, 228, 229, 245, 246
Ashuanipi River, 219, 229, 235, 245
Assinica Lac, 67, 68
Astray Lake, 223, 225, 229, 235, 245
Athabasca Lake, 92, 94, 113-134, 162
Athabasca River, 113-134, 124, 162, 164, 169, 188
Atikonak Lake, 229, 238, 240, 241
Atikonak River, 228
Attawapiskat Lake, 45, 50, 53, 56-59
Attawapiskat River, 45, 50, 56-58
Attikamagen Lake, 232, 234
Attwood River, 50, 51, 59
Aylmer Lake, 121, 160-162, 176, 178, 180-182
Back River, 102, 116, 161, 176-184
Baillie River, 177-181, 183
Baker Lake, 109, 183

Beaulieu River, 157, 160
Beechey Lake, 177, 181, 182
Bell River (Quebec), 65, 66, 68, 69, 71, 72
Bell River (Yukon), 187, 188, 193-199
Beverly Lake, 101-103, 106, 107, 179, 184
Bienville Lake, 78
Big Salmon River, 187, 189, 206
Blackstone River, 150, 151
Bonnet Plume River, 150, 152, 153
Broadback River, 65, 66, 68, 71, 72, 74, 75
Burnside River, 169, 175, 176
Burntwood River, 88-90, 94
Cadillac Lake, 63, 65
Campbell Lake, 102, 106, 161, 163, 183
Camsell River, 122, 132, 156-158, 172
Carnwath River, 166
Cat Lake, 46, 53, 56, 59-61
Chamouchouane River, 31, 70-72, 75, 218
Chantrey Inlet, 156, 180-182, 184
Chesterfield Inlet, 102, 104, 107, 109, 110, 112
Chibougamau Lake, 67, 71-73
Chibougamau River 65-67, 71
Chivelston Lake, 49, 56, 59
Choiseul Lac, 66, 67
Churchill River, 81, 83, 84, 88, 89, 91, 92, 94, 95, 109, 115, 117, 124
Clearwater River (Quebec), 76, 79
Clearwater River (Saskatchewan), 113, 117, 118, 169
Clearwater River (Ungava), 213, 217, 218
Clinton-Colden Lake, 101,

103, 105, 121, 160, 161, 163, 173, 178, 180
Cochrane River, 92-98, 109, 111
Consul River, 102, 178, 179
Contwoyto Lake, 175
Contwoyto River, 177
Coppermine River, 92, 96, 101, 102, 116, 131, 132, 156, 158-162, 168-171, 173, 175, 176
Courageous Lake, 105, 158, 159, 172, 173
Cree Lake, 123
Cree River, 118, 123
Croker River, 168
Cross Lake, 81, 88, 89
Damant Lake, 105, 106, 162
Dease Lake, 136-139, 140, 141, 202, 209-211
Dease River (British Columbia), 135-138, 140, 202, 209-211
Dease River (NWT), 131, 132, 156, 169, 170
Deer River, 89
De Pas River, 221, 223, 232-234
Dismal Lakes, 156, 169, 171
Drowning River, 43, 54, 55
Dubawnt Lake, 96, 109
Dubawnt River, 83, 98, 101, 105, 107, 109, 111, 117, 162, 163, 173, 179, 184
Du Sable River, 218, 220
Eabamet Lake, 47, 58, 59
Eabamet River, 45, 49, 56, 57
Eastmain River, 69-71, 74-77, 218, 219
Echimamish River, 60, 81, 83-88, 96
Eileen Lakes, 103, 108, 162, 163
Ekwan River, 57, 58
Elk River, 101, 105, 162, 173

Ellice River, 177, 183
Ennadai Lake, 109
Esnagami Lake, 55
Esnagi Lake, 32
Eyeberry Lake, 106
Fawn River, 60, 62
Ferguson Lake, 98, 109, 111
Ferguson River, 97, 98, 109
Finlay River, 123, 125-129, 209
Firedrake Lake, 105, 162
Firth River, 165
Flat River, 141-144
Fond du Lac River, 92, 94, 118, 121-123, 163
Fort George River, 75, 78, 79, 220
Fort Nelson River, 125, 126, 132, 133, 135, 137, 138, 142-144, 157, 193, 197
Frances River, 135, 138, 139, 190, 202, 209
Fraser River (Labrador) 225, 230
Frederick House River, 36-39, 41
Garry Lakes, 102, 179-182, 184
George River, 213, 221, 223, 227, 231-235
Gods Lake, 60, 85, 86, 88
Gods River, 87
Goéland, Lac au, 65, 67-69, 72
Goose River, 236
Gouin Reservoir, 67, 72, 73
Grand River, 225, 227-230, 235, 236, 240
Gras, Lac de, 168, 171, 173, 175
Grass River, 89
Grassy River, 37
Great Bear Lake, 102, 117, 120, 122, 128, 131, 132, 138, 155-158, 169, 170, 172, 173, 198
Great Bear River, 120-122, 128, 132, 138, 155-157
Great Slave Lake, 113-134

Great Whale River, 78, 79

Groundhog River, 35-38, 41, 45, 54

Gwillem Lake, 67, 68

Hanbury River, 101-106, 159, 161, 163, 173, 179, 180, 183

Hare Indian River, 155, 166

Harricanaw River, 63, 65, 75

Hart River, 150, 151

Hay River, 137, 157, 164

Hayes River (Manitoba), 39, 60, 81, 83-88, 96

Hayes River (NWT), 184

Henik Lakes, 98

Hill River, 84, 85

Hood River, 169, 175

Hornaday River, 166, 168

Horton River, 166

Hyland River, 136, 137, 140

Indin Lake, 159

Iroquois River, 166

Ivanhoe River, 35, 37

Kabinakagami River, 31, 43, 54, 55

Kagianagami Lake, 53, 59

Kaleet River, 180

Kamilukuak Lake, 98, 109, 111

Kamilukuak River, 110

Kaminak Lake, 97, 109

Kaminuriak Lake, 98

Kanairiktok River, 225, 234

Kaniapiskau Lake, 71, 78, 218, 220

Kaniapiskau River, 71, 77, 78, 213, 217-220, 246

Kapikotongwa River, 53, 55, 56, 59

Kapuskasing River, 32, 35, 36

Kasba Lake, 94, 97, 109, 111

Kasmere Lake, 94, 96, 97, 111

Kayedon Lake, 53

Kazan River, 83, 96, 98, 101, 107, 109-111, 176

Keele River, 135, 148, 149, 191, 201, 203

Keezhik Lake, 47

Kekek River, 66

Kenemu River, 236

Kenogami River, 32, 43, 46, 54-56

Kenogamissi Lake, 35

Kenojiwan Lake, 52

Kesagami Lake, 39, 43

Kesagami River, 43

Kississing River, 92

Klondike River, 187, 199, 200

Knee Lake, 83, 85-87

Kogaluk River, 213, 215, 216, 225, 231, 232

Kognak River, 98

Koksoak River, 71, 79, 213, 217-219, 221, 223

Korok River, 213, 223, 224

Kunwak River, 110

Kuujjua River, 251

Larch River, 79, 213, 217, 218

Leaf River, 213, 216, 224

Liard River, 121, 122, 125-128, 132, 133, 135-142, 144-146, 157, 187, 188, 190, 193, 197, 202, 209, 210

Lichteneger Lake, 76

Little Nahanni River, 144, 145

Little Whale River, 78

Lloyd Lake, 117

Lockhart River, 105, 106, 157, 158, 160-163, 172, 173, 180-182

Lynx Lake, 106, 162, 163

MacAlpine Lake, 177, 178

MacFarlane River, 118, 121, 123

MacKay Lake, 158, 160, 161, 173, 178, 181, 183

Mackenzie River, 113-134

Macmillan River, 147, 148, 187, 202-205

McPhayden River, 78

Magpie River, 237, 242-244

Maguse River, 98, 111

Maicasagi Lake, 67, 68

Mara River, 175, 176

Marian River, 122, 133, 156-158, 172

Marjorie Lake, 107

Marten River, 31, 71-73, 75

Martin-Drinking River, 45, 56-58

Matagami Lake, 65, 66, 68, 69, 71, 72, 75

Mattagami Lake, 35

Mattagami River, 35-37, 41, 45, 54, 71

Mattawitchewan River, 29, 31

Mégiscane River, 65, 66

Menihek Lake, 78, 219, 229, 245

Mesgouez Lake, 74, 76

Methye Portage, 84, 92, 113, 117, 124

Michikamau Lake, 221, 228, 235

Michipicoten River, 30, 33, 45, 54, 84

Miminiska Lake, 45, 48

Miniss Lake, 49, 51, 59

Minto Lake, 213, 216

Missinaibi Lake, 29, 31, 33, 41

Missinaibi River, 29, 31-34, 40-42, 45, 54, 75, 84, 217, 240

Missisa River, 57

Mistassini Lake, 31, 65, 67, 68, 70-77, 218

Mistassini River, 67

Misticawasse Creek, 74, 76

Moisie River, 219, 227, 229, 237, 240, 244-248

Moose River, 31

Morse River, 180, 184

Mountain River, 149

Nagagami River, 43, 54, 55

Naskaupi River, 221, 227, 228, 235

Nastapoka Islands, 33, 36, 42, 79

Nastapoka River, 79

Natashquan River, 237, 239

Natla River, 149

Nelson River, 60, 81, 84-90

Nemiscau Lake, 31, 65, 68, 69, 71, 72, 74, 75

Nichicun Lake, 70, 75, 219

Nighthawk River, 33, 37

Nipigon Lake, 52

Nipissis River, 245, 246

Nonacho Lake, 162, 163

North Nahanni River, 120, 121, 135, 148

Notakwanon River, 221, 225, 232

Nottaway River, 36, 65, 66, 68, 75

Nowleye Lake, 109, 111

Nueltin Lake, 93, 95-98

Oba River, 31

Obatogamau Lake, 72

Obatogamau River, 66

Ogilvie River, 150, 151

Ogoki River, 43, 45, 51-53, 56, 58, 59

Old Factory River, 77

Ombabika River, 52, 53, 56, 59

Opemisca Lake, 67

Opichuan River, 48, 53, 56, 58, 59

Opinaca River, 76

Ossokmanuan Lake, 228, 229, 240

Otoskwin River, 53, 56-59

Oxford Lake, 81, 83, 86, 88

Ozhiski Lake, 58

Pagawachuan River, 45, 54, 55

Parsnip River, 124-128, 130, 164

Partridge River, 43

Pashkokogan Lake, 49, 50, 52, 53, 56

Payne River, 213, 215, 217

Peace River, 105-107, 115, 118-120, 123-130, 135, 137, 138, 164

Peel River, 116, 125, 126, 129, 131-133, 135, 136, 150-153, 157

Pekans River, 219, 220, 237, 247

Pelly River, 135-137, 149, 187-191, 202-206, 209

Penylan Lake, 106

Perry River, 177, 178

Petawanga Lake, 48

Petit Mécatina River, 237-239

Petitsikapau Lake, 218, 219, 227, 228, 240, 245

Pic River, 54

Pickle Lake, 56, 58, 61

Pike's Portage, 101, 102, 106, 107, 121, 161-163, 181, 182

Pipestone River, 58-60

Pitikigushi River, 52

Pivibiska River, 29, 31

Playgreen Lake, 81, 83

Point Lake, 168, 171-173, 175

Porcupine River, 116, 117, 121, 123, 125, 129, 131, 133, 139, 144, 151, 152, 157, 187, 188, 191, 193, 198, 199

Povungnituk River, 213, 215

Princess Mary Lake, 110

Putahow Lake, 96, 97

Quinze Lake, 40

Quoich River, 101, 112

Rae River, 168

Ram River, 148

Rat River, 121, 125, 129, 131, 133, 135, 150, 152, 153, 157, 187, 194

Redstone River, 135, 148

Reindeer Lake, 83, 90, 92-94, 96-98, 109, 111, 122, 123

Reindeer River, 89, 92, 93, 96, 115, 117

Richmond Gulf, 78-80, 213, 217, 218

Roggan River, 78

Romaine River, 227-229, 237, 238, 240-242

Root River, 46, 47, 49, 58

Ross River, 146, 147, 149, 187, 191, 202, 203, 205, 206
Rupert River, 31, 65, 68, 69, 71-77, 218
Sakami Lake, 76, 77
Savant Lake, 47, 53, 56, 59
Schultz Lake, 102, 103, 180, 183
Seal Lake, 79, 80, 215, 217, 218
Seal River, 92, 95, 96, 98
Sealhole Lake, 96, 98
Selwyn Lake, 101, 105, 107, 108, 110, 162, 184
Severn River, 39, 57, 59, 60, 62, 86
Shamattawa River, 57, 58, 60
Sifton Lake, 101-105
Sikanni Chief River, 125, 132, 133, 138
Simpson River, 179
Sipiwesk Lake, 88, 89
Sisipuk Lake, 89, 92
Sixty Mile River, 187, 200
Slave River, 113-134, 162, 169, 188, 193
Smalltree Lake, 107, 108, 162
Snake River, 150, 153

Snare River, 157-159, 170-172
Snowbird Lake, 97, 109, 111
Snowdrift River, 108, 157, 162, 163, 171
Soper River, 249
South Nahanni River, 122, 135, 140-147, 205
Southern Indian Lake, 92, 94, 95
Split Lake, 89, 90, 109
St.Augustin River, 237, 238
St.Jean River, 227-229, 237, 240-242
St.Joseph Lake, 45-49, 51-53, 56, 58, 59
St.Paul River, 237
Stewart River, 149-152, 187, 189, 194, 200-202
Stikine River, 125, 136-138, 141, 202, 208, 209, 211, 212
Sutton River, 58
Swampy Bay River, 213, 218-220, 245
Tadoule Lake, 95
Takiyuak Lake, 175
Taltson River, 106, 108, 157, 162, 163

Tatonduk River, 187, 199
Tatshenshini River, 207, 208
Tazin River, 162, 163
Témiscamie River, 72, 76
Teslin River, 187, 189, 190, 192, 205, 206, 210
Tha-anne River, 97, 98
Thelon River, 99, 101-103, 105-107, 109, 162, 163, 173, 178-180, 183, 184
Thlewiaza River, 85, 93, 96, 97
Thoa River, 162, 163
Tichégami River, 76, 77
Trout Lake, 60-62
Ugjoktok River, 225, 233
Ungava Crater, 215
Unknown River, 227-229, 240
Wababimiga Lake, 54, 55
Wabakimi Lake, 52
Wabasca River, 130
Wabassinon River, 76, 77
Wabitotem River, 58
Waconichi Lake, 71-74
Waswanipi River, 65-68, 71, 72
Webequie Lake, 58

Western River, 177
Wetetnagami River, 66
Whale River, 213, 220, 227
Wheeler River, 213, 220
Wholdaia Lake, 98, 101, 105, 107-109, 111, 162, 184
Wind River, 126, 132, 150-152, 194
Windigo Lake, 59, 60
Windigo River, 59, 60
Winisk Lake, 57, 58
Winisk River, 46, 57-60
Winter Lake, 158, 159, 169, 170, 172, 175
Wollaston Lake, 92, 94, 97, 118, 121-123, 162, 163
Woollett Lake, 75, 76
Wunnummin Lake, 58-60
Yathkyed Lake, 97, 98, 109, 111
Yellowknife River, 157-159, 169, 171-173
Yukon River, 117, 123, 125, 129, 133, 135, 137, 151, 152, 185-207, 209

INDEX TO ORGANIZATIONS

BOUNDARY SURVEYS

International Boundary Commission, 190
Ontario-Manitoba Boundary Survey 90
Quebec Boundary Survey, 66
U.S.-Canadian Boundary Survey, 191
Yukon-Alaska Boundary Survey, 190, 209

CANADIAN GOVERNMENT

Canadian Fisheries, 41, 54
Canadian Heritage River System, 18
Canadian Wildlife Service, 48, 97, 103, 109, 144, 145, 181
Department of Mines and Resources, 103
Department of the Interior, 93, 102, 121, 126, 132, 249
Dept. of Fisheries and Forests, 130
Dept. of Mines and Natural Resources, 158
Dept. of Public Works, 90
Geographical Branch, Dept. of Mines, 150, 166
Indian Trade Commission, 47
Treaty #8, 119, 126
Treaty #9, 41, 46

CANOE GROUPS

Arctic and Rideau Canoe Club (John Godfrey, Ted Johnson *et al*), 153, 175, 176, 250-54
Bytown Bushwackers, 34, 146
FQCC, 217, 218, 238, 239, 241-43
Hide-Away Canoe Club, 184, 215
Christian Science Brigade, 134
Lakeview High School Outers, 51, 59

Northwest Voyageur Canoe Club of Edmonton, 146
Outdoor Education Club, Technical High School, Prince Albert, Saskatchewan, 95,
Syracuse University Outing Club, 48
Voyageurs (Eric Morse *et al*), 15, 22, 87, 90, 94, 95, 103, 106, 108, 110, 117, 122, 157, 158, 161, 163, 171, 197
Wilderness Canoe Association, 146

CHURCHES

Anglican, 31, 32, 35, 36, 39-41, 45-47, 54, 57, 60, 66, 71, 79, 80, 84, 85, 89, 97, 101, 116, 125, 128, 131, 132, 164, 188, 191, 193-95, 202
Methodist, 84, 89
Roman Catholic, 38-40, 57, 58, 60, 65, 66, 69, 71, 72, 75, 78, 107, 116, 119, 126, 136, 156, 166, 168-70, 181, 193, 218, 227, 228, 240, 242, 245

COMMERCE

British-America Corporation, 191

EDUCATIONAL

Bowdoin College, Maine, 228
Hampshire College, 50
Lakefield College, 149
McGill University, 85, 184, 192
McMaster University, 145
Oxford University Soil Science Labratory, 238
Tokai University Canadian Arctic Research Expedition, 251
Trinity College School, 104

University of Alaska, 197
University of Iowa, 119, 132, 159
University of Minnesota, 181
University of Toronto, 31, 52, 73
University of Waterloo, 218
University of Wisconsin, 109, 161
Whitmore College, 98, 105, 107, 111, 173, 175, 176, 182, 184
York University, 212

GUIDED ADVENTURE

Arctic Barrens Expeditions, 178, 180
Arctic Edge, 149, 153, 165
Canoe Arctic Inc. 183
Canoe Sport British Columbia, 139
Headwaters, 62, 239
North West Expeditions, 147
North Winds, 250
Polar Arctic Expeditions (Bob Dannert), 123, 173, 175, 177, 179, 182
Sunrise County Canoe, 217, 250
Trailhead/Black Feather, 147, 149, 254
Voyageurs North, 51
Wanapitei, 68, 74, 75, 150, 151, 173, 198
Wilderness Way, 50, 53, 57, 59, 76, 77

FUR TRADE

Compagnie du Nord, 69
Hudson's Bay Company, 17, 18, 21, 22, 29-32, 35, 36, 38-41, 43, 45-47, 49, 51, 56, 59, 60, 65, 69-71, 75, 78, 79, 81, 83, 84, 86-92, 96, 97, 101, 115, 116, 118, 119, 121, 124-126, 128, 131, 132, 134, 136, 138, 141, 148, 150, 151, 153, 155, 156, 162, 166, 168, 169, 172, 173, 178, 180, 183, 185, 187, 188, 190, 194, 196, 200, 202, 208, 209, 215, 217-219, 221, 222, 224, 227, 231, 235, 245, 246
North West Company, 35, 39, 69, 81, 84, 92, 115, 118, 124, 130, 140
Revillon Frères, 29, 32, 41, 42, 45, 71, 89, 96, 102, 109

MILITARY AND NAVAL

British Army, 84, 116, 125
Canadian Army, 47, 143, 171, 219
Royal Navy, 84, 116, 123, 131, 156, 159, 169, 175
U.S. Army Engineers, 189

MUSEUMS

American Museum of Natural History, 96, 128, 137, 142, 194, 210
British Museum, 238
Brooklyn Museum, 162
Carnegie Museum, 33, 36, 41, 42, 71, 79, 80, 215, 219, 246
Museum of Natural History, Canada, 92, 96, 128, 137, 142, 194, 210
National Museum, Canada, 80, 87, 103, 109, 165, 179
New Jersey State Museum, 42
Royal Ontario Museum, 73

NATURE

Audubon Club of Chicago, 116,
Illinois Natural History Survey, 55, 178
Kew Gardens, 238
Ontario Breeding Bird Atlas, 62

POLICE

RCMP, 47, 94, 103, 138, 149, 158, 182
RNWMP, 24, 86, 102, 119, 126, 127, 137, 150, 156, 191, 202

PROSPECTING

Cyril Knight Prospecting Company, 80, 98, 221
Labrador Exploration and Mining Company, 241
Mackenzie and Mann Company, 36, 219, 246
Yukon Valley Prospecting-Mining, 126

PROVINCIAL GOVERNMENTS

British Columbia Department of Mines, 209
Manitoba Government, 90
Newfoundland Dept. of Natural Resources, 229
Ontario Lands and Forests, 56, 59, 61
Quebec Forestry, 66

PUBLICATIONS

Explorers Club, 197
Globe and Mail, 215
National Geographic, 123, 175, 193, 215, 230

RAILWAY AND TELEGRAPH

Algoma Central Railway, 36
North Railway Company, 79
Quebec North Shore and Labrador Railway, 243, 244
Western Union Telegraph, 188, 208, 209

SCIENTIFIC

Arctic Institute of North America, 55, 184
Canadian Arctic Expedition, 165, 168, 170
Carnegie Institute, 71
Danish Government Expedition, 109
National Research Council, 184
Peabody Foundation for Archaeology, 72
Radar Exploration, 229
Royal Geographical Society, 229
Science Search, 215
Smithsonian Institution, 39, 116, 136, 193, 234
Viking Fund, 72
Wilkie Foundation, 181

SURVEYS

Crown Lands Commission, Quebec, 237-239, 242, 245
Dominion Land Survey, 65, 107, 189, 199, 206

Dominion Observatory Magnetic Survey, 96
Geological Survey of Canada, 17, 18, 24, 31, 32, 35, 36, 39, 42, 43, 45, 46, 52, 54, 56-58, 61, 63, 65, 68-71, 75, 78, 79, 84, 85, 89, 92, 93, 97, 98, 101-03, 107-09, 116, 119-121, 125-127, 132, 133, 136, 138, 139, 142, 143, 148-50, 152, 157, 158, 162, 164, 165, 168, 170, 171, 181, 190, 191, 193, 194, 200-04, 206, 209, 211, 217, 218, 228, 240, 251, 252
Northern Ontario Land Survey, 17, 21, 32, 36, 40, 41, 52, 54
Ontario Land Survey, 32, 36, 40, 41, 52, 54, 101
Topographical Survey, 93, 103, 121, 127, 133, 190, 201
Wild River Survey of Canada, 18, 21, 24, 34, 51, 53, 57, 62, 75, 106, 117, 123, 139, 148, 149, 151, 152, 155, 159, 165, 172, 198, 200, 202, 205, 206, 211, 232-234, 236, 238, 239, 241, 247, 249

U.S. GOVERNMENT DEPARTMENTS

U.S. Biological Survey, 121, 127, 204

U.S. Coast and Geodetic Survey, 193
U.S. Dept. of Agriculture, 85, 120
U.S. Geological Survey, 139, 190
U.S. Zoological Survey, 116

YOUTH CAMPS

Kandalore, 34, 42, 50, 51, 75, 96
Kapitachouane, 66-68, 74, 75
Keewaydin, 20, 33, 36, 37, 41, 42, 49, 51, 53, 54, 57, 63, 65, 66, 68, 71-74, 76, 77, 79
Keewaydin Wilderness, 67, 68, 73-75, 77
Manitou, 55
Minocqua, 51
North Woods, 106
Onondaga, 34, 104
Owakonze, 49-51, 88, 90, 104
Temagami, 49, 51, 53, 56, 59, 73
Wabun, 48-51, 53, 55, 57, 73, 74
Wanapitei, 34, 37, 42, 43, 55-57, 68, 74, 78, 96, 147, 150, 151, 159, 221, 233
Widjiwagan, 60, 88, 90, 94, 95, 97, 105, 108, 110, 117, 123, 129, 134, 157, 158, 162, 163, 166, 173, 220

ABOUT THE AUTHORS...

A recognized canoeing authority, **Bruce W. Hodgins**, currently Professor of History at Trent University, is the author of many books and articles on the North, canoeing, aboriginal people and comparative federalism. He has led many lengthy canoe trips on northern rivers.

Gwyneth Hoyle, recently retired College Librarian, Trent University, is a research associate with the graduate program of the university's Frost Centre of Canadian Heritage and Development Studies and an experienced canoeist.

Bruce W. Hodgins and Gwyneth Hoyle on the Trent University campus, with the Bata Library on the Otonabee River in the background, Peterborough, Ont., May 1994.